Lecture Notes in Computer Science 15263

The series Lecture Notes in Computer Science (LNCS), including its subseries Lecture Notes in Artificial Intelligence (LNAI) and Lecture Notes in Bioinformatics (LNBI), has established itself as a medium for the publication of new developments in computer science and information technology research, teaching, and education.

LNCS enjoys close cooperation with the computer science R & D community, the series counts many renowned academics among its volume editors and paper authors, and collaborates with prestigious societies. Its mission is to serve this international community by providing an invaluable service, mainly focused on the publication of conference and workshop proceedings and postproceedings. LNCS commenced publication in 1973.

Joaquin Garcia-Alfaro · Ken Barker ·
Guillermo Navarro-Arribas · Cristina Pérez-Solà ·
Sergi Delgado-Segura · Sokratis Katsikas ·
Frédéric Cuppens · Costas Lambrinoudakis ·
Nora Cuppens-Boulahia · Marek Pawlicki ·
Michał Choraś
Editors

Computer Security

ESORICS 2024
International Workshops

DPM, CBT, and CyberICPS
Bydgoszcz, Poland, September 16–20, 2024
Revised Selected Papers, Part I

 Springer

Editors
Joaquin Garcia-Alfaro 🆔
Institut Polytechnique de Paris
Palaiseau, France

Ken Barker
University of Calgary
Calgary, AB, Canada

Guillermo Navarro-Arribas 🆔
Universitat Autònoma de Barcelona
Bellaterra, Spain

Cristina Pérez-Solà 🆔
Universitat Autònoma de Barcelona
Bellaterra, Spain

Sergi Delgado-Segura 🆔
Chaincode Labs
New York, NY, USA

Sokratis Katsikas 🆔
Norwegian University of Science
and Technology - NTNU
Gjøvik, Norway

Frédéric Cuppens
Polytechnique Montréal
Montreal, QC, Canada

Costas Lambrinoudakis 🆔
University of Piraeus
Piraeus, Greece

Nora Cuppens-Boulahia 🆔
Polytechnique Montréal
Montreal, QC, Canada

Marek Pawlicki 🆔
Bydgoszcz University of Science
and Technology
Bydgoszcz, Poland

Michał Choraś 🆔
Bydgoszcz University of Science
and Technology
Bydgoszcz, Poland

ISSN 0302-9743   ISSN 1611-3349 (electronic)
Lecture Notes in Computer Science
ISBN 978-3-031-82348-0   ISBN 978-3-031-82349-7 (eBook)
https://doi.org/10.1007/978-3-031-82349-7

Preface

The 29th edition of the European Symposium on Research in Computer Security (ESORICS) was held in Bydgoszcz, Poland, during September 16–20, 2024. In addition to the main conference, eight workshops were organized and held on September 19–20.

This volume includes the accepted contributions to three of these workshops, as follows:

- the 19th International Workshop on Data Privacy Management (DPM 2024);
- the 8th International Workshop on Cryptocurrencies and Blockchain Technology (CBT 2024);
- the 10th International Workshop on the Security of Industrial Control Systems and of Cyber-Physical Systems (CyberICPS 2024).

While each of the workshops had a high-quality program of its own, the organizers opted to publish the proceedings jointly; these are included in this volume, which contains 33 revised papers. The authors improved and extended the accepted papers based on the reviewers' feedback as well as the discussions at the workshops.

We would like to thank each and every one who was involved in the organization of the ESORICS 2024 workshops. Special thanks go to the ESORICS 2024 Workshop Chairs and to all the workshop organizers and their respective Program Committees who contributed to making the ESORICS 2024 workshops a real success. We would also like to thank the ESORICS 2024 Organizing Committee for supporting the day-to-day operation and execution of the workshops.

December 2024

Joaquin Garcia-Alfaro
Ken Barker
Guillermo Navarro-Arribas
Cristina Pérez-Solà
Sergi Delgado-Segura
Sokratis Katsikas
Frédéric Cuppens
Costas Lambrinoudakis
Nora Cuppens-Boulahia
Marek Pawlicki
Michał Choraś

About This Book

This two-volume set LNCS 15263 and LNCS 15264 constitutes the refereed proceedings of eight International Workshops which were held in conjunction with the 29th European Symposium on Research in Computer Security, ESORICS 2024, in Bydgoszcz, Poland, during September 19–20, 2024.

The papers included in these proceedings stem from the following workshops:

19th International Workshop on Data Privacy Management, DPM 2024, which accepted 7 regular papers and 6 short papers from 24 submissions;

8th International Workshop on Cryptocurrencies and Blockchain Technology, CBT 2024, which accepted 9 regular papers from 17 submissions;

10th International Workshop on the Security of Industrial Control Systems and of Cyber-Physical Systems, CyberICPS 2024, which accepted 9 regular papers from 17 submissions;

2nd International Workshop on Security and Artificial Intelligence, SECAI 2024, which accepted 10 regular papers and 5 short papers from 42 submissions;

4th International Workshop on Computational Methods for Emerging Problems in Disinformation Analysis, DisA 2024, which accepted 4 papers from 8 submissions;

5th International Workshop on Cyber-Physical Security for Critical Infrastructures Protection, CPS4CIP 2024, which accepted 4 papers from 9 submissions.

3rd International Workshop on System Security Assurance, SecAssure 2024, which accepted 8 papers from 14 submissions.

Contents – Part I

CBT Papers

CyberICPS Papers

Contents – Part II

DisA Papers

CPS4CIP Papers

SecAssure Papers

Invited Paper

Establishing Secure and Privacy-Preserving Blockchain Applications Through Real World Cryptography

Pedro Moreno-Sanchez[(✉)]

IMDEA Software Institute, VISA Research, MPI-SP, San Francisco, USA
`pedro.moreno@imdea.org`

1 Introduction

A blockchain is an immutable, append-only data structure (called *ledger*), maintained by a set of participants (called *miners*), using a distributed protocol to reach consensus on the validity of transactions. Although different cryptocurrencies present custom designs to cater different use cases, they all are based on a common principle: maintain a shared, public ledger that contains all the transactions in the past.

While having such a publicly available ledger aids the public verifiability of the transactions contained therein, it is at odds with privacy: Every observer of the ledger can trivially derive who pays what to whom. Yet, privacy is a crucial feature. Users may maintain their transactions hidden (e.g., medical bills or salary); or companies may maintain their businesses hidden from the prying eyes of competitors. Therefore, providing security and privacy simultaneously is an interesting challenge in the realm of cryptocurrencies.

As an illustrative application example, consider the problem of zero-knowledge contingent payments [1]. Alice, an avid fan of brainteasers, has a Sudoku puzzle that they want to know the solution for. To get help solving it, they are willing to pay Bob for the solution. But there are some problems. First, Alice wants Bob to first provide the solution so that they can verify it is correct before paying Bob, whereas Bob insists on not sending the solution to Alice until they get paid (*atomicity*). Second, when Alice pays Bob in a certain cryptocurrency for the solution, they both want that a third party observing the ledger does not learn who pays what to whom (*privacy*). Finally, Alice wants to rely on a payment mechanism that permits them to use any of the existing cryptocurrencies (*interoperability*). In general, it is interesting to develop blockchain applications that provide atomicity, privacy and interoperability guarantees.

Existing works approach these goals from different angles. On the one hand, privacy-focussed cryptocurrencies (e.g., Monero or Zcash) provide certain level of privacy for their transactions. However, they do not offer atomicity guarantees since each transaction is handled separately, and they do not support smart

J. Garcia-Alfaro et al. (Eds.): ESORICS 2024 Workshops, LNCS 15263, pp. 3–6, 2025.
https://doi.org/10.1007/978-3-031-82349-7_1

contracts to encode the application logic within. On the other hand, cryptocurrencies with support for smart contracts (e.g., Ethereum), allows to encode the application logic within a smart contract, enabling atomicity in that all the operations that need to be executed atomically are done so within the same call to the contract. Yet, this approach reveals who pays to whom, and it is restricted to cryptocurrencies with smart contract support.

In this keynote, we present our quest for designing blockchain applications that aim to simultaneously provide atomicity, privacy and interoperability.

2   Our Approach

We consider a blockchain model where a user is represented with a pair of public, private key pair $(\mathbf{pk}, \mathbf{sk})$. A transaction is a simple data structure represented by a tuple $(\mathbf{pk}_A, \mathbf{pk}_B, \alpha)$, denoting that the user represented by $\mathbf{pk}_A$ sends α coins to the user represented by $\mathbf{pk}_B$. Such a transaction is authorized if it is accompanied by a signature from the secret key $\mathbf{sk}_A$ corresponding to $\mathbf{pk}_A$. We call such a simple model $\mathcal{B}_{gen}$. Therefore, developing blockchain applications that work over $\mathcal{B}_{gen}$ would help with interoperability since the minimal functionality required is shared among virtually all existing cryptocurrencies.

Our approach then is twofold. First, we aim at designing cryptographic building blocks that only require interactions with $\mathcal{B}_{gen}$. An illustrative example of this research direction is our work on adaptor signatures [2]. An adaptor signature scheme is an extension of standard digital signatures that ties together the creation of a digital signature (e.g., as required to authorize a transaction) and the leakage of a secret value. Imagine that Bob holds a secret s and Alice wants to pay Bob in exchange for learning s. For that, Alice can rely on adaptor signatures as follows. First, Alice uses their secret key $\mathbf{sk}_A$ to create a *pre-signature* $\hat{\sigma}$ on a transaction that pays Bob. Bob can *adapt* the pre-signature $\hat{\sigma}$ into a valid signature σ using the secret s and publish it in $\mathcal{B}_{gen}$ to receive the payment. After doing so, Alice observes the signature σ previously created by Bob and, using the pre-signature and signature pair $(\hat{\sigma}, \sigma)$, Alice can *extract* the secret s.

Similar to adaptor signatures, we have contributed other cryptographic building blocks that only require interactions with $\mathcal{B}_{gen}$, such as verifiable witness encryption for threshold signatures [3].

Second, building upon the abovementioned cryptographic building blocks, we aim at designing cryptographic protocols that implement the synchronization of blockchain transactions as required by the different blockchain applications. As an illustrative example, we next overview how to design an atomic swap of coins between Alice and Bob using the abovementioned adaptor signatures [4].

In a two-party atomic swap, two users (e.g., Alice and Bob) hold coins in two different blockchains, governed by their private keys $\mathbf{sk}_A$ and $\mathbf{sk}_B$, correspondingly. The goal is to design a protocol to exchange their coins atomically, meaning that Alice transfers their coins to Bob if and only if Bob also transfers their coins to Alice. For that, Alice and Bob can rely on adaptor signatures as follows. Alice computes a fresh secret s and creates a *pre-signature* $\hat{\sigma}_A$ on the transaction that transfer their coins to Bob. Bob, upon receiving $\hat{\sigma}_A$, creates and sends to Alice a *pre-signature* $\hat{\sigma}_B$ on the transaction that transfer their coins to Alice. Alice, who knew the secret s from the beginning, can *adapt* $\hat{\sigma}_B$ into a valid signature σ_B and publish it in $\mathcal{B}_{gen}$ to obtain Bob's coins. When Bob observes σ_B, they can *extract* the secret s using the pair $(\hat{\sigma}_B, \sigma_B)$. Finally, using such a secret s, Bob can *adapt* $\hat{\sigma}_A$ into a valid signature σ_A and publish it in $\mathcal{B}_{gen}$ to obtain the Alice's coins.

Similar to the aforementioned application of two-party atomic swaps, in our research we have shown how to use the building blocks of adaptor signatures and verifiable witness encryption for threshold signatures in other blockchain applications such as payment channels [2], payment channel networks [5], virtual channels [6], coin mixing [7,8], oracle-based contracts [3] and zero-knowledge contingent payments [9].

The design followed by the aforementioned applications requires expertise in both cryptography and (blockchain) systems. Yet, this design comes with several advantages in practice. The thereby designed blockchain applications impose a lower computation and communication overhead on the users than relying on off-the-shelf cryptographic tools such as multi-party computation. It is possible to prove cryptographic properties of these blockchain applications using the cryptographic properties of the corresponding building blocks. This design paves the way for interoperability since only a simple functionality as modeled by $\mathcal{B}_{gen}$ is required. Last, but not least, it helps with privacy since only standard transactions transfering coins among users are published in $\mathcal{B}_{gen}$, thereby hiding the logic of the blockchain application.

Yet, it would be interesting to reduce the number of transactions that these blockchain applications require to include in the $\mathcal{B}_{gen}$, so that the overall overhead in the blockchain is reduced. Towards this goal, we can rely on *payment channels*. A payment channel allows to perform arbitrarily many payments between two users without requiring to include all of them in the blockchain. In a bit more detail, a payment channel can be seen as the digital counterpart of a retailer's gift card. First, both users of the payment channel submit a transaction to the blockchain that locks their coins into a shared account, effectively *opening* the channel. Then, both users can pay to each other *off-chain* by exchanging digitally signed statements of the new balances in the channel. They can repeat this operation arbitrarily many times. Finally, one of the users can *close* the channel by submitting to the blockchain the last agreed statement of their balance.

In summary, in our research towards achieving *security*, *privacy*, and *interoperability* for blockchain applications, we pursue a modular approach where (i) we assume a simple, generic blockchain $\mathcal{B}_{gen}$; (ii) we design cryptographic building blocks that seamlessly operate with $\mathcal{B}_{gen}$; and (iii) we use these building blocks towards designing blockchain applications as cryptographic protocols where users jointly synchronize what transactions and in which order need to be submitted to the blockchain. Additionally, to improve upon privacy and scalability, we also design blockchain applications that interact with payment channels instead of submitting all the transactions to $\mathcal{B}_{gen}$.

Acknowledgements. This work has been partially supported by the ESPADA project (grant PID2022-142290OB-I00) and by the PRODIGY project (grant ED2021-132464B-I00) both from the agency MCIN/AEI/10.13039/501100011033 FEDER, UE, and the European Union NextGenerationEU/ PRTR.

References

1. Maxwell, G.: Zero knowledge contingent payment. https://en.bitcoin.it/wiki/Zero_Knowledge_Contingent_Payment
2. Aumayr, L.: Generalized channels from limited blockchain scripts and adaptor signatures. In: Tibouchi, M., Wang, H. (eds.) ASIACRYPT 2021. Part II, volume 13091 of LNCS, pp. 635–664. Springer, Cham (2021). https://doi.org/10.1007/978-3-030-92075-3_22
3. Madathil, V., Thyagarajan, S.A.K., Vasilopoulos, D., Fournier, L., Malavolta, G., Moreno-Sanchez, P.: Cryptographic oracle-based conditional payments. In: NDSS 2023. The Internet Society, February (2023)
4. Thyagarajan, D.S.K., Malavolta, G., Moreno-Sanchez, P.: Universal atomic swaps: secure exchange of coins across all blockchains. In: IEEE Symposium on Security and Privacy, pp. 1299–1316. IEEE Computer Society Press, May (2022)
5. Malavolta, G., Moreno-Sanchez, P., Schneidewind, C., Kate, A., Maffei, M.: Anonymous multi-hop locks for blockchain scalability and interoperability. In: NDSS 2019. The Internet Society, Februar (2019)
6. Lukas Aumayr, et al.: Bitcoin-compatible virtual channels. In: 2021 IEEE Symposium on Security and Privacy, pp. 901–918. IEEE Computer Society Press (May 2021)
7. Tairi, E., Moreno-Sanchez, P., Maffei, M.: A^2L: Anonymous atomic locks for scalability in payment channel hubs. In: 2021 IEEE Symposium on Security and Privacy, pp. 1834–1851. IEEE Computer Society Press (May 2021)
8. Glaeser, N., Maffei, M., Malavolta,, G., Moreno-Sanchez, P., Tairi, E., Thyagarajan, A.K., Foundations of coin mixing services. In Yin, H., Stavrou, A., Cremers, H., Shi, editors, *ACM CCS 2022*, pp. 1259–1273. ACM Press (November 2022)
9. Castejon-Molina, D., Vasilopoulos, D, Moreno-Sanchez, P.: MixBuy: Contingent payment in the presence of coin mixers. Cryptology ePrint Archive, Report 2024/953 (2024)

DPM Papers

Preface to the Proceedings of DPM 2024

This volume contains the post-proceedings of the 19th International Workshop on Data Privacy Management (DPM 2024), which was organized as a part of the 29th European Symposium on Research in Computer Security (ESORICS 2024). The DPM series started in 2005 when the first workshop took place in Tokyo (Japan). Since that inaugural meeting it has been held in different venues: Atlanta, USA (2006); Istanbul, Turkey (2007); Saint Malo, France (2009); Athens, Greece (2010); Leuven, Belgium (2011); Pisa, Italy (2012); Egham, UK (2013); Wrocław, Poland (2014); Vienna, Austria (2015); Crete, Greece (2016); Oslo, Norway (2017); Barcelona, Spain (2018); Luxembourg, Luxembourg (2019); Guildford, UK (2020); Darmstadt, Germany (2021); Copenhagen, Denmark (2022); and The Hague, The Netherlands (2023).

The 2024 DPM event was held in Bydgoszcz, Poland on September 19th as a part of the ESORICS 2024 workshops. All presentations were in person, and the workshop was structured to allow for a thorough presentation of each contribution's key ideas and allowed for subsequent discussion from attendees that provided new insights on the contributed work and facilitated nascent directions for subsequent work.

We received 24 submissions. All papers were assigned to at least 3 program committee members to provide commentary about each paper, and we are thankful to our PC members who returned all reviews in a timely way. Each submission was evaluated based on its significance, novelty, and technical quality. The program committee performed a thorough single-blind review process, undertook consensus discussions, and selected 7 regular papers and 6 short papers for presentation at the workshop.

The workshop was initiated with a joint session with the 8th International Workshop on Cryptocurrencies and Blockchain Technologies (CBT 2024) where Pedro Moreno-Sánchez from the IMDEA Software Institute provided insights into the cryptographic underpinnings that impact on core technologies that aim to establish secure and privacy-preserving blockchain applications. This was an excellent kick-off to both DPM and CBT because of the interesting overlap between these related technologies and directions. A summary of the talk is also included in this book, as an invited paper authored by Pedro Moreno-Sánchez.

The DPM 2024 workshop held privacy questions at its core and included papers that address traditional challenges associated with cryptographic approaches while seeking to address increasing challenges posed by technologies such as artificial intelligence and machine learning. The workshop papers also had an important goal of understanding the pragmatic challenges of incorporating privacy into real applications to ensure that utility is maintained while privacy is preserved.

We would like to thank everyone who helped to organize the event, including all the members of the organizing committees for both ESORICS 2024 and DPM 2024. Our gratitude goes to Michał Choraś and Sokratis Katsikas, General Chairs of ESORICS 2024, Marek Pawlicki, Workshop Chair of ESORICS 2024, and all the people in the

ESORICS 2024 organization. A very special thank you goes to all the DPM 2024 Program Committee members, additional reviewers, and, most notably, all the authors who submitted papers, and to all the workshop attendees.

We also thank our sponsors for providing support in different forms: *Plan de Recuperación, Transformación y Resiliencia funded* with Next Generation EU funds through the project DANGER INCIBE-C062/23; Spanish Ministry SECURING/NET PID2021-125962OB-C33, and CiberSec+ RED2022-134603-T; Catalan AGAUR SGR2021-00643.

We believe that the papers presented at DPM 2024 will advance our understanding of how to best address the ever-intensifying challenges faced by all who value privacy. The work reported here is both a step forward and a stepping stone to address the next challenges we collectively face.

November 2024   Ken Barker
                                                        Joaquin Garcia-Alfaro
                                                  Guillermo Navarro-Arribas

Organization

19th DPM International Workshop on Data Privacy Management (DPM 2024)

PC Chairs

Ken Barker	University of Calgary, Canada
Joaquin Garcia-Alfaro	Institut Polytechnique de Paris, France
Guillermo Navarro-Arribas	Universitat Autònoma de Barcelona, Spain

Program Committee

Esma Aïmeur	University of Montreal, Canada
Abderrahim Ait Wakrime	Mohammed V University, Morocco
Nora Boulahia-Cuppens	Polytechnique Montréal, Canada
Jordi Casas-Roma	Universitat Autònoma de Barcelona, Spain
Jordi Castellà-Roca	Universitat Rovira i Virgili, Spain
Depeng Chen	Anhui University, China
Mauro Conti	University of Padua, Italy
Mathieu Cunche	University of Lyon, France
Mila Dalla Preda	University of Verona, Italy
Sabrina De Capitani di Vimercati	Universita degli Studi di Milano, Italy
Jose M. De Fuentes	Universidad Carlos III de Madrid, Spain
Josep Domingo-Ferrer	Universitat Rovira i Virgili, Spain
Sebastien Gambs	Université du Québec à Montréal, Canada
Lorena González Manzano	Universidad Carlos III de Madrid, Spain
M. Emre Gursoy	Koç University, Turkey
Guy-Vincent Jourdan	University of Ottawa, Canada
Marc Juarez	University of Edinburgh, UK
Christos Kalloniatis	University of the Aegean, Greece
Bruce Kapron	University of Victoria, Canada
Sokratis Katsikas	Norwegian University of Science and Technology, Norway
Christophe Kiennert	Télécom SudParis, France
Romain Laborde	Paul Sabatier University, France
Patrick Lacharme	ENSICAEN, France
Giovanni Livraga	University of Milan, Italy
Brad Malin	Vanderbilt University, USA

Lukas Malina	Brno University of Technology, Czech Republic
David Megias	Universitat Oberta de Catalunya, Spain
Chris Mitchell	Royal Holloway, University of London, UK
Gerardo Pelosi	Politecnico di Milano, Italy
Cristina Perez-Sola	Universitat Autònoma de Barcelona, Spain
Kai Rannenberg	Goethe University Frankfurt, Germany
Isabel Praça	GECAD/ISEP, Portugal
Ruben Rios	Universidad de Málaga, Spain
Pierangela Samarati	Università degli Studi di Milano, Italy
Vicenç Torra	Umeå University, Sweden
Alexandre Viejo	Universitat Rovira i Virgili, Spain
Isabel Wagner	University of Basel, Switzerland
Jens Weber	University of Victoria, Canada
Lena Wiese	University of Göttingen, Germany
Nicola Zannone	Eindhoven University of Technology, The Netherlands

Additional Reviewers

Haoying Zhang
Chao Yan
Sergio Martínez
Sascha Loebner
Cristòfol Daudén-Esmel
Luis Del Vasto Terrientes

Privacy-Preserving Optimal Parameter Selection for Collaborative Clustering

Maryam Ghasemian and Erman Ayday[✉]

Case Western Reserve University, Cleveland, OH, USA
{maryam.ghasemian,erman.ayday}@case.edu

Abstract. This study investigates the optimal selection of parameters for collaborative clustering while ensuring data privacy. We focus on key clustering algorithms within a collaborative framework, where multiple data owners combine their data. A semi-trusted server assists in recommending the most suitable clustering algorithm and its parameters. Our findings indicate that the privacy parameter (ϵ) minimally impacts the server's recommendations, but an increase in ϵ raises the risk of membership inference attacks, where sensitive information might be inferred. To mitigate these risks, we implement differential privacy techniques, particularly the Randomized Response mechanism, to add noise and protect data privacy. Our approach demonstrates that high-quality clustering can be achieved while maintaining data confidentiality, as evidenced by metrics such as the Adjusted Rand Index and Silhouette Score. This study contributes to privacy-aware data sharing, optimal algorithm and parameter selection, and effective communication between data owners and the server.

Keywords: Clustering · Privacy · Differential Privacy · Membership Inference Attack · Data Mining · Machine Learning

1 Introduction

Clustering, a fundamental technique in unsupervised machine learning, involves identifying patterns in unlabeled data. This process includes feature selection, measuring data similarity, and evaluating algorithms [21,35]. There are several types of clustering algorithms: partitioning based [25,34], distribution based [19, 22], density based [3,6,31], and hierarchical [11,24]. Our study concentrates on selecting the optimal hyperparameters for key representative clustering algorithms from each category, within a privacy-preserving collaborative framework. Specifically, we explore K-Means (partitioning-based), Hierarchical Clustering (HC, hierarchical), Gaussian Mixture Models (GMM, distribution-based), and DBSCAN (density-based).Choosing the right parameters is crucial as it directly impacts the accuracy and effectiveness of the clustering results, thereby influencing the insights derived from the data while maintaining privacy.

Motivated by the fact that clustering algorithm perform better with larger amount of data and that datasets are typically distributed across different parties, cooperative clustering and collaborative clustering [7] techniques have

© The Author(s), under exclusive license to Springer Nature Switzerland AG 2025
J. Garcia-Alfaro et al. (Eds.): ESORICS 2024 Workshops, LNCS 15263, pp. 13–32, 2025.
https://doi.org/10.1007/978-3-031-82349-7_2

been popular. In cooperative clustering, each party generates its own clustering results, and a final clustering is performed via a post-processing step once individual processes are completed. In contrast, collaborative clustering aims to leverage the contributions of multiple parties by exchanging information about local data, current hypothesized clustering, or algorithm parameters to benefit each other's computations. Due to privacy concerns of the parties, privacy-preserving algorithms have been proposed during collaborative clustering, which aim to protect the sensitive information in each parties' local dataset. However, depending on the type of clustering (partitioning-based, distribution-based, density-based, or hierarchical clustering), parties need to decide on some common input parameters. Selection of such parameters significantly effect the accuracy of the clustering algorithm and existing privacy-preserving collaborative clustering techniques assume such parameters are pre-selected. On the other hand, such parameters typically depend on the distribution of the federated dataset of the parties and they should be determined in a privacy-preserving way before the collaborative clustering. In addition, parties also need to decide the type of the clustering algorithm depending on their federated dataset as different types of algorithms perform differently in particular datasets. To fill this gap, we focus on a server-assisted scenario for collaborative clustering, aiming to evaluate server-provided input parameters and clustering algorithms. We experiment with K-Means, Hierarchical Clustering, Gaussian Mixture Models, and DBSCAN using a labeled numeric dataset, assessing results with metrics like Adjusted Rand Index (ARI) and Silhouette Score.

Using a semi-trusted server enhances privacy and helps select optimal clustering algorithms and parameters without burdening data owners with large computational resources. Differential privacy techniques safeguard data throughout the process. Our findings show that this approach effectively maintains data privacy while delivering high-quality clustering, evidenced by ARI and Silhouette Scores. The Randomized Response mechanism efficiently preserves data structure while protecting privacy.

In this work, we make the following contributions to the context of collaborative clustering with hyper parameter recommendation:

1. Privacy-Preserving and Efficient Communication: We introduce a novel privacy-preserving step in the collaborative clustering process, where data owners share parts of their datasets with the server after applying the randomized response (RR) mechanism to add noise to their respective datasets. This step enhances privacy protection by concealing sensitive information while still allowing for meaningful analysis. Additionally, we establish a seamless communication framework between the data owners and the server, ensuring privacy-preserving data sharing. Unlike previous works that primarily rely on pre-selected clustering parameters and then apply encryption techniques in distributed or collaborative clustering, our approach goes beyond by addressing the challenge of parameter selection by determining the optimal clustering algorithm along with the respective hyper-parameters and incorporating the randomized response (RR) mechanism to introduce noise and safeguard sensitive information during data sharing.

2. Optimal Algorithm Selection: The server plays a crucial role in identifying the optimal clustering algorithm and its corresponding hyper-parameters. By employing various methods, the server evaluates different algorithms and provides data owners with recommendations for achieving the best clustering results. This step helps alleviate the burden of algorithm selection and parameter tuning for data owners.
3. Server-Data Owner Interaction: The server communicates chosen algorithms and parameters back to the data owners, ensuring that all parties are aligned with the recommended strategies. This facilitates a coordinated effort that enhances both accuracy and efficiency.

In summary, our study contributes to privacy-aware data sharing, optimal algorithm and hyper-parameter selection, and effective communication between data owners and the server. The results revealed that the amount of noisy data shared and the privacy budget (ϵ) did not significantly affect the server's algorithm and parameter recommendations. However, an increase in the privacy budget was found to elevate the risk of membership inference attacks, suggesting a trade-off between privacy protection and attack vulnerability.

2   Related Work

Our study reviews privacy-preserving approaches in distributed and collaborative clustering, categorized by algorithm types, introduced in Sect. 1. Existing methods typically use predefined algorithms and hyperparameters, while our contribution dynamically identifies optimal clustering algorithms and hyperparameters to enhance collaborative clustering performance in a privacy-aware manner.

Bi et al.'s PriKPM scheme [5] introduces a privacy-preserving k-prototype clustering method using additive secret sharing to handle mixed data types in cloud environments, addressing privacy concerns. This framework ensures clustering privacy through secure processing by dual servers, validated by experiments demonstrating computational efficiency and accuracy.

Wang et al. [33] propose a privacy-preserving k-means clustering model for IoT, using multi-key fully homomorphic encryption for secure cloud-edge computations. The model optimizes resource use and ensures data privacy through secure communication protocols, demonstrating the feasibility of privacy-sensitive cloud-edge collaborations with minimal overhead.

Further contributions include Jagannathan and Wright's [20], as well as Baby et al.'s [4], protocols for privacy-preserving distributed K-Means clustering, designed for data partitioned arbitrarily. These protocols maintain data confidentiality while following the K-Means algorithm's iterative nature, allowing secure computation of cluster centers and distances without data exposure.

Additionally, Lin et al. [22] present an expectation maximization-based strategy for private clustering across distributed sites, utilizing secure summation to protect horizontally partitioned data. Liu et al. [23] offer privacy-preserving

Table 1. Overview of Adversary and System Models in Related Works

Reference	Clustering Algorithm	System Model	Adversary Model	Privacy Technique
Bi et al. [5]	k-Prototype	Cloud-based with dual servers	Semi-honest adversary	Additive Secret Sharing
Wang et al. [33]	k-Means	IoT ecosystem with cloud-edge collaboration	Semi-honest adversary	Multi-Key Fully Homomorphic Encryption
Jagannathan [20], Baby et al. [4]	k-Means	Arbitrarily partitioned data, distributed	Honest-but-curious adversary	Secure Multiparty Computation (SMC)
Lin et al. [22]	Expectation Maximization	Distributed sites with horizontally partitioned data	Honest-but-curious adversary	Secure Summation
Liu et al. [23]	DBSCAN	Distributed with various data partitions	Honest-but-curious adversary	Additive Homomorphic Encryption
Meng et al. [24]	Hierarchical Clustering	Two-party model	Semi-honest adversary	Homomorphic Encryption and Garbled Circuits
Our Work	Multiple (K-Means, HC, GMM, DBSCAN)	Semi-trusted server in collaborative clustering	Semi-honest server, honest-but-curious data owners	Local Differential Privacy, Randomized Response

DBSCAN techniques for data distributed in various ways, employing a Multiplication protocol based on additive homomorphic encryption for secure clustering.

Meng et al. [24] introduce privacy-preserving hierarchical clustering algorithms, emphasizing a two-party model that employs homomorphic encryption and garbled circuits. Their approach provides a dendrogram depicting the clustering process, enriched with detailed merge metadata.

These diverse approaches share a common goal of enhancing privacy in collaborative clustering, yet they employ fixed algorithms and parameters. Our study seeks to advance this domain by focusing on adaptive parameter selection to achieve optimal clustering results, reflecting a significant leap toward balancing privacy preservation and analytical utility in collaborative settings. To provide a clearer comparison of the various approaches, Table 1 summarizes the adversary models and system models considered in the related works discussed above.

3   Background

In this section we review some background and definitions of different clustering algorithms and clustering evaluation metrics as well as the local differential privacy.

3.1 Clustering Algorithms

This study explores four clustering algorithms: partitioning-based, distribution-based, density-based, and hierarchical [3,6,11,19,22,24,25,34]. K-Means, a widely used unsupervised algorithm, partitions data into K non-overlapping clusters by minimizing distances between data points and centroids [25,34]. Gaussian Mixture Models (GMM) handle clusters with varying sizes and correlations by assuming data is generated from a mixture of Gaussian distributions [19,22]. DBSCAN identifies clusters of arbitrary shapes based on data density and automatically detects outliers, without needing to predefine the number of clusters, though it is sensitive to its parameters: neighborhood size (*Eps*) and minimum points (*minpoint*) [3,6]. Hierarchical clustering creates a tree of clusters without a pre-specified number, using either a bottom-up or top-down approach. It is useful for hierarchical data but is computationally intensive and varies with the linkage criterion used [14,15,17,24,36].

Table 2. Table of symbols and notations.

Symbol	Description
D_i	Dataset of each data owner i
ND_i	Noisy data of each data owner i produced as a result of RR
f_{NDi}	Portion of the noisy data, ND_i, shared with server from each data owner i
RR	Randomized Response mechanism
ϵ, eps	epsilon, Privacy Parameter
Eps	Epsilon, Maximum distance between clusters in DBSCAN
k	Number of clusters
ARI	Adjusted Rand Index
CH	Calinski-Harabasz Index
Homo	Homogeneity of the clusters
Comp	Completeness

3.2 Evaluation Metrics for Clustering Algorithms

This section outlines the evaluation metrics used to assess the effectiveness of the proposed privacy-preserving collaborative clustering approach. To measure the performance of our approach, we use the following metrics, each selected for its capability to capture various dimensions of clustering quality and privacy preservation:

Adjusted Rand Index (ARI): Measures the similarity between two clusterings, with scores ranging from -1 (independent clusterings) to 1 (perfect agreement). *Higher* ARI values indicate better clustering performance.

Silhouette Coefficient Score: Evaluates cluster cohesion and separation, with scores ranging from -1 to 1. *Higher* values indicate better-defined clusters.

Calinski-Harabasz Index (CH): Measures clustering quality based on the ratio of between-cluster dispersion to within-cluster dispersion. *Higher* CH values indicate better separation between clusters.

Classification Accuracy: We also added classification accuracy to our evaluation framework, a metric that measures the proportion of correct predictions. Although unusual in unsupervised learning tasks like clustering, it helps evaluate how well cluster assignments match predefined labels when known. This metric is key in scenarios with known data classifications, allowing for direct comparison between our privacy-preserving clusters and actual categories.

Table 2 contains a list of symbols and notations used throughout this paper.

3.3 Local Differential Privacy and Randomized Response Mechanism

Local Differential Privacy (LDP) [8,10] is a more restricted form of traditional differential privacy [9]. Unlike traditional differential privacy, LDP does not rely on a trusted third party and provides a higher level of data protection for users. In LDP, each user modifies their own data before sharing them with a data aggregator. The aggregator only sees the perturbed data, ensuring privacy. An algorithm A satisfies ϵ-local differential privacy (ϵ-LDP) if, for any input values $v1$ and $v2$: $Pr[A(v1) = y] \leq e^\epsilon Pr[A(v2) = y]$, This condition holds true for all possible outputs of the algorithm A. The randomized response mechanism is commonly used to achieve $\epsilon - LDP$ [12]. In this mechanism, an individual reports the true value of a single bit of information with probability p and flips the true value with probability $1 - p$, following the $(ln\frac{p}{1-p}) - LDP$ property. Although initially defined for binary inputs (e.g., yes/no), the randomized response mechanism can be generalized. To achieve ϵ-LDP, the generalized randomized response mechanism [18] shares the correct value with probability $p = \frac{e^\epsilon}{(e^\epsilon+m-1)}$ where m is the number of possible states. Each incorrect value is shared with the probability. $q = \frac{1}{(e^\epsilon+m-1)}$. A data aggregator collects the perturbed values from individuals and aims to calculate the frequency of values in the population while preserving privacy.

4   System and Threat Models

In this section, we provide an explanation of the system and threat model for privacy-preserving hyper-parameter identification for collaborative clustering.

4.1   System Model

In the proposed system model, the party who aims to collaborate in clustering with other data owners is referred to as the "data owner" (or researcher), while the server represents a third party that assists the data owners in identifying the optimal clustering algorithm and hyper-parameters. Our approach focuses on the preliminary stages before actual clustering occurs in a collaborative environment. Our objective is to identify the optimal algorithm and input parameters for collaborative clustering among multiple data owners who wish to maintain data privacy. As discussed, different types of clustering algorithms perform differently depending on the type and distribution of the datasets, and hence it is crucial to identify the optimal clustering algorithm type beforehand. Once these optimal conditions are determined, clustering can then be executed using one of the existing algorithms mentioned in Sect. 3.1. In this context, data owners selectively share differentially private data with a semi-trusted server. This server plays a crucial intermediary role, analyzing the noisy data to recommend the most suitable clustering algorithm and corresponding hyper-parameters for the data received from data owners.

4.2   Threat Model

In this section, we outline the considered threats in our proposed scheme, which involve both the server and the data owners.

Server: In this study, the server is considered semi-honest, indicating it might engage in malicious activities, such as extracting sensitive information from the datasets of the individual parties (data owners), but it honestly follows the protocol execution. The server's role is pivotal, yet poses a risk of privacy violations. Privacy attacks like membership inference [28–30], deanonymization [26,27,29], and attribute inference [13,29] are concerns. Membership inference attacks aim to determine whether a specific record is in the dataset. Deanonymization attacks link anonymized data to actual identities using external information. Attribute inference attacks deduce sensitive attributes from observed data. In our setting, the most relevant is membership inference, where the server tries to determine if a specific record is part of one of the data owners' datasets, leading to privacy breaches. Our proposed scheme prevents this by sharing only a small, differentially-private portion of the dataset (f_{NDi}), which makes deanonymization more complex and significantly reduces the threat of membership inference.

Data Owners: In our system model, we assume that the parties involved in the collaborative clustering are honest but curious. This means that while they trust each other and do not engage in malicious behavior, they may still be interested in learning about each other's data. This assumption is based on the fact that other literature (such as those in Sect. 2) has already addressed the challenges posed by malicious or semi-honest data owners in collaborative clustering using privacy-enhancing techniques like homomorphic encryption. In our work, we specifically focus on the task of selecting the optimal algorithm and hyper-parameters for the clustering process. By concentrating on this aspect, we aim to improve the efficiency and effectiveness of collaborative clustering while assuming a cooperative environment among the data owners.

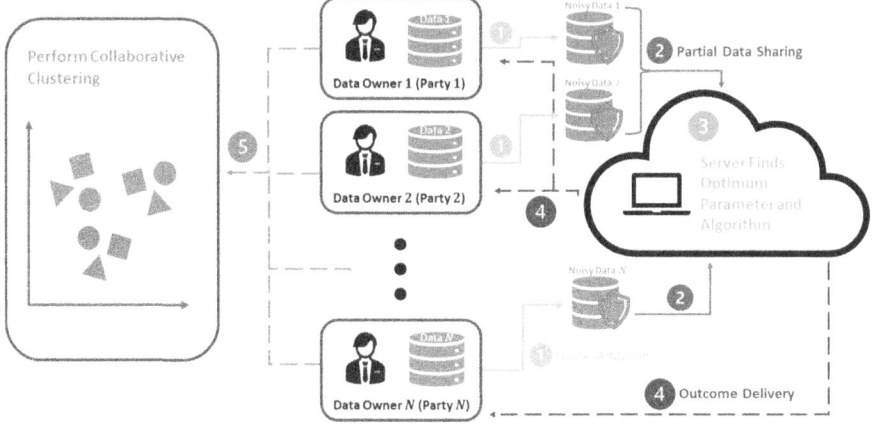

Fig. 1. Comprehensive five-step process, highlighting the interaction between multiple data owners and the server. We show how data are shared, processed for noise addition (to achieve differential privacy), and then utilized in a collaborative clustering algorithm, all while maintaining strict privacy protocols. In step (1), data owners add noise to part of their datasets using randomized response (RR). Data owners send a portion of their noisy data to the server in step (2). In step (3), the server applies various methods to find the optimum algorithm with its corresponding hyper parameter(s), and the server provides its outcome (algorithm and parameter) to the data owners in step (4). Finally, the data owners perform collaborative clustering based on server suggestions in step (5).

5 Proposed Solution and Framework

Our proposed system model and framework, as shown in Figure 1, encompass five fundamental steps:

Step 1-Noise Addition to Datasets: Data owners $(DO_{1 \to N})$ add noise to their datasets (to achieve differential privacy) through randomized response (RR) $(\{D_1, D_2, ..., D_N\} \to \{ND_1, ND_2, ..., ND_N\})$. In this process, we utilize a generalized version of the RR mechanism as mentioned in Sect. 3.3, allowing data owners to use perturbed data directly without encoding. The number of possible states for each feature (attribute) can vary according to the specific domain.

Step 2-Data Sharing with the Server: Data owners transmit a portion of their noisy data (f_{NDi}) to the server. During this step, data owners share their perturbed data with the server, enabling it to analyze the data and provide recommendations for the clustering process.

Step 3-Server-Based Algorithm and Parameter Selection: The server selects the best clustering algorithm and its hyperparameters using collaborative clustering, where multiple data owners keep their data private with the Generalized Randomized Response (RR) mechanism. Each owner sends noisy data to a semi-trusted server, which combines the datasets and uses methods like the elbow method and silhouette method [37] to determine optimal parameters for algorithms such as K-Means, hierarchical clustering, Gaussian mixture models. For DBSCAN, it sets the *Eps* value using the k-Nearest Neighbors algorithm and adjusts the *minpoint* parameter based on data dimensionality, following different recommendations from prior research [14,32].

One of the challenges the server faces is the absence of ground truth data. To address this, the server uses internal performance evaluation metrics that do not require ground truth, such as the Silhouette Coefficient and the Calinski-Harabasz (CH) index. These metrics objectively measure the effectiveness of different algorithms, guiding the server in its selection process.

Here is the selection mechanism that server adapts to select the optimum clustering algorithm and its corresponding parameters for the data it received from data owners: The input to the selection algorithm includes a combined dataset from all data owners (*data*), a list of candidate clustering algorithms (*algorithms*), and a threshold parameter set to 0.1 (α). The output is the optimal clustering algorithm (*best_algorithm*) and its corresponding parameters (*best_parameters*). The procedure begins by initializing *max_silhouette* to $-\infty$, *best_algorithm* to *None*, *best_parameters* to *None*, and *best_ch_index* to $-\infty$. It evaluates all algorithms, updating *max_silhouette* if the Silhouette score is higher. The algorithm then sets a silhouette threshold (*max_silhouette* $- \alpha$) and selects algorithms within this range with the highest CH index, updating *best_algorithm*, *best_parameters*, and *best_ch_index* accordingly.

Step 4-Communication of Recommendations: The server communicates the recommended clustering algorithm and its parameters to the data owners, based on the analysis of the shared data.

Step 5-Execution of Collaborative Clustering: Data owners apply the suggested algorithm and hyper-parameters for collaborative clustering. As discussed in Sect. 2, previous approaches often used encryption for distributed or collaborative clustering. In contrast, this study focuses on selecting the optimal algorithm and hyper-parameters, assuming mutual trust among data owners for clustering on the combined dataset. Further details are provided in Sect. 4.2.

By following these steps, our framework provides recommendations for the optimal clustering algorithm and its hyper-parameters when data owners wish to perform clustering in a collaborative environment.

6 Evaluation

6.1 Datasets

We use the Obesity dataset [2] (2,111 records, 17 features) and the Extended Iris dataset [1] (1,200 rows, 20 features) which is an enhanced version of the classic Iris dataset [16]. The Obesity dataset assesses obesity levels based on diet and physical condition, while the Extended Iris dataset provides detailed biological and ecological information about the iris flower. These datasets were chosen due to their varying characteristics and complexity, which provide a comprehensive evaluation of our proposed approach across different types of data distributions and clustering challenges.

6.2   Metric Significance and Evaluation Approach

ARI, Silhouette Score, classification accuracy, and Calinski-Harabasz Index (CH) provide a comprehensive performance view. ARI and Silhouette Score assess internal cluster consistency and separation, while classification accuracy offers external validation, and CH highlights cluster distinctness. Together, these metrics enable a thorough assessment of both the clustering effectiveness and the impact of privacy-preserving techniques on data utility. In our evaluation, we analyze these metrics under varying conditions of data perturbation and privacy budget settings to explore the trade-offs between clustering quality and privacy preservation. The goal is to achieve optimal hyper-parameter selection that balances these aspects effectively, demonstrating the practical utility of our approach in collaborative clustering scenarios.

6.3   Evaluation Results

The datasets were pre-processed by converting categorical variables to numerical values for analysis. To determine the optimal number of clusters, we applied the elbow and silhouette methods, as detailed in Sect. 5. Our experiments, particularly under varying privacy budgets (ϵ), aimed to identify the most effective method for our data. The results for *dataset 1* are shown in Table 3.

Given that *dataset 1* has 7 clusters and *dataset 2* has 3, our analysis shows that the elbow method outperforms the silhouette method in determining the optimal cluster count. Consequently, we use the elbow method for a more detailed analysis, aiding in the selection of the optimal k for clustering algorithms like K-Means, hierarchical clustering, and Gaussian mixture models.

Table 3. Comparison of Silhouette and Elbow Methods for Predicting the Optimal Number of Clusters (k): It highlights the superior performance of the Elbow method in predicting the optimal cluster count, leading to its selection for further analysis in this study.

ϵ	Baseline K	Silhouette K	Elbow K
0.0010	7	2	8
0.1000	7	2	8
1.00	7	2	8
5.00	7	2	7
10.00	7	2	7

Optimum Input Parameter Selection Results on Noisy Datasets: The experimental findings of this study are illustrated in Table 4 and Fig. 2. Table 4 offers a glimpse into the server's input parameter recommendations, based on the analysis of 10% of the noisy data shared by the data owners, with a noise parameter (ϵ) set at 0.1. Figure 2, on the other hand, showcases the clustering outcomes derived from applying these server recommendations to the combined dataset. Notably, the results from this application highlight the superiority of the K-Means clustering algorithm for the combined dataset, a finding that resonates with the server's initial suggestion regarding the most suitable algorithm and hyper-parameter configuration. These findings and recommendations by the server are not merely data points, but they serve as critical guidance for the data owners. They enable the owners to align their clustering strategies with the server's insights, which are rooted in a meticulous analysis of optimal input parameters. This alignment is key to enhancing the effectiveness and accuracy of the clustering process in a collaborative, privacy-preserving data environment.

Table 4. Server Suggestions for Clustering Input Parameters: Recommendations for various clustering algorithms based on 10% shared noisy data ($\epsilon = 0.1$).

Dataset	Algorithm	Data shared to Server	ϵ	K or Eps	Silhouette	CH
	GMM	10%	0.1	k = 8	0.34	301.30
Dataset #1	DBSCAN	10%	0.1	k = 10, Eps = 1	-	-
	K-Means	**10%**	**0.1**	**k = 8**	**0.36**	**318.13**
	HC	10%	0.1	k = 8	0.31	237.61
	GMM	10%	0.1	k = 3	0.23	46.88
Dataset #2	DBSCAN	10%	0.1	k = 6, Eps = 7	-	-
	K-Means	**10%**	**0.1**	**k = 3**	**0.36**	**61.92**
	HC	10%	0.1	k = 3	0.37	51.57

Effect of Privacy Parameter ϵ: We have examined the influence of different levels of ϵ, which perturb the data through the Randomized Response (RR) mechanism, on the server's ability to suggest input parameters for clustering algorithms. In this experiment, the server receives the same amount of data while varying the value of ϵ, and its suggestions are evaluated on the joint dataset without any noise. Experimental results, as shown in Tables 5 and 6, reveal a notable consistency in the server's recommendations.

Regardless of the ϵ value, the server consistently proposes around 7 clusters for the first dataset (Obesity dataset) and approximately 3 clusters for the second dataset (Extended Iris dataset). This consistency closely aligns with the established ground truth, indicating a marginal effect of the privacy parameter ϵ on the server's cluster count recommendations. However, it is important to note that the actual quality of the clusters formed is subject to the specific clustering algorithm employed. For instance, in the first dataset (Obesity dataset), clustering algorithms demonstrate varied effectiveness influenced by different privacy budgets (ϵ), shown in Table 5. K-Means excel, achieving high ARI values, reaching up to 1.0 when less noise introduced to data (higher ϵ), but maintain low

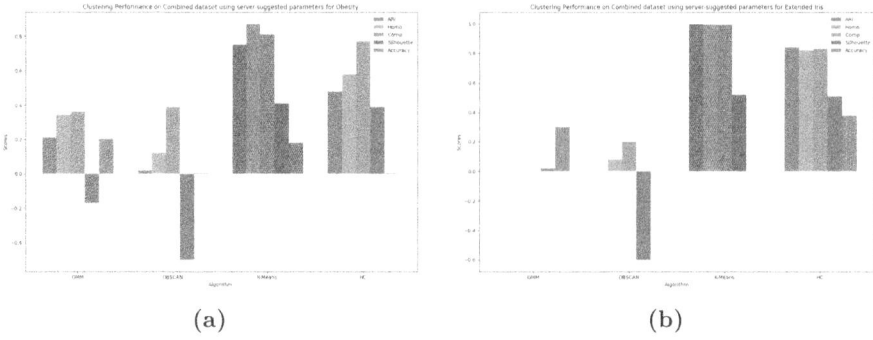

(a)   (b)

Fig. 2. Visual Representation of Clustering Algorithm Performance Across Combined Datasets. This figure illustrates the performance metrics from Table 4 for various clustering algorithms—GMM, DBSCAN, K-Means, and Hierarchical Clustering (HC)—evaluated under conditions of 10% data sharing and a privacy parameter of $\epsilon = 0.1$. Performance metrics including Adjusted Rand Index (ARI), Homogeneity (Homo), Completeness (Comp), Silhouette Score, Calinski-Harabasz Index (CH), and Accuracy are plotted. Algorithms recommended by the server are highlighted with dots, showcasing their superior performance in comparison to others in each dataset scenario.

classification accuracy across all settings, indicating well-defined clusters that do not match predefined labels. Silhouette scores also improve with increased ϵ, suggesting clearer cluster definition. Hierarchical Clustering (HC) shows moderate and stable ARI values around 0.48 but face declines in accuracy under extreme privacy settings, hinting at potential misalignments with actual labels. Gaussian Mixture Models (GMM) record lower ARI and negative silhouette scores, suggesting less effective clustering and poor separation, with fluctuating accuracy that sometimes aligned with class labels under minimal privacy constraints. DBSCAN consistently performs poorly with very low ARI, negative silhouette scores, and minimal accuracy, indicating its unsuitability for this dataset due to its sensitivity to specific parameter settings and data density. In the second dataset (Extended Iris dataset), the performance of clustering algorithms vary significantly under different privacy settings as shown in Table 6. K-Means showcases excellent clustering with ARI values of 0.997 at low and high ϵ levels, though it drops at $\epsilon = 1$, reflecting its sensitivity to privacy settings, despite maintaining high silhouette scores for good cluster separation. However, its consistently low accuracy indicates a misalignment between the clusters and actual class labels. Hierarchical Clustering (HC) remains stable across all metrics and ϵ settings, achieving moderate to high ARI and silhouette scores, and comparatively better accuracy at 0.38, suggesting it aligns more closely with true labels. Gaussian Mixture Models (GMM) exhibit poor performance with negative ARIs and low silhouette scores, with only moderate accuracy, underscoring its challenges in this dataset under privacy constraints. DBSCAN performs poorly, with extremely low ARI, negative silhouette scores, and zero accuracy across all ϵ settings, confirming its unsuitability for the dataset. Overall, the K-Means algorithm excels over others when the server's recommendation was $k = 3$, according to various evaluation metrics. Furthermore, the server's recommendations do not significantly deviate from the original data in both datasets. To understand the behavior of data points in dataset #1, we conducted an analysis by selecting two clusters from the original dataset and applying the RR mechanism with varying ϵ values. This investigation revealed that the RR mechanism effectively maintains the separation between clusters when present.

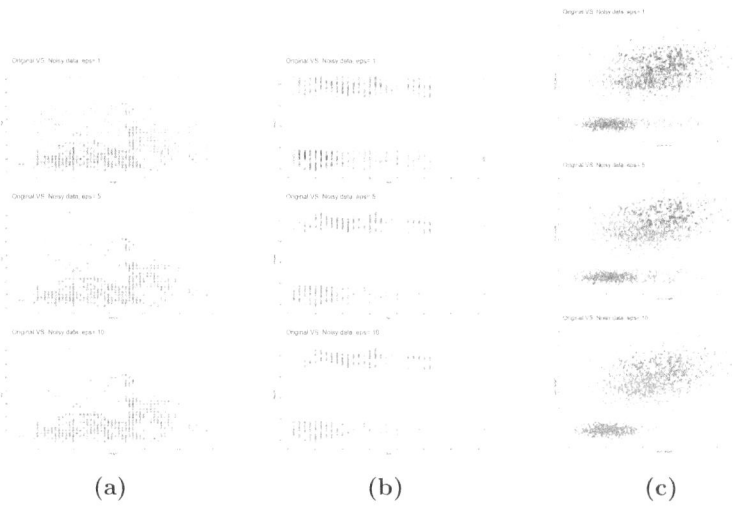

(a)   (b)   (c)

Fig. 3. (a): Contrast in dataset #1 with Overlapping Clusters ($\epsilon = 1, 5, 10$): This part displays the differences between original ('O') and noise-modified ('X') data in closely positioned clusters, colored blue and red. **(b)**: Comparison in dataset #1 with Clear Cluster Gaps ($\epsilon = 1, 5, 10$): Here, the focus is on the impact of the Randomized Response (RR) method on data (original 'O', noisy 'X') in maintaining cluster gaps despite noise variations, balancing privacy with data structure integrity. **(c)**: Original vs. Noisy Data in dataset #2 ($\epsilon = 1, 5, 10$): This section compares original ('O') and noise-affected ('X') data at different privacy levels, using blue, red, and green to show cluster separation effectiveness via the RR mechanism. Note: Plots can be zoomed in for clearer visualization. (Color figure online)

A comparison of Figs. 3a and 3b illustrates that the distinction between two randomly selected clusters is retained even when the data is subjected to different ϵ values. This finding is significant as it demonstrates that despite lower ϵ values possibly leading to a more sparse appearance of the data, the server is still capable of accurately identifying two distinct clusters. This is because the RR mechanism ensures that data points are redistributed within a range akin to their original positions. Furthermore, an analysis of Table 4 shows that the server's recommendations for second dataset closely mirror the original data. An exploration involving a comparison of the original and RR-perturbed data points across different ϵ values, as demonstrated in Fig. 3c, indicates that in two out of the three clusters in dataset #2, data points overlap without a clear gap, while the third cluster's points are notably distanced from the others. This observation reinforces the notion that the RR mechanism is capable of preserving existing gaps between clusters for various ϵ values.

These results underscore the RR mechanism's proficiency in safeguarding the intrinsic structure of the data while incorporating elements of privacy protection. By effectively maintaining the relative distances between data points, the server is enabled to provide precise recommendations for the number of clusters, despite the noise caused by different ϵ values. This highlights the RR mechanism's balance in protecting data privacy while ensuring the accuracy of clustering algorithm suggestions in a privacy-conscious data analysis setting.

Table 5. Differential Impact of Privacy Levels on Clustering Algorithms in the dataset #1. This table explores the performance variations (measured through ARI, Silhouette, and Accuracy) of four distinct clustering algorithms (K-Means, HC, GMM, DBSCAN) at different privacy budget levels ($\epsilon = 0.1, 1, 5$) with a consistent data sharing percentage (10%).

Algorithm	Shared	ϵ	K	ARI	Silhouette	Accuracy
K-Means	10%	0.1	k = 8	0.75	0.41	0.18
K-Means	10%	1	k = 8	0.75	0.41	0.18
K-Means	10%	5	k = 7	1	0.44	0.15
HC	10%	0.1	k = 8	0.481	0.39	0.005
HC	10%	1	k = 7	0.482	0.41	0.17
HC	10%	5	k = 8	0.482	0.41	0.005
GMM	10%	0.1	k = 6	0.185	−0.0143	0.201
GMM	10%	1	k = 8	0.2069	−0.072	0.05
GMM	10%	5	k = 6	0.2008	−0.007	0.14
DBSCAN	10%	0.1	k = 10	0.017	−0.504	0.005
DBSCAN	10%	1	k = 10	0.017	−0.504	0.005
DBSCAN	10%	5	k = 10	0.017	−0.504	0.005

Impact of Shared Data Volume on Server Suggestions: In exploring the influence of shared data volume on clustering algorithm suggestions for both datasets 1 and 2, the results consistently indicate that varying the proportion of data shared with the server does not significantly impact the server's recommendations for clustering input parameters. To investigate this, we conduct experiments where varying amounts of data are shared with the server while keeping the privacy parameter (ϵ) unchanged. This observation is consistent across both datasets and all tested algorithms, as shown in Tables 7 and 8.

Table 6. Influence of Privacy Settings on Clustering Recommendations in the dataset #2. This table details how varying privacy budgets ($\epsilon = 0.1, 1, 5$) affect the recommendations for clustering parameters and subsequent algorithm performance (ARI, Silhouette, and Accuracy) for multiple clustering algorithms (K-Means, HC, GMM, DBSCAN), all with a consistent 10% data sharing arrangement.

Algorithm	Shared	ϵ	K	ARI	Silhouette	Accuracy
K-Means	10%	0.1	k = 3	0.997	0.52	0
K-Means	10%	1	k = 2	0.44	0.57	0.18
K-Means	10%	5	k = 3	0.997	0.52	0
HC	10%	0.1	k = 3	0.84	0.51	0.38
HC	10%	1	k = 3	0.84	0.51	0.38
HC	10%	5	k = 3	0.84	0.51	0.38
GMM	10%	0.1	k = 3	−0.0003	0.021	0.3
GMM	10%	1	k = 2	−0.0004	0.051	0.34
GMM	10%	5	k = 3	−0.0003	0.021	0.3
DBSCAN	10%	0.1	k = 6	0.003	−0.6	0
DBSCAN	10%	1	k = 6	0.003	−0.6	0
DBSCAN	10%	5	k = 6	0.003	−0.6	0

Table 7. Impact of Data Sharing Proportions on Clustering Algorithms' Performance in the dataset #1. This table evaluates how different proportions of data shared with the server (10%, 30%, 50%) influence the clustering outcomes (ARI, Silhouette, and Accuracy) for various algorithms (K-Means, HC, GMM, DBSCAN) at a fixed privacy parameter ($\epsilon = 0.1$).

Algorithm	Shared	ϵ	K	ARI	Silhouette	Accuracy
K-Means	10%	0.1	k = 8	0.75	0.41	0.18
K-Means	30%	0.1	k = 8	0.75	0.41	0.18
K-Means	50%	0.1	k = 8	0.75	0.41	0.18
HC	10%	0.1	k = 8	0.481	0.39	0.005
HC	30%	0.1	k = 8	0.481	0.39	0.005
HC	50%	0.1	k = 8	0.0.481	0.39	0.005
GMM	10%	0.1	k = 6	0.185	−0.143	0.201
GMM	30%	0.1	k = 8	0.175	−0.111	0.18
GMM	50%	0.1	k = 5	0.169	−0.001	0.23
DBSCAN	10%	0.1	k = 10	0.017	−0.504	0.005
DBSCAN	30%	0.1	k = 10	0.017	−0.504	0.005
DBSCAN	50%	0.1	k = 10	0.017	−0.504	0.005

For the first dataset, the K-Means algorithm maintains the same ARI, Silhouette, and Accuracy metrics across different data sharing proportions, suggesting that its performance remains stable despite changes in the volume of data shared. Similarly, Hierarchical Clustering (HC), Gaussian Mixture Models (GMM), and DBSCAN show consistent performance metrics across different data sharing amounts, further supporting the notion that the quality of clustering recommendations does not deteriorate with reduced data sharing. In the second dataset, similar patterns emerge. For instance, the K-Means algorithm and HC adjust their suggested number of clusters slightly depending on the data share, but the overall performance metrics such as ARI and Silhouette remain relatively stable. This trend continues with GMM and DBSCAN, which also show little variation in performance across different data sharing proportions.

These findings suggest that the server is capable of providing robust and reliable recommendations for clustering parameters regardless of the amount of data shared, enabling effective clustering outcomes even when data owners choose to share minimal data. This is particularly advantageous in scenarios where data privacy is a concern, as it allows data owners to restrict the amount of shared data without compromising the effectiveness of the clustering process. Overall, the server's ability to consistently suggest appropriate clustering parameters across varying data proportions demonstrates its effectiveness and reliability in guiding the clustering process under different data availability conditions.

Table 8. Analysis of Server Recommendations for Clustering Parameters Based on Data Sharing Amounts in the second Dataset. This table examines the influence of varying amounts of data shared (10%, 30%, 50%) on server-suggested clustering parameter (k) and their resulting ARI, Silhouette, and Accuracy metrics at a constant privacy parameter ($\epsilon = 0.1$).

Algorithm	Shared	ϵ	K	ARI	Silhouette	Accuracy
K-Means	10%	0.1	k = 3	0.997	0.52	0
K-Means	30%	0.1	k = 2	0.44	0.57	0.18
K-Means	50%	0.1	k = 2	0.44	0.57	0.18
HC	10%	0.1	k = 3	0.84	0.51	0.38
HC	30%	0.1	k = 2	0.55	0.52	0.66
HC	50%	0.1	k = 2	0.55	0.52	0.66
GMM	10%	0.1	k = 3	−0.0003	0.021	0.3
GMM	30%	0.1	k = 2	−0.0004	0.051	0.32
GMM	50%	0.1	k = 2	−0.0004	0.051	0.32
DBSCAN	10%	0.1	k = 6	0.003	−0.6	0
DBSCAN	30%	0.1	k = 6	0.003	−0.6	0
DBSCAN	50%	0.1	k = 6	0.003	−0.6	0

7   Privacy Analysis: Membership Inference Attack

Membership inference attacks (MIA) are techniques used to determine whether specific individual data was included in a dataset. These attacks pose significant privacy risks, especially when datasets contain sensitive information. Our goal is to minimize these risks for individuals whose data is part of a dataset shared with others. To enhance data privacy, only a portion of the dataset, even in its noisy format, is shared with the server. It has been observed that the likelihood of successful membership inference attacks is inversely related to the amount of noise added to the dataset. We divide the data into two groups to assess the impact of these attacks:

Case Group: This group contains data from specific number of individuals (150 for first dataset and 100 for second dataset) and represents the subset of the dataset that is shared with server, thus exposed to potential membership inference attacks.

Control Group: This group includes data that remains entirely internal and is not shared with the server. It serves as a benchmark to gauge the risk of data exposure. We address membership inference attacks by computing a threshold that determines whether an individual's data is likely part of the training dataset based on similarity between shared and unshared data. Similarity exceeding this threshold indicates a risk of data exposure through membership inference.

Our detailed analysis is visually represented in Fig. 4, demonstrating the impact of the privacy parameter (ϵ), with increased ϵ values reducing the noise and thereby increasing the risk of data identification.

Our findings show that as ϵ increases, the risk of membership inference attacks rises, indicating less noise leads to higher identification likelihood. Therefore, limiting shared data and augmenting it with noise is essential to reduce

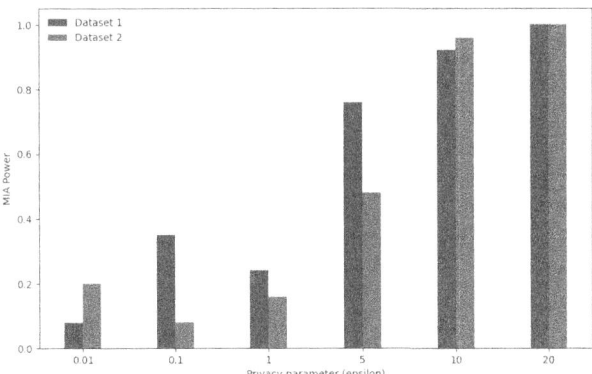

Fig. 4. Analysis of Membership Inference Attack Risks: This figure illustrates the increasing likelihood of data identification in two datasets as privacy parameters (ϵ) increase. The blue bars represent dataset #1, and the green bars represent dataset #2, highlighting the direct correlation between reduced noise levels and heightened data vulnerability. (Color figure online)

these risks, necessitating a strategic approach to balance data utility and privacy in collaborative clustering.

8 Conclusion

This study aims to identify optimal input parameters for four clustering algorithms to facilitate collaborative clustering among multiple data owners. Introducing a semi-trusted third party improves clustering reliability and accuracy by recommending optimal algorithms and parameters. Results show that neither the amount of perturbed data shared nor the privacy budget (ϵ) significantly impacts the server's recommendations.

Furthermore, this study conducts an analysis of membership inference attacks to evaluate the vulnerability of the system. As the privacy budget (ϵ) increases, the power of membership inference attacks also increases. This indicates that higher levels of privacy budget compromise the effectiveness of privacy protection, making it easier for attackers to infer whether an individual's data is part of the shared dataset.

These findings emphasize the need for careful consideration of privacy-preserving mechanisms and the importance of maintaining an appropriate balance between privacy protection and utility. While the server's suggestions for input parameters remain consistent regardless of the amount of perturbed data or the privacy budget, the potential risks associated with membership inference attacks highlight the need to adopt appropriate safeguards and mitigation strategies. Protecting the privacy of individuals and ensuring the security of collaborative clustering processes should be key priorities in future research and system design.

Acknowledgement. The work was partly supported by the National Library of Medicine of the National Institutes of Health under Award Number R01LM013429, the National Science Foundation (NSF) under grant numbers 2141622, 2050410, 2200255, and OAC-2112606, and Cisco Research.

References

1. Extended iris dataset. https://www.kaggle.com/datasets/samybaladram/iris-dataset-extended
2. Estimation of obesity levels based on eating habits and physical condition. UCI Machine Learning Repository (2019). https://doi.org/10.24432/C5H31Z
3. Anikin, I.V., Gazimov, R.M.: Privacy preserving DBSCAN clustering algorithm for vertically partitioned data in distributed systems. In: Proceedings International Siberian Conference Control Communication (SIBCON) (2017)
4. Baby, V., Chandra, N.S.: Distributed threshold k-means clustering for privacy preserving data mining. In: 2016 International Conference on Advances in Computing, Communications and Informatics (ICACCI) (2016)

5. Bi, R., Guo, D., Zhang, Y., Huang, R., Lin, L., Xiong, J.: Outsourced and privacy-preserving collaborative k-prototype clustering for mixed data via additive secret sharing. IEEE Internet Things J. **10**(18), 15810–15821 (2023). https://doi.org/10.1109/JIOT.2023.3266028

6. Bozdemir, B., Canard, S., Ermis, O., Mollering, H., Onen, M., Schneider, T.: Privacy-preserving density-based clustering. In: Proceedings ACM Asia Conference Computer and Communications Security (ASIACCS) (2021)

7. Cornuéjols, A., Wemmert, C., Gançarski, P., Bennani, Y.: Collaborative clustering: why, when, what and how. Inf. Fus. **39**, 81–95 (2018). https://doi.org/10.1016/j.inffus.2017.04.008

8. Costello, C., et al.: Geppetto: versatile verifiable computation. In: Proceedings IEEE Symposium on Security and Privacy (2015)

9. Davidson, S., Khanna, S., Milo, T., Panigrahi, D., Roy, S.: Provenance views for module privacy. In: Proceedings 30th ACM SIGMOD-SIGACT-SIGART Symposium Principles Database Systems (PODS) (2011)

10. Davidson, S., Khanna, S., Roy, S., Stoyanovich, J., Tannen, V., Chen, Y.: On provenance and privacy. In: Proceedings 14th International Conference Database Theory (ICDT) (2011)

11. De, I., Tripathy, A.: A secure two party hierarchical clustering approach for vertically partitioned data set with accuracy measure. In: Thampi, S.M., Abraham, A., Pal, S.K., Rodriguez, J.M.C. (eds.) Recent Advances in Intelligent Informatics, pp. 153–162. Springer, Cham (2014)

12. Dey, S., Zinn, D., Ludäscher, B.: ProPub: towards a declarative approach for publishing customized, policy-aware provenance. In: Proceedings 23rd International Conference Science Statistics Database Management (SSDBM) (2011)

13. Dwork, C., Smith, A., Steinke, T., Ullman, J.: Exposed! a survey of attacks on private data. Annu. Rev. Stat. Appl. **4**, 61–84 (2017)

14. Ester, M., Kriegel, H.P., Sander, J., Xu, X.: A density-based algorithm for discovering clusters in large spatial databases with noise. In: Proceedings International Conference Knowledge Discovery Data Mining (KDD) (1996)

15. Everitt, B.S., Landau, S., Leese, M., Stahl, D.: Cluster Analysis. Wiley (2011)

16. Fisher, R.A.: Iris. UCI Machine Learning Repository (1988). https://doi.org/10.24432/C56C76

17. Fukunaga, K., Hostetler, L.: The estimation of the gradient of a density function, with applications in pattern recognition. IEEE Trans. Inf. Theory (1975)

18. Gymrek, M., McGuire, A.L., Golan, D., Halperin, E., Erlich, Y.: Identifying personal genomes by surname inference. Science **339** (2013)

19. Hamidi, M., Sheikhalishahi, M., Martinelli, F.: Privacy preserving expectation maximization (EM) clustering construction. In: Distributed Computing and Artificial Intelligence, 15th International Conference 15, pp. 255–263 (2019)

20. Jagannathan, G., Wright, R.N.: Privacy-preserving distributed k-means clustering over arbitrarily partitioned data (2005)

21. Jain, A.K., Murty, M.N., Flynn, P.J.: Data clustering: a review. ACM Comput. Surv. **31**(3), 264–323 (1999)

22. Lin, X., Clifton, C., Zhu, M.: Privacy-preserving clustering with distributed EM mixture modeling. Knowl. Inf. Syst. (2005)

23. Liu, J., Xiong, L., Luo, J., Huang, J.Z.: Privacy preserving distributed DBSCAN clustering. Trans. Data Privacy (2013)

24. Meng, X., Papadopoulos, D., Oprea, A., Triandopoulos, N.: Private two-party cluster analysis made formal and scalable. arXiv preprint arXiv:1904.04475v2 (2019)

25. Mohassel, P., Rosulek, M., Trieu, N.: Practical privacy-preserving k-means clustering (2020)
26. Narayanan, A., Shmatikov, V.: Robust de-anonymization of large sparse datasets. In: Proceedings IEEE Symposium Security Privacy (SP) (2008). https://doi.org/10.1109/SP.2008.33
27. Narayanan, A., Shmatikov, V.: De-anonymizing social networks. In: Proceedings 30th IEEE Symposium Security Privacy (SP), pp. 173–187 (2009). https://doi.org/10.1109/SP.2009.22
28. Nergiz, M.E., Atzori, M., Clifton, C.: Hiding the presence of individuals from shared databases. In: Proceedings ACM SIGMOD International Conference Management Data (SIGMOD) (2007). https://doi.org/10.1145/1247480.1247554
29. Power, J., Beresford, A.: SoK: managing risks of linkage attacks on data privacy. In: Proceedings Privacy Enhancement Technologies (PoPETS) (2023). https://doi.org/10.56553/popets-2023-0043
30. Pyrgelis, A., Troncoso, C., De Cristofaro, E.: Measuring membership privacy on aggregate location time-series. Proc. ACM Meas. Anal. Comput. Syst. 4(2) (2020). https://doi.org/10.1145/3392154
31. Rahman, M.S., Basu, A., Kiyomoto, S.: Towards outsourced privacy-preserving multiparty DBSCAN. In: 2017 IEEE 22nd Pacific Rim International Symposium on Dependable Computing (PRDC), pp. 225–226 (2017)
32. Sander, J., Ester, M., Kriegel, H.P., Xu, X.: Density-based clustering in spatial databases: the algorithm GDBSCAN and its applications. Data Min. Knowl. Discov. (1998)
33. Wang, C., Xu, J., Tan, S., Yin, L.: Privacy-preserving cloud-edge collaborative k-means clustering model in IoT. In: Yang, H., Lu, R. (eds.) Front. Cyber Secur., pp. 655–669. Springer, Singapore (2024)
34. Wu, W., Liu, J., Wang, H., Hao, J., Xian, M.: Secure and efficient outsourced k-means clustering using fully homomorphic encryption with ciphertext packing technique. IEEE Trans. Knowl. Data Eng. 33(10), 3424–3437 (2021)
35. Xu, R., Wunsch, D.: Survey of clustering algorithms. IEEE Trans. Neural Netw. 16(3), 645–678 (2005). https://doi.org/10.1109/TNN.2005.845141
36. Xu, X., Ester, M., Kriegel, H.P., Sander, J.: A distribution-based clustering algorithm for mining in large spatial databases. In: Proceedings International Conference Data Engineering (ICDE) (1998)
37. Yuan, C., Yang, H.: Research on k-value selection method of k-means clustering algorithm. J. 2(2), 226–235 (2019)

reteLLMe: Design Rules for Using Large Language Models to Protect the Privacy of Individuals in Their Textual Contributions

Mariem Brahem[1,2], Jasmine Watissee[1,3], Cédric Eichler[1,4], Adrien Boiret[1,4], Nicolas Anciaux[1,2], and Jose Maria de Fuentes[1,5(✉)]

[1] Petscraft project-team, Inria, Paris, France
{mariem.brahem,jasmine.watissee,cedric.eichler,adrien.boiret,
nicolas.anciaux,jose.fuentes}@inria.fr,
{mariem.brahem,nicolas.anciaux}@uvsq.fr
[2] Université Paris Saclay - Versailles, Paris, France
[3] Institut Polytechnique de Paris, Paris, France
jasmine.watissee@polytechnique.edu
[4] INSA Centre Val de Loire, Bourges, France
{cedric.eichler,adrien.boiret}@insa-cvl.fr
[5] Universidad Carlos III de Madrid, Madrid, Spain
josemaria.defuentes@uc3m.es

Abstract. The advanced inference capabilities of Large Language Models (LLMs) pose a significant threat to the privacy of individuals by enabling third parties to accurately infer certain personal attributes (such as gender, age, location, religion, and political opinions) from their writings. Paradoxically, LLMs can also be used to protect individuals by helping them to modify their textual output from certain unwanted inferences, opening the way to new tools. Examples include sanitising online reviews (e.g., of hotels, movies), or sanitising CVs and cover letters. However, how can we avoid miss estimating the risks of inference for LLM-based text sanitisers? Can the protection offered be overestimated? Is the original purpose of the produced text preserved?

To the best of authors knowledge, no previous work has tackled these questions. Thus, in this paper four design rules (collectively referred to as *reteLLMe*) are proposed to minimise these potential issues. We validate these rules and quantify the benefits obtained in a given use case – sanitising hotel reviews. We show that up to 76% of at-risk texts are not flagged as such without fine-tuning. Moreover, classic techniques such as BLEU and ROUGE are shown to be incapable of assessing the amount of purposeful information in a text. Finally, a sanitisation tool based on *reteLLMe* demonstrates superior performance to a state-of-the-art sanitiser, with better results on up to 90% of texts.

Keywords: LLM · Privacy · Inference · Anonymisation

J. Garcia-Alfaro et al. (Eds.): ESORICS 2024 Workshops, LNCS 15263, pp. 33–49, 2025.
https://doi.org/10.1007/978-3-031-82349-7_3

1   Introduction

Large Language Models (LLM) and related generative artificial intelligence techniques are on the rise. They are able to perform complex tasks such as video generation or speech synthesis, to name a few [2].

Despite their countless advantages, LLMs pose a serious threat to privacy by means of inferences [5,19]. Indeed, their ability to accurately predict sensitive attributes (such as age, gender or political beliefs) of the author of a text that is believed to be benign has already been demonstrated [16]. This may lead to the complete deanonymization of the author of a piece of work that was intended to remain unknown, thus leading to undesired consequences.

Conversely, the very same inference capability of LLMs can be applied to mitigate the privacy threat. Previous works have already shown how LLMs can be converted into large-scale anonymizers, thus transforming a piece of data (say text, video, image, etc.) into another one that can reduce the precision of LLM-based inferences [17,18]. Some approaches have also considered the utility of the generated texts as a feature to preserve [4].

There are a number of motivating use cases for such a privacy-preserving use of LLMs. For example, in the context of online reviews, whether for hotels, products, or services, it is essential to protect the anonymity of reviewers to encourage honest and unbiased feedback. Here, a LLM can assist by sanitizing text to conceal Personally Identifiable Information (PII), ensuring consumer opinions are shared without fear of personal exposure. Similarly, in professional environments, such as job applications, ensuring that work-related documents such as reports or cover letters may not leak any highly sensitive information such as religious beliefs or political thoughts could help mitigate discrimination.

A great number of recent efforts revolve around using LLMs as privacy-preserving tools, such as [14,17], to name a few. Although they exhibit promising performance features, their use of LLMs does not follow any particular design criteria. This leads to undesired effects in text utility, user privacy or both. Therefore, it is essential to build those privacy-preserving LLMs in a sound manner, providing reliable evidence of their effectiveness.

To address these issues, this paper proposes a set of design rules (collectively referred to as *reteLLMe*) to build privacy-preserving LLMs and evaluate their efficiency. They provide solid grounds to achieve an optimal transformation of a piece of information while keeping a privacy-utility tradeoff. More specifically, the contributions of this work are as follows:

- We propose a novel problem statement by identifying three main underlying challenges, namely (1) the assessment on a realisic LLM-based attacker, (2) the sanitisation of the piece of information to limit these inferences and (3) the assessment of the utility of the sanitised output to maintain a threshold;
- We provide a set of design rules to address the above challenges;
- We show experimentally the benefit of following these rules, and conversely the impact of ignoring them, in the context of a hotel review sanitiser.

Paper Organization. Section 2 introduces the problem statement. Section 3 introduces the proposed design rules in a case-agnostic fashion. Section 4 describes the application of these rules in the context of sanitising hotel reviews. Section 5 provides an experimental validation and comparison with the state of the art. Section 6 introduces the related work. Lastly, Sect. 7 concludes the paper and points out future work directions.

2   Problem Statement

This paper tackles the intricate task of text sanitisation through the utilization of LLMs to shield sensitive author attributes (e.g., age, gender, etc.). This Section introduces three underlying difficulties of this task (Sects. 2.1, 2.2 and 2.3) and concludes with the problem formulation (Sect. 2.4).

2.1   Difficulty 1: Using LLMs for Privacy Risk Assessment

Recent studies have shown that off-the-shelf LLMs can infer personal information from texts [16]. However, utilizing pre-trained LLMs in a defensive manner to help individuals assess the risk of inference in their texts presents two main obstacles. Firstly, LLMs can sometimes produce inferences as accurate as a random guess, making them unreliable for privacy risk assessments without a mechanism to evaluate the inference likelihood. Secondly, fine-tuning LLMs has shown effectiveness in various contexts, such as reidentifying personal information from anonymized medical documents [18], highlighting the need for considering high-quality and diverse training datasets to accurately estimate privacy risks.

2.2   Difficulty 2: Assessing Text Utility After Sanitisation

Traditional free-text utility metrics like BLEU [11] and ROUGE [8] may be considered in text sanitisation (see e.g., recent preprint [17]). Such metrics are excellent for evaluating summaries by comparing n-gram co-occurrences between texts. However, they fail to differentiate between the loss of utility due to the modification of words and the destruction of relevant information. For example, consider the following fictitious hotel review and its sanitised version:

> [*Original text*] I went there with my husband Francis for the 3rd anniversary of our youngest child. The staff was delightful and the room clean.

> [*Sanitised text*] Family friendly. The staff was delightful and the room clean.

Although the sanitised version retains all the information essential for evaluating the hotel, an n-gram analysis would result in a low utility score with BLEU, of around 0.27. In addition, consider the identifying excerpt:

> [*Privacy-sensitive excerpt*] I went there with my husband Francis for the 3rd anniversary of our youngest child.

The BLEU value for this Privacy-sensitive excerpt is 0.57, which is surprisingly higher than the score for the sanitized text containing the more descriptive hotel review segment. This discrepancy highlights the challenge of accurately assesing the trade-off between privacy and utility.

2.3   Difficulty 3: Optimising the Overall Sanitisation Process

Designing a text sanitisation process that balances the preservation of content utility with a significant reduction in privacy risks is a multifaceted challenge. Indeed, the inference ability of potential adversaries equipped with fine-tuned LLMs and example datasets must be countered. Existing methods, like masking or direct removal of Personally Identifiable Information (PII), either tend to overly sanitise the text, diminishing its original utility, or retain enough information for sensitives to be inferred. For instance, Microsoft's Azure AI solution [1] can identify text segments that might expose PII and health identifiers (PHI). However, recent studies [16] indicate that simply blacking out these segments is not always effective against inferences made by current LLMs. Yet, these approaches often overlook the utility loss associated with de-identification [3].

2.4   Overall Problem Formulation

The challenge in developing an LLM-based text sanitisation tool is to strike a balance between preserving utility and mitigating privacy risks. To our knowledge, this intricate problem remains unsolved. The objective of this article is to provide a set of design rules to address this goal effectively. This complex task can be distilled into three building blocks:

- **Likelihood measure $\Lambda_{\mathcal{A}}$ for inferences**: assesses the validity of the inferred values for a given set $\mathcal{A}$ of sensitive attributes.

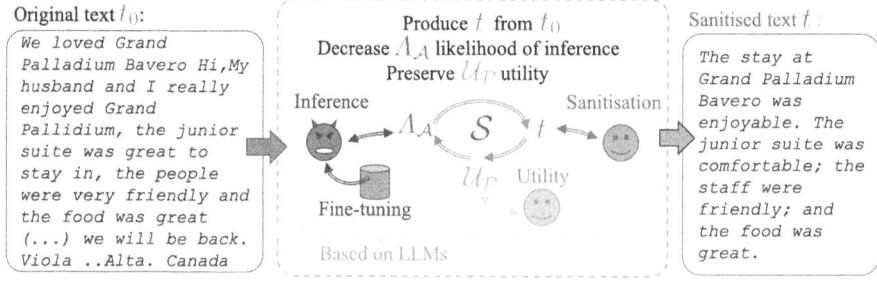

Fig. 1. Main building blocks of a text sanitisation process $\mathcal{S}$ using LLMs

– **Utility measure** $\mathcal{U}_\mathcal{P}$: quantifies the utility of a text based on its alignment with a given purpose $\mathcal{P}$ for which the original text was created.
– **Sanitisation process** $\mathcal{S}_{\Lambda_\mathcal{A},\mathcal{U}_\mathcal{P}}$: transforms the original text into a sanitised text in order to reduce the likelihood of inferences while maintaining utility.

Figure 1 illustrates the overall process and the building blocks for sanitising content using LLMs, from the user text t_0 in input (left) to the sanitised text t in output (right). Our goal is to provide essential guidelines for the design of such LLM-based systems that address the difficulties mentioned above.

3   *reteLLMe* Design Rules

In order to address the problem, clear and effective *design rules* are required. This section introduces these design rules, collectively referred to as *reteLLMe*, organised around the three building blocks they address – inference (Sect. 3.1), utility (Sect. 3.2) and sanitisation (Sect. 3.3).

3.1   Inference Design Rules

The ability of LLMs to make inferences can be regarded as an adversary. The issues raised in Sect. 2.1 require the consideration of a realistic (i.e., sufficiently strong) adversary model suitable for the specific use scenario. An attacker model based on a generic LLM, as considered in recent works [16,17], may underestimate the attacker. This leads to a first practical design rule:

> **Design rule 1: Tailored Adversary LLM.** Avoid using generic attacker models, such as generic LLMs, as this may underestimate accuracy and privacy risks. Instead, employ tailored models such as fine-tuned LLMs.

On the other hand, the capability to infer using LLMs alone is not enough without evaluating the *likelihood* of these inferences. This leads to introduce:

> **Design rule 2: Well-Formed Likelihood Metrics.** The tool must incorporate a well-formed likelihood metrics $\Lambda_\mathcal{A}$ to predict the validity of guesses when truth values are unknown.

These design rules imply an attacker model where $\mathcal{RA}$ (Realistic Adversary) has access to a text t authored by a user u and is interested in a specific set of sensitive attributes $\mathcal{A}$. For each sensitive attribute $A \in \mathcal{A}$ (e.g., Age), D_A represents its domain, and $a_u \in D_A$ denotes its true value for u (e.g., the actual age of u). Using LLMs, $\mathcal{RA}$ produces a_t, the value it inferred from t for each a_u. To represent realistic threats, the adversary is assumed to have access to:

– a dataset D of pre-existing texts written by a set of users U, not including u, for which real values of sensitive attributes $a_{u' \in U}$ are known;

– a likelihood metric $\Lambda_{\mathcal{A}}$ which evaluates the accuracy of guesses about sensitive attributes (i.e., the probability that the inferred value a_t matches the true value a_u).

Designing $\Lambda_{\mathcal{A}}$ is challenging. The likelihood metric estimates the accuracy of each guess made by the attacker. Ideally, a guess represents the probability of its correctness. However, since the truth values of targeted users during the attack are unknown, this probability cannot be analytically computed.

A likelihood metric $\Lambda_{\mathcal{A}}$ is considered well-formed and satisfies design rule 2, if and only if it satisfies the following property: for u the author of text t, $\forall A \in \mathcal{A}$, $\forall \epsilon \in [0,1]$, $\epsilon \mapsto \frac{|\{t \in D: \Lambda_{\mathcal{A}}(a_t) > \epsilon \wedge a_t = a_u\}|}{|\{t \in D: \Lambda_{\mathcal{A}}(a_t) > \epsilon\}|}$ is a monotonically increasing function. It ensures that $\Lambda_{\mathcal{A}}$ can predict whether the probability of a guess being correct is above or below a given threshold. This capability allows an attacker to know whether the inference is plausible and it allows a sanitising tool to alert the user that their text is at risk.

3.2 Utility Assessment Design Rules

We advocate for the adoption of purpose-centric utility metrics alongside inference metrics. The objective is to identify and prioritize information aligned with the intended *purpose* of texts. This leads to the following rule:

> **Design rule 3: Purpose-Centric Utility.** The integration of purpose-centric utility metrics $\mathcal{U}_{\mathcal{P}}$, defined independently of privacy considerations and tailored to the specific purpose of the original text, is essential for maintaining the practical value of LLM-based sanitised outputs.

This guideline entails defining a purpose as a set $\mathcal{P}$ of purpose-related attributes, where each attribute $P \in \mathcal{P}$ represents a category of relevant information regarding the initial purpose for which the text was produced. When a text t produced by sanitising t_0 transmits information about an attribute linked to a purpose $\mathcal{P}$, other users can deduce a value from t. $\mathcal{U}_{\mathcal{P}}$ should evaluate the ability of t to convey *the same* information relevant to the purpose as t_0.

3.3 Sanitisation Design Rules

The process of sanitisation relies on LLMs to transform a text t_0 into a sanitised text t, aiming to reduce privacy risks while maintaining utility. We do not prescribe specific guidelines for the sanitisation process, whether it should be iterative, interactive, or otherwise. The effectiveness of a sanitisation technique hence hinges on the independence between the purpose-centric attributes $\mathcal{P}$ and the sensitive attributes $\mathcal{A}$, leading to a fourth rule:

> **Design rule 4: Privacy-Utility Independence.** Sanitisation techniques must aim to decrease inference likelihood while retaining useful information. The efficiency of the sanitisation process is constrained by the degree of independence between privacy and utility metrics. In case where independence is lacking, residual privacy risks must be carefully evaluated and addressed.

The theoretical feasibility of a perfect sanitiser, which would fully preserve utility while nullifying privacy threats, relies on the independence of relevant information categories between sensitive attributes and purpose-centric ones. However, in practical scenarios where independence is not assured, different trade-offs need exploration, and residual privacy risks must be considered. This underscores the importance of robust privacy risk assessment, as highlighted in Sect. 3.1.

4   Application of *reteLLMe* Design Rules

Demonstrating the suitability of the *reteLLMe* design rules requires instantiating them in a practical scenario. This section shows the instantiation of a sanitiser based on an LLM for sanitising hotel reviews. The scenario and dataset are described in Sect. 4.1. Then the design rules for inference, utility assessment and sanitisation are implemented in Sect. 4.2.

4.1   *"Hotel Reviews Sanitiser"*: Scenario and Dataset Description

We consider a practical application scenario where a sanitisation tool based on *ChatGPT*3.5 is at stake – users enter their hotel review text and the tool rewrites the text to improve privacy while preserving the review utility. This tool could be integrated into commercial platforms such as Booking.com or Airbnb.

To validate our design rules, we use the PAN[1] dataset [13], which provides 4.160 hotel reviews written in English (see an example on left part of Fig. 1). Each one has truth values of two attributes of its author – *gender* (male or female) and *age* ([18, 24], [25, 34], [35, 49], [50, 64] or [65, xx]).

4.2   Implementation and Compliance to Design Rules

The inference values a_t for age (A) and g_t for gender (G) for a text t are produced using a specific prompt. The inference process involves fine-tuning *ChatGPT*3.5 using a random subset of the PAN hotel reviews dataset. Concerning likelihood

---

[1] PAN is an annual competition [12] that provides datasets for different tasks, including author profiling. We are using the 2014 dataset which is the most comprehensive provided for our use. PAN also provides the accuracy achieved by the winners, which will be used for comparison.

values, they are also produced using specific prompts. All prompts are shared in our online repository as stated below.

In what comes to utility, we define a set of purpose-related attributes $\mathcal{P}$ that typically summarise hotel reviews, including general sentiment, specific problem noted, cleanliness, room quality and service standards. Each attribute in $\mathcal{P}$ is categorized into positive (*good*), negative (*bad*), or neutral/missing ($\perp$) values, reflecting its impact on the overall assessment of hotel performance. For each $P \in \mathcal{P}$, we define a binary utility, which is 1 if $ChatGPT3.5$ provides the same answer for t and t_0 (the latter being a non-null value), and 0 otherwise. The overall utility $\mathcal{U}_\mathcal{P}$ is computed as the average of these utilities. Concerning sanitisation, $ChatGPT3.5$ is instructed to eliminate textual elements that could reveal the reviewer's age or gender. Subsequently, the anonymised text is rewritten in a neutral tone to mitigate unintended biases.

All these decisions are in line with design rules: we apply fine-tuning (Design rule 1); the likelihood of each inference is also self-evaluated by $ChatGPT3.5$, and we show experimentally in the next section that the resulting likelihood metric is well-formed (Design rule 2); we score texts depending on their information across purpose-related attributes (Design rule 3) and we balance privacy and utility in sanitized texts (Design rule 4).

5   Assessment of *reteLLMe* Design Rules

This section presents the experimental results on the proposed *reteLLMe* design rules. First, the methodology and experimental settings are discussed in Sect. 5.1. Afterwards, we use the same order as in the previous sections – Sect. 5.2 focuses on the inference process, Sect. 5.3 on utility computation, Sect. 5.4 on the sanitisation effectiveness. Lastly, Sect. 5.5 discusses the results.

5.1   Experimental Settings

Since the attacker model involves fine-tuning which may lead to variations depending on the training dataset, we randomly partition the dataset in four. Each partition is randomly split into two categories, training (H_{840}, approximately 80% of texts) and tests (the remaining 20%). Experiments are run four times on each dataset. Reported results are the average of all experiments.

To generate our prompts, we used well-known techniques (e.g., "Let's play a game...") to force ChatGPT[2] to perform undesired actions [7,16]. To fine-tune ChatGPT, we used OpenAI's dedicated API [10]. To foster further research, our experimental scripts and prompts are publicly released[3].

---

[2] We used $ChatGPT3.5$.
[3] GitHub repository to be added after acceptance.

5.2   Validating reteLLMe Measure for Inference and Likelihood

The goal of this section is to validate the inference module by (i) evaluating the impact of fine-tuning ChatGPT and confirming the strength of the realistic attacker (to assess Design rule 1) and (ii) validating the proposed likelihood metric (to assess Design rule 2).

Attacker Definitions. In accordance with Design rule 1, our experiment considers a (realistic) strong attacker relying on a fine-tuned version of ChatGPT as described above. For comparison, this *strong attacker* is compared to a *weak attacker* that behaves similarly but relies on an off-the-shelf ChatGPT.

Fine-Tuning Design Rule 1. Figure 2 shows the accuracy of the strong attacker and its weak version with respect to a random guess and the best scores in each category of the PAN competition. The random guess ("baseline") has a score of 0.5 for gender as there are only two options (male/female), and 0.2 for the age as there are five ranges (see Sect. 4.1). Thus, the *total* baseline accuracy is 0.1 as the product of the two.

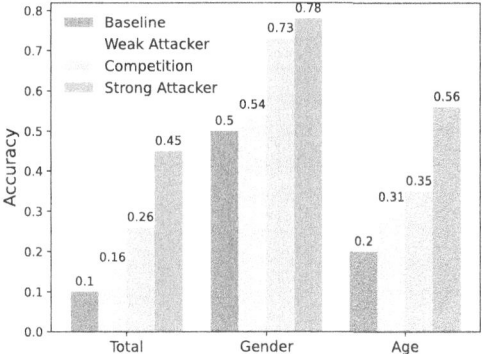

Fig. 2. Accuracy of the weak and strong *reteLLMe*-compliant attackers

Figure 2 shows a significant improvement in the total accuracy from 0.16 to 0.45 with fine-tuning, surpassing both the baseline and the competition results. Furthermore, the comparative analysis between age and gender reveals that the gender category benefits more from fine-tuning than the age category. This could be explained by the differences in the complexity of inferring age, which involves multiple categories, versus gender, which is classified as female or male.

Well-Formed Likelihood Design Rule 2. Figure 3 shows the number of inferences and their average accuracy as a function of their likelihood range. Each attacker provides its own likelihood, so the inferences are partitioned twice according to both. For each likelihood range, the bars show the proportion of inferences (percentage of reviews, left axis) and the curves show their average accuracy (right axis). Note that when no review lies in a likelihood interval, the value of the curve representing accuracy cannot be computed (as in the case of (0,0.6) for gender with the strong attacker).

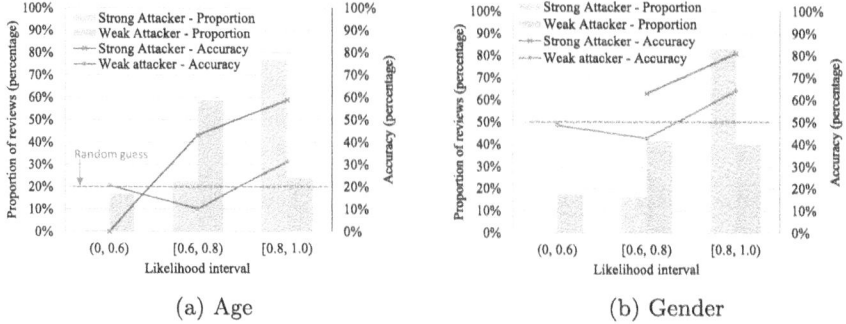

(a) Age   (b) Gender

Fig. 3. Accuracy of inference based on likelihood (original texts)

Accuracy of the strong attacker for age and gender shows a correlation with likelihood (Pearson value of 0.99 for age and 0.96 for gender), as opposed to the weak attacker (age: 0.33, gender: 0.56). In fact, for the strong attacker, the accuracy increases monotonically for increasing likelihood ranges, showing that the likelihood metric is in this setting a well-formed metric (in the sense of Sect. 3.1) that satisfies *Design rule 2*.

Underestimation of Risks Design Rule 1. Beyond the well-formedness, Fig. 3 illustrates the distribution of text accross different likelihood levels. A text is at risk when it falls within a likelihood range where the average accuracy significantly exceeds random guessing. Here, in reality, all texts are at risk. The (realistic) strong attacker, adhering to *reteLLMe* design rules, achieves a likelihood greater than 0.6 for each text, with an average accuracy well above random guessing, even within the [0.6, 0.8) likelihood interval. On the contrary, the weak attacker fails to identify texts with likelihood below 0.8. This discrepancy leads to a significant underestimation of risks: 76% of texts (for age) and 59.5% (for gender) with high inference risks would not be flagged as such.

5.3   Validating *reteLLMe* Measure for Utility

This section validates the purpose-centric *reteLLMe* utility measure presented above (see Sect. 4.2). It first compares the responses obtained using this measure with those provided by humans. It then shows how BLEU and ROUGE behave and concludes on the importance of *Design rule 3*.

Automated Purpose-Related Utility Comparison with Humans. We assign to each review a score out of 10. The score is calculated as the sum of each of the five purpose-related attributes, by assigning 2, 1, and 0 points to each "good", "neutral" and "bad" value respectively. This score is therefore not a measure of the utility of the review (a negative review can be very useful), but simply a way of ranking the reviews from the most positive to the most negative.

Figure 4 shows the distribution of scores for each of the humans and Chat-GPT responses. Each box represents 10% of reviews, from the most positive to the most negative. These three curves show a strong similarity between the humans themselves and between the humans and ChatGPT. This leads to Pearson correlations of 0.8 and 0.82 between each human and ChatGPT. However, it should be noted that the variations in ChatGPT are less uniform than those between humans. Therefore, although imperfect, ChatGPT is a good source of utility in the absence of ground truth.

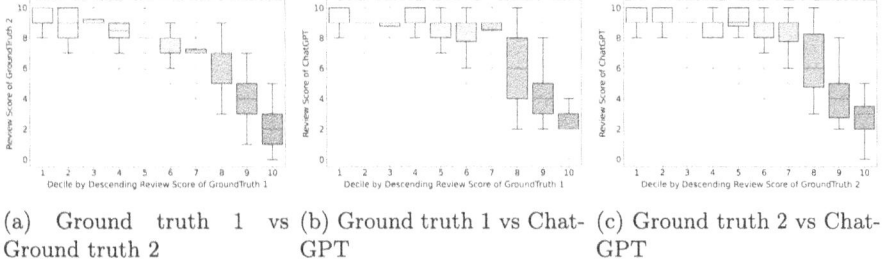

(a) Ground truth 1 vs Ground truth 2

(b) Ground truth 1 vs Chat-GPT

(c) Ground truth 2 vs Chat-GPT

Fig. 4. Human and ChatGPT-based evaluation of purpose-related attributes

BLEU/ROUGE Against Purpose-Related Utility Design Rule 3. To analyse the suitability of BLEU and ROUGE metrics, we examine their alignment with purpose-related utility metric by applying these measures to original hotel reviews (t_0) and sanitised versions (t) and comparing obtained scores with utility preservation according to our proposal.

Figure 5 presents the distribution of BLEU and ROUGE scores, categorized into quintiles with increasing utility preservation. Utility preservation for each sanitized text t compared to original text t_0 is determined by analysing *ChatGPT*3.5's responses to a purpose-related questionnaire using both texts. This involves calculating binary utility $\mathcal{U}_P$ for purpose-related attribute based on *ChatGPT*3.5's responses (which is 1 is same answer is provided, and 1 otherwise) and averaging these values for the five attributes to derive utility preservation (i.e., 1 means fully preserved with same answers to the five purpose-related questions, 0 means answers are all different).

Our results show a significant decorrelation between BLEU/ROUGE scores and utility preservation. Hence, they inadequately assess the purposeful information conveyed in texts, highlighting the negative repercussion of disregarding *Design rule 3.*

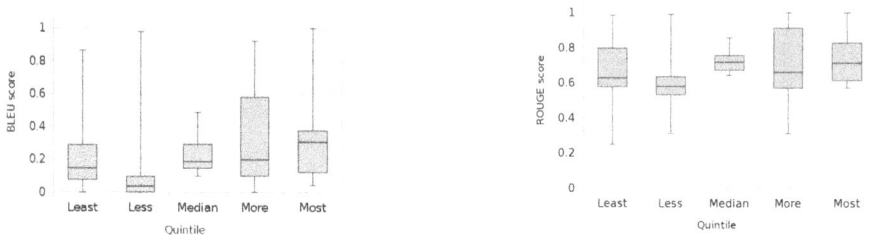

Fig. 5. BLEU/ROUGE scores of sanitised texts ordered by purpose-centric utility

5.4   Sanitisation Effectiveness

We compare our method to the two settings of the anonymiser proposed by Azure, Azure (All entities) and Azure (Three entities) [1]. There are three issues to consider – whereas after sanitisation the inference likelihood is effectively reduced, the inference accuracy is also decreased and the utility is preserved, as needed to satisfy *Design rule 4.*

Decreasing Likelihood. Figure 6 shows the distribution of the inference likelihood for both attributes in the three considered methods. Intuitively, lower likelihood values are preferred from a privacy perspective.

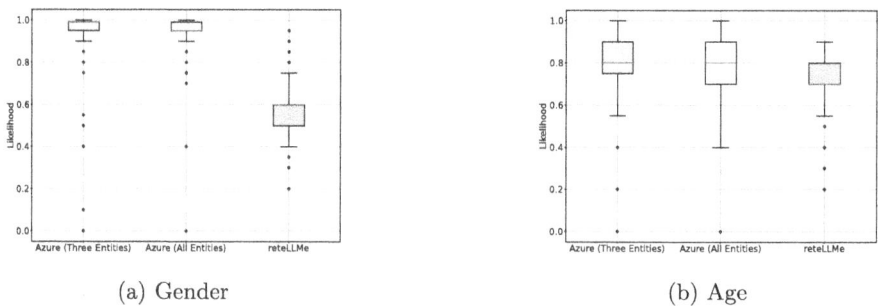

(a) Gender   (b) Age

Fig. 6. Inference likelihood after sanitisation

Figure 6a illustrates the inability of Azure to sanitise gender-related data in both settings, resulting in median likelihood scores of 0.99 and 0.95. Unsurprisingly, the setting removing less data, "Three entities", exhibits the highest likelihood score. On the contrary, *reteLLMe* is significantly more effective to protect this attribute, leading to a median likelihood of 0.6. A similar situation happens for the attribute age (Fig. 6b). Thus, our module outperforms both settings of Azure for the protection of both age and gender attributes.

Decreasing Accuracy. Figure 7 shows the distribution of accuracy values for the three methods. Recall that random guess thresholds are different for age (which is 0.2) and gender (being 0.5). Intuitively, lower likelihood scores lead to smaller accuracy values. Interestingly, *reteLLMe* exhibits good behavior for the highest level of likelihood. Thus, an average accuracy of 0.27 and 0.71 is reached for the age and gender, respectively. For lower likelihood ranges, *reteLLMe* accuracy is closer to a random guess.

As a matter of fact, the amount of texts that remain at risk after sanitisation is largely different. Remarkably, for both attributes and both Azure variants, more than 90% of reviews remain at risk, i.e. belongs to likelihood intervals with an average accuracy significantly more than random guessing (up to 52% average accuracy for age and 78% for gender). When *reteLLMe* is applied, only 11% of reviews are at risk with regard to gender.

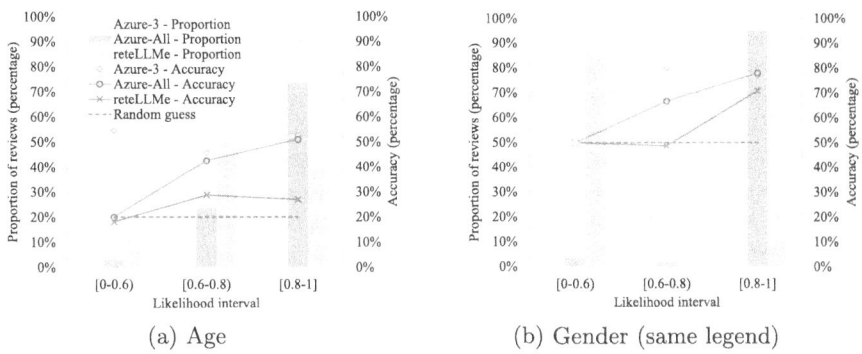

(a) Age   (b) Gender (same legend)

Fig. 7. Accuracy of inference based on likelihood (after sanitisation)

Utility Preservation. Beyond reducing the likelihood of inferences, it is also necessary to ensure that the utility is preserved. Figure 8 shows the distribution of utility preservation across the three methods at stake. The three methods lead to a substantial utility preservation, as the highest amount of records count on the biggest utility preservation figures. Indeed, *reteLLMe*, Azure 3 entities, and Azure all entities preserve between 80% and 100% utility of 71.6%, 70,5%, and 65.6% of texts respectively. Overall and as expected, the "3 entities" setting outperforms the "all entities" setting with regard to utility preservation.

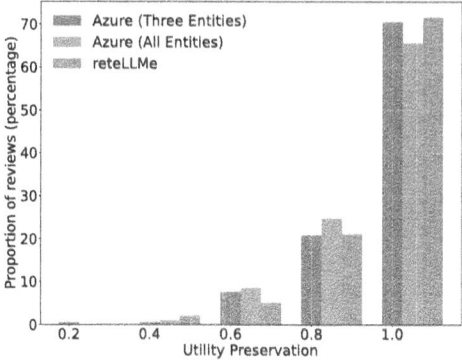

Fig. 8. Distribution of utility preservation

5.5 Discussion

Our experimental results are merely limited to the use-case of hotel reviews with a limited test dataset (4 experiments with 200 texts per experiment). They are however valid to confirm the proposed guidelines.

First, they confirm that LLMs such as ChatGPT can be used as privacy-enhancing tools in an effective manner that outperforms industrial state of the art anonymisers in term of both risk minimization and utility preservation. More importantly, they demonstrate the importance of our design rules.

Indeed, they illustrate the effect of considering a strong adversary by showing how fine-tuning impacts ChatGPT's inference ability. They demonstrate how generic adversaries may severely underestimate privacy risks.

As opposed to the state-of-the-art, they shown that purpose-centric utility metrics are a differentiating factor. Specifically, it is shown that generic metrics such as ROUGE or BLEU may be wholly decorrelated to the amount of purposeful information present in a text.

Our results, however, are limited in that Design rule 4 asked for a sanitisation procedure that decreases the inference likelihood while preserving utility. Nevertheless, our input to ChatGPT does not include the inference likelihood. Our results confirm that even without that input, the inference likelihood and accuracy are severely decreased while the utility is preserved. We argue that this phenomenon cannot be extrapolated to any use case, as it may be due to the very nature of hotel reviews. Nevertheless, our assessment is comprehensive enough to confirm that even the most simplified sanitiser observing this design rule is effective enough.

6 Related Work

The use of LLMs as privacy-enhancing technologies has already attracted some research attention. Indeed, an increasing amount of papers have been produced in the last years. Interested readers may refer to a systematic literature review by Sousa *et al.* [15]. In a nutshell, LLMs seem to be a suitable technology considering the challenges posed by text anonymization, due to the unbounded nature of information related to individuals [9].

[16] was the first study to highlight the critical privacy concerns posed by LLMs beyond the commonly discussed issues related to data memorization. They show that LLMs are able to identify personal data at an unprecedented scale and emphasizes the need for new anonymization techniques to counteract such evolving threats. While the authors effectively illustrate the problem the of inferring personal data from text, they do not propose any solution. Our research builds upon their findings by not only considering these issues but also proposing new guidelines to mitigate the risk of such inferences. Moreover, contrary to our guidelines, they count on a generic attacker – their LLM is not fine-tuned.

A follow-up work by the same authors [17] marks a significant advancement in this domain. They propose an evaluation framework that leverages the capabilities of LLMs for text anonymization. It employs a multiple round process where a LLM adversary analyzes the text for private attribute inference, followed by an anonymizing LLM that modifies the text to obscure identifiable information. Furthermore, this framework introduces a binary "certainty" scoring system discriminating inferences depending on whether they rely on statistical bias or directly identifiable information within texts. We consider that this "certainty" score serves as a metric of inference likelihood. However, [17] does not validate its relation to accuracy. Since statistical analysis may provide accurate guesses, it is not immediate that certainty is a good predictor of accuracy. Beyond the inference likelihood, Staab *et al.* consider utility metrics such as BLEU and ROUGE. Complementarily, they use a "judge" prompt that assesses anonymized texts across three dimensions – readability, meaning, and hallucination. Interestingly, the "meaning" dimension assesses semantic proximity that could be purpose-centric. Since it takes into account *all* information, we argue that it exhibits the same limitations as those discussed in Sect. 2.2 and can never be independent from privacy considerations. This is supported by the observation that BLEU, ROUGE, and judge exhibit the same trends [17].

Another relevant study is [4]. The authors introduce the concept of self disclosure abstraction that allows paraphrasing personal disclosures into more general terms without losing their communicative value, reducing privacy risks while preserving the overall utility (e.g., "Im 16F" to "I'm a teenage girl".) Their methodology involves a fine-tuning strategy to identify instances of self-disclosures which confirms the importance of considering a realistic attacker model as highlighted in our guidelines. However, their approach does not work properly for sensitive attributes which are not directly mentioned in the text, as [16] already proved.

[18] addresses the issue of the de-identification of clinical reports to facilitate data access for research purposes while ensuring patient privacy using the CamemBERT model, a BERT variant specially crafted for French texts. This approach aligns partially with our proposed guidelines. They count on a well-

formed inference likelihood metric. Moreover, their attacker model is concrete enough due to fine-tuning. However, it does not include the notion of utility.

Our work distinguishes itself from recent research by proposing a number of guidelines that have been partially overlooked by previous efforts, as discussed above. To the best of our knowledge, this is the first effort in this direction. Our work has also illustrated which is the impact of not following these guidelines.

7 Conclusion

LLMs have already been shown to be effective to both anonymise and de-anonymise texts. This dual nature gives them an unprecedented ability to be used as privacy-enhancing technology. However, previous attempts have failed to propose such an usage considering the common pitfalls in text utility, inference assessment and sanitisation effectiveness. In this vein, this work has proposed *reteLLMe*, a collection of design rules in this regard. Our assessment in the context of protecting hotel reviews has not only shown the convenience of the proposed rules, but also the negative consequences of disregarding them.

Future work will focus on exploring the suitability of these rules in other contexts. In this vein, the design of well-formed and generalizable purpose-centric utility metrics is envisioned as a critical issue. On the other hand, exploring the impact of LLM-based threats such as privacy leakages [6] in this privacy-enhancing usage is another interesting direction.

Acknowledgement. This work was supported by the French grant iPoP PEPR (ANR-22-PECY-0002). Jose Maria de Fuentes has been partially supported by the Spanish National Cybersecurity Institute (INCIBE) grant APAMciber within the framework of the PRTR funds, financed by the European Union (Next Generation). Jose Maria de Fuentes has also received support from UC3M's Requalification programme, funded by the Spanish Min. de Ciencia, Innovacion y Universidades with EU recovery funds (Convocatoria de la UC3M de Ayudas para la recualificación del sistema universitario español para 2021-2023, de 1 de julio de 2021).

References

1. Azure: What is Azure AI language? (2023). https://learn.microsoft.com/en-us/azure/ai-services/language-service/overview
2. Bai, J., et al.: OFASys: a multi-modal multi-task learning system for building generalist models. arXiv preprint arXiv:2212.04408 (2022)
3. Berthelier, G., Boutet, A., Richard, A.: Toward training NLP models to take into account privacy leakages. In: 2023 IEEE International Conference on Big Data (BigData), pp. 4854–4862. IEEE (2023)
4. Dou, Y., et al.: Reducing privacy risks in online self-disclosures with language models. arXiv preprint arXiv:2311.09538 (2023)
5. Kandpal, N., Pillutla, K., Oprea, A., Kairouz, P., Choquette-Choo, C., Xu, Z.: User inference attacks on LLMs. In: Socially Responsible Language Modelling Research (2023)

6. Kim, S., Yun, S., Lee, H., Gubri, M., Yoon, S., Oh, S.J.: ProPILE: probing privacy leakage in large language models. Adv. Neural Inf. Process. Syst. **36** (2024)
7. Li, H., et al.: Multi-step jailbreaking privacy attacks on ChatGPT. In: Findings of the Association for Computational Linguistics: EMNLP 2023, pp. 4138–4153. Association for Computational Linguistics (2023)
8. Lin, C.Y.: ROUGE: a package for automatic evaluation of summaries. In: Text Summarization Branches Out, pp. 74–81 (2004)
9. Lison, P., Pilán, I., Sánchez, D., Batet, M., Øvrelid, L.: Anonymisation models for text data: state of the art, challenges and future directions. In: Proceedings of the 59th Annual Meeting of the Association for Computational Linguistics and the 11th International Joint Conference on Natural Language Processing (Volume 1: Long Papers), pp. 4188–4203 (2021)
10. OpenAI: OpenAI documentation. https://platform.openai.com/docs/guides
11. Papineni, K., Roukos, S., Ward, T., Zhu, W.J.: Bleu: a method for automatic evaluation of machine translation. In: Proceedings of the 40th Annual Meeting of the Association for Computational Linguistics, pp. 311–318 (2002)
12. Pardo, F.M.R., Rosso, P., Koppel, M., Stamatatos, E., Inches, G.: Overview of the author profiling task at PAN 2013. In: Forner, P., Navigli, R., Tufis, D., Ferro, N. (eds.) Working Notes for CLEF 2013 Conference, Valencia, Spain, September 23-26, 2013. CEUR Workshop Proceedings, vol. 1179. CEUR-WS.org (2013). https://ceur-ws.org/Vol-1179/CLEF2013wn-PAN-RangelEt2013.pdf
13. Rangel Pardo, F., et al.: Overview of the 2nd author profiling task at pan 2014. In: CEUR Workshop Proceedings, vol. 1180, pp. 898–927 (2014)
14. Song, Y., Zhang, J., Tian, Z., Yang, Y., Huang, M., Li, D.: LLM-based privacy data augmentation guided by knowledge distillation with a distribution tutor for medical text classification. arXiv preprint arXiv:2402.16515 (2024)
15. Sousa, S., Kern, R.: How to keep text private? A systematic review of deep learning methods for privacy-preserving natural language processing. Artif. Intell. Rev. **56**(2), 1427–1492 (2023)
16. Staab, R., Vero, M., Balunović, M., Vechev, M.: Beyond memorization: violating privacy via inference with large language models. arXiv preprint arXiv:2310.07298 (2023)
17. Staab, R., Vero, M., Balunović, M., Vechev, M.: Large language models are advanced anonymizers. arXiv preprint arXiv:2402.13846 (2024)
18. Tannier, X., et al.: Development and validation of a natural language processing algorithm to pseudonymize documents in the context of a clinical data warehouse. Methods Inf. Med. (2024)
19. Zhang, X., et al.: PrivacyAsst: safeguarding user privacy in tool-using large language model agents. IEEE Trans. Dependable Secure Comput. (2024)

Plausible Deniability of Redacted Text

Vaibhav Gusain$^{(\boxtimes)}$ ⓘ and Douglas Leith ⓘ

Trinity College Dublin, Dublin, Ireland
gusainv@tcd.ie

Abstract. Providing privacy for natural language text data remains a largely open problem, despite its great practical importance. The current state of the art is manual redaction of sensitive words such as names, addresses etc. In this paper we propose viewing a corpus of text as a probability distribution over sequences of words. A sentence is then one realization from this distribution and redacting words changes the probability distribution. We use the Renyi-divergence divergence as a measure of the distance between two redacted datasets. We show that if enough words are redacted then sensitive redacted text can be made be statistically indistinguishable from non-sensitive redacted text. This can be used to develop efficient redaction strategies, that minimise the amount of redaction while meeting a privacy target.

Keywords: Data Privacy · Natural Language Processing · Text Sanitization

1 Introduction

Training of neural nets such as large language models requires the availability of natural language text training data. In this paper we revisit the question of how to sanitise sensitive text data so that it can be used for model training while preserving privacy. We introduce a new approach for quantitatively estimating the privacy gain from text redaction and demonstrate its usefulness on a wide range of datasets. This can be used to develop efficient redaction strategies, that minimise the amount of redaction while meeting a privacy target. The approach is closely related to differential privacy, but differs in several respects that are important for text data.

There are two main approaches to enhancing privacy when training machine learning models. These approaches are complementary, and both can be used together. One is to add noise to the gradient updates used during training, e.g. see DP-SGD [1,17] and related work. The other is to sanitise the training data itself. Here we focus on the latter.

When the training data is numeric then the addition of appropriate noise, e.g. Laplacian noise scaled proportionally to the differential privacy (DP) "sensitivity" of the data, can be used to enforce differential privacy guarantees [7]. While

---

This work was supported by Science Foundation Ireland grant 16/IA/4610.

J. Garcia-Alfaro et al. (Eds.): ESORICS 2024 Workshops, LNCS 15263, pp. 50–64, 2025.
https://doi.org/10.1007/978-3-031-82349-7_4

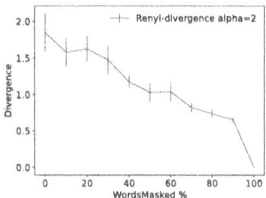

Fig. 1. Measured Renyi vs random redaction level for Medal dataset.

it is tempting to apply this approach to text by mapping the text to a numeric embedding vector, adding noise, and then mapping back to text [5,8,20], this creates a host of unpleasant issues. For example, the nature of the mapping from text to vectors (which texts are mapped to vectors near or far away from one another) directly affects the impact of added noise, and so privacy. However, this is poorly understood, especially for modern embedding approaches based on neural networks. Another deeply problematic issue is that the words in a sentence tend to be correlated in complex ways, making any privacy approach based on individual words tend to overestimate the privacy gained.

In practice, the most popular approach for sanitising text data is redaction i.e. replacing selected words with an uninformative mask token. This is, for example, already widely used to remove personally identifying information (PII), e.g. names and addresses, from documents [12]. However, other aspects of the text data can also be sensitive. For example, the text data may reveal sexual/gender traits, political preferences, health-related information/concerns, social and racial characteristics, etc. of the user population from which the data was gathered. Textual style can also act as a personal fingerprint facilitating de-anonymisation and membership attacks against neural nets trained on this data.

Protecting privacy is especially challenging with text data because simply redacting specified keywords is rarely enough: the surrounding context can easily continue to reveal sensitive information [3]. For example, in the sentence "I am diagnosed with cancer. I have to go to St Lukes for chemotherapy and will probably lose my hair" redacting "cancer" and "chemo" is not sufficient to conceal the cancer diagnosis if St Lukes is known to be a cancer care hospital. If "St Lukes" is also redacted, the combination of "diagnosis" and "lose my hair" is still enough to indicate a cancer diagnosis with high probability.

In summary, there is an urgent need more effective methods for improving the privacy of text data. Given the challenging nature of natural language text, it is probably too much to hope for theoretical guarantees but that should not stop us from trying to develop useful methods motivated by theoretical analysis. In this paper we take a step in that direction. We use redaction to add "noise" to text and by staying within original text domain thereby avoid most of the issues with numerical embeddings, and by working with text corpuses rather than individual words or sentences we can accommodate the word correlations within sentences.

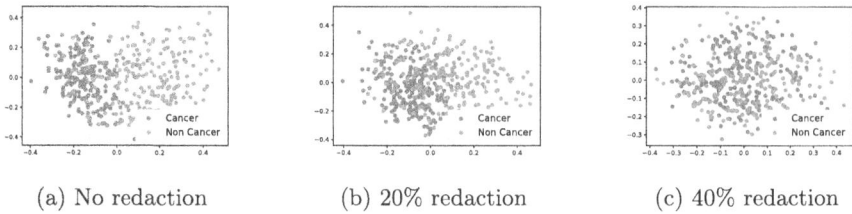

| (a) No redaction | (b) 20% redaction | (c) 40% redaction |

Fig. 2. Illustrating the increasing overlap between the sentence embeddings for cancer and non-cancer text from the Medal dataset as the level of redaction is increased. SentenceBERT embeddings are projected to two dimensions using PCA, random redaction is used.

1.1   Our Approach

A dataset $\mathcal{D}$ is a collection of items. Each item is a sequence $x = (x_1, ..., x_{|x|})$ of words x_t belonging to a fixed vocabulary and with length $|x| \leq N$, N being the maximum admissible length. A redaction policy $\pi_p(x)$ maps sequence x to a new sequence where some words have been redacted i.e. replaced by an uninformative mask token MASK. We will assume that every redaction policy is parameterised by a parameter p taking a value between 0 and 1 such that when $p = 0$ then no words are redacted, when $p = 1$ then every word is redacted. For example, the uniform random $\pi_{rand,p}(x)$ redaction policy redacts each word in sequence x with probability p. Alternatively, we might rank the words in our vocabulary by their sensitivity and redact the top p fraction of these.

Each item x in a dataset is a random draw from a probability distribution $P(x)$ over sequences of words. After redaction, each element x is mapped to a new sequence $redact(x)$ and the redacted dataset becomes a sample from probability distribution $redact(P)$. We measure the distance between two redacted datasets $redact(\mathcal{D}_0)$ and $redact(\mathcal{D}_1)$ by the smallest value of $\epsilon \geq 0$ such that $\tilde{P}_0(y) \leq e^\epsilon \tilde{P}_1(y) + \delta$ and $\tilde{P}_1(y) \leq e^\epsilon \tilde{P}_0(y) + \delta$ where $\tilde{P}_0 := redact(P_0)$ is the probability distribution over token sequences in dataset $redact(\mathcal{D}_0)$, $\tilde{P}_1 = redact(P_1)$ in dataset $redact(\mathcal{D}_1)$ and y is any redacted sequence of words with length $|y| \leq N$.

This distance measure is similar to that used in (ϵ, δ)-differential privacy but with the difference that the set of neighbouring databases now consists of the single database $redact(\mathcal{D}_0)$ rather than all databases differing from $redact(\mathcal{D}_1)$ by a single element. When ϵ, δ are sufficiently small, the publication of private dataset $redact(\mathcal{D}_1)$ then only provides an attacker with limited new information over and above that already available from the public dataset $\mathcal{D}_0$. That is, we gain privacy in the sense of *indistinguishability* between the $redact(\mathcal{D}_0)$ and $redact(\mathcal{D}_1)$ datasets. It will prove convenient to work in terms of the Renyi-divergence

$D_\alpha(\tilde{P}_0||\tilde{P}_1)$ to calculate the distance between the datasets. We then convert this to an (ϵ, δ)-privacy guarantee using equations (2) and (3). See Sect. 4.1 and Sect. 4.2 for more details.

We assume the availability of a "safe" dataset $\mathcal{D}_0$ e.g. a public dataset that is suitably diverse and non-sensitive. Applying redaction policy π_p to both the sensitive dataset $\mathcal{D}_1$ and the safe dataset $\mathcal{D}_0$ then we expect that distance ϵ between the datasets decreases as the level of redaction increases, the distance becoming zero after redaction with $p = 1$.

Figure 1 illustrates this for the Medal dataset of medical records (see below for further details). The original dataset is split into a dataset $\mathcal{D}_1$ of cancer patients and a dataset $\mathcal{D}_0$ of non-cancer patients. Random redaction is used. The figure shows the measured Renyi-Divergence $D_{max}(P_0||P_1)$ between the empirical probability distributions P_0 and P_1 induced by $\mathcal{D}_0$ and $\mathcal{D}_1$ as the level of redaction is varied. As expected, it can be seen that the divergence decreases as the amount of redaction increases i.e. the two datasets become more similar.

Figure 2 illustrates this behaviour more visually. Redacted sentences are mapped to embedding vectors using SentenceBERT [15], the vectors are then projected onto to dimensions using PCA and shown as a scatter plot. It can be seen that without redaction the sentence embeddings have little overlap but as the level of redaction increases the overlap between the embeddings increases, indicating that distinguishing between the two datasets is becoming harder.

We make the following observations. (i) Redaction sanitizes the text data itself (rather then vector embeddings) and so yields a sanitized dataset that can be used for training ML models that take word sequences as input. (ii) By working in terms of the probability distribution over word *sequences* we take account of the correlation between the words in a sentence (the word context) and the associated potential for leakage of sensitive information. (iii) Sanitising the dataset is akin to local differential privacy i.e. the input to a query is perturbed to ensure privacy rather than the output of the query being perturbed. (iv) As the distance ϵ between the sanitized dataset and the safe dataset decreases, privacy increases but of course we expect utility to decrease (the added value of the new dataset decreases).

2   Related Work

The existing literature on enhancing the privacy of text data can be roughly categorised as follows:

Redacting PII. Much of the literature on text redaction has focused on redacting personally identifying information (PII). For example, [12] uses an ensemble of deep learning methods to detect and redact PII information from the medical notes of the patient, [2] considers the discovery of names, home towns, etc. in student discussion boards. Other recent work includes [6,16,21].

Word-Level DP. Word-level DP approaches map an individual word to a vector embedding, add noise and then either map back to a new word or use the noisy embedding directly. See e.g. [5,8,20]. A typical choice of vector embedding

is Glove [14]. The choice of vector embedding has to made up front and its properties affect the privacy gained[1] in ways that remain very poorly understood.
Words are discrete quantities and the impact of quantisation when mapping from
vectors back to words also remains poorly understood. The DP "database" is a
sentence and the words are the database entries. The DP guarantee (modulo concerns regarding the embedding already noted) therefore relates to insensitivity
to an individual word in a sentence. However this DP analysis ignores correlations between the words in a sentence and so can underestimate the information
release. The impact of correlations on DP is well known and was first noted
by [9]. See [10] for further discussion on the deficiencies of word-level DP.

3   Threat Model

We consider the use of natural language text datasets for training machine learning models. We assume that the sensitive dataset itself is stored securely, but
the sanitized/redacted dataset is publicly released. The main threat we consider
is that that the sanitized dataset may be used to infer sensitive user traits e.g.
sexuality, health conditions, political preferences. This is a particularly topical
concern since the development of LLMs is currently being driven by companies
with a commercial interest in identifying user traits e.g. for use in targeting
adverts or other services. We assume that PII (names, addresses etc.) has been
removed, there being many existing techniques for this, see e.g. [6, 16, 21]

4   Preliminaries

The Renyi-divergence of order $\alpha > 1$ between two probability distributions P_0
and P_1 on sample space Y is [13]:

$$D_\alpha(P_0||P_1) = \frac{1}{\alpha - 1} \log \int_Y P_0(x)^\alpha P_1(x)^{1-\alpha} dx \qquad (1)$$

and similarly for $D_\alpha(P_1||P_0)$. When $\alpha = 1$ the Renyi-divergence equals the KL-
divergence [11].

We say that two probability distributions P_0 and P_1 are (ξ, ρ)-zero-
concentrated differentially private when:

$$D_\alpha(P_0||P_1) \leq \xi + \rho\alpha \qquad (2)$$

for all $\alpha > 1$. In the differential privacy literature P_0, respectively P_1, is the probability distribution induced by a randomised mechanism $\mathcal{M}$ applied to dataset
$\mathcal{D}_0$, respectively $\mathcal{D}_1$ [4]. Inequality (2) is then required to hold for all neighbouring datasets $\mathcal{D}_0$, $\mathcal{D}_1$, where datasets are neighbours if they differ by a single

---

[1] Adding noise to an embedding perturbs it to nearby words, the way in which words
are mapped to be close together (or far apart) therefore directly affects the output
of the word-level DP sanitisation process.

element. However, here we will consider other choices for P_0 and P_1. Specifically, they will be the distributions from which two datasets $\mathcal{D}_0$ and $\mathcal{D}_1$ are sampled.

When P_0 and P_1 are (ξ, ρ)-zCDP then from the proof of Lemma 21 in [4],

$$P_1(x) \leq \exp(\epsilon)P_0(x) + \delta \tag{3}$$

for every $\delta > 0$ where $\epsilon = \xi + \rho + 2\sqrt{\rho \log \frac{1}{\delta}}$. We will use (3) to map from Renyi-divergence curves to an (ϵ, δ) privacy guarantee.

4.1 Estimating Renyi-Divergence

To estimate the Renyi-divergence between two datasets we extend the estimator of [13], which is observed to scale well for high dimensional data. We updated the estimator to handle duplicate word-sequences, since these can become common following redaction[2]. In addition, each word sequence is mapped to a vector embedding[3] X_i. These are then fed to the estimator to calculate the Renyi-divergence. We use boot-strapping to calculate confidence intervals for the estimate. Namely, we sample with replacement n times from $redact(\mathcal{D}_0)$ and $redact(\mathcal{D}_1)$, estimate $D_\alpha(P_0||P_1)$ is calculated for each sample and then the mean and standard deviation of these n estimates calculated. We select n by calculating the mean and standard deviation vs n and selecting a value large enough that these are convergent. The mean of the estimated Renyi divergence is shown in our plots with the standard deviation indicated by error bars.

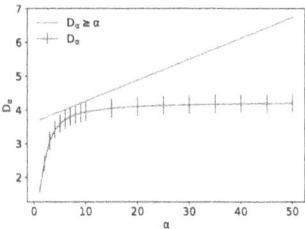

Fig. 3. Divergence vs α for non-redacted cancer and non-cancer text from Medal medical dataset.

---

[2] See Appendix https://anonymous.4open.science/r/appendix_repo-F4CC for more details.

[3] The choice of embedding will, in general, affect the estimated divergence. This can be mitigated by calculating the divergence for many different embeddings and using the worst-case (i.e. largest) value. However, we found the impact to be relatively minor in practice, see Section-6.3, and SentenceBERT [15] to work well.

4.2   Calculating (ϵ,δ)

To calculate ξ and ρ in equation (2), we first calculate D_α for a range of α values[4]. We then find a line that lies above the D_α vs α curve and select ρ as the slope of the line and ξ the intercept. Of course, many lines lie above the D_α curve, so we try to select one such that ρ and ξ are minimised. See for example Fig. 3, which shows D_α vs α for the Medal medical dataset (the blue curve). This curve is upper bounded by the red line. The values of ρ and ξ corresponding to this red line are plugged into equation (3 to obtain the corresponding (ϵ,δ) privacy values.

Note. We use $\delta = 0.00008$ in all of our experiments as it is encouraged to keep $\delta < \frac{1}{n^2}$ where n is the number of input points [1].

5   Experiments

5.1   Datasets

We evaluate performance using the following datasets, each of which we split into "sensitive" and "safe" datasets.

(i) Medal dataset [19][5]. This dataset contains abstracts of medical papers, along with the diseases the abstract talks about. We partition this dataset into text with cancerous and non-cancerous diseases. Each dataset contains 2200 sentences. For our experiments, text with cancerous diseases was chosen to be the sensitive dataset.

(ii) Political dataset- [18][6]. This contains comments on Facebook posts from 412 members of the United States Senate and House. Each comment is labeled with the corresponding Congressperson's party affiliation i.e. S ϵ {democratic, republican} We partition the dataset into text from users with Republican and Democrat political preferences. Each dataset contains 2000 sentences. For our experiments, text from users with Republican political preferences is chosen to be the sensitive dataset.

(iii) Amazon dataset[7]. This dataset contains product reviews from Amazon customers. We selected the reviews which were categorised as "drug-store" and "kitchen-appliances". For our experiments, the dataset with drug-store reviews was chosen to be the sensitive dataset.

(iv) Reddit dataset[8]. This dataset contains post content from the subreddits r/depression and r/SuicideWatch. We partition this data into posts related to suicide and depression. Each dataset contains 2000 sentences. For our experiments, the text from the suicide subreddit was chosen to be the sensitive dataset.

---

[4] We select the range to be large enough that D_α no longer increases as we increase α.

[5] https://huggingface.co/datasets/medal.

[6] Data can be downloaded by following the instructions in the repository https://github.com/xuqiongkai/PATR.

[7] https://huggingface.co/datasets/amazon_reviews_multi.

[8] https://www.kaggle.com/general/256134.

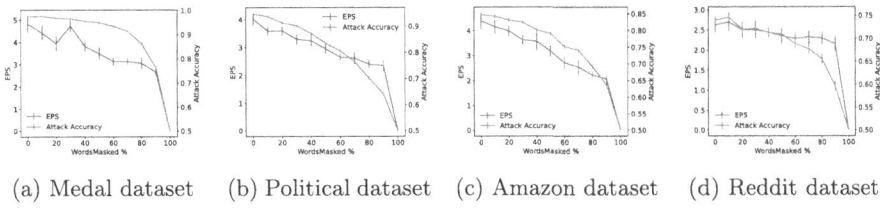

(a) Medal dataset   (b) Political dataset   (c) Amazon dataset   (d) Reddit dataset

Fig. 4. Measured ϵ between redacted sensitive and safe datasets vs redaction level; random redaction. A lower value indicates better privacy. Also shown is the measured accuracy of a classification attack that tries to label which dataset the redacted sensitive text originated from (lower accuracy therefore equals greater privacy, with a classification accuracy of 50% corresponding to a random classifier).

5.2   Enhancing Privacy By Redaction

For each of the datasets we measured the Renyi-divergence as the percentage of words redacted using a random redaction policy was varied from 0 to 100%. The divergence values were then converted to ϵ values as explained previously. The results are shown in Fig. 4.

To help gain confidence that redaction really is improving privacy, we carry out a simple classification attack. The redacted datasets are split into training and test data (90:10 split). A classifier is trained on this data, taking a sequence of words as input and outputting an estimate of whether the sentence came from the safe or sensitive datasets. Since there are only two classes and the data is balanced, a classification accuracy of 50% corresponds to a random classifier. Figure 4 shows how the measured accuracy of this classifier varies with the redaction level for each of the datasets. It can be seen that the accuracy decreases as the redaction level increases, and that this decrease is roughly proportional to the decrease in the measured ϵ value.

5.3   Smarter Redaction

It can be seen from Fig. 4 that when random redaction is used then relatively high levels of redaction are needed to ensure smaller ϵ values. Of course random redaction is rather crude, and smarter redaction approaches (in the sense that they achieve a target ϵ with fewer words redacted) are certainly possible.

We illustrate the scope for smarter redaction via a simple approach based on logistic regression weights. Namely, we took the logistic regression classifier from Sect. 5.2 and ranked the words from the datasets by the magnitude of the weight assigned to them by this classifier. We then redact the top p percent of these words from the datasets when redacting at level p.

Figure 5 plots the measured ϵ between the sensitive and safe datasets as the redaction level is increased in this way. It can be seen that a much lower level of redaction is now needed, compared to Fig. 4, to obtain a given ϵ value. Also shown in Fig. 5 is the measured accuracy of the simple classification attack as

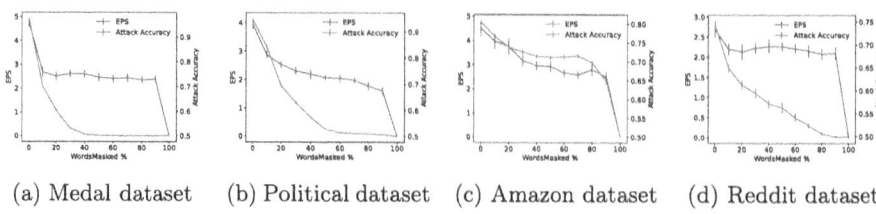

(a) Medal dataset   (b) Political dataset   (c) Amazon dataset   (d) Reddit dataset

Fig. 5. Measured ϵ between redacted sensitive and safe datasets vs redaction level; more efficient redaction strategy. A lower value indicates better privacy. Also shown is the measured accuracy of a classification attack that tries to label which dataset the redacted sensitive text originated from (lower accuracy therefore equals greater privacy, with a classification accuracy of 50% corresponding to a random classifier).

the redaction level is varied and it can be seen that the accuracy also now falls much more rapidly. For example, in Fig. 4(a) a redaction level of around 90% is needed to reduce the accuracy of the attack to 60% (recall an accuracy of 50% corresponds to a random classifier, so 60% represents a high level of privacy), for the Medal dataset while with the smarter redaction strategy a redaction level of around 30% is sufficient to achieve this. Observe also that there is now a clear "knee" in the measured divergence vs redaction level curve, with the knee corresponding a low attack accuracy. It can be seen from Fig. 5 that the behaviour is also similar for the other datasets studied.

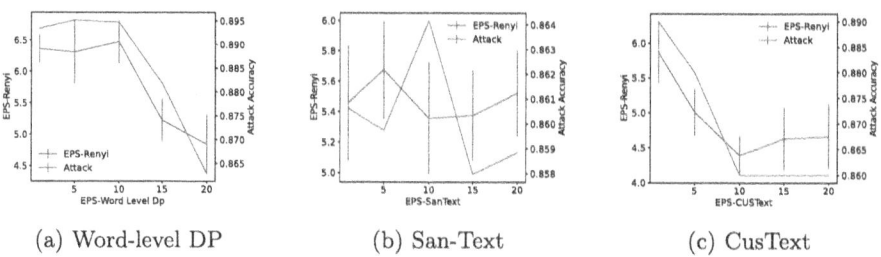

(a) Word-level DP   (b) San-Text   (c) CusText

Fig. 6. Measured ϵ-renyi and attack accuracy for various word-level DP approaches applied to Medal Dataset.

5.4   Word-Level DP

Word-level DP approaches sanitize text by converting each individual word to a vector embedding, adding noise to the embedding, and then mapping the noisy embedding back to a word [5,8,20]. In this section, we compare our approach to word-level DP approaches.

As discussed previously, word-level DP approaches aim to hide the information revealed by the individual words and so can fail to hide information revealed by the sentence as a whole[9].

We illustrate this by conducting the same attack as before on the word-level DP sanitized data, while also checking the ϵ (indicated by ϵ-renyi) between the sensitive and safe datasets. A high attack accuracy indicates that sensitive information is leaked from the sanitized sentences. Similarly, a high ϵ-renyi indicates that there are significant differences between sensitive and non-sensitive datasets.

Figure 8 shows the measured ϵ-renyi for the Medal dataset as the level of noise is increased (indicated by ϵ) for various word-level DP approaches. Also shown is the measured accuracy of our classification attack. It can be seen that even when a great deal of noise is added (low ϵ values), both the ϵ-renyi values and the attack accuracy remain high. Results for other datasets show similar behaviour and are provided in the Appendix[10].

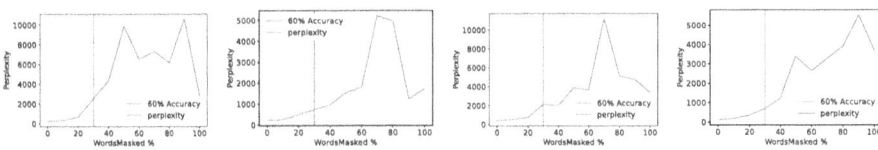

(a) Medal dataset   (b) Political Dataset   (c) Amazon Dataset   (d) Reddit dataset

Fig. 7. Measuring impact of privacy on utility. Next word prediction performance for LSTM trained on redacted dataset. Performance is measured on non-redacted data. The vertical line indicates the redaction level that reduces classification attack accuracy to 60%, taken from Fig. 5.

5.5   Utility Vs Privacy

In general, we expect there to be a trade-off between privacy and utility. By redacting text to make a sensitive training dataset more private, the value of the sensitive training data is likely to be reduced because (i) redaction reduces the textual information contained in the sensitive dataset and (ii) by making the sensitive dataset more similar to an existing safe public dataset the added value over only using the public data for training is reduced.

To investigate this trade-off we trained a next-word-prediction model using PyTorch. A standard LSTM-RNN model[11] was used with two layers, each layer

---

[9] In particular, the DP analysis ignores correlations between the words in a sentence and so may greatly underestimate the information release. The impact of correlations on DP is well known and was first noted by [9].

[10] https://anonymous.4open.science/r/appendix_repo-F4CC.

[11] Training code can be found at: https://github.com/pytorch/examples/tree/main/word_language_model.

having 200 hidden states and an input Embedding layer. The model has 4,041,675 parameters. A dictionary of all words was created from the dataset and input text was vectorized by replacing each word with its corresponding index in the dictionary. The model was trained using a negative log-likelihood loss.

The sensitive dataset was divided into a train-validation (90:10) split. The training data was redacted while validation data was not redacted. The model was then trained on the redacted training data and was tested against the held-out validation data. The model performance was evaluated by the measured perplexity (ppl) on the validation set, the lower the value of perplexity the better the model is at predicting a given sequence.

Figure 7 shows the measured perplexity on the validation data of the next word prediction model for each of the datasets studied as the redaction level is varied (for the smarter redaction approach of Sect. 5.3). The vertical line in the plot indicates the point where the measured attack classification accuracy is 60% (taken from Fig. 5). It can be seen as expected, the perplexity increases as the redaction level increases. It can be seen that the perplexity increases with the level of redaction, as expected. However, for redaction levels up to 20–30% the perplexity of the model trained on the redacted dataset remains fairly close to the perplexity of the model trained on non-redacted dataset. A redaction level of 30% is sufficient to bring the attack classification accuracy down to 60% i.e. a good degree of privacy can be obtained while preserving the utility of the dataset for model training.

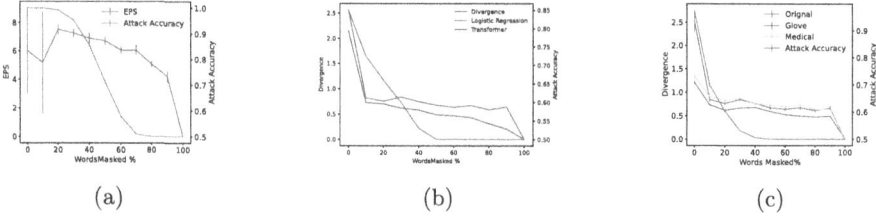

(a)   (b)   (c)

Fig. 8. 8(a) Measured ϵ and attack accuracy for cancer sentences when compared against IMDB reviews.8(b) Measured Renyi-divergence ($\alpha = 2$) and attack accuracy for logistic regression and BERT transformer classification attacks as the redaction level is increased. Medal dataset. 8(c) Measured Renyi-divergence ($\alpha = 2$) with different embeddings: (i) general-purpose sentenceBERT, (ii) fine-tuned medical sentenceBERT, (ii) Glove. Medal dataset.

6   Discussion

6.1   Choice of the Safe Dataset

When the safe dataset is similar to the sensitive dataset, then we can expect that only a small amount of redaction is needed to bring the two datasets closer together. Conversely, we expect that a higher level of redaction is needed to make very disparate datasets similar.

This is illustrated in Fig. 8a, which can be directly compared with Fig. 5a. In both cases the Medal cancer text is the sensitive dataset but in Fig. 8a the safe dataset is IMDB review text while in Fig. 5a it is Medal non-cancer text. It can be seen that with the IMDB data almost 80% of the words need to be redacted to get an attack accuracy close to 50% whereas with the Medal non-cancer text a redaction level of around 50% is sufficient.

The choice of safe dataset is therefore a privacy design parameter that can be used to manage the trade-off between privacy and utility in a fairly transparent manner.

6.2   More Powerful Attacks

It is important to stress that it is the Renyi-divergence that provides a sound measure of privacy, not the accuracy of any specific attack. In the previous sections we use a classification attack based on logistic regression to roughly verify privacy. However, this attack on its own does not provide any privacy guarantee.

For example Fig. 8b shows the attack accuracy and Renyi-divergence as the level of redaction is varied. It can be seen that at redaction levels around 50–80% the attack accuracy is low (close to 50%, the accuracy of a random classifier). However, the Renyi-divergence remains relatively high at around 2.5 at these redaction levels, indicating that the datasets remain dissimilar. We therefore trained a more powerful BERT transformer model and used it to carry out the classification attack. Figure 8b, shows the measured attack accuracy. It can be seen that at 50–80% redaction the attack accuracy now remains relatively high, demonstrating the predictive power of the Renyi-divergence approach.

6.3   Choice of Embedding

The estimator in Sect. 4 maps text to a vector embedding and then estimates the Renyi-divergence between sets of vectors. It therefore depends on the choice of embedding used. It is problematic for a privacy approach to depend on the choice of embedding since (i) the properties of these embeddings remain poorly understood and (ii) an attacker can easily use a different embedding. For example, if a general purpose embedding is used in the Renyi-divergence but the attacker uses a domain specific embedding, a natural concern is that attacker may be able to extract information even when the Renyi-divergence estimate is low.

One of the great advantages of redaction is that it does not depend on the choice of embedding, but rather works directly with the text data[12]. We can then calculate Renyi-divergence estimates for different choices of embeddings and use the largest value to evaluate privacy.

---

[12] And one of the major deficiencies of all approaches tied to a single up front choice of embedding, such as word-level DP approaches.

For example Fig. 8c shows the measured Renyi-divergence estimates for three different choices of embedding: (i) a general-purpose pre-trained sentenceBERT embedding[13], (ii) sentenceBERT after fine-tuning on medical data and (iii) Glove[14] [14]. sentenceBERT is a state of the art transformer embedding, Glove is an older embedding commonly used on word-level DP.

It can be seen from Fig. 8c that the Renyi-divergence estimates for the two sentenceBERT embeddings are almost the same and consistently higher than the Renyi-divergence estimate using Glove i.e. Glove overestimates privacy. The consistency in the divergence estimates between the general purpose and fine-tuned sentenceBERT embedding indicates the robustness of the general purpose sentenceBERT and is why we use it in our earlier plots.

6.4   Limitations

Renyi-divergence is an estimate. Probably the main limitation of our approach is that it uses an estimate of the Renyi-divergence rather than the true value. We partially mitigate this by also estimating confidence intervals. However use of an estimate seems unavoidable since the true divergence cannot be calculated for realistic text data, and for similar reasons theoretical differential privacy guarantees are intractable. We argue that adopting a pragmatic approach and using estimates provides a way forward that is both useful and represents significant progress over the state of the art in text privacy. This is particularly pressing given the prevalence of text data and the current great interest in using it to train large language models.

7   Conclusions

We revisit the question of how to sanitise sensitive text data so that it can be used for model training while preserving privacy. The great majority of the existing literature on privacy enhanced model training gains privacy by adding noise to gradients used for training. The amount of noise added needs to scale with the number of model parameters since the DP sensitivity scales with this. When the number of model parameters is large (as it usually is for language models), the amount of noise needed is considerable and adversely affects model utility. Sampling of the input data can be used to boost privacy, but requires effective anonymisation which can be hard to achieve in practice and reduces the volume of training data available. The data sanitisation approach that we consider complements this line of work and offers new ways to manage the trade-off between privacy and utlity.

---

[13] https://www.sbert.net/.

[14] The embedding vector of each word in a sentence is calculated, and the mean of these vectors is used as the sentence embedding.

References

1. Abadi, M., et al.: Deep learning with differential privacy. In: Proceedings of the 2016 ACM SIGSAC Conference on Computer and Communications Security, pp. 308–318. CCS '16, Association for Computing Machinery, New York, NY, USA (2016). https://doi.org/10.1145/2976749.2978318
2. Bosch, N., Crues, R., Shaik, N., Paquette, L.: Hello, [REDACTED]: protecting student privacy in analyses of online discussion forums. Grantee Submission (2020)
3. Brown, H., Lee, K., Mireshghallah, F., Shokri, R., Tramèr, F.: What does it mean for a language model to preserve privacy? In: 2022 ACM Conference on Fairness, Accountability, and Transparency, pp. 2280–2292. FAccT '22, Association for Computing Machinery, New York, NY, USA (2022). https://doi.org/10.1145/3531146.3534642
4. Bun, M., Steinke, T.: Concentrated differential privacy: simplifications, extensions, and lower bounds (2016)
5. Chen, S., et al.: A customized text sanitization mechanism with differential privacy. In: Findings of the Association for Computational Linguistics: ACL 2023, pp. 5747–5758. Association for Computational Linguistics, Toronto, Canada (2023). https://doi.org/10.18653/v1/2023.findings-acl.355
6. Doudalis, S., Kotsogiannis, I., Haney, S., Machanavajjhala, A., Mehrotra, S.: One-sided differential privacy (2017)
7. Dwork, C., McSherry, F., Nissim, K., Smith, A.: Calibrating noise to sensitivity in private data analysis. In: Halevi, S., Rabin, T. (eds.) Theory of Cryptography, pp. 265–284. Springer, Berlin, Heidelberg (2006)
8. Feyisetan, O., Balle, B., Drake, T., Diethe, T.: Privacy- and utility-preserving textual analysis via calibrated multivariate perturbations. In: Proceedings of the 13th International Conference on Web Search and Data Mining, pp. 178–186. WSDM '20, Association for Computing Machinery, New York, NY, USA (2020). https://doi.org/10.1145/3336191.3371856
9. Kifer, D., Machanavajjhala, A.: No free lunch in data privacy. In: Proceedings of the 2011 ACM SIGMOD International Conference on Management of Data, pp. 193–204. SIGMOD '11, Association for Computing Machinery, New York, NY, USA (2011). https://doi.org/10.1145/1989323.1989345
10. Mattern, J., Weggenmann, B., Kerschbaum, F.: The limits of word level differential privacy. In: Findings of the Association for Computational Linguistics: NAACL 2022, pp. 867–881. Association for Computational Linguistics, Seattle, United States (2022). https://doi.org/10.18653/v1/2022.findings-naacl.65
11. Mironov, I.: Rényi differential privacy. In: 2017 IEEE 30th Computer Security Foundations Symposium (CSF). IEEE (2017). https://doi.org/10.1109/csf.2017.11
12. Murugadoss, K., et al.: Building a best-in-class automated de-identification tool for electronic health records through ensemble learning. medRxiv (2021). https://doi.org/10.1101/2020.12.22.20248270
13. Noshad, M., Moon, K.R., Sekeh, S.Y., Hero, A.O.: Direct estimation of information divergence using nearest neighbor ratios. In: 2017 IEEE International Symposium on Information Theory (ISIT). IEEE (2017). https://doi.org/10.1109/isit.2017.8006659
14. Pennington, J., Socher, R., Manning, C.D.: Glove: global vectors for word representation. In: Empirical Methods in Natural Language Processing (EMNLP), pp. 1532–1543 (2014). http://www.aclweb.org/anthology/D14-1162

15. Reimers, N., Gurevych, I.: Sentence-BERT: sentence embeddings using Siamese BERT-networks (2019)
16. Shi, W., Shea, R., Chen, S., Zhang, C., Jia, R., Yu, Z.: Just fine-tune twice: selective differential privacy for large language models. In: Proceedings of the 2022 Conference on Empirical Methods in Natural Language Processing, pp. 6327–6340. Association for Computational Linguistics, Abu Dhabi, United Arab Emirates (2022). https://aclanthology.org/2022.emnlp-main.425
17. Shokri, R., Shmatikov, V.: Privacy-preserving deep learning. In: Proceedings of the 22nd ACM SIGSAC Conference on Computer and Communications Security, pp. 1310–1321. CCS '15, Association for Computing Machinery, New York, NY, USA (2015). https://doi.org/10.1145/2810103.2813687
18. Voigt, R., Jurgens, D., Prabhakaran, V., Jurafsky, D., Tsvetkov, Y.: RtGender: a corpus for studying differential responses to gender. In: Proceedings of the Eleventh International Conference on Language Resources and Evaluation (LREC 2018). European Language Resources Association (ELRA), Miyazaki, Japan (2018). https://aclanthology.org/L18-1445
19. Wen, Z., Lu, X.H., Reddy, S.: MeDAL: medical abbreviation disambiguation dataset for natural language understanding pretraining. In: Proceedings of the 3rd Clinical Natural Language Processing Workshop. Association for Computational Linguistics (2020). https://doi.org/10.18653/v1/2020.clinicalnlp-1.15
20. Yue, X., Du, M., Wang, T., Li, Y., Sun, H., Chow, S.S.M.: Differential privacy for text analytics via natural text sanitization. In: Findings of the Association for Computational Linguistics: ACL-IJCNLP 2021, pp. 3853–3866. Association for Computational Linguistics (2021). https://doi.org/10.18653/v1/2021.findings-acl.337
21. Zhao, X., Li, L., Wang, Y.X.: Provably confidential language modelling. In: Proceedings of the 2022 Conference of the North American Chapter of the Association for Computational Linguistics: Human Language Technologies, pp. 943–955. Association for Computational Linguistics, Seattle, United States (2022). https://doi.org/10.18653/v1/2022.naacl-main.69

Exploring Distribution Learning of Synthetic Data Generators for Manifolds

Sonakshi Garg$^{(\boxtimes)}$ ⓘ and Vicenç Torra ⓘ

Umeå University, Umeå, Sweden
{sgarg,vtorra}@cs.umu.se

Abstract. In the era of data protection regulations like GDPR, safeguarding sensitive information has become paramount, prompting the exploration of synthetic data generation as a privacy-preserving alternative. Generative Adversarial Networks (GAN) and Variational Autoencoders (VAE), among other tools, have become popular for synthetic data generation. Despite their effectiveness, these models often carry the perception of being black boxes due to their complex learning mechanisms. Understanding the intricate behaviors of data within GAN or VAE poses a significant challenge, particularly with high-dimensional datasets. This is essential from privacy perspective as one can use synthetic data instead of original data and this can be considered as an alternative to anonymization. Our study aims to assess the distribution learning capabilities of synthetic data generators. Our methodology centers on artificially created datasets, such as swish roll and S-curve distributions, which offer easy visualization in $\mathbb{R}^\times$ space. Additionally, we evaluate point datasets containing discontinuous points to determine whether GAN and VAE comprehend the discontinuity behavior of datasets. By evaluating the data processed by GAN and VAE, we aim to reveal their learning capabilities and disentangle the complexities of synthetic data generation. Our research shifts the focus from real-world image datasets to artificially generated datasets, enabling exploration of commonly encountered distributions in low-dimensional spaces. Despite widespread recognition of GAN in image synthesis, achieving satisfactory results often requires employing numerous tricks due to training instability. We found that VAE exhibit a superior understanding of the underlying distribution of points in $\mathbb{R}^\times$ space compared to GAN. This inclination towards VAE arises from their more stable training process, inherent ability to capture latent structures within the data, and faster convergence compared to GAN.

Keywords: Manifold Learning · Privacy · Synthetic Data Generators · Generative Adversarial Networks · Variational Auto Encoder

1 Introduction

In today's data-driven world, privacy concerns, especially under GDPR [6], highlight the need for effective data protection. Two key approaches are data

J. Garcia-Alfaro et al. (Eds.): ESORICS 2024 Workshops, LNCS 15263, pp. 65–76, 2025.
https://doi.org/10.1007/978-3-031-82349-7_5

anonymization [4,19] and synthetic data generation. While data anonymization has been extensively studied, synthetic data generation is a growing field. Generative Adversarial Networks (GANs) [7] and Variational AutoEncoders (VAEs) [10] are prominent methods for this. GANs use adversarial training with a generator and discriminator to create realistic data, whereas VAEs use probabilistic inference to encode and decode data. Both models excel but are often seen as black boxes with limited insight into their internal workings [18].

While GANs and VAEs excel in image synthesis, their black-box nature complicates visualization and understanding, particularly with complex datasets like ImageNet [3]. To address this, our methodology utilizes simpler, artificially created datasets like Swish Roll and S-Curve, which can be easily visualized in lower-dimensional spaces. This approach helps illuminate the learning behavior of these models and their synthetic data generation capabilities. While GANs perform well on some datasets [9], their effectiveness can vary with more complex data distributions [2,14], making simpler datasets ideal for exploring their strengths and limitations. Thus, our research shifts focus to artificially generated datasets, allowing us to explore the learnability of commonly encountered distributions in low-dimensional spaces. Through this endeavor, we seek to enhance understanding of synthetic data generation methods and their applicability across various domains.

We use UMAP [12] leveraging its unique capability of inverse transformation, which is not possible with many other approaches to transform datasets into a latent space, generate synthetic data with GANs and VAEs, and then reconstruct the data using UMAP's inverse transform. This approach allows us to evaluate the performance of both manifold learning and synthetic data generators. Our experiments, including on datasets like Swish Roll and S-Curve, show that VAEs better capture data distribution compared to GANs. We also found that GANs often struggle with instability and require complex optimization. Our research addresses the challenges of visualizing and evaluating synthetic data generation for manifold datasets, which are distinct from traditional image datasets.

The main contributions of the paper are as follows.

1. We explore how synthetic data generators (GANs and VAEs) perform on artificially created datasets, focusing on privacy concerns.
2. Our methodology involves using UMAP to map datasets to a latent space for synthetic data generation and subsequent reconstruction to assess learning capabilities.
3. We evaluate these models on various datasets, including Swish Roll, S-Curve, and image datasets, uncovering challenges and insights.
4. Our findings show that VAEs outperform GANs in capturing data distribution, and we address the difficulties encountered in GAN training.
5. We address challenges in synthetic data generation for high-dimensional manifold datasets, aiming to improve understanding and performance.

2   Preliminaries

In this section we will explain the important concepts that are used in this paper.

2.1   Manifold Learning

Mathematically, a manifold is a topological space locally resembling Euclidean space, meaning it can be approximated by Euclidean space in small neighborhoods. Formally, a manifold is a space where each point has a neighborhood that is homeomorphic to an open subset of n-dimensional Euclidean space.

Definition 1. *(Manifold Learning) Given a finite set of data points $x_1, ... x_n \in \mathbb{R}^D$ be in a D-dimensional space, Manifold learning aims to find the low-dimensional points $y_1, ... y_n \in \mathbb{R}^d$ where $d \ll D$ such that Euclidean relationship between (y_i, y_j) reflects the intrinsic non-linear relationships between (x_i, x_j) [5].*

In manifold learning, the hypothesis is that data points reside on a low-dimensional manifold $\mathbb{R}^d$, embedded within a higher-dimensional ambient space $\mathbb{R}^D$ [20]. The goal is to find a mapping from $\mathbb{R}^D$ to a lower-dimensional space while preserving geometric properties.

2.2   Synthetic Data Generators

Synthetic data generators create data that mimics original data to address privacy concerns and reduce reliance on actual data. Regulatory frameworks like GDPR highlight the importance of data protection. While one method involves anonymizing data, another involves generating synthetic data that replicates original data structures. GANs [7] have recently become popular for this purpose. GANs have been applied in fields like natural language processing and computer vision. The basic GAN architecture, known as Vanilla GAN, generates realistic data across various domains. For more control over output, Conditional GAN (cGAN) [13] allows for conditional image generation based on factors like class labels. Another specialized variant, Deep Convolutional GAN (DCGAN) [16], improves image synthesis by using convolutional layers in both the generator and discriminator, enhancing training stability and capturing spatial hierarchies in images. Conditional Tabular GAN (CTGAN) [21] is a robust GAN variant designed for diverse real-world datasets, capturing data heterogeneity effectively. In addition to GANs, Variational Autoencoders (VAEs) [10] are another prominent generative model family. VAEs are autoencoders that regularize the encoding distribution to ensure a well-structured latent space for generating new data. They are trained to minimize reconstruction error while avoiding overfitting.

3   Methodology

In this section we propose our methodology for visualizing the manifolds to determine whether the manifolds generated using synthetic data generators converge to real data manifolds. We aim to assess the ability of generators to understand and replicate the underlying distribution of the data it is trained on. We describe our methodology with step-by-step explanation as follows.

1. Dataset Selection: Start by selecting a real-world high-dimensional dataset with a manifold structure. For this task, we use the MNIST [3] dataset.

2. Train a Manifold Learning Model: Train Uniform Manifold Approximation and Projection (UMAP) [12] on the chosen dataset to transform it into a lower-dimensional space. UMAP is selected for its ability to preserve both local and global structures, functionality of inverse-transformation and its faster computation compared to t-SNE.

3. Reconstruction to Original Space: Use UMAP's inverse mapping to reconstruct the data back to its original high-dimensional space, ensuring the model handles manifold structures effectively.

4. Generation of Artificial Data: Test the trained model on artificial datasets in $\mathbb{R}^4$ and $\mathbb{R}^2$ to visualize and understand the dataset, the lower-dimensional transformations, and the synthetic data, which is not feasible with high-dimensional real-world data.

5. Test the Manifold Learning Model: Apply the trained manifold learning model to transform artificial datasets into the latent space for visualization. This step assesses the model's ability to preserve proximity between points from high-dimensional to lower-dimensional spaces and allows for performance evaluation of the manifold learning algorithm.

6. Synthetic Data Generators: Introduce generators like GAN and VAE to create synthetic data from the latent space. This step evaluates how well the generated data resembles real data and ensures privacy by retaining data structure while introducing variability to avoid exact replication.

7. Synthetic Data Reconstruction: Use the inverse transformation function to reconstruct synthetic data back to its original dimensional space. Compare the reconstructed data with the original synthetic data to evaluate the accuracy of the reconstruction process.

4   Experimental Setup

In this section we describe the setup of our experiments which includes description of the datasets and some details about the synthetic data generator architectures.

4.1   Datasets Description

We selected various datasets with manifold structures to evaluate our approach comprehensively. Manifold structure represents intricate data distribution patterns in a high-dimensional space that can't be fully captured by traditional linear methods. These include high-dimensional point datasets like Swish Roll [11] and S-curve residing in $\mathbb{R}^4$, and lower-dimensional datasets such as Concentric Circles, Mixture of Gaussian Points, and Two-Half Circles residing in $\mathbb{R}^2$ plane, all generated using the sklearn library [15]. Each dataset consists of 4000 samples with each sample representing a fixed point in $\mathbb{R}^n$. Additionally, we used the MNIST dataset to test manifold learning on real-world complex data distributions. This variety allows us to assess the robustness and effectiveness of our manifold learning techniques and synthetic data generators.

4.2   Architectures

We trained our model using Vanilla GAN, where both the generator and discriminator networks were built. The generator had four dense layers with Leaky ReLU activations and a tanh activation at the output. The discriminator mirrored this setup but used a sigmoid activation at the output. After updating the discriminator, it was frozen, and the generator was trained on fake data, with loss backpropagated to adjust its weights. Next, we used the DCGAN architecture for image synthesis. The DCGAN generator includes dense layers, Batch Normalization, and a Convolution1D layer for upsampling. Unlike traditional GANs, the DCGAN discriminator handles image inputs rather than vectors, and both generated and original images are evaluated by it. Leaky ReLU activations are used in this setup, while the discriminator's operation follows the traditional GAN process.

Alongside Vanilla GAN and DCGAN, we used Conditional Tabular GAN (CTGAN) and Differentially Private GAN (DPGAN) for synthetic data generation. CTGAN was used for its specialization in tabular data, while DPGAN's architecture was employed to ensure differential privacy. This approach allowed us to assess the effectiveness of these GAN variants in generating synthetic data and addressing privacy concerns across different domains. We used VAE for synthetic data generation, featuring an encoder with two dense ReLU layers to produce the mean and log variance of the latent distribution, and a decoder with two dense ReLU layers and a sigmoid output for reconstruction. The sampling layer utilizes the reparameterization trick to generate latent vectors. All models, including VAE, were trained with the Adam optimizer at a learning rate of 10^{-4}.

5   Results and Discussion

In this section, we delve into the outcomes of our experiments and provide comprehensive discussion on them.

5.1   Visualizing Synthetic Generation from S-Curve Transformation

Figure 1 outlines our methodology applied to the S-Curve dataset, beginning with its creation using the 'make-s-curve' function from sklearn. We first transformed this dataset into a 2D plane using a pre-trained UMAP model, originally trained on the MNIST dataset (Fig. 1b). This transformation effectively retained the original shape and geometry of the S-Curve, validating the manifold hypothesis which posits that proximity in high-dimensional space is preserved in lower-dimensional representations. The labeled points in the 2D plane confirm the accurate univariate positioning based on the primary dimensions of the manifold.

Next, we generated synthetic data using a Variational Autoencoder (VAE) trained on the UMAP-transformed data (Fig. 1c). VAEs, known for capturing the underlying distribution of input data, utilized the lower-dimensional structure provided by UMAP to produce synthetic data that mirrors the original dataset's patterns. The latent space representation by the VAE further confirmed its efficacy in capturing the essential features of the S-Curve. Finally, we used the inverse transform functions of UMAP to reconstruct the data in the original space (Fig. 1d). While the reconstructed points generally clustered around the central region, the dispersion was limited, highlighting the challenge of precisely recovering the high-dimensional structure and indicating areas for improvement in the transformation process.

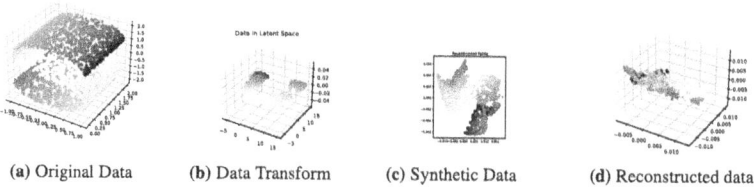

(a) Original Data   (b) Data Transform   (c) Synthetic Data   (d) Reconstructed data

Fig. 1. S-Curve Dataset

5.2   Unrolling the Swish Roll: Exploring Manifold Transformation

Fig. 2 shows the Swish roll dataset, initially visualized in Fig. 2(a). Transforming this data into 2D using UMAP (Fig. 2b) reveals its intricate structure and relationships, illustrating manifold learning principles. UMAP effectively captures and preserves the dataset's complex high-dimensional patterns in a lower-dimensional space, highlighting its utility for creating meaningful data representations. In Fig. 2(c), synthetic data generated by VAE from UMAP-transformed points displays distinct labels and closely mimics the original data, with minor dissimilarities indicating noise for privacy. This highlights VAE's effectiveness in capturing the original data's characteristics while preserving privacy. Figure 2(d) shows the reconstruction of original data using the manifold model's inverse transform. Although points cluster by label, overlapping regions complicate accurate reconstruction, reflecting challenges in handling high-dimensional data with noise and overlapping surfaces.

5.3   Understanding 2D Point Datasets

In our analysis of synthetic data generators, we applied our methodology to 2D point datasets. Figure 3(a) shows Gaussian clusters generated using sklearn's make-blobs function, with three clusters having a standard deviation of 0.2. We then used a VAE to replicate this data, as seen in Fig. 3(b). The VAE-generated points form three distinct clusters, though some points are stretched within each cluster. This indicates the VAE's success in producing data similar to the original while preserving privacy through slight dissimilarities. The VAE effectively learns and reproduces the discontinuous nature of the original data points, despite not following a continuous pattern. This contrasts with findings in [17], where the model struggled with data discontinuity due to assumptions of a continuous latent space.

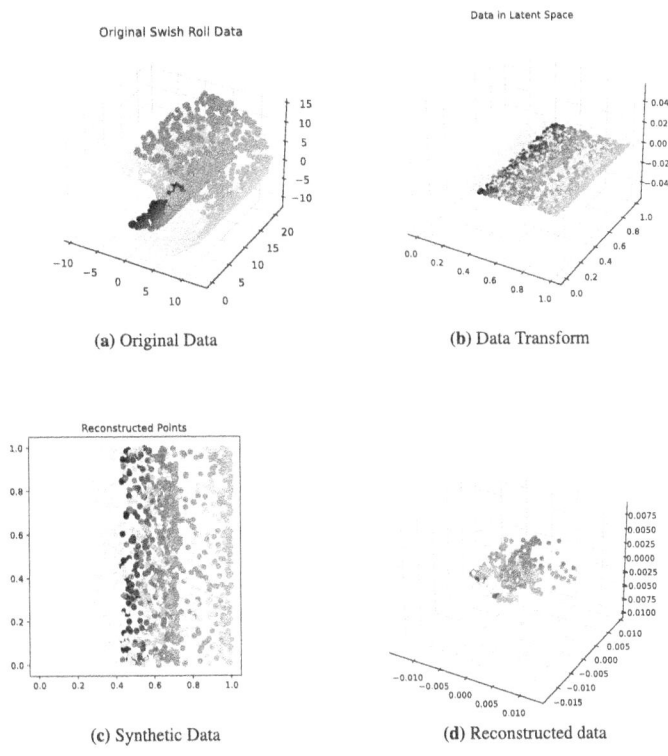

(a) Original Data   (b) Data Transform

(c) Synthetic Data   (d) Reconstructed data

Fig. 2. Swish Roll Dataset

In Fig. 4, we observe a similar pattern with the concentric circles dataset and the two half circles dataset. In both visualizations, the original datasets exhibit a discontinuous nature with distinct geometrical patterns. This process ensures that the privacy of the original data's structure and geometry is maintained while generating synthetic data. The produced synthetic data closely resembles the structure and geometry of the original datasets while incorporating some variation. This behavior arises because the VAE learns the distribution of the data and generates new points based on this learned distribution, thereby pre-

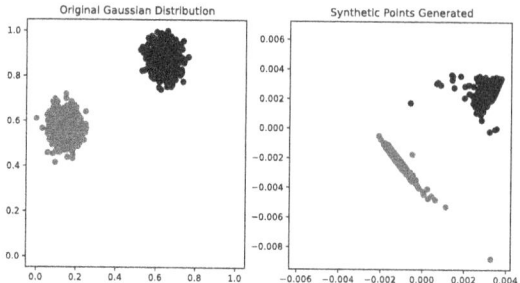

Fig. 3. Mix of Gaussian Points

serving the essential characteristics of the original data while introducing slight deviations.

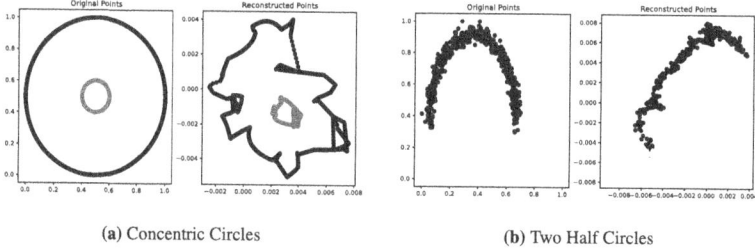

(a) Concentric Circles   **(b)** Two Half Circles

Fig. 4. Concentric and Two Half Circles

5.4   Visualizing Real-World Data

We explored the capabilities of manifold learning and synthetic data generators using the MNIST dataset, a widely-used real-world dataset in machine learning. Firstly, we visualized the original MNIST dataset, consisting of 70,000 hand-written digit images sized at 28x28 pixels, as shown in Fig. 5(a). Next, we trans-formed this data into a 2D latent space using manifold learning, resulting in well-separated clusters representing different digits, as depicted in Fig. 5(b). We then generated synthetic data from this transformed data using a VAE, shown in Fig. 5(c), where the data points appear clustered closely together. The recon-structed data, seen in Fig. 5(d), closely resembles the original data. However, when dealing with real-world image datasets like MNIST, we can only visualize the original and reconstructed data. Once the data is transformed into a latent space, visualization is limited to observing if the data points are well-separated according to their labels. This black-box-like mechanism of synthetic data gen-erators makes it difficult to visualize how the geometry of data points changes at each step. This is why we used artificially created datasets in 4D and 2D planes, allowing us to visualize the workings of synthetic data generators more effectively.

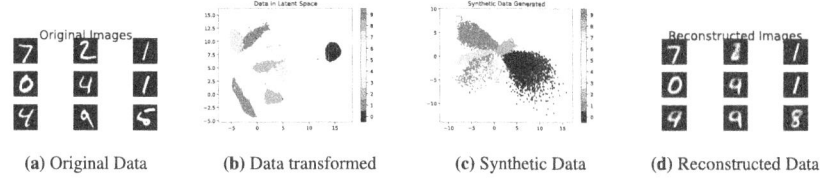

(a) Original Data   (b) Data transformed   (c) Synthetic Data   (d) Reconstructed Data

Fig. 5. MNIST Dataset

5.5   Privacy Risk Assessment in VAE

We extended our privacy analysis of VAEs by adding new artificial points to the original S-Curve dataset and examining the VAE's ability to regenerate these points. Figure 6(a) shows the original data with 10% additional points arranged along a straight line, marked in red and green. Figure 6(b) displays the synthetic data generated by the VAE, which accurately regenerates the added points. This demonstrates the VAE's proficiency in learning and generalizing from the dataset, effectively capturing the underlying structure, including the newly introduced points. When the added points are numerous and systematically distributed, as in Fig. 6(a), the model's ability to regenerate them in Fig. 6(b) indicates that it has effectively learned the underlying structure of the data, including the newly introduced points. This capability highlights the VAE's proficiency in learning and generalizing from the dataset, ensuring that it can produce realistic synthetic data while preserving the distribution of added data points.

If the VAE regenerates very few newly added points precisely at their original locations, it indicates a potential privacy leak due to memorization of individual samples rather than learning general patterns. Figures 6(c) and 6(d) illustrate this scenario. In Fig. 6(c), only 0.01% of points are newly added and strategically placed. In Fig. 6(d), the synthetic data shows these points in different locations, indicating the VAE did not memorize the specific data samples but learned general patterns instead. The scattered positions of the newly added points demonstrate that the VAE preserves the overall S-curve structure without retaining exact data points, reducing the risk of privacy leakage. In Fig. 6(c), the three newly added points (two green and one red) coincide with the S-Curve data points but are not regenerated at the same positions by the VAE, indicating they were not memorized. Instead, these points are scattered across the S-Curve structure. Figure 6(d) shows that while the VAE preserves the overall S-shape, it does not retain the exact positions of individual data points, as evidenced by the color spectrum. This observation is crucial for privacy, demonstrating that the VAE does not memorize specific, potentially sensitive information, thereby reducing the risk of privacy leakage.

This visualization assesses privacy risks in VAE data generation. Accurate regeneration of specific, newly added points by the VAE suggests memorization of exact details rather than learning general patterns, potentially leading to privacy breaches. Ensuring the VAE does not memorize individual data points is crucial for maintaining privacy and avoiding the revelation of sensitive information.

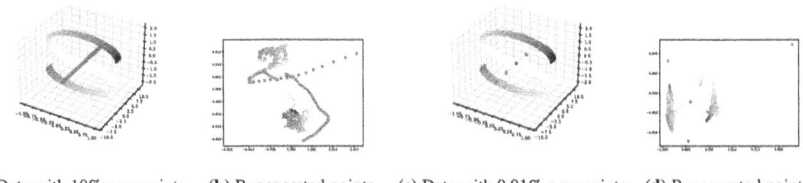

(a) Data with 10% new points   (b) Regenerated points   (c) Data with 0.01% new points   (d) Regenerated points

Fig. 6. Privacy Risk Assessment in VAE

5.6   Visualization with Diverse GAN Architectures

We tested various GANs for synthetic data generation, including Vanilla GAN, DCGAN, CTGAN, and DPGAN. Starting with Vanilla GAN on the S-Curve dataset, as shown in Fig. 7(a), we found that it performed poorly, with generated data being far from the original points. This indicates that Vanilla GAN struggled with the 3D point data's intrinsic dimensionality. We tested various GANs on all datasets, but obtained similar results across them. For simplicity, we are only presenting the findings for the S-Curve dataset. We applied DCGAN to the Swish Roll dataset (Fig. 7(b)), finding that while the generated points overlapped with the original, they were disorganized. Using CTGAN on the S-Curve dataset (Fig. 7(c)), the generated points also showed significant overlap with the original data, and the latent space representation was scattered, highlighting CTGAN's difficulty in capturing the 3D geometry.

We tested DPGAN on the Swish Roll dataset (Fig. 7(d)), but found that the generated points were scattered and lacked geometric fidelity. GANs, known for their instability and slow convergence [7,16] compared to VAEs [1], struggled with manifold data. This led us to favor VAE, which provided more reliable results. Unlike GANs, which often face mode collapse, VAE effectively captured the diverse structures in our datasets [8], making it the preferred choice for our synthetic data generation. This discrepancy sheds light on why GAN struggled with our manifold data, which consists of data points in $\mathbb{R}^n$ space rather than images.

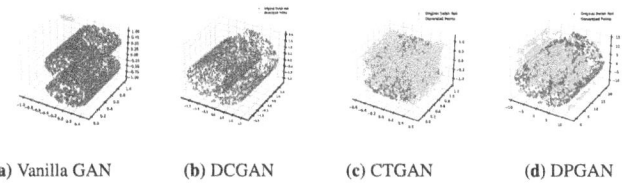

(a) Vanilla GAN   (b) DCGAN   (c) CTGAN   (d) DPGAN

Fig. 7. Results with other types of GAN

6 Conclusion and Future Works

In this study, we examined the effectiveness of synthetic data generators, GAN and VAE, for privacy-preserving data. Given their black-box nature and challenges with high-dimensional data, we used artificially created datasets in $\mathbb{R}^n$ and applied UMAP for data transformation. This approach allows us to visualize and evaluate the performance of GAN and VAE throughout their training, providing clearer insights into their learning capabilities. Our findings indicate that VAE demonstrate a superior ability to understand and learn the intrinsic structure of our artificial point dataset compared to GAN. Furthermore, when attempting to reconstruct the original data using inverse transformation, we observed interesting outcomes. For instance, in the case of the swish roll dataset, the data points were clustered according to their labels, while in the s-curve dataset, the produced samples were situated between the clusters of data. This outcome leads to generalization of data which is promising from a privacy perspective, as the generated data samples fall within the range of the original data points without fully revealing their exact shape and structure. However, the effectiveness of this process depends on the compression and inverse transformation techniques employed. Nevertheless, privacy always comes at the cost of utility. Future research could focus on developing techniques that offer both efficient transformation and inverse transformation with minimal loss. Additionally, there is a need for synthetic data generators tailored specifically for point datasets in $\mathbb{R}^n$ rather than images, which could further enhance privacy-preserving data generation techniques.

References

1. Bond-Taylor, S., Leach, A., Long, Y., Willcocks, C.G.: Deep generative modelling: a comparative review of vaes, gans, normalizing flows, energy-based and autoregressive models. IEEE Trans. Pattern Anal. Mach. Intell. **44**(11), 7327–7347 (2021)
2. Brock, A., Donahue, J., Simonyan, K.: Large scale gan training for high fidelity natural image synthesis. arXiv preprint arXiv:1809.11096 (2018)
3. Deng, J., Dong, W., Socher, R., Li, L.J., Li, K., Fei-Fei, L.: Imagenet: a large-scale hierarchical image database. In: 2009 IEEE Conference on Computer Vision and Pattern Recognition, pp. 248–255. IEEE (2009)
4. Dwork, C.: Differential privacy. In: International colloquium on automata, languages, and programming, pp. 1–12. Springer (2006)

5. Garg, S., Torra, V.: K-anonymous privacy preserving manifold learning. In: The 20th International Conference on Security and Cryptography, Rome, Italy, v July 2023. vol. 1, pp. 37–48 (2023)
6. GDPR:EU: Gdpr compliance(2020). https://gdpr.eu/
7. Goodfellow, I., et al.: Generative adversarial networks. Commun. ACM **63**(11), 139–144 (2020)
8. Huang, H., Yu, P.S., Wang, C.: An introduction to image synthesis with generative adversarial nets. arXiv preprint arXiv:1803.04469 (2018)
9. Karras, T., Aila, T., Laine, S., Lehtinen, J.: Progressive growing of gans for improved quality, stability, and variation. arXiv preprint arXiv:1710.10196 (2017)
10. Kingma, D.P., Welling, M., et al.: An introduction to variational autoencoders. Foundat. Trends® Mac. Learn. **12**(4), 307–392 (2019)
11. Marsland, S.: Machine learning: an algorithmic perspective. Chapman and Hall/CRC (2011)
12. McInnes, L., Healy, J., Melville, J.: Umap: uniform manifold approximation and projection for dimension reduction. arXiv preprint arXiv:1802.03426 (2018)
13. Mirza, M., Osindero, S.: Conditional generative adversarial nets. arXiv preprint arXiv:1411.1784 (2014)
14. Odena, A., Olah, C., Shlens, J.: Conditional image synthesis with auxiliary classifier gans. In: International Conference on Machine Learning, pp. 2642–2651. PMLR (2017)
15. Pedregosa, F., et al.: Scikit-learn: machine learning in python. J. Mach. Learn. Res. **12**, 2825–2830 (2011)
16. Radford, A., Metz, L., Chintala, S.: Unsupervised representation learning with deep convolutional generative adversarial networks. arXiv preprint arXiv:1511.06434 (2015)
17. Rege, A., Monteleoni, C.: Evaluating the distribution learning capabilities of gans. arXiv preprint arXiv:1907.02662 (2019)
18. Savage, N.: Breaking into the black box of artificial intelligence (2022)
19. Sweeney, L.: k-anonymity: a model for protecting privacy. Internat. J. Uncertain. Fuzziness Knowl.-Based Syst. **10**(05), 557–570 (2002)
20. Tenenbaum, J.B., Silva, V.d., Langford, J.C.: A global geometric framework for nonlinear dimensionality reduction. Science **290**(5500), 2319–2323 (2000)
21. Xu, L., Skoularidou, M., Cuesta-Infante, A., Veeramachaneni, K.: Modeling tabular data using conditional gan. Adv. Neural Inform. Process. Syst. **32** (2019)

HEDAS: Secure and Efficient Distributed OLAP Using Fully Homomorphic Encryption

Yu Tian[1], Tianxiang Shen[1], Qi Hu[1], Wei Chen[1], Heming Cui[1,3], and Ji Qi[2(✉)]

[1] The University of Hong Kong, Hong Kong, China
{tianyuk,txshen2,h3009790,h3011068,heming}@cs.hku.hk
[2] Institute of Software, Chinese Academy of Sciences, Beijing, China
qiji@iscas.ac.cn
[3] Shanghai AI Laboratory, Shanghai, China

Abstract. The popularity of cloud computing has revolutionized Online Analytical Processing (OLAP), yet risks of privacy leakage limit the use of public clouds in security-critical scenarios, such as healthcare and finance. Fully Homomorphic Encryption (FHE) is a promising solution that enables computations on encrypted data without decryption. However, the performance overhead of FHE hinders its practical use in OLAP. Existing FHE-based OLAP systems primarily focus on single-machine optimization and lack proper co-design with OLAP characteristics, leading to suboptimal effectiveness. Our key idea is to distribute FHE-based OLAP across multiple machines, inspired by the MapReduce model, to reduce end-to-end latency.

In this paper, we propose HEDASHEDAS stands for Homomorphic Encryption-based Distributed Analytical System, the first distributed FHE-based OLAP system that achieves secure and efficient OLAP. HEDAS effectively addresses the limitations of FHE by introducing the *pre-group* operation and two key stages: *Secure Map (SMap)* and *Secure Reduce (SReduce)*. These stages securely and efficiently execute filtering and aggregation operations in OLAP. By leveraging the MapReduce model, HEDAS effectively distributes FHE-based OLAP across multiple machines, achieving a notable reduction ($\sim$44.1%) in end-to-end latency using four computing nodes, with further reductions as the number of computing nodes increases. Additionally, two case studies are conducted to address the optimization of the filter bottleneck within HEDAS, and evaluation experiments demonstrate the efficiency and scalability of HEDAS compared to the state-of-the-art single-machine FHE-based OLAP system.

Keywords: Fully homomorphic encryption (FHE) · Online analytical processing (OLAP) · MapReduce

J. Garcia-Alfaro et al. (Eds.): ESORICS 2024 Workshops, LNCS 15263, pp. 77–93, 2025.
https://doi.org/10.1007/978-3-031-82349-7_6

1   Introduction

The widespread adoption of cloud computing has revolutionized database systems, including Online Analytical Processing (OLAP) [8], yet concerns about privacy breaches have restricted the applicability of public clouds in scenarios where data confidentiality is of utmost importance [26,41,42]. While the public cloud can provide OLAP with scalability and flexibility advantages, industries such as healthcare and finance face the requirement to safeguard sensitive data of patients and customers in compliance with regulations and to maintain trust.

To ensure the security of data on public clouds, traditional encryption techniques (e.g., AES [38] and RSA [35]) are unsuitable for OLAP scenarios due to their inability to perform computations and analysis on encrypted data. Instead, Fully Homomorphic Encryption (FHE) [14] overcomes this limitation by enabling computations on encrypted data without the need for decryption, thereby allowing the utilization of cloud computing resources while preserving data confidentiality. As a result, there has been a surge in research efforts to design FHE-based OLAP systems [2,34].

However, although FHE is utilized in some OLAP systems to meet security requirements, it suffers from substantial performance overhead. For instance, when executing the CKKS algorithm [5] on CPU, it typically incurs a computational complexity overhead of $\sim 10^4$-$10^5 \times$ compared to plaintext computations.

Much existing work has explored ways to accelerate FHE-based OLAP systems; however, they haven't fully satisfied the performance requirements for practical applications. There exists two major categories of work, one focusing on single-machine optimization by improving FHE algorithms [2,33,34,36], and the other utilizing heterogeneous computing acceleration units (e.g., GPU [40,43] and FPGA [27]) to enhance the performance of critical analytic operators under FHE. While these methods achieved notable performance improvements, they solely focus on the single-machine level and lack deep integration with the characteristics of OLAP. OLAP applications are commonly deployed in a distributed manner, such as data lakes [21] and data warehouses [1], providing an opportunity to leverage the distributed workload computation capabilities across multiple machines.

One strawman approach to scaling existing FHE-based OLAP systems in a distributed manner is by utilizing the classical MapReduce model [11], a well-established practice in distributed data processing, making it an ideal choice for our early exploration. As shown in the left part of Fig. 1, the MapReduce model consists of a coordinator node and multiple worker nodes responsible for task assignment and data processing, respectively. MapReduce abstracts the data processing into two stages: Map and Reduce. During the Map stage, each worker node processes a portion of the data and generates intermediate key-value results, which involves filtering out unnecessary data that doesn't meet the specified conditions. Subsequently, the system groups the intermediate results with the same key to the corresponding Reduce node, known as the data shuffle. The Reduce nodes then aggregate the intermediate results and produce the final results. Compared to single-machine processing, MapReduce provides a scalable and fault-tolerant distributed abstraction, effectively utilizing the computing resources of multi-node clusters.

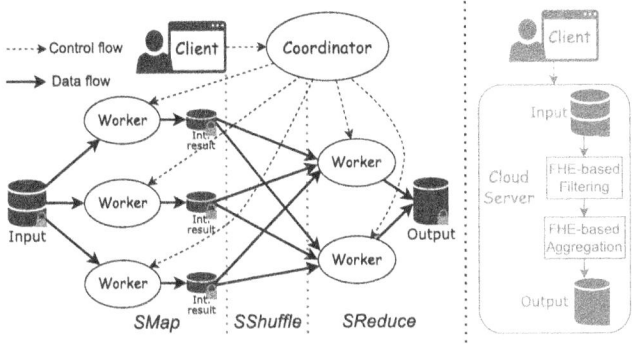

Fig. 1. An overview of the HEDAS model compared to single-machine processing.

However, directly extending FHE-based OLAP systems using the MapReduce model is non-trivial, as it introduces new challenges. Specifically, (1) the result of FHE comparison is encrypted randomly, making it impossible to group the intermediate results, rendering the data shuffle in the MapReduce model impractical. When performing OLAP on a single machine, there is no requirement to handle partial data, eliminating the necessity for data shuffle. On the contrary, in a distributed MapReduce model, it becomes essential to shuffle intermediate results after filtering; otherwise, subsequent aggregation operations cannot be performed. (2) Even if we can employ the MapReduce model, the filtering operation based on FHE comparison becomes a significant bottleneck due to its slow performance. It involves FHE subtraction, FHE most significant bit (MSB) extraction, FHE transformation to generate an encrypted 0/1 vector filter, and vector multiplication between the filter and the data entries [2]. This process is significantly time-consuming, approximately taking 99.96% of the overall time, and it is impossible to filter out unnecessary data based on the encrypted result filter, resulting in the need to process the entire dataset.

To address these challenges, we propose HEDAS, the first distributed FHE-based OLAP system in the MapReduce style that enables secure and efficient OLAP operations. Our first insight is that by employing a pre-group operation which splits the query based on grouping attributes before assigning map tasks, HEDAS can effectively overcome the limitation of FHE filtering that doesn't support shuffling on encrypted intermediate results. By introducing two MapReduce-like stages, *Secure Map (SMap)* and *Secure Reduce (SReduce)*, HEDAS securely and efficiently executes filtering and aggregation operations in OLAP. To address the performance bottleneck associated with filtering, our second insight is to employ a design that separates data retrieval and aggregation computations. This design was inspired by the recognition that not all scenarios require the highest level of security assurance and that trade-offs between security and cost are necessary. We conducted two case studies utilizing widely accepted methods, CryptDB's index and a kind of HashFilter index, as alternatives to the FHE comparison indexing method to explore the optimization of the filter bottleneck.

We built HEDAS on top of HE³DB [2], a state-of-the-art single-machine FHE-based encrypted database framework that enables secure OLAP querying. To evaluate the performance of HEDAS, we conducted experiments using the TPC-H benchmark [10]. The evaluation results demonstrate the following:

- HEDAS is efficient. It significantly reduces end-to-end latency by 44.1% compared to HE³DB with four computing nodes. Additionally, the two case-study systems, HEDAS-CryptDB and HEDAS-HashFilter, achieve further 96.7% and 97.1% reductions in latency respectively, effectively mitigating the performance bottleneck of filtering.
- HEDAS is scalable. The improvements become more pronounced as the number of computing nodes increases, benefiting from the distributed computing capabilities of the MapReduce model.

In summary, our work makes the following contributions: (1) We introduce the pre-group operation and SMap/SReduce stages with FHE and OLAP co-design, effectively enabling distributed computation in FHE-based OLAP systems. (2) We present an index-computation separation architecture and conduct two case studies to address the filtering bottleneck. (3) Through evaluation experiments, we demonstrate the significant latency improvements of HEDAS compared to the state-of-the-art single-machine FHE-based OLAP system.

2   Background and Related Work

2.1   Homomorphic Encryption (HE)

Homomorphic Encryption (HE) [35] is a cryptographic technique that enables computations on encrypted data without decryption. In general, HE involves an encryption function $E(m)$ that encrypts a message m into a ciphertext c and a decryption function $D(c)$ that decrypts c back into the original m. The homomorphic property enables the computation of a function f on encrypted data c_1 and c_2, resulting in an encrypted result $f(c_1, c_2)$ which is equal to $E(g(m_1, m_2))$, where g is the corresponding function that operates on plaintext.

HE can be categorized into three types: partially homomorphic encryption (PHE), somewhat homomorphic encryption (SWHE), and fully homomorphic encryption (FHE). PHE supports only one type of operation (addition or multiplication), while SWHE supports both types of operation but with limited depth. FHE, on the other hand, supports an arbitrary number of addition and multiplication computations on encrypted data, making it the most powerful and versatile type of HE.

Since the introduction of FHE [14], numerous FHE schemes with distinct characteristics have been proposed [4–6,13,15]. There are also many open-source libraries that implement some of the FHE types mentioned above, such as

Microsoft SEAL [37], IBM HElib [18], and TFHEpp [24]. However, FHE introduces significant computational complexity ($\sim 10^4$-$10^5 \times$) and memory overhead ($\sim 10^3$-$10^4 \times$), limiting its practical application in real-world scenarios.

2.2 Secure OLAP Systems

We categorize the existing secure OLAP systems into three categories: FHE-based systems, systems based on specific cryptographic primitives, and TEE-based systems. In Table 1, we compare HEDAS with these systems.

Table 1. Comparison of HEDAS and related secure OLAP systems. **Pattern-Security** indicates whether the system can protect data access patterns, **HW-Independent** indicates whether the system is independent of specific hardware security features (e.g., TEEs), and ✗*denotes partial support for pattern security.

System	FHE-Support	Distributed	Pattern-Security	HW-Independent
CryptDB [32]	✗	✗	✗	✓
Opaque [44]	✗	✓	✗*	✗
Arx [31]	✗	✓	✗*	✓
Seabed [28]	✗	✓	✗*	✓
SAGMA [17]	✗	✓	✗*	✓
HEDA [34]	✓	✗	✓	✓
HE^{3}DB [2]	✓	✗	✓	✓
HEDAS	✓	✓	✓	✓

FHE-Based Secure OLAP Systems. FHE-based secure OLAP systems [2, 34] leverage the power of FHE to enable the execution of complex analytical queries on encrypted data while preserving data confidentiality. These systems provide robust protection against data leakage and even safeguard data access patterns, owing to the strong security guarantees provided by FHE. However, the performance of these systems is limited by the computational complexity and memory overhead of FHE, and they only focus on single-machine scenarios, which restricts their scalability and efficiency when handling large datasets.

Secure OLAP Systems Based on Specific Cryptographic Primitives. In addition to FHE, other cryptographic techniques can be used for secure OLAP computations, such as Deterministic Encryption (DET), Order-Preserving Encryption (OPE)/Order-Revealing Encryption (ORE), Searchable Encryption (SE), and Partial Homomorphic Encryption (PHE). By leveraging these cryptographic primitives, it is also possible to build secure OLAP systems capable of performing queries on encrypted data (e.g., CryptDB [32]). However, these encryption schemes have security limitations that may result in data access pattern leakage [19,20], and they have limitations in scenarios involving complex computation schemes on encrypted data. Although the successors, such as Arx [31], Seabed [28] and SAGMA [17], have addressed some of these issues, they still cannot provide the same level of strong security guarantees as FHE.

TEE-Based Secure OLAP Systems. Another approach to secure OLAP is leveraging Trusted Execution Environments (TEEs) provided by specific hardware. TEEs, such as Intel SGX [9] and ARM TrustZone [30], create secure enclaves within the hardware to protect sensitive data and computations. Secure OLAP systems that utilize TEEs, such as Opaque [44], provide high expressiveness with moderate performance overhead. However, TEEs are susceptible to side-channel attacks [12,22,25,39], which can be exploited by malicious insiders. Additionally, TEEs face challenges related to portability, as different hardware platforms have varying TEE implementations. Therefore, the limitations of TEEs restrict their adoption in high-security OLAP systems.

2.3   FHE Acceleration Techniques

In recent years, significant efforts have been made to accelerate FHE computations using various techniques, resulting in notable performance improvements, including methods based on GPUs [40,43], FPGAs [27], and ASICs [33,36]. We argue that these acceleration methods are complementary to our approach and can be combined to enhance the performance of FHE. On one hand, while accelerators like GPUs provide increased processing power, their capabilities are still limited. Therefore, distributed computing methods are necessary to meet the demands of large-scale data processing in OLAP. On the other hand, for each node participating in distributed OLAP computations, we can choose the appropriate acceleration methods to improve performance. In this work, we focused on optimizing FHE-based OLAP through distributed computing and didn't take these acceleration techniques into consideration.

3   Overview

3.1   System Model

Inspired by the MapReduce model, the HEDAS system also consists of three primary components: the client, the coordinator, and the worker, as depicted in Fig. 1 and Fig. 2. The coordinator and worker nodes are deployed in the cloud, with a single coordinator overseeing task scheduling and multiple workers dedicated to parallel task processing. Each cloud machine stores a portion of the encrypted data and can deploy multiple workers to leverage multi-core parallelism. Specifically, each type of component is described as follows:

Client. The client is the owner of the original plaintext dataset and holds the private key. Its responsibilities include encrypting the dataset, generating the encrypted attributes table, and uploading them to the coordinator. It also encrypts the query parameters, sends the query request to the coordinator, and decrypts the encrypted query results returned by the coordinator.

Coordinator. The coordinator is responsible for three main tasks: (1) Horizontally sharding the encrypted dataset and distributing it across multiple cloud machines. (2) Conducting pre-group operations based on the query and the attributes table. (3) Assigning tasks to worker nodes.

Worker. The worker nodes are responsible for processing the tasks assigned by the coordinator, which involves filtering and aggregating the encrypted data based on the query parameters.

3.2   Threat Model

Our security goal is to protect the security of the outsourced dataset in an honest-but-curious public cloud environment, and our threat model is similar to previous work [2,17,32,34], achieving the same level of security as HE^{3}DB [2]. We assume that the cloud service platform honestly follows our workflow to execute computations, but it may attempt to infer as much security information as possible from the dataset within a probabilistic polynomial time. Additionally, we assume that the client does not disclose any information or private keys. In our model, we categorize the information as public or confidential, as follows:

– Public information: the encrypted dataset, the encrypted attributes table, evaluation keys, the size of the dataset, the encrypted query parameters, and the query pattern (including aggregation function types, the number of query predicates, and the logical connections between predicates).
– Confidential information: the private key, the original plaintext dataset, and the plaintext query parameters.

3.3   The Pre-group Operation

Traditionally, in the MapReduce model, the GROUP BY operation is performed after the map operations and before the reduce operations, which is known as data shuffle. However, when using FHE, the intermediate results generated by Map workers are encrypted randomly, making it impossible to determine which group the data belongs to. As a result, the traditional data shuffle approach is not feasible in FHE-based systems.

To address this issue, we propose the pre-group operation, conducted by the coordinator, which splits the query with the GROUP BY operation into numerous subqueries based on the attributes table. The attributes table is an encrypted set-like structure generated by the client, which contains all the distinct values

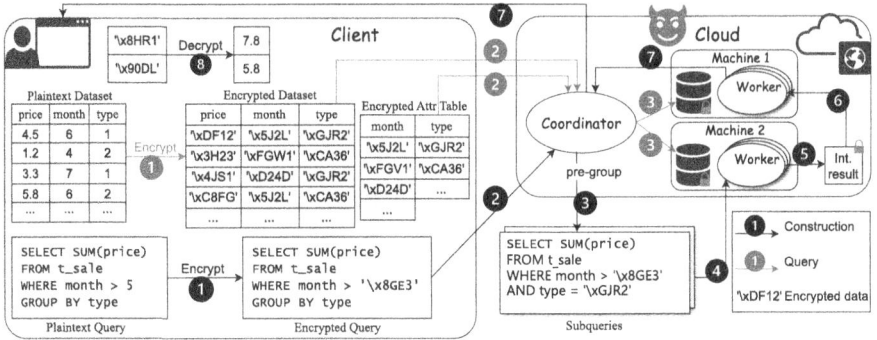

Fig. 2. The system workflow of HEDAS.(Color figure online)

of the grouping attribute. Each subquery replaces the GROUP BY operation with a homomorphic equal comparison corresponding to a specific group. By introducing the pre-group operation, the GROUP BY operation is performed before assigning the map tasks, resulting in a change in the shuffle model: the intermediate results produced by a Map worker now correspond to a single group, referred to as *Secure Shuffle (SShuffle)*.

We argue that the pre-group operation does not leak the data access pattern, because the GROUP BY attribute values are FHE-encrypted in the attributes table, and each query with a GROUP BY operation is split into a predetermined number of subqueries using the same attributes table. Consequently, attacks based on data access pattern analysis [19,20] are ineffective against this scheme.

3.4   SMap and SReduce

The FHE-based OLAP process can be logically divided into two main steps: filtering and aggregation. During the filtering step, data is retrieved based on the WHERE conditions. However, unlike traditional OLAP indexing, FHE-based filtering cannot reduce the amount of data that needs to be processed. Instead, as shown in Fig. 3, it generates a filter represented as an encrypted $0/1$ vector to indicate whether the data satisfies the WHERE conditions. Then the data vector needs to be multiplied with the filter to aggregate the portion that satisfies the WHERE conditions. Therefore, shuffling the intermediate result immediately after the filtering step would require transmitting unnecessary data, resulting in increased communication overhead.

To address this communication overhead, we reorganize the processing into two stages *Secure Map (SMap)* and *Secure Reduce (SReduce)*. We first divide the aggregation into two parts: pre-aggregation and post-aggregation. Pre-aggregation involves locally aggregating the partially filtered results, reducing the amount of data transferred without increasing the computational complexity. By combining filtering and pre-aggregation, we create the SMap stage. Post-

---

Algorithm 1: System Construction

Input: Original plaintext dataset D_{pl}

// Step ❶: Encrypt dataset and generate attributes table

1 $pk \leftarrow$ GetEncryptionKey(); $ek \leftarrow$ GenerateEvalKey(pk);

2 $D_{en} \leftarrow$ Encrypt(D_{pl},pk); $attr\_table \leftarrow$ GenerateAttributeTable(D_{pl},pk);

// Step ❷: Send encrypted data and attributes table to coordinator

3 SendInitData(D_{en}, $attr\_table$, ek);

// Step ❸: Shard encrypted data and distribute to cloud machines

4 $machine\_num \leftarrow$ GetMachineNum();

5 $shards\_array[] \leftarrow$ DataSharding(D_{en},$machine\_num$);

6 **For each cloud machine** m_i; **do**

7 | SendShard($shards\_array[m_i]$);

---

aggregation occurs after data shuffling and is responsible for aggregating the intermediate pre-aggregated results, forming the SReduce stage.

4 System Workflow

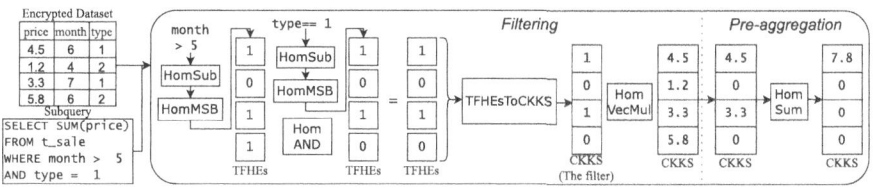

Fig. 3. The processing details of an SMap task.

As depicted in Fig. 2, the HEDAS system consists of two main phases: system construction and query processing. The system construction phase aims to establish a secure OLAP system on the public cloud and prepare the sharded encrypted data. Meanwhile, the query processing phase is responsible for executing secure queries and returning the encrypted query results.

4.1 System Construction

The system construction phase comprises 3 steps, as outlined by the red marks in Fig. 2 and Algorithm 1:

In the system construction phase, the client first encrypts the data and generates the encrypted attributes table (step ❶), then uploads them to the coordinator on the cloud (step ❷). The attributes table is an encrypted structure consisting of all the distinct attribute values, which is utilized for the pre-group

---

Algorithm 2: Query Processing

Input: Plain text query scheme QS with plaintext filtering predicate
        parameters P_{pl} and GROUP BY attribute G

// Step ❶: Encrypt query parameters

1 $pk \leftarrow$ GetEncryptionKey(); $P_{en} \leftarrow$ Encrypt(P_{pl},pk);

// Step ❷: Send query with encrypted parameters to coordinator

2 SendQuery(QS, P_{en}, G);

// Step ❸: pre-group operation

3 $attr\_table \leftarrow$ GetAttributeTable();

4 $sub\_queries[] \leftarrow$ PreGroup(QS, P_{en}, G, $attr\_table$);

// Step ❹: Assign SMap tasks to worker nodes

5 **While SMap not finished; do**

6 | $worker \leftarrow$ WaitWorker(); $SMap\_task \leftarrow$ GetSMapTask($sub\_queries$);

7 | AssignTask($worker$, $SMap\_task$);

// Step ❺: Workers process SMap tasks

8 $SMap\_task \leftarrow$ RequestSMapTask();

9 $int\_result \leftarrow$ DoSMapTask($SMap\_task$); CacheIntResult(int_result);

// Step ❻: Assign SReduce tasks

10 **While SReduce not finished; do**

11 | $worker \leftarrow$ WaitWorker(); $SReduce\_task \leftarrow$ GetSReduceTask();

12 | AssignTask($worker$, $SReduce\_task$);

// Step ❼: Workers process SReduce tasks

13 $SReduce\_task \leftarrow$ RequestSReduceTask();

14 $int\_results \leftarrow$ GetIntResults($SReduce\_task.key$);

15 $partial\_result \leftarrow$ DoSReduceTask($SReduce\_task$, $int\_results$);

16 SendResultToCoordinator($partial\_result$);

// Step ❽: Coordinator collects and returns the final result

17 $result \leftarrow$ CollectAllResults(); ReturnResult($result$);

---

operation described in §3.3. After receiving the encrypted data and the attributes table, the coordinator horizontally partitions the encrypted data into data shards and distributes them across multiple machines (step ❸).

4.2   Query Processing

The query processing phase consists of 8 steps, as outlined by the black marks in Fig. 2 and Algorithm 2:

During the query processing phase, the client first encrypts the query parameters (step ❶) and sends the encrypted query to the coordinator (step ❷). The coordinator then performs pre-group operations (step ❸) to generate subqueries based on the GROUP BY attribute and the corresponding attribute table. For more details on pre-group, please refer to §3.3.

After the pre-group separation, the coordinator assigns tasks to worker nodes, which are divided into two stages: SMap and SReduce. The details of the SMap and SReduce stages are described in §3.4.

In the SMap stage, the coordinator assigns the data shard addresses and sub-query parameters (including the specially encrypted GROUP BY attribute) to the map workers (step ❹). Each worker performs the filtering and pre-aggregation operations on the assigned data shard and caches the intermediate results (step ❺). To minimize communication overhead, the coordinator attempts to assign the data shard on the same machine. Once the workers complete their tasks, they inform the coordinator with the addresses of the cached intermediate results.

In the SReduce stage, the coordinator assigns the post-aggregation tasks to the reduce workers (step ❻), which is similar to the reduce operation in the MapReduce model. In SReduce, the key argument corresponds to the encrypted GROUP BY attribute, and the value argument represents the intermediate pre-aggregated results. The reduce workers fetch the intermediate results from the map workers as part of the SShuffle process and perform the post-aggregation operation. After all the workers complete their SReduce tasks, the coordinator collects the final results and sends them back to the client (step ❼).

After all, the client decrypts and obtains the final query results (step ❽).

5 Case Studies

As mentioned in §3.4, the OLAP process can be logically divided into two stages: indexing/filtering data and aggregation computation. Traditionally, as depicted in Fig. 3, FHE-based filtering involves utilizing TFHE [7] for homomorphic sub-traction on all data entries, performing homomorphic most significant bit (MSB) extraction [2], conducting homomorphic bitwise AND operations, transforming the results into CKKS [5] format to generate an encrypted 0/1 vector filter (i.e., 'TFHEsToCKKS' in Fig. 3), and performing homomorphic vector multiplication between the filter and the data. This process is highly time-consuming and acts as a significant performance bottleneck, taking up approximately 99.96% of the overall time, although it provides exceptional security guarantees.

We argue that not all scenarios require such a high computational cost to maintain security. In cases where accessing the auxiliary database for attacks is challenging, it is feasible to adopt widely accepted indexing schemes, such as CryptDB-like schemes or HashFilter schemes. While these schemes may result in some access pattern leakage, they can significantly reduce the filtering cost. Therefore, we conducted two case studies to replace the FHE-based filtering scheme in HEDAS with CryptDB's indexing method and a kind of HashFilter-based indexing method to alleviate the performance bottleneck.

5.1 Case Study 1: CryptDB-Based Indexing

CryptDB [32] is a secure OLAP system that relies on specific cryptographic primitives. Its indexing mechanism utilizes DET, OPE, and SE within an onion-like multi-layered encryption model to automatically adapt to various query requirements. In our case study, we applied CryptDB's onion-like indexing method to HEDAS, replacing the FHE-based filtering approach. This modified system is referred to as HEDAS-CryptDB. The workflow of HEDAS-CryptDB is mostly identical to that of HEDAS, with the pre-group operation removed and regular data shuffle employed, because the use of DET and OPE allows for conventional data shuffling.

5.2   Case Study 2: HashFilter-Based Indexing

HashFilter-based indexing is a straightforward and efficient method that uses a hash function to map data to a fixed-size space for rapid data retrieval, and further enhances the indexing process by employing filters (e.g., Bloom filter [3]) to quickly eliminate data that does not meet specific conditions. Drawing on previous research [16,29], we propose a tree-like index structure based on the one-way hash function and the Bloom filter to accelerate the retrieval of encrypted data. To address the issue of false positives caused by the Bloom filter, we introduce a timely verification mechanism based on the characteristics of the tree structure to promptly eliminate such occurrences. In this case study, we integrate this indexing method into HEDAS, replacing the FHE-based filtering approach, referred to as HEDAS-HashFilter. The workflow of HEDAS-HashFilter closely resembles that of HEDAS-CryptDB.

Table 2. Latency breakdown analysis for 4 systems with 256 rows, where N/A indicates not applicable.

System	Filtering(s)	Aggregation(ms)		Shuffle(ms)	Total Latency(s)
		Pre-aggregation(ms)	Post-aggregation(ms)		
HE^{3}DB	286.59($\pm$0.60)	87.35($\pm$0.14)		N/A	286.67($\pm$0.60)
HEDAS	154.39($\pm$25.36)	67.90($\pm$5.25)	2.12($\pm$0.02)	65.09($\pm$2.25)	168.29($\pm$27.89)
HEDAS-CryptDB	0.81($\pm$0.04)	66.46($\pm$3.22)	0.90($\pm$0.40)	60.92($\pm$4.06)	6.80($\pm$1.24)
HEDAS-HashFilter	0.53($\pm$0.06)	69.94($\pm$6.16)	1.15($\pm$0.47)	64.67($\pm$4.22)	6.72($\pm$0.30)

6   Evaluation

6.1   Experiment Setup

We implemented HEDAS using the HE^{3}DB [2] framework and utilized the Microsoft SEAL [37], OpenPEGASUS [23], and TFHEpp [24] libraries for specific functions. We then conducted two case studies on the HEDAS system. Our compilation environment was GCC 11.4.0 with the -O3 optimization level and C++17 standard. The runtime environment consisted of 10 machines with identical configurations, each equipped with a 2.60GHz Intel E5-2690 V3 CPU, 64GB memory, 40Gbps NIC, and 24 cores. The average ping latency between the nodes was ~0.102ms. We used the same benchmark as HE^{3}DB, which is a subset of the TPC-H [10] queries, and adopted identical encryption parameters as HE^{3}DB, ensuring that the encryption overhead mirrored that of HE^{3}DB. For latency, we utilize the same metric as HE^{3}DB, which logs the timestamp of critical points in the query process and calculates the time span for each part.

Throughout our experiments, we aim to explore the following three research questions:

- To what extent can HEDAS's performance be improved compared to the state-of-the-art single-machine system?
- How much additional performance improvement can be achieved by changing the filtering method?
- How does HEDAS's performance vary as the number of computing nodes increases?

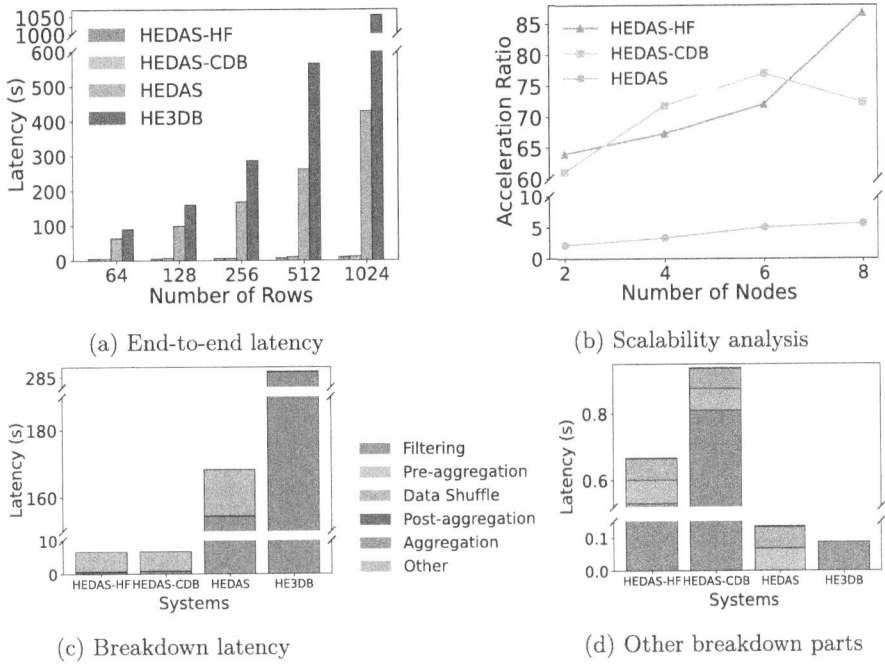

(a) End-to-end latency

(b) Scalability analysis

(c) Breakdown latency

(d) Other breakdown parts

Fig. 4. Evaluation results of HEDAS, HEDAS-CryptDB (CDB), HEDAS-HashFilter (HF), and HE^{3}DB.

6.2 End-to-End Performance

We evaluated to compare the performance of HEDAS, HEDAS-CryptDB, and HEDAS-HashFilter on 4 computing nodes, using HE^{3}DB running on a single machine as the baseline, and the TPC-H query 6 was used as the test case.

The results, as illustrated in Fig. 4a, demonstrate that HEDAS achieves significantly lower latency compared to HE^{3}DB, ranging from 40.8% to 71.6%.

HEDAS-CryptDB and HEDAS-HashFilter further reduce the latency, achieving 2.56% to 9.47% and 2.33% to 8.97% of HEDAS's latency, respectively. These findings strongly indicate that HEDAS outperforms HE³DB in terms of end-to-end latency, and additional performance improvements can be achieved by changing the indexing method, although they trade off security guarantees.

6.3 Breakdown Analysis

To further conduct a comprehensive analysis of the performance improvements, we performed a latency breakdown analysis on a dataset of 256 rows using 4 nodes across the 4 systems, as illustrated in Fig. 4c and summarized in Table 2. For HEDAS, HEDAS-CryptDB, and HEDAS-HashFilter, we divided the query process into four parts: filtering, pre-aggregation, shuffle, and post-aggregation. Additionally, there is also an 'other' part, including time for waiting, data loading, and other overheads. In the case of HE³DB, the query process was divided into two parts: filtering and aggregation. Notably, Table 2 reveals that the Filtering part consumes significantly more time compared to other parts across all systems. Consequently, for better comparability, the breakdown of the remaining parts is also presented in Fig. 4d.

The results demonstrate that when comparing HEDAS and HE³DB, although HEDAS introduces an additional shuffle communication part, the parallel execution effectively distributes the computational overhead, resulting in a significant reduction in the latency of both the filtering and aggregation parts, reducing approximately 46.1% and 19.8% of HE³DB's latency, respectively. Regarding the comparison between the two case study systems (i.e., HEDAS-CryptDB and HEDAS-HashFilter) and HEDAS, it is observed that the latency of the filtering part is significantly decreased in both cases, accounting for approximately 99.7% and 99.8% reduction of HEDAS's latency, respectively. Consequently, changing the filtering method proves to be an effective approach to addressing the performance bottleneck associated with FHE-based filtering.

6.4 Scalability Analysis

To evaluate the scalability of HEDAS, we conducted performance experiments on HEDAS and the two case study systems using varying numbers of computing nodes, as shown in Fig. 4b.

The results demonstrate that the performance of HEDAS exhibits a clear increasing trend as the number of computing nodes increases, indicating good scalability. However, it is observed that as the number of computing nodes continues to increase, the growth rate of HEDAS's performance slightly diminishes. We attribute this phenomenon to the increasing network overhead. Regarding the two case study systems, both HEDAS-CryptDB and HEDAS-HashFilter demonstrate good scalability with similar acceleration ratios. However, their acceleration ratios show more fluctuation compared to HEDAS, potentially due to their faster but erratic speed.

7   Conclusion

In this work, we propose HEDAS, the first distributed FHE-based OLAP system in the MapReduce style, enabling secure and efficient OLAP operations. By introducing the pre-group operation and the SMap and SReduce stages, HEDAS effectively addresses the limitations of FHE in distributed OLAP scenarios. To address the performance bottleneck of FHE-based filtering, we present an index-computation separation architecture and conduct two case studies replacing the FHE-based filtering method in HEDAS. Our experimental results demonstrate that HEDAS outperforms the state-of-the-art single-machine FHE-based OLAP system by leveraging the parallel execution capabilities of the MapReduce model, and the case study systems exhibit even better performance improvements. Additionally, our scalability experiments confirm that HEDAS exhibits good scalability, further validating its potential for handling larger workloads. In conclusion, HEDAS successfully addresses the challenges of secure and efficient OLAP operations in the public cloud and provides a promising solution.

Acknowledgments. The work is supported in part by National Key R&D Program of China (2022ZD0160201), HK RIF (R7030-22), HK ITF (GHP/169/20SZ), the Huawei Flagship Research Grant in 2023, HK RGC GRF (Ref.: 17208223 and 17204424), National Key R&D Program of China (2023YFB4503902), the HKU-CAS Joint Laboratory for Intelligent System Software, and the Shanghai Artificial Intelligence Laboratory.

References

1. Akinde, M.O., Böhlen, M.H., Johnson, T., Lakshmanan, L.V., Srivastava, D.: Efficient OLAP query processing in distributed data warehouses. Inf. Syst. **28**(1–2), 111–135 (2003)
2. Bian, S., et al.: HE3DB: an efficient and elastic encrypted database via arithmetic-and-logic fully homomorphic encryption. In: Proceedings of the 2023 ACM SIGSAC Conference on Computer and Communications Security, pp. 2930–2944 (2023)
3. Bloom, B.H.: Space/time trade-offs in hash coding with allowable errors. Commun. ACM **13**(7), 422–426 (1970)
4. Brakerski, Z., Gentry, C., Vaikuntanathan, V.: (leveled) fully homomorphic encryption without bootstrapping. ACM Trans. Comput. Theory (TOCT) **6**(3), 1–36 (2014)
5. Cheon, J.H., Kim, A., Kim, M., Song, Y.: Homomorphic encryption for arithmetic of approximate numbers. In: Advances in Cryptology–ASIACRYPT 2017: 23rd International Conference on the Theory and Applications of Cryptology and Information Security, Hong Kong, China, December 3-7, 2017, Proceedings, Part I 23, pp. 409–437. Springer (2017)
6. Chillotti, I., Gama, N., Georgieva, M., Izabachene, M.: Faster fully homomorphic encryption: Bootstrapping in less than 0.1 seconds. In: Advances in Cryptology–ASIACRYPT 2016: 22nd International Conference on the Theory and Application of Cryptology and Information Security, Hanoi, Vietnam, December 4-8, 2016, Proceedings, Part I 22, pp. 3–33. Springer (2016)

7. Chillotti, I., Gama, N., Georgieva, M., Izabachène, M.: TFHE: fast fully homomorphic encryption over the torus. J. Cryptol. **33**(1), 34–91 (2020)

8. Codd, E.F.: Providing OLAP (on-line analytical processing) to user-analysts: an it mandate (1993). http://www.arborsoft.com/papers/coddTOC.html

9. Costan, V., Devadas, S.: Intel SGX explained. Cryptology ePrint Archive (2016)

10. Council, T.P.P.: TPC BENCHMARK^{TM}h standard specification, Technical report, Transaction Processing Performance Council, San Francisco, CA (2022)

11. Dean, J., Ghemawat, S.: MapReduce: simplified data processing on large clusters. Commun. ACM **51**(1), 107–113 (2008)

12. Disselkoen, C., Kohlbrenner, D., Porter, L., Tullsen, D.: Prime+ Abort: a Timer-FreeHigh-Precision L3 cache attack using intel TSX. In: 26th USENIX Security Symposium (USENIX Security 17), pp. 51–67 (2017)

13. Fan, J., Vercauteren, F.: Somewhat practical fully homomorphic encryption. Cryptology ePrint Archive (2012)

14. Gentry, C.: Fully homomorphic encryption using ideal lattices. In: Proceedings of the Forty-First Annual ACM Symposium on Theory of Computing, pp. 169–178 (2009)

15. Gentry, C., Sahai, A., Waters, B.: Homomorphic encryption from learning with errors: conceptually-simpler, asymptotically-faster, attribute-based. In: Advances in Cryptology–CRYPTO 2013: 33rd Annual Cryptology Conference, Santa Barbara, CA, USA, August 18-22, 2013. Proceedings, Part I, pp. 75–92. Springer (2013)

16. Goh, E.J.: Secure indexes. Cryptology ePrint Archive (2003)

17. Hackenjos, T., Hahn, F., Kerschbaum, F.: SAGMA: secure aggregation grouped by multiple attributes. In: Proceedings of the 2020 ACM SIGMOD International Conference on Management of Data, pp. 587–601 (2020)

18. IBM: HElib (2021). https://github.com/homenc/HElib

19. Islam, M.S., Kuzu, M., Kantarcioglu, M.: Access pattern disclosure on searchable encryption: ramification, attack and mitigation. In: NDSS, vol. 20, p. 12. Citeseer (2012)

20. Kellaris, G., Kollios, G., Nissim, K., O'neill, A.: Generic attacks on secure outsourced databases. In: Proceedings of the 2016 ACM SIGSAC Conference on Computer and Communications Security, pp. 1329–1340 (2016)

21. Latreche, O., Boukraa, D.: Self-service, on-demand creation of OLAP cubes over big data: a metadata-driven approach. In: 2020 IEEE International Conference on Big Data (Big Data), pp. 2907–2914. IEEE (2020)

22. Lee, S., Shih, M.W., Gera, P., Kim, T., Kim, H., Peinado, M.: Inferring fine-grained control flow inside SGX enclaves with branch shadowing. In: 26th USENIX Security Symposium (USENIX Security 17), pp. 557–574 (2017)

23. Lu, W.J., Huang, Z., Hong, C., Ma, Y., Qu, H.: Pegasus: bridging polynomial and non-polynomial evaluations in homomorphic encryption. In: 2021 IEEE Symposium on Security and Privacy (SP), pp. 1057–1073. IEEE (2021)

24. Matsuoka, K.: TFHEpp: pure C++ implementation of TFHE cryptosystem (2020). https://github.com/virtualsecureplatform/TFHEpp

25. Moghimi, A., Irazoqui, G., Eisenbarth, T.: Cachezoom: how SGX amplifies the power of cache attacks. In: Cryptographic Hardware and Embedded Systems–CHES 2017: 19th International Conference, Taipei, Taiwan, September 25-28, 2017, Proceedings, pp. 69–90. Springer (2017)

26. Mulazzani, M., Schrittwieser, S., Leithner, M., Huber, M., Weippl, E.: Dark clouds on the horizon: using cloud storage as attack vector and online slack space. In: 20th USENIX Security Symposium (USENIX Security 11) (2011)

27. Nam, K., Oh, H., Moon, H., Paek, Y.: Accelerating n-bit operations over TFHE on commodity CPU-FPGA. In: Proceedings of the 41st IEEE/ACM International Conference on Computer-Aided Design, pp. 1–9 (2022)
28. Papadimitriou, A., et al.: Big data analytics over encrypted datasets with seabed. In: 12th USENIX Symposium on Operating Systems Design and Implementation (OSDI 16), pp. 587–602 (2016)
29. Pappas, V., et al.: Blind seer: a scalable private DBMS. In: 2014 IEEE Symposium on Security and Privacy, pp. 359–374. IEEE (2014)
30. Pinto, S., Santos, N.: Demystifying arm TrustZone: a comprehensive survey. ACM Comput. Surv. (CSUR) **51**(6), 1–36 (2019)
31. Poddar, R., Boelter, T., Popa, R.A.: Arx: an encrypted database using semantically secure encryption. Cryptology ePrint Archive (2016)
32. Popa, R.A., Redfield, C.M., Zeldovich, N., Balakrishnan, H.: CryptDB: protecting confidentiality with encrypted query processing. In: Proceedings of the Twenty-Third ACM Symposium on Operating Systems Principles, pp. 85–100 (2011)
33. Reagen, B., et al.: Cheetah: optimizing and accelerating homomorphic encryption for private inference. In: 2021 IEEE International Symposium on High-Performance Computer Architecture (HPCA), pp. 26–39. IEEE (2021)
34. Ren, X., et al.: HEDA: multi-attribute unbounded aggregation over homomorphically encrypted database. Proc. VLDB Endow. **16**(4), 601–614 (2022)
35. Rivest, R.L., Shamir, A., Adleman, L.: A method for obtaining digital signatures and public-key cryptosystems. Commun. ACM **21**(2), 120–126 (1978)
36. Samardzic, N., et al.: F1: a fast and programmable accelerator for fully homomorphic encryption. In: MICRO-54: 54th Annual IEEE/ACM International Symposium on Microarchitecture, pp. 238–252 (2021)
37. Microsoft SEAL (release 3.7), microsoft Research, Redmond, WA (2021). https://github.com/Microsoft/SEAL
38. National Institute of Standards and Technology: Advanced encryption standard. NIST FIPS PUB 197 (2001)
39. Wang, W., et al.: Leaky cauldron on the dark land: understanding memory side-channel hazards in SGX. In: Proceedings of the 2017 ACM SIGSAC Conference on Computer and Communications Security, pp. 2421–2434 (2017)
40. Wang, Z., et al.: HE-booster: an efficient polynomial arithmetic acceleration on GPUs for fully homomorphic encryption. IEEE Trans. Parallel Distrib. Syst. **34**(4), 1067–1081 (2023)
41. Xiao, L., Xu, D., Xie, C., Mandayam, N.B., Poor, H.V.: Cloud storage defense against advanced persistent threats: a prospect theoretic study. IEEE J. Sel. Areas Commun. **35**(3), 534–544 (2017)
42. Xue, K., Chen, W., Li, W., Hong, J., Hong, P.: Combining data owner-side and cloud-side access control for encrypted cloud storage. IEEE Trans. Inf. Forensics Secur. **13**(8), 2062–2074 (2018)
43. Yang, H., Shen, S., Dai, W., Zhou, L., Liu, Z., Zhao, Y.: Phantom: a CUDA-accelerated word-wise homomorphic encryption library. IEEE Trans. Dependable Sec. Comput. (2024)
44. Zheng, W., Dave, A., Beekman, J.G., Popa, R.A., Gonzalez, J.E., Stoica, I.: Opaque: an oblivious and encrypted distributed analytics platform. In: 14th USENIX Symposium on Networked Systems Design and Implementation (NSDI 17), pp. 283–298 (2017)

Card-Based Cryptographic Protocols for Three-Input Functions with a Standard Deck of Cards Using Private Operations

Naoki Kobayashi and Yoshifumi Manabe$^{(\boxtimes)}$ [ORCID]

School of Informatics, Kogakuin University, Shinjuku, Tokyo 163-8677, Japan
manabe@cc.kogakuin.ac.jp

Abstract. This paper shows card-based cryptographic protocols to calculate several Boolean functions with a standard deck of cards using private operations. They are multi-party secure computations executed by multiple semi-honest players without computers. The protocols use private operations that are executed by a player at a place where the other players cannot see. Most card-based cryptographic protocols use a special deck of cards that consists of many cards with two kinds of marks. Though these protocols are simple and efficient, the users need to prepare such special cards. Few protocols were shown that use a standard deck of playing cards, though the protocols with a standard deck of cards can be easily executed in our daily lives. It was shown that logical AND, logical XOR, and copy protocols can be executed with the minimum number of cards. However, the protocols for complicated functions are not known. This paper shows that by using private operations, all of the following Boolean functions can be calculated without additional cards other than the input cards: (1) any three input Boolean functions, (2) half adder and full adder, and (3) any n-input symmetric Boolean functions. The results show the effectiveness of private operations in card-based cryptographic protocols.

Keywords: card-based cryptographic protocols · multi-party secure computation · Boolean functions · half adder · symmetric functions · private operations · standard deck of cards

1 Introduction

1.1 Overview of Card-Based Cryptographic Protocols

Card-based cryptographic protocols [26,28] were proposed in which physical cards are used instead of computers to securely compute values. They can be used when computers cannot be used or users cannot trust the software on the computer. Also, the protocols are easy to understand, thus the protocols can be used to teach the basics of cryptography [4,21] to accelerate the social implementation of advanced cryptography [6]. den Boer [3] first showed a five-card protocol

J. Garcia-Alfaro et al. (Eds.): ESORICS 2024 Workshops, LNCS 15263, pp. 94–111, 2025.
https://doi.org/10.1007/978-3-031-82349-7_7

to securely compute the logical AND of two inputs. Since then, many protocols have been proposed to realize primitives to compute any Boolean functions [8,11,29,34,37,38,47,48] and computate a specific class of Boolean functions [1,2,5,7,13–15,18,22,25,35,36,40,41,44–46,50,51].

This paper considers computations of (1) any three input Boolean functions, (2) half adder and full adder, and (3) any n-input symmetric Boolean functions. No additional cards are necessary to calculate these functions with a standard deck of cards when we use private operations.

Note that in this paper, all players are assumed to be semi-honest. Few works are done for the case when some players are malicious or make mistakes [10,16,24,27,30,49].

1.2 Standard Deck of Cards

Most of the above works are based on a two-color card model. In the two-color card model, there are two kinds of cards, ♣ and ♡. Cards of the same marks cannot be distinguished. In addition, the back of both types of cards is ?. It is impossible to determine the mark in the back of a given card of ?. Though the model is simple, such special cards are not available in our daily lives.

To solve the problem, card-based cryptographic protocols using a standard deck of playing cards were shown [9,12,13,17,19,20,23,30,31,33,47]. Playing cards are available at many houses and are easy to buy. The standard deck of playing cards is also used for zero-knowledge proof of puzzle solutions [39,42]. This paper discusses protocols to calculate logical functions. Niemi and Renvall first showed protocols that use a standard deck of playing cards [33]. They showed logical XOR, logical AND, and copy protocols since any Boolean functions can be realized by a combination of these protocols. Their protocols are 'Las Vegas' type protocols, that is, the execution times of the protocols are not limited. The protocols are expected to terminate within a finite time and the efficiency of these protocols is evaluated by the expected execution time. However, if the sequence of the random numbers is bad, the protocols do not terminate forever. Mizuki showed fixed time logical XOR, logical AND, and copy protocols [23]. Though the number of cards used by the XOR protocol is the minimum, the ones used by the logical AND and copy protocols are not the minimum. Koch et al. showed a four-card 'Las Vegas' type AND protocol and it is impossible to obtain a four-card finite time protocol with the model without private operations [9]. Koyama et al. showed a three-input 'Las Vegas' type AND protocol with the minimum number of cards [12]. Koyama et al. showed an efficient 'Las Vegas' type copy protocol [13]. Shinagawa and Mizuki showed protocols to compute any n-variable function using a standard deck of playing cards and a deck of UNO[1] cards [47]. Miyahara et al. showed a protocol that solves Yao's millionares' problem using a standard deck of playing cards [19]. Miyahara and Mizuki showed new protocols that use a special primitive that opens the suit of a playing card [20]. This paper discusses protocols that publically or privately open the cards. Another class of

---

[1] https://www.letsplayuno.com.

protocols is considered, in which each player knows his/her private data, and the player privately inputs the data to the protocol. Nakai et al. showed AND, XOR, and majority protocols [31].

1.3   Private Operations

Randomization or a private operation is the most important primitive in these card-based protocols. If every primitive executed in a card-based protocol is deterministic and public, the relationship between the private input values and the output values is known to the players. When the output values are disclosed, the private input values can be known to the players from the relationship. Thus, all protocols need some random or private operation.

First, public randomization primitives have been discussed then recently, private operations are considered. Many protocols use random bisection cuts [29], which randomly execute swapping two decks of cards or not swapping. If the random value used in the randomization is disclosed, the secret input value is known to the players. If some player privately brings a high-speed camera, the random value selected by the randomization might be known by analyzing the image. Though the size of a high-speed camera is very large, the size might become very small shortly. To prepare for the situation, we need to consider using private operations.

Operations that a player executes in a place where the other players cannot see are called private operations. These operations are considered to be executed under the table or in the back. Private operations are shown to be the most powerful primitives in card-based cryptographic protocols. They were first introduced to solve the millionaires' problem [32]. Using three private operations shown later, committed-input and committed-output logical AND, logical XOR, and copy protocols can be achieved with the minimum number of cards on the two-color card model [37].

For the primitives of logical AND, logical XOR, and copy operation, the minimum number of cards is achieved with a standard deck of cards using private operations [17]. So the research question is whether we can achieve the minimum number of cards for complicated calculations.

1.4   Our Results

This paper shows new card-based protocols with a standard deck of cards using private operations to calculate (1) any three input Boolean functions, (2) half adder and full adder, and (3) any n-input symmetric Boolean functions. All of these protocols need no additional cards other than the input cards. Thus these protocols are optimal in regard to the number of cards.

In Sect. 2 basic definitions and the private operations introduced by [37] are shown. Then, the sub-protocols shown in [17] and used in this paper are stated. Section 3 shows protocols to calculate three input Boolean functions. Section 4 shows protocols to calculate half and full adder, and n-input symmetric Boolean functions. Section 5 concludes the paper.

2   Preliminaries

2.1   Basic Notations

This section gives the notations and basic definitions of card-based protocols with a standard deck of cards. A deck of playing cards consists of 52 distinct mark cards, which are named as 1 to 52. The number of each card (for example, 1 is the ace of spade and 52 is the king of club) is common knowledge among the players. The back of all cards is the same $\boxed{?}$. It is impossible to determine the mark in the back of a given card of $\boxed{?}$.

One-bit data is represented by two cards as follows: $\boxed{i}\,\boxed{j} = 0$ and $\boxed{j}\,\boxed{i} = 1$ if $i < j$.

One pair of cards that represents one bit $x \in \{0, 1\}$, whose face is down, is called a commitment of x, and denoted as $commit(x)$. It is written as $\underbrace{\boxed{?}\,\boxed{?}}_{x}$.

The base of a commitment is the pair of cards used for the commitment. If card i and $j(i < j)$ are used to set $commit(x)$ (That is, set $\boxed{i}\,\boxed{j}$ if $x = 0$ and set $\boxed{j}\,\boxed{i}$ if $x = 1$), the commitment is written as $commit(x)^{\{i,j\}}$ and written as $\underbrace{\boxed{?}\,\boxed{?}}_{x^{\{i,j\}}}$. When the base information is obvious or unnecessary, it is not written.

Note that when these two cards are swapped, $commit(\bar{x})^{\{i,j\}}$ can be obtained. Thus, logical negation can be computed without private operations.

A set of cards placed in a row is called a sequence of cards. A sequence of cards S whose length is n is denoted as $S = s_1, s_2, \ldots, s_n$, where s_i is i-th card of the sequence. $S = \underbrace{\boxed{?}}_{s_1}\,\underbrace{\boxed{?}}_{s_2}\,\underbrace{\boxed{?}}_{s_3} \ldots, \underbrace{\boxed{?}}_{s_n}$. A sequence whose length is even is called an even sequence. $S_1 || S_2$ is a concatenation of sequence S_1 and S_2.

All protocols are executed by two players, Alice and Bob. The players are semi-honest, that is, they obey the rules of the protocols but try to obtain secret values.

The inputs of the protocols are given in a committed manner, that is, the players do not know the input values. If a player knows his secure input value x, the player just makes a commitment of x, and the protocols in this paper can be used. The output of the protocol must be given in a committed format so that the result can be used as an input to further computation. If the players need to obtain the output value, they just open the committed output. Thus committed output is desirable.

A protocol is secure when the following two conditions are satisfied: (1) If the output cards are not opened, each player obtains no information about the private input values from the view of the protocol for the player (the sequence of the cards opened to the player). (2) When the output cards are opened, each player obtains no additional information about the private input values other than the information by the output of the protocol. For example, if the output cards of an AND protocol for input x and y are opened and the value is 1, the players can know that $x = 1$ and $y = 1$. If the output value is 0, the players must not know whether the input (x, y) is $(0, 0)$, $(0, 1)$, or $(1, 0)$.

The following protocols use random numbers. Random numbers can be generated without computers using coin-flipping or some similar methods. During the protocol executions, cards are sent and received between the players. The communication is executed by sending the cards between the players to avoid information leakage during the communication. If the players are not in the same place during the protocol execution, a trusted third party (for example, the post office) is necessary to send and receive cards between players.

2.2   Private Operations

We show three private operations introduced in [37]: private random bisection cuts, private reverse cuts, and private reveals.

Primitive 1 *(Private random bisection cut)*
   A private random bisection cut is the following operation on an even sequence $S_0 = s_1, s_2, \ldots, s_{2m}$. A player selects a random bit $b \in \{0, 1\}$ and outputs

$$S_1 = \begin{cases} S_0 & \text{if } b = 0 \\ s_{m+1}, s_{m+2}, \ldots, s_{2m}, s_1, s_2, \ldots, s_m & \text{if } b = 1 \end{cases}$$

The player executes this operation in a place where the other players cannot see. The player must not disclose the bit b.

Note that if the private random cut is executed when $m = 1$ and $S_0 = commit(x)$, given $S_0 = \boxed{?}\boxed{?}$, The player's output $S_1 = \boxed{?}\boxed{?}$, which is $\boxed{?}\boxed{?}$
$$\underbrace{}_{x} \qquad \underbrace{}_{x \oplus b} \qquad \underbrace{}_{x}$$

or $\boxed{?}\boxed{?}$.
$\underbrace{}_{\overline{x}}$

Note that a private random bisection cut is the same as the random bisection cut [29], but the operation is executed in a hidden place.

Primitive 2 *(Private reverse cut, Private reverse selection)*
   A private reverse cut is the following operation on an even sequence $S_2 = s_1, s_2, \ldots, s_{2m}$ and a bit $b \in \{0, 1\}$. A player outputs

$$S_3 = \begin{cases} S_2 & \text{if } b = 0 \\ s_{m+1}, s_{m+2}, \ldots, s_{2m}, s_1, s_2, \ldots, s_m & \text{if } b = 1 \end{cases}$$

The player executes this operation in a place where the other players cannot see. The player must not disclose b.

Note that the bit b is not newly selected by the player. This is the difference between the primitive in Primitive 1, where a random bit must be newly selected by the player.

Note that in some protocols below, selecting left m cards is executed after a private reverse cut. The sequence of these two operations is called a private reverse selection. A private reverse selection is the following procedure on an even sequence $S_2 = s_1, s_2, \ldots, s_{2m}$ and a bit $b \in \{0, 1\}$. A player outputs

$$S_3 = \begin{cases} s_1, s_2, \ldots, s_m & \text{if } b = 0 \\ s_{m+1}, s_{m+2}, \ldots, s_{2m} & \text{if } b = 1 \end{cases}$$

Primitive 3 *(Private reveal). A player privately opens a given committed bit. The player must not disclose the obtained value.*

Using the obtained value, the player privately sets a sequence of cards.

Consider the case when Alice executes a private random bisection cut on $commit(x)$ and Bob executes a private reveal on the bit. Since the committed bit is randomized by the bit b selected by Alice, the opened bit is $x \oplus b$. Even if Bob privately opens the cards, Bob obtains no information about x if b is randomly selected and not disclosed by Alice. Bob must not disclose the obtained value. If Bob discloses the obtained value to Alice, Alice knows the value of the committed bit.

2.3 Opaque Commitment Pair

An opaque commitment pair is defined as a useful situation to design a secure protocol using a standard deck of cards [23]. It is a pair of commitments whose bases are unknown to a player. Let us consider the following two commitments using cards i, j, i' and j'. The left (right) commitment has value x (y), respectively, but it is unknown that (1) the left (right) commitment is made using i and j (i' and j'), respectively, or (2) the left (right) commitment is made using i' and j' (i and j), respectively. Such a pair of commitments is called an opaque commitment pair and written as $commit(x)^{\{i,j\},\{i',j'\}} || commit(y)^{\{i,j\},\{i',j'\}}$.

The protocols in this paper use a little different kind of pair, called semi-opaque commitment pair. A player thinks a pair is an opaque commitment pair but another player knows the bases of the commitments. Let us consider the case when a protocol is executed by Alice and Bob. Bob privately makes the pair of commitments with the knowledge of x and y. For example, Bob randomly selects a bit $b \in \{0, 1\}$ and

$$S = \begin{cases} commit(x)^{\{i,j\}} || commit(y)^{\{i',j'\}} & \text{if } b = 0 \\ commit(x)^{\{i',j'\}} || commit(y)^{\{i,j\}} & \text{if } b = 1 \end{cases}$$

then $S = commit(x)^{\{i,j\},\{i',j'\}} || commit(y)^{\{i,j\},\{i',j'\}}$ for Alice. Such a pair is called a semi-opaque commitment pair and written as $commit(x)^{\{i,j\},\{i',j'\}|Alice} || commit(y)^{\{i,j\},\{i',j'\}|Alice}$, where the name(s) of the players who think the pair is a opaque commitment pair is written. Note that a name is not written does not mean the player knows the bases of the commitments. For example, the above example says nothing about whether Bob knows the bases or not. Note that the name of the player is written with the initial when it is not ambiguous.

2.4   Space and Time Complexities

The space complexity of card-based protocols is evaluated by the number of cards. Minimizing the number of cards is discussed in many works.

The number of rounds was proposed as a criterion to evaluate the time complexity of card-based protocols using private operations [38]. The first round begins from the initial state. The first round is (possibly parallel) local executions by each player using the cards initially given to each player. It ends at the instant when no further local execution is possible without receiving cards from another player. The local executions in each round include sending cards to some other players but do not include receiving cards. The result of every private execution is known to the player. For example, shuffling whose result is unknown to the player himself is not executed. Since the private operations are executed in a place where the other players cannot see, it is hard to force the player to execute such operations whose result is unknown to the player. The $i(> 1)$-th round begins with receiving all the cards sent during the $(i-1)$-th round. Each player executes local executions using the received cards and the cards left to the player at the end of the $(i-1)$-th round. Each player executes local executions until no further local execution is possible without receiving cards from another player. The number of rounds of a protocol is the maximum number of rounds necessary to output the result among all possible inputs and random values. If the local execution needs many operations, for example, $O(n)$ operations where n is the size of the problem, we might need another criterion to consider the cost of local executions.

Let us show an example of a protocol execution, its space complexity, and time complexity.

Protocol 1 *(XOR protocol) [17]*
   Input: $commit(x)^{\{1,2\}}$ and $commit(y)^{\{3,4\}}$.
   Output: $commit(x \oplus y)^{\{1,2\}}$.

1. *Alice executes a private random bisection cut on $commit(x)^{\{1,2\}}$ and $commit(y)^{\{3,4\}}$ using the same random bit $b \in \{0,1\}$. The result is $commit(x \oplus b)^{\{1,2\}}$ and $commit(y \oplus b)^{\{3,4\}}$. Alice sends these cards to Bob.*
2. *Bob executes a private reveal on $commit(y \oplus b)^{\{3,4\}}$. Bob sees $y \oplus b$. Bob executes a private reverse cut on $commit(x \oplus b)^{\{1,2\}}$ using $y \oplus b$. The result is $commit((x \oplus b) \oplus (y \oplus b))^{\{1,2\}} = commit(x \oplus y)^{\{1,2\}}$.*

The number of cards is four since no cards are used other than the inputs.

Let us consider the time complexity of the protocol. The first round ends at the instant when Alice sends $commit(x \oplus b)^{\{1,2\}}$ and $commit(y \oplus b)^{\{3,4\}}$ to Bob. The second round begins with receiving the cards by Bob. The number of rounds of this protocol is two.

Since each operation is relatively simple, the dominating time to execute protocols with private operations is the time to send cards between players and set up so that the cards are not seen by the other players. Thus the number of rounds is the criterion to evaluate the time complexity of card-based protocols with private operations.

2.5   Protocols for AND, Copy, and Other Boolean Functions

This subsection shows the sub-protocols presented in [17] used in this paper's protocols. The correctness proof is shown in [17].

AND Protocol. Before showing the AND protocol, a subprotocol to fix the base of commitments is shown.

Protocol 2 *(Base-fixed protocol) [17]*
    Input: $commit(x)^{\{1,2\},\{3,4\}|A}||commit(y)^{\{1,2\},\{3,4\}|A}$.
(Note: y is a private value that must not be known to the players)
    Output: $commit(x)^{\{1,2\}}$.

1. *Bob executes a private random bisection cut on both pairs using two distinct random bits $br_1, br_2 \in \{0,1\}$. The result $S_1 = commit(x \oplus br_1)^{\{1,2\},\{3,4\}|A}||commit(y \oplus br_2)^{\{1,2\},\{3,4\}|A}$. Bob sends S_1 to Alice.*
2. *Alice executes a private reveal on S_1. Alice sees $x \oplus br_1$ and $y \oplus br_2$. If the base of the left pair is $\{1,2\}$, Alice just faces down the left pair and the cards, S_2, are the result. Otherwise, the base of the right pair is $\{1,2\}$. Alice makes $S_2 = commit(x \oplus br_1)^{\{1,2\}}$ using the right cards. Alice sends S_2 to Bob.*
3. *Bob executes a private reverse cut using br_1 on S_2. The result is $commit(x)^{\{1,2\}}$.*

Using the base-fixed protocol, the AND protocol in [17] is shown below.

Protocol 3 *(AND protocol) [17]*
    Input: $commit(x)^{\{1,2\}}$ and $commit(y)^{\{3,4\}}$.
    Output: $commit(x \wedge y)^{\{1,2\}}$.

1. *Alice executes a private random bisection cut on $commit(x)^{\{1,2\}}$ using random bit a_1. Alice sends the results, $S_1 = commit(x \oplus a_1)^{\{1,2\}}$ and $S_2 = commit(y)^{\{3,4\}}$ to Bob.*
2. *Bob executes a private reveal on S_1. Bob sees $x \oplus a_1$. Bob privately sets*

$$S_{3,0} = \begin{cases} commit(0)^{\{1,2\}}||commit(y)^{\{3,4\}} & \text{if } x \oplus a_1 = 0 \\ commit(y)^{\{3,4\}}||commit(0)^{\{1,2\}} & \text{if } x \oplus a_1 = 1 \end{cases}$$

Bob sends $S_{3,0}$ to Alice.
3. *Alice executes private random bisection cuts on each of pairs in $S_{3,0}$ using two distinct random bits a_2 and a_3. Let the result be $S_{3,1}$.*

$$S_{3,1} = \begin{cases} commit(0 \oplus a_2)^{\{1,2\}}||commit(y \oplus a_3)^{\{3,4\}} & \text{if } x \oplus a_1 = 0 \\ commit(y \oplus a_2)^{\{3,4\}}||commit(0 \oplus a_3)^{\{1,2\}} & \text{if } x \oplus a_1 = 1 \end{cases}$$

Alice sends $S_{3,1}$ to Bob.

4. *Bob randomly selects bit $b_1 \in \{0,1\}$. Bob reveals $S_{3,1}$ and exchanges the bases of the two commitments if $b_1 = 1$. Let the result be $S_{3,2}$.*

$$S_{3,2} = \begin{cases} commit(0 \oplus a_2)^{\{1,2\},\{3,4\}|A}||commit(y \oplus a_3)^{\{1,2\},\{3,4\}|A} & \text{if } x \oplus a_1 = 0 \\ commit(y \oplus a_2)^{\{1,2\},\{3,4\}|A}||commit(0 \oplus a_3)^{\{1,2\},\{3,4\}|A} & \text{if } x \oplus a_1 = 1 \end{cases}$$

Bob sends $S_{3,2}$ to Alice.

5. *Alice executes private reverse cuts on the two pairs of $S_{3,2}$ using a_2 and a_3, respectively. Let the result be S_4.*

$$S_4 = \begin{cases} commit(0)^{\{1,2\},\{3,4\}|A}||commit(y)^{\{1,2\},\{3,4\}|A} & \text{if } x \oplus a_1 = 0 \\ commit(y)^{\{1,2\},\{3,4\}|A}||commit(0)^{\{1,2\},\{3,4\}|A} & \text{if } x \oplus a_1 = 1 \end{cases}$$

Alice then executes a private reverse selection on S_4 using a_1. Let S_5 be the result and the remaining two cards be S_6. The result $S_5 = commit(y)^{\{1,2\},\{3,4\}|A}$ if $(a_1 = 0$ and $x \oplus a_1 = 1)$ or $(a_1 = 1$ and $x \oplus a_1 = 0)$. The condition equals $x = 1$.
$S_5 = commit(0)^{\{1,2\},\{3,4\}|A}$ if $(a_1 = 0$ and $x \oplus a_1 = 0)$ or $(a_1 = 1$ and $x \oplus a_1 = 1)$. The condition equals $x = 0$. Thus,

$$S_5 = \begin{cases} commit(y)^{\{1,2\},\{3,4\}|A} & \text{if } x = 1 \\ commit(0)^{\{1,2\},\{3,4\}|A} & \text{if } x = 0 \end{cases}$$

$$= commit(x \wedge y)^{\{1,2\},\{3,4\}|A}$$

Alice sends S_5 and S_6 to Bob.
6. *Bob and Alice execute Protocol 2 (Base-fixed protocol) to $S_5||S_6$. Then they obtain $commit(x \wedge y)^{\{1,2\}}$.*

COPY Protocol

Protocol 4 *(Copy protocol) [17]*
   Input: $commit(x)^{\{1,2\}}$ and two new cards 3 and 4.
   Output: $commit(x)^{\{1,2\}}$ and $commit(x)^{\{3,4\}}$

1. *Alice executes a private random bisection cut on $commit(x)^{\{1,2\}}$. Let b be the random bit Alice selects. Alice sends the result, $commit(x \oplus b)^{\{1,2\}}$, to Bob.*
2. *Bob executes a private reveal on $commit(x \oplus b)^{\{1,2\}}$ and sees $x \oplus b$. Bob privately makes $commit(x \oplus b)^{\{3,4\}}$. Bob sends $commit(x \oplus b)^{\{1,2\}}$ and $commit(x \oplus b)^{\{3,4\}}$ to Alice.*
3. *Alice executes a private reverse cut on each of the pairs using b. The result is $commit(x)^{\{1,2\}}$ and $commit(x)^{\{3,4\}}$.*

The protocol is three rounds.

Preserving an Input. In the above protocols to calculate Boolean functions, the input commitment values are lost. If the input is not lost, the input commitment can be used as an input to another calculation. Thus input preserving calculation is discussed [34,37].

In the XOR protocol, $commit(y \oplus b)^{\{3,4\}}$ is no longer necessary after Bob sets the result. Thus, Bob can send back $commit(y \oplus b)^{\{3,4\}}$ to Alice. Then, Alice can recover $commit(y)^{\{3,4\}}$ using the private reverse cut. In this modified protocol, the output is $commit(x \oplus y)^{\{1,2\}}$ and $commit(y)^{\{3,4\}}$ without additional cards. By exchanging the roles of x and y, the output can be $commit(x \oplus y)^{\{3,4\}}$ and $commit(x)^{\{1,2\}}$.

An input preserving AND protocol can be obtained using the idea in [34]. When we execute the AND protocol, two cards are selected by Alice at the final step. The remaining two cards are used to recover an input value. The unused two cards' value is

$$\begin{cases} 0 \text{ if } x = 1 \\ y \text{ if } x = 0 \end{cases}$$

thus the output is $commit(\overline{x} \wedge y)$.

Execute the above input preserving XOR protocol for these two output values so that the input $x \wedge y$ is preserved. The output of the XOR protocol is $(x \wedge y) \oplus (\overline{x} \wedge y) = y$. Thus, input y can be recovered without additional cards. By executing a base-fixed protocol, the output can be $commit(x \wedge y)^{\{1,2\}}$ and $commit(y)^{\{3,4\}}$.

n-Input Boolean Functions. Since any 2-input Boolean function, NOT, and COPY can be executed, any n-input Boolean function can be calculated by the combination of the above protocols using $2n + 4$ cards by the idea in [34,37].

Any Boolean function $f(x_1, x_2, \ldots, x_n)$ can be represented as follows:
$$f(x_1, x_2, \ldots, x_n) = \overline{x}_1 \wedge \overline{x}_2 \wedge \cdots \overline{x}_n \wedge f(0,0,\ldots,0) \oplus x_1 \wedge \overline{x}_2 \wedge \cdots \overline{x}_n \wedge f(1,0,\ldots,0) \oplus \overline{x}_1 \wedge x_2 \wedge \cdots \overline{x}_n \wedge f(0,1,\ldots,0) \oplus \cdots \oplus x_1 \wedge x_2 \wedge \cdots x_n \wedge f(1,1,\ldots,1).$$

Since the terms with $f(i_1, i_2, \ldots, i_n) = 0$ can be removed, this function f can be written as $f = \bigoplus_{i=1}^{k} v_1^i \wedge v_2^i \wedge \cdots \wedge v_n^i$, where $v_j^i = x_j$ or $\overline{x}_j$. Let us write $T_i = v_1^i \wedge v_2^i \wedge \cdots \wedge v_n^i$. The number of terms $k(< 2^n)$ depends on f.

Protocol 5 *(Protocol for any n-variable Boolean function [17]*
Input: $commit(x_i)^{\{2i+3,2i+4\}}(i = 1,2,\ldots,n)$.
Output: $commit(f(x_1, x_2, \ldots, x_n))^{\{1,2\}}$.
The additional four cards (two pairs of cards) 1,2,3, and 4 are used as follows.
1 and 2 store the intermediate value to compute f.
3 and 4 store the intermediate value to compute T_i.

Execute the following steps for $i = 1, 2, \ldots, k$.

1. *Copy v_1^i from the input $commit(x_1)$ as $commit(v_1^i)^{\{3,4\}}$. (Note that if v_1^i is $\overline{x}_1$, NOT is taken after the copy).*

2. *For* $j = 2, \ldots, n$, *execute the following procedure: Execute the input preserving AND protocol to* $commit(\cdot)^{\{3,4\}}$ *and* $commit(v_j^i)$ *so that input* $commit(v_j^i)$ *is preserved. The result is stored as* $commit(\cdot)^{\{3,4\}}$. *(Note that if* v_j^i *is* $\bar{x}_j$, *NOT is taken before the AND protocol, and NOT is taken again for the preserved input.)*

   At the end of this step, T_i *is obtained as* $commit(v_1^i \wedge v_2^i \wedge \cdots \wedge v_n^i)^{\{3,4\}}$.

3. *If* $i = 1$, *copy* $commit(\cdot)^{\{3,4\}}$ *to* $commit(\cdot)^{\{1,2\}}$. *If* $i > 1$, *apply the XOR protocol between* $commit(\cdot)^{\{3,4\}}$ *and* $commit(\cdot)^{\{1,2\}}$. *The result is stored as* $commit(\cdot)^{\{1,2\}}$.

At the end of the protocol, $commit(f(x_1, x_2, \ldots x_n))^{\{1,2\}}$ *is obtained.*

3   Protocols for Three-Input Boolean Functions

This section shows protocols for three input Boolean functions. The arguments to show the protocols with six cards are just the same as the one in [35]. The main difference is that logical AND can be calculated by four cards using private operations. In our protocols, no additional cards are necessary other than the cards for inputs.

There are $2^{2^3} = 256$ different functions with three inputs. However, some of these functions are equivalent by replacing variables and taking negations. NPN-classification [43] was considered to reduce the number of different functions considering the equivalence class of functions. The rules of NPN-classification are as follows.

1. Negation of input variables (Example: $x_i \leftrightarrow \overline{x_i}$).
2. Permutations of input variables (Example: $x_i \leftrightarrow x_j$).
3. Negation of the output ($f \leftrightarrow \bar{f}$).

For example, consider $f_1(x_1, x_2, x_3) = (x_1 \wedge x_2) \vee x_3$. Several functions in the same equivalence class that includes f_1 are: $f_2 = (\overline{x_1} \wedge \overline{x_2}) \vee x_3$, $f_3 = (\overline{x_1} \wedge \overline{x_3}) \vee x_2$, $f_4 = \bar{f_3}$, and so on.

Input negation and output negation can be executed by card-based protocols without increasing the number of cards. They are executed by just swapping input cards or output cards. Permutations of input variables can also be executed without increasing the number of cards. They can be achieved by just changing the positions of the input values. Therefore, all functions in the same NPN equivalence class can be calculated with the same number of cards.

Theorem 1. *Any three input Boolean functions can be securely calculated without additional cards other than the input cards with a standard deck of cards when we use private operations.*

Proof. When the number of inputs is 3, there are the following 14 NPN-representative functions [43]. (Note that x, y, and z are used to represent input variables.)

1. $NPN_1 = 1$
2. $NPN_2 = x$
3. $NPN_3 = x \vee y$
4. $NPN_4 = x \oplus y$
5. $NPN_5 = x \wedge y \wedge z$
6. $NPN_6 = (x \wedge y \wedge z) \vee (\overline{x} \wedge \overline{y} \wedge \overline{z})$
7. $NPN_7 = (x \wedge y) \vee (x \wedge z)$
8. $NPN_8 = (x \wedge y) \vee (\overline{x} \wedge \overline{y} \wedge z)$
9. $NPN_9 = (x \wedge y \wedge \overline{z}) \vee (x \wedge \overline{y} \wedge z) \vee (\overline{x} \wedge y \wedge z)$
10. $NPN_{10} = (x \wedge \overline{y} \wedge \overline{z}) \vee (\overline{x} \wedge y \wedge \overline{z}) \vee (\overline{x} \wedge \overline{y} \wedge z) \vee (x \wedge y \wedge z) = x \oplus y \oplus z$.
11. $NPN_{11} = (x \wedge y) \vee (x \wedge z) \vee (y \wedge z)$
12. $NPN_{12} = (x \wedge \overline{z}) \vee (y \wedge z)$
13. $NPN_{13} = (x \wedge y \wedge z) \vee (x \wedge \overline{y} \wedge \overline{z})$
14. $NPN_{14} = (x \wedge y) \vee (x \wedge z) \vee (\overline{x} \wedge \overline{y} \wedge \overline{z})$

Among these 14 functions, NPN_1 - NPN_4 depend on less than three inputs. These functions can be calculated without additional cards [17]. We show a calculation protocol for each of the remaining functions. Note that the output is $commit(f)^{\{1,2\}}$ when the inputs are $commit(x)^{\{1,2\}}$, $commit(y)^{\{3,4\}}$, and $commit(z)^{\{5,6\}}$.

For NPN_5, $x \wedge y$ can be calculated without additional cards. Then $x \wedge y \wedge z$ can be calculated without additional cards other than the input cards, $x \wedge y$ and z.

NPN_7 can be represented as $NPN_7 = x \wedge (y \vee z)$, thus this function can also be calculated without additional cards.

NPN_{10} can be calculated as $(x \oplus y) \oplus z$ without additional cards.

NPN_{13} can be represented as $NPN_{13} = x \wedge (\overline{y \oplus z})$, thus this function can also be calculated without additional cards.

NPN_{14} can be represented as $NPN_{14} = \overline{x} \oplus (y \vee z)$, thus this function can also be calculated without additional cards.

NPN_6 can be represented as $NPN_6 = (\overline{x \oplus y}) \wedge (\overline{x \oplus z})$. First, calculate $commit(x \oplus y)^{\{3,4\}}$ with preserving input $commit(x)^{\{1,2\}}$. Then calculate $commit(x \oplus z)^{\{1,2\}}$. Then NOT is applied to each result. Next, calculate AND to these results.

NPN_8 can be represented as $NPN_8 = (\overline{x \oplus y}) \wedge (y \vee z)$. First, calculate $commit(x \oplus y)^{\{1,2\}}$ with preserving input $commit(y)^{\{3,4\}}$. Then NOT is applied to the result. Then calculate $commit(y \vee z)^{\{3,4\}}$. Next, calculate AND to these results.

NPN_9 can be represented as $NPN_9 = (\overline{x \oplus y \oplus z}) \wedge (x \vee z)$. First, calculate $commit(x \oplus y)^{\{3,4\}}$ with preserving input $commit(x)^{\{1,2\}}$. Next, calculate $commit((x \oplus y) \oplus z)^{\{3,4\}}$ with preserving $commit(z)^{\{5,6\}}$. Then NOT is applied to the result. Next, calculate $commit(x \vee z)^{\{1,2\}}$. Next, calculate AND to these results.

NPN_{12} can be calculated as follows. First, calculate $commit(x \wedge \overline{z})^{\{1,2\}}$ with preserving input $commit(z)^{\{5,6\}}$. Next, calculate $commit(y \wedge z)^{\{3,4\}}$. Then, calculate OR to these results by using the AND protocol.

NPN_{11} can be represented as

$$NPN_{11} = \begin{cases} z & \text{if } x \oplus y = 1 \\ x & \text{if } x \oplus y = 0 \end{cases}$$

Since this equation is similar to the AND equation, the function can be calculated by modifying the AND protocol as follows.

1. Alice and Bob calculate $commit(x \oplus y)^{\{3,4\}}$ with preserving input $commit(x)^{\{1,2\}}$.
2. Alice executes private random bisection cut on $commit(x \oplus y)^{\{3,4\}}$, $commit(x)^{\{1,2\}}$, and $commit(z)^{\{5,6\}}$ using different random bit $a_1, a_2, a_3 \in \{0,1\}$. Alice sends the result $commit(x \oplus y \oplus a_1)^{\{3,4\}}$, $commit(x \oplus a_2)^{\{1,2\}}$, and $commit(z \oplus a_3)^{\{5,6\}}$ to Bob.
3. Bob privately select a bit $b_1 \in \{0,1\}$ and exchanges the bases of $commit(x \oplus a_2)^{\{1,2\}}$ and $commit(z \oplus a_3)^{\{5,6\}}$ if $b_1 = 1$. Though Bob sees the committed values, Bob obtains no information about x and z since Alice randomized the values. Bob sends $commit(x \oplus a_2)^{\{1,2\},\{5,6\}|A}||commit(z \oplus a_3)^{\{1,2\},\{5,6\}|A}$ to Alice.
4. Alice executes private reverse cuts to the sequence using a_2 and a_3. Alice sends the result $commit(x)^{\{1,2\},\{5,6\}|A}||commit(z)^{\{1,2\},\{5,6\}|A}$ to Bob.
5. Bob executes private reveal on $commit(x \oplus y \oplus a_1)$. Bob sets

$$S_2 = \begin{cases} commit(z)^{\{1,2\},\{5,6\}|A}||commit(x)^{\{1,2\},\{5,6\}|A} & \text{if } x \oplus y \oplus a_1 = 1 \\ commit(x)^{\{1,2\},\{5,6\}|A}||commit(z)^{\{1,2\},\{5,6\}|A} & \text{if } x \oplus y \oplus a_1 = 0 \end{cases}$$

6. Alice executes a private reverse cut on S_2 using the bit a_1 generated in the private random bisection cut. Let the obtained sequence be S_3. S_3 is $commit(z)^{\{1,2\},\{5,6\}|A}||commit(x)^{\{1,2\},\{5,6\}|A}$ if $(x \oplus y \oplus a_1 = 1$ and $a_1 = 0)$ or $(x \oplus y \oplus a_1 = 0$ and $a_1 = 1)$. The case equals to $x \oplus y = 1$. The output is $commit(x)^{\{1,2\},\{5,6\}|A}||commit(z)^{\{1,2\},\{5,6\}|A}$ if $(x \oplus y \oplus a_1 = 1$ and $a_1 = 1)$ or $(x \oplus y \oplus a_1 = 0$ and $a_1 = 0)$. The case equals to $x \oplus y = 0$. Thus the result is

$$S_3 = \begin{cases} commit(z)^{\{1,2\},\{5,6\}|A}||commit(x)^{\{1,2\},\{5,6\}|A} & \text{if } x \oplus y = 1 \\ commit(x)^{\{1,2\},\{5,6\}|A}||commit(z)^{\{1,2\},\{5,6\}|A} & \text{if } x \oplus y = 0 \end{cases}$$

Note that the left pair has the value of the result.

7. Alice and Bob execute base-fixed protocol on S_3. They obtain

$$\begin{cases} commit(z)^{\{1,2\}} & \text{if } x \oplus y = 1 \\ commit(x)^{\{1,2\}} & \text{if } x \oplus y = 0 \end{cases}$$

Therefore, NPN_{11} can also be calculated without additional cards.   □

4   Half Adder, Full Adder, and Symmetric Functions

This section first shows a realization of half adder and full adder. In our protocols, no additional cards are necessary other than the cards for inputs.

The input and output of the secure half adder are as follows:

- Input: $commit(x)^{\{1,2\}}$ and $commit(y)^{\{3,4\}}$
- Output: $S = commit(x \oplus y)^{\{3,4\}}$ and $C = commit(x \wedge y)^{\{1,2\}}$

The half adder is realized by the following steps, whose idea is just the same as the one in [34].

1. Execute XOR protocol with preserving input x. Thus $commit(x)^{\{1,2\}}$ and $commit(x \oplus y)^{\{3,4\}}$ are obtained.
2. Obtain $commit(\overline{x \oplus y})^{\{3,4\}}$ by swapping the two cards of $commot(x \oplus y)^{\{3,4\}}$.
3. Execute AND protocol to $commit(x)^{\{1,2\}}$ and $commit(\overline{x \oplus y})^{\{3,4\}}$ with preserving input $commit(\overline{x \oplus y})^{\{3,4\}}$. Thus $commit(\overline{x \oplus y})^{\{3,4\}}$ and $commit(x \wedge \overline{(x \oplus y)})^{\{1,2\}} = commit(x \wedge y)^{\{1,2\}}$ are obtained.
4. Obtain $commit(x \oplus y)^{\{1,2\}}$ by swapping the two cards of $commit(\overline{x \oplus y})^{\{1,2\}}$.

No additional cards are necessary other than the four input cards.

The input and output of the secure full adder are as follows:

- Input: $commit(C_I)^{\{1,2\}}$, $commit(x)^{\{3,4\}}$, and $commit(y)^{\{5,6\}}$.
- Output: $C_O = commit((x \wedge y) \vee (x \wedge C_I) \vee (y \wedge C_I))^{\{1,2\}}$ and $S = commit(x \oplus y \oplus C_I)^{\{3,4\}}$.

Since the half adder can be calculated without additional cards, the full adder can also be calculated without additional cards by the following protocol.

1. Add C_I and x using the half adder. The outputs are $commit(x \oplus c_I)^{\{3,4\}}$ and $commit(x \wedge C_I)^{\{1,2\}}$.
2. Add $commit(y)^{\{5,6\}}$ to the result $commit(x \oplus C_I)^{\{3,4\}}$ using the half adder. The outputs are $commit(x \oplus y \oplus C_I)^{\{3,4\}}$ and $commit(y \wedge (x \oplus C_I))^{\{5,6\}}$.
3. Execute OR protocol to $commit(y \wedge (x \oplus C_I))^{\{5,6\}}$ and $commit(x \wedge C_I)^{\{1,2\}}$. Since $(y \wedge (x \oplus C_I)) \vee (x \wedge C_I) = (x \wedge y) \vee (x \wedge C_I) \vee (y \wedge C_I)$, the carry C_O is obtained by the base of $\{1, 2\}$.

Using the half adder and full adder, calculation of symmetric function can be done by the technique in [34]. n-input symmetric function $f(x_1, x_2, \ldots, x_n)$ depends only on the number of variables such that $x_i = 1$. Let $Y = \sum_{i=1}^{n} x_i$. Then the function f can be written as $f(x_1, x_2, \ldots, x_n) = g(Y)$. When Y is given by a binary representation, $Y = y_k y_{k-1} \ldots y_1$, g can be written as $g(y_1, y_2, \ldots, y_k)$, where $k = \lfloor \log n \rfloor + 1$.

Given input $x_1, x_2, \ldots, x_n$, first, obtain the sum of these inputs using the half adder and full adder protocols without additional cards. The sum is obtained as $y_1, y_2, \ldots, y_k$. Then, calculate g using y_i. When $n \leq 7$, $k \leq 3$, thus any three input Boolean function g can be calculated without additional cards. When $n \geq 8$, Y is represented with $k = \lfloor \log n \rfloor + 1$ bits. Since $n - k \geq 4$, at least 8 input cards are unused after y_is are calculated. Any Boolean function can be calculated with four additional cards, thus g can be calculated without additional cards other than the input cards.

Theorem 2. *Any symmetric Boolean function can be securely calculated without additional cards other than the input cards when we use private operations.*

5   Conclusion

This paper showed card-based cryptographic protocols to calculate three input Boolean functions, half adder, full adder, and symmetric functions with a standard deck of cards using private operations. These results show the effectiveness of private operations.

One of the important open problems is obtaining another class of Boolean functions that can be calculated without additional cards using private operations. However, it seems very difficult to achieve all four-input Boolean functions without additional cards.

References

1. Abe, Y., Hayashi, Y.I., Mizuki, T., Sone, H.: Five-card and computations in committed format using only uniform cyclic shuffles. New Gener. Comput. **39**(1), 97–114 (2021)
2. Abe, Y., Mizuki, T., Sone, H.: Committed-format and protocol using only random cuts. Nat. Comput., 1–7 (2021)
3. den Boer, B.: More efficient match-making and satisfiability the five card trick. In: Quisquater, J.-J., Vandewalle, J. (eds.) EUROCRYPT 1989. LNCS, vol. 434, pp. 208–217. Springer, Heidelberg (1990). https://doi.org/10.1007/3-540-46885-4_23
4. Cheung, E., Hawthorne, C., Lee, P.: CS 758 project: secure computation with playing cards (2013). http://cdchawthorne.com/writings/secure_playing_cards.pdf
5. Francis, D., Aljunid, S.R., Nishida, T., Hayashi, Y., Mizuki, T., Sone, H.: Necessary and sufficient numbers of cards for securely computing two-bit output functions. In: Proceedings of Second International Conference on Cryptology and Malicious Security (Mycrypt 2016). LNCS, vol. 10311, pp. 193–211 (2017)
6. Hanaoka, G., et al.: Physical and visual cryptography to accelerate social implementation of advanced cryptographic technologies. IEICE Trans. Fundam. Electron. Commun. Comput. Sci., 214–228 (2023) (In Japanese)
7. Isuzugawa, R., Toyoda, K., Sasaki, Y., Miyahara, D., Mizuki, T.: A card-minimal three-input and protocol using two shuffles. In: Proceedings of 27th International Computing and Combinatorics Conference (COCOON 2021). LNCS, vol. 13025, pp. 668–679. Springer (2021)
8. Kastner, J., et al.: The minimum number of cards in practical card-based protocols. In: Proceedings of Asiacrypt 2017, Part III. LNCS, vol. 10626, pp. 126–155 (2017)
9. Koch, A., Schrempp, M., Kirsten, M.: Card-based cryptography meets formal verification. N. Gener. Comput. **39**(1), 115–158 (2021)
10. Koch, A., Walzer, S.: Foundations for actively secure card-based cryptography. In: Proceedings of 10th International Conference on Fun with Algorithms (FUN 2020). Schloss Dagstuhl-Leibniz-Zentrum für Informatik (2020)

11. Koch, A., Walzer, S., Härtel, K.: Card-based cryptographic protocols using a minimal number of cards. In: Proceedings of Asiacrypt 2015. LNCS, vol. 9452, pp. 783–807 (2015)
12. Koyama, H., Miyahara, D., Mizuki, T., Sone, H.: A secure three-input and protocol with a standard deck of minimal cards. In: Santhanam, R., Musatov, D. (eds.) Proceedings of 16th International Computer Science Symposium in Russia (CSR 2021). LNCS, vol. 12730, pp. 242–256. Springer, Cham (2021)
13. Koyama, H., Toyoda, K., Miyahara, D., Mizuki, T.: New card-based copy protocols using only random cuts. In: Proceedings of the 8th ACM on ASIA Public-Key Cryptography Workshop, pp. 13–22. APKC '21, Association for Computing Machinery, New York, NY, USA (2021)
14. Kuzuma, T., Isuzugawa, R., Toyoda, K., Miyahara, D., Mizuki, T.: Card-based single-shuffle protocols for secure multiple-input AND and XOR computations. In: Proceedings of the 9th ACM on ASIA Public-Key Cryptography Workshop, pp. 51–58 (2022)
15. Manabe, Y., Ono, H.: Card-based cryptographic protocols for three-input functions using private operations. In: Flocchini, P., Moura, L. (eds.) IWOCA 2021. LNCS, vol. 12757, pp. 469–484. Springer, Cham (2021). https://doi.org/10.1007/978-3-030-79987-8_33
16. Manabe, Y., Ono, H.: Card-based cryptographic protocols with malicious players using private operations. N. Gener. Comput. **40**(1), 67–93 (2022)
17. Manabe, Y., Ono, H.: Card-based cryptographic protocols with a standard deck of cards using private operations. New Gener. Comput. **42**, 305–329 (2024)
18. Marcedone, A., Wen, Z., Shi, E.: Secure dating with four or fewer cards. IACR Cryptology ePrint Archive, Report 2015/1031 (2015)
19. Miyahara, D., Hayashi, Y.I., Mizuki, T., Sone, H.: Practical card-based implementations of Yao's millionaire protocol. Theoret. Comput. Sci. **803**, 207–221 (2020)
20. Miyahara, D., Mizuki, T.: Secure computations through checking suits of playing cards. In: Proceedings of International Workshop on Frontiers in Algorithmic Wisdom (IJTCS-FAW 2022). LNCS, vol. 13461, pp. 110–128. Springer (2022)
21. Mizuki, T.: Applications of card-based cryptography to education. In: IEICE Technical Report ISEC2016-53, pp. 13–17 (2016) (In Japanese)
22. Mizuki, T.: Card-based protocols for securely computing the conjunction of multiple variables. Theoret. Comput. Sci. **622**, 34–44 (2016)
23. Mizuki, T.: Efficient and secure multiparty computations using a standard deck of playing cards. In: Foresti, S., Persiano, G. (eds.) CANS 2016. LNCS, vol. 10052, pp. 484–499. Springer, Cham (2016). https://doi.org/10.1007/978-3-319-48965-0_29
24. Mizuki, T., Komano, Y.: Information leakage due to operative errors in card-based protocols. Inf. Comput. **285**, 104910 (2022)
25. Mizuki, T., Kumamoto, M., Sone, H.: The five-card trick can be done with four cards. In: Proceedings of Asiacrypt 2012. LNCS, vol. 7658, pp. 598–606 (2012)
26. Mizuki, T., Shizuya, H.: A formalization of card-based cryptographic protocols via abstract machine. Int. J. Inf. Secur. **13**(1), 15–23 (2014)
27. Mizuki, T., Shizuya, H.: Practical card-based cryptography. In: Proceedings of 7th International Conference on Fun with Algorithms (FUN2014). LNCS, vol. 8496, pp. 313–324 (2014)
28. Mizuki, T., Shizuya, H.: Computational model of card-based cryptographic protocols and its applications. IEICE Trans. Fundam. Electron. Commun. Comput. Sci. **100**(1), 3–11 (2017)

29. Mizuki, T., Sone, H.: Six-card secure AND and four-card secure XOR. In: Deng, X., Hopcroft, J.E., Xue, J. (eds.) FAW 2009. LNCS, vol. 5598, pp. 358–369. Springer, Heidelberg (2009). https://doi.org/10.1007/978-3-642-02270-8_36

30. Morooka, T., Manabe, Y., Shinagawa, K.: Malicious player card-based cryptographic protocols with a standard deck of cards using private operations. In: Proceedings of 18th International Conference on Information Security Practice and Experience (ISPEC 2023). LNCS, vol. 14341, pp. 332–346. Springer, Singapore (2023)

31. Nakai, T., Iwanari, K., Ono, T., Abe, Y., Watanabe, Y., Iwamoto, M.: Card-based cryptography with a standard deck of cards, revisited: efficient protocols in the private model. New Gener. Comput. (2024)

32. Nakai, T., Misawa, Y., Tokushige, Y., Iwamoto, M., Ohta, K.: How to solve millionaires' problem with two kinds of cards. N. Gener. Comput. **39**(1), 73–96 (2021)

33. Niemi, V., Renvall, A.: Solitaire zero-knowledge. Fundam. Informaticae **38**(1, 2), 181–188 (1999)

34. Nishida, T., Hayashi, Y., Mizuki, T., Sone, H.: Card-based protocols for any Boolean function. In: Jain, R., Jain, S., Stephan, F. (eds.) TAMC 2015. LNCS, vol. 9076, pp. 110–121. Springer, Cham (2015). https://doi.org/10.1007/978-3-319-17142-5_11

35. Nishida, T., Hayashi, Y., Mizuki, T., Sone, H.: Securely computing three-input functions with eight cards. IEICE Trans. Fundam. Electron. Commun. Comput. Sci. **98**(6), 1145–1152 (2015)

36. Nishimura, A., Nishida, T., Hayashi, Y., Mizuki, T., Sone, H.: Card-based protocols using unequal division shuffles. Soft. Comput. **22**(2), 361–371 (2018)

37. Ono, H., Manabe, Y.: Card-based cryptographic logical computations using private operations. N. Gener. Comput. **39**(1), 19–40 (2021)

38. Ono, H., Manabe, Y.: Minimum round card-based cryptographic protocols using private operations. Cryptography **5**(3) (2021)

39. Ruangwises, S.: Two standard decks of playing cards are sufficient for a ZKP for sudoku. N. Gener. Comput. **40**(1), 49–65 (2022)

40. Ruangwises, S., Itoh, T.: AND protocols using only uniform shuffles. In: van Bevern, R., Kucherov, G. (eds.) CSR 2019. LNCS, vol. 11532, pp. 349–358. Springer, Cham (2019). https://doi.org/10.1007/978-3-030-19955-5_30

41. Ruangwises, S., Itoh, T.: Securely computing the n-variable equality function with 2n cards. Theoret. Comput. Sci. **887**, 99–110 (2021)

42. Ruangwises, S., Itoh, T.: Physical ZKP for Makaro using a standard deck of cards. In: Proceedings of 17th International Conference on Theory and Applications of Models of Computation (TAMC 2022). LNCS, vol. 13571, pp. 43–54. Springer (2022)

43. Sasao, T., Butler, J.T.: Progress in Applications of Boolean Functions. Morgan and Claypool Publishers (2010)

44. Shikata, H., Miyahara, D., Mizuki, T.: Few-helping-card protocols for some wider class of symmetric Boolean functions with arbitrary ranges. In: Proceedings of the 10th ACM International Workshop on ASIA Public-Key Cryptography (APKC), pp. 33–41 (2023)

45. Shikata, H., Toyoda, K., Miyahara, D., Mizuki, T.: Card-minimal protocols for symmetric Boolean functions of more than seven inputs. In: Seidl, H., Liu, Z., Pasareanu, C.S. (eds.) Proceedings of 18th International Conference on Theoretical Aspects of Computing (ICTAC 2022). LNCS, vol. 13572, pp. 388–406. Springer, Cham (2022)

46. Shinagawa, K., Mizuki, T.: The six-card trick: secure computation of three-input equality. In: Proceedings of 21st International Conference on Information Security and Cryptology (ICISC 2018). LNCS, vol. 11396, pp. 123–131 (2018)
47. Shinagawa, K., Mizuki, T.: Secure computation of any Boolean function based on any deck of cards. In: Chen, Y., Deng, X., Lu, M. (eds.) FAW 2019. LNCS, vol. 11458, pp. 63–75. Springer, Cham (2019). https://doi.org/10.1007/978-3-030-18126-0_6
48. Shinagawa, K., Nuida, K.: A single shuffle is enough for secure card-based computation of any Boolean circuit. Discret. Appl. Math. **289**, 248–261 (2021)
49. Takashima, K., Miyahara, D., Mizuki, T., Sone, H.: Actively revealing card attack on card-based protocols. Nat. Comput. **21**(4), 615–628 (2022)
50. Toyoda, K., Miyahara, D., Mizuki, T., Sone, H.: Six-card finite-runtime XOR protocol with only random cut. In: Proceedings of the 7th ACM Workshop on ASIA Public-Key Cryptography, pp. 2–8 (2020)
51. Yoshida, T., Tanaka, K., Nakabayashi, K., Chida, E., Mizuki, T.: Upper bounds on the number of shuffles for two-helping-card multi-input and protocols. In: Proceedings of 22nd International Conference on Cryptology and Network Security (CANS 2023). LNCS, vol. 14342, pp. 211–231. Springer (2023)

Grid-Based Decompositions for Spatial Data Under Local Differential Privacy

Berkay Kemal Balioglu, Alireza Khodaie, Ameer Taweel,
and M.Emre Gursoy[✉]

Department of Computer Engineering, Koç University, Istanbul, Turkey
{bbalioglu23,akhodaie22,ataweel20,emregursoy}@ku.edu.tr

Abstract. Local differential privacy (LDP) has recently emerged as a popular privacy standard. With the growing popularity of LDP, recent works have applied LDP to spatial data, and grid-based decompositions have been a common building block in DP and LDP. In this paper, we study three grid-based decomposition methods for spatial data under LDP: Uniform Grid (UG), PrivAG, and AAG. UG is a static approach that consists of equal-sized cells. To enable data-dependent decomposition, PrivAG was proposed by Yang et al. (2022). To advance the state-of-the-art in adaptive grids, this paper proposes the Advanced Adaptive Grid (AAG) method. For each grid cell, following the intuition that the cell's intra-cell density distribution will be affected by its neighbors, AAG performs uneven cell divisions depending on the neighboring cells' densities. We experimentally compare UG, PrivAG, and AAG using three real-world location datasets, varying privacy budgets, and query sizes. Results show that AAG provides higher utility than PrivAG, demonstrating the superiority of our proposed approach. Furthermore, when the grid size is chosen optimally in UG, AAG still beats UG for small queries, but UG beats AAG for large (coarse-grained) queries.

Keywords: Local differential privacy · location privacy · spatial grids · location-based services · spatial data management

1 Introduction

Large volumes of spatial data are nowadays available for collection and analysis, thanks to the popularity of smartphones, connected cars, location-based services (LBS), and social networks. Ensuring the privacy of spatial data is imperative since it contains sensitive information about individuals, such as their home and work addresses, frequently visited locations, and personal habits. Hence, users are reluctant to share their location data with untrusted data collectors. In recent years, local differential privacy (LDP) has become a widely accepted standard for privacy protection and deployed in products of various companies such as Apple, Google, and Microsoft [2,4,6,7]. With the growing popularity of LDP, several recent works have applied LDP to spatial data and LBS [1,

J. Garcia-Alfaro et al. (Eds.): ESORICS 2024 Workshops, LNCS 15263, pp. 112–123, 2025.
https://doi.org/10.1007/978-3-031-82349-7_8

5,9,11,13,14]. However, in many applications of DP and LDP to spatial data, the data needs to be discretized so that the input and output domains of the privacy mechanisms are discrete and finite. Grid-based decompositions, which decompose the overall geospatial area Ω into non-overlapping cells, are a popular method for this purpose. After a grid is laid, the user's location can be discretized by determining which cell it falls inside. Indeed, uniform and adaptive grids have been widely used in the DP and LDP literature for trajectory collection and sharing [5,13], range query answering [10], synthetic data generation [8], and so forth.

A uniform grid (UG) partitions the geospatial area Ω into $N \times M$ cells of equal size. However, since the uniform grid does not adapt to the underlying data distribution [10,13], it may result in a poor partitioning when certain regions of Ω have too high or too low density. To enable density-dependent decomposition of Ω, the adaptive grid approach was proposed [8,10,13]. Its main idea is to first lay a uniform grid $\mathcal{G}_1$ over the given Ω, and according to the cell density estimations obtained from a portion of the users, further divide each individual cell (i.e., adapt the grid). To the best of our knowledge, the most recent adaptive grid approach in LDP is PrivAG by Yang et al. [13].

In this paper, we propose Advanced Adaptive Grid (AAG). In PrivAG, when a certain cell $C_k \in \mathcal{G}_1$ needs to be divided further, this division is done evenly. In AAG, we propose to perform this division by taking into account C_k's neighbor cells because C_k's intra-cell density distribution is likely to mimic its neighbors' densities. For example, if C_k's right neighbor is dense but the left neighbor is sparse, then the intra-cell density of C_k is likely to be skewed towards the right. Following this intuition, we perform an uneven division which is weighted proportional to the neighbors' densities. Furthermore, we propose heuristic strategies to handle edge cells and corner cells that lack one or more neighbors. In addition, motivated by our observation that the parameter choices in PrivAG yield cell counts too similar to $\mathcal{G}_1$, we propose new parameter values for AAG.

We experimentally compare UG, PrivAG, and AAG using three real-world location datasets (Gowalla, Porto, Foursquare) by measuring their Average Query Errors (AQE) in answering spatial density queries with different privacy budgets ε and query sizes ρ. We find that the AQEs of UG are heavily dependent on the grid size, i.e., it performs well when the grid size is chosen optimally, but poorly otherwise. Comparing UG with optimal grid sizes against PrivAG and AAG, we observe that: (i) AAG is preferable to PrivAG across all ε and ρ, demonstrating that AAG improves the state-of-the-art in adaptive grids in LDP, (ii) AAG is the best approach when ρ is small but UG is the best approach when ρ is large.

2   Background

Let $\mathcal{U} = \{u_1, u_2, u_3, ...\}$ denote the set of users where $|\mathcal{U}|$ is the total number of users, and let the two-dimensional geospatial area be denoted by Ω. For each user u_i, the user's true location is represented by l_i, such that $l_i \in \Omega$ and l_i consists of a pair of *(latitude, longitude)* coordinates. We assume that the boundaries of the overall domain Ω are not privacy-sensitive, and can be known by all parties. Yet, each user's location is privacy-sensitive and must be protected.

Local differential privacy (LDP) is a widely accepted standard for safeguarding privacy. In LDP, users' data is perturbed on their devices before being collected by the aggregator (also called the "server"). After collecting perturbed data, the server uses estimation methods to recover statistics pertaining to the general population. However, since each user's data is perturbed, the server cannot infer exact information about a specific user. In our context, since each user's location l_i needs to be protected, we define LDP as follows.

Definition 1 (ε-LDP). A randomized algorithm Ψ satisfies ε-local differential privacy (ε-LDP), where $\varepsilon > 0$, if and only if for any two inputs l_i, l_i^*:

$$\forall y \in Range(\Psi) : \quad \frac{Pr[\Psi(l_i) = y]}{Pr[\Psi(l_i^*) = y]} \leq e^\varepsilon \tag{1}$$

where $Range(\Psi)$ stands for the set of all possible outputs of the algorithm Ψ.

ε-LDP ensures that having observed the output y, the server (or any other party who observed y) is not able to distinguish whether the original location of the user was l_i or l_i^* with probability more than the odds ratio controlled by e^ε. The strength of the privacy protection is controlled by the parameter ε, commonly known as the *privacy budget*. Lower ε yields stronger privacy.

Numerous LDP protocols have been proposed to minimize utility loss and/or communication cost under various conditions. In this paper, we use a state-of-the-art protocol called *Optimized Local Hashing (OLH)* [12] due to its high utility and low communication cost [3,7]. Similar to other LDP protocols, OLH consists of two main components: (i) user-side encoding and perturbation on users' devices, and (ii) server-side estimation after collecting perturbed data from the user population. Due to the page limit, we refer the reader to [12] for the components' technical descriptions. Note that although we use OLH as the LDP protocol, the grid methods are not specific to OLH. Other protocols such as GRR, RAPPOR, OUE, and the Staircase Mechanism can also be used [11,12].

3   Grid-Based Decompositions Under LDP

We first describe the Uniform Grid (UG) approach in Sect. 3.1, then the existing adaptive grid approach called PrivAG [13] in Sect. 3.2, and finally our novel Advanced Adaptive Grid approach called AAG in Sect. 3.3.

3.1   Uniform Grid (UG)

A uniform grid partitions the geospatial area Ω into $N \times M$ cells of equal size. We denote this grid by $\mathcal{G}_{uni} = (C_1, C_2, ..., C_{N \times M})$ where each $C_j \in \mathcal{G}$ is one cell. The geographic coverage of all cells are disjoint from one another. User u_i

---

Algorithm 1. Collecting location data with LDP using a grid

1: **Input:** Users $\mathcal{U}$, grid $\mathcal{G}$, privacy budget ε
2: **Output:** Densities of each cell in $\mathcal{G}$
3:
4: ▷ **User-side discretization and perturbation**
5: **for** each user $u_i \in \mathcal{U}$ **do**
6:     **for** each cell $C_j \in \mathcal{G}$ **do**
7:         **if** l_i falls inside C_j **then**
8:             Set user's true cell as: $C_i \leftarrow C_j$
9:             **break**
10:     Execute user-side OLH with true value = C_i, domain = $\mathcal{G}$, and budget = ε
11:     Send the resulting tuple $\langle H_u, x'_u \rangle$ to the server
12:
13: ▷ **Server-side estimation**
14: Server receives $\langle H_u, x'_u \rangle$ from all $u_i \in \mathcal{U}$
15: **for** each cell $C_j \in \mathcal{G}$ **do**
16:     Compute $Sup(C_j)$ as the number of tuples for which $x'_u = H_u(C_j)$
17:     Compute $\Phi(C_j)$ using the server-side estimation of OLH
18: **return** $\Phi(C_1)$, $\Phi(C_2)$, ... for all $C_j \in \mathcal{G}$

---

with location l_i discretizes his/her location by finding which $C_i \in \mathcal{G}$ their l_i falls inside. Then, to satisfy LDP, the cell information C_i needs to be perturbed. Hence, we feed C_i into the OLH protocol with the appropriate parameters.

An overview of LDP location data collection using $\mathcal{G}_{uni}$ is shown in Algorithm 1. For each user u_i with location l_i, the user first finds their true cell C_i, i.e., which cell in the grid their location falls inside (lines 6-9). Then, the user executes the OLH protocol by treating their true value as C_i, the domain of the protocol as $\mathcal{G}_{uni} = (C_1, C_2, ..., C_{N \times M})$, and using the privacy budget ε. Since l_i is discretized as C_i, the domain of OLH is also discretized: $\mathcal{D} = \mathcal{G}_{uni} = (C_1, C_2, ..., C_{N \times M})$, instead of using a continuous domain $\mathcal{D} = \Omega$. Each user sends the OLH protocol output to the server. The server receives the outputs from all users and then estimates the density of each cell $C_j \in \mathcal{G}_{uni}$ (lines 15-17) using the server-side estimation procedure of OLH.

3.2   Existing Adaptive Grid: PrivAG

UG is a static approach that does not adapt to the underlying data distribution [10,13]. It may result in a poor partitioning of Ω when certain regions have too high or too low density. For example, when a cell is too crowded, then further partitioning it into smaller cells enables a better understanding of the detailed data distribution *within* that cell. Yet, the uniform grid is not able to achieve this. On the other hand, if a certain region of Ω is sparse, then the cells in that region will have zero or near-zero density, and the uniform grid will be over-partitioning that region. Over-partitioned cells lead to utility loss since their estimated densities are non-zero due to LDP perturbation, leading to fictitious

---

Algorithm 2. Algorithmic summary of the PrivAG approach

1: **Input:** Users $\mathcal{U}$, parameters α and σ, privacy budget ε
2: **Output:** Densities of each cell in adaptive grid $\mathcal{G}_{ag}$
3:
4: ▷ **First phase of PrivAG**
5: Server computes g_1 and divides $\mathcal{U}$ into $\mathcal{U}_1$ and $\mathcal{U}_2$ such that $|\mathcal{U}_1| = \sigma \times |\mathcal{U}|$
6: Server lays $g_1 \times g_1$ uniform grid $\mathcal{G}_1$ on Ω
7: Call Algorithm 1 with $\mathcal{U}_1$, $\mathcal{G}_1$ and ε to obtain $\Phi(C_1)$, $\Phi(C_2)$, ... for all $C_k \in \mathcal{G}_1$
8:
9: ▷ **Second phase of PrivAG**
10: **for** each cell $C_k \in \mathcal{G}_1$ **do**
11:    Compute g_2^k and divide C_k into $g_2^k \times g_2^k$ cells of equal size
12: Let $\mathcal{G}_{ag}$ denote the resulting grid after the above divisions
13: Call Algorithm 1 with $\mathcal{U}_2$, $\mathcal{G}_{ag}$ and ε to obtain $\Phi(C_1)$, $\Phi(C_2)$, ... for all cells in $\mathcal{G}_{ag}$

---

and skewed results. To enable data-dependent decompositions, the adaptive grid approach was proposed in DP and LDP [10,13]. Its main idea is to first lay a uniform grid $\mathcal{G}_1$ over the given Ω, and according to the cell density estimations obtained from users, further divide each individual cell (i.e., adapt the grid).

To the best of our knowledge, the most recent adaptive grid approach in LDP is PrivAG, proposed by Yang et al. [13]. An algorithmic overview of PrivAG is given in Algorithm 2. In PrivAG, the server first divides the set of users $\mathcal{U}$ into two groups: $\mathcal{U}_1$ and $\mathcal{U}_2$. Then, the server constructs a uniform grid $\mathcal{G}_1$ of size $g_1 \times g_1$ and broadcasts $\mathcal{G}_1$ to users in $\mathcal{U}_1$. Based on $\mathcal{G}_1$, users in $\mathcal{U}_1$ discretize their locations and use OLH to send their perturbed outcomes to the server. The server estimates the densities of each cell in $\mathcal{G}_1$. Then, for each cell $C_k \in \mathcal{G}_1$, the server further partitions C_k into $g_2^k \times g_2^k$ cells, where g_2^k depends on $\Phi(C_k)$ and other parameters. After all cells are partitioned according to their g_2^k, the resulting adaptive grid $\mathcal{G}_{ag}$ is obtained. Then, $\mathcal{G}_{ag}$ is advertised to users in $\mathcal{U}_2$ and desired statistics are obtained using $\mathcal{G}_{ag}$, e.g., cell densities. Since the values of g_1 and g_2^k have an important impact on the final grid, Yang et al. propose guidelines for choosing them in [13].

3.3   Proposed Approach: Advanced Adaptive Grid (AAG)

We propose the Advanced Adaptive Grid (AAG) approach which advances PrivAG. Consider Fig. 1, which exemplifies a uniform grid with user densities written inside the cells (on the left), PrivAG (in the middle), and AAG (on the right). Say that the first phase of PrivAG laid a 3×3 uniform grid $\mathcal{G}_1$ on Ω, and the resulting densities of cells are shown on the left of Fig. 1. In its second phase, PrivAG iterates through each $C_k \in \mathcal{G}_1$ and decides how to further divide C_k. Say that in the current iteration, C_k is the middle cell in Fig. 1, and it is found that $g_2 = 2$. Then, PrivAG divides the middle cell into $2 \times 2 = 4$ equally sized cells. Our intuition is that the division of this middle cell into equal-sized cells is suboptimal. This is because there are 10.000 users in the upper neighbor whereas 50.000 users in the lower neighbor. Furthermore, there are 2.000 users in the left neighbor whereas 4.000 users in the right neighbor. Based on these neighbor cells' densities, it is likely that the bottom right corner of C_k is denser whereas the upper left corner is more sparse, because the intra-cell distribution is likely to be affected by neighbor cells. According to the original intuition behind adaptive grids [10,13], it is desirable to have many small cells in dense areas but few large cells in sparse areas. Hence, instead of dividing C_k evenly (as done in PrivAG), AAG proposes to divide the cell by taking into account the neighbors' densities. Therefore, the vertical division of the cell is done with the ratio 1-to-5 which is proportional to the densities of the upper and lower neighbors (10.000 vs 50.000), whereas the horizontal division is done with the ratio 1-to-2 which is proportional to the left and right neighbors (2.000 vs 4.000). The result is shown on the right of Fig. 1.

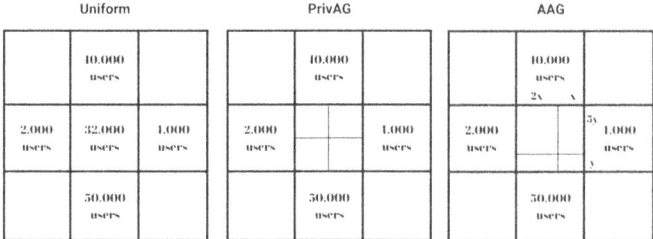

Fig. 1. Difference between PrivAG and AAG

We give an algorithmic overview of our proposed AAG approach in Algorithm 3. The first phase of AAG is identical to PrivAG, i.e., it lays a $g_1 \times g_1$ uniform grid $\mathcal{G}_1$ on Ω and obtains the cell densities $\Phi(C_1)$, $\Phi(C_2)$, ... for all $C_k \in \mathcal{G}_1$ using ε-LDP. The core difference lies in the second phase. After computing g_2^k, instead of dividing cell C_k uniformly, AAG first calculates the horizontal split location using the densities of the left and right neighbors. Denoting the left neighbor of C_k by C_k^L and the right neighbor of C_k by C_k^R, the horizontal split location $hsplit$ is calculated as:

$$hsplit = \frac{\Phi(C_k^R)}{\Phi(C_k^L) + \Phi(C_k^R)} \times (\text{width of } C_k) \qquad (2)$$

Similarly, to calculate the vertical split location, the densities of the upper and lower neighbors are used. Denoting the upper neighbor of C_k by C_k^U and the lower neighbor of C_k by C_k^B, the vertical split location $vsplit$ is calculated as:

$$vsplit = \frac{\Phi(C_k^B)}{\Phi(C_k^U) + \Phi(C_k^B)} \times (\text{height of } C_k) \qquad (3)$$

Then, C_k is divided horizontally using $hsplit$ and vertically using $vsplit$. As a result, four subcells of C_k are obtained. If $g_2^k > 2$, then each of the four

---

Algorithm 3. Algorithmic summary of the AAG approach

1: **Input:** Users $\mathcal{U}$, parameters α and σ, privacy budget ε
2: **Output:** Densities of each cell in adaptive grid $\mathcal{G}_{aag}$
3:
4: ▷ **First phase of AAG**
5: The first phase of AAG is the same as PrivAG
6:
7: ▷ **Second phase of AAG**
8: **for** each cell $C_k \in \mathcal{G}_1$ **do**
9:     Compute *hsplit* and *vsplit* for C_k according to Equations 2 and 3
10:     Divide C_k into four subcells using *hsplit* and *vsplit*
11:     **if** $g_2^k > 2$ **then**
12:         Uniformly divide each subcell into $\frac{g_2^k - 1}{2}$ pieces horizontally and vertically
13: Let $\mathcal{G}_{aag}$ denote the resulting grid after the above divisions
14: Call Algorithm 1 with $\mathcal{U}_2$, $\mathcal{G}_{aag}$ and ε to obtain $\Phi(C_1)$, $\Phi(C_2)$, .. for all cells in $\mathcal{G}_{aag}$

---

subcells needs to be further divided. This further division is done uniformly, i.e., uniformly into $(g_2^k - 1)/2$ pieces horizontally and $(g_2^k - 1)/2$ pieces vertically, to make sure that C_k is divided into $g_2^k \times g_2^k$ subcells overall.

Handling Edge and Corner Cells. When C_k is a cell that is located on one of the edges or corners of $\mathcal{G}_1$, it will lack one or more neighbors. For example, consider the top left cell in Fig. 1, which is a corner cell. This cell has a lower neighbor and a right neighbor, therefore $\Phi(C_k^B)$ and $\Phi(C_k^R)$ can be found. However, it does not have an upper neighbor or a left neighbor, therefore $\Phi(C_k^U)$ and $\Phi(C_k^L)$ are not available. Similarly, if a cell is an edge cell, then it has three neighbors but it lacks one neighbor. For cells that lack one or more neighbors, computing their *hsplit* and *vsplit* locations via Eqs. 2 and 3 using zero densities for the missing neighbors leads to erroneous results. To address this problem, we perform the following. If any of the neighbors of the current cell C_k is missing, then C_k uses its own density $\Phi(C_k)$ in place of the missing neighbor's density. For example, for the top left cell which lacks an upper neighbor and left neighbor, instead of assuming $\Phi(C_k^U) = 0$ and $\Phi(C_k^L) = 0$, we enforce: $\Phi(C_k^U) = \Phi(C_k)$ and $\Phi(C_k^L) = \Phi(C_k)$.

Choice of g_1 **and** g_2^k. PrivAG has two parameters (α and σ) which affect the values of g_1 and g_2^k. As we experimented with PrivAG and AAG, we observed that the recommended values for the α and σ parameters in PrivAG yield $\mathcal{G}_{aag}$ with cell counts that are similar to the initial uniform grid $\mathcal{G}_1$, which diminishes the benefits of using an adaptive grid. To address this problem, we propose to use different values for the α and σ parameters in AAG, leading to different choices of g_1 and g_2^k. Our choices aim to obtain an increased number of cell divisions in dense regions so that dense regions can be partitioned and represented in more detail, but without causing excessively large g_2^k. Specifically, as opposed to the default values of α and σ in PrivAG, we use $\alpha = 0.25$ and $\sigma = 0.5$ in AAG.

4   Experiments and Discussion

4.1   Experiment Setup and Datasets

In this section, we experimentally compare the three grid-based decomposition methods (UG, PrivAG, AAG). We implemented all algorithms and methods in Python. We use three real-world location datasets in our experiments: Gowalla, Porto, and Foursquare. To account for LDP randomness, each experiment is repeated 10 times and the average results are reported.

Gowalla: Gowalla was a location-based social networking site where users shared their locations via check-ins. From the full dataset, we extracted check-ins made in the United States, between longitudes -124.26 and -71.87 and latitudes 25.45 and 47.44. Consequently, we have 3,451,190 remaining locations.

Porto: The Porto dataset contains trips of 442 taxis driving in the city of Porto. It was released as part of the Taxi Service Prediction Competition in ECML-PKDD. The original dataset contains full taxi trips, i.e., trajectories with multiple location readings per trip. We pre-processed it by keeping only one randomly sampled location from each trip and treated them as the current locations of users $\mathcal{U}$. We only used the locations between longitudes -8.691294 and -8.552009 and latitudes 41.138351 and 41.185935, corresponding to the city of Porto. This resulted in 1,620,157 remaining locations.

Foursquare: The Foursquare dataset contains location check-ins of social media users in Tokyo, between April 2012 and February 2013. We used this dataset without pre-processing. In total, the dataset contains 573,703 locations.

Following previous works, we use spatial density queries for utility measurement [1,8,10,13]. A spatial density query q with geospatial area denoted by $A(q)$ is a query of the form: "How many users are located within $A(q)$"? Let ans_q denote the ground truth answer of q and ans_q' denote the version estimated using LDP grids. We generate $\gamma = 500$ number of random queries $q_1, q_2, \ldots$ with different $A(q_i)$ and compute their ans_{q_i} and ans_{q_i}'. Then, we measure the average error between ans_{q_i} and ans_{q_i}' using the AQE metric:

$$AQE = \frac{1}{\gamma} * \sum_{i=1}^{\gamma} \frac{|ans_{q_i} - ans_{q_i}'|}{max\{ans_{q_i}, b\}} \tag{4}$$

Here, b denotes a bound to mitigate the dominating effect of queries with extremely low ans_{q_i} [8]. We set the value of b as: $b = 2\% \times |\mathcal{U}|$.

4.2   Comparison of Grid Approaches

In this section, we compare the three grid approaches (UG, PrivAG, AAG) using different-sized random queries. To do so, we enforce that the random queries we generate for calculating AQE have size: $A(q) = \rho \times \Omega$, where $\rho \in (0, 1]$ is the query size parameter. In Table 1, we fix $\varepsilon = 1$ and vary the value of ρ between 0.005% and 0.5%. Note that these are relatively low values of ρ, i.e., the generated queries are small. We use the **bold** notation in Table 1 when comparing the two adaptive grid approaches (PrivAG vs AAG), i.e., the one that yields lower AQE is written in bold. This helps to demonstrate the improvement of AAG compared to PrivAG. We use the grey cell background to denote the best-performing approach when comparing all three (UG vs PrivAG vs AAG).

Table 1. AQEs with varying query sizes ρ, fixed $\varepsilon = 1$.

Dataset	Method	$\rho = 0.005\%$	$\rho = 0.01\%$	$\rho = 0.05\%$	$\rho = 0.1\%$	$\rho = 0.5\%$
	UG	0.0034	0.0067	0.0279	0.0485	0.120
Gowalla	PrivAG	0.0039	0.0077	0.0374	0.0728	0.305
	AAG	**0.0023**	**0.0051**	**0.0236**	**0.0460**	**0.185**
	UG	0.0028	0.0045	0.0180	0.0321	0.082
Porto	PrivAG	0.0034	0.0056	0.0283	0.0540	0.205
	AAG	**0.0025**	**0.0045**	**0.0247**	**0.0501**	**0.195**
	UG	0.0032	0.0054	0.0243	0.0416	0.126
Foursquare	PrivAG	0.0036	0.0062	0.0291	0.0547	0.203
	AAG	**0.0025**	**0.0043**	**0.0234**	**0.0450**	**0.177**

The results in Table 1 show that AAG achieves lower error compared to PrivAG in all settings. In addition, AAG also achieves lower error compared to UG in the majority of settings. However, as ρ increases, UG starts performing better than AAG. This implies that for fine-grained density modeling and small-sized queries, AAG is the best approach. This is an intuitive result, considering that AAG excels in dividing dense areas in a detailed fashion. Yet, for more coarse (high-level) density statistics, UG can perform better. Another observation we make from Table 1 is that when ρ increases, the errors also increase. This is because increasing ρ causes the intersection between $A(q_i)$ and various cells to increase, therefore ans_{q_i} and ans'_{q_i} become larger. Hence, overall noise amount increases as well, and among the two factors in the denominator of Eq. 4, ans_{q_i} starts to dominate rather than b. Consequently, higher AQEs are obtained.

4.3   Impact of the Privacy Budget ε

In this section, we keep the query sizes ρ fixed and vary the privacy budgets ε between 0.5 and 5. We selected this range of ε values since they are parallel to the commonly used values in the LDP literature. Table 2 provides the results with $\rho = 0.01\%$ and Table 3 provides the results with $\rho = 4\%$. In both tables, we use the same bold and grey color highlight strategies that we used in the previous section. According to the results in Table 2, when $\rho = 0.01\%$, AAG is the best approach. It yields the lowest AQEs across all ε. On the other hand, when $\rho = 4\%$, UG becomes the best approach as shown in Table 3. This is parallel to the results reported in the previous section. When $\rho = 4\%$, although AAG consistently beats PrivAG, it cannot reach UG's low AQE values.

Table 2. AQEs with varying privacy budgets ε, fixed $\rho = 0.01\%$.

Dataset	Method	$\varepsilon = 0.5$	$\varepsilon = 1$	$\varepsilon = 3$	$\varepsilon = 5$
	UG	0.0070	0.0066	0.0064	0.0056
Gowalla	PrivAG	0.0075	0.0077	0.0072	0.0062
	AAG	**0.0047**	**0.0051**	**0.0049**	**0.0041**
	UG	0.0048	0.0045	0.0045	0.0045
Porto	PrivAG	0.0058	0.0056	0.0059	0.0060
	AAG	**0.0048**	**0.0045**	**0.0049**	**0.0049**
	UG	0.0055	0.0054	0.0051	0.0048
Foursquare	PrivAG	0.0060	0.0062	0.0061	0.0069
	AAG	**0.0044**	**0.0043**	**0.0040**	**0.0047**

Table 3. AQEs with varying privacy budgets ε, fixed $\rho = 4\%$.

Dataset	Method	$\varepsilon = 0.5$	$\varepsilon = 1$	$\varepsilon = 3$	$\varepsilon = 5$
	UG	0.28	0.23	0.17	0.19
Gowalla	PrivAG	1.09	1.15	1.08	0.98
	AAG	**0.68**	**0.71**	**0.68**	**0.76**
	UG	0.16	0.12	0.10	0.09
Porto	PrivAG	0.77	0.76	0.71	0.71
	AAG	**0.49**	**0.49**	**0.62**	**0.63**
	UG	0.26	0.19	0.16	0.16
Foursquare	PrivAG	0.69	0.63	0.75	0.69
	AAG	**0.61**	**0.56**	**0.55**	**0.51**

In both tables, we observe that as ε increases, AQEs of UG decrease. This is an intuitive result since higher ε means less perturbation caused by LDP, therefore results are more accurate. On the other hand, this trend does not always hold for PrivAG and AAG. For example, despite increasing ε, there are cases in PrivAG and AAG in which AQE values increase. This is because ε is used in the choice of g_1 and g_2^k. Hence, changing ε also changes the grid structures in PrivAG and AAG. These structural changes may affect ans_q' positively or negatively, and LDP perturbation is no longer the only factor in the accuracy of ans_q'. Thus, we do not see a consistent trend between ε and AQE in PrivAG and AAG. On the other hand, this observation shows that if the choices of g_1 and g_2^k are made in a more optimized fashion, especially in high ε regions, there is potential to improve utility, which can be an avenue for future work.

Combining all experiment results, we arrive at the following take-away messages: (i) AAG is preferable to PrivAG across all ε and ρ, (ii) AAG is the best approach when ρ is small, e.g., for computing answers to small queries or for detailed statistics, and (iii) UG is the best approach when ρ is large, e.g., for computing answers to large queries or for coarse statistics.

5   Conclusion

In this paper, we studied three grid-based decomposition approaches under LDP: UG, PrivAG, and AAG. Our proposed AAG approach advances the state-of-the-art adaptive grid approach (PrivAG) by performing cell divisions according to neighboring cells' densities. We experimentally compared UG, PrivAG, and AAG using three datasets and multiple ε and ρ values. We observed that AAG always beats PrivAG, and it also beats UG when ρ is small. However, when ρ is large, UG with a near-optimal choice of grid size becomes better than AAG. Note that the utility improvement of AAG comes at no additional LDP cost for users since UG, PrivAG, and AAG are compared using the same ε budgets.

Overall, considering the use of grids in the DP and LDP literature as well as the utility improvement offered by AAG, our work enables potential utility improvements in various LDP tasks such as density estimation and visualization, query answering, trajectory collection and sharing, and synthetic data generation [5,8,13]. In future work, we plan to integrate AAG into such downstream tasks. Furthermore, we plan to compare UG, PrivAG, and AAG against tree-based decompositions. Finally, we will investigate methods to improve PrivAG and AAG's utility especially in high ε regimes.

Acknowledgments. This study was supported by Scientific and Technological Research Council of Türkiye (TUBITAK) under Grant Number 121E303. The authors thank TUBITAK for their support.

References

1. Alptekin, E., Gursoy, M.E.: Building quadtrees for spatial data under local differential privacy. In: Atluri, V., Ferrara, A.L. (eds.) Data and Applications Security and Privacy XXXVII: 37th Annual IFIP WG 11.3 Conference, DBSec 2023, Sophia-Antipolis, France, July 19–21, 2023, Proceedings, pp. 22–39. Springer Nature Switzerland, Cham (2023). https://doi.org/10.1007/978-3-031-37586-6_2

2. Cormode, G., Jha, S., Kulkarni, T., Li, N., Srivastava, D., Wang, T.: Privacy at scale: Local differential privacy in practice. In: Proceedings of the 2018 International Conference on Management of Data, pp. 1655–1658. ACM (2018)
3. Cormode, G., Maddock, S., Maple, C.: Frequency estimation under local differential privacy. Proc. VLDB Endowm. **14**(11), 2046–2058 (2021)
4. Ding, B., Kulkarni, J., Yekhanin, S.: Collecting telemetry data privately. In: Advances in Neural Information Processing Systems, pp. 3571–3580 (2017)
5. Du, Y.: Ldptrace: locally differentially private trajectory synthesis. Proc. VLDB Endowment **16**(8), 1897–1909 (2023)
6. Erlingsson, Ú., Pihur, V., Korolova, A.: Rappor: randomized aggregatable privacy-preserving ordinal response. In: Proceedings of the 2014 ACM SIGSAC Conference on Computer and Communications Security, pp. 1054–1067. ACM (2014)
7. Gursoy, M.E., Liu, L., Chow, K.H., Truex, S., Wei, W.: An adversarial approach to protocol analysis and selection in local differential privacy. IEEE Trans. Inf. Forensics Secur. **17**, 1785–1799 (2022)
8. Gursoy, M.E., Liu, L., Truex, S., Yu, L., Wei, W.: Utility-aware synthesis of differentially private and attack-resilient location traces. In: Proceedings of the 2018 ACM SIGSAC Conference on Computer and Communications Security, pp. 196–211 (2018)
9. Hong, D., Jung, W., Shim, K.: Collecting geospatial data under local differential privacy with improving frequency estimation. IEEE Trans. Knowl. Data Eng. 1–12 (2022). https://doi.org/10.1109/TKDE.2022.3181049
10. Qardaji, W., Yang, W., Li, N.: Differentially private grids for geospatial data. In: 2013 IEEE 29th International Conference on Data Engineering (ICDE), pp. 757–768. IEEE (2013)
11. Wang, H., Hong, H., Xiong, L., Qin, Z., Hong, Y.: L-srr: Local differential privacy for location-based services with staircase randomized response. In: Proceedings of the 2022 ACM SIGSAC Conference on Computer and Communications Security, p. 2809–2823. Association for Computing Machinery, New York, NY, USA (2022)
12. Wang, T., Blocki, J., Li, N., Jha, S.: Locally differentially private protocols for frequency estimation. In: Proceedings of the 26th USENIX Security Symposium, pp. 729–745 (2017)
13. Yang, J., Cheng, X., Su, S., Sun, H., Chen, C.: Collecting individual trajectories under local differential privacy. In: 2022 23rd IEEE International Conference on Mobile Data Management (MDM), pp. 99–108. IEEE (2022)
14. Zhang, Y., Ye, Q., Chen, R., Hu, H., Han, Q.: Trajectory data collection with local differential privacy. Proc. VLDB Endowment **16**(10), 2591–2604 (2023)

Balancing Privacy and Utility in Multivariate Time-Series Classification

Adrian-Silviu Roman$^{(\boxtimes)}$, Béla Genge , and Piroska Haller

George Emil Palade University of Medicine, Pharmacy, Science and Technology of
Targu Mures, Targu Mures, Mures 540142, Romania
{adrian.roman,bela.genge,piroska.haller}@umfst.ro

Abstract. In the modern era, characterized by the widespread presence of sensor-based systems, ensuring time-series data privacy without compromising utility has emerged as a significant challenge. While current strategies for safeguarding time-series data prioritize either input data protection or privacy-preserving classification models, they often fall short in assessing the balance between data privacy and utility, particularly when strong adversary classification models are involved. Our approach introduces a novel protection technique specifically designed for multivariate Time-Series Classification. This technique involves perturbing the data by distributing the noise among features using a feature importance-based approach, thus securing the data while preserving its analytical value. We propose a dual-model evaluation system consisting of two supervised classifiers, a Privacy-Breaking Classifier and a Utility-Focused Classifier. These are designed to respectively assess the potential for privacy breaches and the extent of data utility preservation in the context of protected time-series data. The experimental results demonstrate the effectiveness and viability of our methodology. Our approach provides a framework for evaluating the privacy and utility levels of time-series data. Additionally, it guides the selection of an appropriate perturbation level to ensure both aspects are adequately addressed.

Keywords: Utility-preserving data privacy · Time-series classification · Local differential privacy · Automotive systems

1   Introduction

Data collected from sensor-based systems, such as automotive vehicles, wearable devices, or smart grids, is often transmitted over the Internet to centralized databases for analysis and processing by third-party systems (e.g., traffic monitoring conducted by authorities or insurance companies). While time-series data itself does not explicitly contain personally identifiable information (e.g., names, e-mails), they may expose user-related details (e.g., geolocation and biometrics) or lead to user identification or re-identification (e.g., by data classification) [6,12]. Protecting sensor data from both "honest-but-curious" data processors

© The Author(s), under exclusive license to Springer Nature Switzerland AG 2025
J. Garcia-Alfaro et al. (Eds.): ESORICS 2024 Workshops, LNCS 15263, pp. 124–136, 2025.
https://doi.org/10.1007/978-3-031-82349-7_9

and malicious actors is crucial. To address these concerns, data can be distorted or aggregated to enforce privacy without losing its utility.

While methods exist to safeguard data collected from sensors during transmission to third-party systems [10], ensuring data privacy poses additional challenges. When applying data protection mechanisms, monitoring and retaining data usefulness is essential to ensure that enough information is preserved for effective analysis. Typically, evaluating data utility (i.e., the usefulness of data) involves measuring how well a selected data privacy method preserves aggregate statistical information. However, when addressing the classification of time-series data, relying exclusively on aggregate statistical information derived from protected data might not adequately capture the extent to which the data achieves a balance between privacy and utility. In the field of time-series data classification, data privacy predominantly relies on two primary methodologies: (i) secure input data through diverse techniques such as perturbation, encryption, deidentification, data transformation, machine learning methodologies (e.g., using deep autoencoders) [11,14]; and (ii) employing classification models that preserve privacy, thereby securing the training data against potential adversaries [1].

The proposed approach introduces a time-series data protection mechanism tailored for multivariate data, which can be implemented at the device level and is designed to neutralize adversaries using powerful classifiers. This mechanism is configurable to achieve the desired balance between privacy and utility. To summarize, the research presented in this paper advances the state of the art from several perspectives:

– We formulate the problem of balancing privacy and utility in the context of multivariate Time-Series Classification (TSC), using a dual-model, consisting of two opposing classifiers, a Privacy-Breaking Classifier (PBC) and a Utility-Focused Classifier (UFC);
– We propose a protection technique independent of the perturbation type, applying the perturbation to multivariate time-series data and utilizing feature importance to distribute the noise;
– We introduce the *classification utility-privacy balance* score, $\mathcal{B}_{UP}$, and a methodology for determining the appropriate value of the applied perturbation, to achieve the desired level of utility and privacy;
– We demonstrate the effectiveness and viability of the proposed methodology by enforcing a Local Differential Privacy (LDP) perturbation on two well-known driver datasets [9,15], and compare the results with the outcomes of uniformly applying the same perturbation across all features.

The remainder of this paper is organized as follows. Section 2 describes the addressed problem, and it introduces the basic concepts and terminology. Section 3 presents an in-depth description of the proposed approach. This is followed by extensive experimental results in Sect. 4. The paper concludes in Sect. 5.

2   Problem Definition and Basic Concepts

Consider data collected from sensors, temporarily stored at the device level, and sent as data streams to a central data warehouse for classification. The objective is to protect the multivariate time-series data from a privacy-breaking adversary classifier while preserving data utility. Furthermore, we impose the restriction that no dimensionality reduction methods are permitted, ensuring that the full set of features is maintained.

Within this setting, two distinct types of classifiers are evaluated: (i) a UFC, for identifying non-user related data patterns, and (ii) a PBC, designed to determine the identity of the users. The objective of this research is to propose a protection mechanism at the device level, such that the Utility-Focused Classi-fierUFC provides suitable detection accuracy while the accuracy of the Privacy-Breaking Classifier (PBC) is as low as possible.

Classification Model Generation. The process of generating the Utility-Focused Classifier (UFC) model assumes a secure environment without any device-level perturbations. In both the training and testing phases of construct-ing the Utility-Focused Classifier (UFC)s, data labels for each batch of records are stored in the data warehouse. After constructing the Utility-Focused Clas-sifier (UFC) models, there is the possibility to remove the data labels from the database. No label information is shared with third-party systems. Moreover, during the prediction phase, no explicit information that could identify the user is transmitted to the central database, or recorded in any form. This procedure serves as a fundamental privacy protection strategy.

Adversarial Model. We examine the scenario in which the attacker possesses access to all potential data sources, containing both the training dataset with labels, the unlabeled data collected from the devices, and other observable, non-perturbed data. Consequently, the attacker is capable of constructing a Privacy-Breaking Classifier (PBC) that promptly and accurately re-identifies users based on intercepted data. Another potential privacy breach is associated with "honest-but-curious" entities, such as a data analyst who has access to all the data needed to construct a classifier that compromises privacy.

Local W-Event Level Differential Privacy for Time Series. To demon-strate the proposed approach, we choose LDP as the time series perturbation method. This involves applying LDP perturbation per feature for each batch of w data values. The *w-event-level* DP perturbation [8] provides privacy protection to any sequence of w consecutive events and represents a compromise between the *user* and the *event-level privacy*. To perturb the data at the device level we utilize the local *w-event-level* DP [13]. The size of the noise is determined by the privacy budget ϵ and the sensitivity [3]. Introducing noise into the data through a mechanism that satisfies ϵ-differential privacy is achieved using the

Laplace mechanism, as proposed by Dwork et al. [3]. Data collected from sensors is multivariate, meaning the resulting time-series data has numerous attributes or features. We apply the w-event LDP separately for each feature.

Privacy and Utility Measurements. To validate the proposed approach in the context of TSC, we use the classification accuracy of the PBC as a measure of privacy protection. Similarly, the classification accuracy of the UFC measures the data utility. Additionally, we employ the Mean Average Error (MAE) to further assess the utility of the perturbed data, a metric commonly used for comparing time series perturbation methods [16]: $MAE = \frac{1}{N} \sum_{i \in N} |V_i - V_i'|$, where N is the number of values of the time series, V is the original set of values, and V' is the perturbed data.

3   Proposed Approach

Time-series data, continuously collected from sensors, is perceived as infinite data streams, with each distinct value representing an event generated by the user (such as an event indicating "the driver u traveled at speed s at time t"). Further, we introduce our proposed approach for protecting the sensitive data encapsulated in these events.

We propose a time-series perturbation method suitable for multivariate time-series data that outperforms the uniform distribution of perturbation across all features. Our approach is designed to be independent of the specific perturbation method used, ensuring robustness and flexibility in handling diverse types of time-series data. Additionally, the method is developed for locally applied perturbation at the device level.

Let the continually collected data, consisting of records with d features, be stored locally on the device and then transmitted in groups of w records to a central location for processing. Thus, let $\mathbf{X}_i^t$ be the time-series data collected for a period of time and stored locally at time t, on the sensor-based device i. $\mathbf{X}_i^t$ is represented as a matrix of w rows and d columns. Each column denotes measurements associated with a particular attribute/feature.

TSC refers to the task of assigning a label or category to a given time-series data based on its patterns, trends, or features. A classifier model produces a function $f : \mathbb{R}^{w \cdot d} \longrightarrow \mathcal{C}, \mathcal{C} = \{1, ..., n\}$, where w is the number of records, d is the number of features and n the number of categories, that is applied to any input $\mathbf{X}$. The function $f(\mathbf{X})$ is regarded as an estimate of the category that $\mathbf{X}$ belongs to [5]. Let f_p and f_u be two classification functions, $f_p : \mathbb{R}^{w \cdot d} \longrightarrow \mathcal{C}_u$ and $f_u : \mathbb{R}^{w \cdot d} \longrightarrow \mathcal{C}_p$ that output the class that $\mathbf{X}_i^t$ belongs to, in case of the Privacy-Breaking Classifier (PBC), and Utility-Focused Classifier (UFC), respectively. $f_p(\mathbf{X}_i^t)$ is the Privacy-Breaking Classifier (PBC) classifier that breaks the user privacy by identifying the set of collected values as belonging to a user from a specified class $\mathcal{C}_p$, and $f_u(\mathbf{X}_i^t)$, the Utility-Focused Classifier (UFC), classifies the non-sensitive information from a class $\mathcal{C}_u$.

In the training and testing phases of building the UFC, for each $\mathbf{X}_i^t$ an id of the device or/and of the user is also collected and stored, with the objective of labeling the data. Let $\mathbf{Y}_{pi}^t$ be the label information for the user identification, and let $\mathbf{Y}_{ui}^t$ be the label for non-user-related data classification. In the prediction phases, as a fundamental measure to preserve privacy, no data that could identify individuals or devices is transmitted to the central data warehouse.

The objective is to perturb time-series data $\mathbf{X}_i^t$ with a mechanism $\mathcal{M}$ such that two conditions are met: the classification accuracy of f_p on the perturbed data is minimum, and, simultaneously, the classification accuracy of f_u on the perturbed data is maximum.

Let the classification accuracy, which shows the number of correct classifications, for the two classifiers f_u and f_p be defined as follows:

$$\mathcal{A}_u = \frac{1}{N \cdot T} \sum_{i=1}^{N} \sum_{t=1}^{T} \mathbb{I}(\mathbf{Y}_{ui}^t = f_u(\mathbf{X}_i^t)), \mathcal{A}_p = \frac{1}{N \cdot T} \sum_{i=1}^{N} \sum_{t=1}^{T} \mathbb{I}(\mathbf{Y}_{pi}^t = f_p(\mathbf{X}_i^t)), \quad (1)$$

where $\mathcal{A}_u$ is the accuracy of f_u, $\mathcal{A}_p$ is the accuracy of f_p, N is the number of sensor-based devices, T the number of data batches collected, and $\mathbb{I}(c)$ the binary indicator function returning 1 iff the condition c is true, and returns 0 otherwise. Furthermore, the classification accuracy for the perturbed data is defined as:

$$\mathcal{A}_u'(\theta) = \frac{1}{N \cdot T} \sum_{i=1}^{N} \sum_{t=1}^{T} \mathbb{I}(\mathbf{Y}_{ui}^t = f_u(\mathcal{M}(\mathbf{X}_i^t; \theta))), \text{and} \quad (2)$$

$$\mathcal{A}_p'(\theta) = \frac{1}{N \cdot T} \sum_{i=1}^{N} \sum_{t=1}^{T} \mathbb{I}(\mathbf{Y}_{pi}^t = f_p(\mathcal{M}(\mathbf{X}_i^t; \theta))). \quad (3)$$

where $\mathcal{M}$ is the perturbation mechanism, $\mathcal{M} : \mathbb{R}^{w \cdot d} \longrightarrow \mathbb{R}^{w \cdot d}$, and θ is the set of perturbation parameters (e.g., ϵ for LDP).

Thus, the data perturbation objective is bounded by the following conditions:

$$\mathcal{A}_p'(\theta) \ll \mathcal{A}_p \text{ and } \mathcal{A}_u'(\theta) \approx \mathcal{A}_u, \quad (4)$$

such that the accuracy of PBC is significantly diminished when data is perturbed, while the accuracy of the UFC for perturbed data remains close to the accuracy of the classification on non-perturbed data.

Achieving a balance between privacy and utility presents a significant challenge, particularly when considering classification tasks involving two opposing classifiers. We introduce $\mathcal{B}_{UP}$, the *classification utility-privacy balance*, as a measure for balancing privacy and utility in the proposed classification problem, computed as follows:

$$\mathcal{B}_{UP}(\theta) = 1 - \frac{\mathcal{A}_u'(\theta)}{\mathcal{A}_u} \cdot \left(1 - \frac{\mathcal{A}_p'(\theta)}{\mathcal{A}_p}\right). \quad (5)$$

The score $\mathcal{B}_{UP}$ is positive and close to zero when the perturbation successfully meets the specified objectives from Eq. 4. This indicates that the accuracy of the UFC with perturbed data is close to its accuracy with unperturbed data, while the accuracy of the PBC with perturbed data is significantly lower than its accuracy with unperturbed data. A negative $\mathcal{B}_{UP}$ value signifies that the chosen perturbation has increased the accuracy of the PBC, representing the worst-case scenario.

The proposed method for finding the perturbation parameters consists of the following steps: (i) compute feature importance for the two classifications (Utility-Focused Classifier (UFC) and Privacy-Breaking Classifier (PBC)); (ii) cluster features based on the computed importance coefficients; (iii) distribute and apply the perturbation to the features of the time-series data $\mathbf{X}_i^t$; (iv) select the perturbation parameter set θ^* such that $\mathcal{B}_{UP}(\theta)$ is minimum:

$$\theta^* = argmin_\theta \{\mathcal{B}_{UP}(\theta)|\mathcal{B}_{UP}(\theta) > 0\}. \tag{6}$$

3.1 Feature Importance Computation and Feature Clustering

Feature importance computation [2] estimates the relative significance of features within a dataset for a specific classification. One notable benefit of employing feature importance computation techniques lies in assessing feature significance without requiring prior knowledge of the adversarial model. Consequently, this computation is conducted solely based on available data labels and by anticipating potential classifications.

We propose using the Random Forest (RF) algorithm [2], a popular technique for feature ranking and feature importance computation, to identify the features that hold the most relevance for classifications. For the current research, we selected the impurity-based feature importance (e.g., Gini importance [2]).

Let $\mathbf{X}$ be the set of all $\mathbf{X}_i^t$ selected for the training phase. By computing the feature importance for classifying $\mathbf{X}$ on class $\mathcal{C}_p$ using the labels $\mathbf{Y}_p$ and for classifying $\mathbf{X}$ on class $\mathcal{C}_u$ using labels $\mathbf{Y}_u$, we obtain I_p and I_u, the vectors of importance coefficients $(I_{pi}, I_{ui} \in [0,1], i \in \{1, ..., d\})$.

Let $\mathcal{F}$ be the set of selected features from the dataset, $\mathcal{F} = \{F_1, ..., F_i, ...\}$. Based on the computed importance coefficients I_p and I_u, we aim to cluster $\mathcal{F}$ into three subsets: $\mathcal{F}_u$ with features necessary for the utility-focused classification, $\mathcal{F}_p$ with features that play a significant role in resolving the privacy-breaking classification, and $\mathcal{F}_{up}$ with features that are important for both classifications, such that $\mathcal{F} = \mathcal{F}_u \cup \mathcal{F}_p \cup \mathcal{F}_{up}$.

Let $S_{F_i}(I_{ui}, I_{pi})$ be the score of importance coefficients for feature F_i in I_p and I_u, respectively, such that: $S_{F_i}(I_{ui}, I_{pi}) = I_{ui} - I_{pi}$. Further, let the line represented by $S_{F_i}(I_{ui}, I_{pi}) = 0, \forall i \in \{1, ..., d\}$, be the main decision boundary and ρ_I be the distance between the main and secondary decision boundaries. The following rules for clustering are considered:

$$F_i \in \mathcal{F}_u \text{ if } S_{F_i}(I_{ui}, I_{pi}) > \rho_I, F_i \in \mathcal{F}_p \text{ if } S_{F_i}(I_{ui}, I_{pi}) < -\rho_I, \tag{7}$$

$$F_i \in \mathcal{F}_{up} \text{ if } S_{F_i}(I_{ui}, I_{pi}) \in [-\rho_I, \rho_I]. \tag{8}$$

The score $S_{F_i}(I_{ui}, I_{pi})$ determines when a feature shows a significantly greater significance in a classification context compared to another. When $S_{F_i}(I_{ui}, I_{pi}) = 0$, only the features that have the same importance coefficients for both UFC and PBC belong to $\mathcal{F}_{up}$.

3.2 Data Perturbation

The proposed mechanism introduces a global perturbation budget to be divided within the features in $\mathcal{F}$. To achieve the goal of reducing the Privacy-Breaking Classifier (PBC)'s impact while preserving the accuracy of the Utility-Focused Classifier (UFC), we introduce substantial perturbation to features within $\mathcal{F}_p$, moderate perturbation to features within $\mathcal{F}_{up}$, while maintaining the features within the cluster $\mathcal{F}_u$ unmodified.

Consider the mechanism $\mathcal{M}$ of perturbing $\mathbf{X}_i^t$ a composition of d mechanisms $\mathcal{M}_i$, one for each feature F_i in clusters $\mathcal{F}_p$, $\mathcal{F}_{up}$ and $\mathcal{F}_u$. Let the total perturbation budget β_T be allocated to $\mathcal{M}$ and distributed to mechanisms $\mathcal{M}_i$, based on the membership in clusters $\mathcal{F}_p$, $\mathcal{F}_{up}$ and $\mathcal{F}_u$. Let β_p, β_{up}, and β_u be the cumulative privacy budgets for features in clusters $\mathcal{F}_p$, $\mathcal{F}_{up}$ and $\mathcal{F}_u$, respectively, such that:

$$\beta_p = \alpha_p \cdot \beta_T, \beta_{up} = \alpha_{up} \cdot \beta_T, \beta_u = 0, \text{ and } \alpha_p + \alpha_{up} = 1, \text{ with } \alpha_p, \alpha_{up} \in [0,1], \tag{9}$$

where α_p and α_{up} are the perturbation budget distribution parameters. Within each cluster, budgets are uniformly distributed such that: $\beta_{pi} = \frac{\alpha_p \cdot \beta_T}{|\mathcal{F}_p|}$, and $\beta_{upi} = \frac{\alpha_{up} \cdot \beta_T}{|\mathcal{F}_{up}|}$, where β_{pi} is the privacy budget allocated for each $F_i \in \mathcal{F}_p$, β_{upi} the budget allocated for each $F_i \in \mathcal{F}_{up}$, and $|\mathcal{F}_p|$, $|\mathcal{F}_{up}|$ the number of features in clusters $\mathcal{F}_p$ and $\mathcal{F}_{up}$. Additionally, the imposed requirement is that the perturbation applied to features in $\mathcal{F}_p$ be higher or equal to the one applied to features in $\mathcal{F}_{up}$. When the data perturbation is proportional to the allocated budget we enforce that $\beta_{pi} \geq \beta_{upi}$, otherwise $\beta_{pi} \leq \beta_{upi}$.

A possible perturbation method to be applied in the proposed context involves implementing the w-event level LDP (described in Sect. 2) to features in clusters $\mathcal{F}_p$ and $\mathcal{F}_{up}$. The selection of perturbation budget parameters α_p and α_{up} needs to account for the number of features in the cluster. The challenge lies in identifying ρ_I, which defines the feature clustering (Sect. 3.1), along with β_T, α_p, α_{up}, to ensure that $\mathcal{B}_{UP}(\theta)$, with $\theta = \{\rho_I, \beta_T, \alpha_p, \alpha_{up}\}$, is minimized while remaining positive. Further, the experiments confirm that suitable values for the perturbation parameters can be identified and that the $\mathcal{B}_{UP}$ score effectively indicates the appropriate size of the perturbation.

4 Experimental Results

To demonstrate the validity of the proposed approach, we focused the experiments on two datasets collected from automotive vehicles, the UAH-Driveset

[15], and, the HCRL Driving Dataset [9]. For benchmarking the driver identification classification, we utilized the LSTM-based approach, as proposed by
Karim *et al.* [7].

Recall that the work at hand addresses two objectives: to protect sensitive
information while concurrently preserving data utility in the context of multivariate TSC. We examine two distinct scenarios: (i) driver detection as PBC
with road type detection as UFC, which we term *driver-vs-road-type classification*; and (ii) driver detection functioning as the PBC and behavior detection
operating as the UFC, a setup we refer to as *driver-vs-behavior classification*.

The first experimental stage involved constructing classification models
specifically trained to identify the driver, determine driver behavior, and categorize road types. These models utilized the FCN-LSTM architecture [7] and
were trained on non-perturbed data from the selected datasets. The datasets
were preprocessed following the same procedures proposed by El Mekki *et al.*
[4]. The obtained results represented the accuracy achieved by the classification
models in various tasks.

To evaluate the impact of distributing perturbation unequally between features, as outlined in Sect. 3.2, we initially explored a scenario where features were
not clustered, with each feature receiving an identical amount of perturbation.
This approach was a direct extension of perturbation methods originally designed
for univariate data, specifically the w-event LDP [8,13]. In this case, $\epsilon_i = \epsilon_j$ for
all $i, j \in \{1, ..., d\}$, and the total privacy budget for all features was $\epsilon_T = \sum_{i=0}^{d} \epsilon_i$.
The budget ϵ_i for each feature F_i was uniformly distributed among the values
belonging to the same feature, according to the formula $w \cdot \Delta g / \epsilon_i$ proposed by
Kellaris et al. [8] for w-event LDP, where Δg represents the data sensitivity.
The noise was generated using the Laplace mechanism [3] and applied to data
batches of $w = 60$ records of sensor values. Figure 1 and Table 1 demonstrate
that applying an equal perturbation to all features fulfills the objectives stated
in Eq. 4. However, in all cases, the accuracy $\mathcal{A}'_p(\theta)$ of the PBC remained close
to $\mathcal{A}'_u(\theta)$ for smaller perturbations, where $\mathcal{A}'_u(\theta) \approx \mathcal{A}_u$.

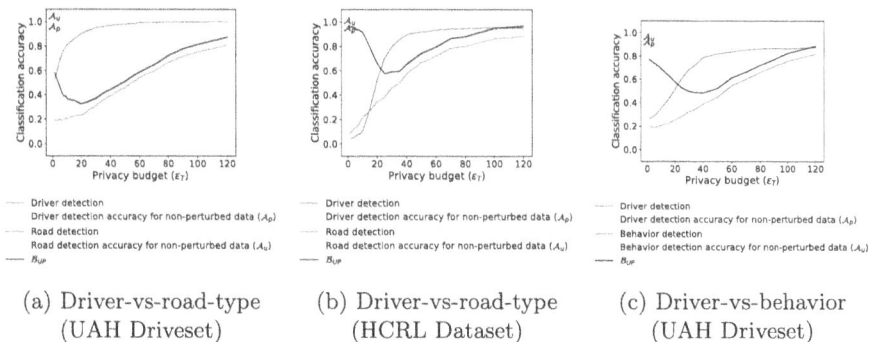

(a) Driver-vs-road-type
(UAH Driveset)

(b) Driver-vs-road-type
(HCRL Dataset)

(c) Driver-vs-behavior
(UAH Driveset)

Fig. 1. Classification accuracy with equally distributed perturbation for all features.

Furthermore, the experiments involved computing feature importance to evaluate the relevance of each feature for driver detection and non-driver-related data classification. Subsequently, features were clustered (Fig. 2) in $\mathcal{F}_p$, $\mathcal{F}_{up}$, and $\mathcal{F}_u$, according to the rules described in Sect. 3.1, considering the computed feature importance for driver identification and behavior/road type detection, respectively. Features in $\mathcal{F}_p$ and $\mathcal{F}_{up}$ were perturbed, as described in Sect. 3.2, using the same w-event LDP method, with variable privacy budget for each cluster.

The proposed approach for distributing the perturbation is based on a set of parameters, including the clustering parameter ρ_I, the privacy budget ϵ_T, and the cluster privacy budget distribution parameters α_p and α_{up}. We analyzed the number of features in each cluster to determine potential values for ρ_I. Our criteria ensured that there is at least one feature in both $\mathcal{F}_u$ and $\mathcal{F}_p$ and that the number of features in $\mathcal{F}_{up}$ is less than the sum of the features in $\mathcal{F}_p$ and $\mathcal{F}_u$ to maintain manageable uncertainty. For the cluster privacy budget distribution parameters α_p and α_{up}, we followed the condition that $\frac{\alpha_p}{|\mathcal{F}_p|} \leq \frac{\alpha_{up}}{|\mathcal{F}_{up}|}$. The considered values for ρ_I, α_p, and α_{up} are listed in Table 1.

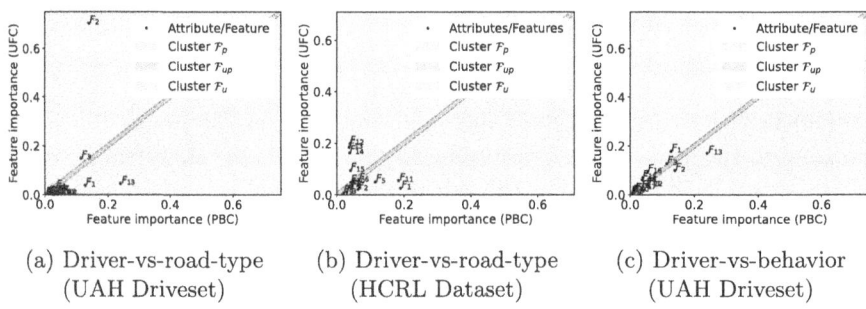

(a) Driver-vs-road-type   (b) Driver-vs-road-type   (c) Driver-vs-behavior
    (UAH Driveset)   (HCRL Dataset)   (UAH Driveset)

Fig. 2. Feature clustering based on feature importance coefficients for two classifications (UFC and PBC), conducted using Random Forest with Gini importance ($\rho_I = 0.01$).

The perturbed data was verified against previously trained classification models to determine an appropriate perturbation level ϵ_T, aiming to achieve the desired levels of privacy and utility while adhering to the established constraints. Figure 3 shows the classification accuracy for the considered parameter values in the case of *driver-vs-road-type classification*. The findings, as presented in Table 1 (with the best results highlighted in bold), demonstrated that certain parameter settings for the proposed approach produced superior outcomes compared to uniformly distributing noise across all features, aligning with the objectives outlined in Eq. 4. The overall performance evaluation was based on the calculation of the classification utility-privacy balance, $\mathcal{B}_{UP}(\theta)$.

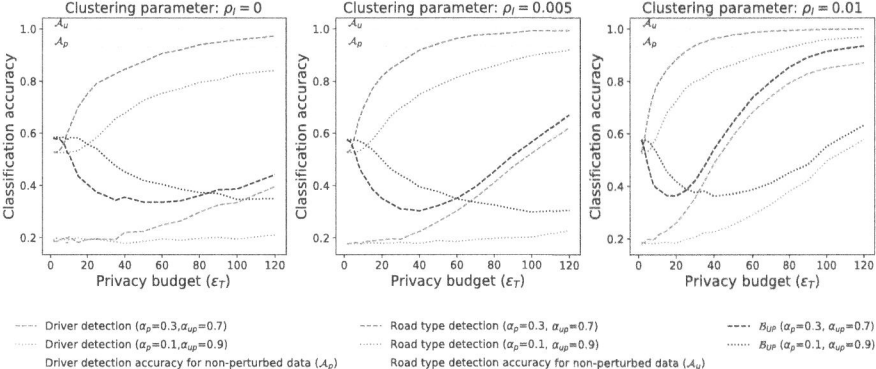

Fig. 3. Driver-vs-road-type classification accuracy on perturbed data (UAH dataset).

For the *driver-vs-road-type* classification using the UAH dataset, the accuracy $\mathcal{A}'_p(\theta)$ of the PBC was lower than the reference accuracy, while the classification accuracy $\mathcal{A}'_u(\theta)$ of the UFC is higher. The minimum value of $\mathcal{B}_{UP}(\theta)$ was achieved when clustering resulted in a large number of features in $\mathcal{F}_p$ and a small number of features in $\mathcal{F}_{up}$ and $\mathcal{F}_u$. This configuration allocated most of the perturbation to the features in $\mathcal{F}_p$, amplified by the large number of features in this cluster. Additionally, the MAE value was lower than the reference, indicating higher data utility. The privacy budget ϵ_T in this scenario was significantly higher ($\epsilon_T = 100$ compared to $\epsilon_T = 15$) than the proposed approach, indicating an overall lower perturbation. For the HCRL dataset, in the same type of classification, the best results were obtained when the clustering ($\rho_I = 0$) did not include features in $\mathcal{F}_{up}$.

In the case of the *driver-vs-behavior* classification, both classifiers relied on a similar set of features (Fig. 2c). However, the results showed that data protection was possible under the considered constraints with $\rho_I = 0$, $\alpha_p = 0.3$, $\alpha_p = 0.7$, and $\epsilon_T = 50$. Similar accuracy for PBC and UFC were obtained for significantly lower perturbation ($\epsilon_T = 50$ compared to $\epsilon_T = 30$).

Table 1. Classification accuracy for perturbed data using the proposed approach.

Dataset	Classification scenario	Perturbation approach	Clustering parameter (ρ_l)	# of features per cluster ($\mathcal{F}_p, \mathcal{F}_{up}, \mathcal{F}_u$)	Perturbation parameters (α_p, α_{up})	$\min(\mathcal{B}_{UP})$	c_T	$A'_p(\theta)$	$A'_u(\theta)$	MAE
UAH [15]	Driver-vs-road-type	w-event LDP [8,13] (no clustering)	-	-	-	0.3348	15	0.2103	0.8610	1.0170
		w-event LDP (feature clustering, **proposed method**)	0	{15,0,2}	{0.3,0.7}	0.3357	60	0.2480	0.9058	0.7424
					{0.1,0.9}	0.3459	100	0.1941	0.8266	1.3350
			0.005	{12,3,2}	{0.3,0.7}	0.3022	40	0.2227	0.9175	0.6038
					{0.1,0.9}	**0.2973**	**100**	0.2012	0.8967	0.6921
			0.01	{10,5,2}	{0.3,0.7}	0.3630	20	0.2564	0.8831	0.8141
					{0.1,0.9}	0.3623	40	0.2253	0.8415	1.0194
HCRL [9]	Driver-vs-road-type	w-event LDP [8,13] (no clustering)	-	-	-	0.5683	30	0.4356	0.7941	0.5291
		w-event LDP (feature clustering, **proposed method**)	0	{10,0,5}	{0.3,0.7}	0.5765	60	0.4613	0.8235	0.4306
					{0.15,0.85}	**0.5629**	**1200**	0.4377	0.8076	0.4302
			0.01	{9,2,4}	{0.3,0.7}	0.5785	60	0.4635	0.8235	0.4304
					{0.15,0.85}	0.5749	100	0.3755	0.6945	0.5168
			0.015	{7,4,4}	{0.3,0.7}	0.5803	40	0.3841	0.6968	0.4946
					{0.15,0.85}	0.5707	90	0.4263	0.7750	0.4428
UAH [15]	Driver-vs-behavior	w-event LDP [8,13] (no clustering)	-	-	-	0.4859	30	0.3090	0.6844	0.5077
		w-event LDP (feature clustering, **proposed method**)	0	{9,0,8}	**{0.3,0.7}**	**0.4692**	**50**	0.3181	0.7220	0.3651
					{0.15,0.85}	0.4834	100	0.3305	0.7175	0.3655
			0.005	{6,6,5}	{0.3,0.7}	0.4986	20	0.3759	0.7545	0.4110
					{0.15,0.85}	0.5426	20	0.4000	0.7201	0.5002
			0.01	{4,8,5}	{0.3,0.7}	0.4836	25	0.3714	0.7707	0.3609
					{0.15,0.85}	0.4965	20	0.3480	0.7207	0.4458

5   Conclusion

In conclusion, our research aimed to reach a balance between data privacy and utility when dealing with protected time-series data in the context of TSC. The proposed methodology offers several significant advantages: it results in a lower $\mathcal{A}'_p$ (accuracy of PBC), a higher $\mathcal{A}'_u$ (accuracy of UFC), and improved utility, as quantified by MAE. Further benefits of this approach are: (i) certain features ($\mathcal{F}_u$, crucial for utility classification) remain unperturbed, thereby preserving their utility for a variety of data processing activities beyond classification; (ii) the perturbation budget is significantly higher, resulting in lower noise when clustering is employed to achieve comparable privacy and utility objectives.

We introduced the *classification utility-privacy balance* score, $\mathcal{B}_{UP}$, which provides a detailed assessment of the privacy and utility achieved by the selected parameter set. This score maximizes the distance between $\mathcal{A}'_u(\theta)$ and $\mathcal{A}'_p(\theta)$, effectively balancing the trade-offs. However, alternative perturbation parameters may be selected if the accuracy of PBC or UFC is prioritized. Depending on specific requirements, such as maximizing the classification accuracy for PBC or maintaining the classification accuracy for UFC below a predetermined threshold, different perturbation parameters can be chosen.

References

1. Abadi, M., et al.: Deep learning with differential privacy. In: Proceedings of the 2016 ACM SIGSAC Conference on Computer and Communications Security, pp. 308–318 (2016)
2. Breiman, L.: Random forests. Mach. Learn. **45**, 5–32 (2001)
3. Dwork, C., McSherry, F., Nissim, K., Smith, A.: Calibrating noise to sensitivity in private data analysis. In: Halevi, S., Rabin, T. (eds.) Theory of Cryptography, pp. 265–284. Springer Berlin Heidelberg, Berlin, Heidelberg (2006). https://doi.org/10.1007/11681878_14
4. El Mekki, A., Bouhoute, A., Berrada, I.: Improving driver identification for the next-generation of in-vehicle software systems. IEEE Trans. Veh. Technol. **68**(8), 7406–7415 (2019)
5. Goodfellow, I., Bengio, Y., Courville, A.: Deep learning. MIT press (2016)
6. Hallac, D., et al.: Driver identification using automobile sensor data from a single turn, pp. 953–958 (11 2016)
7. Karim, F., Majumdar, S., Darabi, H., Chen, S.: Lstm fully convolutional networks for time series classification. IEEE access **6**, 1662–1669 (2017)
8. Kellaris, G., Papadopoulos, S., Xiao, X., Papadias, D.: Differentially private event sequences over infinite streams. Proc. VLDB Endow. **7**(12), 1155–1166 (aug 2014)
9. Kwak, B.I., Woo, J., Kim, H.K.: Know your master: Driver profiling-based anti-theft method. In: PST 2016 (2016)
10. Lyu, L., He, X., Law, Y.W., Palaniswami, M.: Privacy-preserving collaborative deep learning with application to human activity recognition, pp. 1219–1228 (11 2017)
11. Malekzadeh, M., Clegg, R.G., Cavallaro, A., Haddadi, H.: Mobile sensor data anonymization. In: Proceedings of the International Conference on Internet of Things Design and Implementation, pp. 49–58 (2019)

12. Mekruksavanich, S., Jitpattanakul, A.: Biometric user identification based on human activity recognition using wearable sensors: An experiment using deep learning models. Electronics **10**(3), 308 (2021)
13. Ren, X., Shi, L., Yu, W., Yang, S., Zhao, C., Xu, Z.: Ldp-ids: Local differential privacy for infinite data streams. In: Proceedings of the 2022 International Conference on Management of data, pp. 1064–1077 (2022)
14. Roman, A.S., Genge, B., Duka, A.V., Haller, P.: Privacy-preserving tampering detection in automotive systems. Electronics **10**(24) (2021)
15. Romera, E., Bergasa, L.M., Arroyo, R.: Need data for driver behaviour analysis? presenting the public uah-driveset. In: 2016 IEEE 19th International Conference on Intelligent Transportation Systems (ITSC), pp. 387–392. IEEE (2016)
16. Wang, H., Xu, Z.: Cts-dp: publishing correlated time-series data via differential privacy. Knowl.-Based Syst. **122**, 167–179 (2017)

Dynamic k-Anonymity for Electronic Health Records: A Topological Framework

Arjhun Swaminathan[1,2]($\boxtimes$) and Mete Akgün[1,2]

[1] Medical Data Privacy and Privacy Preserving Machine Learning, Department of
Computer Science, University of Tübingen, Tübingen, Germany
{mete.akguen,arjhun.swaminathan}@uni-tuebingen.de
[2] Institute for Bioinformatics and Medical Informatics, Tübingen, Germany

Abstract. With the rapid digitization of Electronic Health Records
(EHRs), fast and adaptive data anonymization methods have become
increasingly important. While tools from topological data analysis
(TDA) have been proposed to anonymize static datasets—allowing the
creation of multiple generalizations for different anonymization needs
from a single computation—the application to dynamic datasets remains
unexplored. To address this, our work adapts existing methodologies to
the dynamic setting. We develop an improved version of weighted persistence barcodes that track higher-dimensional holes in data, allowing us
to edit persistence information on the fly. Additionally, we introduce filtration trimming, a novel technique designed to update persistence data
quickly with minimal computing effort when data is added. Our work
represents a significant advancement in healthcare data privacy, offering
a refined approach to protecting highly sensitive and evolving patient
data through dynamic k-anonymity.

Keywords: Persistence Barcodes · k-anonymity · Dynamic datasets ·
Medical Data Privacy

1 Introduction

In the era of digital transformation, the healthcare sector has accumulated vast
amounts of patient data through EHRs, encompassing demographics, medica-
tions, diagnoses, progress notes, and medical history. By 2019, 96% of general
practitioners in the EU had adopted EHRs[1]. This shift coincides with strict privacy regulations like the GDPR[2], which mandate de-identification or anonymization of sensitive data before processing.

Healthcare providers face the challenge of utilizing this rich data for improved
healthcare while ensuring patient privacy. Anonymizing EHRs before public or
third-party access enables researchers to conduct large-scale studies, aid in public

---

[1] eHealth adoption in primary healthcare in the EU is on the rise, European Commission.

[2] General Data Protection Regulation ((EU) 2016/679).

J. Garcia-Alfaro et al. (Eds.): ESORICS 2024 Workshops, LNCS 15263, pp. 137–152, 2025.
https://doi.org/10.1007/978-3-031-82349-7_10

health monitoring and develop crucial medical treatments without compromising privacy. The primary technique for anonymizing EHRs has been k-anonymity [30,37], but it is vulnerable to attacks like background knowledge attacks [22, 34], attribute disclosure attacks [21], membership inference attacks, and linkage attacks [18], as highlighted by Sweeney's analysis of the 1990 U.S. Census data [36]. To address these limitations, l-diversity [22,45] and t-closeness [21] were developed to enhance k-anonymity. Despite its computational challenges and NP-hardness [25], k-anonymity remains widely used [2,24,28,38,40–42].

Differential privacy, another key privacy technique, adds noise to data to ensure that the omission of a single entry does not significantly alter analysis results [11]. It protects against linkage and dataset reconstruction attacks [12] and is used in various fields, such as privacy-preserving data sharing in GWAS studies [1,14] and health recommender systems [39]. However, differential privacy is analysis-sensitive—the amount of noise added to the data depends on the type of queries or computations executed on it. k-anonymity often emerges as a more general alternative for various applications.

Amongst numerous techniques that achieve k-anonymity, [33] stands out, being the only topologically informed method. It is particularly notable for its unique ability to compute multiple generalizations for different k values without the need to rerun the algorithm for each generalization or each k. This in turn allows for stronger privacy measures such as l-diversity and t-closeness to be applied. This remarkable efficiency is achieved through a single computation of a weighted persistence barcode, using scalable algorithms [3,9,23]. However, the method has a critical limitation - it is limited to static datasets. This is a significant drawback in time sensitive fields such as healthcare where data is frequently republished, often with alterations. When handling the dynamic nature of data in such cases, [33] would require a complete re-computation of the weighted persistence barcode for the dataset, leading to significant computational strain.

1.1   Our Contribution and Paper Structure

In our work, we address the major limitation identified in [33] by developing a method that removes the need for complete re-computation of persistent homology when the data changes. We introduce the concept of *hole-weighted persistence barcodes*, a new approach to track the evolution of higher-dimensional holes in the data. This innovation allows us to manage data removal, addition, and updating in dynamic datasets efficiently.

For data removal and updating, our algorithm changes the existing hole-weighted persistence barcodes directly, thus avoiding the need to recalculate persistent homology with every change in the dataset. When new data is added, we use *filtration trimming*, a novel technique which significantly reduces the number of persistent homology re-computations needed. Our proof of concept experimental evaluation using [3] on simulated data exhibits a significant reduction in the number of re-computations needed for data additions compared to [33].

We chose to evaluate our method against Speranzon et al. [33] because of its pioneering role in topology-informed k-anonymity and its unique advantages. To the best of our knowledge, our work is the first topologically-informed anonymization method for dynamic data.

The remainder of the paper is structured as follows. In Sect. 2, we review k-anonymity and other preliminaries. In Sect. 3, we discuss related work, with a focus on [33]. In Sect. 4, we propose our methodology, proposing hole-weighted persistence barcodes, and inductively describing handling of addition, deletion and updating of data. We conclude in Sect. 5.

2   Preliminaries

2.1   k-anonymity

When employing k-anonymity, one aims to work with datasets whose attributes are categorized into identifiers, quasi-identifiers, and sensitive data, as described in Table 1.

- **Identifiers:** These are attributes like name or Social Security number that can directly identify an individual. These are typically de-identified before data publishing to protect the privacy of individuals.
- **Quasi-identifiers:** These are attributes $A_1, A_2, \ldots, A_M$ such as age, gender, or zip code that cannot individually identify an individual but can do so when combined together.
- **Sensitive data:** These are attributes like medical conditions or salary, which are sensitive information one intends to keep private.

Table 1. Table illustrating the classification of data attributes into identifiers (to be de-identified prior to publication), quasi-identifiers, and sensitive data.

Name	Admission Date	Age	Blood Pressure	Diagnosis
Maria	02.10.2022	23	121 mm Hg	Anxiety
Priya	05.10.2022	44	97 mm Hg	UTI
Ahmed	03.01.2023	21	95 mm Hg	–
Aiden	05.02.2023	41	100 mm Hg	Asthma

Identifiers	Quasi-identifiers	Sensitive Data

The table of quasi-identifiers is denoted by $T(A_1, A_2, \ldots, A_M)$ consisting of N rows, where A_i are attributes that can take numeric or categorical value. Then the ith sample's j^{th} quasi-identifier data is denoted as T_{ij}. Another table $\bar{T} = (\bar{A}_1, \bar{A}_2, \ldots, \bar{A}_M)$ consisting of N rows is said to be a generalization $\bar{T}$ of T if for all i, j, $T_{ij} \subset \bar{T}_{ij}$.

Table 2. Here, T represents the original data table, $\bar{T}$ is the 2-anonymous generalization of T, while $\bar{T}^*$ is an over-generalization of T and $\bar{T}$.

T			$\bar{T}$			$\bar{T}^*$		
02.10.2022	23	121	2022	20-50	95-125	****	**	***
05.10.2022	44	97	2022	20-50	95-125	****	**	**
03.01.2023	21	95	2023	*1	70-100	****	**	**
05.02.2023	41	100	2023	*1	70-100	****	**	***

Definition 1 (k-anonymity [30]). *Consider a generalization $\bar{T}$ of T. $\bar{T}$ is said to have the k-anonymity property if every row in $\bar{T}$ appears at least k times in $\bar{T}$.*

An illustration of k-anonymity is described in Table 2. The objective of k-anonymity is to transform a given table T with quasi-identifiers into a generalized table that satisfies the k-anonymity property. There exist multiple generalizations that achieve k-anonymity, but we aim to minimize data loss, so the anonymized data is private, but also usable for further analysis. A common first step used to achieve k-anonymity, is mapping data to a metric space, and forming a point cloud with the data. This allows for geometric structures to be defined to create generalizations.

Definition 2 (Embedded Point Cloud [33]). *Consider a table of quasi-identifiers T containing M attributes and N samples. An embedded point cloud $P_T \in \mathbb{R}^M$ is formed by treating each row of T as a point in $\mathbb{R}^M$, such that $P_T = \{p_1, p_2, \ldots, p_N\}$, where p_i corresponds to the ith row of T. This data is generally standardized along every attribute.*

3   Related Work

3.1   k-anonymity in Practice

The implementation of k-anonymity involves techniques like data generalization, fragmentation, and microaggregation, each with its own distinct advantages. Generalization can use predefined intervals (hierarchy-based) such as [19,30] or runtime-determined intervals (recoding-based) like Mondrian [20,33], and our approach. Data fragmentation separates quasi-identifier data from sensitive information [45], while microaggregation forms clusters with a minimum of k-similar records [10,24,31,32].

k-anonymity is applied in various fields. During COVID-19, contact-tracing apps used Bluetooth Low Energy (BLE) to maintain user privacy [2,28,38,40]. These contract tracing applications anonymize data via encrypted beacon IDs or hash-based representations of user contacts, ensuring users were indistinguishable from at least k-1 others. In location-based services (LBS), spatial cloaking [15,16,26] reduces location accuracy to ensure each request is indistinguishable from k-1 others, using trusted anonymizers. Other applications include road networks [27], autonomous vehicles [42], crowd-sensing [43], and data publishing for research [41].

The utility of k-anonymity to safeguard dynamic datasets has been explored in various studies, each offering vastly different methodologies to ours limiting direct comparability. The seminal work by [5] established a method for efficiently updating k-anonymized frameworks with the addition of new data entries, although it does not address deletions or modifications. In contrast, m-invariance [46] utilizes counterfeit data to preserve privacy when data is either added or removed. Alternatively, [29] employs micro-aggregation to manage changes including additions, deletions, and updates, which is fundamentally different from generalization-based approaches.

Unique in its application, [33] employs topological information to achieve k-anonymity. This method not only supports the generation of multiple generalizations but also caters to varied k-anonymity requirements in a single computation.

3.2   Topology-Based k-anonymity

We now briefly discuss the theoretical framework developed by [33], which enables the application of persistent homology to the k-anonymity problem to derive an optimal generalization for a database with minimal loss. We will discuss application to numerical data, as in the foundational work, and this can be extended to categorical data using *generalization trees*.

Definition 3 (Anonymity Complex [33]). *Given an embedded point cloud P_T derived from a table T of quasi-identifiers, an anonymity complex $\mathcal{C}^\epsilon(P_T)$ is the Čech complex [17] defined over P_T comprising of simplices [17], each having vertices that correspond to points in P_T. A k-simplex is included in $\mathcal{C}^\epsilon(P_T)$ iff the ϵ-ball neighborhoods around its $k+1$ vertices share at least one common point.*

Definition 4 (k-anonymity Complex [33]). *An anonymity complex $\mathcal{C}^\epsilon(P_T)$ is termed a k-anonymity complex if the following conditions are met:*

1. *$\bigcup S_l = P_T$, where S_l is an l-simplex with $l \geq k-1$.*
2. *$S_{l_1} \cap S_{l_2} = \emptyset$ for all $l_1 \neq l_2$.*
3. *For every p_i in P_T, p_i belongs to some S_l.*

The smallest ϵ for which $\mathcal{C}^\epsilon(P_T)$ satisfies these conditions is termed the global generalization strategy for parameter k, and is denoted by ϵ_k. Other ϵ that satisfies these conditions are other generalizations. We call the sequence of subcomplexes $\phi \subseteq \mathcal{C}^{\epsilon_1}(P_T) \subseteq \ldots \subseteq \mathcal{C}^{\epsilon_n}(P_T)$, where $\epsilon_i < \epsilon_j$ if $i < j$, a filtration.

Notably, it was demonstrated in [33] that an anonymity complex $\mathcal{C}^{\epsilon_k}(P_T)$ is a k-anonymity complex iff it has trivial homology groups $H_n(\mathcal{C}^{\epsilon_k}(P_T)) = 0$ for all $n > 0$.

By mapping T into an embedded point cloud P_T and constructing a Čech filtration as illustrated in Fig. 1, we aim to find the smallest ϵ-value, ϵ_k, that forms

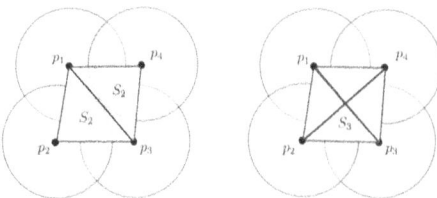

Fig. 1. A comparative visualization of two filtration levels, ϵ_1 and ϵ_2, showcasing the formation of a 3-simplex, S_3, at $\epsilon_2 > \epsilon_1$. While the points do not form a 3-anonymity complex at ϵ_1, they successfully form a 4-anonymity complex at ϵ_2.

a k-anonymity complex $\mathcal{C}^{\epsilon_k}(P_T)$. Simplices S_l in the complex form when their $l + 1$ vertices have overlapping ϵ_k-ball neighborhoods. However, these simplices do not represent the anonymized equivalence classes. Instead, equivalence classes are defined by computing the circumcenter and circumcircle radius r of each simplex. The equivalence class for a simplex is the higher-dimensional hypercube centered at the circumcenter with side length $2r$. This method generalizes the data, distinguishing equivalence classes from the simplices.

Weighted Persistence Barcodes. To identify the optimal generalization strategy ϵ_k for a specific k-anonymity problem, [33] introduced weighted persistence barcodes, as shown in Fig. 2. We replicated this using *PHAT* [3]. Unlike traditional persistence barcodes, the weighted versions feature bars with varying thickness, determined by the number of vertices in each H_0 component.

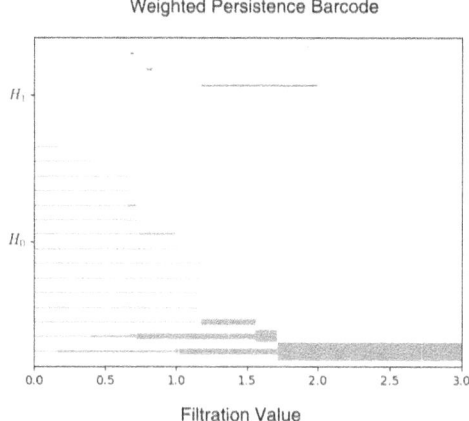

Fig. 2. The weighted persistence barcode describing the merging of components and formation of holes on a simulated dataset consisting of 15 samples and 2 quasi-identifiers.

The goal is to find filtration values where all H_0 bars have a thickness of k, and higher-order homology groups are trivial, indicating a viable k-anonymity complex. These regions are potential generalization values ϵ_k. The number of equivalence classes in a generalization relates to the maximal simplices [17] covering the complex at specific filtration values. Thus, a single persistence barcode calculation for a dataset can identify multiple generalizations for any k, which other algorithms cannot achieve [10, 19, 20, 24, 29–32, 45].

The smallest viable generalization is optimal, and for stronger properties like l-diversity and t-closeness, other generalizations can be used.

Computational Constraints. Although [33] stands out amongst other methods of anonymization with its unique advantages, it comes at a cost since computing persistent homology is a costly operation. When limited to static datasets, the method needs to recompute the persistent homology for the entire data when any change occurs in the dataset. In the worst case scenario, this comes at a computational cost of $\mathcal{O}(\sum_i^M ({}^N C_i)^3)$ where N denotes the number of points, and M the number of quasi-identifiers [6, 8, 13].

4   Proposed Method

In this section, we introduce our methodology to utilize persistence information to anonymize dynamic datasets. Recalculating persistent homology with every dataset change is computationally impractical. Our goal is to efficiently use existing persistence barcode information and extract insights as the data evolves. We address data removal, addition, and updating scenarios inductively.

First, we introduce hole-weighted persistence barcodes that help avoid recomputing persistent homology when data is removed. Next, we introduce *filtration trimming*, a technique that significantly reduces the number of persistent homology recomputations made when additional data is added. Finally we discuss data updates, where the stability of persistence diagrams help avoid recomputations.

4.1   Hole-Weighted Persistence Barcodes

To capture information about holes across the filtration, we enhance weighted persistence barcodes from [33] to include both component and cycle information. This non-trivial task is detailed in Algorithm 1, which tracks the birth and progression of topological holes. Specifically, we track a k-dimensional hole from its birth ϵ_{birth} to its death ϵ_{death}. We do this by constructing a graph of simplices and using breadth-first search (BFS) [4] to find loops. Persistence data $\mathcal{P}$ will represent simplex formations and corresponding filtration values.

Figure 3 simulated using persistence information with the help of [3] demonstrates that in contrast to the growing thickness of bars in H_0, bars for holes decrease in weight over time due to the ongoing filling of these holes.

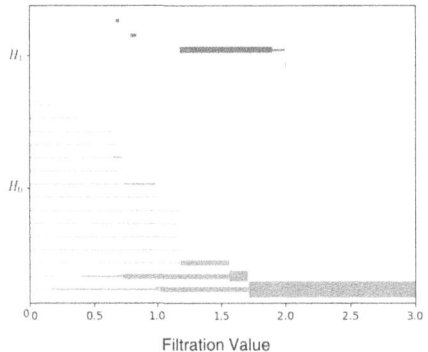

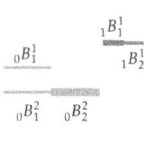

Fig. 3. Hole-weighted persistence barcode describing the merging of components and evolution of holes demonstrated on simulated data comprising 15 samples and 2 quasi-identifiers.

Fig. 4. Visual representation of the notation used.

We now establish our notation to describe hole-weighted persistence barcodes as visualized in Fig. 4. Let's represent each component in H_n as $_nB^i$. Each component $_nB^i$ comprises a series of bars represented as $(_nB^i_1, _nB^i_2, \ldots, nB^i_{n_i})$. Here, $_nB^i_j$ denotes the jth bar in the component $_nB^i$. n_i represents the number of bars in the ith n-dimensional component.

Further deconstructing, each bar, $_nB^i_j$, is represented as a tuple: $_nB^i_j = (_nb^i_j, _nd^i_j, _nw^i_j, _nV^i_j)$, where:

- $_nb^i_j$ denotes the birth of a topological hole.
- $_nd^i_j$ denotes the death of a topological hole.
- $_nw^i_j$ represents the number of vertices forming the hole.
- $_nV^i_j$ is the set of vertices that form the hole.

To ensure chronological coherence, we maintain that for every $j < n$, the relation $_nd^i_j = _nb^i_{j+1}$ holds true. This alignment presents a sequential understanding of the evolution of topological holes over time.

4.2 Data Removal

Healthcare data management is subject to strict regulations, often requiring time-bound consent for patient information. As a result, healthcare institutions periodically delete patient data from their databases. To handle this removal of data efficiently, we directly modify hole-weighted persistence barcodes instead of recomputing persistent homology across the filtration of the updated data. Without loss of generality, we detail the removal of vertex v_r from the data in Algorithm 2. It is worth noting that we wouldn't need to track holes for further updates in the data since the algorithm inherently produces the hole-weighted persistence barcode associated with the updated data.

Algorithm 1. Tracking k-dimensional holes in a filtration

Require: Persistence data $\mathcal{P}$, ϵ_{birth}, ϵ_{death}.
Ensure: Updated hole-weighted persistence barcode $\mathcal{B}$.
 1: Let $V_I \leftarrow [v_1, v_2, \dots, v_{k+1}]$ be the simplex forming at ϵ_{birth}.
 2: Initialize $S_k \leftarrow$ all k-simplices from $\mathcal{P}$ formed at or before ϵ_{birth}.
 3: Initialize an undirected graph $G(V, E)$ where $V = S_k$.
 4: **for** each pair of simplices $s_1, s_2 \in S_k$ **do**
 5:     **if** $s_1 \cap s_2$ has k vertices **then**
 6:         Add edge (s_1, s_2) to E.
 7:     **end if**
 8: **end for**
 9: $G' \leftarrow$ component of G containing V_I.
10: $L \leftarrow$ BFS(G') to identify all loops.
11: **for** each loop $l \in L$ **do**
12:     $\Delta_l \leftarrow \bigcup_{s \in l} s$
13:     **if** NOT $\exists s \in \mathcal{P}$ such that s formed before ϵ_{birth} and $s = \Delta_l$ **then**
14:         Mark Δ_l as a hole.
15:     **end if**
16: **end for**
17: **for** each k-simplex s formed after ϵ_{birth} and before ϵ_{death} **do**
18:     **if** $s \subseteq \Delta_l$ **then**
19:         Add s as a vertex to G'.
20:         **for** each $s_{G'} \in G'$ **do**
21:             **if** $s \cap s_{G'}$ has k vertices **then**
22:                 Add edge $(s, s_{G'})$ to G'.
23:             **end if**
24:         **end for**
25:         $L' \leftarrow$ loops in Δ_L using BFS(G') such that $s \not\subseteq \Delta_{L'}$.
26:         Update Δ_L with $\Delta_{L'}$.
27:     **end if**
28: **end for**
29: **return** $\mathcal{B}$ updated based on changes to Δ_L.

Algorithmic Complexity. In the worst-case scenario, where the dataset forms a fully connected graph, the BFS algorithm employed for generating the hole-weighted persistence barcode incurs a computational complexity of $\mathcal{O}(\sum_i^M ({}^N C_i)^3)$, where N represents the number of data points and M the dimension of the space the points reside in. This complexity is analogous to that of computing persistent homology for the dataset as discussed earlier in Sect. 3. Consequently, the cumulative complexity for both computing the persistence information and generating the hole-weighted persistence barcode is $\mathcal{O}(2\sum_i^M ({}^N C_i)^3)$, in comparison to the $\mathcal{O}(\sum_i^M ({}^N C_i)^3)$ required solely for computing persistence information.

However, an important distinction arises in the context of data removal. While recalculating persistent homology after each data point removal remains computationally intensive, modifying the existing hole-weighted persistence barcode is considerably more efficient, with a complexity of only $\mathcal{O}(N)$. After under-

Algorithm 2. Data removal

Require: Persistence data $\mathcal{P}$, vertex v_r to be removed.
Ensure: Updated hole-weighted persistence barcode.
1: Collect all $_0B^r$ where $_0d_1^r$ is the shortest distance between v_r and any other point.
2: Remove any one component $_0B^{\tilde{r}}$ that contains only one bar $_0B_1^{\tilde{r}}$.
3: **if** $_0V_1^{\tilde{r}} = [v_l] \neq [v_r]$ **then**
4:     **for** $_0B^{\tilde{r}}$ with $_0V_1^{\tilde{r}} = [v_r]$ **do**
5:         Replace every occurrence of v_r with v_l and vice versa.
6:     **end for**
7: **end if**
8: **for** each bar $_0B_j^i$ in every component **do**
9:     **if** v_r is a member of $_0V_j^i$ **then**
10:        **if** 1-simplex $[v_t, v_r]$ forms at b_j^i and $v_t \in {_0V_j^i}$ **then**
11:            $\mathbf{d} \leftarrow \min\{\|v_r - v_s\| \mid v_s \notin {_0V_j^i}\}$.
12:            Adjust $_0b_j^i$ by adding $\mathbf{d}$.
13:        **end if**
14:        Remove v_r from $_0V_j^i$.
15:        Update $_0w_j^i = {_0w_j^i} - 1$.
16:     **end if**
17: **end for**
18: **for** each component $_{k\geq1}B^i$ **do**
19:     **if** $v_r \in {_kV_j^i}$ **then**
20:        Remove $_kB_j^i$.
21:     **end if**
22: **end for**
23: **for** each component without bars **do**
24:     Remove the component.
25: **end for**
26: Relabel the persistence barcode to reflect changes.
27: **return** Updated hole-weighted persistence barcode.

---

going K successive data removal operations, [33] would incur a computational complexity of $\mathcal{O}(\sum_{J=N-K}^{N} \sum_i^M ({}^J C_i)^3)$. In contrast, our approach maintains a more manageable complexity of $\mathcal{O}(2 \sum_i^M ({}^N C_i)^3 + KN)$.

4.3   Data Addition

The continuous flow of new data in the healthcare sector highlights the need to regularly update medical datasets. Regular updates help capture changes in patient profiles and medical treatments, improving diagnostic and therapeutic strategies. However, this continuous addition of data presents a challenge: maintaining the privacy of individuals while ensuring k-anonymity. Each new entry can potentially compromise existing anonymizations.

Addressing the complexities of data addition, our concern is the recalibration of persistence barcodes without the need to compute the persistence information for the entire Cêch filtration. We demonstrate that the addition of a single point does not demand a comprehensive homology computation in Algorithm 3. Instead, updates primarily occur in the local vicinity of the added point. By leveraging the persistent homology computations from the static data, we only recompute specific trimmed segments influenced by the new data. This methodology promotes computational efficiency by reducing redundant calculations.

When introducing a new point, v_{N+1}, we first identify the circumcenters of all simplices that include v_{N+1} up to dimension M within its local neighbourhood. Here, M represents the number of quasi-identifiers. Subsequently, we calculate the distances between these circumcenters and v_{N+1}, sorting them in $\delta = \{\delta_1, \delta_2, \ldots, \}$ where, for $i < j$, $\delta_i < \delta_j$.

Algorithm 3. Data addition

Require: δ, Persistence data $\mathcal{P}$.
Ensure: Updated persistence barcode.
1: Add new component $_0B_1^{N+1} = (0, \min(\delta), 1, [v_{N+1}])$.
2: **for** any one v_l such that $\|v_l - v_{N+1}\| = \min(\delta)$ **do**
3:     Find bar $_0B_j^l$ such that $_0b_j^l \leq \min(\delta) \leq {}_0d_j^l$ where $v_l \in {}_0V_j^l$.
4:     Set $_0B_j^l = (_0b_j^l, \min(\delta), {}_0w_j^l, {}_0V_j^l)$
5:     Set $_0B_{j_+}^l = (\min(\delta), {}_0d_j^l, {}_0w_j^l + 1, {}_0V_j^l \cup [v_{N+1}])$
6: **end for**
7: Identify all δ_i with $i > 1$ and compute persistence in ascending order of δ_i.
8: Determine homology changes as compared to previous persistence information and denote as $\tilde{\delta} = \{\tilde{\delta}_1, \ldots, \tilde{\delta}_k\}$.
9: **for** each $0 \leq i < k$ **do**
10:    Compute persistent homology using the updatable SNF for the filtrations:

$$\mathcal{C}^{\tilde{\delta}_i} \to \mathcal{C}^{\epsilon_i^1} \to \ldots \to \mathcal{C}^{\epsilon_i^k} \to \mathcal{C}^{\tilde{\delta}_{i+1}}$$

11:    **if** $H_k(\mathcal{C}^{\epsilon_i^t})$ matches the previous persistence information for any k at ϵ_i^t **then**
12:        Move to next filtration
13:    **end if**
14: **end for**
15: Relabel indices as per component and bar order.
16: **return** Updated persistence barcode

Algorithmic Complexity. Calculating a simplex's circumcenter is an $\mathcal{O}(t)$ operation using Welzl's recursive algorithm [44], where t is the dimensionality of the simplex. Assuming we have $\bar{T}$ simplices around the added point, calculating the circumcenters of $\bar{T}$ t-dimensional simplices has a complexity of only $\mathcal{O}\left({}^{\bar{T}}C_{\bar{T}/2}(t/2)\right)$. A key insight emerges from this: computing circumcenters around our new data point is considerably less resource-intensive than computing the persistent homology for an entire filtration.

Table 3. Filtration Lengths and Trimmed Filtration Lengths for Simulated Data with 2 Quasi-identifiers.

Data Points	Added Points	Filtration Length	Trimmed Length
10	1	231	19
10	2	298	20
10	5	575	45
20	1	1561	347
20	5	2625	386
20	10	4525	1115
50	1	22151	3301
50	5	27775	3792
50	10	36050	3374
100	1	171801	15379
100	5	193025	17263
100	10	221925	18760
100	25	325625	19242

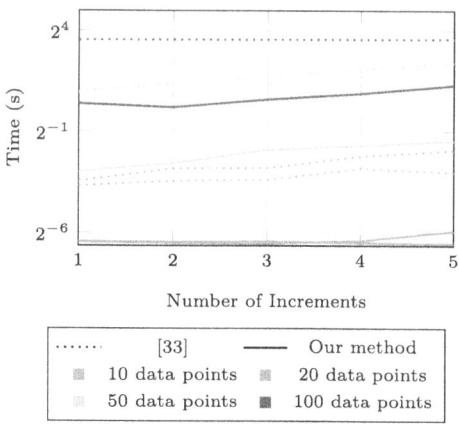

Fig. 5. Comparison of methods when data points are increased by 10% of the original dataset at each step. The time required to compute persistent homology on full and trimmed filtration lengths is plotted.

The parameter δ and its reduction $\tilde{\delta}$ has proven instrumental in our algorithmic approach to trimming the filtration length in our Cêch filtration, as shown in Table 3 and Fig. 5, generated using [3]. Here we measure the filtration lengths when additional data is added, and after we perform filtration trimming. The runtimes reported are total persistent homology computation times for the respective filtration lengths. This streamlined process, even with the addition of extra data points, dramatically cuts down on computational overhead, especially when considering larger datasets. For our experiments, we worked with data simulated using two quasi-identifiers to maintain simplicity.

4.4 Data Updatability

In rare cases when EHR data entries are modified, whether to refine diagnoses or correct data, it raises challenges for maintaining k-anonymity.

Based on the findings from [7], minor data perturbations have minimal impact on persistent homology. This suggests a practical approach: for slight data modifications, first check if the current anonymized dataset meets k-anonymity standards. If not, manage changes using protocols for data removal and addition. If the data is minimally altered and k-anonymity is satisfied, updating the hole-weighted persistence barcode is straightforward. If a component or hole arises due to the formation of a simplex $[\ldots, v_u, \ldots]$ with v_u being the adjusted data, we modify the associated bar by computing the circumcenter of the simplex.

Table 4. Comparison of various k-anonymity methods.

Method	Technique Applied	Handles Categorical Data	Multiple Generalisa-tions	Multiple Anonymiza-tions	Adaptability to Dynamic Databases
[20]	Recoding-based	✗	✗	✗	✗
[19]	Recoding/Hierarchy-based	✓	✗	✗	✗
[35]	Recoding/Hierarchy-based	✓	✗	✗	✗
[5]	Recoding-based	✗	✗	✗	partially
[46]	Recoding/Hierarchy-based	✓	✗	✗	✓
[29]	Microaggregation	✓	✗	✗	✓
[33]	Recoding-based	✗	✓	✓	✗
Our Method	Recoding-based	✗	✓	✓	✓

4.5   Comparison with Related Literature

Below, in Table 4, we present a comprehensive comparison between our method and established k-anonymity techniques against key criteria. These were chosen to highlight the strengths and potential areas for improvement of our approach relative to the current state-of-the-art. Our work, and [33] stand out as the only two topology-informed methods, that can generate multiple generalizations for multiple anonymization criteria with a single computation. Additionally, our method's ability to handle dynamic data allows us to adapt not only to changing data but also to evolving privacy requirements.

5   Conclusion and Future Work

In conclusion, our work substantially advances the application of TDA techniques for privacy-preserving dynamic data publishing in the context of EHRs. Previous work in the field focused on static datasets [33] and required computation of persistent homology on the whole dataset whenever data is updated. Our methodology extends this by addressing key challenges in dynamic databases, including data removal, addition, and updatability, enabling rapid adaptability without the need for extensive recomputation of persistent homology for updated data. Our solution can adapt not only to dynamic data, but dynamic privacy demands without requiring additional computational strain.

For data removal, we have innovatively utilized hole-weighted persistence barcodes, constructed through a breadth-first search algorithm on a graph derived from existing persistence data. This approach allows for systematic editing of the barcodes upon data removal. In the case of data addition, we have refined the process by trimming the Cêch filtration, thus significantly reducing the number of persistent homology recomputations required, as our experiments have demonstrated. Regarding data updatability, we focused on the stability of persistence diagrams and computed a limited number of simplex circumcenters, avoiding expensive persistent homology re-computations.

Our approach enhances the balance between data utility, anonymization flexibility and patient privacy, which is crucial in the context of rapid EHR adoption and stringent regulations like the GDPR. Although our work primarily addresses numerical data, extending these methodologies to include categorical data using zigzag persistent homology is a promising direction for future research. Moreover, incorporating more robust privacy measures such as l-diversity and t-closeness could enhance the algorithm. As tools for persistence computations continue to evolve, the scalability and practical applicability of our approach are expected to increase, providing greater utility across various applications.

Availability of Software Code. Our code to implement hole-weighted persistence barcodes is available at the URL: https://github.com/mdppml/dynamic-topological-k-anonymity.git

Acknowledgments. This research was supported by the German Ministry of Research and Education (BMBF), project number 01ZZ2010. We thank Saradha Senthil Velu for their invaluable discussions that helped in formulating the ideas presented in the paper.

References

1. Akgün, M., Bayrak, A.O., Ozer, B., Sağıroğlu, M.Ş: Privacy preserving processing of genomic data: A survey. J. Biomed. Inform. **56**, 103–111 (2015)
2. Ali, J., Dyo, V.: Cross hashing: Anonymizing encounters in decentralised contact tracing protocols. In: 2021 International Conference on Information Networking (ICOIN), pp. 181–185. IEEE (2021)
3. Bauer, U., Kerber, M., Reininghaus, J., Wagner, H.: Phat-persistent homology algorithms toolbox. J. Symb. Comput. **78**, 76–90 (2017)
4. Bundy, A., Wallen, L.: Breadth-first search. Catalogue of artificial intelligence tools pp. 13–13 (1984)
5. Byun, J.-W., Sohn, Y., Bertino, E., Li, N.: Secure anonymization for incremental datasets. In: Jonker, W., Petković, M. (eds.) SDM 2006. LNCS, vol. 4165, pp. 48–63. Springer, Heidelberg (2006). https://doi.org/10.1007/11844662_4
6. Carlsson, G., De Silva, V., Morozov, D.: Zigzag persistent homology and real-valued functions. In: Proceedings of the Twenty-fifth Annual Symposium on Computational Geometry, pp. 247–256 (2009)
7. Cohen-Steiner, D., Edelsbrunner, H., Harer, J.: Stability of persistence diagrams. In: Proceedings of the Twenty-first Annual Symposium on Computational Geometry, pp. 263–271 (2005)
8. Cohen-Steiner, D., Edelsbrunner, H., Harer, J.: Extending persistence using poincaré and lefschetz duality. Found. Comput. Math. **9**(1), 79–103 (2009)
9. Cohen-Steiner, D., Edelsbrunner, H., Morozov, D.: Vines and vineyards by updating persistence in linear time. In: Proceedings of the Twenty-second Annual Symposium on Computational Geometry, pp. 119–126 (2006)

10. Domingo-Ferrer, J., Torra, V.: Ordinal, continuous and heterogeneous k-anonymity through microaggregation. Data Min. Knowl. Disc. **11**, 195–212 (2005)
11. Dwork, C.: Differential privacy. In: International colloquium on automata, languages, and programming, pp. 1–12. Springer (2006)
12. Dwork, C., Roth, A., et al.: The algorithmic foundations of differential privacy. Found. Trends® Theor. Comput. Sci. **9**(3–4), 211–407 (2014)
13. Edelsbrunner, L.: Zomorodian: topological persistence and simplification. Discr. Comput. Geometry **28**, 511–533 (2002)
14. Fienberg, S.E., Slavkovic, A., Uhler, C.: Privacy preserving gwas data sharing. In: 2011 IEEE 11th International Conference on Data Mining Workshops, pp. 628–635. IEEE (2011)
15. Gedik, B., Liu, L.: Protecting location privacy with personalized k-anonymity: architecture and algorithms. IEEE Trans. Mob. Comput. **7**(1), 1–18 (2007)
16. Gruteser, M., Grunwald, D.: Anonymous usage of location-based services through spatial and temporal cloaking. In: Proceedings of the 1st International Conference on Mobile Systems, Applications and Services, pp. 31–42 (2003)
17. Hatcher, A.: Algebraic topology
18. Kitamura, K., Irvan, M., Shigetomi Yamaguchi, R.: Disclosure of multiple" patient characteristics" format statistics leaks quasi-identifier linkage. In: Proceedings of the 9th ACM International Workshop on Security and Privacy Analytics, pp. 15–25 (2023)
19. LeFevre, K., DeWitt, D.J., Ramakrishnan, R.: Incognito: Efficient full-domain k-anonymity. In: Proceedings of the 2005 ACM SIGMOD International Conference on Management of Data, pp. 49–60 (2005)
20. LeFevre, K., DeWitt, D.J., Ramakrishnan, R.: Mondrian multidimensional k-anonymity. In: 22nd International Conference on Data Engineering (ICDE'06), pp. 25–25. IEEE (2006)
21. Li, N., Li, T., Venkatasubramanian, S.: t-closeness: Privacy beyond k-anonymity and l-diversity. In: 2007 IEEE 23rd International Conference on Data Engineering, pp. 106–115. IEEE (2006)
22. Machanavajjhala, A., Kifer, D., Gehrke, J., Venkitasubramaniam, M.: l-diversity: privacy beyond k-anonymity. ACM Trans. Knowl. Discov. Data (TKDD) **1**(1), 3–es (2007)
23. Maria, C., Boissonnat, J.-D., Glisse, M., Yvinec, M.: The Gudhi Library: Simplicial Complexes and Persistent Homology. In: Hong, H., Yap, C. (eds.) ICMS 2014. LNCS, vol. 8592, pp. 167–174. Springer, Heidelberg (2014). https://doi.org/10.1007/978-3-662-44199-2_28
24. Mayer, R., Karlowicz, A., Hittmeir, M.: K-anonymity on metagenomic features in microbiome databases. In: Proceedings of the 18th International Conference on Availability, Reliability and Security, pp. 1–11 (2023)
25. Meyerson, A., Williams, R.: On the complexity of optimal k-anonymity. In: Proceedings of the Twenty-third ACM SIGMOD-SIGACT-SIGART Symposium on Principles of Database Systems, pp. 223–228 (2004)
26. Mokbel, M.F., Chow, C.Y., Aref, W.G.: The new casper: query processing for location services without compromising privacy. In: VLDB. vol. 6, pp. 763–774 (2006)
27. Mouratidis, K., Yiu, M.L.: Anonymous query processing in road networks. IEEE Trans. Knowl. Data Eng. **22**(1), 2–15 (2009)
28. Park, J., Ahmed, E., Asif, H., Vaidya, J., Singh, V.: Privacy attitudes and covid symptom tracking apps: Understanding active boundary management by users. In: International Conference on Information, pp. 332–346. Springer (2022)

29. Salas, J., Torra, V.: A General Algorithm for k-anonymity on Dynamic Databases. In: Garcia-Alfaro, J., Herrera-Joancomartí, J., Livraga, G., Rios, R. (eds.) DPM/CBT -2018. LNCS, vol. 11025, pp. 407–414. Springer, Cham (2018). https://doi.org/10.1007/978-3-030-00305-0_28

30. Samarati, P.: Protecting respondents identities in microdata release. IEEE Trans. Knowl. Data Eng. **13**(6), 1010–1027 (2001)

31. Soria-Comas, J., Domingo-Ferrer, J.: Probabilistic k-anonymity through microaggregation and data swapping. In: 2012 IEEE International Conference on Fuzzy Systems, pp. 1–8. IEEE (2012)

32. Soria-Comas, J., Domingo-Ferrer, J., Sánchez, D., Martínez, S.: Enhancing data utility in differential privacy via microaggregation-based k-anonymity. VLDB J. **23**(5), 771–794 (2014)

33. Speranzon, A., Bopardikar, S.D.: An algebraic topological perspective to privacy. In: 2016 American Control Conference (ACC), pp. 2086–2091. IEEE (2016)

34. Sun, Y., Yin, L., Liu, L., Xin, S.: Toward inference attacks for k-anonymity. Pers. Ubiquit. Comput. **18**, 1871–1880 (2014)

35. Sweeney, L.: Guaranteeing anonymity when sharing medical data, the datafly system. In: Proceedings of the AMIA Annual Fall Symposium, p. 51. American Medical Informatics Association (1997)

36. Sweeney, L.: Simple demographics often identify people uniquely. Health (San Francisco) **671**(2000), 1–34 (2000)

37. Sweeney, L.: Achieving k-anonymity privacy protection using generalization and suppression. Internat. J. Uncertain. Fuzz. Knowl.-Based Syst. **10**(05), 571–588 (2002)

38. Tedeschi, P., Bakiras, S., Di Pietro, R.: Iotrace: a flexible, efficient, and privacy-preserving iot-enabled architecture for contact tracing. IEEE Commun. Mag. **59**(6), 82–88 (2021)

39. Valdez, A.C., Ziefle, M.: The users' perspective on the privacy-utility trade-offs in health recommender systems. Int. J. Hum Comput Stud. **121**, 108–121 (2019)

40. Vaudenay, S.: Analysis of dp3t-between scylla and charybdis (2020)

41. Verdonck, J., De Boeck, K., Willocx, M., Lapon, J., Naessens, V.: A hybrid anonymization pipeline to improve the privacy-utility balance in sensitive datasets for ml purposes. In: Proceedings of the 18th International Conference on Availability, Reliability and Security, pp. 1–11 (2023)

42. Wang, J., Cai, Z., Yu, J.: Achieving personalized k-anonymity-based content privacy for autonomous vehicles in cps. IEEE Trans. Industr. Inf. **16**(6), 4242–4251 (2019)

43. Wang, X., Liu, Z., Tian, X., Gan, X., Guan, Y., Wang, X.: Incentivizing crowd-sensing with location-privacy preserving. IEEE Trans. Wireless Commun. **16**(10), 6940–6952 (2017)

44. Welzl, E.: Smallest enclosing disks (balls and ellipsoids). In: Maurer, H. (ed.) New Results and New Trends in Computer Science. LNCS, vol. 555, pp. 359–370. Springer, Heidelberg (1991). https://doi.org/10.1007/BFb0038202

45. Xiao, X., Tao, Y.: Anatomy: Simple and effective privacy preservation. In: Proceedings of the 32nd International Conference on Very Large Data Bases, pp. 139–150 (2006)

46. Xiao, X., Tao, Y.: M-invariance: towards privacy preserving re-publication of dynamic datasets. In: Proceedings of the 2007 ACM SIGMOD International Conference on Management of Data, pp. 689–700 (2007)

Using Static Code Analysis for GDPR Compliance Checks

Andreas M. Binder$^{(\boxtimes)}$ (ID) and Immanuel Kunz (ID)

Fraunhofer AISEC, Garching, München, Germany
{andreas.binder,immanuel.kunz}@aisec.fraunhofer.de

Abstract. Ensuring compliance with the General Data Protection Regulation (GDPR) remains a labor-intensive activity, especially in large applications. Moreover, legal experts often do not have the technical knowledge to assess source code. Privacy threat modeling can be used to systematically guide the assessment of privacy threats in designs and code, but it is time-intensive and needs to be redone for changes. In this paper, we build on an existing approach to automate privacy threat modelling using static code analysis and extend it for GDPR compliance checks. We first derive code properties from individual GDPR articles, implement them in a static code analysis tool, and propose queries for the automated analysis of source code. Finally, we evaluate the results using a novel test suite.

Keywords: Static Code Analysis · Privacy Threat Modeling · GDPR Compliance Engineering

1 Introduction

The General Data Protection Regulation (GDPR) [6] of the European Union has established a high bar for data protection in software products that process personal data. Due to lacking knowledge about the legal texts and their implications, implementing these legal requirements remains a challenge for software engineers. Especially in large software systems with ongoing changes, ensuring compliance to data protection regulations is a difficult task.

There are numerous approaches for implementing privacy-friendly software, like checklists [1, 11], Privacy Design Strategies [10] and Privacy Design Patterns [2], but approaches to automatically verify compliance with data protection regulations, like the GDPR, are currently missing. Privacy threat modeling methods such as LINDDUN [5, 15] can uncover non-compliance issues using a data flow diagram, but they focus on basic GDPR principles like data minimization and do not cover specific articles of the GDPR. Creating a data flow diagram and performing threat modeling require a comprehensive understanding of the system and significant effort, and errors can affect the accuracy and reliability of the process. Additionally, threat modeling is a manual and time-consuming process,

J. Garcia-Alfaro et al. (Eds.): ESORICS 2024 Workshops, LNCS 15263, pp. 153–169, 2025.
https://doi.org/10.1007/978-3-031-82349-7_11

making it difficult to integrate into the short sprints of agile software development [8]. In comparison, automated approaches realized through static code analysis offer an effective way to reduce effort and can be well integrated into agile software development cycles. However, existing tools cannot check source code for compliance with individual articles of the GDPR. For example, there are tools that attempt to uncover data flows of personal data [3,14] or that check source code for compliance with an individually defined privacy policy [7,13]. As existing tools do not offer the possibility to check source code for compliance with indvidual articles of the GDPR, manual assessment is still being used. As a result, legal experts, who may not have the necessary expertise in understanding source code and software architectures, are required to support the development process and ensure that the software complies with legal requirements.

In this paper, we present a tool for static code analysis, which enables a (semi-)automated check of source code for GDPR compliance. With this tool we want to address the time-consuming and error-prone process of verifying compliance of source code with data protection requirements. To this end, we first create a generic example (Sect. 3), which is used to derive workflows that a service provider can implement to comply with selected articles of the GDPR. In the same section, we analyze the properties of these workflows and derive source code properties from them, for example data flows and database operations. Based on the resulting properties, in Sect. 4 an existing static code analysis tool (the Privacy Property Graph (PPG) [12]) is extended to allow mapping of all necessary code properties on the graph. Subsequently, compliance checks are developed using reusable queries in the Cypher query language that enable automated verification of the source code via the PPG. In summary, the following contributions are presented:

- A translation of GDPR articles to low-level code properties that can be identified in a static code analysis
- An extension of an existing static code analysis tool for the automated detection of the identified code properties, in the form of a code property graph
- Reusable queries in the Cypher language to automatically check the graph for indications of (non-)compliance with the GDPR articles.

2   Background and Related Work

Code property graphs (CPGs) are representations of source code that allow the analysis of large source code projects [16]. They include nodes that represent elements of the source code and edges that put the nodes into relation. Properties that CPGs can depict include the program's syntactic structure, its control flow, data flows, as well as program dependencies. In the context of privacy analysis, the representation of data flows in a Data Flow Graph (DFG) is essential to track the flow of personal data. The resulting graph can be stored in a graph database and can then be queried using a query language manually or automatically. This way, problematic data usage patterns can be uncovered.

Banse et al. [4] have extended a CPG library for the analysis of distributed cloud applications. Kunz et al. [12], have then built on this work to also cover the analysis of privacy threats, called the Privacy Property Graph (PPG). The PPG focuses on the automatic detection of LINDDUN threats [5]. Yet, LINDDUN does not directly address compliance with individual GDPR articles but only addresses high-level data protection principles, like data transparency.

The Privacy Flow Graph [14] focuses on visualizing personal data flows to support, e.g., privacy impact assessments. It analyzes source code to uncover data flows of personal data, presenting them in a graphical format. The graphical representation of the data flows can help auditors to uncover problematic data flows. An automated GDPR compliance check, however, is not addressed. Hjerppe et al. [9] use an Abstract Syntax Tree to track personal data via annotations made by developers in code to automate the creation of a privacy policy. Through the help of annotations the authors pointed out that it is easier to spot personal data processing and storage. Their aim is to support the documentation of personal data processing and facilitate the development of tooling as we propose it in this paper.

Ferrara et al. [7] also explore static code analysis for GDPR checks, but focus on detecting data leaks. Their approach is based on custom policies that define allowed data flows. Commercial tools include Privado [13], which is partly open-source and also uses custom rules to define (non-)compliant program behavior.

Each approach facilitates GDPR compliance checks but a considerable gap remains in the automated code-level check of specific GDPR articles. In this paper we build on the PPG as it already addresses privacy threats on code-level, is open source, and easily extendable.

3   Approach: Extraction of Code Properties

In this section we present our approach for automated GDPR compliance checks. We derive code properties from GDPR articles, which can be detected through static code analysis. Since the articles of the GDPR are defined in an abstract manner, it can be challenging to translate them to the implementation-level. To bridge the gap between the abstract level and concrete implementation suggestions, we introduce a generic example service. This service is designed as a typical client-server architecture, making it a representative model for many types of services that process personal data and are subject to the GDPR.

A complete analysis of the GDPR is not in scope of this paper and is not meaningful as many articles specify authority competences (Art. 51–59), remedies, liabilities, and penalties (Art. 77–84), as well as other provisions that are not reflected in source code. In this paper, we focus on articles that often imply direct interaction of users with their data, i.e. access (Art. 15), rectification (Art. 16), erasure (Art. 17), and portability (Art. 20). Note, however, that the PPG already largely covers Art. 15 which is why we focus on Articles 16, 17 and 20 in the following. We expect that future work can build on the results to verify compliance with many other articles, such as identifying automated decision-making (Art. 22) and determining flows to geolocations outside the EU (Art. 44).

Running Example: The Online Notepad. The example depicted in Fig. 1 is an online notepad where registered users can store and retrieve personal notes. Through a web app, users can interact with the online notepad and view all their data, such as notes and account information, which is stored in the database. The management server receives requests from users, converts them into database queries, and sends the results back to the web app. Additionally, the management server sends headlines of the notes and user interaction frequencies to an external provider for advertising purposes. This example reflects a commonly used client-server architecture, which we use in the following to derive code properties. All communication between the parties is assumed to be handled via REST interfaces and the HTTP protocol. Furthermore, all communication to external parties is assumed to be done via the management server, i.e. from the data controller. The limitations of this assumption including reliance on the HTTP protocol for general applicability are discussed in Sect. 5.4.

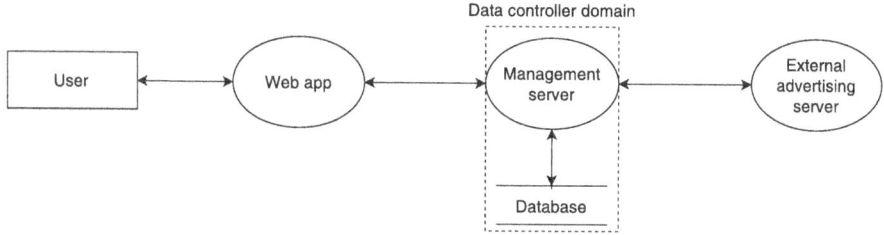

Fig. 1. Data flow diagram of the running example: The *User* entity can interact with the *Web app* provided by the data controller, which in turn communicates with a *Management server*. This server processes the incoming data and may use the *Database* to store, retrieve or delete data. The *Management server* and the *Database* are representing the domain of the data controller, which shares data with a third party's advertising server (*External advertising server*). All data flows between the elements are realized with the HTTP protocol.

In the following we analyze Articles 16, 17 and 20 in the context of the running example to derive code properties.

3.1 Article 16 Right to Rectification

Article 16 states that the data subject has the right to request rectification of his personal data by the data controller and to complete personal data that is incomplete with additional data.

For the running example, the online notepad service can adopt this workflow to comply with Article 16:

1. The user can edit or complete his personal data within the *Web app* via a user interface. The changes are then passed to a function linked to the user interface.

2. After changing personal data, the *Web app* communicates these changes to a specified REST interface of the *Management server* using a PUT HTTP call (e.g. via URL path /user/user_id).
3. The *Management server* processes the incoming data and initiates the re-save by forwarding the user's rectified data to the *Database* via an update database query.

The following **code properties** can be derived:

1. **Prop-data-flow**: A directed, chronological data flow for each personal datum, starting from the property marked as *(*Entry point)* to the component labeled *(*Exit point)*
2. **Prop-ui-editing-form**: An editing form in the client's code that allows editing personal data *(*Entry point)*.
3. **Prop-put-http-request**: A PUT HttpRequest in the client's code that addresses an HttpEndpoint specified on the server.
4. **Prop-put-http-endpoint**: An HttpEndpoint in the server's code, which is addressed by the client program's HTTP PUT request.
5. **Prop-update-database-operation**: A DatabaseOperation in the server's code that performs an update of already stored data *(*Exit point)*.

3.2 Article 17 Right to Erasure

Paragraph 1. Article 17(1) states that the data subject has the right to request an erasure of his personal data by the data controller. The grounds can be, for example, a revocation of consent to the processing or the unlawful processing of data.

For the running example, the online notepad service can adopt this workflow to comply with Article 17(1):

1. The user requests the deletion (e.g. of a personal note) within the *Web app* via an UI-element, e.g. a button, which triggers the function described in the next steps.
2. The *Web app* communicates the deletion request to a specified REST interface of the *Management server* using a HTTP call of type DELETE, e.g. using the URL path /user/user_id/notes/note_id
3. The *Management server* processes the incoming request and initiates the deletion of the corresponding database entry via a delete query.

Paragraph 2. The second paragraph states that if the data controller discloses personal data to a further data processor and an erasure of the data has taken place in accordance with paragraph 1, the other data processors shall be informed that the data subject has requested an erasure.

For the running example, the online notepad service can adopt this workflow to comply with Article 17(2):

1. The user requests deletion (e.g. of a personal note) from the *Web app* via an UI-Element, e.g. a button, which invokes a function call, that triggers the process described in the next steps.
2. The *Web app* communicates the deletion request to a specified REST interface of the *Management server* using an HTTP call of type DELETE, e.g. using the URL path `/user/user_id/notes/note_id`.
3. The *Management server* informs all other data processors who have received personal data of the user (in the case of the running example the *External advertising server* received headlines of the notes). This is realized via an HTTP call of type DELETE, which is called from the *Management server*.

Derived Code Properties. Since the paragraphs 1 and 2 of Article 17 are closely related to each other, the code properties are nearly the same, except one difference, which can be seen in the following derived **code properties**:

1. **Prop-data-flow**
2. **Prop-ui-button-linked-function** *(*Entry point)*
3. **Prop-delete-http-request**
4. **Prop-delete-http-endpoint**
5. (only for Article 17(1)): (**Prop-delete-database-operation**): A `Database-Operation` in the server's code that performs a deletion of the stored data *(*Exit point).*
6. (only for Article 17(2)): **Prop-delete-http-request-extern**: A DELETE `HttpRequest` in the server code targets a REST interface not maintained or run by the service provider *(*Exit point).*

3.3   Article 20 Right to Data Portability

Paragraph 1. Article 20(1) states that the data subject has the right to receive his personal data in a structured, commonly used, machine-readable format, which allows the transmission of his personal data to another data controller. This right is given to the person if consent to the processing of the data was given and the processing of the data is automated.

The workflow we expect the notepad service provider to implement assumes that consent for data processing has been obtained and the processing is automated. For the running example, the online notepad service can adopt this workflow to comply with Article 20(1):

1. The user can request via a form in the *Web app* that the service provider delivers the user's personal data in a machine-readable format (e.g. CSV or JSON). The form is linked to a function, which initiates the process described in the next steps.
2. The *Web app* communicates this request to a specified REST interface on the *Management server* using an HTTP call of type GET, for example with the URL path `/user/user_id`.
3. The *Management server* queries all the user's personal data, which are stored in the *Database*, using a database read query.

4. The *Management server* passes the user's personal data to the *Web app* by answering the HTTP request.
5. The *Web app* saves the user's personal data to a file that is machine-readable. E.g. the file format is JSON or CSV.

The following **code properties** can be derived:

1. **Prop-data-flow**
2. **Prop-ui-button-linked-function** *(*Entry point)*
3. **Prop-get-http-request**
4. **Prop-get-http-endpoint**
5. **Prop-retrieve-database-operation**: A `DatabaseOperation` in the server's code that retrieves all stored data from the database.
6. **Prop-json-data-format**: The personal data is in a machine-readable format (e.g. JSON).
7. **Prop-data-storage** *(*Exit point)*

Paragraph 2. Article 20(2) states that the data subject has the right to request the data controller to transfer his personal data directly to another data controller.

For the running example, the online notepad service can adopt this workflow to comply with Article 20(2):

1. The user can request the transferral of his personal data in a machine-readable format (e.g. JSON) to another data controller via a form in the *Web app*. The submission of the form triggers a function executing the process described in the next steps.
2. The *Web app* communicates this request to a specified REST interface on the *Management server* using an HTTP call of type GET, for example with the URL path `/user/user_id?destination=example_destination`
3. *Management server* queries all the user's personal data, which are stored in the *Database*, using a database read query.
4. The *Management server* converts all personal data into JSON format.
5. The *Management server* passes the data in a machine-readable format to the specified destination of the user by addressing a REST interface via a POST HTTP call.

The following **code properties** can be derived:

1. **Prop-data-flow**
2. **Prop-ui-button-linked-function** *(*Entry point)*
3. **Prop-get-http-request**
4. **Prop-get-http-endpoint**
5. **Prop-retrieve-database-operation**
6. **Prop-json-data-conversion**
7. **Prop-post-http-request-extern**: A POST HTTP request in the server code targets a REST interface not maintained or run by the service provider *(*Exit point)*.

4   Implementation

Various tools could be used for the implementation of the compliance checks. In this implementation we leverage the PPG [12] which already provides support for many of the code properties identified in Sect. 3. We thus map out the gaps between the PPG implementation and the code properties identified above and implement them. In Sect. 4.1 we present the modifications we applied to enrich the graph with the properties of interest. In Sect. 4.2, we develop reusable queries, which check the compliance of programs to the respective articles from Sect. 3. Thereby, generic and reusable queries are written, which are applicable across applications and programming languages. The enhancements of the PPG as well as the evaluation test suite (Sect. 5.1) are published in the PPG open-source repository[1].

4.1   Enhancements of the PPG

The PPG creates the graph by first applying the underlying CPG library to it and it then adds further nodes and edges through dedicated *passes*. Each pass analyzes the source code and the code property graph that already has been created for it (see Sect. 2), and modifies it further, e.g., to add nodes and edges for HTTP connections or database operations.

To implement the missing code properties, we create such passes or extend already existing ones. The resulting graph is stored in a Neo4j database which provides the SQL-like Cypher language to query the database.

Firstly, the *DatabaseOperationPass* needs to be enhanced to enable the PPG to identify and integrate various database operations into the graph. This involves introducing a new type property for 'DatabaseQuery' nodes to differentiate among query types such as CREATE, READ, UPDATE, DELETE, and UNKNOWN (e.g. the called function executes an arbitrary database query, which cannot be assessed before runtime).

Secondly, for the detection of HTTP requests and endpoints, the *HttpRequestPass* must be extended. This involves creating 'HttpRequest' and 'HttpEndpoint' nodes, with additional capabilities to recognize PUT and DELETE requests and endpoints. An important addition is the 'url' property for 'HttpRequest' nodes for the identification of destination URLs in HTTP requests.

Lastly, a significant enhancement involves the introduction of the *FileWritePass* to detect file write operations. This requires the creation of a new 'FileWrite' class in the CloudPG ontology, representing an abstraction for all function calls that write to a file, regardless of the programming language. This class should link to the respective 'CallExpression' node performing the file write operation. Moreover, language-specific passes are needed for different programming languages to accurately detect file write operations.

---

[1] Currently open pull request in repository: https://github.com/clouditor/cloud-property-graph.

4.2   Development of Compliance Checks

Having extended the PPG with passes that add further code properties to the generated graph, we describe in this section how the graph can be used to check for compliance to the respective articles (semi-)automatically. Users of these compliance checks could be developers, designers, auditors, and privacy experts. The queries are designed to be applicable to various software structures and application types.

A key objective in crafting these queries is to minimize false-negative results, i.e. false indications about a program's compliance. However, given the complexity of unambiguously determining compliance, our goal is to design queries to report more false positives (incorrect non-compliance) rather than false negatives (incorrect compliance). This approach ensures that compliance is only indicated when there is a strong likelihood of its veracity. It is better if users who analyze the results filter out false-positive results than to overlook an actual non-compliance that may lead to costly design and implementation changes later (see also Sect. 5.4).

These queries enable automatic non-compliance checks through the Neo4j API, which interacts directly with the Neo4j database. They can be executed directly on the database. Additionally, these queries can also be used for manual compliance checks using the Neo4j UI.

Preliminary Steps. To automatically verify if source code complies with the GDPR through static code analysis, personal data must be identifiable. We propose that personal data be annotated in the code with labels, such as `Pseudo-Identifier`. This label has to be added to every variable declaration that already contains or will contain personal data when executing the software. This step has to be executed first in order to be able to track personal data flows in the following and subsequently analyzing them.

Article 16 Right to Rectification. We assume compliance with Article 16 if a user can modify any of his stored personal data (Sect. 3.1). We check for every flow of personal data that is stored in a database, if another data flow exists, starting from a PUT HTTP request. This PUT HTTP request must then lead to a PUT HTTP endpoint on the server, which receives the personal data and then leads to a database update query. Also it must be ensured that the database update query is performed at the the same database in which the personal datum was initially stored. We show the developed query, checking for all derived code properties (Sect. 3.1) in Listing 1.1 and a plot of the data flows described above in Fig. 2.

Note that in the Cypher queries we use the term *path* to denote a path of data flows throughout the program. To query the graph and uncover these paths, we use Neo4j's query language Cypher. It uses round brackets to denote nodes and their types ((:Expression)), dashes for undirected edges (–), arrows for directed edges (->), and square brackets in between dashes to denote edge types (-[:ANONYMIZES]-). The *-operator denotes a path of arbitrary length[2].

```
MATCH path1=(ps1:PseudoIdentifier)--()-[:DFG*]->(hr1:HttpRequest {name:
    'POST'}) -[:TO]->(he1:HttpEndpoint)--()-[:DFG*]->(d1:DatabaseQuery {
    type:  'CREATE'})
WHERE NOT EXISTS
{MATCH path2=(ps1)--()-[:DFG*]->(hr3:HttpRequest {name: 'PUT'}) -[:TO]->(
    he3:HttpEndpoint {method:  'PUT'})--()-[:DFG*]->(d2:DatabaseQuery)
    WHERE (d2.type='UPDATE')/(d2.type='DELETE') AND (d1)-[:STORAGE]->(:
        DatabaseStorage)<-[:STORAGE]-(d2)}
RETURN path1
```

Listing 1.1. Cypher query which identifies non-compliant Article 16 and 17 personal data flows. `path1` traces all tagged personal data in a database. `path2` follows `path1` data leading to an update (Art. 16) or delete (Art. 17) query in the same database. If `path2` is absent, indicating non-compliance, `path1` is returned.

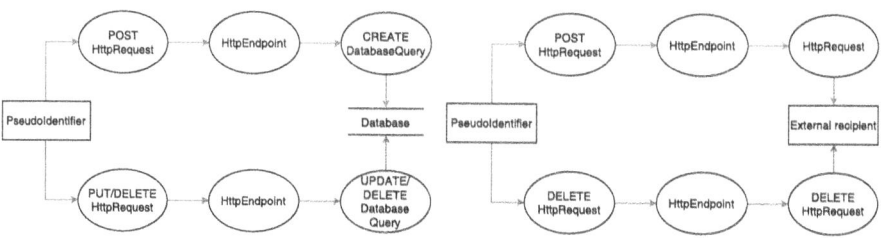

Fig. 2. Diagram consisting of two data flow diagrams – Left data flow diagram: Illustrating `path1` (in blue) and `path2` (in red) data flows for assessing non-compliance with Articles 16 and 17. Right Data flow diagram: Shows two data flows `path1` (blue) and `path2` (red) of the query for the non-compliance check of Article 17(2).

Article 17 Right to Erasure. The first paragraph describes that it must be possible for the user to request the deletion of his stored personal data. We check for each flow of personal data to a database, if another data flow exists starting with a HTTP DELETE request. This HTTP DELETE request must lead to an HTTP endpoint at the server, which receives the personal data leading to a database delete operation within the same database in which the personal datum was initially stored. The respective query, which checks for all derived code properties (Sect. 3.2), can be seen in Listing 1.1. A plot of the data flows described above can be seen in Fig. 2.

The second paragraph describes that the data controller informs the other recipients of the personal data as soon as the user requests deletion. We identify all data flows that are communicating personal data to an external party. Note that a communication to an external party can be detected via the PPG because the source code of the external party is not known and therefore the

---

[2] See https://neo4j.com/developer/cypher/querying.

PPG does not create an `HttpEndpoint` node and connects it via a `TO` edge to the `HttpRequest`. Knowing all data flows, communicating personal data to an external data recipient, we check whether the external data receiver is informed about the deletion request. This is the case if another data flow for every personal datum exists starting from HTTP delete request. This HTTP delete request must then lead to an HTTP endpoint on the server that receives the personal data and informs all external recipients of the data about the deletion via an HTTP delete request. We list the developed query, checking for all derived code properties (Sect. 3.2) in Listing 1.2 and the plot of the data flows described above in Fig. 2.

```
MATCH (hr1:HttpRequest), path1=(ps1:PseudoIdentifier)--()-[:DFG*]->(hr1)
WHERE NOT (hr1)-[:TO]-(:HttpEndpoint) AND NOT EXISTS
{MATCH path2=(ps1)--()-[:DFG*]->(hr2:HttpRequest {name: 'DELETE'})-[:TO
    ]-(he2:HttpEndpoint {method: 'DELETE'})--()-[:DFG*]->(hr3:
    HttpRequest)
        WHERE (hr3.name='DELETE') AND (hr3.url = hr1.url) AND NOT (hr3)-[:TO
            ]-(:HttpEndpoint)}
RETURN path1
```

Listing 1.2. Cypher query detects Article 17(2) non-compliance in data flows. `path1` tracks personal data with `PseudoIdentifier` shared with external parties. `path2` traces notifications to these parties about deletion requests. Absence of `path2` signals non-compliance, returning `path1`.

Article 20 Right to Data Portability. The first paragraph states that the user has the right to receive his stored personal data in a machine-readable format. We check whether for each personal datum stored in the database a data flow, starting from a HTTP request of type GET exists. This HTTP request then in turn leads to an HTTP endpoint, leading to a database query that loads the personal data from the same database, where it was initially stored and returns it to the client. Returning data is indicated by HTTP status code OK (200). Additionally, we verify if the data returns to the user through a file creation process involving the personal data, presuming the file's machine-readability. The developed query, checking for all derived code properties (Sect. 3.3) is shown in Listing 1.3 and a plot of the data flows described above is illustrated in Fig. 3.

```
MATCH path1=(psi:PseudoIdentifier)--()-[:DFG*]->(hr1:HttpRequest {name:
    ''POST''})-[:TO]->(he1:HttpEndpoint)-[:DFG*]->(d1:DatabaseQuery {type
    :"CREATE"})
WHERE NOT EXISTS
{MATCH path2=(psi)--()-[:DFG*]->(hr2:HttpRequest {name: ''GET''})-[:TO
    ]->(he2:HttpEndpoint {method: ''GET''})-[:DFG*]->(d2:DatabaseQuery {
    type:"READ"})-[:DFG*]->({name: ''HttpStatus.OK''}),
    path3=(:FileWrite)-[:CALLS]->(m:MemberCallExpression)-[:ARGUMENTS
        ]->(:Node)<-[:DFG*]-(hr2)
        WHERE (d1)-[:STORAGE]->(:DatabaseStorage)<-[:STORAGE]-(d2)}
RETURN path1
```

Listing 1.3. Cypher query that detects Article 20(1) non-compliant personal data flows. `path1` maps tagged personal data stored in a database. `path2` traces these data flows to a query retrieving the data from the same database. `path3` finds member call expressions using this data to create a files on the disk. Non-compliance returns `path1` if `path2` or `path3` are missing.

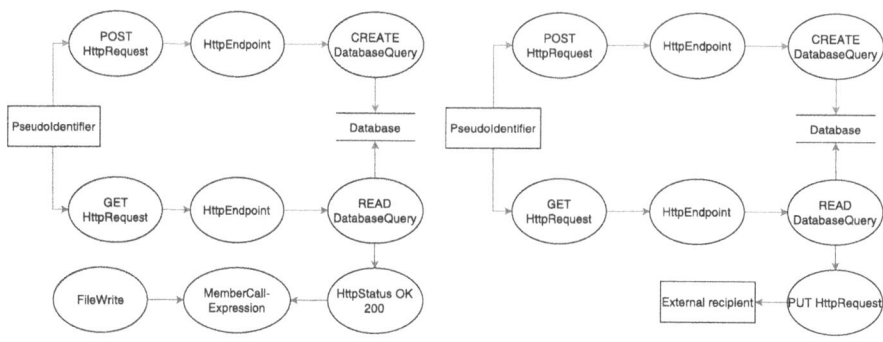

Fig. 3. Diagram consisting of two data flow diagrams – Left data flow diagram: Shows the three data flows `path1` (blue), `path2` (red) and `path3` (purple) of the query for the non-compliance check of Article 20(1). Right data flow diagram: Illustrating the two data flows `path1` (blue) and `path2` (red) of the query for the non-compliance check of Article 20(2).

The second paragraph specifies that the user can also arrange that the personal data is transmitted directly from the data controller itself to another data controller in a machine-readable format. We check for every personal data that is stored in the database if there exists a data flow that leads an HTTP request of type GET. This HTTP request then leads to an HTTP endpoint, which subsequently leads to a database query that loads the personal data from the same database. Furthermore, we investigate whether the personal data loaded from the database is now passed to an HttpRequest of type PUT, which does not have an HTTP endpoint and thus communicates to an external recipient. The query, checking for all derived code properties (Sect. 3.3) is shown in Listing 1.4 and the data flow is illustrated in Fig. 3.

```
MATCH path1=(psi:PseudoIdentifier)--()-[:DFG*]->(hr1:HttpRequest {name:
    ''POST"}) -[:TO]->(he1:HttpEndpoint)--()-[:DFG*]->(d1:DatabaseQuery {
    type: ''CREATE"})
WHERE NOT EXISTS
{MATCH path2=(psi)--()-[:DFG*]->(hr2:HttpRequest {name: ''GET"}) -[:TO
    ]->(he2:HttpEndpoint)--()-[:DFG*]->(d2:DatabaseQuery {type:"READ"})
    -[:DFG*]->(hr3:HttpRequest {name: ''PUT"})
    WHERE NOT (hr3) -[:TO] -(:HttpEndpoint) AND (d1) -[:STORAGE]->(:
        DatabaseStorage)<-[:STORAGE]-(d2)}
RETURN path1
```

Listing 1.4. Cypher query that identifies Article 20(2) non-compliant data flows. `path1` tracks tagged personal data in a database. `path2` traces data flows from `path1` to a query that loads and sends this data via HTTP to an external party. `path1` indicates non-compliance if `path2` is absent.

5   Evaluation and Discussion

5.1   Accuracy

For assessing the accuracy of detecting (non-)compliance using our queries, we developed a dedicated test suite, as no such test suite existed for GDPR-specific code samples. It comprises 19 test cases split into two categories, i.e., for testing compliance and for testing non-compliance. The tests are based on scenarios and code properties from Sect. 3. Each test case in our suite is structured as a Python program, consisting of a client and a server, performing communication with each other. Additionally, each case includes a configuration file with simulated deployment data, like mock databases. The PPG is then used to generate a code property graph from the Python code and storing the results in a Neo4j database. The Cypher queries presented in Sect. 4.2 are then executed and compared against expected results. For instance, the Article 16 test case models a client-server interaction handling personal data, with a focus on data rectification, and aims to ensure no data flow contravenes Article 16 of the GDPR.

Our findings, summarized in Table 1, indicate the test suite's effectiveness in detecting non-compliances, albeit with some false positives and a false negative. The causes of these inaccuracies and potential improvements are discussed in Sect. 5.4. This test suite offers a foundation for future research to refine static analysis tools and discuss the implications of the GDPR on code level.

Table 1. Results of the evaluation of the compliance checks using the implemented test suite: ■ = Expected result, successful detection of (non-)compliance; □ = False positive; □ = False negative

Art.16	Art.17(1)	Art.17(2)	Art.19	Art.20(1)	Art.20(2)
■ □	■ □	■ □	■ □	■ □ □	■ □

5.2   Performance

As the evaluation of the original PPG shows [12], its performance primarily depends on used passes instead of memory, retrieval of results or the pure parsing of the code. Therefore, we evaluate the impact of newly written or modified passes on the execution time of the PPG. For this purpose, the software state of the PPG before the extension of the passes is first applied to the Python code of one test case of Article 20(1). This test case contains HTTP requests, database operations and a write file call and thus triggers the DatabaseOperationPass, HttpRequestPass and FileWritePass, which were extended in the scope of this paper. Finally, the PPG and the extensions are applied to the same code part and the results are compared. The benchmark involves 20 iterations, including one warm-up iteration not counted in the final measurement. We used a MacBook Pro with Intel Core i7 processor of 2018 with 16gb of RAM for the evaluation.

Before extending passes, execution times varied from 685 ms to 875 ms, averaging 742 ms (SD = 28 ms). After extensions, times ranged from 777 ms to 879 ms, with an average of 839ms (SD = 26 ms), marking a 97 ms increase. Despite the rise, we would argue that this difference is negligible, since the execution of the tool is generally not time-critical.

5.3   Reduction of Effort Through Automation

Compliance verification usually involves manual review of code and documentation, a process that often is labor-intensive and error-prone. By automating compliance checks, a more consistent and in-depth analysis is possible that allows legal experts to make better informed decisions and allows to retest applications quickly for potential non-compliances.

For programmers, the usage of automated compliance checks reduces the effort required by developers in two key ways. Due to the automated compliance checks, programmers receive immediate feedback on GDPR compliance of their code. This immediate response makes it easier for developers to address compliance issues as they code, rather than having to revisit large sections of the codebase for compliance reviews at a later stage. Automated compliance checks significantly streamline the interaction between legal professionals and programmers by reducing the need for extensive explanations, how a certain article can be reflected into source code, which is also necessary after changes made to the software. Typically, translating complex legal requirements of GDPR into a language that is understandable to programmers can be a challenging and time-consuming process. With automated checks, this translation is inherent in the PPG and highlights affected data flows.

In order to use the automated compliance checks, it is first necessary to setup the PPG, create new passes, if certain programming languages or libraries are not yet supported and to train developers to correctly insert `PseudoIdentifier` labels in code. We do not discuss the effort related to these steps, since these are introduced by the usage of the PPG itself and not from the compliance checks. A discussion of these aspects can be found in the paper of Kunz et al. [12].

5.4   Limitations

In this paper, we have derived code properties based on an example scenario. While the example is designed in a generic way to achieve broad applicability, there is a possibility that the example might not encompass the full landscape of real-world application variations. E.g., our current implementation focuses on communication over HTTP, but also other communication protocols are used in practice, like HTTPS, FTP, Telnet or SMTP. To enable the detection of these protocols as well, additional passes for each respective protocol need to be added to the PPG and the queries must be adjusted. Another limitation is that the proposed workflows represent only one approach to achieve GDPR compliance for the constructed running example. Often, multiple options exist for complying with GDPR articles, such as Article 17's right to data deletion: Our workflow assumes user-initiated deletion via an UI interaction, but alternative compliant methods, like email requests, exist. The construction of the running example and the derivation of code properties from proposed workflows thus can lead to false negatives.

Another limitation of our approach is that while it ensures the elements required for GDPR compliance are present at the process level, it does not guarantee the correctness of their implementation. For example, in the case of the right to rectification (Art. 16), our approach can verify that an data flow to an update operation exists, but it cannot ensure that the operation correctly updates the intended rows in the database, potentially leading to incorrect or incomplete updates.

Another limitation to note is that our implementation heavily relies on the implementation of the *CPG* and the PPG. This reliance inherently means that the accuracy and effectiveness of our work depends on the correct implementation of these tools. More significantly, any inherent limitations or shortcomings present within the *CPG* and PPG approaches could be replicated in our own implementation and can lead to false results in non-compliance detection. An example, which leads to false positive results, arises from how the PPG handles annotations in the source code. It creates a separate graph node for each *PseudoIdentifier* annotation. Consequently, identical personal data processed in different files results in multiple nodes, potentially missing necessary data flows for compliance. For example let us consider a web app with distinct user registration and data editing pages, both handling the same personal data, but recognized as separate by the PPG. This could falsely indicate non-compliance (false positive) in some scenarios. A proposed solution is to assign a unique ID to each *PseudoIdentifier* annotation, allowing the PPG to merge identical data annotations into a single node, reducing false positives.

Another limitation involves the query for Article 20(1) non-compliance detection. The current focus is on storage of personal data in a file, presuming a machine-readable format (code property **Prop-json-data-format**). However, without validating this property, the query might overlook scenarios where data is not stored in a JSON format, leading to false negatives. Addressing this, we suggest developing a new pass that abstracts file descriptor opening, verifying if a file is in a machine-readable format.

Also annotating personal data in the code is crucial for successful compliance checks. This allows the PPG to store and check associated nodes. However, human errors in labeling can lead to false positives and negatives. Training for developers on what should be considered "personal data" is thus essential.

Furthermore, the accuracy of compliance check results, as evaluated by our self-implemented test suite, may have inherent biases due to the limited variety of code examples tested. We thus plan to enrich the test suite with diverse test cases, addressing various compliance scenarios (see Sect. 6).

6   Conclusion

In this paper, we introduced an innovative method for automated GDPR compliance checks using a code property graph. First, we have translated GDPR requirements into code properties that can be automatically detected. We then extended an existing static code analysis tool [12] to incorporate these properties, enabling automated verification. Our tool can thus integrate into automated software development workflows and assist legal experts in compliance assessment. Testing with a 19-case test suite confirmed the tool's effectiveness and practicality in identifying compliant and non-compliant code segments.

In future work we will refine the tool by expanding the test suite for more complex cases, improving reliability in detecting GDPR issues, and minimizing errors. Finally, we want to extend our tool to cover more GDPR articles.

Acknowledgments. This work was partly funded by the German Federal Ministry for Economic Affairs and Climate Action, within the project ToHyVe.

References

1. GDPR checklist for data controllers. https://gdpr.eu/checklist/. Accessed Mar 25 2024
2. Al-Momani, A.A., et al.: Land of the lost: privacy patterns' forgotten properties: enhancing selection-support for privacy patterns. In: Proceedings of the 36th Annual ACM Symposium on Applied Computing, pp. 1217–1225 (2021)
3. Arzt, S., Huber, S., Rasthofer, S., Bodden, E.: Denial-of-app attack: Inhibiting the installation of android apps on stock phones. In: Proceedings of the ACM Conference on Computer and Communications Security (2014)
4. Banse, C., Kunz, I., Schneider, A., Weiss, K.: Cloud property graph: connecting cloud security assessments with static code analysis. In: IEEE International Conference on Cloud Computing, CLOUD 2021-Sept, pp. 13–19 (2021)
5. Deng, M., Wuyts, K., Scandariato, R., Preneel, B., Joosen, W.: A privacy threat analysis framework: supporting the elicitation and fulfillment of privacy requirements. Requirements Eng. **16**(1), 3–32 (2011)
6. Parliament, E., Council, E.: General data protection regulation: GDPR. Off. J. Europ. Union **119**, 1–88 (2016)
7. Ferrara, P., Olivieri, L., Spoto, F.: Tailoring Taint Analysis to GDPR. Springer International Publishing, Cham (2018)
8. Galvez, R., Gurses, S.: The odyssey: modeling privacy threats in a brave new world. In: IEEE European Symposium on Security and Privacy Workshops (EuroS&PW), pp. 87–94 (2018)
9. Hjerppe, K., Ruohonen, J., Leppänen, V.: Annotation-based static analysis for personal data protection. In: Friedewald, M., Önen, M., Lievens, E., Krenn, S., Fricker, S. (eds.) Privacy and Identity Management. Data for Better Living: AI and Privacy: 14th IFIP WG 9.2, 9.6/11.7, 11.6/SIG 9.2.2 International Summer School, Windisch, Switzerland, August 19–23, 2019, Revised Selected Papers, pp. 343–358. Springer International Publishing, Cham (2020). https://doi.org/10.1007/978-3-030-42504-3_22
10. Hoepman, J.-H.: Privacy design strategies. In: Cuppens-Boulahia, N., Cuppens, F., Jajodia, S., Abou El Kalam, A., Sans, T. (eds.) SEC 2014. IAICT, vol. 428, pp. 446–459. Springer, Heidelberg (2014). https://doi.org/10.1007/978-3-642-55415-5_38
11. Edward Kost. 10-step checklist: Gdpr compliance guide. https://www.upguard.com/blog/how-to-be-gdpr-compliant. Accessed 25 Mar 2024

12. Kunz, I., Weiss, K., Schneider, A., Banse, C.: Privacy property graph: towards automated privacy threat modeling via static graph-based analysis. Proc. Priv. Enhancing Technol. **2023**(2), 171–187 (2023). https://doi.org/10.56553/popets-2023-0046
13. Prashant, M.: Launching privado open source for privacy compliance and data security. https://privado.ai/post/launching-privado-open-source-for-privacy-compliance-and-data-security. Accessed 19 Apr 2023
14. Tang, F., Østvold, B.M.: Using, A.S.P., the Privacy Flow-Graph. MSR4P&S,: Association for Computing Machinery, p. 2022. NY, USA, New York (2022)
15. Wuyts, K., Sion, L., Joosen, W.: Linddun go: A lightweight approach to privacy threat modeling. In: 2020 IEEE European Symposium on Security and Privacy Workshops (EuroS&PW), pp. 302–309. IEEE (2020)
16. Yamaguchi, F., Golde, N., Arp, D., Rieck, K.: Modeling and discovering vulnerabilities with code property graphs. In: Proceedings - IEEE Symposium on Security and Privacy, pp. 590–604 (2014)

Privacy-Preserving Tabular Data Generation: Systematic Literature Review

Pablo Sanchez-Serrano[(✉)] [iD], Ruben Rios [iD], and Isaac Agudo [iD]

Network, Information and Computer Security (NICS) Lab, University of Malaga,
Málaga, Spain
{pablosanserr,ruben.rdp,isaac}@uma.es

Abstract. There is a wide range of tabular data of great value to science, economy and social progress. When sharing such data, privacy must be taken into account. Traditionally, this has been addressed through anonymization. However, in recent years, with the growth of AI, the possibility of using generative models has emerged as a way to generate synthetic data that guarantees privacy while maintaining their utility. This systematic literature review aims to identify and classify existing privacy-preserving tabular generative models in order to create a taxonomy of solutions. In addition, we analyze the privacy metrics and techniques they use, and identify possible unexplored lines of research.

Keywords: Synthetic data · Privacy · Tabular data

1 Introduction

There is a wide variety of tabular data, including medical records, financial transactions, and demographic details. This data holds immense value for scientific, economic and social progress, as it can be used to identify patterns, facilitate decision-making and disseminate knowledge. However, the sharing of this data raises privacy concerns, given that it often contains PII (personally identifiable information).

Traditional methods for protecting privacy in tabular data include [20]: data pseudonymization, which replaces PII with fake identifiers, and data anonymization, which involves generalization, suppression and perturbation techniques that modify attributes in the dataset to obtain a supposedly anonymous dataset. To decrease the risk of re-identification some models like k-anonymity, l-diversity and t-closeness have been proposed. Recently, generative models have emerged as a way to guarantee the privacy of datasets [9]. These models generate synthetic data from real datasets, mimicking the statistical properties of the training data.

When dealing with synthetic datasets, there are significant differences in the amount of knowledge and access available to different users (see Fig. 1). This involves a range of privacy challenges that need to be considered. Users further to the right of the diagram show a higher level of difficulty in discerning which data were used to generate the synthetic data. The number of barriers will be

J. Garcia-Alfaro et al. (Eds.): ESORICS 2024 Workshops, LNCS 15263, pp. 170–180, 2025.
https://doi.org/10.1007/978-3-031-82349-7_12

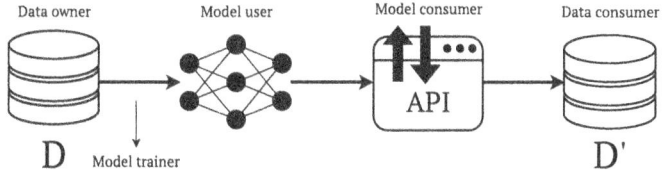

Fig. 1. Different levels of knowledge and access to the trained model.

higher the further to the right the user is located, i.e. the less knowledge and access the user has.

A *model trainer* uses the real data (D) given by the data owner to train a generative model. The model trainer must be careful with possible data leakage due to errors or intermediate outputs. The model trainer could also be malicious, or the data owners may not trust the data owner. Security mechanisms such as homomorphic encryption [3] or federated learning [36] should be implemented. Once the model is trained, the user can have different levels of access to the model. We refer to the user with full access to the model as the *model user*. Despite having completed the training phase, it may be possible to obtain information about D from the model [38]. Conversely, a *model consumer* can only generate samples from the model using an API, but do not have access to the trained model. The amount of information available to this type of users depends on the API. A first-level API allows unlimited samples generation, leading to honest-but-curious users who seeks information while respecting established protocols. On the other hand, a second-level API has some restrictions on data generation, i.e. limited number of requests or attributes that are not allowed to be generated. Membership Inference Attacks (MIAs) [26] can exploit the lack of restrictions on data generation. MIAs take advantage of differences in how models respond to queries from members inside and outside of the training dataset. Finally, the *data consumer* only has access to a synthetic dataset (D') generated by the model, and is unable to generate samples by himself. Although more challenging, it is possible to obtain information about D from D' [4].

The contributions of this paper can be summarized as follows:

1. The use of a systematic methodology to provide an overview of privacy techniques used in tabular data generative models.
2. A collection of 24 systematically selected papers.
3. A collection of privacy metrics for in tabular data generative models.
4. A taxonomy of privacy-preserving generative models for tabular data.

This works is organized as follows. Section 2 introduces the methodology and how the papers were selected. Section 3 discusses the different ways to measure privacy in tabular data generation and explains the techniques used to ensure privacy collected from the selected papers. Section 4 provides a taxonomy of generative models for tabular data, giving an order and clarifying the differences between them. Finally, Sect. 5 draws conclusions and outlines possible lines of future research based on the observations made in the paper.

2   Systematic Literature Review

A Systematic Literature Review (SLR) is a rigorous approach to reviewing and synthesizing research literature on a specific topic. This methodology is designed to provide a comprehensive, unbiased and reproducible summary of existing research. The PICOC framework is employed to define the scope and focus of our study. It involves three main steps: planning, conducting and reporting.

2.1   Planning

This SLR is performed to answer the following questions:

1. What are the main techniques used to guarantee privacy in generative models for tabular data?
2. How can we measure the privacy of generative models for tabular data?

PICOC terms help to define a list of keywords, as shown in Table 1. Using these keywords we can create a search query (see Definition 1), which addresses our research questions.

Table 1. Keyword list created from PICOC terms.

Keywords	Synonyms	PICOC
Tabular data	Database, Dataset	Population
Privacy techniques	Data masking, Differential privacy, Masked data, Privacy approach, Privacy methods, Privacy-preserving, k-anonymity, l-diversity, t-closeness	Intervention
Generative model	Data synthesis, Synthesizer, Synthetic data generation, Synthetic generator	Comparison
Benchmark		Outcome
Privacy metric	Anonymity metric	Outcome
Utility metric	Data quality, Data utility, ML efficacy, Usefulness of data	Outcome

Definition 1 (Search Query). *("Tabular data" OR "Database" OR "Dataset") AND ("Privacy techniques" OR "Data masking" OR "Differential privacy" OR "Masked data" OR "Privacy approach" OR "Privacy methods" OR "Privacy-preserving" OR "k-anonymity" OR "l-diversity" OR "t-closeness") AND ("Generative model" OR "Data synthesis" OR "Synthesizer" OR "Synthetic data generation" OR "Synthetic generator") AND ("Benchmark" OR "Privacy metric" OR "Anonymity metric" OR "Utility metric" OR "Data quality" OR "Data utility" OR "ML efficacy" OR "Usefulness of data")*

The next step is to define which digital libraries use to search. We selected IEEE Digital Library, ISI Web of Science and Scopus. There might be duplicate papers but this will be taken into account in the conducting phase.

To refine the search and ensure the inclusion of high-quality and relevant studies, the following exclusion criteria are applied: (i) accepted papers should address privacy for generative AI models for tabular data, (ii) surveys or reviews will be discarded, (iii) only articles, conference papers, proceedings or journals will be considered, (iv) a minimum number of citations is required. Papers published before 2022 should have at least 20 citations. Papers from 2022 are required to include a minimum of 10 citations. Papers from 2023 or 2024 must have a minimum of 5 citations. To sum up, these are the exclusion criteria:

- The paper does not discuss privacy
- The paper does not discuss AI
- The paper does not focus on tabular data
- It is a survey/review
- It is not an article, conference paper, proceeding or journal
- It has not enough citations
- It is not published in English

After an initial filtering using the exclusion criteria, a checklist of five questions (listed below) with specific criteria is established. There are three possible scores for each criterion: Yes (1 point), Partially (0.5 points), or No. Thus, 5 points is the maximum score. Papers that reach 3 points are finally selected.

1. Does the article propose a new AI model for tabular data generation?
2. Does the article propose new attacks to privacy in generative models?
3. Does the paper propose a model practical implementation?
4. Does the model include techniques to provide privacy?
5. Does the article discuss how to measure privacy for tabular generative data models? Does it also include a way to measure utility?

2.2   Conducting

The first step is to perform a search using the query string presented in Sect. 2.1. Initially, a total of 977 papers were found. From this list of papers, 36 were duplicated, giving a total of 941 unique papers. To provide a clearer understanding of the evolution of research on this topic, Fig. 2 illustrates the number of papers published each year. The graph shows a growth in the number of papers over the years. Although the number of papers published in 2024 is lower than in previous years, the reason is that the current writing date is mid 2024.

This is the moment to apply the exclusion criteria presented in Sect. 2.1. All papers are reviewed, focusing on the title, keywords, and abstract. At the end of this process, 61 papers are accepted.

After an initial filtering, it is time to apply the Quality Assessment Checklist presented in Sect. 2.1. During this step, potential papers are added through snowballing. The papers added in this way are also submitted to Quality Assessment

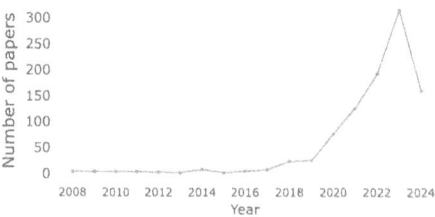

Fig. 2. Number of papers found

Table 2. Reference list of papers.

Years	Papers
2017	[15]
2019	[2, 11, 34]
2020	[12, 33]
2021	[5, 6, 13, 27]
2022	[8, 16, 28, 30–32]
2023	[14, 17–19, 22, 29, 35]
2024	[37]

Checklist. During the conducting process, a backward snowballing (or backward reference searching) is performed. This involves looking through the references listed in the selected papers to find older studies that the key papers have cited, which might also be relevant in the research topic. At the end of this process, a final list of 24 papers are selected. The reference list of papers is shown in Table 2. As with the papers found with the query (Fig. 2) there is an increase in the number of selected papers over the years, except in 2024.

2.3   Reporting

In this section, we extract some statistical data about the selected articles. The information extracted from the papers is discussed in the following sections.

Out of the 24 selected papers, 17 papers propose a new model for privacy-preserving tabular data generation. There are two papers that propose two

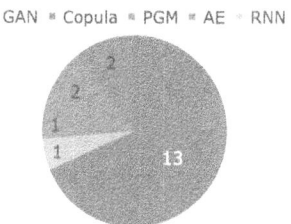

Fig. 3. Model family distribution, in which models are grouped according to their nature or type.

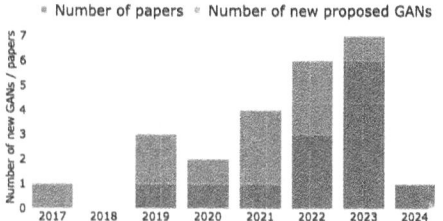

Fig. 4. Evolution of the GANs proposed in the selected papers compared to the number of selected papers.

models, for a total of 19 proposed models. Figure 3 shows the different types of model families collected. This chart will be useful in establishing a taxonomy of different generative models. There is a clear predominance of GANs over the others.

Figure 4 compares the years of creation of GANs with the years of publication of all selected papers. It can be seen that the growth of interest in GANs follows the growth of interest in the research area. This shows that GANs are the type of generative models that are most often used to generate tabular data with privacy guarantees.

3   Measuring Privacy in Tabular Data Generation

There are several ways to measure privacy in generative models for tabular data. Some traditional privacy techniques, such as k-anonymity or t-closeness, can also implicitly act as privacy measures. Among the selected papers, differential privacy stands out.

Differential privacy [7] is a mathematical framework designed to provide privacy guarantees for data entries within a dataset. Differential privacy ensures that the inclusion or exclusion of a single individual's data does not significantly affect the outcome of any analysis, thereby protecting the individual's privacy.

Definition 2 (Neighboring Datasets). *Two datasets, D and D', are neighboring, if and only if D' differs from D in only one entry.*

Definition 3 ((ε, δ)-Differential Privacy). *For a non-negative privacy budget ε and a non-negative relaxation term δ, an algorithm, M, satisfies (ε, δ)-differential privacy if for any pair of neighboring datasets D, D' and $S \subseteq Range(M)$*

$$Pr[M(D) \in S] \leq exp(\varepsilon) \cdot Pr[M(D') \in S] + \delta \tag{1}$$

where Pr is taken with respect to the randomness of M. δ is a relaxation term to ε-differential privacy. There are a variety of techniques for achieving differential privacy. Essentially, the algorithm M perturbs the input with some noise distribution, i.e. normal distribution, based on ε and δ.

The following expression is obtained by clearing ε from expression 1:

$$\varepsilon \geq ln\left(\frac{Pr[M(D) \in S] - \delta}{Pr[M(D') \in S]}\right) \tag{2}$$

A lower value of ε implies a higher level of privacy because inequality 2 is more restrictive. However, decreasing ε increases the noise that needs to be added to satisfy Definition 3.

There are some variations or extensions of the definition of differential privacy, such as RDP (Rényi Differential Privacy) [21], LDP (Local Differential Privacy) or CDP (Concentrated Differential Privacy).

Privacy accounting concept indicates that there is a need of some "accountant" procedure that computes the privacy cost at each access to the training data, and accumulates this cost as the training progress [1]. The privacy analysis of our some differential privacy techniques employs the moments accountant approach to keep track of the privacy cost in multiple iterations. This concept can also be used to measure privacy degradation with increasing number of queries. One way to compensate for this progressive loss of privacy would be to progressively increase the noise.

There are several techniques to ensure differential privacy, such as Differentially Private Expectation Maximization (DP-EM) [25], Private Aggregation of Teacher Ensembles (PATE) [23,24] or Differentially Private Stochastic Gradient Descent (DP-SGD) [1]. In general, they all involve the addition of noise in one way or another.

Similar to differential privacy, there is also the concept of identifiability [33]. This framework is used to measure and limit the risk of re-identification. There are also other ways to measure privacy for those models that do not theoretically guarantee privacy, but rather focus on an empirical approach to measure privacy. These focus on performing attacks to see how effective they are. The most common is the Membership Inference Attack (MIA) [26].

SELENA [30] is a ensemble method that combines Split-AI and Self-Distillation to mitigate MIAs. Although SELENA is primarily designed for supervised classification tasks, it could be used as a component of a generative model. For example, SELENA could be used in GANs to protect the discriminator from revealing membership information about the training data. SELENA trains submodels on random data subsets and uses adaptive inference to ensure similar behavior on member and non-member inputs, significantly reducing MIA risks.

4   A Taxonomy for Tabular Data Generative Models

This section categorizes tabular data generative models from selected papers (see Fig. 5). Due to length restrictions, the taxonomy focuses on GANs with privacy guarantees. However, other types of models were found:

- Autoencoders (AEs) : DP-SYN [2]
- Probabilistic Graphical Models (PGMs) : PrivMRF [5] and PrivIncr [18]
- Recurrent Neural Networks (RNNs) : Conditional-LSTM [22]
- Copula-based models : LoCop and DR_LoCop [32]

The white boxes in Fig. 5 represent each of the 13 models, while the gray boxes represent the categories into which the different models fall. Note that DP-GAN, whose connector is shown as a dotted line, is a particular case. Although it is possible to introduce conditions on one of its components [13], it does not fall within the definition of a conditional GAN. Therefore, it is placed in the category of non-conditional GANs. Models that were originally designed to generate EHR (Electronic Health Record) data are in a green box. Similarly, those GANs that integrate an autoencoder as a component of their model are in a blue box.

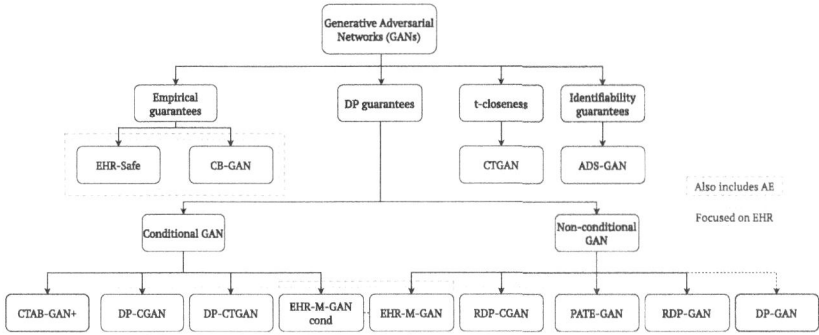

Fig. 5. Privacy-preserving tabular data GAN taxonomy

4.1 Generative Adversarial Networks (GAN)

A generative adversarial network (GAN) [10] is a type of machine learning framework where two neural networks are trained simultaneously in a zero-sum game setting. GANs have established themselves as one of the state-of-the-art generative models. GANs consists of two adversarial models:

– Generator G: takes random noise as input and generates samples. It aims to generate data that imitates a given dataset.
– Discriminator D: attempts to differentiate between real data samples taken from the training dataset and fake data samples generated by the generator. It outputs a probability indicating if a given sample is real or fake.

The generator tries to fool the discriminator by generating realistic data. The discriminator tries to become better at distinguishing real data from fake data. This creates a minimax game between them. The generator aims to maximize the probability of the discriminator misclassifying its outputs as real, and the discriminator aims to minimize the probability of incorrectly classifying real data as fake and vice versa.

There is a wide variety of GANs, each one specialized in generating certain kinds of data, such as images, video, network trafic, tabular data, etc.

Conditional GANs. There is no control on the process of data generation in a standard GAN. It generates synthetic data from the real data without allowing any further conditions or requirements. Conditional Generative Adversarial Networks (CGANs) are used to address this problem. With CGANs, a condition can be included to control the data generation process. The following types of CGANs are designed to generate tabular data ensuring differential privacy:

– CTAB-GAN+ [37]: It is a general purpose model trained with DP-SGD to impose strict privacy guarantees and leverage the RDP for privacy accounting because it provides stricter bounds on the privacy budget.

- DP-CGAN [29]: It is focused on EHR data generation. This model uses standard differential privacy.
- DP-CTGAN [8]: It is focused on EHR data generation. This model also uses standard differential privacy. Has a federated learning-oriented variant, FDP-CTGAN.
- EHR-M-GAN cond [17]: It is a conditional variation of EHR-M-GAN. It is focused con EHR data generation. It uses a dual variational autoencoder (dual-VAE) as a part of its architecture. DP-SGD is used to guarantee privacy.

Non-Conditional GANs. There are other ways to create synthetic data with privacy assurances beyond CGANs. The following GAN models provide privacy guarantees but are not conditional:

- EHR-M-GAN [17]: It is focused con EHR data generation. It uses a dual variational autoencoder (dual-VAE) as a part of its architecture. It uses DP-SGD to guarantee privacy.
- DP-GAN [13]: One of the components is a conditional network, but it is not a conditional GAN as CGANs are defined. This model uses standard differential privacy.
- PATE-GAN [34]: This model modify the discriminator to be differentially private using a modified version of PATE framework.
- RDP-CGAN [31]: It is a convolutional GAN focused on EHR data. To ensure privacy, this model uses RDP.
- RDP-GAN [19]: This model uses RDP to ensure privacy. It is a general purpose model.

5   Conclusions

This paper provides an overview of the state of the art in privacy-preserving tabular data generation. From a total of 941 unique papers, we selected 24 papers to answer two research questions: "What are the main techniques used to guarantee privacy in generative models for tabular data?" and "How can we measure the privacy of generative models for tabular data?". For the first question, we found that although there is a wide range of generative models in the literature, GAN is the predominant model for synthetic tabular data generation, and the most used application scenario is the protection of medical records. Regarding the second question, most models focus on providing differential privacy guarantees, either its standard definition or some variants. However, we also found some models that do not theoretically guarantee privacy, but rather focus on an empirical approach to measure privacy. As future work, we plan to identify other generative models where the community has not yet begun to discuss privacy risks, and analyze the reasons for this, in order to incorporate privacy guarantees into these models.

Acknowledgments. This work has been partially supported by project PID2022-139268OB-I00, financed by MCIN/AEI /10.13039/501100011033 / FEDER, UE and project TED2021-129830B-I00, financed by MCIN/AEI /10.13039/501100011033/ Next-GenerationEU/PRTR.

References

1. Abadi, M., et al.: Deep learning with differential privacy. In: Conference on Computer and Communications Security (CCS), pp. 308–318. ACM (2016)
2. Abay, N.C., Zhou, Y., Kantarcioglu, M., Thuraisingham, B., Sweeney, L.: Privacy preserving synthetic data release using deep learning. In: Berlingerio, M., Bonchi, F., Gärtner, T., Hurley, N., Ifrim, G. (eds.) ECML PKDD 2018. LNCS (LNAI), vol. 11051, pp. 510–526. Springer, Cham (2019). https://doi.org/10.1007/978-3-030-10925-7_31
3. Armknecht, F., Boyd, C., Carr, C., Gjøsteen, K., Jäschke, A., Reuter, C.A., Strand, M.: A Guide to Fully Homomorphic Encryption. Cryptology ePrint Archive, Paper 2015/1192 (2015)
4. van Breugel, B., Sun, H., Qian, Z., van der Schaar, M.: Membership inference attacks against synthetic data through overfitting detection (2023). https://arxiv.org/abs/2302.12580
5. Cai, K., Lei, X., Wei, J., Xiao, X.: Data synthesis via differentially private markov random fields. Proc. VLDB Endow. **14**(11), 2190–2202 (2021)
6. Domingo-Ferrer, J., Muralidhar, K., Bras-Amorós, M.: General confidentiality and utility metrics for privacy-preserving data publishing based on the permutation model. IEEE Trans. Depend. Secure Comput. **18**(5), 2506–2517 (2021)
7. Dwork, C.: Differential privacy. In: Automata. Languages and Programming, pp. 1–12. Springer, Berlin, Heidelberg (2006)
8. Fang, M.L., Dhami, D.S., Kersting, K.: DP-CTGAN: differentially private medical data generation using CTGANs. In: Artificial Intelligence in Medicine, pp. 178–188. Springer (2022)
9. Figueira, A., Vaz, B.: Survey on Synthetic Data Generation, Evaluation Methods and GANs. Mathematics **10**(15) (2022)
10. Goodfellow, I., et al.: Generative adversarial networks. Commun. ACM **63**(11), 139–144 (2020)
11. Hittmeir, M., Ekelhart, A., Mayer, R.: Utility and privacy assessments of synthetic data for regression tasks. In: IEEE Conference on Big Data, pp. 5763–5772 (2019)
12. Hittmeir, M., Mayer, R., Ekelhart, A.: A baseline for attribute disclosure risk in synthetic data. In: ACM Conference on Data and Application Security and Privacy (CODASPY), pp. 133–143. ACM (2020)
13. Ho, S., Qu, Y., Gu, B., Gao, L., Li, J., Xiang, Y.: DP-GAN: differentially private consecutive data publishing using generative adversarial nets. J. Netw. Comput. Appl. **185**, 103066 (2021)
14. Hu, R., Li, D., Ng, S.K., Zheng, Z.: CB-GAN: generate sensitive data with a convolutional bidirectional generative adversarial networks. In: Database Systems for Advanced Applications, pp. 159–174. Springer Nature (2023)
15. Jia, R., Sangogboye, F.C., Hong, T., Spanos, C., Kjærgaard, M.B.: PAD: protecting anonymity in publishing building related datasets. In: ACM Conference on Systems for Energy-Efficient Built Environments (BuildSys). ACM (2017)
16. Kotal, A., Piplai, A., Chukkapalli, S.S.L., Joshi, A.: PriveTAB: secure and privacy-preserving sharing of tabular data. In: International Workshop on Security and Privacy Analytics (IWSPA), pp. 35–45. ACM (2022)
17. Li, J., Cairns, B.J., Li, J., Zhu, T.: Generating synthetic mixed-type longitudinal electronic health records for artificial intelligent applications. NPJ Digit. Med. **6**(1), 98 (2023)

18. Liu, G., et al.: Multi-dimensional data publishing with local differential privacy. In: EDBT, pp. 183–194 (2023)
19. Ma, C., et al.: RDP-GAN: a Rényi-differential privacy based generative adversarial network. IEEE Trans. Depend. Secure Comput. **20**(6), 4838–4852 (2023)
20. Majeed, A., Lee, S.: Anonymization techniques for privacy preserving data publishing: a comprehensive survey. IEEE Access **9**, 8512–8545 (2021)
21. Mironov, I.: Rényi differential privacy. In: IEEE Computer Security Foundations Symposium (CSF), pp. 263–275 (2017)
22. Mosquera, L., El Emam, K., Ding, L., et al.: A method for generating synthetic longitudinal health data. BMC Med. Res. Methodol. **23**(1), 67 (2023)
23. Papernot, N., Abadi, M., Úlfar Erlingsson, Goodfellow, I., et al.: Semi-supervised Knowledge Transfer for Deep Learning from Private Training Data (2017)
24. Papernot, N., Song, S., Mironov, I., Raghunathan, A., Talwar, K., Úlfar Erlingsson: scalable private learning with PATE. In: International Conference on Learning Representations (ICLR) (2018)
25. Park, M., Foulds, J., Choudhary, K., Welling, M.: DP-EM: differentially private expectation maximization. In: International Conference on Artificial Intelligence and Statistics, vol. 54, pp. 896–904. PMLR (2017)
26. Shokri, R., Stronati, M., Song, C., Shmatikov, V.: Membership inference attacks against machine learning models. In: Symposium on Security and Privacy (IEEE S&P), pp. 3–18 (2017)
27. Song, L., Mittal, P.: Systematic evaluation of privacy risks of machine learning models. In: 30th USENIX Security Symposium, pp. 2615–2632 (2021)
28. Stadler, T., Oprisanu, B., Troncoso, C.: Synthetic Data – anonymisation groundhog day. In: 31st USENIX Security Symposium, pp. 1451–1468. Boston, MA (2022)
29. Sun, C., van Soest, J., Dumontier, M.: Generating synthetic personal health data using conditional generative adversarial networks combining with differential privacy. J. Biomed. Inform. **143**, 104404 (2023)
30. Tang, X., Mahloujifar, S., Song, L., Shejwalkar, V., Nasr, M., et al.: Mitigating membership inference attacks by self-distillation through a novel ensemble architecture. In: 31st USENIX Security Symposium, pp. 1433–1450 (2022)
31. Torfi, A., Fox, E.A., Reddy, C.K.: Differentially private synthetic medical data generation using convolutional GANs. Inf. Sci. **586**, 485–500 (2022)
32. Wang, T., Yang, X., Ren, X., Yu, W., Yang, S.: Locally private high-dimensional crowdsourced data release based on copula functions. IEEE Trans. Serv. Comput. **15**(2), 778–792 (2022)
33. Yoon, J., Drumright, L.N., van der Schaar, M.: Anonymization through data synthesis using generative adversarial networks (ADS-GAN). IEEE J. Biomed. Health Inform. **24**(8), 2378–2388 (2020)
34. Yoon, J., Jordon, J., van der Schaar, M.: PATE-GAN: generating synthetic data with differential privacy guarantees. In: International Conference on Learning Representations (ICLR) (2019)
35. Yoon, J., Mizrahi, M., Ghalaty, N.F., et al.: EHR-Safe: generating high-fidelity and privacy-preserving synthetic electronic health records. NPJ Digit. Med. **6**(1), 141 (2023)
36. Zhang, C., Xie, Y., Bai, H., Yu, B., Li, W., Gao, Y.: A survey on federated learning. Knowl.-Based Syst. **216**, 106775 (2021)
37. Zhao, Z., Kunar, A., Birke, R., Van der Scheer, H., Chen, L.Y.: CTAB-GAN+: enhancing tabular data synthesis. Front. Big Data **6** (2024)
38. Zhu, L., Liu, Z., Han, S.: Deep leakage from gradients. In: Advances in Neural Information Processing Systems, vol. 32. Curran Associates, Inc. (2019)

A DPIA Repository for Interdisciplinary Data Protection Research

Laurens Sion$^{(\boxtimes)}$, Dimitri Van Landuyt , and Wouter Joosen

DistriNet, KU Leuven, 3001 Leuven, Belgium
{laurens.sion,dimitri.landuyt,wouter.joosen}@kuleuven.be

Abstract. Any data collection or processing activity that incurs significant risk requires a Data Protection Impact Assessment (DPIA), which is a comprehensive, analytical evaluation of the risks of violating fundamental data protection rights. While performing a DPIA is considered a cornerstone activity for demonstrating GDPR compliance and adherence to data protection by design principles, they are rarely made public by organizations. Although DPIAs have received considerable attention from a wide range of inter-disciplinary research perspectives, this attention remains fragmented and a solid comparative basis does not yet exist.

In this paper, we present our efforts in establishing an open repository that indexes common and representative DPIAs. Starting from clearly-defined inclusion requirements for representative cases, we present the outcome of the first two years of consolidation efforts: a repository indexing 130 DPIAs. Finally, we discuss how this repository enables inter-disciplinary DPIA research, on comparing and evaluating diverse DPIA approaches, models, and tools. The resulting repository is a valuable resource for researchers across disciplines, to spark debate on DPIA goals andquality, and to evaluate different DPIA methodologies, approaches, and tools.

Keywords: data protection · DPIA · privacy · repository

1 Introduction

With its introduction in 2018, the GDPR has re-affirmed the importance of addressing privacy and data protection concerns early in the design and development of software-intensive systems that collect or process personal data. One of its obligations in cases with high risk –but a good practice regardless– is to perform a Data Protection Impact Assessment (DPIA). This activity starts with systematically describing the data processing operations and then involves an in-depth assessment of the risks they pose to data subjects' rights and freedoms.

While many national supervisory authorities provide guidance, advice, and templates for DPIA reports; these resources remain more generic in nature and do not provide normative illustrations of the potential or desired results of such an assessment in practice. Hence, it is hard for organizations to gain an appreciation of the expected outcomes of a concrete DPIA in terms of detail and depth.

J. Garcia-Alfaro et al. (Eds.): ESORICS 2024 Workshops, LNCS 15263, pp. 181–192, 2025.
https://doi.org/10.1007/978-3-031-82349-7_13

Many scientific communities have made efforts to center their collective focus on exemplars [23,33], common and public data sets, problem characterizations [24], and reference benchmarks [17,35,40]. The establishment and consolidation of common, accessible resources is essential to create a community effect, to foster discussion, and to enable empirical research efforts.

Similar efforts however are severely lacking in the research on DPIAs. In recent years, many tools [8,34], guidelines [4,9–11,16], templates [3], commercial offerings [1,5,27,28,32] and academic studies have emerged. In the work-up towards the GDPR, the Article 29 Working Party [4] has established a number of criteria and guidelines for DPIAs, but these are still relatively open-ended. While all of these elements add value towards providing guidance, a common baseline or shared understanding in terms of, for example, the degree of completeness or level of detail is lacking. This problem is exacerbated by the fact that organizations rarely publish outcomes: DPIAs are a risk analysis activity that may convey sensitive details about the organizations.

To address these limitations, we present the approach and results of establishing a public repository of DPIAs, currently consisting of 130 DPIAs.[1] We discuss the goals, inclusion criteria, and desired attributes of representative cases.

2   Related Work

Performing a DPIA is necessary in data processing operations that are "*likely to result in a high risk to the rights and freedoms of natural persons*" (Art. 35(1)) and is a generally accepted technique for a controller to meet its obligations to appropriately manage risk [4], regardless of necessity. DPIAs can be used to assess a single processing operation, multiple similar or related ones, or to assess the data protection impact of a specific technology or product. A wide range of approaches, tools, methodologies, and recommendations [25] have been discussed.

Domain-specific approaches and cases. A number of approaches have been proposed to conduct a DPIA in specific application domains. One area of active focus is the performance of DPIA in health-related systems. Georgiou et al. [19] discuss the application of the CNIL methodology for a DPIA of cloud-based health applications. Várkonyi and Gradišek [37] use a DPIA to assess the risks inherent to the use of Artificial Intelligence (AI) in an e-health context. Conte et al. [13] present a case study called Health360 involving the application of a DPIA to Electronic Health Records. Alnemr et al. [2] have presented a dedicated approach and tool (DPIAT) for performing DPIAs in cloud applications. Bisztray et al. [6] present an in-depth analysis of the applicability of two DPIA approaches to biometric-based authentication systems. Other applications of DPIAs focus on cyber-physical systems [22], big data applications [20], the use of AI [37] or biometrics [6], smart cities [7], smart grids [30], but also vertical application domains and sectors such as that of charities [21]. Vandercruysse

---

[1] This repository is available at https://dpiarepository.distrinet-research.be.

et al. [36] discuss the merits of applying DPIAs to particular enabling technologies and even hardware-based systems.

Methodologies, approaches and tools. The performance of DPIA is traditionally decoupled from the software development life-cycle, performed by a more compliance-oriented stakeholder such as a data protection officer (DPO). This decoupling is generally undesirable as contemporary development (agile development, CI/CD) is highly incremental which leads to the DPIA itself becoming outdated very quickly. To avoid such a divergence, a number of tools and techniques have recently emerged. Among these are model-based approaches that involve the creation of intermediate artifacts [8, 12, 14, 26, 34], but also machine-readable representations such as the Data Privacy Vocabulary (DPV) [29]. Some tools and approaches [15] even focus on integrating these activities with the source code.

Field studies. Wright et al. [39] have performed an in-depth comparison of the adoption and implementation of Privacy Impact Assessment (PIA) activities in six different countries, focusing on both differences and commonalities. Their study highlights the value of a PIA as an activity, and emphasizes that these activities are ideally not performed one-off, but part of a more continuous process. The PIA report itself in that sense as an artifact is just one element of the broader context of a PIA, and the process (e.g., accountability, internal review, etc.) is considered equally important. The descriptive field study of van Puijenbroek and Hoepman [31] focuses on practitioners in the Netherlands. It illustrates the diversity of application domains, in approaches and methodologies (specifying operations and assessing risk) and highlights the current lack of harmonization and more concrete reproducible guidelines. Friedewald et al. [18] share experiences gained from several specific and practical DPIA efforts and highlight the value of more interdisciplinary effort (e.g., through more extensive integration of DPIA outcomes in technology-centric risk assessment approaches and tools).

3   Requirements for a DPIA repository

We first list and articulate the main requirements for the open shared DPIA repository presented in this article. Section 4 further motivates these requirements on a per-stakeholder basis.

1 *Quality assessment and control.* The DPIA reports selected for the repository should include mature DPIA examples of high quality.
2 *Case inclusion and coverage.*
   2.a *Representativeness.* The repository should include representative examples of typical or common application cases, and these should not be artificial.
   2.b *Diversity.* The repository should contain a wide range of DPIAs for a variety of data processing operation types.
3 *Methodological Coverage.*

3.a *Representativeness.* The repository should include DPIAs resulting from sufficiently representative methodologies that are used in practice.

3.b *Diversity.* The repository should have examples of DPIA outcomes of different methodologies and approaches.

4 *Alternative DPIA artifact for a single case.* In addition to accepting intermediate artifacts contributing to the establishment of a single DPIA entry, the repository should provide support for accepting different or alternative DPIA outcomes (models, spreadsheets, etc.) for the same case.

5 *Multiple DPIA artifact versions over time.* The repository should support keeping track of different versions of the DPIA artifacts over time.

4   Motivating Use Cases

An open, shared, and accessible repository of DPIA outcomes supports and strengthens interdisciplinary scientific research, but has purposes beyond purely research. This section discusses the motivating use cases[2] for different types of stakeholders.

Practitioners currently lack access to rich and normative DPIA examples. Even for examples that are available, information is lacking on the quality and this prohibits them from selecting cases that can be considered normative and positive. Practitioners require access to enriched examples, to allow them to better grasp what is expected of them, in terms of comprehensiveness, detail, and argumentation (req 1). In addition, an open, diverse, and representative collection of DPIAs allows practitioners to search for the most relevant examples based on similarity to their applications (req 2.a).

DPIA Researchers can study the diversity in approaches on how to structure and motivate different data processing operations (req 3.b) and explore and evaluate scientific hypotheses (for example, completeness in terms of covering the WP29 criteria [4]). Furthermore, it allows the development of quality criteria of DPIAs (e.g., comprehensiveness and depth of the analysis) (req 3.b). Alternative artifacts (req 4) for a single case also enable comparative evaluation of the quality of the DPIA outcomes, while, inclusion of multiple versions (req 5) enables longitudinal analysis. Once there is consensus about the quality of individual artifacts, it paves the way for nominating exemplary and normative reference cases.

Software vendors and service providers can access DPIA outcomes to help determine what information to provide to their customers for DPIA efforts and to assist them in performing DPIAs involving their products or services (req 1 and 2.a).

Data subjects will benefit from a public DPIA repository to gain insight and appreciation for the measures taken by organizations that process their personal data and, ideally, to demand similar efforts from other organizations

---

[2] References to numbered requirements from Sect. 3 are included between brackets.

that process their data (req 1 and 2.a). For concerned data subjects, including a DPIA in a public repository, and opening it up to public scrutiny can increase trust in the organization's intentions towards respecting key data subjects' rights and freedoms.

5 A Community Repository of DPIA

This section elaborates on the repository of DPIAs in four parts: the implementation, the DPIA meta-data, and the current set, and operating the repository.

5.1 Design and Implementation of the Repository

This section elaborates on the development of the repository itself to host those DPIAs and their metadata. The main criteria are the following: (i) prefer static sites to avoid complex hosting requirements; (ii) provide support for processing/hosting collections of items; (iii) enable the custom specification of metadata or properties; (iv) input data should be structured in an accessible format (e.g., CSV, YAML, etc.); and (v) be relatively easy to customize the output.

The framework we encountered that best meets these criteria is *Collection-Builder* [38], an open source framework for creating digital collections that leverages the Jekyll static site generator. This makes it especially to create the DPIA index in a publicly-available repository on, for example, GitHub or GitLab.

Only a few implementation steps are needed to customize the output of the collection items to provide all the additional attributes (Sect. 5.2) on the generated DPIA entry pages. The largest effort involves populating and enriching the collection items with their metadata.

5.2 DPIA attributes

We enrich the collected DPIAs with a rich set of meta-data attributes. This allows users to perform search queries and supports advanced navigation of the repository. The attributes are grouped into the following categories (Tables 1 and 2): (i) the described processing operations, (ii) the involved organizations, (iii) the DPIA report or artifacts, and (iv) coverage of the WP29 DPIA criteria [4].

5.3 Current Set of DPIAS

At the initial release of the DPIA repository in 2022, it consisted of 25 entries. This amount has grown throughout 2023 to 41 and currently contains 130 DPIAs.

The initial set of DPIAs was gathered by conducting search queries for 'data protection impact assessment' and 'data protection impact assessment report' and through further snowballing (by including related DPIAs when they were encountered). These queries were constrained to PDF, further discarding templates and guidelines in the search results. These results are then further

Table 1. Overview of DPIA attributes

I. INTRINSIC COMPLEXITY OF THE PROCESSING OPERATION	
1	**Indirect collection**	The amount of indirect collections of personal data.
2	**Disclosure**	The amount of disclosures of personal data to other parties.
3	**Automated decision-making**	The amount of automated decision-making activities that occur.
4	**Sensitive personal data**	The amount of sensitive types of personal data are processed as part of the data processing operations.
5	**Sensitive personal data types**	The concrete types of sensitive personal data that are processed.
6	**Data subjects**	The amount of data subject types considered and a characterisation (e.g., adults and minors).
7	**Types of data subjects**	The concrete types of data subjects involved in the data processing operations.
8	**Cross-border transfers**	The amount of cross-border data transfers involved in the data processing operations.
9	**Processing size**	The size of the described processing operations in terms of the amount of different processing operations.

II. INVOLVED ORGANIZATIONS	
1	**Controller**	The amount of controllers.
2	**Processor**	The amount of (sub-)processors.
3	**Controller countries**	The countries where the controllers are established.
4	**Processor countries**	The countries where the (sub-)processors are established.
5	**Organization types**	The types of involved organizations (e.g., government, company)
6	**Joint controllership**	Whether multiple controllers are involved in the processing operation as joint controllers.
7	**Representatives**	The amount of organizations involved in the processing that need to have representatives in the EU.

III. REGARDING THE DPIA ARTIFACT	
1	**Year**	The year of the DPIA. This is the year when finished, not when the assessment started.
2	**Language**	The language in which the DPIA is available.
3	**Report size**	The size of the PDF report in number of pages.
4	**Scope**	The scope: a single processing operation, multiple similar processing operations, or a technology product?
5	**Template**	The particular template used to create the DPIA.
6	**Method**	The methodology used to perform the DPIA.
7	**Tool execution**	The application or framework used to perform the DPIA.
8	**Performed by**	Who performed the DPIA.
9	**Artifact type**	Type of artifact (e.g., PDF, spreadsheet, model).
10	**Version**	The version of the DPIA.
11	**Processing ID**	An ID for the processing that can be used to link multiple repository entries to the same case.

complemented with DPIAs encountered by the authors. This initial set is to be expanded as part of a continuing community effort over time.

The collection is not yet representative for the full range of published DPIAs, or the diversity of methods and approaches that we aim at covering. In addition,

Table 2. Overview of DPIA attributes (continued)

IV. WP29 DPIA criteria	
1 **Processing description**	Contains a systematic description of the processing. This can be further broken down into: (i) the nature, scope, context, and purposes; (ii) the personal data, recipients, and period of storing; (iii) the processing operations; (iv) the assets (hardware, software, people, etc.); and (v) compliance with codes of conduct.
2 **Necessity and proportionality (processing)**	The DPIA describes measures contributing to the proportionality and the necessity of the processing. This can be further broken down into: (i) specified, explicit and legitimate purposes; (ii) the lawfulness of the processing. (iii) what is necessary data. and (iv) storage limitations.
3 **Necessity and proportionality (data subject rights)**	The DPIA describes measures contributing to the rights of data subjects. This can be further broken down into: (i) information provided to the data subject; (ii) right of access and data portability; (iii) rectification and erasure; (iv) objection and restriction of processing; (v) relationships with processors; (vi) safeguards surrounding international transfer(s); and (vii) prior consultation.
4 **Risk to the rights and freedoms of data subjects**	The DPIA describes the risks (origin, nature, particularity, and severity). This can be further broken down into: (i) the risk sources; (ii) the potential impacts to data subjects' rights and freedoms; and (iii) the estimated likelihood and severity of those risks.
5 **Risk to the rights and freedoms of data subjects (measures)**	The report describes specific measures to treat those risks (mitigate, reduce, manage).
6 **Interested parties**	The DPIA describes the involved interested parties. This can be further broken down into: (i) the DPO advice; and (ii) views of data subjects or their representatives.

the complete determination of the different attributes outlined in Sect. 5.2 is a still a work in progress as this will –amongst other efforts– require the peer review for quality control (outlined in Sect. 5.4). Nonetheless, we argue that this is a significant and relevant stepping stone towards fostering the open collaboration and the community effect that is required for this endeavor. In the next section, we outline our vision on how the repository can be operated in support of this.

5.4 Operating the DPIA repository

This section briefly outlines the operation of the repository. Although the current version of the repository is not yet the result of a peer review process, we have anticipated and designed an explicit process for community interaction and peer review of the DPIAs.

Table 3. Qualitative assessment of requirement coverage

Requirement (Attributes)	Rationale
1 Quality (IV.1–6)	The quality of the selected DPIAs in the repository is mainly ensured through the process for including new DPIAs. Quality assessment and peer review ensures that new submissions to the repository are of sufficient quality and are paired with rich meta-data in terms of the attributes from Table 1. The WP29 DPIA criteria are a good set of independent properties to assess the quality of the DPIA report in terms their coverage (as described in the DPIA).
2.a Case representativeness (I.1–9, II.1–7)	The representativeness of the cases described in the DPIAs submitted to the repository can be assessed using the DPIA attributes of categories I and II. These are assessed as part of the submission process to ensure the described processing operations are representative.
2.b Case diversity (I.1–9, II.1–7)	The diversity of cases in the repository cannot be assessed for an individual DPIA, but needs to be continually assessed in terms of the attributes of categories I and II to ensure that the set of DPIAs in the repository contains enough variation over these attributes.
3.a Method representativeness (III.4–8)	The method representativeness can mainly be assessed through the artifact properties, to the extent that they document or describe the process that was followed. The procedure for including new DPIA can ensure that the followed methodologies are relevant and representative.
3.b Method diversity (III.4–9)	The diversity in methods is assessed over the repository in terms of the attributes in category III.
4 Artifact types (III.5–7, III.9–11)	The repository supports capturing multiple different artifact types as separate entries and link them to the same processing operations (III.11)
5 Artifact versioning (III.10–11)	The version information and link to the same processing operation that is being described allows the repository to capture longitudinal information of how a processing operation is described in different DPIAs over time.

Submission. Upon submission, the properties, involved artifacts, diversity and representativeness (req 2.b and 2.a) are verified.

Review. The second phase entails the community review of the attributes by other legal stakeholders to ensure agreement and correctness. This review enables more extensive discussions in terms of the quality and the identification of exemplary DPIAs in terms of, for example, the comprehensiveness and depth of their system description or legal rationale.

Publication & Maintenance. After inclusion and publication, repository management will be a continuous effort to maintain data quality.

6   Conclusion

In this paper, we highlight the current lack of high-quality, normative examples and rich, realistic application cases and discuss how it impedes scientific research on DPIAs. We particularly motivate the value of a public and accessible collection of DPIA artifacts for a variety of stakeholders, ranging from practitioners and technology providers, to tool developers, to DPIA researchers, and to data subjects.

As the main contribution, we present the design and implementation of a DPIA repository, open for collaboration and community contribution and report its current state. Having been maintained for two years, the repository currently consists of 130 DPIAs. Table 3 discusses how the requirements (Sect. 3) can be attained through the repository (Sect. 5) and its operation.

This paper is a first necessary stepping stone in a longer-term community-building effort on maintaining and enriching the overall repository of DPIAs. We strongly believe that interdisciplinary collaboration will be required to further grow this collection not just in size, but also in terms of documented attributes, intermediate and alternative representations, etc. As a secondary effect of this effort, we argue that a public, comparative repository may also nudge organizations into further increasing their DPIA efforts, to publish high-quality DPIAs, thereby further increasing the transparency of their data processing operations and reducing overall data protections risks. Finally, to further illustrate the scientific value of the repository, we highlight that we are currently conducting an in-depth comparative evaluation of a model-driven DPIA framework called DPMF [34] using DPIA artifacts selected entirely from the repository.

Acknowledgments. This research is partially funded by the Research Fund KU Leuven and Cybersecurity Research Program Flanders.

Disclosure of Interests. The authors have no competing interests to declare that are relevant to the content of this article.

References

1. Akarion AG: Niobase: Master the GDPR. https://niobase.com/en/ (2019)
2. Alnemr, R., et al.: A data protection impact assessment methodology for cloud. In: Berendt, B., Engel, T., Ikonomou, D., Le Métayer, D., Schiffner, S. (eds.) Privacy Technologies and Policy, pp. 60–92. Springer International Publishing, Cham (2016). https://doi.org/10.1007/978-3-319-31456-3_4
3. Article 29 Working Party: opinion 07/2013 on the data protection impact assessment template for smart grid and smart metering systems (2013)
4. Article 29 Working Party: guidelines on data protection impact assessment (DPIA) (WP248 rev.01) (2017)
5. AvePoint: AvePoint Privacy Impact Assessment System: comply with GDPR and other key data protection regulations (2019). https://www.avepoint.com/privacy-impact-assessment/

6. Bisztray, T., Gruschka, N., Mavroeidis, V., Fritsch, L.: Data protection impact assessment in identity control management with a focus on biometrics. In: Open Identity Summit 2020. Lecture Notes in Informatics, Gesellschaft für Informatik e.V. (2020)
7. Calvi, A.: Gender, data protection & the smart city: exploring the role of DPIA in achieving equality goals **19**(3), 24–47 (2022)
8. CNIL: PIA: Analyse d'impact sur la protection des données (Privacy Impact Assessment). Commission Nationale de l'Informatique et des Libertés (2018). https://www.cnil.fr/en/open-source-pia-software-helps-carry-out-data-protection-impact-assesment
9. CNIL: Privacy Impact Assessment (PIA) 1: Methodology. Commission Nationale de l'Informatique et des Libertés (2018). https://www.cnil.fr/sites/default/files/atoms/files/cnil-pia-1-en-methodology.pdf
10. CNIL: Privacy Impact Assessment (PIA) 2: Template. Commission Nationale de l'Informatique et des Libertés (2018). https://www.cnil.fr/sites/default/files/atoms/files/cnil-pia-2-en-templates.pdf
11. CNIL: Privacy Impact Assessment (PIA) 3: Knowledge Bases. Commission Nationale de l'Informatique et des Libertés (2018). https://www.cnil.fr/sites/default/files/atoms/files/cnil-pia-3-en-knowledgebases.pdf
12. Coles, J., Faily, S., Ki-Aries, D.: Tool-supporting data protection impact assessments with Cairis. In: 2018 IEEE 5th International Workshop on Evolving Security & Privacy Requirements Engineering (ESPRE), pp. 21–27. IEEE (2018)
13. Conte, R., Sansone, F., Tonacci, A., Pala, A.P.: Privacy-by-design and minimization within a small electronic health record: the health360 case study. Appl. Sci. **12**(17) (2022). https://www.mdpi.com/2076-3417/12/17/8441
14. Dashti, S., Ranise, S.: Tool-assisted risk analysis for data protection impact assessment. In: Friedewald, M., Önen, M., Lievens, E., Krenn, S., Fricker, S. (eds.) Privacy and Identity Management. Data for Better Living: AI and Privacy: 14th IFIP WG 9.2, 9.6/11.7, 11.6/SIG 9.2.2 International Summer School, Windisch, Switzerland, August 19–23, 2019, Revised Selected Papers, pp. 308–324. Springer International Publishing, Cham (2020). https://doi.org/10.1007/978-3-030-42504-3_20
15. Ethyca: Fides: the open-source language for data privacy. https://ethyca.com/fides
16. European Data Protection Supervisor: Accountability on the ground part II: Data Protection Impact Assessments & Prior Consultation (2018)
17. Ficco, M., Rak, M., Venticinque, S., Tasquier, L., Aversano, G.: Cloud evaluation: benchmarking and monitoring. In: Quantitative Assessments of Distributed Systems, pp. 175–199 (2015)
18. Friedewald, M., Schiering, I., Martin, N., Hallinan, D.: Data protection impact assessments in practice: experiences from case studies. In: Katsikas, S., et al. (eds.) Computer Security. ESORICS 2021 International Workshops: CyberICPS, SECPRE, ADIoT, SPOSE, CPS4CIP, and CDT&SECOMANE, Darmstadt, Germany, October 4–8, 2021, Revised Selected Papers, pp. 424–443. Springer International Publishing, Cham (2022). https://doi.org/10.1007/978-3-030-95484-0_25
19. Georgiou, D., Lambrinoudakis, C.: Data protection impact assessment (DPIA) for cloud-based health organizations. Future Internet **13**(3) (2021). https://www.mdpi.com/1999-5903/13/3/66
20. Gruschka, N., Mavroeidis, V., Vishi, K., Jensen, M.: Privacy issues and data protection in big data: a case study analysis under GDPR. In: 2018 IEEE International Conference on Big Data (Big Data), pp. 5027–5033 (2018)

21. Henriksen-Bulmer, J., Faily, S., Jeary, S.: Implementing GDPR in the charity sector: a case study. In: Kosta, E., Pierson, J., Slamanig, D., Fischer-Hübner, S., Krenn, S. (eds.) Privacy and Identity Management. Fairness, Accountability, and Transparency in the Age of Big Data: 13th IFIP WG 9.2, 9.6/11.7, 11.6/SIG 9.2.2 International Summer School, Vienna, Austria, August 20-24, 2018, Revised Selected Papers, pp. 173–188. Springer International Publishing, Cham (2019). https://doi.org/10.1007/978-3-030-16744-8_12
22. Henriksen-Bulmer, J., Faily, S., Jeary, S.: DPIA in context: applying DPIA to assess privacy risks of cyber physical systems. Future internet **12**(5), 93 (2020)
23. Iftikhar, M.U., Ramachandran, G.S., Bollansée, P., Weyns, D., Hughes, D.: DeltaioT: a self-adaptive internet of things exemplar. In: 12th International Symposium on Software Engineering for Adaptive and Self-Managing Systems (SEAMS) (2017)
24. Katz, S., Mezini, M., Kienzle, J. (eds.): Transactions on Aspect-Oriented Software Development VII. LNCS, vol. 6210. Springer, Heidelberg (2010). https://doi.org/10.1007/978-3-642-16086-8
25. Kloza, D., et al.: Data protection impact assessments in the European union: complementing the new legal framework towards a more robust protection of individuals (2017)
26. Meis, R.: Problem-based privacy analysis (ProPAn) – a computer-aided privacy requirements engineering method. Ph.D. thesis (2018)
27. Nymity: Automate the entire PIA process and provide better response time to the business with improved business engagement. https://www.nymity.com/wp-content/uploads/Nymity-PIA-DPIA-Datasheet.pdf (2019)
28. OneTrust: OneTrust privacy management software. https://www.onetrust.com/solutions/privacy-compliance/ (2019)
29. Pandit, H.J., Esteves, B., Krog, G.P., Ryan, P., Golpayegani, D., Flake, J.: Data Privacy Vocabulary (DPV) – version 2 (2024)
30. Piatkowska, E., Bajraktari, A., Chhajed, D., Smith, P.: Tool support for data protection impact assessment in the smart grid **134**(1), 26–29 (2017)
31. van Puijenbroek, J., Hoepman, J.H.: Privacy impact assessments in practice: Outcome of a descriptive field research in the Netherlands (2017)
32. RealDPG: RealDPG features and benefits. https://www.realdpg.com/en/features-benefits (2019)
33. Shin, Y.J., Liu, L., Hyun, S., Bae, D.H.: Platooning LEGOs: an open physical exemplar for engineering self-adaptive cyber-physical systems-of-systems. In: 2021 International Symposium on Software Engineering for Adaptive and Self-Managing Systems (SEAMS), pp. 231–237. IEEE (2021)
34. Sion, L., Dewitte, P., Van Landuyt, D., Wuyts, K., Valcke, P., Joosen, W.: DPMF: a modeling framework for data protection by design. Enterprise Modelling Inf. Syst. Archit. (EMISAJ) **15**, 10–1 (2020)
35. Van Landuyt, D., Levrau, M., Reniers, V., Joosen, W.: An e-commerce benchmark for evaluating performance trade-offs in document stores. In: Proceedings of the 26th International Conference on Big Data Analytics and Knowledge Discovery (2024)
36. Vandercruysse, L., Buts, C., Dooms, M.: Beyond data controllership: merits of a generic DPIA by hardware and technology suppliers. Eur. Data Prot. L. Rev. **6**, 133 (2020)
37. Várkonyi, G.G., Gradišek, A.: Data protection impact assessment case study for a research project using artificial intelligence on patient data. Informatica **44**(4) (2020)

38. Williamson, E.P., Becker, D., Wikle, O.: CollectionBuilder-CSV (2021). https://github.com/CollectionBuilder/collectionbuilder-csv
39. Wright, D., Finn, R., Rodrigues, R.: A comparative analysis of privacy impact assessment in six countries $\mathbf{9}$(1) (2013)
40. Zhang, C., Lu, J., Xu, P., Chen, Y.: UniBench: a benchmark for multi-model database management systems. In: Technology Conference on Performance Evaluation and Benchmarking, pp. 7–23. Springer (2018)

Secrecy and Sensitivity: Privacy-Performance Trade-Offs in Encrypted Traffic Classification

Spencer Giddens[1], Raphael Labaca-Castro[2(✉)], Dan Zhao[3], Sandra Guasch[2], Parth Mishra[2], and Nicolas Gama[2]

[1] University of Notre Dame, Notre Dame, IN, USA
`sgiddens@nd.edu`
[2] SandboxAQ, Palo Alto, CA, USA
{`raphael.labaca,sandra.guasch,parth.mishra,nicolas.gama`}`@sandboxaq.com`
[3] New York University, New York, NY, USA
`dz1158@nyu.edu`

Abstract. As datasets and models grow in size and complexity to increase performance, the risks associated with sensitive data also grow. Differential privacy (DP) offers a framework for designing mechanisms that provide a degree of privacy that can help conceal sensitive features or information. However, different domains and applications can naturally exhibit different rates of trade-offs between privacy and performance depending on their characteristics. In contrast to well-studied areas (e.g., healthcare), one relatively unexplored domain is network traffic analysis where the data contains sensitive information on users' communications. In this paper, we apply DP to various machine learning models trained to classify between encrypted and non-encrypted packets from network traffic; we emphasize that our goal is to examine a relatively unexplored area to analyze the trade-offs between privacy and performance when the data contains both encrypted and un-encrypted observations. We show how varying model architecture and feature sets can be a relatively simple way to achieve more optimal performance-privacy trade-offs; we also compare and contextualize reasonable privacy budgets from our analysis in the network traffic domain against those in other more well-studied domains.

Keywords: network traffic classification · differential privacy · privacy budget · performance evaluation

1 Introduction

Network traffic analysis is a key component of infrastructure security—proper identification of network protocols can facilitate network sizing and enable the

---

S. Giddens and R. Labaca-Castro—Joint first author

S. Giddens and D. Zhao—This publication is a result of the work done during their stay at SandboxAQ.

© The Author(s), under exclusive license to Springer Nature Switzerland AG 2025
J. Garcia-Alfaro et al. (Eds.): ESORICS 2024 Workshops, LNCS 15263, pp. 193–202, 2025.
https://doi.org/10.1007/978-3-031-82349-7_14

detection of anomalous connections, revealing ongoing attacks or insecure protocols within the network.

A unique challenge for training machine learning (ML) models on network traffic data lies with the data itself, which contains sensitive information such as IPs, ports, protocols, or clear-text payloads. If these models are shared across different parties, it is imperative that no sensitive information on the underlying data is leaked.

In this paper, we explore the trade-offs of applying differential privacy (DP) [9] to a ML model to protect the privacy of the data used to train it, in the context of network traffic classification into plain and encrypted traffic. The main reason behind it is to be able to detect the use of unsecure protocols and unencrypted communications within an infrastructure, which may have security and legal/compliance consequences. Although the use of zero-trust architectures and encrypted communications by default is increasing, there may be environments where these are still not enforced due to the increased management and configuration complexity, and the potential penalisation in performance.

By varying the choice of model architecture and features used, we study the privacy-performance trade-offs of training both the DP and non-DP versions of models and show how these changes, along with the underlying domain and data characteristics, can considerably impact the selection of reasonable privacy budgets.

2 Background

2.1 Network Traffic

Data is carried over computer networks in the form of discrete network packets where each packet carries protocol-dependent headers along with information in its payload. These packets then constitute a tuple-like structure consisting of multiple fields of information including source and destination IP addresses, ports, and other data relevant to network protocols. These packets are our fundamental unit of information as we classify between encrypted and un-encrypted/plain traffic.

Although deterministic solutions already exist for distinguishing between plain and encrypted traffic based on the protocol, entropy calculation, ports, and other features, these solutions do not work well in corner cases especially when compressed data is evaluated. Compressed values present higher entropy and therefore are often indistinguishable from encrypted data. Any solution relying on only such a metric would be prone to higher false positive values. This is our main motivation for using machine learning for this classification.

We note that if a compressed file is sent over an un-encrypted protocol we consider it plain.

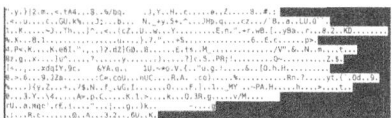

(a) An example of a plain network packet: a data unit transmitted over a computer network without any additional headers, encapsulation, or encryption.

(b) An example of an encrypted network packet: a packet that has been encoded or scrambled to protect content from unauthorized access or interception.

Fig. 1. An illustration of the two types of packets: encrypted and un-encrypted (or plain).

2.2 Differential Privacy (DP)

Differential privacy, intuitively, ensures that for any given individual in a dataset, the output of a DP-satisfying mechanism will be similar whether the individual's data is included in the mechanism input or not. Those protected by DP guarantees (i.e., the entity whose presence is to be concealed) are known as privacy units and can represent any entity in the data (e.g., a user). In this paper, our privacy unit is a network packet or the information in said packet. We first formalize the notion of DP.

Definition 1 $((\varepsilon, \delta)$**-differential privacy)** [8] *A randomized mechanism* $\mathcal{M}$ *satisfies* (ε, δ)*-DP if for all* $S \subset \text{Range}(\mathcal{M})$ *and all neighboring datasets* D *and* $\tilde{D}$ *(datasets differing by a single individual),*

$$P(\mathcal{M}(D) \in S) \leq e^{\varepsilon} P(\mathcal{M}(\tilde{D}) \in S) + \delta, \tag{1}$$

where $\varepsilon > 0$ *and* $\delta \in [0, 1)$ *are privacy budget parameters. When* $\delta = 0$*, we denote this as* ε*-DP.*

The degree of similarity between neighboring datasets for a DP mechanism is governed by ε; smaller values correspond to more privacy and vice versa. The parameter δ is commonly viewed as the probability with which ε-DP fails and is usually set on the order of $o(1/\text{poly}(n))$, where n is the size of the dataset. DP's popularity can be largely attributed to its strong theoretical properties, relative ease of use, and overall flexibility. We refer to [10] for a more comprehensive review.

2.3 Related Work

Ad hoc anonymization methods alone have been insufficient to ensure privacy for sensitive datasets [1,15]. Sweeney [21] linked public voter records to anonymized health records from Massachusetts state employees to identify then-governor William Weld's health records. A similar attack [15] shut down the Netflix Prize competition after individuals in the anonymized competition dataset were partially de-identified. Even summary statistics of anonymized data have proven insecure as attacks on 2010 US Census statistics were able to reconstruct 46% of the records [6].

Models trained on sensitive data are also susceptible to attacks. [19] showed that, by using a black-box "target model" to synthesize training data and using those to train "shadow models" replicating the target model, an attacker can use the shadow models and synthesized data to infer membership of a given record in the training dataset for the target model. [24] demonstrated (approximate) attribute inference is also possible using membership inference as a subroutine. If attackers have additional information (e.g., model parameters), more attacks are possible [19,24]. DP makes no assumptions on the methods used by attackers to reveal an individual's presence in a sensitive dataset. [22] proved that an attacker's membership inference (MI) advantage Adv_{MI} (i.e., the difference between the attacker's true and false positive rates) is bounded by $Adv_{MI} \leq e^{\varepsilon} - 1$. Even for larger ε where theoretical MI advantage bounds no longer hold, [13] demonstrated that DP still limits state-of-the-art MI attack success rates in practice. [2] explored the use of DP to train a deep neural network to classify encrypted network traffic into classes of interest but do not attempt to classify between encrypted and plain data or study performance-privacy trade-offs using reasonable privacy budgets. [17] uses a convolutional neural network to classify traffic flows into different categories and applications. However, given that the payload is not used for the training, the authors do not consider including privacy-protection techniques such as DP to protect the training data.

2.4   DP in Network Analysis

As described in Sect. 2.2, DP provides mathematically rigorous privacy guarantees to the data which, in this context, we use to try and protect sensitive data that is commonly exchanged throughout our networks. One problem with network data is that sensitive information might be exposed while travelling the network, for example behind TLS terminations in enterprise infrastructures. If attributes can be inferred from the data, user information such as visited websites, financial transactions, or even passwords can be revealed. Other domain-specific peculiarities include the possible existence of more efficient DP mechanisms when portions of the network data are already encrypted or applying DP to an online stream of network packet time-series data among others—all relatively unexplored areas which we leave as part of our future work.

3   Methodology

The goal is to train a binary classifier using two sets of features, with and without DP in the model being trained, to distinguish between encrypted and unencrypted network traffic. These two sets of features can be characterized by two approaches towards where the most useful network data lies: namely *header-based*, in which information about the network packet header is extracted, and *payload-based*, that focuses in calculating metrics that characterize the network payload. We train *vanilla* versions of these models (without DP guarantees) as baselines to compare against their differentially private versions.

3.1 Approach

To classify network traffic into *encrypted* and *non-encrypted* (or plain) data, we pursue two strategies, each characterized by a different set of explanatory variables in classifying network data: a *header-based* approach and a *payload-based* approach. In the former, a number of features are extracted from the header of the packet, while, in the latter, information from the payload itself is used to calculate randomness metrics as our features.

Our privacy-preserving versions of both random forest and logistic regression models are implemented in Python via IBM's DP library, *diffprivlib* [12]. These are produced with ε-DP guarantees for various values of ε. As the dataset considered for this paper is already public, our main focus is to explore the privacy-utility trade-off to determine a reasonable domain-specific value for the privacy budget ε that balances DP guarantees and model performance. To have a fair comparison between vanilla and DP models, especially given the additional privacy budget allocation that would be necessary for hyper-parameter tuning, we train each model with its default settings.

Header-based. In this approach, the features are extracted from the header of the network packets in the dataset 3.2 including multiple fields of network protocols found in the network and transport layers. These features are calculated through a custom network dissector tool, which provides a serialized representation before entering into a pre-processing pipeline that processes the data in a way to mitigate inconsistencies produced during the data capturing process from network interfaces such as invalid or incomplete packets.

Payload-based. A payload-based approach is characterized by the hypothesis that the entropy of encrypted data will be higher than that of equal-length plain data. Inspired by [4], we use the statistics from randomness tests conducted on the payload data as features to train our classifiers. The payload is first extracted using a custom extraction algorithm before being passed into a module that conducts randomness tests on the payload including entropy, chi-squared, and arithmetic average, which are used as the key features in our payload-based approach.

Model Choices. We train random forest, decision tree, AdaBoost, and logistic regression models as our base models. Due to our specific domain and dataset, we favored tree-based approaches that tend to be well-suited with both numerical and categorical data. Likewise, we also chose to evaluate an AdaBoost algorithm since weak learners behave similar to decision trees using a single split. Due to the nature of the network data and its heterogeneity across different network environments it might be useful to leverage its iterate methods to improve overall performance. Finally, we explore the logistic regression model as a simple binary algorithm to benchmark against previous models accordingly.

3.2   Dataset

The dataset [18] consists of network data captures in PCAP format collected between July 3rd at 9AM to July 7th at 5PM in 2017 and has been used relatively frequently in the field of network traffic applications [17,20,23]. The data is labeled as encrypted or un-encrypted (plain) before being divided into train/test splits. The training set consists of ~1.26 million packets while the test set has ~350,000 with approximately equal representation between the encrypted/un-encrypted classes.

4   Evaluation

We evaluate the performance and trade-offs of our models with and without DP using both the feature and payload-based approaches with a 70%/30% train-test data split. Vanilla (without DP) random forests, decision trees, AdaBoost, and logistic regression models are trained; these classifiers were then evaluated via prediction accuracy and F1-score on the test set. Then, for each $\varepsilon \in \{10^{-7}, 10^{-6.5}, \ldots, 10^3\}$, we train 30 random forests and logistic regression models satisfying ε-DP, and calculate their accuracy and F1-scores on the test set for comparison.

Header-based Approach. Figure 2 shows the results of our DP simulations. As expected, the average performance of the privacy-preserving models approaches the performance of non-DP models as ε increases. For the DP version of logistic regression, its performance approaches that of the non-DP version starting from $\varepsilon = 10^2$ onward. While theoretical privacy guarantees at these ε values are weak, [13] demonstrated that even at this large of a privacy budget, practical privacy benefits can still be realized. For the header-based approach, the random forest model appears to be more promising with only a slight performance loss. The performance metrics level off beginning around $\varepsilon = 10^{-4}$. Though at this ε we see on average a 10% performance loss, the privacy guarantees at this level are strong. Based on [22], an attacker's membership inference advantage can be at most $e^{0.0001} - 1 \approx 0.0001$, guaranteeing that an attacker's ability to infer whether any given network packet is in the training set is barely better than random guessing. Based on these results, a DP version of the random forest with the header-based approach works best.

Likely, part of the difference in the behaviour of DP random forest and DP logistic regression is due to the choice of hyperparameters such as regularization or tree depth, which poses a trade-off since hyperparameter tuning requires spending part of the privacy budget. In the case of DL logistic regression, the regularization parameter may be too large compared to the signal when computing the loss function for lower values of ϵ. In the case of DP random forest, the tree depth is limited in order to limit the privacy budget required for fitting, which puts a cap on the maximum accuracy that can be achieved for larger values of ϵ.

Payload-based Approach. In Fig. 2, for the payload-based approach, in contrast to the header-based comparisons, both the DP logistic regression and DP random forest reach their best performance levels at smaller values of ε. DP logistic regression begins performing similarly to its vanilla counterpart around $\varepsilon = 10^{-3}$, while the performance of DP random forest levels off at around $\varepsilon = 10^{-4.5}$. In fact, for $\varepsilon \geq 10^{-2}$, DP logistic regression even outperforms DP random forest for the payload-based approach. These values of ε all represent strong theoretical privacy guarantees against membership inference attacks.

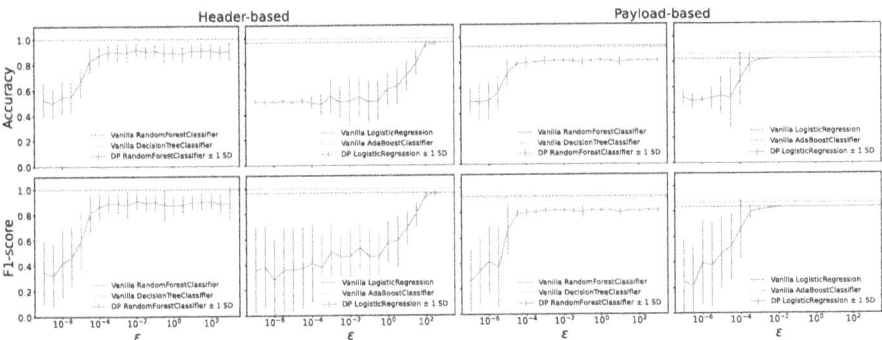

Fig. 2. Comparison of model performance between vanilla classifiers and classifiers trained with ε-DP guarantees across a range of ε privacy budget values. Both the accuracy and the F1-score are shown. The first two columns show model results from the header-based approach, while the last two pertain to the payload-based approach. The solid lines represent the average metric value over 30 seeds and the error bars represent one standard deviation in each direction. Dotted lines indicate the non-DP models' performance.

4.1   Privacy Budget ε Comparisons with Other Domains

We compare the minimum ε reasonable privacy budgets from our network traffic domain to DP models in more common, well-studied domains in finance and healthcare (Table 1).

For our purposes, we define a "reasonable privacy budget" to be a value ε at which an ε-DP classifier achieves performance that is both better than a baseline fully-random classifier and as close as possible to the performance of its analogous vanilla (non-DP) classifier. For example, a reasonable privacy budget for the DP random forest classifiers in Fig. 2 would be $\varepsilon \geq 10^{-4}$. To ensure a fair comparison, we took a random sub-sample of our network traffic data of approximately the same size and class distribution and re-ran our DP model simulations. In this circumstance, the payload-based approach achieves reasonably good utility for ε values comparable to the finance domain, while the header-based approach struggles to obtain better-than-baseline performance for any ε in $[5,11]$, possibly due to the dimensionality of feature sets used. Though the healthcare domain results are not directly comparable to ours due to differences in the types of differential privacy and ML models used, we believe

Table 1. Comparison of privacy budgets (smallest values of ε achieving acceptable utility) between our network traffic domain and other domains in other works. For a fair comparison, we adjusted the size of our training dataset to match the size of datasets from these other domains; therefore, the reasonable budgets shown for the network traffic domain here differ from those in Fig. 2.

Domain	Dataset	Model Type	Reasonable Budget	References
Finance	Adult [7]	Logistic regression	$\varepsilon \geq 0.1$	[5]
Finance	Adult [7]	Decision tree	$\varepsilon \geq 1$	[11]
Healthcare	eICU [16]	Deep learning	$\varepsilon \geq 2.88$	[3]
Healthcare	Pneumonia [14]	Deep learning	$\varepsilon \geq 2.69$	[25]
Network traffic	PCAP data [18]	Logistic regression (payload)	$\varepsilon \geq 0.45$	This paper
Network traffic	PCAP data [18]	Random forest (payload)	$\varepsilon \geq 0.01$	This paper

these comparisons give additional perspective and highlight the importance of better understanding reasonable privacy budgets with respect to the particular data-generating process and characteristics of each domain.

Since our results can be used to understand which models perform better with a given privacy budget in the context of network classification, they can be used as a starting point for systems and future research dealing with classification problems with similar datasets and features, although additional fine-tuning may still be required due to the differences in specific scenarios.

5   Conclusion

In this paper, we explored the performance/privacy trade-offs in the network security domain and assessed how these trade-offs vary with the choice of features and model architecture as well as against other more well-studied domains. A better understanding of these trade-offs between performance and privacy guarantees can derive easy and efficient ways to protect sensitive data and still preserve performance. Our future work hopes to build upon this by developing more efficient privacy-preserving mechanisms such as studying DP guarantees for only protecting/concealing un-encrypted observations in datasets with both encrypted and un-encrypted data.

References

1. Ahn, S.: Whose genome is it anyway?: re-identification and privacy protection in public and participatory genomics. The San Diego Law Rev. **52**, 751 (2015)
2. Akbari, I., Tahoun, E.: PrivPkt: privacy preserving collaborative encrypted traffic classification. ResearchGate (2020). https://doi.org/10.13140/RG.2.2.22431.59046
3. Beaulieu-Jones, B.K., Yuan, W., Finlayson, S.G., Wu, Z.S.: Privacy-preserving distributed deep learning for clinical data (2018)

4. Cha, S., Kim, H.: Detecting encrypted traffic: a machine learning approach. In: Information Security Applications: 17th International Workshop, WISA 2016, Jeju Island, Korea, August 25-27, 2016, Revised Selected Papers 17, pp. 54–65. Springer (2017)

5. Chaudhuri, K., Monteleoni, C., Sarwate, A.D.: Differentially private empirical risk minimization. J. Mach. Learn. Res. **12**(29), 1069–1109 (2011). http://jmlr.org/papers/v12/chaudhuri11a.html

6. Desfontaines, D.: Demystifying the us census Bureau's reconstruction attack. https://desfontain.es/privacy/us-census-reconstruction-attack.html   (2021). Accessed 5 Sept 2023

7. Dua, D., Graff, C.: UCI machine learning repository (2017). http://archive.ics.uci.edu/ml

8. Dwork, C., Kenthapadi, K., McSherry, F., Mironov, I., Naor, M.: Our data, ourselves: privacy via distributed noise generation. In: Vaudenay, S. (ed.) EUROCRYPT 2006. LNCS, vol. 4004, pp. 486–503. Springer, Heidelberg (2006). https://doi.org/10.1007/11761679_29

9. Dwork, C., McSherry, F., Nissim, K., Smith, A.: Calibrating noise to sensitivity in private data analysis. In: Halevi, S., Rabin, T. (eds.) Theory of Cryptography, pp. 265–284. Springer Berlin Heidelberg, Berlin, Heidelberg (2006). https://doi.org/10.1007/11681878-14

10. Dwork, C., Roth, A.: The algorithmic foundations of differential privacy. Found. Trends Theor. Comput. Sci. **9**(3–4), 211–407 (2014). https://doi.org/10.1561/0400000042

11. Friedman, A., Schuster, A.: Data mining with differential privacy. In: Proceedings of the 16th ACM SIGKDD International Conference on Knowledge Discovery and Data Mining, pp. 493–502. KDD '10, Association for Computing Machinery, New York, NY, USA (2010). https://doi.org/10.1145/1835804.1835868

12. Holohan, N., Braghin, S., Mac Aonghusa, P., Levacher, K.: Diffprivlib: the IBM differential privacy library. ArXiv e-prints 1907.02444 [cs.CR] (2019)

13. Jayaraman, B., Evans, D.: Evaluating differentially private machine learning in practice. In: 28th USENIX Security Symposium (USENIX Security 19), pp. 1895–1912. USENIX Association, Santa Clara, CA (2019). https://www.usenix.org/conference/usenixsecurity19/presentation/jayaraman

14. Kermany, D.S., et al.: Identifying medical diagnoses and treatable diseases by image-based deep learning. Cell **172**(5) (2018). https://doi.org/10.1016/j.cell.2018.02.010

15. Narayanan, A., Shmatikov, V.: Robust de-anonymization of large sparse datasets. In: 2008 IEEE Symposium on Security and Privacy (SP 2008), pp. 111–125 (2008). https://doi.org/10.1109/SP.2008.33

16. Pollard, T.J., Johnson, A.E., Raffa, J.D., Celi, L.A., Mark, R.G., Badawi, O.: The eICU collaborative research database, a freely available multi-center database for critical care research. Sci. Data **5** (2018)

17. Shapira, T., Shavitt, Y.: FlowPic: encrypted internet traffic classification is as easy as image recognition. In: IEEE INFOCOM 2019-IEEE Conference on Computer Communications Workshops (INFOCOM WKSHPS), pp. 680–687. IEEE (2019)

18. Sharafaldin, I., Lashkari, A.H., Ghorbani, A.A.: Toward generating a new intrusion detection dataset and intrusion traffic characterization. ICISSp **1**, 108–116 (2018)

19. Shokri, R., Stronati, M., Song, C., Shmatikov, V.: Membership inference attacks against machine learning models. In: 2017 IEEE Symposium on Security and Privacy (SP), pp. 3–18 (2017). https://doi.org/10.1109/SP.2017.41

20. Singh, R., Srivastav, G.: Novel framework for anomaly detection using machine learning technique on CIC-IDS2017 dataset. In: 2021 International Conference on Technological Advancements and Innovations (ICTAI), pp. 632–636. IEEE (2021)
21. Sweeney, L.: Only you, your doctor, and many others may know. Technol. Sci. (2015). https://techscience.org/a/2015092903/
22. Yeom, S., Giacomelli, I., Fredrikson, M., Jha, S.: Privacy risk in machine learning: analyzing the connection to overfitting. In: 2018 IEEE 31st Computer Security Foundations Symposium (CSF), pp. 268–282 (2018). https://doi.org/10.1109/CSF.2018.00027
23. Yulianto, A., Sukarno, P., Suwastika, N.A.: Improving AdaBoost-based intrusion detection system (IDS) performance on CIC IDS 2017 dataset. J. Phys.: Conf. Ser. **1192**, 012018. IOP Publishing (2019)
24. Zhao, B.Z.H., et al.: On the (in)feasibility of attribute inference attacks on machine learning models. In: 2021 IEEE European Symposium on Security and Privacy, pp. 232–251 (2021). https://doi.org/10.1109/EuroSP51992.2021.00025
25. Ziller, A., Usynin, D., Braren, R., Makowski, M., Rueckert, D., Kaissis, G.: Medical imaging deep learning with differential privacy. Sci. Rep. **11**(13524) (2021). https://doi.org/10.1038/s41598-021-93030-0

CBT Papers

Preface to the Proceedings of CBT 2024

This volume contains the post-proceedings of the 8th International Workshop on Cryptocurrencies and Blockchain Technology (CBT 2024), which was organized as part of the 29th European Symposium on Research in Computer Security (ESORICS 2024).

The CBT workshop started in 2017 with the aim to provide a forum for researchers with a specific focus on the use of cryptocurrencies and blockchain technologies in areas such as the identification and tracking of distributed autonomous organizations. Papers published in previous venues carefully analyzed current issues in such domains and proposed scientific updates to consolidate security and privacy in the blockchain research area. Since that inaugural workshop in Oslo, Norway (2017), CBT has been held in different venues: Barcelona, Spain (2018); Luxembourg, Luxembourg (2019); Guildford, UK (2020); Darmstadt, Germany (2021); Copenhagen, Denmark (2022); and The Hague, The Netherlands (2023).

The 2024 edition of CBT took place in Bydgoszcz, Poland on September 19th as part of the ESORICS 2024 workshops. All presentations were in person, featuring a format that provided ample time for each contributor to present their work in depth. This setup encouraged active discussion among attendees, sparking fresh insights into the presented research and paving the way for future explorations in the field.

The workshop received 17 submissions, each assigned to three program committee members who provided detailed feedback through double-blind reviews. We are grateful to our committee members for their timely and thorough reviews. Submissions were assessed on their significance, innovation, and technical quality, resulting in consensus-driven discussions by the program committee. Ultimately, 9 regular papers were selected for presentation.

The workshop was initiated with a joint session with the 19th International Workshop on Data Privacy Management (DPM 2024) where Pedro Moreno-Sánchez (from the IMDEA Software Institute) provided insights into the cryptographic underpinnings that impact the core technologies that aim to establish secure and privacy-preserving blockchain applications. This was an excellent kick-off to both DPM and CBT given the interesting overlap between these related technologies and directions.

We would like to thank everyone who helped with the event organization, including all the members of the organizing committees for both ESORICS 2024 and CBT 2024. Our gratitude goes to Michał Choraś and Sokratis Katsikas, General Chairs of ESORICS 2024, Marek Pawlicki, Workshop Chair of ESORICS 2024, and everyone in the ESORICS 2024 organization. A very special thank you goes to all the CBT 2024 Program Committee members, additional reviewers, and, most notably, all the authors who submitted papers, and all the workshop attendees.

We also thank our sponsors for providing support in different forms: *Plan de Recuperación, Transformación y Resiliencia* funded with Next Generation EU funds through the project DANGER INCIBE-C062/23; and Spanish Ministry SECURING/NET PID2021-125962OB-C33 and SECURING/CYBER PID2021-125962OB-C31.

The contributions presented at CBT 2024 represent a meaningful advance in our understanding of blockchain technology's challenges and potential solutions. We believe that this work not only marks significant progress but also serves as a foundation for addressing upcoming challenges in the field.

November 2024

Sergi Delgado-Segura
Cristina Pérez-Solà

Organization

Route Discovery in Private Payment Channel Networks

Zeta Avarikioti[1], Mahsa Bastankhah[2], Mohammad Ali Maddah-Ali[3],
Krzysztof Pietrzak[4], Jakub Svoboda[4], and Michelle Yeo[5(✉)]

[1] TU Wien, Vienna, Austria
georgia.avarikioti@tuwien.ac.at
[2] Princeton University, Princeton, USA
mb6458@princeton.edu
[3] University of Minnesota Twin Cities, Minneapolis, USA
maddah@umn.edu
[4] Institute of Science and Technology Austria, Klosterneuburg, Austria
{krzysztof.pietrzak,jakub.svoboda}@ist.ac.at
[5] National University of Singapore, Singapore, Singapore
mxyeo@nus.edu.sg

Abstract. In this work, we explore route discovery in private payment channel networks. We first determine what "ideal" privacy for a routing protocol means in this setting. We observe that protocols achieving this strong privacy definition exist by leveraging Multi-Party Computation but they are inherently inefficient as they must involve the entire network. We then present protocols with weaker privacy guarantees but much better efficiency (involving only a small fraction of the nodes). The core idea is that both sender and receiver gossip a message which propagates through the network, and the moment any node in the network receives both messages, a path is found. In our first protocol the message is always sent to all neighbouring nodes with a delay proportional to the fees of that edge. In our second protocol the message is only sent to one neighbour chosen randomly with a probability proportional to its degree. We additionally propose a more realistic notion of privacy in order to measure the privacy leakage of our protocols in practice. Our realistic notion of privacy challenges an adversary that join the network with a fixed budget to create channels to guess the sender and receiver of a transaction upon receiving messages from our protocols. Simulations of our protocols on the Lightning network topology (for random transactions and uniform fees) show that 1) forming edges with high degree nodes is a more effective attack strategy for the adversary, 2) there is a tradeoff between the number of nodes involved in our protocols (privacy) and the optimality of the discovered path, and 3) our protocols involve a very small fraction of the network on average.

Keywords: Payment Channel Networks · Privacy · Bitcoin · Route Discovery · Lightning Network

ⓒ The Author(s), under exclusive license to Springer Nature Switzerland AG 2025
J. Garcia-Alfaro et al. (Eds.): ESORICS 2024 Workshops, LNCS 15263, pp. 207–223, 2025.
https://doi.org/10.1007/978-3-031-82349-7_15

1 Introduction

Payment channel networks (PCNs) is one of the most promising approaches to scale cryptocurrencies like Bitcoin [18]. PCNs allow any pair of users to set up a payment channel with each other, thereby enabling an unlimited number of costless off-chain transactions between them. Users who are not directly connected with a payment channel can still transact with each other by routing the transaction through intermediate nodes in the network. These intermediate nodes typically charge a fee for forwarding these transactions. There are several PCN proposals [2,5,10,11,20,26]; the most widely used being the Bitcoin Lightning Network [20].

To route a transaction in a PCN from sender to receiver, a two-step process is necessary (but sometimes executed in parallel): (a) finding the optimal route or *route discovery*, which typically means finding the shortest or cheapest path from sender to receiver, and (b) executing the transaction payment in an atomic fashion, i.e., the transaction is either executed or aborted in all the channels of the path, so no party can lose money. The route discovery problem focuses on the first step, and thus the goal is to find the optimal route from sender to receiver in an efficient and privacy-preserving manner, while the atomic execution of transactions is not considered. This is a well-researched problem with several existing solutions [15,19,21,24,25,28]. However all these solutions assume that the *entire topology of the PCN is known* by at least one party (for instance the users who download the entire network [29] or trampoline nodes [21]).

Recently, however, the Bitcoin protocol upgraded to taproot [8] that uses Schnorr signatures [16] to aggregate public keys and signatures, making a transaction involving multiple users indistinguishable from a transaction involving just two users on the blockchain. As a result, the users of the Lightning Network can now form *private channels*, leading eventually to a private payment channel network with unknown topology. This in turn affects heavily the route discovery process as all existing algorithms utilize the known PCN topology. Hence, *designing route discovery algorithms suitable for private PCNs is paramount.*

Our Contribution. In this work, we consider for the first time the problem of route discovery in private PCNs where the capacities, fees, and even the mere *existence* of channels can be (partially) unknown. In particular, the route discovery protocols we propose do not assume any knowledge about the network other than the minimal requirement that nodes know about their own channels (i.e., their balances, fees, and local neighborhood).

Our objective is to construct protocols that are *efficient, private, and optimal* in terms of minimal fees. We identify several key challenges: (a) we observe that in this setting, the only strategy a sender and receiver can follow to find an (optimal) route is to send exploratory messages through the network. However, this may incur high communication overhead. (b) To find the optimal path with certainty, all nodes should be involved in the route discovery process, again leading the high communication overhead. (c) To achieve ideal privacy, nodes that end up in a payment path should not learn any information beyond the amount and the nodes right before and after them in the path; even the sender and receiver jointly should not learn the users on a path other than their direct neighbours. Thus, no information can be leaked on the PCNs topology but even simple topology hiding broadcast protocols are highly inefficient [3,17]. (d) If ideal privacy is out of reach, there is no practical notion of privacy for PCNs to measure the possible privacy leakage.

We explain how we address these key challenges below. At its core, we exploit a trade-off between the number of involved nodes (which defines efficiency and affects privacy) and how cheap the discovered route is (optimality). To practically measure the privacy leakage, we present a novel game for route discovery protocols over arbitrary networks. In detail, our contributions are:

- (Ideal and Practical Notion) We put forward a security notion for private route discovery in Sect. 3 and give a feasibility result using multi-party computation (MPC). Our notion is inspired by security notions from topology hiding MPC. This solution is inefficient, not just because MPC computations are expensive, but also because it must involve the *entire* network (and this inherent for any protocol achieving our ideal notion, confirming challenge (c)). To account for the inefficiency of our ideal security notion, we also define a practical notion of privacy in Sect. 3.3 inspired by metrics used in information retrieval (addressing challenge (d)). We empirically analyse our protocols with respect to our practical privacy notion.
- (Practical Protocols) We present a family of route discovery protocols on private PCNs in Sect. 4 that are much more efficient, involving a small fraction of the network (addressing challenges (a) and (b)). These protocols work by propagating exploratory messages from the sender and receiver through the PCN. The first protocol we propose is Forward-to-All where nodes forward messages on all their edges but each edge has a delay that is proportional to its fee. In our second protocol Degree-Proportional Random Walk nodes just send messages to one neighbour, chosen randomly with a probability proportional to their degree. Forward-to-All always finds the shortest path, but it involves a larger fraction of the network than Degree-Proportional Random Walk.
- (Simulations) We simulated our protocols on the Lightning Network and a certain class of graphs (Barabási–Albert) that are used to model PCNs in Sect. 5. Our simulation show that Forward-to-All typically involves around 3% of nodes in Lightning, while Degree-Proportional Random Walk only involves around 0.1%, and the discovered paths are around twice as long as the optimal ones.
- (Analysis) We also prove some analytical bounds in Sect. 5 for our algorithms on particular classes of graphs.

In the following, we use the terms user, node, and party interchangeably.

2   Model and Definitions

We model a payment channel network (PCN) as a directed graph $G = (V, E)$ where each node in the set V represents a user in the PCN and an edge (u, v) in the set E indicates an open channel between the users u and v in V. We denote with $f_{u,v}(.)$ the fee function, i.e., u charges $f_{u,v}(x)$ to transfer x coins over the channel (u, v). In existing PCNs like the Lightning Network, $f_{u,v}(.)$ is set by u.

The route discovery problem in a PCN represents the task of finding the path with the smallest aggregated fees, or the cheapest path, in a PCN for a given pair of sender/receiver nodes $u_s, u_r \in V$ and amount x, i.e., a path $(u_0 = u_s, u_1, \ldots, u_\ell = u_r)$, minimizing the aggregated fees $\sum_{i=1}^{\ell} f_{u_{i-1}, u_i}(x + \phi_{i-1})$, where ϕ_i, $i = 0, \ldots, \ell - 1$, is the aggregated fees that nodes $u_{i+1}, u_{i+2}, \ldots, u_{\ell-1}$ charge. Since the receiver u_ℓ is the last node in the path, $\phi_{\ell-1} = 0$. We use the notation $\mathsf{shortestPath}_G(u_s, u_r, x) \mapsto \{u_0 = u_s, u_1, \ldots, u_{\ell-1}, u_\ell = u_r\}$ to describe the functionality that takes two nodes u_s and u_r and a transaction amount x as inputs and outputs the cheapest path between those two nodes.

Network model. We assume a synchronous network model, i.e., there exists some known finite time bound Δ and the adversary cannot delay delivery of any message sent by honest parties for a larger than Δ time period. We further assume all users only have local knowledge of the topology of the payment channel network with the addition of an estimate of the degree of their neighbours, i.e., each node u only knows their set of immediate neighbours and an estimate of the degree of each neighbour in that set.

3   Ideal and Practical Privacy Notions

We first define an ideal notion of privacy for route discovery and outline how to construct protocols achieving this notion, albeit very impractical ones.

Ideal privacy for PCNs means that each party only learns the bare minimum information required to participate in the transaction: its predecessor and successor on the payment path and the amount to be transferred. This information is minimal, assuming that users know at the very least the current balances on their own channels (as in the Lightning Network). In this case they learn the predecessor, successor, and amount of a transaction they were involved in by simply comparing the balances on their channels before and after the transaction.

We only consider path finding protocols Π, which always find the cheapest path. Defining ideal privacy for protocols that do not necessarily output the cheapest path is more complex because the privacy loss depends on the discovered path. We also only consider passive adversaries, that is, an adversary can corrupt users and learn their internal state, but not make them deviate from honestly executing the protocol (e.g., by providing wrong or inconsistent input).

Our privacy notion is inspired by the Indistinguishability under Chosen Topology Attack (IND-CTA) security definition from work on topology-hiding multiparty computation [17], and it is defined as follows: We consider an adversary that initially chooses two networks and a transaction for each of them, and also a subset of nodes to corrupt. We then require that given the view of the corrupted nodes after the path finding protocols has been executed on one of the two networks, an adversary cannot determine which. Of course we must require that the adversary chooses the networks, transactions, and corrupted nodes such that the corrupted nodes have the same neighbours and fee functions, and the final output of the corrupted nodes (either they are not on the path, and if, they learn their predecessor, successor and amount to be transferred) is identical in both cases; otherwise distinguishing between both networks is trivial for any protocol as one can distinguish using just the initial view and final output of the protocol. We give a more formal definition below.

3.1 The Ideal Privacy Security Game

We consider a security game involving an adversary $\mathcal{A}$ against a path-finding protocol Π. The protocol is run by the players V on a network $G = (V, E)$. Each player initially gets as inputs its neighbours and fee functions.

When the protocol starts, two players u_s, u_r get as extra input (u_s, u_r, x) informing them they are, respectively, the sender and the receiver of some amount x. The correctness we require from our protocol is that every $u \notin$ shortestPath$_{G^b}(u_s^b, u_r^b, x)$ outputs $\bot$, while every u on the path outputs its predecessor, successor and amount they transfer in this optimal path. The security game goes as follows:

- $\mathcal{A}$ chooses the following for $i \in \{0, 1\}$:
    1. A network (directed graph) $G^i = (V^i, E^i)$, where every edge (u, v) is labelled with a fee function $f_{u,v}^i(.)$.
    2. A sender and receiver pair (u_s^i, u_r^i) and amount x.
  $\mathcal{A}$ chooses a subset $S \subset V^0 \cap V^1$ of nodes to corrupt. These nodes must have the same neighbourhood and fee functions in both networks, and their final output (predecessor, successor and amount) must be identical.
- We choose a random bit $b \in \{0, 1\}$ and run Π on G^b (with input (u_s^b, u_r^b, x)).
- $\mathcal{A}$ gets the transcripts of the corrupted nodes.
- $\mathcal{A}$ outputs a bit b'. If $b' = b$, $\mathcal{A}$ wins the game.

Let us call a path finding protocol Π ϵ-private if $\mathcal{A}$ wins the above game with probability at most $1/2 + \epsilon$, and private if it is ϵ secure for some negligible ϵ.

3.2 Protocols with Ideal Privacy from MPC

If we assume a trusted third party $\mathcal{T}$ (that cannot be corrupted by the adversary and has a channel to every node in the network), the design of a private path-finding protocol is not challenging. In particular, each party in the network can send their data to $\mathcal{T}$, which will then locally compute the cheapest path and send the output, i.e., either $\bot$ or the amount, successor and predecessor in the cheapest path, to every party.

To design a protocol without a trusted third party, we can instantiate $\mathcal{T}$ using a multi-party computation (MPC) protocol. As here the users need to share pairwise channels, they need to know about the other users, which means in our security definition we need the users V^1 and V^2 in the two networks to be identical $V^1 \equiv V^2$. Our security notion is inspired by notions from topology-hiding MPC, where the goal is to hide the topology of the communication channels. Instead, we assume pairwise channels but want to hide the topology of the payment network. But of course we could also use a topology-hiding MPC to instantiate $\mathcal{T}$, in which case we would only require communication channels between users that share a channel. In this setting, one could potentially also achieve security when $V^1 \neq V^2$ as nodes would only talk to their neighbours, and for the corrupted nodes, these are identical.

3.3   A Practical Notion of Privacy

Here we outline the following game as well as some metrics to measure the privacy of any route discovery protocol over an arbitrary network. The game is played with an adversary $\mathcal{A}$ over an arbitrary network $G = (V, E)$. The adversary $\mathcal{A}$ is given some budget $B \in \mathbb{N}$ and $\mathcal{A}$ can corrupt (as defined in Sect. 3.1) any number of nodes in the network such that the total number of edges incident to these nodes is no greater than B. Here we emphasise two pertinent aspects of the corruption process: first, when $\mathcal{A}$ corrupts a node, *all* of the node's channels must be added to the total count, and second, we do not double count channels that have already been accounted for (which is the case where $\mathcal{A}$ corrupts two neighbouring nodes). The constraint on the number of edges the adversary can create captures the notion that creating new nodes (i.e., wallets) in a PCN is cheap, however, creating new edges (i.e., channels) comes with some fixed cost.

   We denote by Π a route discovery protocol run by a pair of honest nodes (a source and a sink) over the graph G which may contain outputs (henceforth called messages) for both honest and adversarial nodes in the process of running the protocol. The goal of the adversary is to correctly identify the source or sink of Π upon receiving a set of messages from Π.

Estimators. Let $\mathcal{M}$ denote the space of all messages adversarial nodes may receive in process of honest nodes running Π. An *estimator* is simply a function g that takes as input a set of messages M such that each message in the set is from $\mathcal{M}$ and outputs a pair of nodes in V. That is, given a set of messages from Π, the adversary outputs a guess of the nodes that are the source and sink of the route finding protocol Π.

Privacy Metrics. We adopt a similar approach as in [30] and use *recall* to measure the privacy our of route discovery protocols. Recall is a common performance metric used in information retrieval to evaluate estimators in classification settings. Let $M_{(u,v)}$ denote the set of messages the adversary receives that originates from a pair of honest nodes $u, v \in V$ running an instance of Π. The recall of an estimator g is defined as the number of classifications for the pair (u, v) where either u is classified as the source or v is classified as the sink over the total number of instances where Π is run between u as source and v as sink. Formally,

$$Rec_{g,(u,v)} = \mathbb{1}\{g(M_{(u,v)}) = (u, \cdot) \vee g(M_{(u,v)}) = (\cdot, v)\} \tag{1}$$

We note that it is common to average as well as macro-average the recall over all honest nodes to get the macro-averaged expected recall $\mathbb{E}[Rec_g] = \frac{1}{|V \times V|} \sum_{(u,v) \in V \times V} \mathbb{E}[Rec_{g,(u,v)}]$.

4   A Family of Protocols

Consider a sender $u_s \in V$ who wants to transfer x coins to a receiver $u_r \in V$ and thus needs to know a path for the transaction, ideally the cheapest one. Next, we present a family of exploratory route discovery protocols that provide solutions to this problem. At its core, these protocols employ local probing: nodes send exploratory messages (originating at the sender and receiver) to their neighbours who in turn propagate them. Our protocols only require nodes to know their incident channels, and some also require a degree estimate of each neighbour.

The protocols run in three phases, (1) *exploration*, which runs until the first node receives both messages, i.e., the one originating at the sender and the receiver, (2) *notification*, where the relevant nodes are informed that a path was found and (3) *stopping*, where the nodes currently participating in the exploration phase are informed so they do not propagate messages further. Phase (1) is running slow, i.e., messages are propagated with some delay which should be significantly larger than the typical network delay, while in phase (2) and (3) messages are relayed immediately. The main reason we need Phase (1) to be slow is so the messages in the stopping phase can easily "catch up" to the nodes which are in the exploration phase. This further helps to improve correctness and even privacy.

Our protocols differ only on the proportion of nodes each node forwards the message to. On one extreme, we have Forward-to-All that involves nodes sending exploratory messages to all their neighbours, where each message is delayed for some time proportional to the fees. As a result, the optimal path is always discovered, and moreover, the first path that is found is also the cheapest one. On the other end of the spectrum, we have a more parsimonious protocol, namely Degree-Proportional Random Walk, that only involves sending messages to one neighbour. In this case, we expect fewer nodes to be involved in the discovery process but the optimal path may not be discovered.

As the protocols in the family are similar, we first present a generic overview of Forward-to-All, and then briefly describe how to modify it to get Degree-Proportional Random Walk. We then suggest some improvements to boost the privacy of this family of protocols. For clarity of exposition, we leave the detailed description of our protocols to Appendix A in our extended technical report [4].

4.1   Forward-To-All Exploration Phase

In this protocol, both the sender u_s and receiver u_r create messages with a special identifier (so intermediate nodes who receive messages from u_s and u_r can associate them together), an amount x that u_s wants to send to u_r, as well as a tag Sender or Receiver which specifies whether they are sending or receiving the transaction. The sender and receiver then propagate these messages through the graph by sending these messages to all their neighbours who then in turn propagate the message to all their neighbours. At every step of the propagation, the nodes update the transaction amount adding their desired fees for routing the transaction, and only forward the message after some time period has elapsed that is proportional to their desired fees. All nodes store the messages they received, as well as an id (not to be confused with identifier) of the node that sent them the message. The precise rule and fee computation differs, however, depending on whether a node gets a message from the sender or the receiver.

Fee Computation for Messages from Receiver. Apart from the receiver, each intermediate node u_i upon receiving a message with the Receiver tag from another node u_{i+1}, updates the transaction amount to add a fee for sending the transaction amount along the channel (u_i, u_{i+1}). This is to reflect the fee u_i would charge for forwarding the transaction to u_{i+1}. Figure 1 illustrates this process where the receiver u_r sends a message with the transaction amount x to all of u_r's neighbours. Upon receiving the message from u_r, u_{i+1} adds a fee of $f_{u_{i+1},u_r}(x)$ to the transaction x. Messages with this updated transaction amount of $x + f_{u_{i+1},u_r}(x)$ would be sent to all of u_{i+1}'s neighbours.

Fee Computation for Messages from Sender. The fee computation for the sender and the nodes that receive messages with the Sender tag is trickier. Although the sender knows the transaction amount x, they do not know the total amount they would have to send at the end of the protocol as it would include the fees along the path which is still unknown. Thus the sender would have to add an estimate of the total fee of the path, δ, to the transaction amount in their initial message. Each node that receives a message with the Sender tag, updates the transaction amount to subtract a fee for each edge they propagate the message to. This is to account for the fees the node will charge to forward the transaction. For instance in Fig. 1, the node u_{i-1}, upon receiving a message with transaction amount $x + \delta$, subtracts $f_{u_{i-1},v}(x + \delta)$ from the transaction amount before forwarding the message with this new transaction amount to the node v. The node u_{i-1} does the same but subtracts $f_{u_{i-1},u_i}(x + \delta)$ from the transaction amount before sending the message to u_i.

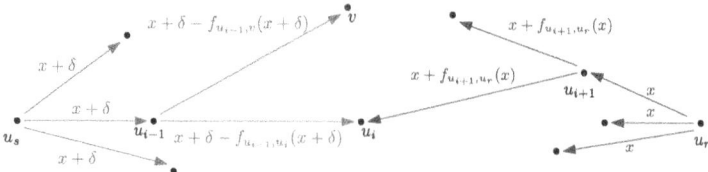

Fig. 1. Propagating exploratory messages from sender and receiver in the Forward-to-All protocol. Each directed edge (u, v) is labelled with the transaction amount in the message that u sends to v.

Delay Time Computation. Let d be a publicly available delay function that maps fees to delay times. Let $d_{u,v}$ denote the delay time for the total fee for sending an arbitrary but fixed amount x over the channel (u,v), i.e., $d_{u,v} = d(f_{u,v}(x))$. Every node (except the sender and receiver) computes a delay time with the delay function d and the fees computed as described above. In Fig. 1 for instance, since the sender u_s and receiver u_r do not have fees, u_s and u_r will send their exploratory messages immediately. The node u_{i+1} will wait d_{u_{i+1},u_r} before forwarding the message to u_i, and u_{i-1} will wait d_{u_{i-1},u_i} before forwarding the message to u_i.

4.2   Forward-to-All Notification Phase

Upon receiving a new message, a node checks its identifier with the identifiers of the stored messages to see if the message identifiers can be associated together. When a node u_i finds an association of identifiers that indicate two messages are from the sender and receiver of a given sender-receiver pair, u_i begins a process of notifying both sender and receiver that a path exists between them. We denote the two nodes that sent u_i the associated sender and receiver messages by u_{i-1} and u_{i+1}, respectively. We also denote the transaction amounts in these messages as x_s and x_r respectively. Then, u_i immediately sends u_{i-1} a message with the identifier and amount x_s (resp. x_r to u_{i+1}). Both u_{i-1} and u_{i+1} then identify the nodes that sent them the messages with the same identifier and forward these messages to these nodes. Refer to Fig. 2 for an illustration of the process.

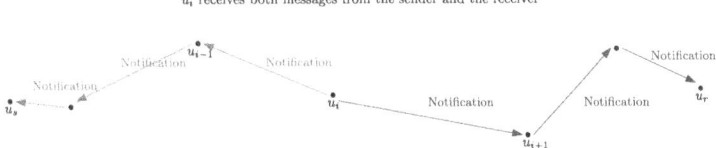

Fig. 2. Sending informative messages back to sender and receiver.

This process repeats itself until the sender and receiver get the message. At this point, the sender has enough information to proceed with the transaction. In particular, the sender can easily compute the total fee of the path from $x, x+\delta, x_s$ and x_r (communicated by the receiver).

Optimality of the Discovered Route. Using delay guarantees that in Forward-to-All, either the notification message corresponding to the shortest path (subject to the accuracy of the fee estimation of the sender) always reaches the sender first, or the sender can find out if someone on the path deviated from the delay protocol. For example, let L^* be the optimal path from u_s to u_r and L' be a strictly more expensive path. Suppose several adversarial nodes on L' immediately forward messages without delay and as a result, u_s receives the notification message from an intermediate node on L' first. Since u_s knows the time they sent the first exploratory messages, u_s can extract the fees from the message received and check if the total delay time on this path is larger than the difference of the current time and the time u_s sent the first exploratory messages.

4.3 Forward-to-All Stopping Phase

When both sender and receiver are aware that a path exists between them and the sender is satisfied with the cost of the path, both sender and receiver can stop the protocol by sending a *stop message* with their identifiers to the nodes they sent the exploratory messages to. Nodes that have not yet sent the exploratory message to their neighbours would, upon receiving the stop message with the identifier, stop the message propagation. Nodes that have already send the exploratory messages would forward the stop message to the neighbours they sent the exploratory message to. This process is fast and thus will reach the slow propagation of the exploratory messages.

4.4 Degree-Proportional Random Walk

The Degree-Proportional Random Walk protocol is analagous to the Forward-to-All protocol with the exception that each node only forwards the message to *one* neighbour. Specifically, each node chooses a neighbour to forward the message to randomly with probability proportional to its degree. Thus, the messages are propagated according to two weighted random walks on the network, one starting from the sender and the other from the receiver, with the weight of any directed edge (u, v) corresponding to the degree of v. We observe that due to the probabilistic nature of Degree-Proportional Random Walk, optimality of the discovered path is not guaranteed unlike in Forward-to-All.

4.5 Improving Privacy

From the messages that originate at the sender and receiver and propagate through the network, we only need the property that one can efficiently recognise when a message from both is received. The simplest solution is to simply sample some random nonce I and propagate it together with a one bit tag specifying whether it is a sender or receiver originating message.

These messages are, however, completely linkable. This is unfortunate as it means that even if many path finding protocols are executed over the network at the same time, a potential adversary that controls some nodes in the network will still recognize with certainty which messages belong to the same path finding request. Thus, we do not leverage the fact that many protocols are running at the same time to improve privacy.

Making Messages Unlinkeable using Bilinear Maps. We can improve unlinkability by using a bilinear map [12] $e : G_1 \times G_2 \to G_T$ (such a map allows "for one multiplication in the exponent" as $e(g_1^a, g_2^b) = g_T^{a \cdot b}$ where g_1, g_2, g_T are generators of G_1, G_2, G_T) for a group where the DDH assumption holds in G_1

and G_2. Concretely, the sender and receiver sample a random x and then the sender, for every outgoing edge, samples a random r and propagates $(g_1^{x \cdot r} g_1^r)$ as the identifier, while the receiver propagates $(g_2^{r'/x}, g_2^{r'})$.

A node that receives $(g_1^{x \cdot r}, g_1^r)$ (similarly for the receiver tuples) propagates it only after re-randomizing it by exponentiating both elements with some fresh r' which gives a tuple $(g_1^{x \cdot r''}, g_1^{r''})$ where $r'' = r \cdot r'$. This way an adversary (who does not know x) will not be able to distinguish a pair of tuples of the form $(g_1^{x \cdot r}, g_1^r), (g_1^{x \cdot r'}, g_1^{r'})$ from random, and thus cannot decide whether they belong to the same instantiation of the path finding protocol. We stress that the unlinkeability is limited as it only holds if the adversary has access to messages originating either only at the sender or only at the receiver. This is inherent as we need parties who receive tuples (a, b) and (a', b') originating at both to efficiently recognize a path is found by checking whether $e(a, a') = e(b, b')$ as

$$(a, b) = (g_1^{x \cdot r}, g_1^r), (a', b') = (g_2^{r'/x}, g_2^{r'}) \Rightarrow e(a, a') = e(b, b') = g_T^{r \cdot r'}$$

Quantising the Transaction and Encrypting the Fees. Messages that contain the exact transaction amount are also linkable, even when fees are added, as the fees are typically miniscule compared to the transaction amount. To reduce this linkability (at the cost of fee accuracy), the sender and receiver can quantise the amount of the transaction by rounding it up to a predefined value (for instance, a power of 2). Then, instead of adding the fees to the quantised transaction amount, nodes encrypt their fees using an additive homomorphic encryption scheme such as additive ElGamal encryption. If several protocols are running simultaneously on the network, nodes will see many messages with the same quantised transaction amount, effectively reducing linkeability.

5   Analysis and Evaluation

In this section, we empirically study the *efficiency, optimality* and *privacy* of our family of protocols described in Sect. 4 on a recent snapshot (September 2021) of the Lightning network [9], which comprises of 13780 nodes and 63518 channels. We parameterise our family of protocols by $\beta \in (0, 1]$ which represents the proportion (rounded up to the nearest integer) of neighbouring nodes in the Degree-Proportional Random Walk protocol that any node chooses to pass messages to. We note that $\beta = 1$ corresponds to Forward-to-All. In our experiments using the Lightning network, we chose 1000 random pairs of sender and receivers and ran our protocols for selected values of β with these random pairs. Our choices of β can be seen in Table 1 which also presents a summary of our results.

5.1   Efficiency

We measure the efficiency of our protocols by the communication overhead. This is measured by the average number of involved nodes in one route discovery attempt, i.e., the number of nodes that receive at least one message in any given run of our protocol. As we can see from the second column of Table 1, the expected number of involved nodes in a single route discovery attempt ranges from 16 (0.1% of the network) to 459 (3% of the network) with the smallest value corresponding to sending messages to just 1 neighbour and the largest value corresponding to Forward-to-All.

We are also interested to see how our protocols perform as the Lightning Network scales in size. To do so, we perform simulations of our protocols on Barabási–Albert (BA) graphs. The BA model [7] is a popular algorithm to create scale free networks using a preferential attachment mechanism. Many real world networks, including the Lightning network, are characterized as scale-free [6,22]. Figure 3 presents the average communication overhead as well as the average ratio of the length of the found path over the optimal path. Our empirical simulations show that the communication overhead for the BA graph with 20000 nodes is similarly low (2%) when compared to the Lightning Network. We finally complement our empirical analysis with a theorem (proof in Appendix D of [4]) which states that for BA graphs the communication overhead of the Degree-Proportional Random Walk protocol scales sublinearly in the number of nodes n.

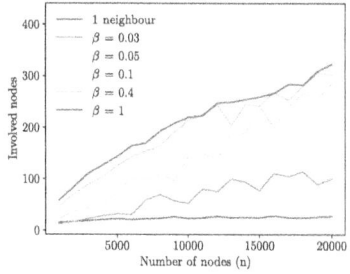
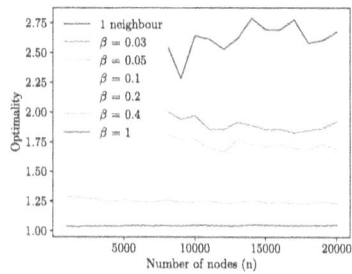

(a) Communication overhead

(b) Ratio of length of found path to length of optimal path

Fig. 3. Efficiency and optimality of our routing algorithms on Barabasi-Albert graphs

Theorem 1. *The expected number of involved nodes in the Degree-Proportional Random Walk protocol on a BA graph with n nodes is $O(\sqrt{n} \cdot \frac{\log^2 n}{\log \log n})$.*

5.2 Optimality

The fee-proportional delay function that we described in the Notification Phase of Sect. 4 guarantees that the first message that reaches the sender and the receiver corresponds to the shortest path in Forward-to-All. There is no such guarantee, however, for our protocols in the case where $\beta < 1$ due to its probabilistic nature. To measure the optimality of the discovered path for our protocols when $\beta < 1$, we look at the average ratio of the discovered path length over the length of the shortest path for various choices of β in the 1000 runs as described above. In the third column of Table 1, we observe that protocols with $\beta < 1$ return longer paths on average compared to Forward-to-All, as expected. However, even for small values of β, e.g., $\beta = 0.01$, the average ratio is no more than 2.

Table 1. Summary of the efficiency, optimality and privacy of our protocols on the Lightning Network, run with budget 0.15 in our estimation of recall.

β	# involved nodes	$\frac{len(\text{found path})}{len(\text{shortest path})}$	Recall
only 1 neighbour	16	3.36	0.129
1%	34	1.54	0.129
10%	86	1.14	0.191
20%	133	1.10	0.249
40%	277	1.07	0.29
80%	431	1.01	0.371
100%	459	1	0.43

5.3 Privacy

We empirically measure the privacy of our protocols using the notion of recall as defined in Sect. 3.3. We stress that there are two integral components of our notion of recall. The first is the corruption strategy of the adversary, which is used by the adversary to choose nodes up to the corruption budget B to corrupt. The second is the choice of estimator the adversary uses to guess the source and sink of an instance of the route discovery protocol. We will first describe 3 corruption strategies, and then define the first spy estimator. We further show that the first spy estimator is in general a good guessing heuristic for the adversary.

Corruption strategies. The first strategy, called *random corruption*, involves choosing nodes at random in the network to corrupt (and all their edges) until the total number of corrupted edges is less the adversarial budget B. In the second strategy, termed *well-connected corruption*, we first sort the nodes in the network based on their degree and then sequentially corrupt nodes in descending order to their degree until the budget is depleted. The intuition behind this strategy is that high-degree nodes tend to serve as hubs that route a large proportion of the transactions in the Lightning Network [1,9]. However, this strategy assumes the adversary has *full* knowledge of the degree of all nodes in the network, which is not the case in private PCNs. To achieve similar results with only local knowledge of the graph, we introduce our third strategy, called *random hub corruption*. In this strategy, the adversary starts with a random node, but instead of corrupting the node, it randomly corrupts one of its neighbours. This process continues until the budget is depleted. Intuitively, the majority of nodes in a PCN are users that are connected to high-degree hub nodes. As such, there is a high chance that a random neighbour of a selected node is a hub node. An algorithmic description of all 3 corruption strategies is given in Appendix B.1 in our extended version [4].

First spy estimator. The choice of estimator in our experiments is the *first-spy estimator* [30], which is simply guessing the first honest node that passes a message from the protocol to any adversarial node as the source. We justify our choice of estimator with the following lemma (proof in Appendix B.2 in our extended version [4]) which shows that the first spy estimator is optimal in a restricted setting where messages are not re-randomised, sender and receivers are randomly chosen, and timing assumptions are not taken into account.

Lemma 1. *For Degree-Proportional Random Walk (without re-randomisation), when sender-receiver pairs are chosen uniformly and independently from honest nodes and both propagate their messages independently and randomly, the first spy estimator is the Maximum a Posteriori (MAP) estimator.*

We stress that our theoretical results hold in a restricted setting which does not mirror the realistic setting which we run our experiments on. Indeed in Appendix B.4 in our full paper [4], we highlight some limitations to the first spy estimator under more realistic assumptions. Nevertheless, we believe it is a good first step guessing heuristic and we leave developing stronger theoretical results in the realistic setting as an interesting direction of future work.

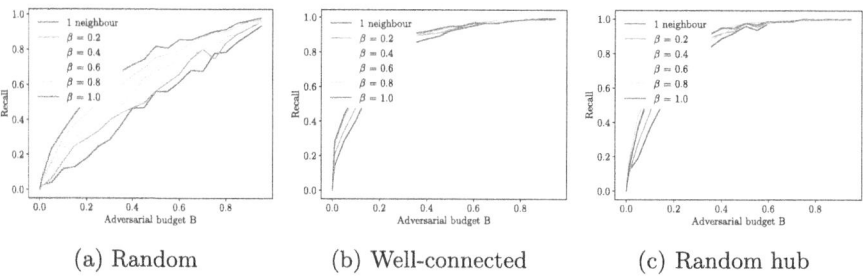

(a) Random   (b) Well-connected   (c) Random hub

Fig. 4. Average recall over 1000 random runs of the protocols in the Lightning network for different corruption strategies

Average Recall. Figure 4 presents the average recall for each of the corruption strategies given the first spy estimator over 1000 runs of each protocol. The well-connected and random hub corruption strategies perform strictly better in terms of recall for all β values compared to random corruption. Moreover, random hub corruption performs almost equally well compared to well-connected corruption and thus is a good choice to use in practice when there is only partial information known about node degrees. Finally, our plots show that the adversary achieves the highest average recall with Forward-to-All and the lowest with Degree-Proportional Random Walk.

Optimality and Efficiency/Privacy Trade-off. In Forward-to-All, nodes forward messages to all their neighbours, and as a result a large fraction of the network is involved in the route-discovery process, which as we see in Sect. 5.1 and Sect. 5.3 has negative impact on the efficiency and privacy of the protocol. On the other hand, reaching every node is the only way to guarantee the shortest path is always found. In Degree-Proportional Random Walk, each node just forwards messages to one neighbour and thus only a very small fraction of the graph is involved. However, as we see from Sect. 5.1 the paths are longer on average. We note that β values in between these extremes allow users to trade off between optimality and efficiency/privacy.

6 Related Work

Existing work on route discovery in PCNs can be broadly classified into two categories: solutions which focus on efficiency, and solutions which focus on privacy.

On the efficiency front, Flare [21] and SilentWhispers [15] route payments through highly connected nodes to improve the scalability of route discovery. SpeedyMurmurs [24] and VOUTE [23] employ a similar routing technique called prefix embeddings, which makes the process even faster. These solutions require nodes to have global knowledge of the network, whereas we present a protocol that does not require any knowledge of the PCN topology. Spider Network [25] splits payments into smaller units and routes them over multiple paths using waterfilling. However, this does not guarantee the discovery of an optimal path, whereas our protocol guarantees optimality by adding a fee-proportional delay in the route discovery process. Flash [31] uses a modified max-flow algorithm to find the optimal path, but also requires nodes to have global knowledge of the network. Perun [2] avoids routing through intermediaries altogether by introducing the notion of virtual channels. However, this does not solve the route discovery problem.

On the privacy front, MAPPCN [29] focuses on anonymity and privacy during transaction execution, but does not address the issue of route discovery as users are required to know the payment path. LightPIR [19] uses private information retrieval to perform private route discovery efficiently, but does not account for optimality in the case of private channels. In contrast, our protocols employ local probing, thus our solutions are still optimal even with private channels. Recently, [27] uses MPC to perform privacy preserving routing of transactions, however it is only limited to fixed star graph topologies. Finally, [13,14] present routing protocols that also do not assume information about the topology of the involved PCN, but lack formal definitions of privacy and evaluation metrics.

7   Conclusion

We presented route discovery protocols that are suitable for private PCNs. We first formalized the ideal notion of privacy in PCNs, and showed that ideal privacy is feasible yet inefficient. We then presented a family of practical route discovery protocols which trade off between optimality and efficiency/privacy. To evaluate their privacy leakage, we introduced and leveraged a novel practical notion of privacy.

The simulation of our protocols on the Lighting Network and Barabási–Albert graphs validates our approach, unveiling the aforementioned trade-off. We also observe that our protocols involve a very small fraction of the network on average, showcasing we can indeed design efficient and private routing algorithms that rely on minimal to no assumptions on the topology of the PCN with almost optimal results. From our simulations on Lightning we further deduce that an effective strategy for an adversary is to connect with high-degree nodes, i.e., payment hubs. We also discover through our empirical simulations on large Barabási–Albert graphs that the efficiency and privacy of our algorithms perform much better on average compared to our theoretical upper bound, which demonstrates that our algorithms also scale efficiently with the size of PCNs.

Acknowledgements. This work was supported in part by the ERC CoG 863818 (ForM-SMArt), Austrian Science Fund (FWF) 10.55776/COE12, and MOE-T2EP20122-0014 (Data-Driven Distributed Algorithms) grants.

References

1. Lightning network search and analysis engine. https://1ml.com/
2. Perun: Virtual payment hubs over cryptocurrencies. In: IEEE S&P (2017)
3. Akavia, A., LaVigne, R., Moran, T.: Topology-hiding computation on all graphs. J. Cryptol., 176–227 (2020)
4. Avarikioti, Z., Bastankhah, M., Maddah-Ali, M.A., Pietrzak, K., Svoboda, J., Yeo, M.: Route discovery in private payment channel networks. IACR Cryptol. ePrint Arch., 1539 (2021)
5. Avarikioti, Z., Kogias, E.K., Wattenhofer, R., Zindros, D.: Brick: asynchronous incentive-compatible payment channels. In: FC (2021)
6. Barabási, A.L., Albert, R., Jeong, H.: Scale-free characteristics of random networks: the topology of the world-wide web. Phys. A: Stat. Mech. Its Appl., 69–77 (2000)
7. Barabási, A.L., Pósfai, M.: Network Science. Cambridge University Press, Cambridge (2016). http://barabasi.com/networksciencebook/
8. Bitcoin community: Bitcoin core 0.21.0-based taproot client 0.1. https://bitcointaproot.cc/ (2021)
9. Decker, C.: Lightning network research; topology, datasets. https://github.com/lnresearch/topology. Accessed 01 Oct 2022
10. Decker, C., Russell, R., Osuntokun, O.: eltoo: A simple layer2 protocol for bitcoin (2018). https://blockstream.com/eltoo.pdf
11. Decker, C., Wattenhofer, R.: A fast and scalable payment network with bitcoin duplex micropayment channels. In: Stabilization, Safety, and Security of Distributed Systems, pp. 3–18. Springer (2015)

12. Galbraith, S.D., Paterson, K.G., Smart, N.P.: Pairings for cryptographers. Discret. Appl. Math. **156**(16), 3113–3121 (2008)
13. Grunspan, C., Lehéricy, G., Pérez-Marco, R.: Ant routing scalability for the lightning network. CoRR abs/2002.01374 (2020)
14. Grunspan, C., Pérez-Marco, R.: Ant routing algorithm for the lightning network. CoRR abs/1807.00151 (2018)
15. Malavolta, G., Moreno-Sanchez, P., Kate, A., Maffei, M.: SilentWhispers: enforcing security and privacy in decentralized credit networks. In: NDSS (2017)
16. Maxwell, G., Poelstra, A., Seurin, Y., Wuille, P.: Simple Schnorr multi-signatures with applications to bitcoin. Des. Codes Cryptogr. **87**(9), 2139–2164 (2019)
17. Moran, T., Orlov, I., Richelson, S.: Topology-hiding computation. In: Dodis, Y., Nielsen, J.B. (eds.) Theory of Cryptography: 12th Theory of Cryptography Conference, TCC 2015, Warsaw, Poland, March 23-25, 2015, Proceedings, Part I, pp. 159–181. Springer, Berlin, Heidelberg (2015). https://doi.org/10.1007/978-3-662-46494-6_8
18. Nakamoto, S.: Bitcoin: a peer-to-peer electronic cash system (2008)
19. Pietrzak, K., Salem, I., Schmid, S., Yeo, M.: LightPIR: privacy-preserving route discovery for payment channel networks. In: Proceedings of IFIP Networking (2021)
20. Poon, J., Dryja, T.: The bitcoin lightning network: Scalable off-chain instant payments (2016)
21. Prihodko, P., Zhigulin, S., Sahno, M., Ostrovskiy, A., Osuntokun, O.: Flare: an approach to routing in lightning network. White Paper (2016)
22. Rohrer, E., Malliaris, J., Tschorsch, F.: Discharged payment channels: quantifying the lightning network's resilience to topology-based attacks. In: 2019 IEEE EuroS&P Workshop. IEEE (2019)
23. Roos, S., Beck, M., Strufe, T.: Voute-virtual overlays using tree embeddings. arXiv 1601.06119 (2016)
24. Roos, S., Moreno-Sanchez, P., Kate, A., Goldberg, I.: Settling payments fast and private: efficient decentralized routing for path-based transactions. arXiv: 1709.05748 (2017)
25. Sivaraman, V., Venkatakrishnan, S.B., Alizadeh, M., Fanti, G., Viswanath, P.: Routing cryptocurrency with the spider network. In: Proceedings of 17th ACM Workshop on Hot Topics in Networks, pp. 29–35 (2018)
26. Spilman, J.: Anti dos for tx replacement. https://lists.linuxfoundation.org/pipermail/bitcoin-dev/2013-April/002433.html. Accessed 22 Nov 2020
27. Tiwari, S., Yeo, M., Avarikioti, Z., Salem, I., Pietrzak, K., Schmid, S.: Wiser: increasing throughput in payment channel networks with transaction aggregation. CoRR abs/2205.11597 (2022)
28. Tochner, S., Zohar, A., Schmid, S.: Route hijacking and dos in off-chain networks. In: AFT (2020)
29. Tripathy, S., Mohanty, S.K.: MAPPCN: multi-hop anonymous and privacy-preserving payment channel network. In: Bernhard, M., et al. (eds.) Financial Cryptography and Data Security: FC 2020 International Workshops, AsiaUSEC, CoDeFi, VOTING, and WTSC, Kota Kinabalu, Malaysia, February 14, 2020, Revised Selected Papers, pp. 481–495. Springer International Publishing, Cham (2020). https://doi.org/10.1007/978-3-030-54455-3_34
30. Venkatakrishnan, S.B., Fanti, G., Viswanath, P.: Dandelion: redesigning the bitcoin network for anonymity. Proc. ACM Meas. Anal. Comput. Syst. **1**(1) (2017)
31. Wang, P., Xu, H., Jin, X., Wang, T.: Flash: efficient dynamic routing for offchain networks. In: International Conference on Emerging Networking Experiments and Technologies, pp. 370–381 (2019)

A Comparative Study of Rust Smart Contract SDKs for Application-Specific Blockchains

Jan Vanhoof$^{(\boxtimes)}$ and Tom Van Cutsem

DistriNet, KU Leuven, Leuven, Belgium
{jan.vanhoof1,tom.vancutsem}@kuleuven.be

Abstract. This paper reports on a comparative study of two recent software development kits (SDKs) for so-called "Application-specific Blockchains" that support development of smart contracts in general-purpose languages. Specifically we report on the similarities and differences between Cosmwasm and Polkadot smart contracts written in the Rust programming language.

To help guide our comparative study we start from a representative set of Solidity smart contracts, namely an English auction contract and a Non-Fungible Token (NFT) contract. Both contracts offer insights into the requirements that must be offered by a smart contract SDK. We develop a concrete baseline for comparison between Cosmwasm and Polkadot by translating the two Solidity contracts into Rust, using the respective SDKs.

Our comparison defines a starting point for better understanding the design space of smart contract SDKs, and what the advantages and disadvantages are of different API interfaces and execution models.

Keywords: Smart contracts · API design · Rust

1 Introduction

The Ethereum [5] blockchain pioneered the concept of a "programmable" blockchain by allowing users to deploy small programs on the blockchain, so-called *smart contracts*. Such smart contracts have been widely adopted for use cases ranging from creating custom (fungible and non-fungible) tokens, auctions, decentralized exchanges and community-controlled token vaults (DAOs).

Despite the widespread adoption, smart contracts in Ethereum remain mostly limited to small-scale programs (both in program size as well as in runtime execution). The most widely used smart contract language, Solidity, is a domain-specific language designed specifically to write logic to execute on the Ethereum Virtual Machine (EVM). Despite its domain-specific design, programs written in Solidity are prone to a wide range of vulnerabilities, many of which have led to large financial losses [2].

© The Author(s), under exclusive license to Springer Nature Switzerland AG 2025
J. Garcia-Alfaro et al. (Eds.): ESORICS 2024 Workshops, LNCS 15263, pp. 224–241, 2025.
https://doi.org/10.1007/978-3-031-82349-7_16

In addition, Ethereum has been a victim of its own success, with network congestion leading to more and more smart contracts competing for limited transaction throughput and block storage, leading to large "gas fees" (transaction costs), rendering many use cases too expensive to run as contracts on the blockchain.

In response to these issues, *application-specific* blockchains, also called "Appchains", have arisen. In contrast to Ethereum where all contracts share a single common blockchain, appchains support multiple independent blockchains that each support one, or a few, application use cases. To avoid weakened security or interoperability, most appchain platforms offer built-in ways for these separate chains to interconnect, enabling shared security and transferability across chains, to varying degrees.

Another distinguishing feature of appchain platforms compared to Ethereum and its EVM, is their support for a general-purpose runtime environment to host and execute smart contract code. Here, WebAssembly [9] is a widely used choice because of its performance, portability across operating systems and instruction sets, sandboxed execution environment, and common compilation target for a large number of source languages.

WebAssembly is a portable bytecode format, but does not natively support the features required to implement smart contracts and to interact with a blockchain environment. Appchains must thus make an API available to the WebAssembly code, and this API is usually exposed to the higher-level source language in the form of a Software Development Kit (SDK) that helps developers design, deploy and debug high-level contract code. The Rust programming language is a widely adopted language for this purpose, because of its combination of generating efficient code, small binaries, and expressive type system and memory-safe programming model.

In this paper we perform a comparative study of the execution layer for the two most popular appchain platforms, namely Cosmwasm and Polkadot.[1] Both appchains offer a Rust SDK for developing WebAssembly-based smart contracts (Sect. 2). To help guide our comparative study we start from a representative set of Solidity smart contracts, namely an English auction contract and a Non-Fungible Token (NFT) contract (Sect. 3). Both contracts offer insights into the requirements that must be offered by a smart contract SDK (Sect. 4). We develop a concrete baseline for comparison between Cosmwasm and Polkadot by translating the two Solidity contracts into Rust, using the respective appchain SDKs (Sect. 5). Our comparison provides a starting point for better understanding the design space of smart contract SDKs, and what the advantages and disadvantages are of different API interfaces and execution models (Sect. 6).

---

[1] One metric for popularity is to look at active contributors to code repositories on GitHub, linked to appchain-related projects. According to Electric Capital's yearly Web3 Developer Report at https://www.developerreport.com/ the top four projects based on total number of contributors on Dec. 31, 2023 were Ethereum, Polkadot, Polygon and Cosmos. Of these four only Polkadot and Cosmos are appchain projects (Polygon is an Ethereum side-chain and reuses the EVM for compatibility).

2   Background on Application-Specific Blockchains

Figure 1 offers a high-level overview of how smart contracts are compiled and deployed in Ethereum, Cosmwasm and Polkadot.

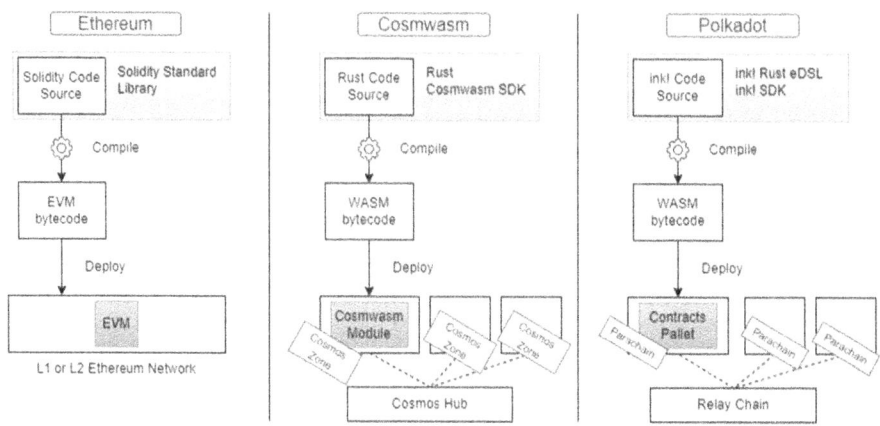

Fig. 1. Overview of smart contract compilation and deployment across different blockchains

Cosmos [10] is a network of interoperable blockchains, called Cosmos zones, built on the CometBFT consensus protocol. The project also offers the Cosmos SDK to allow blockchain developers to easily set up their own blockchain. Cosmwasm is a separate open source project to add support for WebAssembly-based smart contracts to any blockchain built with the Cosmos SDK. In addition, Cosmwasm is also the name of a public blockchain with built-in support for deploying WebAssembly smart contracts, similar to the public Ethereum network. Cosmos zones can communicate via a Cosmos hub, a central Cosmos network designed to relay messages, by using the Inter Blockchain Protocol (IBC).

Polkadot [14] is a multi-chain blockchain platform that offers a "relay chain" to which custom appchains, called "parachains", can be connected. Through this relay chain, parachains can communicate with each other via Cross-Chain Messages (XCM). To be allowed to connect to the relay chain, each parachain needs to participate in an auction and bid to get a slot as these are limited. Nodes of the relay chain will also serve as validators for the parachain to increase security. A custom Polkadot runtime can be composed of pallets (similar to modules). One of those pallets, the contracts pallet, supports ink!, an embedded domain-specific language (eDSL) in Rust that compiles to WebAssembly.

3   Running Example: NFT Auction

To be able to compare differences between the appchains, we will use two representative contracts, as most real world use cases don't consist of just one smart contract, but multiple which call each other. The first is an NFT Contract (ERC721), the second an NFT auction (English Auction), both based on examples from Solidity by Example [12]. The interaction between the two contracts and their participants is visualized in Fig. 2.

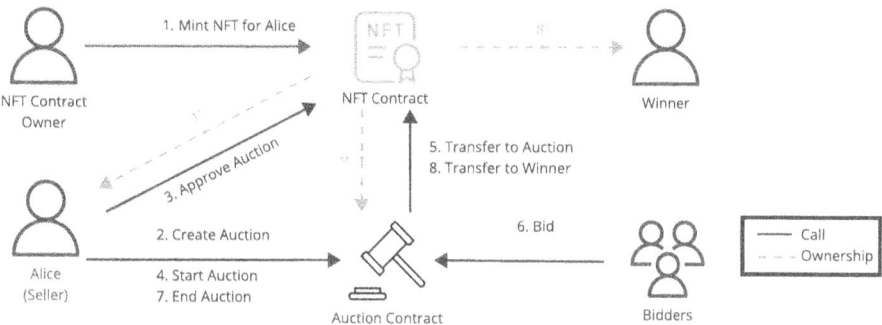

Fig. 2. Interaction Diagram of an NFT auction example

The interaction flow is as follows: *1.* The NFT Contract Owner Mints a new NFT for Alice. *2.* Alice creates a new NFT Auction Contract to sell the NFT. *3.* Alice adds the NFT Auction Contract as approver of the NFT. *4.* Alice starts the auction which triggers *5.*, the NFT Auction contract makes itself, as approver, the new owner of the NFT. *6.* Multiple bidders make a bid for the NFT. *7.* Alice ends the auction when the deadline has been reached which triggers *8.*, the NFT is transferred to the Winner (the person with the highest bid) and Alice gets the highest bid transferred to her account (not visualized).

3.1   The NFT Contract

For the NFT contract we use a simplified NFT contract based on the ERC721 standard [8]. Anyone can instantiate a new NFT Contract and becomes automatically the NFT contract owner. Only the contract owner is allowed to Mint new NFTs for a specified NFT owner. The NFT owner can allow another party to manage this specific NFT via the Approve action. Either the NFT owner or the approved party can transfer the ownership of the NFT to someone else with the Transfer action. Anyone can query the smart contract to check who the owner is of a specific NFT (OwnerOf), which NFTs belong to a certain owner (BalanceOf) and can request who the approver is for an NFT (Approved).

The NFT contract and its available methods are represented in Table 1.

Table 1. NFT Contract Methods

Action	Role	Conditions (NFT Contract nc, NFT n, Caller c)
Instantiate	Contract Owner	{}
Mint	Contract Owner	{nc.Owner == c}
Approve	Seller	{n.Owner == c}
Transfer	Seller or Approver	{n.Owner == c OR c ∈ n.Approved}
OwnerOf	Anyone	{}
BalanceOf	Anyone	{}
Approved	Anyone	{}

3.2 The Auction Contract

The second smart contract is an English auction. An NFT owner (Seller) can create a new auction and becomes owner of the contract. After granting approval to the NFT contract to manage the NFT, the seller can Start the auction. At this moment the end time of the auction is determined and the auction contract will take ownership of the NFT until the auction ends. Once started, everyone can bid on the NFT using the Bid method with funds attached. A bid is accepted if it is higher than the current highest bid and the auction has not ended. Previous bidders, except the current highest bidder, can Withdraw their previous bids. When the set amount of time has passed, anyone can End the auction. The contract will check if the minimum bid, set at creation, was reached and if so it transfers the NFT to the highest bidder and the seller is payed out. If the minimum bid was not reached, the NFT is returned to the seller.

Table 2 summarizes the methods provided by the NFT Auction contract.

Table 2. NFT Auction Contract Methods

Action	Role	Conditions (Auction a, NFT n, Caller c, Bid b)
Instantiate	Seller	{}
Start	Seller	{a.Owner == c AND a ∈ n.Approved)}
Bid	Anyone	{a.Started AND a.EndTime > now AND b.Value > a.StartBid}
Withdraw	Anyone	{c != a.HighestBidder}
End	Anyone	{a.Started AND a.EndTime <= now}

4 Smart Contract Framework Requirements

To be able to implement the smart contracts defined in Sect. 3, the appchain platform needs to fulfill certain requirements in its smart contract framework. We will give an overview of these requirements in this section.

Message Endpoints. Each contract requires at least one accessible message endpoint for users and other contracts to interact with it.

Identification. A user or contract needs to be identifiable to be able to link their digital assets (fungible or non-fungible) to them. Most blockchains represent user or contract identity with an address, based on the public key of the user or contract. Identification is used in the example contracts to assign ownership, transfer funds and for the auction contract to call the NFT contract.

Ownership. Different digital assets, like fungible tokens, non-fungible tokens, but also smart contracts can be owned by a user or contract. This implies that only that user or contract has the exclusive authority to transfer or use the assets. In the auction example, ownership is used to determine who owns the smart contracts, who owns the NFT and for the balance of native tokens of each party.

Access Control. Some actions can only be performed by users who fulfill certain conditions, e.g., the user needs to be owner or approver of a token to transfer it. How can a smart contract enforce this? In the example only the NFT owner and the NFT approver are allowed to transfer the NFT.

Transactionality. In many situations a set of actions must either all succeed or all fail. How does the framework enable a smart contract to enforce this kind of atomicity rules? At the end of the auction, the NFT is sent to highest bidder and the funds are transferred to the seller. If either of these actions should fail, both action are reverted.

Persisting State. Most smart contracts need to be able to maintain a persistent state across different function calls. State is required in the auction example in many cases, for example to keep track of which NFTs there are and who owns them. Or who placed already a bid in the auction and for what value.

Token Transfer. Blockchains typically have a cryptocurrency, which is the native asset which can be traded with other users. This can be used to pay for a service like the execution of a contract or to buy a digital asset. There are also non-native tokens, which are non-unique (fungible) and can be exchanged in a similar way. The example makes use of native tokens to place a bid in the auction and to pay out to the seller.

Contract Metadata. A contract needs to be able to acquire some information about itself relative to the blockchain which is not maintained in its own state. Examples of this are the contract address and the token balance of the contract. The auction contract needs to know its own address to transfer the NFT or transfer native tokens.

Blockchain State. Smart contracts must be able to inspect the current state of the blockchain, like the current block height, look up previous transactions or access some other functionality offered by the blockchain like address validation. Address validation is required in the example to validate addresses passed in function parameters.

Notion of Time. This can be considered as part of the Blockchain State but it deserves some extra attention. Real world use cases require a notion of time. A smart contract could base itself on the current block height, but that's not always an accurate measurement. Therefore most blockchains encode the current real world time as a timestamp in the blocks. This notion of time is required in the NFT auction contract to be able to determine whether the auction has ended.

Call Smart Contracts. Smart contracts need to be able to interact with other contracts for many different reasons, size limitations of a contract, dynamic adaptability, interacting with already existing contracts, ... By calling a smart contract we mean executing a method on the smart contract which changes the state of the contract. The auction smart contract needs to be able to call the NFT smart contract to transfer the NFT for which the auction was created.

Query Smart Contracts. Similar to calling smart contracts, a contract needs to be able to query the current state of an existing contract. A query will not change the state of the other contract. This can be used by the auction contract to check whether the NFT is actually owned by the seller.

Events. The decentralized application (dApp) ecosystem consists of more than components on the blockchain. To communicate with external applications, smart contracts emit events to notify that something noteworthy has happened.

5   Analysis of Appchain Rust SDKs Based on Smart Contract Requirements

To be able to understand how different appchain SDKs support the requirements that we put forward in Sect. 4, we implemented the NFT Auction presented in Sect. 3 in both Cosmwasm and Polkadot.[2] In this section we will elaborate on how each technology handles smart contracts with its provided smart contract SDK.

---

[2] The source code of the smart contracts is available at https://github.com/JvHKuL/RustSDKCompare.

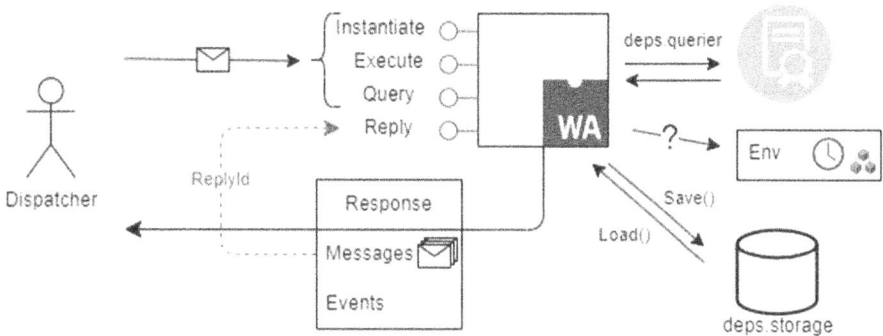

Fig. 3. Key interfaces of a Cosmwasm contract

5.1   Smart Contracts in Cosmwasm

Figure 3 offers an overview of the key interfaces for a smart contract in Cosmwasm.

Cosmwasm is a module that can be used in any Cosmos appchain, but there already exists an appchain with the same name, Cosmwasm, that allows you to deploy your own smart contracts on a publicly hosted shared blockchain, similar to e.g. the Ethereum mainnet. At the moment Rust is the main programming language for Cosmwasm. Although the normal Rust compiler is used to compile the Rust code to WebAssembly, Cosmwasm does impose certain interface requirements for it to be compatible with the module. Cosmwasm offers different Rust crates to facilitate this setup and a `cosmwasm-check` utility to validate the compatibility of the resulting contract.

Listing 1.1. Cosmwasm contract entry point signatures

```
1  #[entry_point]
2  pub fn instantiate (Depsmut, Env, MessageInfo, InitMsg) ->
3      StdResult<Response>
4  #[entry_point]
5  pub fn execute (DepsMut, Env, MessageInfo, ExecuteMsg) ->
6      StdResult<Response>
7  #[entry_point]
8  pub fn query (Deps, Env, QueryMsg) -> StdResult<Binary>
9  #[entry_point]
10 pub fn reply(DepsMut, Env, Reply) -> StdResult<Response>
```

Each contract exposes so called "entry points" for the appchain to interact with it. Cosmwasm defines four basic entry points, `instantiate`, `execute`, `query` and `reply` (Listing 1.1). A valid Cosmwasm smart contract expects at least an `instantiate` entry point.

In Cosmwasm the bytecode of a contract is first uploaded to the blockchain. This code can then be instantiated via the `instantiate` entry point, resulting in a new instance of the contract with its own address and state.

The `execute` function is used to execute smart contract code that can alter the state of the contract or blockchain.

The `query` function is used to query the state of the smart contract or blockchain, without altering it.

`Deps(Mut)` is a utility parameter to communicate with the outer world. It allows querying and updating the contract state, querying (not changing) other contracts' state, and gives access to an API object with a couple of helper functions for dealing with Cosmwasm addresses.

`Env` represents the blockchain state when the message is executed. It contains the chain height and id, current timestamp, and the address of the called contract.

`MessageInfo` contains the address of caller and the native tokens that were sent with the request.

All functions return a `StdResult<Response>` returning either a value of type `Response` or an `Error`.

Contrary to Solidity, Cosmwasm doesn't allow the exposure of custom functions as entry point. Instead Custom Message types are used to make the distinction between what action needs to be triggered on the contract. This forces the developer to declare a new message type for each functionality the smart contract needs to expose and avoids accidental exposure of functions. A message enters the contract via one of the three basic entry points and is then dispatched to the proper internal function based on the received message type.

Cosmwasm was designed this way because it follows the actor model [1]. Instead of directly executing calls on other contracts or appchain modules, a contract must return a message via the response to a dispatcher, which resides in the appchain. The dispatcher will then send the message to the proper contract or module. The resulting response will then be relayed back to the original contract. This approach has multiple advantages. There is loose coupling between the contracts: only the exchanged data format, the message, needs to be agreed upon. It avoids one of the most common problems in Solidity smart contracts, the re-entrancy attack [2], by only sequentially treating calls in a contract, guaranteeing that its state is finalized before a new message is processed. Cosmwasm assures the atomic execution of the messages and their submessages by creating a save point when a new external transaction is processed and performing optimistic updates. If all goes well, the transaction is committed, if it fails, a rollback is performed.

We will now analyse how the Cosmwasm SDK satisfies the requirements offered in Sect. 4.

Message Endpoints. Cosmwasm offers predefined message endpoints, called "entry points", primarily `initiate`, `execute`, `query` and `reply`. Rust enumerations are used to distinguish different actions to be performed.

Identification. Users and contracts are identified by their address. They have a predefined prefix based on the appchain.

Ownership. A distinction needs to be made between the ownership of native tokens, a contract, or digital assets like NFTs. Native token ownership is handled by a balance per account (address). For contract ownership the `cw-ownable` utility crate provides macros to extend `execute` and `query` messages with default values and functions to set and validate the current ownership of a contract. Digital asset ownership is managed by the contract itself, typically by maintaining a mapping between the owner address and the asset.

Access Control. Access control for the owner is done via the previously mentioned `cw-ownable` utility functions, specifically `cw_ownable::assert_owner`, which will throw a predefined `OwnershipError`. For other roles this is done by the contract itself with conditional statements and internally stored role information. In both cases the contract gets the caller information from the `MessageInfo` parameter of the called function.

Transactionality. Atomicity is guaranteed by the hosting environment via the optimistic update and rollback mechanism. If a contract calls another contract, and that call fails, the main contract can decide whether its state is still committed or not. If there is a failure in the main contract, the state of both the main contract and all called contracts is rolled back.

Persisting State. Cosmwasm advises to use the `cw-storage-plus` package which offers different classes that offer an abstraction on top of the standard `Storage` class. It offers an `Item` class to store basic types or `structs` and also a `Map`. Important to note is that the developer is responsible for the loading and saving of these classes to and from persistent storage. However there are a variety of functions provided to hide this, e.g. a closure can be used to update a value in the storage with loading and saving done automatically. (See Listing 1.2)

Listing 1.2. Cosmwasm storage handling using a closure

```
1 pub owned_tokens_count: Map<'a, &'a Addr, u32>
2 owned_tokens_count: Map::new(owned_tokens_count_key)
3 ...
4 self.owned_tokens_count
5     .update(deps.storage, &owner_addr, |old| match old {
6         Some(x) => Ok::<u32, ContractError>(x + 1),
7         None => Ok(1),
8     })?;
```

Token Transfer. In CosmWasm, contracts are not called when tokens are sent to them, but they can query their current balance via the `deps.querier` parameter. Native tokens can be sent with a contract call. To access the amount sent, the contract can query the `info.funds` parameter. Transferring tokens from the contract to another address is done via a `BankMessage` attached to the response, following the actor model. See Listing 1.3 for an example of the latter.

Listing 1.3. A token transfer using the Cosmwasm SDK

```
1 let bank_msg = BankMsg::Send {
2     to_address: caller.to_string(),
3     amount: vec![coin.to_owned()],
4 };
5 let resp = Response::new().add_message(bank_msg);
6 Ok(resp)
```

Contract Metadata. The contract can find its own address in the `Env` parameter. Token balance for any address can be queried by sending a `BankQuery` through `deps.querier`.

Blockchain State and Notion of Time. Information about the current state of the blockchain is available in the `Env` parameter. This information includes block height and the timestamp of the block. Cosmwasm offers also an API, `deps.api`, to check the validity of an address.

Call Smart Contracts. Calling another contract or module is done by adding a new `ExecuteMessage` to the response of the current message. See Listing 1.4 for an example. To act on the result of the call, the message is encapsulated in a submessage with the identifier of the current function and added to the response. The dispatcher will send the result back to the `reply` entry point on the original contract, where the reply is dispatched to the correct code based on the identifier that was provided in the submessage.

Listing 1.4. Calling another contract using the Cosmwasm SDK

```
1 let erc_transfer_msg = erc721::ExecuteMsg::TransferNft {
2     recipient: env.contract.address.to_string(),
3     token_id: nft_id,
4 };
5 let erc_transfer_msg = WasmMsg::Execute {
6     contract_addr: nft_contract.into_string(),
7     msg: to_json_binary(&erc_transfer_msg)?,
8     funds: vec![],
9 };
10 let resp = Response::new().add_message(erc_transfer_msg);
11 Ok(resp)
```

Query Smart Contracts. Querying other contracts or modules can be done via `deps.querier`. (See Listing 1.5)

Listing 1.5. Querying the state of another contract using the Cosmwasm SDK

```
1  let resp: erc721::OwnerOfResponse = deps.querier.query_wasm_smart(
2              nft_contract_addr.to_owned(),
3              &erc721::QueryMsg::OwnerOf { token_id: 1 },
4      )?;
```

Events. Events are attached to the response of the current message, similar to a BankMsg for a token transfer, and will then be published by the appchain.

5.2   Smart Contracts in Polkadot

The ink! framework is an embedded domain-specific language (eDSL) to write smart contracts in Rust that compile to WebAssembly. Figure 4 offers an overview of the key interfaces using the ink! eDSL.

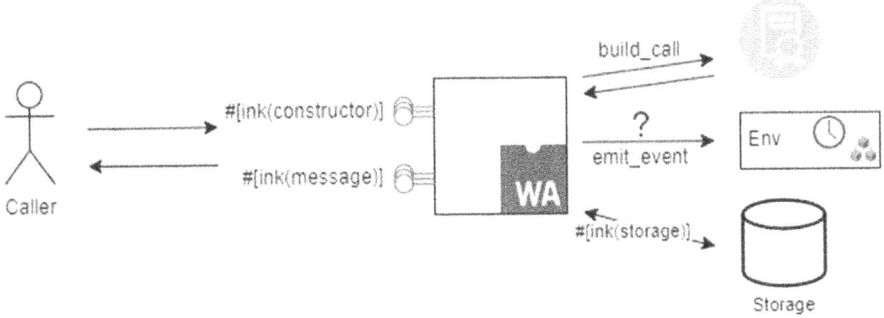

Fig. 4. Key interfaces of a smart contract on a Polkadot parachain using the ink! eDSL

ink! offers its own CLI tool, cargo-contract, for setting up new contracts, compiling them, but also for interacting with the application-specific chain (called "parachain" in Polkadot).

The ink! eDSL uses Rust macros intensively to hide the complex underlying mechanics and make it more user-friendly. Each ink! smart contract is preceded by the #[ink::contract] macro and requires at least the following elements: exactly one struct with the #[ink(storage)] tag for storing the state of the contract, at least one function with the #[ink(constructor)] tag for initializing the contract on creation and at least one function with the #[ink(message)] tag which defines an entry point for the contract.

In Polkadot the bytecode of a contract is first uploaded to the blockchain. A new instance of the smart contract can then be created by initiating it with one of the defined constructors.

The messages that can be sent to the contract are defined as functions of the storage struct, which is a very common pattern in Rust. (See Listing 1.6)

Listing 1.6. Structure of an NFT smart contract implemented with the ink! eDSL

```
1  #[ink::contract]
2  mod erc721 {
3      #[ink(storage)]
4      #[derive(Default)]
5      pub struct Erc721 {
6          token_owner: Mapping<TokenId, AccountId>,
7          ...
8      }
9      impl Erc721 {
10         #[ink(constructor)]
11         pub fn new() -> Self {...}
12         #[ink(message)]
13         pub fn balance_of(&self, owner: AccountId) -> u32 {...}
14         #[ink(message)]
15         pub fn transfer_from(&mut self, from: AccountId,
16                              to: AccountId, id: TokenId,
17         ) -> Result<(), Error> {...}
18     }
19 }
```

Interaction with the blockchain environment is done via environment functions which are available via a public crate function `Self::env()` in the constructor or on `self.env()` for other methods.

ink! uses a synchronous approach to call or query other contracts which can be done in 2 different ways: using contract references or using a builder API.

To use contract references the contract to be called needs to be imported in the caller's project and the contract needs to be instantiated from that project. This can not be used to interact with contracts previously deployed on-chain.

The builder API can be used to call any smart contract compatible with the contracts pallet. However, the API is low-level and as the interface of the other contract is not imported, it is not type-checked. See Listing 1.7 for an example.

Listing 1.7. Calling an external contract in ink! using the Builder API

```
1  let _my_return_value = build_call::<DefaultEnvironment>()
2      .call(self.nft) //Contract address
3      .call_v1()
4      .gas_limit(0)
5      .exec_input(
6          ExecutionInput::new(Selector::new(ink::selector_bytes!(
7          "transfer_from")))
8              .push_arg(self.seller) //sender
9              .push_arg(self.env().account_id()) //address(this)
10             .push_arg(self.nft_id), //nftId
11     )
12     .returns::<ink::MessageResult<()>>()
13     .invoke();
```

We now analyse how the ink! eDSL covers the requirements from Sect. 4.

Message Endpoints. A smart contract in ink! needs to have at least one public function with the #[ink(constructor)] macro for initializing the contract on creation and at least one public function with the #[ink(message)] macro to process state-changing calls and queries without side effects. Each functionality is implemented in a new public function.

Identification. In most Polkadot parachains, user accounts and contracts are identified by a 256-bit AccountId, which is often the public key of a cryptographic key pair.

Ownership. ink! has no built-in support for contract ownership. This means that contract ownership is handled in the same way as digital asset ownership, by storing ownership information in the contract's state. Native tokens are stored per AccountId and can be consulted via the self.env().balance() method.

Access Control. Access control is managed by the contract itself with conditional statements and internally stored role information. The caller AccountId is retrieved via the self.env().caller() method.

Transactionality. ink! uses a synchronous execution model. When the main contract fails, all state changes are rolled back, including contracts called by the main contract. In case the contract calls another contract, and that call fails, the main contract has the option to handle the failure and still commit its own state.

Persisting State. Each contract has exactly one Rust struct with the #[ink(storage)] macro to store the contract state. ink! supports most common data types, provides its own version of String and Vec. It also allows structs and enums to be stored and provides a Mapping type. Initialization of the state is done in the constructors. Loading and saving is handled by the #[ink(message)] macro and is thus transparent for the developer. The macro will determine whether the method is allowed to change the state or not, in case of a query, by analyzing the method interface.

Token Transfer. A method that can receive native tokens must be marked with the #[ink(payable)] macro. The value received with the call can be determined with self.env().transferred_value() and the total contract balance with self.env().balance(). Sending money from the contract is similar with self.env().transfer(receiver_accountId, value).

Contract Metadata. The contract AccountId, balance and the caller of the method are all made available through functions on self.env().

Blockchain State. Blockchain state can be queried through the `self.env()` functions, for example `self.env().block_number()`.

Notion of Time. Like other Blockchain state information, the timestamp of the last block can be found with `self.env().block_timestamp()`.

Call Smart Contracts and Query Smart Contracts. Both call and query are handled in a synchronous manner in ink!, depending on whether the contract is instantiated by the calling contract, it can be included in the project and allows for type checking at compile time. However if a call is to be made to a previously deployed contract, the usage of a low-level builder API is required.

Events. Events are defined by a `struct` with the `#[ink(event)]` macro. And optionally the topic can be specified by `#[ink(topic)]` macro on the event fields, which let the parachain index the events based on the topic. Events are generated via the `self.env().emit_event(...)` function.

6   Qualitative and Quantitative Comparison of the SDKs

We now offer both a qualitative and a quantitative direct comparison between the Cosmwasm and Polkadot SDKs based on our first-hand experience in implementing the example contracts in each SDK. Table 3 summarizes the key differences between the SDKs.

Table 3. Key differences of Rust smart contracts in Cosmwasm and Polkadot SDKs.

Cosmwasm	Polkadot
Fixed set of entry points	Open-ended set of entry points
Asynchronous inter-contract calls (actor model). Type validation at compile time	Synchronous inter-contract calls. Prone to re-entrancy attack
Explicit key-value storage. Developer responsible for saving and loading of state	Implicit storage of a single annotated `struct`
Token transfer via `BankMessage` attached to the `Response`	`payable` attribute required on function to receive funds. Synchronous token transfer via `self.env().transfer()`
Contract ownership with `cw-ownable` crate	No built-in notion of contract ownership
Environment accessed via function parameters	Environment accessed via static functions
Events are attached to the `Response`	Events are emitted via a function call

Our quantitative comparison consists of measuring the total lines of code needed to implement both contracts in each SDK. Table 4 provides an overview of the count of non-comment, non-blank source lines of code (SLOC) of the smart contracts specified in Sect. 3 for Ethereum (Solidity), Cosmwasm (Rust) and Polkadot (Rust with ink! eDSL).[3] We took care to align the example code to have the same functionality, and we excluded any code related to unit tests in the count.

Table 4. Comparison of example smart contract implementation lines of code.

	Ethereum	Cosmwasm	Polkadot
NFT contract	72	313	184
Auction contract	63	318	217
Total	135	631	398

Perhaps unsurprisingly, Ethereum's Solidity language enables the most compact implementation with its tailored design. Both Cosmwasm and Polkadot Rust implementations are significantly larger. Part of this is due to the coding style and formatting rules of the Rust language. In addition, for Polkadot, the macro annotations add verbosity, as well as inter-contract calls with the builder API. Cosmwasm clearly has the most verbose implementation. This is in large part due to its actor model interface, with more lines needed to define custom message types and dispatching logic. However, the small difference in code count between the two example contracts indicates that once the setup is in place, adding extra functionality has less impact on the code count.

A final aspect of our qualitative comparison involves sharing some personal experiences gained from porting the Solidity code to both SDKs:

Documentation. Both Cosmwasm and Polkadot offer tutorials and documentation, but generally the right information is scattered across many sources. The ink! documentation is more comprehensive, but still not complete enough to serve as a single reference. ink!'s extensive usage of Rust macros hides a lot of the complexity and results in a more straightforward migration from Solidity.

Scaffolding. Polkadot offers a sample project to create a new smart contract. In Cosmwasm, a new smart contract project is a normal Rust library project, which needs to be manually customized or a template can be downloaded from https://github.com/CosmWasm/cw-template. We felt that a Cosmwasm project is more elaborate to set up, but once in place it is easy to extend and avoids accidental exposure of unwanted functionality, as each message type needs to be explicitly defined.

---

[3] Tokei, which supports both rust and solidity, was used to perform these measurements. https://github.com/XAMPPRocky/tokei.

Testing. Both SDKs offer frameworks that simulate the appchain and allow for end-to-end testing. We found the Polkadot toolchain to be easier to use. It offers a development node with initialised test accounts and a UI to facilitate contract interactions. The Cosmwasm development node requires more configuration and interaction can happen only via the CLI.

7   Related Work

Other comparative studies of smart contract languages and platforms exist in the literature, but they do not focus specifically on Rust or the SDK aspects of blockchain Dapp development. We review the most relevant studies below.

Bartoletti *et al.* [3] compare a variety of different smart contract languages, but do not focus on the use of Rust and Webassembly as the execution layer. The authors do take into account the security implications of the language design and the tooling ecosystem, which is an aspect we want to consider for Rust SDKs as part of our future work (Sect. 8). Voloder and di Angelo [13] perform a comparative study of different smart contract platforms, but focus on the entire platform instead of the language and SDK aspects. Benahmed *et al.* [4] perform a comparative analysis from the development and performance perspective of the included platforms and only touch lightly on smart contract language design.

8   Conclusion and Future Work

We performed a comparative study of the Rust SDKs for developing smart contracts on the two most popular appchain platforms, Cosmwasm and Polkadot. Our study was guided by 13 requirements gathered from a representative pair of Solidity contracts, namely an English auction contract that can autonomously auction off an NFT (Non-fungible Token) managed by an NFT contract. Translating the two contracts to Rust using the Cosmwasm and Polkadot SDKs provides a baseline comparison on how the SDKs cover these requirements.

Our analysis creates a starting point for better understanding the design space of smart contract SDKs. Cosmwasm and Polkadot clearly occupy opposite points in this space, with Cosmwasm offering a library-based API, programmer-controlled storage and asynchronous inter-contract calls versus Polkadot's eDSL API, transparent storage and synchronous calls.

In future work, we aim to extend this research along three lines. First, we want to gain a deeper understanding of the impact of the SDK design on smart contract correctness (avoiding bugs), modularity (adding or changing functionality), and performance. Second, we want to expand the comparison to include additional use case scenarios (contracts) and other blockchain SDKs that support WebAssembly (candidates include NEAR [11], Internet Computer [7] and Solana [15]). We also want to add a more in-depth section on the usability of the different SDKs and their ecosystems (i.e. user friendliness, available tooling, documentation quality, community support). Third, inspired by research into vulnerabilities in WebAssembly-based contracts [6], we want to extend the comparison from the Rust source code level to the WebAssembly bytecode level in order to understand how the SDKs expose blockchain host functionality to their guest Wasm contract modules.

Acknowledgments. This research is partially funded by the Research Fund KU Leuven, and by the Cybersecurity Research Program Flanders.

References

1. Agha, G.: Actors: a model of concurrent computation in distributed systems. MIT Press (1986)
2. Atzei, N., Bartoletti, M., Cimoli, T.: A survey of attacks on ethereum smart contracts (SoK). In: Maffei, M., Ryan, M. (eds.) POST 2017. LNCS, vol. 10204, pp. 164–186. Springer, Heidelberg (2017). https://doi.org/10.1007/978-3-662-54455-6_8
3. Bartoletti, M., et al.: Smart Contract Languages: A comparative analysis (Apr 2024)
4. Benahmed, S., et al.: A comparative analysis of distributed ledger technologies for smart contract development. In: PIMRC. IEEE (Sep 2019)
5. Buterin, V.: Ethereum: A next-generation smart contract and decentralized application platform. (2014). https://ethereum.org/en/whitepaper/
6. Chen, W., Sun, Z., Wang, H., Luo, X., Cai, H., Wu, L.: Wasai: uncovering vulnerabilities in wasm smart contracts. In: ISSTA 2022 (2022)
7. DFINITY Team: The internet computer for geeks. Cryptology ePrint Archive, Paper 2022/087 (2022). https://eprint.iacr.org/2022/087
8. Erc-721: Non-fungible token standard (2018). https://eips.ethereum.org/EIPS/eip-721
9. Haas, A., et al.: Bringing the web up to speed with webassembly. In: PLDI 2017 (2017)
10. Kwon, J., Buchman, E.: Cosmos: A network of distributed ledgers (2016). https://cosmos.network/whitepaper
11. NEAR Foundation: The official near white paper (2021). https://pages.near.org/papers/the-official-near-white-paper/
12. Solidity by example (Jun 2024). https://solidity-by-example.org/
13. Voloder, A., Di Angelo, M.: Comparison of smart contract platforms from the perspective of developers. In: Wang, Q., Feng, J., Zhang, L.J. (eds.) Blockchain – ICBC 2023. Springer (2023)
14. Wood, G.: Polkadot: Vision for a heterogeneous multi-chain framework (2016). https://polkadot.network/whitepaper
15. Yakovenko, A.: Solana: A new architecture for a high performance blockchain. Whitepaper (2018)

Offchain Runtime Verification (for The Tezos Blockchain)

Margarita Capretto[1,2](✉) ⓘ, Martin Ceresa[1] ⓘ, Felipe Gorostiaga[1,3] ⓘ,
Fernando Macias[1] ⓘ, Paloma Pedregal[1] ⓘ, and Cesar Sanchez[1] ⓘ

[1] IMDEA Software Institute, Pozuelo de Alarcón s/n, 28223 Madrid, Spain
margarita.capretto@imdea.org
[2] UPM, Madrid, Spain
[3] CIFASIS, Rosario, Argentina

Abstract. In this paper, we present *offchain runtime verification*, a dynamic analysis technique to inspect blockchain executions without affecting the blockchain itself.

Runtime verification (RV) is a technique that analyzes traces of system execution based on monitors created from system specifications. There are two flavors of RV: online and offline. In online RV, monitors run in tandem with the system, either with their own resources or as code inlined in the system implementation. In offline RV, monitors have a dump of the system trace available. Examples of offline monitoring include post-mortem analysis and log inspection.

We present a novel notion of monitors running offchain while fetching information about the blockchain evolution and its agents (e.g. external users, bakers) to assess security and fairness, assign blame, and compute explanations. Our monitoring infrastructure is both *online*—as the monitors can receive new blocks incrementally—and *offline* since the monitors can query the history of the blockchain. Online queries are necessary because monitors are created after the blockchain has been running and relevant information is discovered online (e.g. who interacted in the past with an address recently discovered to be malicious). We describe in this paper an RV infrastructure for offchain monitoring for the Tezos Blockchain.

1 Introduction

Blockchains [30] running smart contracts [43,45] provide a trusted third party where transactions are persistent and permanent. Smart contracts are immutable pieces of code (the code is the contract) that govern the interaction between agents using a blockchain without requiring a trusted centralized

This work was funded in part by PRODIGY Project (TED2021-132464B-I00)—funded by MCIN/AEI/10.13039/501100011033/ and the European Union NextGenerationEU/PRTR—by DECO Project (PID2022-138072OB-I00)—funded by MCIN/AEI/10.13039/501100011033 and by the ESF—and by a research grant from Nomadic Labs and the Tezos Foundation.

J. Garcia-Alfaro et al. (Eds.): ESORICS 2024 Workshops, LNCS 15263, pp. 242–259, 2025.
https://doi.org/10.1007/978-3-031-82349-7_17

authority. We can use smart contracts to describe sophisticated functionality, enabling many applications like decentralized finances (DeFi), decentralized governance, and Web3. Smart contracts are deterministic, i.e. the effects of executing smart contracts are uniquely determined by the blockchain state and the transactions parameters. Since smart contracts are immutable and they govern the blockchain evolution (including the cryptocurrency exchanged), the correctness of smart contracts is crucial and errors and vulnerabilities can lead to huge losses (e.g. [37]). Both static [1,6,7,11,31,36,42] and dynamic techniques [2,8,14,26] have been proposed to approach the problem of smart contract correctness. Dynamic techniques analyze the evolution of the blockchain. Specifications describe correctness criteria for smart contracts and monitoring code is generated which extends the code of the contract. At runtime, monitors inspect smart contract invocations, detecting violations and reverting illegal executions. This *onchain* monitoring approach requires monitors to be deployed on-chain as part of smart contracts themselves, because otherwise, once smart contracts commit their effects cannot be reverted. Onchain monitoring, in turn, affects the normal execution of smart contracts as monitors consume some gas.

In this paper, we explore an alternative monitoring technique where monitors are deployed in a running system. Additionally, we seek non-intrusive monitors, so that the execution of smart contracts is completely unaffected by the execution of monitors. In these scenarios, monitors only observe a suffix of the system original trace. There are three possible approaches to cope with this lack of past observability: (1) *ignore the missing past* so monitors operate as if they were observing the whole history, which is the simplest approach but can lead to inaccurate results; (2) *encode the lack of knowledge* by modifying the specification [22]; (3) *access a log system* to fetch the missing past and then continue monitoring online with future events. We propose in this paper to follow the third approach by combining *offline* and *online* monitoring.

Runtime verification (RV) is a formal method for analyzing execution traces, one at a time. Traces are evaluated against monitors built from a given formal specification [4,25]. Formal specifications are described using different languages implementing different logics like linear temporal logic [39]. Most RV languages describe a monolithic monitor that processes input events. Another approach is dynamic parametrization, also known as parametric trace slicing, which quantifies over objects and spawns monitors that follow independently the objects observed as in Quantified Event Automata (QEA) [3]. One can think of it as grabbing a magnifying glass when required.

Our approach is based on Stream Runtime Verification (SRV), pioneered by Lola [13], which relates output streams of verdicts to input streams of observations. Originally designed for testing synchronous hardware, SRV has since extended to other applications, including asynchronous and real-time systems (e.g. [18]). HLola [9,19,21] is an implementation of Lola as an embedded DSL in Haskell, which simplifies the specification development and runtime system. HLola leverages Haskell data types for Lola streams. Our main technical contribution is the extension of HLola with functionalities for *retroactive dynamic parametrization*, where parametrized specifications can be specialized with information discovered dynamically (parametrization) and specifications can revisit past events to obtain missing information (retroactivity).

The inspection of the blockchain evolution is a perfect application of retroactive dynamic parametrization. The blockchain state, that is, the state of each smart contract and wallet, is connected to the next state and monitors can observe the whole execution history of the system. The challenge is to design efficient monitoring runtime systems that compute only what is necessary to produce a verdict.

Previous works have already inspected the blockchain evolution, mostly for security concerns within blockchain ecosystems [5,10,12,16,23,24,27,28,28,29, 33,34,38,40,41,44]In general, these works focus on specific problems and are tailored for performance but not correctness. In contrast, our framework is designed to be applied to several scenarios, and it allows writting diverse specifications ensuring that the monitors generated are correct with regard to the specification.

Running Example: Sandwich Attacks. We introduce our running example, a blockchain vulnerability known as sandwich attack. Decentralized Exchanges (exchanges from now on) are a common application ofy blockchains to decentralized finances (DeFi) where users trade tokens directly without intermediaries. Sandwich attacks exploit the delay between transaction submission and transaction execution. When transactions are submitted for execution in blockchains they are first added as requests to a distributed service, known as mempools, containing transaction requests that have not yet been executed. The mempool content is visible to all agents in the blockchain, including malicious actors which inspect the mempool searching for victim transactions. In a sandwich attack, a victim tries to trade a large amount of token **A** for **B** in an exchange which will cause an increase in the price of token **B**. A malicious actor tries to "sandwich" the victim transaction with two additional transactions to profit from the future value increase of **B**. The first transaction, known as the *frontrunning* transaction, buys tokens **B** and is scheduled before the victim transaction. In the second transaction, known as the *backrunning* transaction, the malicious actor sells the purchased tokens **B** at a major price obtaining a profit.

The frontrunning transaction increases the price of token **B** causing the victim transaction to purchase **B** at a higher price than expected. Since token prices often fluctuate, the price of a given token when a transaction is submitted might differ from the actual transaction execution. Hence, most exchanges offer a way to define price ranges where token purchases can occur, which limits the amount of tokens **B** that the malicious actor can buy in the frontrunning transaction. This limits malicious actor's profits, but it does not prevent sandwich attacks from happening.

Consider a user trading a large amount of Tezos (XTZ) for USDT on an exchange. A malicious account can perform a sandwich attack purchasing USDT with XTZ in the same exchange right before the victim's transaction, and then selling USDT for XTZ right after.

In the remainder of the paper, we focus on detecting sandwich attacks against a specific account, denoted by a. We say that an account is *malicious* if it performs a sandwich attack to account a. We also identify *suspicious* wallets as those that interacted directly with malicious accounts.

We implemented retroactive dynamic parametrization in HLola and report the result of applying our implementation to detect sandwich attacks in the Tezos blockchain [17]. An early prototype of this technique [35] was already used to efficiently detect distributed denial of service attacks in realistic network traffic. The contributions of this paper are:

– A new monitoring technique and its application for inspecting blockchain histories, described in Sect. 3.
– A demonstration of how to apply the features of our framework to detect sandwich attacks, identify involved actors, and compute attackers' profits and victims' losses, shown in Sect. 4.
– Further applications of our monitoring framework, presented in Sect. 5.

2   Preliminaries

We introduce now necessary concepts of Blockchains and SRV.

Blockchains. Blockchains [30] were introduced as distributed infrastructures that eliminate the need of trust third parties in electronic payment systems. Modern blockchains incorporate smart contracts [43,45], stateful programs stored in blockchains controlling the functionality of blockchain transactions. Users interact with blockchains by invoking smart contracts. Blockchain "actors" (users and smart contracts) are identified by their *account*. We refer to accounts managed by end-users as *wallets*.

A *node* is a machine that stores a copy of the blockchain (or at least a portion of it) and keeps its local copy updated by regularly communicating with other nodes in a peer-to-peer network. Public blockchains allow anyone to launch a fully functional node. While nodes hold the entire history of the blockchain, searching this data directly can be slow and resource-intensive. Therefore, there is an ecosystem of tools, called *indexers*, that retrieve information from nodes and process it to allow efficient search. Indexers crawl the whole blockchain and store its data plus some additional information about the evolution of the blockchain, offering an API to query this information. Each API restricts the vision of the blockchain to what can be retrieved by such API language.

Stream Runtime Verification. Stream Runtime Verification (SRV) enriches monitoring algorithms from runtime verification to handle arbitrary data. SRV separates the logic of how data relates over time from the specific operations of each datatype. In this paper, we use the extensible tool HLola [9,19,21], an implementation of Lola [13] developed as an embedded DSL in Haskell.

Lola specifications consist of a set of typed input and output streams that represent the input events observed by the monitor and the intermediate observations and outputs of the monitor, respectively. Specifications are defined as equations that declaratively describe the intended values of every output stream variable in terms of the input and output streams. The set of *stream expressions* of a given type is built from constants and function symbols as constructors, and from *offset expressions* of the form $s[k|d]$ where s is a stream variable, k is an integer number and d is a default value of the type of s.

For example, offset expression `balanceA[-1|0]` represents the value of stream `balanceA` in the previous step of time with `0` as the value used at the initial instant. We define a stream `balA_ok` which checks that the `balance` of account A is always above a predefined threshold of `100` tokens:

```
1 input Int balanceA
2 output Bool balA_ok = balanceA[now] > 100
```

Given values of the input streams, the formal semantics of a Lola specification is defined denotationally as the unique collection of streams of values satisfying all equations.

One of the benefits of the extensible tool HLola is its ability to define templates for stream definitions using *static parametrization*. These templates act as abstractions, hiding specific concrete values, which are instantiated in static time by the compiler. Following the previous example, we can define a more generic version of the stream `balA_ok` as follows:

```
1 input Int balanceA
2 output Bool balA_checker <Int threshold> = balanceA[now] > threshold
3 output Bool balA_ok = (balA_checker 100)[now]
```

However, static parametrization cannot handle parameters whose values are discovered at runtime. The values of all parameters must be determined before the monitor starts executing. Users must ensure that the resulting specification contains a finite number of streams.

3   System Architecture

Our solution is composed of a monitor generated from an HLola specification and an external component interfacing with Tezos nodes and indexers called *adapter*. When monitors start execution, we start an adapter process in charge of receiving data from the Tezos blockchain and formatting it for the monitor input. Once the monitor is online, up and running, it can send parametrized queries to the adapter to fetch subtraces of the blockchain history. The adapter can perform complex requests to the Tezos indexer, i.e. filtering and formatting the received data before redirecting the result to the monitor. Through the use of the adapter, monitors efficiently obtain newly relevant data that was previously omitted or they can process blocks that were added to the blockchain before the monitor was launched. The adapter allows monitors to be agnostic to the blockchain used, the indexer and the format of the data, so this architecture can be used (adapting the adapter) to other blockchains like Ethereum. Figure 1 shows this architecture.

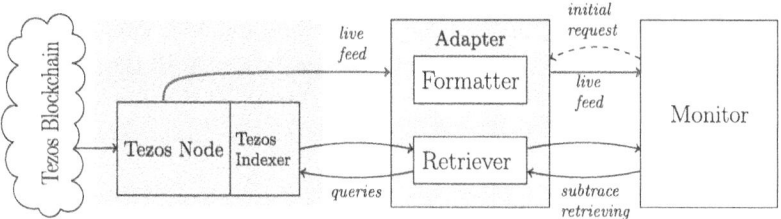

Fig. 1. Offchain monitoring system architecture

4 Features

In this section, we present the features of our framework and demonstrate how to apply them for effective monitoring, including to detect sandwich attacks, identify malicious and suspicious actors, and calculate attackers' profits.

4.1 Monitor Side Features

Nested Monitors. Nested monitors [20] allow using SRV specifications as data functions inside other specifications. Nested specifications are created and executed dynamically. A nested monitor receives a finite subtrace of the system original trace as input, typically obtained using HLola operator $s[:n]$, which creates a list with the next n values of stream s.

To define a *nested* specification, we need to provide a name so we can refer to it later on and add an extra clause: return x when y where x is a stream of any type and y is a **Boolean** stream. The type of the stream x determines the type of the value returned when the specification is invoked dynamically. The Boolean stream y dictates when the nested specification finishes. The nested monitor returns the value of x at the first instant at which y becomes **true**(without needing to inspect the rest of the list), or the last value of x if y is never **true**. Nested specifications can be parametric, parameters are declared after its name. We can execute nested specifications by using the HLola function runSpec specifying the parameters and the input streams with which the nested monitor will be executed.

Example 1. The following specification calculates whether a transaction in the input stream tx is the frontrunning transaction of a sandwich attack against account a.

Blockchain traces may contain many trading operations involving the same pair of tokens. In a sandwich attack, the frontrunning and backrunning transactions must occur close in time to the victim transaction. For simplicity, we consider an operation to be part of a potential sandwich attack if both the suspected frontrunning and backrunning transactions occur within 10 transactions apart from the victim transaction. We define a stream frontruns which first checks if tokens are traded in the transaction using function tradeTokens. If so, the monitor invokes the nested specification frontrunspec with the current transaction (tx[now]) as the parameter **ftx**, and the next 20 events of tx (tx[:20]) as the input stream tx of the nested monitor.

```
1 use innerspec frontrunspec
2 input Transaction tx
3 output Bool frontruns = if tradeTokens tx[now]
4                         then runSpec (frontrunspec tx[now] tx[:20])
5                         else False
```

We use if · then · else · instead of the Boolean operator (&&) to stress the fact that the nested specification is only executed when tokens are traded. The nested specification frontrunspec defines three streams.

- Stream counter counts the number of transactions processed. We use it to guarantee that the victim transaction is among the first 10 transactions, and that the backrunning transaction occurs within 10 transactions of the victim transaction.
- Stream victim stores the position in the input trace of a potential victim transaction (a transaction where account a trades tokens in the same exchange as the frontrunning transaction).
- Stream attack indicates if an attack occurred (the client from the frontrunning transaction swapped tokens back at most 10 transactions after the victim transaction).

```
 1  innerspec Bool frontrunspec <Transaction ftx>
 2  input Transaction tx
 3  const a = "tz123"
 4  output Int counter = counter[-1|0] + 1
 5  output Int victim =
 6    if counter[now] < 11 &&  tradeTokens tx[now]
 7       && exchange tx[now] == exchange ftx && client tx[now] == a
 8       && token1 tx[now] == token1 ftx && token2 tx[now] == token2 ftx
 9    then counter[now]
10    else -1
11  output Bool attack =
12    victim[now] != -1 && counter[now] < victim[now] + 11
13    && tradeTokens tx[now] && exchange tx[now] == exchange ftx
14    && client tx[now] == client ftx
15    && token1 tx[now] == token2 ftx && token2 tx[now] == token1 ftx
16  return attack when attack
```

In a transaction where tokens are traded, the client of a transaction is the account that traded the tokens, the exchange of a transaction is the exchange where the trade happened, and token1 and token2 of a transaction are the traded tokens. We can further extend the above specification with a stream called malicious to track accounts that performed sandwich attacks against a.

```
 6  output (Set Account) malicious = if frontruns[now]
 7    then insert (client tx[now]) malicious[-1|empty]
 8    else malicious[-1|empty]
```

Retroactive Nested Monitors. Although nested monitors can detect sandwich attacks, this approach can be very inefficient. In a blockchain history, the number of times account a trades tokens (and can be victim of a sandwich attack) is significantly smaller than the total number of transactions where tokens are traded. This leads to a large number of unnecessary nested monitors being created. To address this inefficiency, we propose creating nested monitors only when account a trades tokens. This implies ignoring relevant transactions and later accessing them to search for potential frontrunning transactions. We achieve this *retroactive* search by implementing a function pastRetriever that invokes the adapter (see Sect. 3) to retrieve a specified number of past events.

The following specification checks whether the current transaction corresponds to address a trading tokens, and triggers the finer analysis of the surrounding transactions when necessary.

```
1  use innerspec tradersSpec
2  input Transaction tx
3  const a = "tz123"
4  output Bool attacked =
5    if tradeTokens tx[now] && client tx[now] == a then
6      let fRunners = runSpec ((tradersSpec e t1 t2) (pastRetriever 10))
7          bRunners = runSpec ((tradersSpec e t2 t1) tx[:10]) in
8          not (null (intersection fRunners bRunners))
9    else False
10   where e = exchange tx[now]
11         t1 = token1 tx[now]
12         t2 = token2 tx[now]
```

Within the 10 previous transactions, nested specification tradersSpec computes all accounts that made the same trade as a. On the subsequent 10 transactions, nested specification tradersSpec computes all accounts that did the opposite trade. Finally, the specification checks whether any account appears in both sets. We use if · then · else False (&&) to stress the fact that the nested specification is executed only when a trades tokens.

The nested specification tradersSpec identifies all accounts that trade two specific tokens in a given exchange, as follows:

```
1  innerspec (Set Account) tradersSpec <Account e> <Token t1> <Token t2>
2  input Transaction tx
3  output (Set Account) traders =
4    if tradeTokens tx[now] && exchange tx[now] == e
5       && token1 tx[now] == t1 && token2 tx[now] == t2
6    then insert (client tx[now]) traders[-1|emptySet]
7    else traders[-1|emptySet]
8  return traders when False
```

The above specification finds all transactions that are victims of a sandwich attack at most 10 transactions *after* it happens. Also, the nested monitors in this example are created, executed and destroyed only for every transaction where a exchanges tokens.

(Forward) Dynamic Parametrization. Since we have an efficient way of detecting sandwich attacks and malicious accounts, we can move on to identifying suspicious wallets, defined as those that interact with the malicious account performing the sandwich attack. The following specification computes all wallets that interact with a given account:

```
1  input Transaction tx
2  output (Set Wallet) fellows <Account a> =
3    union (wallets a tx[now]) fellows[-1|empty]
```

The auxiliary function `wallets a tx` returns all wallets that sent tokens to account `a` during the execution of transaction `tx`. To identify all suspicious wallets, we need to instantiate the parametrized stream `fellows` with all malicious accounts. However, malicious accounts are only found after they perform a sandwich attack, which cannot be determined statically.

We can instantiate a parametric stream over values discovered dynamically while processing the input trace using the HLola operator `over`. The `over` operator takes two arguments: (1) a parametric stream `strm`, and (2) a stream `params` of sets of values. The resulting expression is a map where at any point in time the keys are the elements in `params[now]`, and the value associated to each key is the instantiation of `strm` over the key. For a complete description on how this operator is implemented in the tool HLola, see [35]. In our case, we can parametrize the parametric stream `fellows` over the values of stream `malicious`:

```
1  output (Set Wallets) suspicious = foldl union empty
2    (elems (fellows 'over' malicious))
```

Here, `elems m` returns the list of values in map `m`, and function `foldl f l` aggregates the elements in list `l` using `f` to combine them. To compute all suspicious wallets, we join the suspicious wallets related to each malicious account. This specification follows each account independently.

When a new value is added to the set of parameters (the stream `malicious` in our case), we spawn a new monitor parametrized with the discovered value. The newly created nested monitor executes alongside the monitor that created it, as long as its associated parameters remain part of the set represented by stream `malicious`.

The nested monitors used for forward dynamic parametrization process the same events as the root monitor, but it is often the case that only some of the events are relevant to a specific parametrized stream. We can use subtracing to redefine stream `suspicious` as follows:

```
1  output (Set Wallets) suspicious = foldl union empty
2    (elems (fellows 'over' malicious 'updating' (accounts tx[now])))
```

where `accounts` returns the set of all accounts involved in a transaction. The `updating` operator lets us specify the parameters of the monitors that have to process the current event.

In the example above, the monitor follows the dynamically parametrized stream once the parameter has been discovered (like in Lola2.0 [15] or in quantified event automata QEA [3]). However, monitoring a stream only after its parameter is discovered has its limitations, for example that the beginning prefix of the trace is ignored. In our example, this means that the monitor cannot discover wallets that interacted with a malicious account before the malicious account is identified, e.g. before a sandwich attacker reveals its identity.

We could still use *forward dynamic parametrization* to identify all wallets that ever interacted with malicious accounts, regardless of when the interaction happened. To achieve this, we need to follow all created accounts, tracked by stream `allaccounts`, and then, at every instant, keep only the wallets related to the malicious accounts discovered so far, using the stream `malicious`.

```
1 output (Set Account) allaccounts =
2   union (createdAccounts tx[now]) allaccounts[-1|empty]

3 output (Set Wallet) suspicious = foldl union empty
4   (elems (filterWithKey ismalicious
5     (suspicious ‘over‘ allaccounts ‘updating‘ (accounts tx[now]))))
6   where ismalicious k _ = member k malicious[now]
```

The function `filterWithKey p m` filters all the key-values in map `m` that satisfy the predicate `p`. Although this specification is correct, if most accounts are not malicious, this forward monitor follows many accounts unnecessarily.

However, as part of our infrastructure we have the node and indexer storing the past events of the trace, so we can combine *retroactive nested monitors* with *dynamic parametrization* when a new parameter is discovered, effectively implementing *retroactive dynamic parametrization*.

Retroactive Dynamic Parametrization. Retroactive dynamic parametrization [35] is a technique that allows monitors to revisit the past of the trace whenever a new parameter is discovered, initialize the parametric stream with the retrieved information and continue monitoring online from that point onward. This nested monitor behaves exactly as a forward parametrized monitor where an oracle had correctly guessed which parameters would be found to be useful and which parameters can be ignored. Retroactive dynamic parametrization is implemented by adding a new clause `withInit` to the `over` operator. This clause allows specifying an *initializer*, which initializes the nested monitor with events taken from the trace up to the current point. Typically, an initializer involves calling an external program (see Sect. 3) that interacts with an offline infrastructure to efficiently retrieve relevant past trace elements based on the discovered parameter.

We can use *retroactive* monitoring to only create the dynamic parameters when the corresponding account is malicious, and use the retroactive capability to inspect the past of the trace and see which wallets interacted with them in the past. We redefine the stream suspicious accordingly.

```
1 output (Set Wallets) suspicious = foldl union empty
2 (elems (suspicious 'over' malicious 'updating' accs 'withInit' initer))
3 where accs = accounts tx[now]
```

The new over expression specifies an initializer initer (whose definition is not shown in the specification) that calls the adapter to retrieve the past of the corresponding parameter. The adapter uses the indexer to efficiently retrieve only the events in the past relevant to the current account.

4.2 Execution Simulation

To further analyze sandwich attacks, one could be interested in determining the profit obtained by the attacker. This requires reasoning about what would have happened if the invocations to the blockchain had been different. In our example, we are interested in comparing what did happen (in particular the legitimate exchange invocation) with what would have happened if the attack had not existed. For these questions, our monitoring infrastructure introduces a simple *simulation* framework.

The blockchain state is public and the code of smart contracts code is available, and evaluation frameworks are typically provided by the blockchain developers (using the exact same code that bakers execute). We use the official Tezos interpreter in our monitoring infrastructure to perform a small-step execution machine of alternative executions and observe the blockchain intermediate states. We have developed two basic building blocks:

- **Data crawler:** for a given set of operations (blocks or groups) the data crawler queries the blockchain extracting which contracts were involved in the set of transactions requested.
- **Simulation:** given a set of contracts and their state, execute a sequence of grouped transactions in order.

This allows monitors to simulate operations that happened in the blockchain and also to explore alternative histories. To simulate operations that happened, we first get the required information to execute the operations, that is, the invoking smart contract and its state, plus all other invoked smart contracts and their states. Since we know what happened because it is publicly available on the blockchain node, we can determine the smart contracts involved in a given transaction. Once we have the initial states of every contract involved, we can just execute one transaction at a time replicating the behavior executed by the blockchain.

If we diverge from transactions that happened, as it would happen if we are executing hypothetical scenarios, we may get into missing some contract states. To explore alternative histories, we first obtained the contracts that were called during a possible execution. Then, we perform a hypothetical execution, which may lead to the invocation of smart contracts whose storages were not fetched. We detect the address of the missing contract, add it to the list of required addresses for execution using the data crawler and iterate until we finish execution.

We can extend our running example about detecting sandwich attacks computing the damage suffered by the victim simulating an alternative execution in which the sandwich attack does not exist and comparing the hypothetical and the real balance of the victim.

```
1  input Transaction tx
2  input Double balanceA
3  const a = "tz123"
4  output Double stolen =
5    if attacked[now]
6    then (getBalance a (simulate txs')) - balanceA[now]
7    else 0
8    where txs' = filter (not frontruns) (pastRetriever 10)
9          frontruns t = client t /= a && exchange t == exchange tx[now]
10         && tokens1 t == tokens1 tx[now] && tokens2 t == tokens2 tx[now]
```

In the example above, we only expose the difference between the real and alternative balances of the victim. To precisely quantify how much the attacker stole, the monitor can also inspect manually the valuable items (as tokens) and describe the computation as an arithmetic expression. In summary, previous specifications detect and extract transactions causing sandwich attacks, filter them and observe the state of the blockchain as if these transactions had not been executed.

5   Case Studies

1. Detecting Sandwich Attacks. We used our framework to implement a retroactive dynamic monitor for the detection of sandwich attacks, identification of malicious addresses and quantification of the losses incurred.

The monitor receives a stream of transactions from the Tezos blockchain and searches for possible sandwich attacks. In this case study, we set the victim account a to an exchange aggregator smart contract known as *3route v4*.

We executed the monitor starting from block 5,200,000 in the Tezos main net until block 5,250,000. Retroactive parametrization allows us to start the monitor at any point in the blockchain and find fund transfers that happened before the monitor was launched. The table in Fig. 2 sums up the results obtained.

Number of monitored blocks	50,000
Number of transactions in monitored blocks	2,624,594
Number of transactions since the beginning of the blockchain	288,705,340
Number of calls to 3route v4	2,278
Number of attacks	39
Number of malicious accounts	3
Number of suspicious accounts	97
Number of suspicious wallets	5

Fig. 2. Summary of sandwich attack monitoring.

Thanks to retroactive monitoring, we obtained the suspect accounts without analyzing every transaction. Instead of following 288 million transactions, the monitor only queries the adapter for the past transactions when a specific target is dynamically obtained, in the infrequent event where a suspicious account is found. Furthermore, the search for the frontrunning and backrunning transactions is only performed when the monitor detects a call to the exchange aggregator, which occurred only in 0,08% of the monitored transactions.

2. Clustering. In this case study, we consider that an address that performs front-running is a *malicious* address, and we mark the addresses that transferred cryptocurrency in the past to a malicious address as the potential source of funds is a *suspicious* address. We leave out of the search addresses that transferred funds to suspicious accounts.

When we start to follow indirectly related addresses, we find that they form *clusters* of heavily-interacting accounts with prominent addresses that act as interconnecting hubs between clusters. The flexibility of HLola allowed us to develop several implementations of clustering algorithms to discover the degree of suspiciousness of a wallet with respect to a malicious account based on how many times they interact (directly or indirectly), how many funds they exchange (directly or indirectly), and how many intermediaries are in their relation.

3. Juster. Juster is a decentralized application that allows Tezos users to bet on events that represent the changes of certain cryptocurrency prices within a given time interval. Users get a reward if their predictions are correct and lose their bet otherwise. For example, users can bet that the value of the Tezos cryptocurrency XTZ will rise by 10% or more in the following day. The Juster administrator opens events on which the users can bet and closes them after the betting interval ends, distributing the earnings accordingly.

We define an HLola monitor for the Juster platform assessing that:

(1) all closed events were previously open and no open event is reopened;
(2) there are less than 100 open events at any given time.

The monitor receives events tagged with an identifier `eventId` and with the kind of event which can be either `Open` or `Close`. We define the specification in HLola:

```
1  input EventId eventId
2  input Operation operation

3  define {EventId} open_events =
4    if operation[now] == Open
5      then insert(eventId[now], openevents[-1|{}])
6    else if operation[now] == Close
7      then delete(eventId[now], openevents[-1|{}])
8    else openevents[-1|{}]

9  output Bool few_events = size(openevents[now]) < 100

10 output Bool right_order =
11   (operation[now] == Close) == member(eventId[now], openevents[-1|{}])
```

4. BFS Vs DFS in Tezos. Tezos is a self-amending blockchain that provides a mechanism to change its rules through regular protocol upgrades. Protocol Florence [32], modified the execution order of operations between smart contracts, switching from a breadth-first search (BFS) to a more conventional depth-first search (DFS) algorithm. This change in the execution order can potentially impact transactions outcomes. In this case study, we identified those transactions that could have behaved differently under the two execution orders.

A naive approach is to simulate each transaction under both execution orders and compare the results. However, this approach is very inefficient for the entire blockchain because simulating requires access to all invoked smart contracts and their states (see Sect. 4.2). Fortunately, most transactions are guaranteed to behave the same under BFS and DFS without simulation, because the execution order only affects if some smart contract is invoked twice and the order of the calls differs between execution orders. This is because the state of a contract only varies when the contract is invoked. The difference in the call order to a smart contract can be detected by inspecting the transaction call graph (a directed tree where nodes are labeled with smart contracts and edges represent calls).

Unfortunately, indexers do not store the transactions call graph, but only the call sequence. For each transaction, the monitor creates all possible call graphs that can generate the given call sequence when traversed with the corresponding execution order. If in one of the call graphs, the call order for a smart contract differs between BFS and DFS, the monitor marks that the transaction must be simulated.

For this case study, we considered all 34,856,986 transactions corresponding to the years 2021 and 2022. We used the adapter to retrieve from the indexer only those transactions in which some smart contract is called more than once, obtaining 1,260,145 transactions. For each transaction, then the adapter produces only its identifier, call sequence, and the execution order used when executing it. As the actual name and address of the smart contract invoked is irrelevant in this case, to save space, the formater assigns to each smart contract in a given transaction a unique small identifier. Finally, the monitor received all 1,260,145 transactions and detected that only 599,684 (out of 34,856,986) require simulation to determine behavioral differences under the other execution order.

6 Conclusions

We presented in this paper a framework for the offchain runtime verification of blockchains, and more specifically, for the Tezos Blockchain. Offchain monitoring allows us to create monitors which receive new blocks (as in online monitoring) and can perform retroactive queries to the past of the blockchain (as in offline monitoring). The retroactive feature is useful both for requesting information about the past, before the monitoring was created, and to lazily evaluate events that most of the time are irrelevant for the monitor.

We described our implementation based on stream runtime verification, and in particular on the HLola language, and several cases studies including the detection of sandwich attacks. Future work includes more advanced case studies and more quantitative evaluation and comparison with other frameworks, which was beyond the scope of this work. Additionally, we plan to make the monitoring front-end available as a service, enabling its application for other blockchains.

References

1. Ahrendt, W., Bubel, R.: Functional verification of smart contracts via strong data integrity. In: Margaria, T., Steffen, B. (eds.) ISoLA 2020. LNCS, vol. 12478, pp. 9–24. Springer, Cham (2020). https://doi.org/10.1007/978-3-030-61467-6_2
2. Azzopardi, S., Ellul, J., Pace, G.J.: Monitoring smart contracts: ContractLarva and open challenges beyond. In: Colombo, C., Leucker, M. (eds.) RV 2018. LNCS, vol. 11237, pp. 113–137. Springer, Cham (2018). https://doi.org/10.1007/978-3-030-03769-7_8
3. Barringer, H., Falcone, Y., Havelund, K., Reger, G., Rydeheard, D.: Quantified event automata: towards expressive and efficient runtime monitors. In: Giannakopoulou, D., Méry, D. (eds.) FM 2012. LNCS, vol. 7436, pp. 68–84. Springer, Heidelberg (2012). https://doi.org/10.1007/978-3-642-32759-9_9
4. Bartocci, E., Falcone, Y. (eds.): Lectures on Runtime Verification - Introductory and Advanced Topics, LNCS, vol. 10457. Springer (2018). https://doi.org/10.1007/978-3-319-75632-5
5. Bartoletti, M., Pes, B., Serusi, S.: Data mining for detecting bitcoin ponzi schemes. In: CVCBT 2018, pp. 75–84 (2018)
6. Bernardo, B., Cauderlier, R., Hu, Z., Pesin, B., Tesson, J.: Mi-Cho-Coq, a framework for certifying Tezos smart contracts. arXiv abs/1909.08671 (2019). http://arxiv.org/abs/1909.08671
7. Bhargavan, K., et al.: Formal verification of smart contracts: short paper. In: Proceedings of PLAS@CCS 2016, pp. 91–96. ACM (2016)
8. Capretto, M., Ceresa, M., Sánchez, C.: Transaction monitoring of smart contracts. In: Proceedings of RV 2022. LNCS, vol. 13498, pp. 162–180. Springer (2022). https://doi.org/10.1007/978-3-031-17196-3_9

9. Ceresa, M., Gorostiaga, F., Sánchez, C.: Declarative stream runtime verification (hLola). In: Oliveira, B.C.S. (ed.) APLAS 2020. LNCS, vol. 12470, pp. 25–43. Springer, Cham (2020). https://doi.org/10.1007/978-3-030-64437-6_2
10. Christin, N.: Traveling the silk road: a measurement analysis of a large anonymous online marketplace. In: Proceedings of ACM WWW 2013, pp. 213–224 (2013)
11. Conchon, S., Korneva, A., Zaïdi, F.: Verifying smart contracts with cubicle. In: Sekerinski, E., et al. (eds.) FM 2019. LNCS, vol. 12232, pp. 312–324. Springer, Cham (2020). https://doi.org/10.1007/978-3-030-54994-7_23
12. Conti, M., Gangwal, A., Ruj, S.: On the economic significance of ransomware campaigns: a bitcoin transactions perspective. Comput. Secur. **79**, 162–189 (2018)
13. D'Angelo, B., Sankaranarayanan, S., Sánchez, C., Robinson, W., Finkbeiner, B., Sipma, H.B., Mehrotra, S., Manna, Z.: LOLA: Runtime monitoring of synchronous systems. In: Proceedingd of TIME 2005, pp. 166–174. IEEE CS Press (2005)
14. Ellul, J., Pace, G.J.: Runtime verification of Ethereum smart contracts. In: Proceedings of EDCC 2018, pp. 158–163. IEEE Computer Society (2018)
15. Faymonville, P., et al.: StreamLAB: stream-based monitoring of cyber-physical systems. In: Dillig, I., Tasiran, S. (eds.) CAV 2019. LNCS, vol. 11561, pp. 421–431. Springer, Cham (2019). https://doi.org/10.1007/978-3-030-25540-4_24
16. Gomez, G., Moreno-Sanchez, P., Caballero, J.: Watch your back: Identifying cyber-crime financial relationships in bitcoin through back-and-forth exploration. In: Proceedings of ACM CCS 2022, pp. 1291–1305 (2022)
17. Goodman, L.M.: Tezos – A self-amending crypto-ledger (2014). https://www.tezos.com/whitepaper.pdf
18. Gorostiaga, F., Sánchez, C.: Striver: stream runtime verification for real-time event-streams. In: Colombo, C., Leucker, M. (eds.) RV 2018. LNCS, vol. 11237, pp. 282–298. Springer, Cham (2018). https://doi.org/10.1007/978-3-030-03769-7_16
19. Gorostiaga, F., Sánchez, C.: Stream runtime verification of real-time event streams with the Striver language. Int. J. Softw. Tools Technol. Transfer **23**(2), 157–183 (2021). https://doi.org/10.1007/s10009-021-00605-3
20. Gorostiaga, F., Sánchez, C.: Nested monitors: monitors as expressions to build monitors. In: Feng, L., Fisman, D. (eds.) RV 2021. LNCS, vol. 12974, pp. 164–183. Springer, Cham (2021). https://doi.org/10.1007/978-3-030-88494-9_9
21. Gorostiaga, F., Sánchez, C.: Stream runtime verification of real-time event streams with the Striver language. Int. J. Softw. Tools Technol. Transfer **23**(2), 157–183 (2021). https://doi.org/10.1007/s10009-021-00605-3
22. Gorostiaga, F., Sánchez, C.: Monitorability of expressive verdicts. In: Proceedings of NFM 2022. LNCS, vol. 13260, pp. 693–712. Springer (2022). https://doi.org/10.1007/978-3-031-06773-0_37
23. Huang, D.Y., Aliapoulios, M.M., Li, V.G., Invernizzi, L., Bursztein, E., McRoberts, K., Levin, J., Levchenko, K., Snoeren, A.C., McCoy, D.: Tracking ransomware end-to-end. In: 2018 IEEE Symposium on Security and Privacy (SP), pp. 618–631
24. Lee, S., et al.: Cybercriminal minds: an investigative study of cryptocurrency abuses in the dark web. In: Proceedings of NDSS 2019
25. Leucker, M., Schallhart, C.: A brief account of runtime verification. J. Logic Algebr. Progr. **78**(5), 293–303 (2009)
26. Li, A., Choi, J.A., an. Long: Securing smart contract with runtime validation. In: Proceedings of ACM PLDI 2020, pp. 438–453. ACM (2020)
27. Liao, K., Zhao, Z., Doupe, A., Ahn, G.J.: Behind closed doors: measurement and analysis of cryptolocker ransoms in bitcoin. In: 2016 APWG Symposium on Electronic Crime Research (eCrime), pp. 1–13

28. Meiklejohn, S., et al.: A fistful of bitcoins: characterizing payments among men with no names. Commun. ACM **59**(4), 86–93 (2016)
29. Möser, M., Böhme, R., Breuker, D.: An inquiry into money laundering tools in the bitcoin ecosystem. In: 2013 APWG eCrime Researchers Summit, pp. 1–14
30. Nakamoto, S.: Bitcoin: a peer-to-peer electronic cash system (2008). https://bitcoin.org/bitcoin.pdf
31. Nehaï, Z., Bobot, F.: Deductive proof of industrial smart contracts using Why3. In: Sekerinski, E., et al. (eds.) FM 2019. LNCS, vol. 12232, pp. 299–311. Springer, Cham (2020). https://doi.org/10.1007/978-3-030-54994-7_22
32. Nomadic Labs: Protocol florence. https://tezos.gitlab.io/protocols/009_florence.html. Accessed 6 June 2024
33. Paquet-Clouston, M., Haslhofer, B., Dupont, B.: Ransomware payments in the Bitcoin ecosystem. J. Cybersecur. **5**(1), tyz003 (2019)
34. Paquet-Clouston, M., Romiti, M., Haslhofer, B., Charvat, T.: Spams meet cryptocurrencies: sextortion in the bitcoin ecosystem. In: AFT 2019, pp. 76–88
35. Pedregal, P., Gorostiaga, F., Sánchez, C.: A stream runtime verification tool with nested and retroactive parametrization. In: Proceedings of RV2023. LNCS, vol. 14245, pp. 351–362. Springer (2023). https://doi.org/10.1007/978-3-031-44267-4_19
36. Permenev, A., Dimitrov, D., Tsankov, P., Drachsler-Cohen, D., Vechev, M.: VerX: Safety verification of smart contracts. In: Proceedings of S&P 2020, pp. 1661–1677. IEEE (2020)
37. Phil, D.: Analysis of the DAO exploit (2016). https://hackingdistributed.com/2016/06/18/analysis-of-the-dao-exploit/
38. Pletinckx, S., Trap, C., Doerr, C.: Malware coordination using the blockchain: an analysis of the cerber ransomware. In: CNS 2018. pp. 1–9 (2018)
39. Pnueli, A.: The temporal logic of programs. In: Proceedings of FOCS 2077, pp. 46–67. IEEE CS Press (1977)
40. Ron, D., Shamir, A.: How did dread pirate roberts acquire and protect his bitcoin wealth? In: Böhme, R., Brenner, M., Moore, T., Smith, M. (eds.) FC 2014. LNCS, vol. 8438, pp. 3–15. Springer, Heidelberg (2014). https://doi.org/10.1007/978-3-662-44774-1_1
41. Spagnuolo, M., Maggi, F., Zanero, S.: BitIodine: extracting intelligence from the bitcoin network. In: Christin, N., Safavi-Naini, R. (eds.) FC 2014. LNCS, vol. 8437, pp. 457–468. Springer, Heidelberg (2014). https://doi.org/10.1007/978-3-662-45472-5_29
42. Stephens, J., Ferles, K., Mariano, B., Lahiri, S., Dillig, I.: SmartPulse: automated checking of temporal properties in smart contracts. In: Proceedings of S&P 2021. IEEE (2021)
43. Szabo, N.: Smart contracts: building blocks for digital markets. Extropy **18**, 28 (1996)
44. Tekiner, E., Acar, A., Uluagac, A.S., Kirda, E., Selcuk, A.A.: SOK: cryptojacking malware. In: IEEE EuroS&P 2021, pp. 120–139
45. Wood, G.: Ethereum: a secure decentralised generalised transaction ledger. Ethereum Project Yellow Paper **151**, 1–32 (2014)

Quantifying Liveness and Safety
of Avalanche's Snowball

Quentin Kniep[1], Maxime Laval[2], Jakub Sliwinski[1(✉)], and Roger Wattenhofer[1]

[1] ETH Zurich, Zurich, Switzerland
{qkniep,jsliwinski,wattenhofer}@ethz.ch
[2] EPFL, Lausanne, Switzerland
maxime.laval@epfl.ch

Abstract. This work examines the resilience properties of the Snowball and Avalanche protocols that underlie the popular Avalanche blockchain. We experimentally quantify the resilience of Snowball using a simulation implemented in Rust, where the adversary strategically rebalances the network to delay termination.

We show that in a network of n nodes of equal stake, the adversary is able to break liveness when controlling $\Omega(\sqrt{n})$ nodes. Specifically, for $n = 2000$, a simple adversary controlling 5.2% of stake can successfully attack liveness. When the adversary is given additional information about the state of the network (without any communication or other advantages), the stake needed for a successful attack is as little as 2.8%.

We show that the adversary can break safety in time exponentially dependent on their stake, and inversely linearly related to the size of the network, e.g. in 265 rounds in expectation when the adversary controls 25% of a network of 3000.

We conclude that Snowball and Avalanche are akin to Byzantine reliable broadcast protocols as opposed to consensus.

1 Introduction

The Avalanche protocol [13] advertises exceptional performance in terms of transaction throughput and latency. The Avalanche blockchain based on the protocol has certainly gained significant attention and support within the cryptocurrency community, as evidenced by the remarkable market capitalization of its native token amounting to \$10B[1]. The media prominence and monetary value firmly place Avalanche among the most popular and successful blockchain systems.

The protocol is built on a simple mechanism that operates by repeatedly sampling random nodes of the network in order to gauge the system's support of a given decision and confirm transactions. Conceptually, the underlying Snowball protocol can be compared to a voting process for a binary choice concerning a transaction. The protocol description promises to swiftly converge to a final decision from a network state initially divided equally between two alternatives.

---

[1] https://coinmarketcap.com (Accessed: June 19 2024).

© The Author(s), under exclusive license to Springer Nature Switzerland AG 2025
J. Garcia-Alfaro et al. (Eds.): ESORICS 2024 Workshops, LNCS 15263, pp. 260–275, 2025.
https://doi.org/10.1007/978-3-031-82349-7_18

With the aid of a directed acyclic graph (DAG), Avalanche forms a partial order of transactions instead of the total order that is established by usual blockchain protocols, like Bitcoin [12] or Ethereum [6]. Thus when transactions on Avalanche are accepted, validators are able to execute them in different orders based on their current view of the DAG, as long as those transactions are not causally dependent on each other. In theory, such structure can allow for a higher degree of parallelism in the transaction confirmation process, which can lead to a higher throughput than traditional blockchain protocols.

The ideas that form Avalanche stand in contrast to other Proof-of-Stake and BFT-based consensus protocols such as Ethereum 2.0. While the whitepaper [13] claims excellent resilience, it only proves the protocol's liveness in presence of up to $\mathcal{O}(\sqrt{n})$ malicious parties, where n represents the total number of validators (or stake supply). However, usually Proof-of-Stake protocols ensure the upper bound resilience of $\frac{n}{3}$ in partial synchrony.

Another detail that stands out in the description of Avalanche, is how it defines its guarantees with respect to "virtuous" transactions, i.e. assuming there's no conflicting alternative in the system. Remarkably, broadcast-based payment systems [4,9] are inherently reliant on such an assumption, and as such are fundamentally weaker than consensus protocols.

The lack of clarity about the Avalanche family of protocols begs the question: how resilient Snowball and Avalanche really are? Does the unusual consideration of "virtuous" transactions indicate a fundamental limitation?

Our Contribution. We examine the resilience properties of the Snowball and Avalanche protocols.

We experimentally exhibit the resilience of Snowball against attacks from adversarial nodes. Our simulation showcases that in a system of n nodes (or stake supply), the adversary can indefinitely halt the Snowball protocol when controlling a stake of $\Omega(\sqrt{n})$, or less than 2% in some experimental scenarios. Furthermore, we examine a strategy for an adversary to violate safety by getting a single validator to finalize an output distinct from the rest of the network. The expected duration of the safety attack depends exponentially on the stake controlled by the adversary, and is inversely linear to the size of the network. For example, at 25% adversarial stake in a network of 3000, safety can be violated after 265 rounds in expectation.

We discuss how these considerations translate to the Avalanche protocol based on Snowball.

Finally, we draw parallels between Avalanche and broadcast-based payment systems, and conclude that Avalanche is fundamentally weaker than usual consensus protocols.

2 Background

Avalanche's blockchain platform consists of three distinct built-in blockchains: The Exchange Chain (X-Chain), the Contract Chain (C-Chain) and the Platform Chain (P-Chain) [14].

The **X-Chain** is responsible for processing simple transactions on the network, such as transfers of the native AVAX token. It is based on the Avalanche protocol with the DAG that runs multiple instances of the Snowball algorithm and only partially orders transactions.

The **C-Chain** is responsible for executing general smart contracts compatible with the Ethereum Virtual Machine (EVM). In contrast to the X-Chain, C-Chain uses the Snowman protocol which ensures a total order of all transactions.

The **P-Chain** processes various platform-level operations, such as creation of new blockchains and sub-networks, validator (de-)registration, or staking operations. It also uses Snowman.

The Avalanche protocol introduced in the Ava Labs whitepaper, which is also mainly marketed and presented in online materials, is used as the basis of X-Chain. Interestingly, the Snowman protocol, which supports the C-Chain and P-Chain, is almost absent from documentation and marketing, and remains outside the scope of this work.

2.1   Validators

Participants in the Avalanche protocol are called validators or nodes. Validators following the protocol are called honest. As a blockchain protocol, Avalanche aims to be resilient to validators deviating from the protocol, which are called malicious, or collectively as the adversary.

Avalanche employs a Proof-of-Stake mechanism to control the ability of malicious validators joining the system. Validators need to acquire AVAX tokens (2,000 minimum) and deposit them using the Avalanche platform to actively participate in the agreement process. Validators are associated with, and weighted by, the amounts of deposited tokens, called their *stake*. Typically, Proof-of-Stake blockchains aim to be resilient to the adversary that is able to acquire a stake smaller than $1/3$ of the total tokens (which is the theoretical maximum in harsh network conditions).

2.2   UTXO Model

Avalanche uses the Unspent Transaction Output (UTXO) model, as initially introduced in Bitcoin [12]. In the model, a transaction contains a set of inputs, a set of outputs, and a digital signature. Each input of a transaction corresponds to a specific output from a previous transaction. Transactions are issued by users, processed by the system, and as a result are accepted or rejected by the system.

Two transactions including the same input are *conflicting*, and only one transaction from such a pair can be accepted by the system.

The balance of a user is determined by the set of outputs transferred to that user in previously accepted transactions and not yet used as inputs for newer transactions. A valid transaction is also signed with keys corresponding to the relevant inputs.

In contrast to most blockchains such as Bitcoin, Avalanche does not necessitate a total order of all transactions. Instead, transactions in Avalanche form a directed acyclic graph (DAG) resulting in a partial order. A transaction tx' depends on tx if tx' consumes an output of tx. In this case, every validator needs to process tx before processing tx'. Validators can execute transactions that are not dependent on each other in any order.

3   Snowball

The Snowball protocol serves as the foundational component of the Avalanche blockchain. It is based on continuously querying random sets of k validators regarding their current "approval" regarding a transaction, denoted as T.

When performing a query on $k = 20$ nodes within a Snowball instance, the selection probability of a node is proportional to the stake of the node. Intuitively, the influence of validators in validating transactions, quantified by the probability of them being queried, is determined by their stake.

Validators maintain a confidence value for each binary choice: Blue if they prefer to accept transaction T, Red if they reject transaction T. When a validator queried k other nodes and saw at least α for either Red or Blue, we say that this color received a *chit*, and the confidence value for that color is incremented by one. When queried, a validator will either respond Blue if the confidence value for Blue is higher, or Red if the confidence value for Red is higher. A color is accepted by a node if for at least β consecutive rounds of querying it received a chit. The logic of Snowball is illustrated in Fig. 1.

3.1   Safety

Intuitively, safety properties can be understood as "bad" things not happening. In our context, the main safety property is ensuring that two honest nodes cannot perceive two conflicting transactions as accepted. The Avalanche whitepaper outlines the definition of safety as follows:

P1. Safety: When decisions are made by any two honest nodes, they decide on conflicting transactions with negligible probability ($\leq \varepsilon$).

Here ε represents the safety failure probability, with the specific value dependent on the maximum number f of adversarial nodes, which is not explicitly stated in the formal definition provided by the Avalanche whitepaper.

3.2   Liveness

Liveness refers to the continued operation of the system. In our context, liveness mainly refers to ensuring that all honest nodes eventually decide to accept or reject a transaction within a reasonable time frame.

According to the whitepaper, Avalanche has the following liveness guarantees:
P2. Liveness (Upper Bound): Snow protocols terminate with a strictly positive probability within t_{max} rounds. **P3. Liveness (Strong Form):** If $f \in \mathcal{O}(\sqrt{n})$, then the snow protocol terminates with high probability ($\geq 1 - \varepsilon$) in $\mathcal{O}(\log(n))$ rounds.

$k, \alpha, \beta \leftarrow 20, 15, 20$ ▷ *Protocol parameters*

function SNOWBALL($V, v_{\text{self}}, c_{\text{init}}$)
    $c_{\text{pref}} \leftarrow c_{\text{init}}$
    $c_{\text{last}} \leftarrow c_{\text{init}}$
    $confidence \leftarrow [0, 0]$
    $counter \leftarrow 0$

    while $counter < \beta$ **do**
        $V_{\text{query}} \leftarrow$ SAMPLEVAL($V \setminus \{v_{\text{self}}\}, k$)   ▷ *Weighted by stake with replacement.*
        $R \leftarrow$ QUERY(V_{query}) ▷ *Query each with v_{self}, c_{pref}; R is multiset of responses.*
        for $i \in \{0, 1\}$ **do**
            if $|[r \in R \mid r = i]| \geq \alpha$ **then**
                if $c_{\text{last}} \neq i$ **then**
                    $counter \leftarrow 0$
                $confidence[i] \leftarrow confidence[i] + 1$
                if $confidence[i] > confidence[1 - i]$ **then**
                    $c_{\text{pref}} \leftarrow i$
                $c_{\text{last}} \leftarrow i$
                $counter \leftarrow counter + 1$
    return c_{last}

function RESPONDTOQUERY($querier, c_{\text{querier}}$)
    if $c_{\text{pref}} = \bot$ **then**
        $c_{\text{pref}} \leftarrow c_{\text{querier}}$
    return c_{pref}

Fig. 1. Snowball algorithm.

However, it is specified later in the whitepaper that P2 holds only under the assumption that initially, one proposal has at least $\frac{\alpha}{k}$ support in the network, for which there is no guarantee.

4   Simulation

To test resilience of Snowball, we perform a local simulation of the protocol using a Rust implementation [3]. As the base implementation of Snowball (c.f. Figure 1) we use the `avalanche-consensus` Rust library[2], which is a translation of the Snowball Go code that is part of the official Avalanche implementation[3] and is maintained by the Ava Labs team.

The simulation involves a network of multiple honest nodes executing the protocol correctly, aiming to achieve agreement on a binary decision. Malicious nodes collude to perform the considered attacks. In our experimental scenarios, the stake is equally divided among validators.

---

[2] https://crates.io/crates/avalanche-consensus.
[3] https://github.com/ava-labs/avalanchego.

4.1   Network Assumptions

Distributed protocols might require various network reliability assumptions to work correctly. Many blockchain protocols guarantee safety in harsh network conditions, such as those of partially synchronous models, where messages can be greatly delayed.

In our simulation we make the strongest network reliability assumptions possible, where every message arrives with the same, known latency. We deny the adversary any communication advantage whatsoever, including advantages often practically achievable by an attacker in the real world, such as performing queries faster, or performing more queries.

In synchronous rounds, nodes query other nodes, as described by the Snowball protocol. Between rounds, the nodes update their preferred color with which they respond to the queries.

4.2   Adversary Information

To perform the attacks, the adversary needs information about the other nodes' preferred color. We call the adversary *naive* if the adversary simply queries honest nodes in line with the protocol and updates his estimation of the colors preferred by the honest nodes according to the query results.

We also consider an adversary that possesses accurate information about the numbers of nodes preferring Red/Blue in the current round, and call that adversary *informed*.

4.3   Liveness Attack

When attacking the liveness property, the adversary aims to delay the decision of honest nodes by keeping the network split equally between Red and Blue. The attack strategy we consider is straightforward. When the adversary is queried, it responds with the color that is less preferred among all honest validators. By doing so, the adversary aims to bring the network split between the Red and Blue decisions closer to the even 50-50 split. This is shown in Fig. 2.

n, f ▷ *Network parameters.*
μ_{estimate} ▷ *Current estimate of network-wide preference towards 1.*

function RESPONDTOQUERY($v_{\text{query}}, c_{\text{querier}}$)
   if $\mu_{\text{estimate}} < 0.5$ **then**
     return 1
   return 0

Fig. 2. Adversary strategy for liveness attack.

For a given experimental scenario, we consider the attack successful if in more than 5 out of 10 simulation runs, no validator has terminated with a decision after 100,000 rounds. We note that if a round of querying took about 1 s, 100,000 rounds would correspond to over a day.

We perform binary search with respect to the adversary stake to find the minimal fraction of total stake for which the adversary is successful. Figure 3 shows the minimum percentage of stake the adversary needs to attack the liveness of the protocol. It can be seen to decrease significantly with increasing number of total nodes in the network, showing the sub-linear security bound.

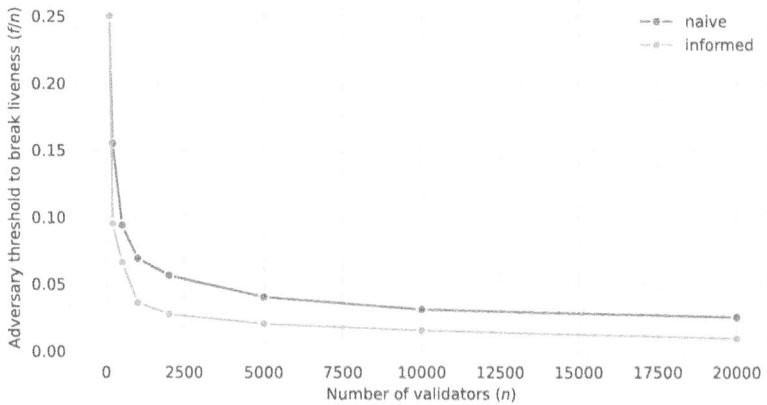

Fig. 3. Minimum fraction of stake needed by the adversary to successfully attack liveness, plotted against the number of nodes in the network with equal stake.

4.4 Safety Attack

In this scenario, the adversary aims to break the safety property of the protocol by causing some honest nodes to accept conflicting transactions.

The adversarial strategy we consider starts with maintaining a modified liveness attack. While the honest nodes are divided between Red and Blue, denote by μ the fraction of honest nodes that prefer Red. Then, the fraction of honest nodes that prefer Blue is $1 - \mu$. The adversary attempts to keep the numbers of honest nodes preferring Red and Blue close to the $\mu : Red, 1 - \mu : Blue$ split by replying to queries with colors that sway the honest nodes towards this split. Additionally, the adversary chooses a set of honest nodes to queries of which the adversary responds exclusively with Red. By employing this approach, the attacker can significantly increase the likelihood of the targeted nodes finalizing with the color Red after some time, while at the same time keeping the rest of the network from deciding in either direction. Once some targeted node accepts Red, the adversary replies to all queries with the color Blue, such that the rest of the network accepts Blue. As a result, the adversary produces a safety violation, as the targeted node decides differently to the rest of the network.

Figure 4 describes the adversarial strategy for the considered safety attack.

n, f ▷ *Network parameters.*
V_{target} ▷ *Validators targeted in the safety attack.*
$\mu_{estimate}$ ▷ *Current estimate of network-wide preference towards 1.*
μ_{target} ▷ *Target split to maintain before finalization.*
fin ▷ *Indicator if some targeted validator has finalized.*

function RESPONDTOQUERY($v_{query}, c_{querier}$)
   if fin **then**
      return 0
   else if $v_{query} \in V_{target}$ **then**
      return 1

   if $\mu_{estimate} < \mu_{target}$ **then**   ▷ *Otherwise, continue with regular liveness attack.*
      return 1
   return 0

Fig. 4. Adversary strategy for safety attack.

4.5   Safety Attack Analysis

Consider the attack where a single node is targeted. Denote the number of adversarial nodes by f and the number of nodes in total by n. Assuming that the adversary can maintain the honest nodes split of $\mu : Red,\ 1 - \mu : Blue$, in expectation we observe the following: when the targeted node queries, it receives a percentage of $\mu(1 - \frac{f}{n}) + \frac{f}{n}$ responses for Red, while other nodes receive $\geq \mu(1 - \frac{f}{n})$ fraction of responses for Red, depending on the adversary. For example, with 30% adversary stake and a split of 69.4% Red and 30.6% Blue among honest nodes, the targeted node has a probability $p = 0.694 \cdot 0.7 + 0.3 = 0.7858$ of receiving a Red response when querying. Consequently, the targeted node can finalize Red with some probability, which eventually occurs.

Once this happens, the adversary replies to all queries with Blue. Since $\mu(1 - \frac{f}{n}) = 0.694 \cdot 0.7 = 0.4858 < 0.5$, it is very likely that all honest nodes flip to Blue and later accept Blue. In general, if $\mu(1 - \frac{f}{n}) < 0.5$, the adversary still has the ability to sway the network towards accepting Blue.

We now compute the probability that the targeted node converges to Red, given that it sees an average proportion of $\mu(1 - \frac{f}{n}) + \frac{f}{n}$ of responses in favor of Red when querying. Recall that when querying $k = 20$ other nodes, a validator increments its successive success counter, denoted as "counter", only if a color receives at least $\alpha = 15$ votes, and if this color is the same as the currently preferred color. Otherwise, the success counter is reset to 0.

Let the random variable X denote the number of participants who prefer Red in a sample of size $k = 20$. We want to calculate the probability distribution $P(X \geq \alpha) = 1 - P(X < 15)$. We can model this using a binomial distribution with parameters $p = \mu(1 - \frac{f}{n}) + \frac{f}{n}$ for the targeted node and $p = \mu(1 - \frac{f}{n})$ for the other nodes. Thus, we have:

$$P(X \geq \alpha) = 1 - P(X < \alpha) = 1 - F(\alpha - 1, k, p) = 1 - \sum_{i=0}^{\alpha-1} \binom{k}{i} p^i (1-p)^{k-i}$$

Here, $F(\alpha - 1, k, p)$ represents the cumulative distribution function (CDF) of the binomial distribution. For our previous example, where $\mu = 0.694$, for honest nodes other than the attack target, we can calculate the probability $P(X \geq \alpha)$, which represents the chance of reaching the α majority threshold for the color Red when querying. Plugging in the probability to receive a response supporting Red in a single round $p = 0.4858$ from above, we get $P(X \geq \alpha) = 1 - F(14, 20, 0.4858) \approx 0.015$. On the other hand, the targeted node that has a probability $p = 0.7858$ to get a Red response, and so $p_\alpha = P(X \geq \alpha) = 1 - F(14, 20, 0.7858) \approx 0.756$. This means that our targeted node has a $p_\alpha \approx 75.6\%$ chance of reaching the α majority for Red when querying $k = 20$ other nodes, whereas other honest nodes only have a 1.5% chance of the same. Consider the expected number of iterations needed to obtain $\beta = 20$ consecutive successes of reaching the $\alpha = 15$ majority for a color. Let X_β represent the number of trials required to achieve β consecutive successes, with the probability of one success being p_α. From [8], we can use the following formulas:

$$\mathbb{E}[X_\beta] = \frac{1 - p_\alpha^\beta}{(1 - p_\alpha)p_\alpha^\beta}$$

$$\mathbb{V}ar[X_\beta] = \frac{1 - (2\beta + 1)(1 - p_\alpha)p_\alpha^\beta - p_\alpha^{2\beta+1}}{(1 - p_\alpha)^2 p_\alpha^{2\beta}}$$

For the example where $p_\alpha = 0.756$ for the targeted node, we obtain:

$$\mathbb{E}[X_{20}] \approx 1095$$

$$\sigma = \sqrt{\mathbb{V}ar[X_{20}]} \approx 1078$$

On average, the targeted node needs to query 1,095 times with a standard deviation of 1,078. We confirmed the expected results experimentally.

The effectiveness of the attack can be greatly increased by targeting a large number of nodes rather than just one. Let X_β^k be the number of trials required for any target node among k targeted nodes to achieve β consecutive successes. Assuming the β successes to be equally probable to conclude in every round after 19, and assuming the constant network split maintained by the adversary, the expected number $\mathbb{E}[X_\beta^k]$ is $\frac{\mathbb{E}[X_\beta - 19]}{k} + 19$. We have simulated some experimental scenarios, such as targeting 1000 nodes with $n = 3000$ and the adversarial stake of $f = 750$, where the results matched our expectation.

With increasing total number of nodes n, the adversary can target more nodes. While in our experiments we successfully targeted over $0.3n$ of $n = 3000$ nodes, future work is needed to understand how big the share of targeted nodes can be in an optimal strategy and with increasing n. In summary, the strength

Table 1. Summary of the expected safety attack results for different percentages of adversarial stake and corresponding stable network splits. The second column shows the maximally imbalanced but stable split of honest validators that the adversary is able to maintain. $\mathbb{E}[X_{20}^{1000}]$ is the expected length of the safety attack when 1000 nodes are targeted.

Adversary	Honest Split	p_α	$\mathbb{E}[X_{20}]$	σ	$\approx \mathbb{E}[X_{20}^{1000}]$
30%	69.4% - 30.6%	0.756	1,095	1,078	20
25%	64.8% - 35.2%	0.560	245,562	245,544	265
20%	60.7% - 39.3%	0.364	9.4e+8	9.4e+8	940,000
10%	54.0% - 46.0%	0.101	8.4e+19	8.4e+19	8.4e+16
5%	51.2% - 48.8%	0.043	2.5e+27	2.5e+27	2.5e+24

of the attack corresponds exponentially to the share of the adversary stake. On the other hand, the expected required duration of the attack is inversely linear to the overall number of nodes n, as the number of targeted nodes can increase roughly linearly with n. Table 1 summarizes the effectiveness of the safety attack for adversaries of different strengths.

5   Avalanche Protocol

In this section, we explain how the Avalanche protocol builds on Snowball to incorporate optimizations and additional features.

5.1   DAG

To enhance the throughput and enable parallel processing of transactions, the Avalanche protocol builds a directed acyclic graph (DAG) for transactions, instead of a linear chain. Each transaction is represented as a node in the DAG. Furthermore, transactions in the DAG are interconnected through parent-child relationships: A transaction T refers to older transactions known as its parents $\mathsf{Parents}(T)$. We denote the parent relation $T' \in \mathsf{Parents}(T)$ by $T' \leftarrow T$. If T'' is reachable by parent links from T, we say that T'' is an ancestor of T, or $T'' \in \mathsf{Ancestors}(T)$, and that T is a descendant of T'', or $T \in \mathsf{Descendants}(T'')$.

5.2   Vertex

In order to limit the coordination overhead, a node in the Avalanche DAG is not an individual transaction but rather a batch of transactions known as a *vertex*. A vote for a vertex is considered a vote for all transactions contained within that vertex. This allows Avalanche to facilitate efficient queries, while still maintaining confidence levels and a conflict set for each individual transaction.

When a vertex is accepted, all transactions within it are accepted. When a vertex is rejected, valid transactions in that vertex may be batched into a new vertex, by removing the non-preferred transactions that resulted in the vertex getting rejected. When a node creates a vertex V, it chooses parents for V that are currently preferred.

When a user submits a payload transaction tx, a node creates a transaction $T\langle tx, \mathcal{D}\rangle$ for that payload. It includes the payload tx, along with the set of UTXO IDs that will be consumed if the transaction is accepted, and the list $\mathcal{D}$ of dependencies on which this transaction relies. Each dependency must be accepted before this transaction can be accepted. The node then batches this transaction $T\langle tx, \mathcal{D}\rangle$ with other pending transactions into a vertex. The node assigns one or more parents to this vertex, allowing it to be added to the DAG. We define an Avalanche transaction T as preferred if it is the preferred transaction in its conflict set P_T. In other words, if transaction T has the highest confidence among other conflicting transactions. Each node u calculates the confidence value for each transaction T denoted by $d_u[T]$. This confidence value is defined as the sum of the chits received by T and all its descendants [13]: $d[T] = \sum_{T' \in \mathcal{T}_u : T \in \mathsf{Descendants}(T')} c_{u,T'}$. Here, $\mathcal{T}_u$ represents all the transactions currently known by node u in its view of the DAG, and $c_{u,T'}$ represents the chit received by transaction T'. $c_{u,T}$ can only take two values: 0 or 1. Node u queries transaction T only once, as the votes on the descendants of T also serve as queries and votes on T. Specifically:

$$c_{u,T} = \begin{cases} 1 & \text{transaction } T \text{ received a chit when } u \text{ queried for it} \\ 0 & \text{otherwise} \end{cases}$$

As a reminder, receiving a chit for transaction T means that node u received an approval rate of at least $\alpha = 15$ when it queried $k = 20$ other nodes to determine if T was their preferred transaction. The confidence value of T (and thus its status as accepted or rejected) is then updated based on the queries made on its descendants.

We say that a transaction T is strongly preferred if T is preferred and all its ancestors are also preferred in their respective conflict sets. An Avalanche transaction T is considered virtuous if it conflicts with no other transactions or if it is strongly preferred. Consequently, a virtuous vertex is a vertex where all its transactions are virtuous. Similarly, a preferred or strongly preferred vertex is one where all its transactions are preferred or strongly preferred, respectively. The parents of a vertex are randomly chosen from the *virtuous frontier* set $\mathcal{VF}$, which consists of the vertices at the frontier of the DAG that are considered virtuous:

$$\mathcal{VF} = \{\, T \in \mathcal{T} \mid \mathsf{virtuous}(T) \wedge \neg\, \mathsf{virtuous}(T')\ \forall T' \in \mathcal{T} : T \leftarrow T'\}$$

The notation $\mathsf{virtuous}(T)$ indicates that T is virtuous. In other words, $\mathcal{VF}$ is the set of vertices that are virtuous, and have no virtuous children.

5.3   From Snowball to Avalanche

The Avalanche protocol runs a Snowball instance on the conflict set of each transaction T once a node hears about a new transaction that gets appended to the DAG. This means that when a new transaction T is received, a validator will query k other random nodes to determine if T is their preferred transaction. The queried nodes will respond positively only if transaction T and its ancestors in the DAG are also their preferred transactions within their respective conflict sets. Instead of querying a Snowball instance for each individual transaction, Avalanche batches transactions into a vertex and instantiates a Snowball instance for that vertex, checking if all the transactions within that vertex and its ancestors are valid.

When a node is queried about the preference of transaction T and its ancestors, it provides not just a binary vote as in Snowball, but rather responds with its entire virtuous frontier $\mathcal{VF}$ based on its local view. This allows the respondents to specify which ancestors are not preferred if T is not strongly preferred. The querying node u collects the virtuous frontier of the k queried nodes. For each virtuous frontier $\mathcal{VF}'$ sent by a node w as a vote, we add the transactions T' from $\mathcal{VF}'$ and the ancestors of T' to a set $\mathcal{G}[T, w]$, which represents the positively reported transactions of w when asked to vote for T. We then count how many times node w, when queried for T, has acknowledged a transaction T' as virtuous, and store this in the counter $ack[T, T']$. We then run a Snowball instance for every $ack[T, T']$: If $ack[T, T']$ received more than α votes it indicates that the α majority of the k queried validator agree that T' is preferred. We then increase the consecutive counter for T' if it was also the preferred transaction in the last vote. The above procedure of voting on a vertex containing a single transaction can be generalized for vertices containing multiple transactions.

Finally, there are two ways in which a vertex V, and consequently all the transactions it contains $T \in V$, can be accepted, provided that all the ancestors of V have also been accepted. The first way is if none of its transactions $T \in V$ conflict with any other transactions, and the vertex V received β_1 consecutive successes. In this case, the vertex and all its transactions are accepted by node u. The second way is if some transactions $T \in V$ have other transactions in their conflict sets, and the vertex V receives β_2 consecutive successes. In this case, the node accepts the vertex V and all its transactions. The Avalanche protocol denotes β_1 as `betaVirtuous` and β_2 as `betaRogue`, and naturally $\beta_1 < \beta_2$.

5.4   Liveness Attack

Suppose that two transactions (both with accepted virtuous ancestors) T batched in vertex V and T' batched in vertex V' are conflicting. Recall that the Snowball liveness attack consisted of a strategy where the adversary tried to ensure that the split between Red and Blue was always close enough to 50% each. Here, the approach is similar, except that we have to ensure that, on average, 50% of the network has V in their virtuous frontier or as an ancestor of their virtuous frontier, and the other 50% of the nodes have V' in their virtuous frontier or as an ancestor of their virtuous frontier. The binary attack can be transposed to one where the adversaries responds with the virtuous frontier $\mathcal{VF}$, with V an ancestor of the nodes in $\mathcal{VF}$, or responds with the virtuous frontier $\mathcal{VF}'$, with V' an ancestor of the nodes in $\mathcal{VF}'$. The intuition behind this attack is that half of the nodes will adopt a virtuous frontier that contains vertex V as a virtuous vertex, and the other half of the nodes will adopt a virtuous frontier that contains V' as a virtuous node. At every iteration of the loop, the adversary needs to maintain those two conflicting virtuous frontiers $\mathcal{VF}$ and $\mathcal{VF}'$, grow the DAG such that some new valid vertices are appended to the conflicting $\mathcal{VF}$ and $\mathcal{VF}'$, and respond accordingly with either one of the virtuous forests using the same technique that was used for the Snowball liveness attack.

5.5   Safety Attack

The safety attack from Snowball to Avalanche can be transposed in the same way as was explained above for the liveness attack. Similarly, we will try to maintain a network split that does not converge: μ of nodes will prefer a virtuous frontier $\mathcal{VF}$ that contains v as an ancestor, and ν of nodes will prefer a virtuous frontier $\mathcal{VF}'$ that contains v' as an ancestor. For one targeted node, the adversary will respond exclusively with the virtuous frontier $\mathcal{VF}$ instead of trying to maintain a split. This way, we can make the targeted node to accept vertex v while all the other nodes are still undecided. Once this is done, the adversary can unanimously respond with virtuous frontier $\mathcal{VF}'$ to make the rest of the nodes accept v' in order to break safety. Such an attack can be instantiated by any adversary that creates conflicting (double spending) transactions T and T', batch them in nodes v and v' and conducts the attack to make some nodes accept T, and some other nodes accept T' thus resulting in a successful double spending.

6   Consensus or Broadcast

Consensus is a property that allows multiple parties to reach agreement on transactions, either accepting or rejecting them. In the context of blockchain systems, consensus can be defined by the following set of properties:

Definition 1. *Each honest validator observes some transaction from a set of conflicting transactions $\{t_0, t_1, \ldots\}$. **Consensus** satisfies the following properties:*

  Totality: *If some honest validator accepts a transaction, every honest validator will eventually accept the same transaction.*
  Agreement: *No two honest validator accept conflicting transactions.*
  Validity: *If every honest validator observes the same transaction (there are no conflicting transactions), this transaction will be accepted by all honest validators.*
  Termination: *Some transaction from the set will eventually be accepted by honest validators.*

As implied by Agreement and Termination, a consensus protocol enables nodes to reach an agreement on conflicting transactions, where multiple valid transactions consuming the same input are involved. In such cases, all nodes should unanimously accept one of the conflicting transactions.

As we have established, the Avalanche protocol features a relatively weak, sublinear resilience to liveness attacks involving conflicting transactions. To address this issue, Avalanche introduces the term of virtuous transactions, which can enjoy better guarantees. In other words, even for a relatively small adversary, Avalanche does not satisfy the Termination property, and only guarantees termination if the Validity condition is also met: all honest validators observe just one valid transaction and no conflicting ones.

The termination property becomes crucial in scenarios involving smart contracts, where conflicting transactions may arise, such as two users attempting to purchase the same product. To address this limitation, the Avalanche team introduced a different solution for the C-Chain and P-Chain, specifically designed to execute smart contracts required for such blockchain applications.

As described by [9], consensus is not necessary for payment systems, and indeed there exist payment systems providing similar guarantees to Avalanche, while also unable to support general applications such as smart contracts: broadcast-based payment systems [4,5,7,11,15]. The provided guarantees of a Byzantine reliable broadcast can be defined as follows:

Definition 2. *Each honest validator observes some transaction from a set of conflicting transactions* $\{t_0, t_1, \dots\}$. ***Byzantine reliable broadcast*** *satisfies the properties of Consensus, without the Termination property.*

Thus, referring to Avalanche as a consensus protocol can be misleading, as it is more akin to broadcast-based payment systems. While the performance of Avalanche is given prominence, a different solution has been used as required by the C-Chain and P-Chain.

7 Related Work

Amores-Sesar et al. [2] analyze the Avalanche protocol. They explain the protocol with pseudocode and introduce a property of Avalanche that was omitted here: No-op transactions which are stateless transactions are added into the DAG by the nodes to make sure we always make progress on the finalization of older transactions. The paper introduces a liveness attack (different from ours) that could be possible if the naive way of voting for a transaction and its ancestors with just a binary yes/no vote was implemented. However, this is not the case, as emphasized at the end of the paper with the pseudocode involving the virtuous frontier concept.

Ash Ketchum and Misty Williams [10] raise concerns similar to ours in their recent write-up, that Avalanche is not a consensus protocol.

Most recently, a follow-up analysis by Amores-Sesar et al. [1] formalized the need for at least $\Omega(\log n + \beta)$ rounds for consensus with the Snow family of protocols. They then proposed a specific modification of Snowflake and Snowball implementing this change.

8   Conclusion

In this paper, we have examined the resilience properties of Avalanche and its underlying Snowball protocol. We have experimentally evaluated simple strategies for a potential adversary. To quantify the efficacy of these attacks, we have conducted simulations and evaluated the ratio of stake the adversary needs to control to launch successful attacks on liveness and safety.

Our analysis revealed that an adversary with a small fraction of the stake can indefinitely keep the network in a state where it cannot finalize a transaction. With some probability depending on the stake and the size of the network, the adversary can also convince some node to finalize a transaction that is then rejected by other honest parties, which can result in a double spending attack.

Through our analysis, we have demonstrated that the Snowball protocol - the foundation of Avalanche - is vulnerable, when conflicting transactions are present. The weak resilience when conflicting transactions are present is a critical limitation, as it makes the protocol unable to support general smart contracts. This explains why Avalanche actually uses a different protocol, called Snowman, which uses a linear blockchain (instead of a DAG) in order to totally order those transactions, unlike what is done for payments [14].

Future Work. The basis of our attacks relies on the presence of conflicting transactions. Future work could analyze how Avalanche distinguishes unique transactions, and determine the feasibility for an adversary to arbitrarily create conflicting transaction from another transaction T broadcast by an honest node, for example, by creating a copy with different parents in the DAG.

References

1. Amores-Sesar, I., Cachin, C., Schneider, P.: An analysis of Avalanche consensus. In: International Colloquium on Structural Information and Communication Complexity, pp. 27–44. Springer (2024). https://doi.org/10.1007/978-3-031-60603-8_2
2. Amores-Sesar, I., Cachin, C., Tedeschi, E.: When is spring coming? a security analysis of Avalanche consensus. arXiv preprint arXiv:2210.03423 (2022)
3. Anonymized for double-blind review: Git repository (2024)
4. Baudet, M., Danezis, G., Sonnino, A.: Fastpay: High-performance byzantine fault tolerant settlement. In: Proceedings of the 2nd ACM Conference on Advances in Financial Technologies, pp. 163–177 (2020)
5. Baudet, M., Sonnino, A., Kelkar, M., Danezis, G.: Zef: low-latency, scalable, private payments. In: Proceedings of the 22nd Workshop on Privacy in the Electronic Society, pp. 1–16 (2023)
6. Buterin, V.: Ethereum: A next-generation smart contract and decentralized application platform (2014). https://ethereum.org/content/whitepaper/whitepaper-pdf/Ethereum_Whitepaper_-_Buterin_2014.pdf
7. Collins, D., et al.: Online payments by merely broadcasting messages. In: 2020 50th Annual IEEE/IFIP International Conference on Dependable Systems and Networks (DSN), pp. 26–38. IEEE (2020)

8. Drekic, S., Spivey, M.Z.: On the number of trials needed to obtain k consecutive successes. Stat. Prob. Lett. **176**, 109132 (2021)
9. Guerraoui, R., Kuznetsov, P., Monti, M., Pavlovič, M., Seredinschi, D.A.: The consensus number of a cryptocurrency. In: Proceedings of the 2019 ACM Symposium on Principles of Distributed Computing - PODC '19 (2019)
10. Ketchum, A., Williams, M.: On pseudo-profound bullshit in the avalanche whitepaper (2019)
11. Mathys, M., Schmid, R., Sliwinski, J., Wattenhofer, R.: A limitlessly scalable transaction system. In: 6th International Workshop on Cryptocurrencies and Blockchain Technology (CBT), Copenhagen, Denmark (September 2022)
12. Nakamoto, S.: Bitcoin: A peer-to-peer electronic cash system (2008). https://bitcoin.org/bitcoin.pdf
13. Rocket, T., Yin, M., Sekniqi, K., van Renesse, R., Sirer, E.G.: Scalable and probabilistic leaderless BFT consensus through metastability. arXiv preprint arXiv:1906.08936 (2019)
14. Sekniqi, K., Laine, D., Buttolph, S., Sirer, E.G.: Avalanche platform. Netw. Distrib, Ledgers (2020)
15. Sliwinski, J., Wattenhofer, R.: Asynchronous proof-of-stake. In: 23rd International Symposium on Stabilization, Safety, and Security of Distributed Systems (SSS) (November 2021)

We Will DAG You

Ignacio Amores-Sesar[1]([envelope])[ID] and Christian Cachin[2][ID]

[1] University of Aarhus, Aarhus University IT - Byen Katrinebjerg, Hopper Building, Åbogade 34, 8200 Aarhus, Denmark
amores-sesar@cs.au.dk
[2] University of Bern, Neubrückstrasse 10, 3012 Berne, Switzerland
christian.cachin@unibe.ch

Abstract. Protocols based on directed acyclic graphs (DAG) have been proposed as potential solution to the latency and throughput limitations of traditional consensus protocols. However, their adoption has been hindered by security concerns and a lack of a solid foundation to guarantee improvements in both throughput and latency. In this paper, we present a construction that rigorously demonstrates how DAG-based protocols can achieve superior throughput and latency compared to chain-based consensus protocols, all while maintaining the same level of security guarantees.

Keywords: Consensus · Chain · DAG · Security · Latency · Throughput

1 Introduction

In the ever-evolving landscape of distributed systems, achieving consensus among a set of processes has become a fundamental challenge that has garnered significant attention in recent years. Consensus protocols are a universal primitive in distributed computing, ensuring that a network of interconnected processes can collectively agree on a shared state despite potential failures or malicious actors. However, as the demands on distributed systems continue to grow, the need for consensus protocols that can deliver both higher throughput and lower latency has become increasingly pressing. This need is particularly relevant in permissionless consensus protocols as used by cryptocurrencies and blockchain protocols, which face stringent demands on their throughput and latency.

Traditional consensus protocols have exhibited considerable advancements in both throughput and latency since the first practical consensus protocols [7,12]. One of the most promising lines of work are DAG consensus protocols as introduced by the "All you need is DAG" paper [10] and subsequently extended by Narwhal and Tusk [8], Bullshark [22], and Cordial Miners [11]. A common characteristic of these protocols is their capacity to enable every participant to generate blocks that reference previous blocks, forming a *directed acyclic graph (DAG)*. In permissionless protocols like Bitcoin [14], every process (miner) can create

---

I. Amores-Sesar — The work has been done while at the University of Bern.

J. Garcia-Alfaro et al. (Eds.): ESORICS 2024 Workshops, LNCS 15263, pp. 276–291, 2025.
https://doi.org/10.1007/978-3-031-82349-7_19

a block upon successfully solving the cryptographic puzzle. Therefore, the concept of constructing a DAG that is later ordered, as proposed by Keidar et al. [10], holds the potential to enhance the throughput and latency of permissionless consensus protocols. In essence, DAG protocols may surpass traditional permissionless consensus protocols, which form a chain.

The evident approach to improving the throughput of chain protocols is to increase the block ratio, i.e., the number of blocks produced per unit of time, effectively accelerating the execution of the protocol as there is less time between created blocks. This goal can be pursued by lowering the difficulty in *Proof-of-Work* (*PoW*) protocols. However, increasing the block ratio may harm the protocol since it elevates the likelihood of forks—situations where two different processes create blocks extending the chain. An abandoned block is one that is never output by the protocol; whenever a chain protocol forks, an abandoned block is produced. Therefore, despite the increased number of generated blocks, the number of abandoned blocks concurrently rises, adversely affecting the protocol's throughput. Moreover, it is imperative to recognize that the block ratio cannot be augmented arbitrarily without compromising the protocol's security.

In this paper, we introduce a construction that takes as input a DAG-based protocol or a chain protocol Π, which may produce abandoned blocks and produces a new DAG protocol Π' with the property that every created block is eventually output. Specifically, Π' creates the same number of blocks as the base protocol Π and outputs *every* created block of Π. We show that the safety and liveness of Π' reduces to the safety and liveness of Π. In simpler terms, Π' is as safe and live as Π. Furthermore, we establish that Π' has lower or equal *latency* as Π while achieving strictly higher *throughput*. Our main contribution lies in a formal proof that chain protocols cannot achieve optimal throughput, i.e., for any chain protocol Π, there is a DAG protocol Π' that is safe and life under the same assumptions as Π, with the same or better latency and better throughput.

2 Related Work

DAG protocols represent a recent breakthrough within the domain of permissioned consensus protocols [8,10,11,22]. While DAG protocols have been previously introduced in the permissionless context, their adoption and success have been somewhat restrained due to their inherent complexity when compared to traditional chain protocols. Several well-known DAG protocols have exhibited vulnerabilities, highlighting challenges in their success. For instance, IOTA [18], one of the pioneering DAG protocols, has been susceptible to vulnerabilities such as Parasite-chain attacks [17,18]. Another promising protocol, GhostDAG [20], has also revealed vulnerabilities in its design [13]. Even Avalanche [19], the most successful DAG protocol in terms of market capitalization, originally had vulnerabilities in its design [3].

An intriguing DAG protocol to note is Conflux [13], which leverages the GHOST consensus rule [21] and augments blocks with additional references to transform a chain protocol into a DAG. Li et al. [13] have demonstrated that Conflux's security is directly inherited from the security of GHOST. However, it is worth mentioning that the GHOST protocol has exhibited lower resilience than other consensus protocols in the presence of network malfunctions [4,15].

Our contribution to this landscape is a formal proof of the superior performance of DAG protocols, facilitated by a construction that can be conceptualized as an extension of the Conflux construction [13]. Specifically, when we instantiate the throughput closure using GHOST [21], we arrive at Conflux [13].

3   Abstractions

We consider a set of n *processes* $\mathcal{P} = \{P_1, P_2, \ldots\}$ that interact with each other by exchanging messages through the network. A protocol Π for $\mathcal{P}$ consists of a collection of programs with instructions for all processes. In particular we are interested in the study of *chain protocol* and *DAG protocol* protocols, i.e., protocol that rely on a chain or a DAG to deliver blocks. These two concepts are formally defined below.

Chain and DAG protocols are pivotal tools employed to establish robust and secure ledgers, and as such, they must adhere to specific fundamental requirements.

Traditionally, the gold standard concept is *atomic broadcast* [6], which ensures that all processes deliver the same set of transactions in the same order. In this paper, we consider a variant of this abstraction that includes the concept of a *block* in the interface and properties [2]. Processes broadcast transactions and deliver blocks using the events *bab-broadcast(tx)* and *bab-deliver(b)*, respectively, where block b contains a sequence of transactions $[tx_1, \ldots, tx_m]$. The protocol outputs an additional event *bab-mined(b, P)*, which signals that block b has been *mined* by process P, where P is defined as the *miner* of b. The event *bab-mined(b, P)* can be understood as the creation of block b by process P. Notice that *bab-mined(b, P)* signals only the creation of a block and not its delivery. In addition to predicate $VT()$ that determines the validity of a transaction, we also equip our protocol with a validity predicate $VB()$ to be applied to blocks. These predicates and function are determined by the higher-level application or protocol.

Definition 1. *A protocol implements* block-based atomic broadcast *with validity predicates* $VT()$ *and* $VB()$ *if it satisfies the following properties, except with negligible probability:*

Validity: *If a correct process invokes a* bab-broadcast(tx), *then every correct process eventually outputs* bab-deliver(b), *for some block b that contains tx.*
No duplication: *No correct process outputs* bab-deliver(b) *more than once.*
Integrity: *If a correct process outputs* bab-deliver(b), *then it has previously output* bab-mined(b, ·) *exactly once.*
Agreement: *If some correct process outputs* bab-deliver(b), *then eventually every correct process outputs* bab-deliver(b).
Total order: *Let b and b′ be blocks, and P_i and P_j correct processes that both output* bab-deliver(b) *and* bab-deliver(b′). P_i *delivers b before b′ if and only if P_j delivers b before b′.*

External validity: *If a correct process outputs bab-deliver(b), then $VB(b) =$* TRUE.

The block-based atomic broadcast abstraction can be implemented by protocols based on different approaches. These differences are not captured in Definition 1, but can still be relevant for the performance of the protocol. The two families of protocols of interest for this paper are *chain protocol* and *DAG protocol* protocols. The distinguishing factor between them lies in the set of references to previously mined blocks. Specifically, for a given block b, we denote the set of *bab-mined* blocks referenced by b as *parents(b)*, commonly known as the *parents* of b. Furthermore, the set of *bab-mined* blocks reachable through references from b is represented as *ancestors(b)* and is often referred to as the *ancestors* of b. A block b is a *descendant* of its ancestors. A block with no descendants is also called *leaf*.

Definition 2. (Chain Protocol, DAG Protocol). *A block-based atomic broadcast protocol Π is a DAG protocol protocol if Π-mined blocks contain references to other Π-mined blocks, meaning that the set of references is not empty. Π is a chain protocol protocol if every Π-mined block refers to exactly one Π-mined block and for every honest process P_i there is a Π-delivered block b such that every Π-delivered by P_i is b or in ancestors(b). In essence, Π-delivered blocks form a chain.*

Fig. 1 illustrates an example of both chain and DAG protocols.

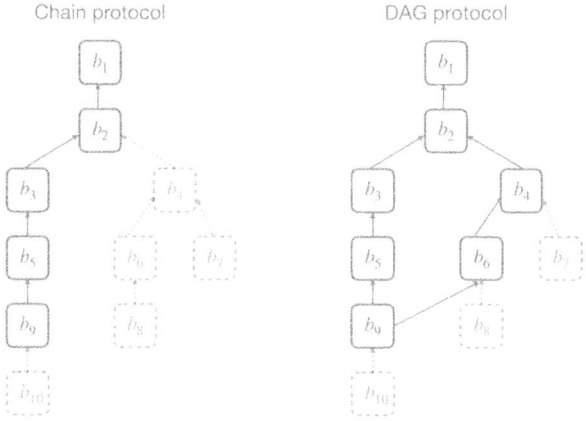

Fig. 1. Comparison between a chain protocol and a DAG protocol. Blocks in blue (continuous lines) are the *bab-delivered* blocks, whereas grey (dashed) blocks are *bab-mined* but not *bab-delivered*. The protocol on the left is a chain protocol; each block refers to exactly one block, and there is a block (b_9) such that every currently *bab-delivered* block is b_9 or an ancestor of it. The protocol on the right is a DAG protocol; block b_9 references multiple blocks.

To set the stage, we make the assumption that both chain and DAG protocols begin with an initial, hard-coded block referred to as the *genesis* block. This genesis block is special in that it possesses an empty set of references. It is important to note that, according to Definition 2, chain protocols inherently are DAG protocols. The blocks mined in chain protocols produce a *tree*, a particular kind of DAG. Therefore, for the remainder of this paper, we will use the term "DAG protocol" to encompass both DAG protocol and chain protocols, acknowledging this inclusion.

One significant implication of abstracting DAG protocols as block-based atomic broadcast (Definition 1) is that the protocol must define a function that operates on DAG that produces a list of delivered blocks. It is worth mentioning that certain DAG protocols, such as the original Avalanche protocol [3,19], do not output an ordered list of transactions but the list output by different processes may differ up to permutation. While DAG protocols can also be modeled as generic broadcast [16], situations arise where complete transaction ordering, as seen in calls to smart contracts, becomes necessary. For the purposes of this paper, we focus on protocols that can be effectively modeled as block-based atomic broadcast, i.e., protocols that achieve total order. The results we derive in this context generalize straightforwardly to protocols modeled as generic broadcasts.

4   Model

DAG protocols base their security on different techniques such as *proof of work* (*PoW*), *proof of stake* (*PoS*) [9], *proof of space-time* (*PoST*) [1], or *proof of elapsed time* (*PoET*) [5]. For the sake of simplicity, we use the PoW terminology. Nevertheless, our model does not use explicit properties of PoW and, thus, includes all these techniques.

Processes. Consistent with prior research, our protocol operates without explicit knowledge of the number or identities of the processes. The processes themselves remain unaware of these details as well. We assume a static network consisting of n processes, where up to f processes are to be corrupted by the adversary, thereby exhibiting arbitrary behavior. We do not assume any general bound on f. The construction introduced in this paper takes a protocol Π as input; we leave the bound on f vary based on the input protocol Π.

Blocks. A transaction tx, comprises a set of *inputs*, a set of *outputs*, and a collection of digital signatures, as in Bitcoin [14]. Transactions have size $|tx|$, and they are grouped into blocks, as introduced in Definition 1. Each block encompasses a specific number of transactions, denoted as m, a number of references to previously *bab-mined* blocks, quantified as n_{refs}, and further parameters essential for the proper execution of protocol Π. It is noteworthy that the size of a reference, represented as $|ref|$, is significantly smaller than that of a transaction, for simplicity, we consider it to be negligible. We reiterate that protocol Π defines external validity predicates, $VT()$ and $VB()$, responsible for determining the *validity* of a transaction or block.

Network. A *diffusion functionality* implements communication among the processes, which is structured into *synchronous* rounds. The functionality keeps a distinct $RECEIVE_i$ string for each process P_i and makes it available to P_i at the start of every round. The purpose of the string $RECEIVE_i$ is to serve as a repository for all the messages received by P_i.

When a process, say P_i, instructs the diffusion functionality to *broadcast* a set of messages, it signifies that P_i has "completed its round". In response, the functionality marks P_i as having completed its operations for that specific round. The adversary, whose actions are described in detail below, possesses the ability to access the string of any process at any point during the execution. Additionally, the adversary can observe every message broadcast by any process instantaneously. Furthermore, the adversary has the capability to insert messages directly and selectively into $RECEIVE_i$ for any process P_i, ensuring that only P_i receives the message at the outset of the following round. This behavior models what is often termed a *rushing* adversary.

Once all non-corrupted processes have concluded their respective rounds, the diffusion functionality aggregates all messages that were broadcast by non-corrupted processes during that round. These aggregated messages are then appended to the $RECEIVE_i$ strings for all processes, this is the reason of the name *synchronous* rounds. Subsequently, each non-corrupted process updates its local view at the conclusion of every round. If a non-corrupted process Π-mines a block in round r, all processes receive the Π-mined block by the subsequent round $r+1$.

Furthermore, even if the adversary causes a block to be received selectively by only some non-corrupted processes in round r, the block is received by all non-corrupted processes by round $r+2$. The update of the local view also encompasses the Π-delivery of blocks that meet given criteria defined by protocol Π.

Adversary. The adversary can corrupt up to f processes at the beginning of the execution. These corrupted processes may deviate arbitrarily from the protocol, adhering to the instructions from the adversary. Additionally, the adversary wields control over the *diffusion functionality*. The adversary can schedule the delivery of messages, read the contents of the $RECEIVE_i$ string for every process at any point during the execution, and directly write messages into the $RECEIVE_i$ of any process. The adversary signals the conclusion of her round by transmitting a specially designated message.

Round Structure. At the beginning of the round, process P_i reads the messages in its input string $RECEIVE_i$. Then, P_i proceeds to update its internal state in accordance with the received messages and performs a set of actions defined by protocol Π. Such actions include the Π-delivery of blocks. P_i concludes the round by broadcasting a set of messages to the other processes.

4.1   Abandoned Blocks

Definition 3. *An* execution *is a history with an entry for each round containing the actions, a list of received messages, and a list of sent messages by each process in that round.*

Since executions are not bounded, an event may be theoretically possible, but its occurrence might have a probability of zero. For instance, consider an algorithm that continuously flips an unbiased coin indefinitely. There could be an execution where all outcomes are heads, but the probability of this specific sequence of events happening is zero, as it is the limit of an infinite execution.

To circumvent these issues, we introduce the concept of a *partial execution*.

Definition 4. *Given a protocol Π, the set of λ-partial executions Φ_λ is defined to be the set of λ-prefixes of all executions of protocol Π. A partial execution is an execution that belongs to Φ_λ for some $\lambda \in \mathbb{N}$.*

Definition 5. *Given an execution $\mathcal{E}$ of a block-based atomic broadcast protocol Π, an* abandoned *block in $\mathcal{E}$ is an honestly bab-mined block b such that b is not bab-delivered in $\mathcal{E}$.*

It is important to note that the validity property defined in block-based atomic broadcast (Definition 1) does not guarantee that every *bab-mined* block will eventually be *bab-delivered*. Instead, this property ensures that for each *bab-broadcast* transaction, there exists at least one *bab-delivered* block that contains it. The concept of abandoned blocks is a significant concern in the context of such protocols. Abandoned blocks have been honestly *bab-mined* but are never *bab-delivered*. The existence of abandoned blocks can severely impact the performance of a chain protocol or DAG protocol.

Definition 6. *A protocol Π permits abandoned blocks if there exist a block b and a partial execution $\mathcal{E}$ such that: b is abandoned in any extension of $\mathcal{E}$.*

Remark 1. Note that given a protocol that permits abandoned blocks, the probability, taken over the randomness of the protocol, of having at least one abandoned block in execution is greater than zero since partial executions happen with non-zero probability.

Determining whether a given protocol Π permits abandoned blocks or not can be a challenging task and, in some cases, may not be computable due to the need to simulate potentially infinitely long executions. However, for certain protocols like Bitcoin [14], the existence of abandoned blocks is a direct consequence of forks occurring among honest miners. This phenomenon is formalized in the following definition.

Definition 7. *Given an execution $\mathcal{E}$ of a given protocol Π, a round r forked if protocol Π outputs two events bab-mined(b, P_i) and bab-mined(b', P_j) in round r at two distinct honest processes P_i and P_j. A protocol with a forked round in at least one partial execution is a forkable protocol.*

Lemma 1. *A forkable chain protocol Π permits abandoned blocks.*

Proof. Given a forkable protocol Π, there exist a round r in which two different honest processes output events *bab-mined*(b, P_i) and *bab-mined*(b', P_j). In particular, $b \neq b'$ because their miners are different. Π is also a chain protocol. thus both b and b' have a unique reference to previously *bab-mined* blocks, so they cannot reference each other. Another implication of Π being a chain protocol is that at any point in the execution of the protocol, there exists a *bab-mined* block b^* such that every *bab-delivered* is in *ancestors*(b^*). Since every block only contains a single reference and b and b' do not refer to each other, we conclude that no honest processes can *bab-deliver* both b and b' simultaneously.

Transactions that were originally included in abandoned blocks must be re-included in subsequent blocks to maintain the validity property (Definition 1). This re-inclusion consumes space in new blocks and has implications for both latency and throughput, as we formalize below.

4.2   Throughput and Latency

Definition 8. *Given a block-based atomic broadcast protocol Π, an adversary $\mathcal{A}$, and an execution $\mathcal{E}$, we define the* throughput *of Π in the presence of $\mathcal{A}$ in execution $\mathcal{E}$ as the average number of bab-delivered blocks per round, and we denote by* throughput$(\Pi, \mathcal{A}, \mathcal{E})$.

Definition 9. *Given a block-based atomic broadcast protocol Π, the* throughput *of Π is defined to be* throughput$(\Pi) := \inf_{\mathcal{A}} \mathrm{E}[\text{throughput}(\Pi, \mathcal{A}, \mathcal{E})]$, *i.e., the infimum over all the possible adversaries $\mathcal{A}$ of the average over the randomness Π of* throughput$(\Pi, \mathcal{A}, \mathcal{E})$ *over all the possible executions.*

Definition 10. *The* goodput *of protocol Π is defined to be the throughput of Π in the presence of an adversary that follows the instructions of the protocol, i.e., the processes controlled by the adversary behave honestly.*

Throughput, as defined above, should be considered as a metric of the average yield of the capacity in the worst adversarial case. *Goodput* should instead be understood as a metric of the capacity of the protocol without an adversary interfering in the protocol.

Definition 11. *Given a block-based atomic broadcast protocol Π, an adversary $\mathcal{A}$, an execution $\mathcal{E}$, and a transaction tx, we define* latency *of tx in the presence of adversary $\mathcal{A}$ in execution $\mathcal{E}$ as the number of rounds since tx is bab-broadcast until the first block containing tx is bab-delivered, and we denote it by* latency$(\Pi, \mathcal{A}, \mathcal{E}, tx)$. *We define the* latency *of Π to be the average number of rounds over the transactions tx in execution $\mathcal{E}$, since tx is bab-broadcast until the first block containing tx is bab-delivered and denote it by* latency$(\Pi, \mathcal{A}, \mathcal{E})$.

Definition 12. *Given a block-based atomic broadcast protocol Π, The* latency *of protocol Π is defined as* latency$(\Pi) = \sup_{\mathcal{A}} \mathrm{E}[\mathrm{latency}(\Pi, \mathcal{A}, \mathcal{E})]$, *i.e., the supremum over all the possible adversaries $\mathcal{A}$ of the average over the randomness of the protocol of the* latency$(\Pi, \mathcal{A}, \mathcal{E})$ *over the possible executions $\mathcal{E}$.*

Latency is the other traditional measure of performance of the protocol. Intuitively, latency is a metric for the response time of the protocol, reflecting the amount of time needed until an operation is executed.

5   The Throughput Closure

We introduce a novel construction designed to enhance a given DAG protocol Π. This construction produces a DAG protocol, which we call *the throughput closure of Π* and denote by Π'. Protocol Π' possesses the unique property of ensuring that every honestly *bab-mined* block is eventually *bab-delivered*. The mechanism by which protocol Π' accomplishes this feat involves the incorporation of additional references to blocks. For any given block b, protocol Π' defines the set *abandoned*(b) as the collection of valid blocks that will not be Π-delivered if b is to be Π-delivered. The block mining and delivery routines of the throughput closure Π' are built on top of their counterparts in Π. We recall that chain protocols are a subset of DAG protocols and the differences between chain protocols and general DAG protocols are the main interest of this paper.

Overview. As shown in Algorithm 1, when an honest process P_i Π-mines a block b, process P_i also Π'-mines the same block. However, in Π', the block b includes an additional set of references to the blocks in the set *abandoned*(b).

The modified delivery routine operates as follows: when a block b would be Π-delivered, all valid blocks in the set *abandoned*(b) are Π'-delivered in a fixed topological order immediately before b. This topological sort allows to order non Π-delivered blocks with respect to Π-delivered blocks deterministically according to the references included in the Π-delivered blocks. This is a crucial aspect as establishing a total order in a DAG can be generally challenging due to different processes having different partial views of the DAG. The topological sort τ ensure that all processes that have received block b agree on the same order. Note that the construction is independent of weather the event Π-deliver is deterministic or not. A canonical example for *topological sort* τ is to order the blocks in *abandoned*(b) according to their *depth* in the DAG, distance to genesis, breaking the ties according to the hash of the block. Note that if an adversary creates a block with low depth, it will be only Π-delivered when deeper block references it, thus the adversarial block is Π'-delivered concurrently with deeper blocks.

Constructing the set *abandoned*(b), even when it can be computed, may be challenging task, as we explained above. However, given a chain protocol Π the set *abandoned*(b) becomes trivial to compute as it is formed by every block that is not an ancestor of b. Furthermore, the set *abandoned*(b) is the set of leaves of the DAG, with the exception of b. As an illustrative example, Fig. 2 shows the application of this construction within the context of Bitcoin. If we consider Π to be GHOST protocol [21], we recreate the Conflux protocol [13]. Referencing the leaves in the DAG is the correct method for referring to the set $abandoned(b)$, as this set is formed by the leaves in the DAG when the input protocol Π is a chain protocol. The same approach can be considered with DAG protocols. This approach is computationally feasible even in scenarios in which the set $abandoned(b)$ may not be computable, however, some blocks may be referenced when there is no need, adding redundancy of references. Further insights into this alternative approach are provided below.

Algorithm 1. Protocol Π' for process P_i.

Implements: block-based atomic broadcast Π'
Uses: block-based atomic broadcast Π
       topological sort τ

   State:
1:    $\mathcal{D}' \leftarrow \emptyset$
2:    $b'_\ell \leftarrow [\,]$

3: **upon event** Π'-$broadcast(tx)$ **do**
4:    **invoke** Π-$broadcast(tx)$

5: **upon event** Π-$mined(b, P_j)$ **do**
6:    **if** $P_i = P_j$ **then**
7:        $weak \leftarrow leaves(abandoned(b, \mathcal{D}'))$
8:        $b' \leftarrow b$
9:        $b'.\text{wrefs} \leftarrow weak$
10:      $\mathcal{D}' \leftarrow \mathcal{D}' \cup \{b'\}$
11:      **invoke** Π'-$mined(b', P_i)$

12: **upon event** Π'-$mined(b', P_j)$ **do**
13:    **if** $VB'(b')$ **then**
14:        $\mathcal{D}' \leftarrow \mathcal{D}' \cup \{b'\}$

15: **upon event** Π-$deliver(b)$ **do**
16:    $ready \leftarrow ancestors'(b') \setminus ancestors'(b'_\ell)$
17:    $b'_\ell \leftarrow b'$
18:    **for** $b^* \in \tau(ready)$ **do**
19:        **invoke** Π'-$deliver(b^*)$

20: **function** $abandoned(b, \mathcal{D}')$:
21:    **return** $\{b' \in \mathcal{D}' : b' \notin ancestors'(b) \wedge incompatible(b, b')\}$

22: **function** $VB'(b')$:
23:    **return** $VB(b) \wedge \exists\, tx \in b' : undelivered(tx)$

Algorithm 2. Greedy approach for process P_i.

24: **upon event** $\Pi\text{-}mined(b, P_j)$ **do**   // Greedy approach
25:     **if** $P_i = P_j$ **then**
26:         $b' \leftarrow b$
27:         $weak \leftarrow leaves(\{b' \in \mathcal{D}' : b' \notin ancestors(b')\})$
28:         $b'.refs \leftarrow b'.refs \| weak$
29:         $\mathcal{D}' \leftarrow \mathcal{D}' \cup \{b'\}$
30:     **invoke** $\Pi'\text{-}mined(b', P_i)$

Detailed Description. We describe the execution of the protocol from the perspective of an honest process P_i. When honest process P_i Π'-*broadcasts* a transaction tx, it invokes Π-*broadcast*(tx) (L3–4). Notably, the broadcast of transactions occurs exactly as it does in protocol Π. When P_i triggers event Π-*mined*(b, P_i) (L5–11), it initially computes the set *abandoned*(b) locally. To Π'-*mine* a new block b', P_i augments b by adding extra references to the set *abandoned*(b) (L7–9). Subsequently, P_i adds b' to the set of mined blocks $\mathcal{D}'$ (L10) and triggers the event Π'-*mined*(b', P_i) (L11).

When event Π'-*mined*(b', P_j) is triggered, P_i verifies the Π'-validity of b' and incorporates it into its local view (L12–14). So far, the execution of Π' closely parallels that of Π. However, the key distinction lies in the delivery of blocks (L15–19). When event Π-*deliver*(b) occurs, P_i searches for the block b' associated with b. P_i then assembles the set *ready*, which comprises the blocks to be Π'-*delivered* (L16). This set is computed as the set-difference between the ancestors of block b' and the ancestors of the last delivered block b'_l. P_i subsequently updates the last delivered block to be b' (L17). Finally, P_i applies a topological sorting algorithm τ to the set *ready* and Π'-delivers them accordingly (L18–19).

A block b' is deemed valid (L22–23) within protocol Π' if it satisfies two conditions: firstly, its associated block b must be Π-*valid*, and secondly, it must contain at least one Π'-valid transaction. Algorithm 2 presents a greedy version of *abandoned*(b). In this approach, a process P_i adds references to b' for every block that is not already an ancestor of b within protocol Π. This greedy approach solves the computational complexity of determining the set *abandoned*(b) at the expense of an excess of references.

The throughput closure mirrors protocol Π when the set *abandoned*(b) is empty for every block, indicating that the protocol does not permit the existence of abandoned blocks. However, if Π permits abandoned blocks, then there exists some executions of Π with a block b such that *abandoned*$(b) \neq \emptyset$, and the throughput closure diverges from the original protocol. The implementation of the throughput closure does entail an increase in local computation for processes. Specifically, processes need to scan the DAG and append a set of references to all leaves in *abandoned*(b) to the currently mined block b. The computational complexity of determining *abandoned*(b) can vary depending on the protocol, as discussed earlier. However, in the case of chain protocols, this set is relatively straightforward to compute. A process simply adds references to every leaf of a chain that has not been referenced by an ancestor.

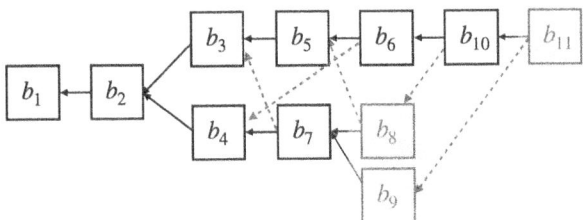

Fig. 2. An example of our construction applied to Nakamoto consensus. The full lines denote the references of the Nakamoto consensus and the blue dashed lines denote the extra references included by the throughput closure. According to Nakamoto consensus, the main chain is the chain $b_1 \cdots b_{11}$ and blocks b_4, b_7, b_8, and b_9 are abandoned. Looking at b_{11}, the set $abandoned(b_{11})$ is formed by block b_9. Blocks b_4, b_7, and b_8 are not part of the $abandoned(b_{11})$ because b_{10} already references them. When delivering b_{11}, block b_9 would be delivered between b_{10} and b_{11}.

6   Analysis

6.1   Security Analysis

Theorem 1. *Given protocol DAG protocol Π implementing block-based atomic broadcast, its throughput closure Π' also implements block-based atomic broadcast.*

Proof. We demonstrate that the throughput closure Π' implements block-based atomic broadcast by leveraging the fact that Π does. Throughout this proof, we assume the perspective of an honest process P_i.

Validity: Assume that an honest process P_j Π'-*broadcasts* a given transaction tx. By construction, process P_j does so by invoking Π-*broadcast* transaction tx (L3–4). The validity property of protocol Π guarantees that process P_i eventually Π-*delivers* a block b containing transaction tx. Process P_i, by definition of the protocol, Π'-*delivers* the block b' consisting of block b with the addition of the extra set of references (L15–19). If every transaction contained in b' is invalid, the block is not Π'-*deliver*. In the case of block b', the validity check can only fail if transaction tx fails the validity predicate. Since tx is Π'-*broadcast*, the external validity predicate is satisfied unless some block containing tx has been Π'*delivered*.

We conclude that for any honestly Π'-*broadcast* transaction tx, P_i eventually Π'-*delivers* a block b' containing tx, thus validity property of protocol Π' is satisfied.

Integrity: Process P_i only Π'-*delivers* blocks that it Π'-*delivers* or ancestors of those contained in the set $\mathcal{D}$ (L15–19). A block b' enters the set $\mathcal{D}$ only after an invokation of Π-*mined*(b, P_j). We conclude that every Π'-*delivers* has previously been Π'-*mined*.

Agreement: Consider a block b' that is Π'-*delivered* by process P_i. We consider two different cases: when b whether b is Π-*delivered* or not. On the one hand, if b is Π-*delivered* by process P_i, every honest process eventually Π-*delivers* b, thus Π'-*delivers* b' as a consequence (L15–19). On the other hand, if block bl' is Π'-*delivered* as a consequence of another block b^* is Π'-*delivered*. The same reasoning as above applies to block b^*, which implies the eventual Π'-*delivery* of block b'.

Total order: Consider two Π'*mined* blocks b'_1 and b'_2 and two honest processes P_i and P_j that $\Pi' - deliver$ both blocks. We distinguish four cases depending on whether blocks b_1 and b_2 are Π-*delivered* or not.

Assume that both b_1 and b_2 are Π-*delivered*. Note that in the view of any honest process the order in which blocks b_1 and b_2 are Π-*delivered* is the same as blocks b'_1 and b'_2 are Π'-*delivered* (L15–19). Due to the total order property of protocol Π, process P_i Π-*delivers* block b_1 and b_2 in the same order as process P_j, thus both processes Π'-*deliver* blocks b_1 and b_2.

If either b'_1 or b'_2 are Π'-*delivered* as a consequence of another block b_3 being Π-*delivered*. Since the set of blocks that are Π'-*delivered* as consequence of block b'_3 are Π'-*delivered* immediately before b'_3, any block b' Π'-*delivered* before (after) b' is also Π'-*delivered* before (after) the set of blocks Π'-*delivered* as a consequence of b'. The same reasoning as above applies to this case. We conclude that P_i also Π'*delivers* both b'_1 or b'_2 in the same order as P_j.

The only case left is when both b'_1 and b'_2 are Π'-*delivered* as a consequence of two blocks b'_3 and b'_4 being Π'-*delivered*. If b'_3 and b'_4 are different the case is the same as before. If b'_3 and b'_4, both P_i and P_j use the topological order to determine in which order to Π'-*delivered*. Since the topological sorting is deterministic and depends only on block b'_3, both P_i and P_j Π'-*deliver* b'_1 and b'_2 in the same order.

External Validity: The external validity property is imposed by lines L22–23.

Theorem 1 states that the throughput closure Π' maintains the exact same safety and liveness properties the original protocol Π. In other words, no other points of attack have been introduced to the core functionality. Studying the incentives of the protocols and its behavior in the rational setting is left as future work.

6.2   Throughput and Latency

In this section, we delve into a comparative analysis of the performance aspects, through throughput and latency, between Π' and Π. It is important to note that both throughput and latency definitions take into account adversarial behavior, and the connection between the adversarial behavior of Π' and Π is discussed in the following remark.

Remark 2. Note that given an adversary $\mathcal{A}'$ for protocol Π', an adversary $\mathcal{A}$ for protocol Π can be constructed by merely removing the extra references from any block that $\mathcal{A}'$ Π'-mines. Additionally, given an adversary $\mathcal{A}$ for protocol Π, it can also be regarded as an adversary for protocol Π', as every action taken by $\mathcal{A}$ in protocol Π is allowed in protocol Π'.

Definition 13. *Given an execution $\mathcal{E}'$ and an adversary $\mathcal{A}'$ for protocol Π', we define the equivalent execution of protocol Π as the execution $\mathcal{E}'$ without the extra references in each block and adversary $\mathcal{A}$, as discussed in Remark 2.*

Lemma 2. *Given a DAG protocol Π, its throughput closure Π' achieves the same or lower latency as Π.*

Proof. Consider an execution $\mathcal{E}'$, an adversary $\mathcal{A}'$ for protocol Π', and a transaction tx that has not already been Π'-delivered. Denote by $\mathcal{E}$ the equivalent execution (Definition 13) of protocol Π. Note that by definition of Π', tx has not been Π-delivered either (L15). Protocol Π' has two different mechanisms to Π'-deliver(tx).

On the one hand, if an event Π-deliver(b) for a block b containing tx is triggered, then b is Π'-delivered (L15). In this case, latency(Π', $\mathcal{A}'$, $\mathcal{E}'$, tx) is the same as latency(Π, $\mathcal{A}$, $\mathcal{E}$, tx).

On the other hand, if an event Π-deliver(b') for a block b' that does not contains tx but is descendent of a block b containing tx., then block b' is Π'-delivered immediately before b (L16). In this case, latency(Π', $\mathcal{A}'$, $\mathcal{E}'$, tx) is strictly smaller than latency(Π, $\mathcal{A}$, $\mathcal{E}$, tx).

We conclude that for every adversary, execution, and transaction, the latency of protocol latency(Π', $\mathcal{A}'$, $\mathcal{E}'$, tx) $\leq$ latency(Π, $\mathcal{A}$, $\mathcal{E}$, tx). Hence, latency(Π') $\leq$ latency(Π)

The next result clarifies the motivation for the term throughput closure.

Lemma 3. *Given a DAG protocol Π, then throughput(Π') $\geq$ throughput(Π), and if Π permits abandoned blocks, then throughput(Π') $>$ throughput(Π).*

Proof. Consider an execution $\mathcal{E}'$, an adversary $\mathcal{A}'$ for protocol Π', and a transaction tx that has not already been Π'-delivered. Denote by $\mathcal{E}$ the equivalent execution (Definition 13) of protocol Π.

On the one hand, if there is no abandoned block in the execution $\mathcal{E}'$, then, the set abandoned(b') is empty for every block b'. Thus, no extra reference is added at any point in the execution of Π' the executions $\mathcal{E}$ and $\mathcal{E}'$ identical. We conclude that throughput(Π, $\mathcal{A}'$, $\mathcal{E}$) = throughput(Π', $\mathcal{A}$, $\mathcal{E}$).

On the other hand, if there exists at least one abandoned block b' in execution $\mathcal{E}'$, then, the set abandoned(b^*) is not empty for some block b^* that is eventually Π'-delivered. When b^* is Π'delivered so is b' (L16).

We conclude that $throughput(\Pi', \mathcal{A}', \mathcal{E}') \geq throughput(\Pi', \mathcal{A}, \mathcal{E})$ for every possible adversary $\mathcal{A}'$ and execution $\mathcal{E}'$, thus $throughput(\Pi') \geq throughput(\Pi')$. Furthermore, if Π permits abandoned blocks, there exists an λ-partial execution with a block b that is abandoned in all its extensions. This means that the probability, over the randomness of the protocol, of having an abandoned block is strictly greater than zero (Remark 1). Thus, $\mathrm{E}[throughput(\Pi', \mathcal{A}', \mathcal{E}')] > \mathrm{E}[throughput(\Pi, \mathcal{A}, \mathcal{E})]$ for at least some adversary $\mathcal{A}'$. We conclude by noticing that if an adversary $\mathcal{A}^*$ prevents the exclusion of abandoned blocks, then $throughput(\Pi', \mathcal{A}^*, \mathcal{E}') > throughput(\Pi', \mathcal{A}', \mathcal{E}')$. Hence, we conclude that

$$throughput(\Pi') = \inf_{\mathcal{A}'} \mathrm{E}[throughput(\Pi', \mathcal{A}', \mathcal{E}')]$$
$$> \inf_{\mathcal{A}} \mathrm{E}[throughput(\Pi, \mathcal{A}, \mathcal{E})] = throughput(\Pi).$$

Corollary 1. *Given a DAG protocol Π, then $goodput(\Pi') \geq goodput(\Pi)$. Furthermore, if Π allows for the existence of abandoned blocks, then $goodput(\Pi') > goodput(\Pi)$.*

Proof. Consider the proof of Lemma 3 limited to adversaries that follow the instructions of the protocol.

Note that every chain protocol trivially permits abandoned block. We can finally conclude that DAG protocols are strictly better then chain protocols.

Theorem 2. *Given a chain protocol Π, there exists a DAG protocol Π' such that: $latency(\Pi') \leq latency(\Pi)$ and $throughput(\Pi') > throughput(\Pi)$.*

Proof. Lemma 1 states that a chain protocol Π permits abandoned blocks. Theorem 1 demonstrates that its throughput closure Π' implements block-based atomic broadcast. Lemma 3 shows that $throughput(\Pi') > throughput(\Pi)$. Finally, Lemma 2 establishes that $latency(\Pi') \leq latency(\Pi)$.

References

1. Chia network. https://docs.chia.net/docs/01introduction/what-is-chia
2. Alpos, O., Amores-Sesar, I., Cachin, C., Yeo, M.: Eating sandwiches: modular and lightweight elimination of transaction reordering attacks. In: 27th International Conference on Principles of Distributed Systems (OPODIS 2023). Leibniz International Proceedings in Informatics (LIPIcs), vol. 286, pp. 12:1–12:22. Schloss Dagstuhl – Leibniz-Zentrum für Informatik (2024). https://drops.dagstuhl.de/entities/document/10.4230/LIPIcs.OPODIS.2023.12
3. Amores-Sesar, I., Cachin, C., Tedeschi, E.: When is spring coming? A security analysis of avalanche consensus. In: OPODIS. LIPIcs, vol. 253, pp. 10:1–10:22. Schloss Dagstuhl - Leibniz-Zentrum für Informatik (2022)
4. Bagaria, V.K., Kannan, S., Tse, D., Fanti, G., Viswanath, P.: Prism: Deconstructing the blockchain to approach physical limits. In: CCS, pp. 585–602. ACM (2019)

5. Bowman, M., Das, D., Mandal, A., Montgomery, H.: On elapsed time consensus protocols. In: Adhikari, A., Küsters, R., Preneel, B. (eds.) INDOCRYPT 2021. LNCS, vol. 13143, pp. 559–583. Springer, Cham (2021). https://doi.org/10.1007/978-3-030-92518-5_25

6. Cachin, C., Guerraoui, R., Rodrigues, L.E.T.: Introduction to Reliable and Secure Distributed Programming (2. ed.). Springer (2011)

7. Castro, M., Liskov, B.: Practical byzantine fault tolerance and proactive recovery. ACM Trans. Comput. Syst. **20**(4), 398–461 (2002)

8. Danezis, G., Kokoris-Kogias, L., Sonnino, A., Spiegelman, A.: Narwhal and tusk: a dag-based mempool and efficient BFT consensus. In: EuroSys, pp. 34–50. ACM (2022)

9. David, B., Gaži, P., Kiayias, A., Russell, A.: Ouroboros praos: an adaptively-secure, semi-synchronous proof-of-stake blockchain. In: Nielsen, J.B., Rijmen, V. (eds.) EUROCRYPT 2018. LNCS, vol. 10821, pp. 66–98. Springer, Cham (2018). https://doi.org/10.1007/978-3-319-78375-8_3

10. Keidar, I., Kokoris-Kogias, E., Naor, O., Spiegelman, A.: All you need is DAG. In: PODC, pp. 165–175. ACM (2021)

11. Keidar, I., Naor, O., Poupko, O., Shapiro, E.: Cordial miners: fast and efficient consensus for every eventuality. In: DISC, LIPIcs, vol. 281, pp. 26:1–26:22. Schloss Dagstuhl - Leibniz-Zentrum für Informatik (2023)

12. Lamport, L.: The part-time parliament. ACM Trans. Comput. Syst. **16**(2), 133–169 (1998)

13. Li, C., et al.: A decentralized blockchain with high throughput and fast confirmation. In: USENIX Annual Technical Conference, pp. 515–528. USENIX Association (2020)

14. Nakamoto, S.: Bitcoin: A peer-to-peer electronic cash system. Whitepaper (2009). http://bitcoin.org/bitcoin.pdf

15. Natoli, C., Gramoli, V.: The balance attack or why forkable blockchains are ill-suited for consortium. In: DSN, pp. 579–590. IEEE Computer Society (2017)

16. Pedone, F., Schiper, A.: Generic broadcast. In: Jayanti, P. (ed.) DISC 1999. LNCS, vol. 1693, pp. 94–106. Springer, Heidelberg (1999). https://doi.org/10.1007/3-540-48169-9_7

17. Penzkofer, A., Kusmierz, B., Capossele, A., Sanders, W., Saa, O.: Parasite chain detection in the IOTA protocol. CoRR abs/ arXiv: 2004.13409 (2020)

18. Popov, S., Saa, O., Finardi, P.: Equilibria in the tangle. Comput. Ind. Eng. **136**, 160–172 (2019)

19. Rocket, T., Yin, M., Sekniqi, K., van Renesse, R., Sirer, E.G.: Scalable and probabilistic leaderless BFT consensus through metastability. CoRR abs/ arXiv: 1906.08936 (2019)

20. Sompolinsky, Y., Wyborski, S., Zohar, A.: PHANTOM GHOSTDAG: a scalable generalization of nakamoto consensus: September 2, 2021. In: AFT, pp. 57–70. ACM (2021)

21. Sompolinsky, Y., Zohar, A.: Secure high-rate transaction processing in bitcoin. In: Böhme, R., Okamoto, T. (eds.) FC 2015. LNCS, vol. 8975, pp. 507–527. Springer, Heidelberg (2015). https://doi.org/10.1007/978-3-662-47854-7_32

22. Spiegelman, A., Giridharan, N., Sonnino, A., Kokoris-Kogias, L.: Bullshark: DAG BFT protocols made practical. In: CCS, pp. 2705–2718. ACM (2022)

Assessing the Impact of Sanctions in the Crypto Ecosystem: Effective Measures or Ineffective Deterrents?

Francesco Zola(✉)[iD], Jon Ander Medina[iD], and Raúl Orduna[iD]

Vicomtech Foundation, Basque Research and Technology Alliance (BRTA),
Paseo Mikeletegi, 57, Donostia 20009, Spain
{fzola,jmedina,rorduna}@vicomtech.org

Abstract. Regulatory authorities aim to tackle illegal activities by targeting the economic incentives that drive such behaviour. This is typically achieved through the implementation of financial sanctions against the entities involved in the crimes. However, the rise of cryptocurrencies has presented new challenges, allowing entities to evade these sanctions and continue criminal operations. Consequently, enforcement measures have been expanded to include crypto assets information of sanctioned entities. Yet, due to the nature of the crypto ecosystem, blocking or freezing these digital assets is harder and, in some cases, such as with Bitcoin, unfeasible. Therefore, sanctions serve merely as deterrents. For this reason, in this study, we aim to assess the impact of these sanctions on entities' crypto activities, particularly those related to the Bitcoin ecosystem. Our objective is to shed light on the validity and effectiveness (or lack thereof) of such countermeasures. Specifically, we analyse the transactions and the amount of USD moved by punished entities that possess crypto addresses after being sanctioned by the authority agency. Results indicate that while sanctions have been effective for half of the examined entities, the others continue to move funds through sanctioned addresses. Furthermore, punished entities demonstrate a preference for utilising rapid exchange services to convert their funds, rather than employing dedicated money laundering services. To the best of our knowledge, this study offers valuable insights into how entities use crypto assets to circumvent sanctions.

Keywords: Sanctions circumvention · Money laundering · Flow analysis · Behavioural analysis · Cryptocurrency · Traceability

1 Introduction

Understanding the multidimensional nature of crime is crucial for developing effective strategies to prevent and combat these illicit activities. Crimes often manifest in various forms and domains, like drug trafficking, human trafficking, and other types of organised crime. Nevertheless, in all these cases, the main

J. Garcia-Alfaro et al. (Eds.): ESORICS 2024 Workshops, LNCS 15263, pp. 292–308, 2025.
https://doi.org/10.1007/978-3-031-82349-7_20

goal of the criminal networks is still to make a profit [23]. For this reason, disrupting the economic incentives driving illicit behaviour has become the primary objective in tackling these crimes [29]. This task requires cooperation and coordination among governments, law enforcement agencies, financial institutions, regulatory bodies, and other stakeholders at national and international levels.

This is the case of authority agencies such as the Office of Foreign Assets Control (OFAC)[1], Office of Financial Sanctions Implementation (OFSI)[2], European External Action Service (EEAS)[3] and United Nations Security Council (UNSC)[4], that aim to implement and enforce financial sanctions directly to the entity behind some violations and crimes. In fact, these agencies have the authority to freeze, block or restrict access to sanctioned entities' assets such as banking accounts, real estate, vessels, etc.

However, with the advent of virtual currencies such as cryptocurrencies, stablecoins, and Non-Fungible Tokens (NFTs), sanctioned entities have discovered new opportunities for circumventing sanctions and continuing their illicit activities [30]. These digital assets promote decentralization and offer varying degrees of anonymity or pseudo-anonymity, creating a borderless ecosystem ideal for the proliferation of illicit activities [14,25]. According to *"The 2024 Crypto Crime Report"* [12], although illicit crypto-transactions constitute less than 0.5% of the total on-chain transaction volume, they accounted for nearly 40 billion USD in 2022 and over 24 billion USD in 2023.

The significant size of the crypto market, the opportunities crypto assets present, and their proven involvement in illicit activities [9,16] have raised concerns about ensuring compliance with existing financial regulations. While some countries such as Tunisia, Nepal, Libya, Iraq, Bolivia, and Algeria have banned the use of cryptocurrency [7], others have directed their effort to implement new frameworks and technology to increase their control degree over the crypto ecosystem. Thus, regulatory agencies have intensified their enforcement actions against sanctioned entities, including tracking information about their crypto assets whenever possible. However, due to the nature of the crypto ecosystem, they still face limitations in blocking these digital assets. As a result, sanctions solely serve as a deterrent, aiming to discourage other individuals and companies from engaging in transactions with punished entities. Yet, this limitation makes crypto assets the perfect facilitator for ongoing illicit operations and circumventing sanctions.

For this reason, in this work, we aim to examine the impact these sanctions generate in the crypto activities of punished entities and their related violations. Our objective is to evaluate the validity and effectiveness (or lack thereof) of such countermeasures. Specifically, we analyse the transactions and the amount of USD moved by punished entities that possess crypto addresses before and after being sanctioned by the authority agency. Furthermore, we investigate which

---

[1] https://ofac.treasury.gov/.

[2] https://sanctionssearchapp.ofsi.hmtreasury.gov.uk/.

[3] https://www.eeas.europa.eu/.

[4] https://www.un.org/securitycouncil/content/un-sc-consolidated-list.

type of known crypto entities (Exchange, Mixers, Gambling, etc.) are typically engaged with by the punished entities post-sanction. Thus, we investigate if they are attempting to connect with other entities involved in illicit operations or are employing strategies such as money laundering, on-ramps and off-ramps operations, funding raise campaigns, etc.

More specifically, this work analyses entities (individuals and companies) sanctioned by the OFAC agency that have information about Bitcoin (BTC) assets. These decisions were taken for two specific reasons: a) Bitcoin (together with stablecoins) is widely recognised among the most popular cryptocurrencies for illicit activities [12], primarily due to its high market value and accessibility, even for users without technical background; b) other authority agencies (OFSI, EEAS, UNSC) do not have a comprehensive list of sanctioned crypto-related entities or do not release it publicly.

The results suggest that sanctions have been effective for roughly half of the sanctioned entities, while the others continue to engage in transactions through sanctioned Bitcoin addresses. Additionally, sanctioned entities prefer to directly convert their cryptocurrencies using dedicated services (*Exchanges*), rather than apply money laundering strategies using services like *Mixers* or *Gambling*.

To the best of our knowledge, this study offers a first step towards determining the effectiveness of sanctions within the crypto ecosystem and how sanctioned entities used them to circumvent sanctions.

2 Background

This section presents an overview of the crypto ecosystem, showing regulations, directives, and literature approaches. Specifically, in Sect. 2.1 a review of European Union regulations related to the crypto ecosystem is presented, while Sect. 2.2 is focused on presenting the United States OFAC agency and its crypto sanctions. Finally, Sect. 2.3 describes related research in the field.

2.1 EU Directive Review

As mentioned, crypto assets can be harder (or in some cases unfeasible) to freeze or block directly. However, governments and regulatory authorities worldwide have been increasingly implementing measures to monitor and regulate crypto markets to tackle concerns related to illicit activities. Thus, these regulations aim to facilitate the imposition of sanctions when necessary.

The European Union (EU) has established and reviewed several directives aimed at tackling issues such as money laundering, fraud, terrorism financing, and other emerging challenges related to non-cash payments. For instance, in 2015, the 5th Anti-Money Laundering Directive (5AMLD) [1] was introduced to address new trends in terrorist financing, building upon the provisions of the 4AMLD. Notably, under the 5AMLD, the role of cryptocurrency Exchanges has changed, they are now considered equivalent to financial institutions. Therefore, they are required, among other measures, to adhere to

Know Your Customer (KYC) requirements, implement Anti-Money Launder-ing (AML) mechanisms, and register with national regulatory authorities. This directive has been amended to include provisions regarding information accom-panying transfers of funds and certain crypto-assets, through the Regulation (EU) 2023/1113 [6]. The amendment fosters international cooperation within the Financial Action Task Force (FATF) and the global implementation of its recommendations [4]. Furthermore, it sets the obligation for virtual asset service providers (VASPs) and crypto asset service providers (CASPs) to collect infor-mation about the person who uses their services. Together with these directives, another pivotal regulation is the Markets in Crypto-Assets (MiCA) [5], which clearly distinguishes between different types of crypto-assets (asset-referenced tokens, electronic money or e-money, and other crypto assets). It then imposes constraints on CASPs to ensure market integrity and financial stability. One of its key provisions involves significant disclosure and transparency rules aimed at better informing consumers about associated risks, as well as mandating the implementation of security measures and anti-money laundering compliance.

Fraud and counterfeiting of non-cash means of payment is regulated through the EU directive 2019/713 [3]. The framework establishes measures aimed at preventing and detecting fraud and counterfeiting of non-cash payment instru-ments, such as security requirements for payment service providers, customer authentication procedures, and usage of secure technologies (encryption and tok-enization). This directive aimed to cover also new types of non-cash payment instruments such as e-money and virtual currencies, since they have a significant cross-border dimension. Another interesting EU framework, although it doesn't specifically mention digital currency or cryptocurrencies due to its general aim, is the Directive (EU) 2017/1371 [2] that defines legal framework and measures to combat any fraud against the financial interests of EU.

Despite the revision, update, and implementation of these policies, freezing or blocking crypto assets remains harder to accomplish by technical design. Its boundary-less structure, the availability of services in jurisdictions where these policies don't apply, or in countries unwilling to cooperate in criminal investi-gations, the anonymity of users, and the ease of conducting transactions - these properties collectively enable users to circumvent sanctions and persist in their illicit activities.

2.2   US Office of Foreign Assets Control

The Office of Foreign Assets Control (OFAC) is part of the Department of the United States (US) Treasury, and it is in charge of implementing economic and trade sanctions in accordance with US foreign policy and national security objec-tives. These sanctions are directed towards specific foreign countries and regimes, terrorists, international narcotics traffickers, individuals involved in the prolif-eration of weapons of mass destruction, and other actors posing threats to the national security, foreign policy, or economy of the United States. These actors and their blocked assets are included in a *Specially Designated Nationals and*

Blocked Persons (SDN) list[5]. Consequently, US individuals and companies are generally prohibited from dealing with them. The actors reported in the SDN list, which we refer to as *entities* in this paper, are sanctioned due to the violation of one (or more) Executive Orders and/or Code of Federal Regulations (CFR)[6]. Since 2018, OFAC has included cryptocurrency-related information in the SDN list as blocked assets for sanctioned entities whenever such information is available. In some cases, one entity can have multiple sanctioned addresses. To date, the violations that have led to sanctions against entities with crypto addresses involved, are detailed in Table 1 in this paper.

Table 1. Violations reported in the SDN list that have generated sanctions against cryptocurrency related entities.

#	Code	Description	Executive Order N.
1	CYBER2	Malicious Cyber Activities	13694, 13757
2	DPKR3	Blocking Property of the Government of North Korea	13722
3	DPKR4	Additional Sanctions With Respect to North Korea	13810
4	ELECTION	Foreign Interference in the US Election	13848
5	IFSR	Iranian Financial Sanctions Regulations	31 CFR part 561
6	ILLICTI-DRUGS	Illicit Drug Trade	14059
7	IRGC	Iranian Financial Sanctions	31 CFR Part 561
8	NPWMD	Weapons of Mass Destruction Proliferators Sanctions	31 CFR part 544
9	RUSSIA	Blocking Harmful Activities of the Russian Federation	14024
10	SDGT	Narcotics Trafficking Sanctions	31 CFR part 594
11	SDNTK	Foreign Narcotics Kingpin Sanctions	31 CFR part 598

2.3 Cryptocurrency and Cybercrime

Cryptocurrencies have created a convenient ecosystem for the permanence and movement of illicit cybercrime-related activities, with currencies such as Bitcoin, Ethereum, and Monero becoming their operational space. The evolution of illicit activities within the cryptocurrency ecosystem has been studied extensively [11,13]. For instance, Hornuf et al. [17] analysed cybercrime related to Ethereum transactions. In particular, they identified over 1.78 million transactions related to 19 categories of cybercrime, with losses amounting to $1.65 billion up to the year 2021, posing the focus on estimating how these cybercrimes impact victims' risk-taking, risk-adjusted returns, and investor behaviour. In the same line, in [26], authors employ the Generalized Autoregressive Score (GAS) model to examine the impact of cybercrime on cryptocurrency returns in South Africa. On the other hand, in [10], authors attempted to correlate the expansion

---

[5] https://sanctionssearch.ofac.treas.gov/.

[6] https://ofac.treasury.gov/specially-designated-nationals-list-sdn-list/program-tag-definitions-for-ofac-sanctions-lists.

of ransomware activities with transactions performed in these cryptocurrencies between 2015 and 2020. However, although it is clear that these cryptocurrencies facilitate the growth of ransomware revenue [12], authors did not find an evident correlation. In [8], traditional machine learning algorithms are used to detect illegal activities using a Bitcoin dataset, while in [19] graph-based networks are used for a similar task. Similar applications are also explored in [20] for defining a method to identify and trace illicit activities in the Ethereum blockchain.

Among the most relevant cybercrimes, cryptocurrencies have become the perfect solution for laundering illegal funds [27]. By fostering decentralization, user anonymity, and the ease of making cross-border transactions, they have led to the proliferation of dedicated services. Achraf Guidara [16] examines the relationship between cryptocurrencies and money laundering, emphasising the urgent need to develop a robust and internationally coordinated regulatory framework to mitigate these risks. In [21], 182 Bitcoin addresses belonging to 56 members of the Conti ransomware group are analysed with the aim of identifying if money laundering mechanisms are applied. They conclude that cryptocurrency exchanges and dark web services are involved in 71% and 30% of transactions, respectively, while only 8% utilized mixers. These findings challenge the prevailing notion that cybercriminals employ sophisticated methods, highlighting instead the simplicity of their tactics [22].

At the same time, as introduced in the previous sections, the lack of market control has turned these cryptocurrencies into a means of evading sanctions, allowing entities to continue their illicit activities. For this reason, in this work, we aim to analyse how punished entities use crypto assets to circumvent sanctions and whether they also employ laundering mechanisms to increase their anonymity.

3   Experimental Framework

In this section, the dataset and the approach followed in this study are presented. More specifically, Sect. 3.1 reviews the sanctioned list used, while Sect. 3.2 introduces the Bitcoin dataset. Finally, the guidelines and key concepts used during the experiments are reported in Sect. 3.3.

3.1   Sanctions List

As of February 2024, the SDN list contains information about 600 crypto addresses related to 17 different cryptocurrencies, as shown in Fig. 1a. The figure shows that the majority of reported addresses ($\sim 65\%$) belong to the Bitcoin (BTC) network, while another $\sim 25\%$ are from Ethereum (ETH). The remaining addresses, representing just 10%, are divided across 15 cryptocurrencies. Furthermore, analysing the composition of the sanctioned entities (Fig. 1b) that belong to the top-5 sanctioned cryptocurrencies, it becomes evident that while there are more punished individuals than companies for both BTC and ETH, companies possess a greater number of punished addresses. These results lead us to focus the analysis only on the BTC-related entities, as anticipated in Sect. 2.2. In particular, this constraint leaves us to study 43 out of the 56 available entities in the SDN list.

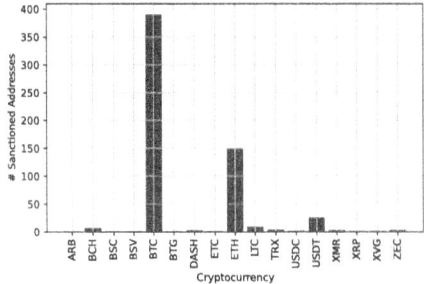 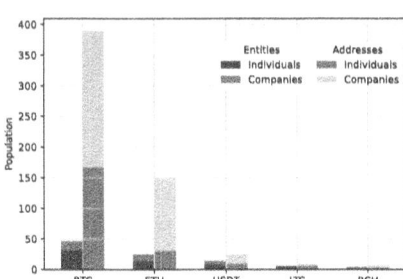

(a) Distribution of sanctioned cryptocurrencies in the SDN list.

(b) Addresses and entities distribution in the SDN list (top-5 populated cryptocurrencies).

Fig. 1. Overall statistics of sanctioned entities with cryptocurrency information extracted from the SDN list (February 2024).

Figure 2a details that most of the BTC-related sanctioned entities (both companies and individuals) are located in China and Russia. In fact, of the 43 punished entities, 13 are from China and 10 from Russia ($\sim 54\%$). In both cases, the number of sanctioned individuals overwhelms the number of companies, while there are only sanctioned companies in Canada, the Czech Republic, St. Vincent, and in the regions of Gaza and the Commonwealth of Independent States (CIS). Figure 2b shows the distribution of these sanctioned entities with respect to their violations. It is to be noted that one entity can face sanctions for multiple violations. Consequently, the most prevalent category, with 23 entities, pertains to malicious cyber-enabled activities since they include a broad spectrum of crimes. Furthermore, among the most populated categories, 10 entities are sanctioned for illicit drug trading, while 5 entities are linked to interference in the US election. Finally, Fig. 2c analyses the temporality of these sanctions and the number of entities involved. The figure shows that US authorities led a significant operation on illicit drug trading in October 2023, resulting in the sanctioning of 6 entities. Another interesting finding is that sanctioning operations against specific violations tend to occur only on specific dates. Specifically, violations related to *CYBER2, ILLICIT-DRUGS*, and *RUSSIA* are consistently detected over time, while the others are detected only on specific dates.

3.2 Bitcoin Dataset

In this paper, the entire Bitcoin blockchain data until the block 830,000 are downloaded, i.e., all the transactions until February 11th, 2024 (more than 900M

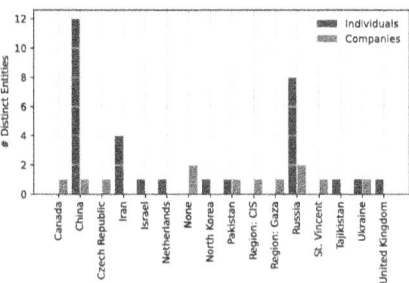

(a) Distribution of BTC-related entities in the SDN list per country/region.

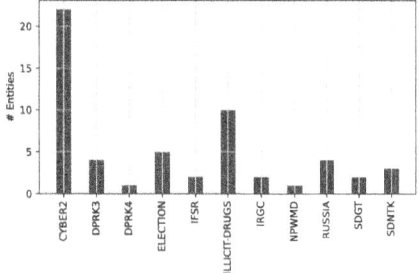

(b) Distribution of BTC-related entities in the SDN list per violation.

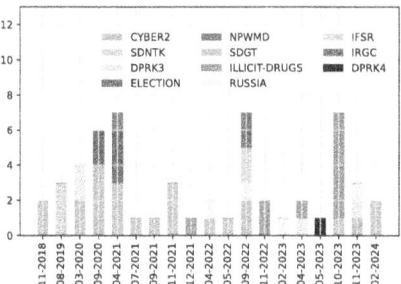

(c) BTC-related entities per violation over time.

Fig. 2. Overview about violations of sanctioned entities with BTC information extracted from the SDN list (February 2024).

transactions). On the other hand, to have more information about real-world entities, labelled (tagged) addresses are gathered from multiple reliable sources, such as WalletExplorer[7] and the tagpacks provided by Graphsense[8]. Indeed, these sources represent valid solutions used in many previous researches [24, 28, 32], and allowed us to gather more than 38M addresses of almost 400 entities labelled as *Exchanges, Gambling, Marketplaces, Mining Pools, Mixers, Services, Trading platforms, eWallet, Ransomware, Sextortion,* and *Extremist*.

3.3 Proposed Analysis

As mentioned in Sect. 3.1, the BTC addresses included in the SDN list represent the starting point of our investigation. More specifically, from each of them, we analyse the address-transaction graph [15, 32]. This graph is directly built using the information available in the BTC blockchain, where nodes are BTC addresses and transactions. Then directed edges (arrows) from addresses to transactions

---

[7] https://www.walletexplorer.com/.
[8] https://graphsense.info/.

represent incoming relations, while edges from transactions to addresses are outgoing relations, as shown in Fig. 3. Furthermore, the edge may incorporate BTC information like amount, fee, timestamps, etc. With these principles, it is possible to define the n-step address-transaction graph of a sanctioned address $X1$, as a graph in which all the paths from $X1$ involve maximum n transactions. Thus, the paths from $X1$ have a maximum length of $2n$ (Fig. 3).

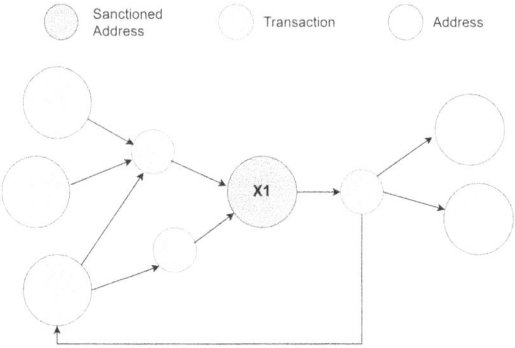

Fig. 3. An example of a _1_-step address-transaction graph

In this work, we present two different analyses: the first one is based on assessing the effectiveness of the sanctions by analysing the activities of the entities (_flow analysis_), and the second has the aim to detect the relations that entities have after being sanctioned (_behavioural analysis_).

For the _flow analysis_, a temporal aspect is introduced in the address-transaction graph. Specifically, for each address of each entity, multiple 1-step address-transaction graphs are created, considering 4 different temporal ranges: a) all the transactions prior to the imposed sanction (_pre-sanction_); b) transactions achieved immediately after the sanctions within the subsequent 7 d (_7 post-sanction_); c) transactions achieved immediately after the sanctions within 30 d post-sanctions (_30 post-sanction_); d) and finally all the activities post-sanctions up to February 11th, 2024 (_up-to-date_). These ranges allow us to evaluate the behaviour of the sanctioned entity and detect how they react to this situation in short, medium, and long terms.

Once these graphs are built, from each one, several metrics such as the number of input and output transactions, the overall balance of the entity after each temporal range, and the amount in USD of money sent and received by the entity (the BTC/USD value is fixed on the day the transaction is performed), are extracted and used for evaluating the trends and the effectiveness of the sanctions. It is to be noted that one entity may possess multiple sanctioned addresses. Therefore, metrics computed from each of its addresses are aggregated to provide a comprehensive overview of the entity's behaviour.

On the other hand, the _behavioural analysis_ is based on analysing a single address-transaction graph for each entity, that is created using data from immediately after the sanctions until the end of the dataset (*up-to-date*). Furthermore, this graph is enriched with real-world entity information, i.e., with labels gathered from the external sources mentioned in Sect. 3.2. This approach enables us to identify whether the sanctioned entity engages in transactions with other known entities, which could include potential actors related to illicit operations (e.g. other sanctioned entities, ransomware, etc.) or it tries to apply strategies for conducting activities such as money laundering (e.g. involving mainly mixers, gambling or other services), on-ramps and off-ramps operations (e.g. involving exchanges), funding raise campaign (e.g. involving mining pool or marketplace). This *behavioural analysis* is performed considering both 1-step and 2-step address-transaction graphs. This approach gives us a deeper view of the entity strategy, since the 1-step analysis only provides information about its direct relations, while the 2-step also includes undirected transactions (reached in two steps).

4   Current Study

In this section, the results obtained in the two proposed analyses are presented. In particular, Sect. 4.1 describes the results obtained analysing transactions and money flow of the entities before and after their sanctions, while Sect. 4.2 details the relations that the sanctioned entities have had with other known type of entities. Finally, discussions and limitations are reported in Sect. 4.3.

4.1   Flow Analysis Results

Fig. 4 shows the number of entities that received and sent money through crypto transactions post-sanctions. Specifically, the figure illustrates that only half of all the sanctioned entities were effectively discouraged from engaging in transactions. In particular, only 21 entities stopped to receive money, and 25 to send funds. On the other hand, the figure reveals that despite the sanctions, some entities (7) continued to move funds within 7 d of the OFAC sanction. For this reason, Fig. 5 enables us to comprehend how these funds are being moved, analysing the balance in terms of BTC held by each entity in its sanctioned addresses before and after the sanctions.

Although Fig. 4 indicates that some entities were not deterred from conducting transactions, Fig. 5 emphasises a general trend of maintaining at least a minimal balance in the sanctioned addresses, excluding the two entities with the highest balance (≥ 50 BTC) who adopted an off-ramp strategy. Yet, the number of entities with a balance of 0 decreased, while the number of entities with a balance in a range > 0 and ≤ 0.1 BTC increased.

Table 2 reports the number of transactions that involve sanctioned entities, categorised by the violation they are convicted of. Additionally, the table includes the USD volume moved by the entities for each violation, both before and after the sanctions. In particular, the volume indicates both incoming and outgoing transactions. Results in Table 2 show that *CYBER2* represents the violation

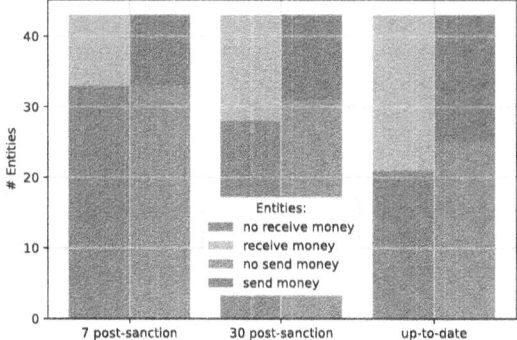

Fig. 4. Number of sanctioned entities that perform transactions (received and sent) in the different post-sanction intervals.

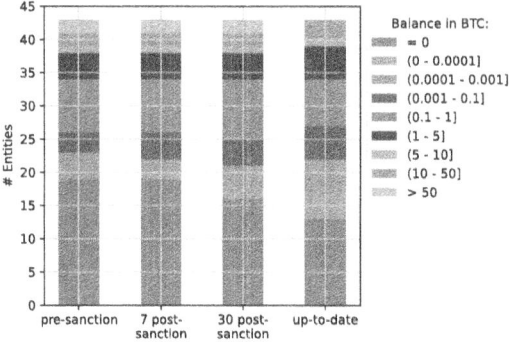

Fig. 5. Entity balance (in BTC) considering the sanctioned addresses at the four stages: *pre-sanction, 7 post-sanction, 30 post-sanction,* and *up-to-date.*

with the highest number of transactions pre-sanction (more than 150K) and the highest USD volume of about 8,300 million. The result is expected since this violation also has the highest number of sanctioned entities (Fig. 2b). However, what is interesting, is that after the sanctions, entities related to this violation still perform 305 transactions for a market of about 3 million USD. On the other hand, entities related to *DPRK3* and *ILLICIT-DRUGS* violations perform a high number of transactions and show a USD volume of 240 million and 120 million pre-sanction, respectively. Although these numbers decrease in the post-sanction phase, they remain consistent, with 209 thousand USD for *DPRK3* and 8 million USD for *ILLICIT-DRUGS*. Also, the market related to *RUSSIA* violation is pretty high pre-sanctions, with almost 40 million USD moved in just 553 transactions. However, it seems strongly affected by the sanctions, resulting in just 4 transactions with an overall amount of 162 USD. Finally, entities related to violations such as *IFSR, IRGC* and *SDGT* are indeed deterred from performing transactions; in fact, they achieve only 1 transaction post-sanctions, moving just a few dollars (or less). Notably, the entities involved in *DPRK4* activities are shut down. More precisely, they have not achieved transactions from May 2023 (Fig. 2c) until the date.

Table 2. Number of transactions achieved and estimation of USD moved before and after the sanctions for each violation.

		# Transactions		USD Volume	
#	Violation	Pre-Sanction	Up-to-date	Pre-Sanction	Up-to-date
1	CYBER2	153 K	305	8,300 M	3 M
2	DPRK3	2 K	63	240 M	209 K
3	DPRK4	62	0	10 M	0
4	ELECTION	46 K	8	6 M	1 K
5	IFSR	182	1	461 K	≤ 1
6	ILLICIT-DRUGS	9 K	747	120 M	8 M
7	IRGC	182	1	461 K	≤ 1
8	NPWMD	97	8	26 K	1 K
9	RUSSIA	553	4	39 M	162
10	SDGT	18 K	1	42 M	103
11	SDNTK	354	42	104 K	12 K

4.2 Behavioural Analysis Results

Table 3 reports the results gathered during the behavioural analysis, involving 1-step and 2-step address-transaction graphs. In particular, by creating a 1-step graph from each of the 43 entities (387 BTC-sanctioned addresses) it is possible to reach about 4K addresses, of which only 340 addresses (8.48%) are related to known entities and have an external label. On the other hand, increasing the analysis considering also undirected connections (2-step address-transaction graphs), it is possible to reach more than 10M addresses, of which just 175,444 (1.67%) are labelled. These outcomes confirm that, although the 1-step analysis has more labelled information, it identifies only 15 known entities of 4 different behaviours, while the 2-step analysis enriches the investigation by uncovering 67 entities with 9 different behaviours.

The results reported in Table 3 highlight that, in both the 1-step and 2-step analyses, the majority of labelled addresses belonged to *Exchanges* with 97% and 86%, respectively. At the same time, in the 2-step analysis, 13.5% of the labelled addresses are linked to 11 crypto services (trading, eWallet, banking, etc.). This enhanced scenario also highlights connections between sanctioned entities and addresses associated with *Sextortion, Ransomware* and *Extremism* crimes.

Table 3. Behavioural analysis of output entities related to sanctioned actors considering 1-step and 2-step address-transaction graphs.

		1-step analysis		2-step analysis	
#	Behaviour	# Distinct Entities	# Distinct Address	# Distinct Entities	# Distinct Address
1	Service	3	5	13	23,727
2	Mixer	1	1	2	14
3	Exchange	9	331	37	151,385
4	OFAC Sanctioned	2	3	6	33
5	Gambling	-	-	1	249
6	Extremism	-	-	1	13
7	Ransomware	-	-	2	9
8	Mining Pool	-	-	4	13
9	Sextortion	-	-	1	1
	Labelled	**15**	**340**	**67**	**175,444**
	No Labelled	-	**3,668**	-	**10,356,787**

4.3 Discussion and Limitations

Discussion. New regulations have started to treat Exchanges as financial services, requiring any Crypto Asset Service Provider or Virtual Asset Service Provider to implement anti-money laundering control measures such as Know Your Customer (KYC) policies. Nevertheless, criminals have started to explore new methods to obtain money fraudulently and to launder and use it, e.g., including dedicated services and other digital assets that current solutions/directives do not adequately supervise. Indeed, these new money laundering methods exploit gaps in existing legislations, which in turn require frequent updates and make them challenging to enforce and follow. In this context, it is crucial to consider and incorporate also technical connectivity to the crypto ecosystem, i.e., ensuring the technology used by both users and service providers is connected and operates under unified legal standards. This alignment will help enforce the law and catch those who commit crimes, making it more difficult for criminals to exploit any legal loopholes.

Aligned with the findings presented in [27], this study, using OFAC information, shows that Bitcoin is among the most used cryptocurrencies for various crimes, not limited to the cyber ecosystem. The results indicate that, despite being sanctioned, entities still perform operations with their blocked or frozen cryptocurrencies without employing complex tactics or dedicated money laundering services in their transactions. In fact, entities prefer to achieve off-ramp activities through known and reliable exchanges. These results are aligned with the outcomes reported in [21,22] regarding ransomware funds. However, the results also show that, in some cases, sanctioned entities maintain relationships with other sanctioned entities or entities involved in other crimes, such as sextortion, ransomware, and extremism.

This paper shows that a 1-step analysis is not sufficient for understanding and tracing the operations of sanctioned entities. Indeed, the analysis reveals that only a few sanctioned entities can be traced to known services, while a 2-step analysis provides enhanced context to their operations. However, although expanding the analysis to include more steps seems beneficial, it should be noted that this approach also introduces more unlabelled addresses, increasing the uncertainty in the "follow-the-money" investigation. Therefore, the number of steps to be included must be determined on a case-by-case basis.

Limitation. When interpreting the results, it is important to take into account some assumptions/constraints considered during this investigation. Firstly, the results of the *behavioural analysis* strongly depend on the quantity and quality of labelled data available in the literature. The outcomes of this work are strictly related to the information provided by the US OFAC authority and need to be verified when information from new authorities becomes available. At the same time, regarding the quantity of the data, as introduced in Sect. 3.2, this work has gathered 38M addresses of almost 400 entities used in many state-of-the-art works [24,28,32]. Yet, these 38M represent only 2.9% of the addresses used in the BTC blockchain, which counts about 1,300M addresses as of February 2024. Additionally, the OFAC SDN list being considered includes 40 sanctioned entities with Bitcoin addresses involved. While one might argue that this number is insufficient for comprehensive trend analysis, it should be noted that this is the maximum number available in the real ecosystem. On the other hand, regarding the quality of the information, we rely on the fact that the labelled datasets are used in many research investigations, as mentioned in Sect. 3.2, and in some cases, they are extracted by tools that are used by LEAs in real investigations [18]. Moreover, although these datasets are generated and gathered from different sources, they do not present inconsistencies among them in the provided data.

Furthermore, it is to be noted that some entities were sanctioned in late 2023 or early 2024, meaning that the gathered crypto transactions (until February 2024) might not fully capture their activities. However, we decided to focus the analysis on the type of violation rather than concrete entities (Table 2). In fact, looking at the distribution analysis provided in Fig. 2c, it is possible to see that the majority of the entities for each violation are prior to May 2023 - excluding the *ILLICIT-DRUGS* crime - allowing us to analyse 9 months of transactions.

Finally, in the context of the 2-step analysis, this study has assumed that there has been no change in ownership of the funds. However, relying just on blockchain information, the validity of this assumption cannot be ensured. Nonetheless, we acknowledge this risk because limiting the analysis solely to 1-step graphs would be excessively restrictive, generating a skewed and poor view of the impact of the sanctions. Furthermore, a change in the ownership of the funds should not generate high-impact deviations in the proposed analysis, since we are just analysing the reached entities using a basic "follow-the-money" approach.

5   Conclusion

The present study represents a first step and provides an interesting yet partial understanding of the impact of sanctions on the crypto ecosystem, with a focus on the Bitcoin cryptocurrency. The first point to emphasise is that sanctions are inherently tied to the prevailing regulations at any given time. As context, this study solely reports on European policies aimed at regulating the crypto market and preventing financial fraud. However, the analysis is conducted using data provided by the US OFAC authority, as it is the only entity that releases a comprehensive list of economically and trade-sanctioned entities.

The *flow analysis* shows that in general, sanctions have been effective on at least half of the sanctioned entities, while the other half has continued to move (receive and send) money through the sanctioned BTC addresses, although they do not show huge changes in their current balance. In particular, sanctions seem to be not very effective against entities related to specific violations, like *CYBER2* and *ILLICIT-DRUGS* which are the ones that still make transactions and move high quantities of USD in proportion with their activities pre-sanctions. On the other hand, the *behavioural analysis* highlights that sanctioned entities tend to prefer reaching out directly to *Exchanges* to convert their cryptos, rather than use dedicated services for money laundering (mixers or gambling).

With the aim of deepening that understanding, further analysis should include heuristics assumptions in the loop [31] as well as automatic labelling strategies to generate clustered entities. Yet, in this way, it would be possible for each punished entity, not only to consider the actual sanctioned addresses reported in the list, but also other addresses that are likely to belong to the same wallet. At the same time, it will be interesting to scale up our approach by incorporating information from other cryptocurrencies (Ethereum) and stablecoins. In fact, as reported in [12], they represent a good alternative - especially in the last three years - through which criminals engage in illicit activities and sanctions circumvention. This approach will allow Law Enforcement Officers to have a complete picture of criminal *modus operandi*.

Acknowledgments. This work has been partially supported by the European Union's Horizon 2020 Research and Innovation Program under the project FALCON (Grant Agreement No. 101121281)

References

1. Directive (eu) 2015/849 of the European parliament and of the council on the prevention of the use of the financial system for the purposes of money laundering or terrorist financing (2015). https://eur-lex.europa.eu/legal-content/EN/TXT/uri=celex%3A32015L0849. Accessed 08 May 2024
2. Directive of the European parliament and of the council on the fight against fraud to the union's financial interests by means of criminal law (2017). https://www.consilium.europa.eu/en/policies/fight-against-terrorism/fight-against-terrorist-financing/. Accessed 08 May 2024

3. Directive of the European parliament and of the council on combating fraud and counterfeiting of non-cash means of payment (2019/713),.https://eur-lex.europa.eu/eli/dir/2019/713/oj, accessed on 08/05/2024
4. International standards on combatting money laundering and the financing of terrorism and proliferation, the FATF recommendations (2023). https://www.fatf-gafi.org/content/dam/fatf-gafi/recommendations/FATF%20Recommendations%202012.pdf.coredownload.inline.pdf, accessed on 08/05/2024
5. Regulation of the European parliament and of the council on markets in crypto-assets (2023). https://eur-lex.europa.eu/legal-content/EN/TXT/?uri=CELEX%3A32023R1114&pk_campaign=todays_OJ&pk_source=EURLEX&pk_medium=TW&pk_keyword=Crypto%20assets&pk_content=Regulation&pk_cid=EURLEX_todaysOJ, accessed on 08/05/2024
6. Regulation of the European parliament and of the council on information accompanying transfers of funds and certain crypto-assets (2023/1113). https://eur-lex.europa.eu/eli/reg/2023/1113/oj, accessed on 08/05/2024
7. Cryptocurrency bans explained: which countries have restricted crypto and why? (2024). https://www.techopedia.com/cryptocurrency-bans-explained-which-countries-have-restricted-crypto. Accessed 25 May 2024
8. Alotibi, J., Almutanni, B., Alsubait, T., Alhakami, H., Baz, A.: Money laundering detection using machine learning and deep learning. Int. J. Adv. Comput. Sci. Appl. **13**(10), 732–738 (2022)
9. Bele, J.L.: Cryptocurrencies as facilitators of cybercrime. In: SHS Web of Conferences, vol. 111, p. 01005. EDP Sciences (2021)
10. Berry, H.S.: The evolution of cryptocurrency and cyber attacks. In: 2022 International Conference on Computer and Applications (ICCA), pp. 1–7 (2022). https://doi.org/10.1109/ICCA56443.2022.10039632
11. Blanchini, M., Cerreta, M., Di Monda, D., Fabbri, M., Raciti, M., Ahmad, H.S., Costa, G.: Supporting criminal investigations on the blockchain: a temporal logic-based approach (2022)
12. Chainalysis Inc.: the 2024 crypto crime report (2024). https://go.chainalysis.com/crypto-crime-2024.html. Accessed 07 Aug 2024
13. Cole, T., Gundur, R.: Virtual currency, cryptoassets, and cybercrime. In: Oxford Research Encyclopedia of Criminology and Criminal Justice (2024)
14. Connolly, L.Y., Wall, D.S.: The rise of crypto-ransomware in a changing cybercrime landscape: taxonomising countermeasures. Comput. Secur. **87**, 101568 (2019)
15. Fleder, M., Kester, M.S., Pillai, S.: Bitcoin transaction graph analysis. arXiv preprint arXiv:1502.01657 (2015)
16. Guidara, A.: Cryptocurrency and money laundering: a literature review. Corp. Law Gov. Rev. **4**(2), 36–41 (2022)
17. Hornuf, L., Momtaz, P.P., Nam, R.J., Yuan, Y.: Cybercrime on the ethereum blockchain (2023)
18. Iknaio: blockchain analytics pilot in bavaria (2022). https://www.ikna.io/2022/06/22/ZCB.html. Accessed 23 May 2024
19. Japinye, A.: Integrating machine learning in anti-money laundering through crypto: a comprehensive performance review. Eur. J. Account. Audit. Finan. Res. **12**(4), 54–80 (2024)
20. Lin, D., Wu, J., Yu, Y., Fu, Q., Zheng, Z., Yang, C.: DenseFlow: spotting cryptocurrency money laundering in Ethereum transaction graphs. In: Proceedings of the ACM on Web Conference 2024, pp. 4429–4438. WWW 2024, Association for Computing Machinery, New York, NY, USA (2024). https://doi.org/10.1145/3589334.3645692

21. Nazzari, M.: From payday to payoff: exploring the money laundering strategies of cybercriminals. Trends Organ. Crime, 1–18 (2023). https://doi.org/10.1007/s12117-023-09505-1
22. Nazzari, M.: Lost in the maze: disentangling the behavioral variety of money laundering. Eur. J. Crim. Policy Res., 1–19 (2023). https://doi.org/10.1007/s10610-023-09572-8
23. Neumann, M., Elsenbroich, C.: Introduction: the societal dimensions of organized crime. Trends Organized Crime **20**, 1–15 (2017)
24. Paquet-Clouston, M., Haslhofer, B., Dupont, B.: Ransomware payments in the bitcoin ecosystem. J. Cybersec. **5**(1), tyz003 (2019)
25. Reddy, E., Minnaar, A.: Cryptocurrency: a tool and target for cybercrime (2018)
26. Sanusi, K.A., Dickason-Koekemoer, Z.: Cryptocurrency returns, cybercrime and stock market volatility: gas and regime switching approaches. Int. J. Econ. Financ. Issues **12**(6), 52 (2022)
27. Soudijn, M.: Encounters with professional money launderers; an analysis of financial transactions as reported by gatekeepers. Eur. J. Crim. Policy Res., 1–14 (2024). https://doi.org/10.1007/s10610-024-09588-8
28. Tovanich, N., Cazabet, R.: Fingerprinting bitcoin entities using money flow representation learning. Appl. Netw. Sci. **8**(1), 63 (2023)
29. Viscusi, W.K.: Market incentives for criminal behavior. In: The Black Youth Employment Crisis, pp. 301–351. University of Chicago Press (1986)
30. Wardani, A., Ali, M., Barkhuizen, J.: Money laundering through cryptocurrency and its arrangements in money laundering act. Lex Publica **9**(2), 49–66 (2022)
31. Zhang, Y., Wang, J., Luo, J.: Heuristic-based address clustering in bitcoin. IEEE Access **8**, 210582–210591 (2020)
32. Zola, F., Eguimendia, M., Bruse, J.L., Urrutia, R.O.: Cascading machine learning to attack bitcoin anonymity. In: 2019 IEEE International Conference on Blockchain (Blockchain), pp. 10–17. IEEE (2019)

Practical Implementation of Pairing-Based zkSNARK in Bitcoin Script

Federico Barbacovi, Enrique Larraia, Paul Germouty$^{(\boxtimes)}$, and Wei Zhang

nChain, London, UK
{f.barbacovi,e.larraia,w.zhang}@nchain.com, germouty.paul@orange.fr

Abstract. Groth16 is a pairing-based zero-knowledge proof scheme that has a constant proof size and an efficient verification algorithm. Bitcoin Script is a stack-based low-level programming language that is used to lock and unlock bitcoins. In this paper, we present a practical implementation of the Groth16 verifier in Bitcoin Script deployable on the mainnet of a Bitcoin blockchain called BSV. Our result paves the way for a framework of verifiable computation on Bitcoin: a Groth16 proof is generated for the correctness of an off-chain computation and is verified in Bitcoin Script on-chain. This approach not only offers privacy but also scalability. Moreover, this approach enables smart contract capability on Bitcoin which was previously thought rather limited if not non-existent.

Keywords: Bitcoin · Smart Contract · Zero-Knowledge Proof

1 Introduction

Zero-knowledge proofs (ZKPs) have been widely adopted to enhance blockchain technology. For example, zCash [36] and Firo [16] use ZKPs for user privacy, and Ethereum uses ZKPs for scalability [14]. Bitcoin, on the other hand, is thought to have limitations that make ZKP integration much more difficult, one of which is the Bitcoin scripting language. Due to its stack-based structure and primitive set of opcodes, it is rather difficult to implement the complex mathematical functions required by most ZKPs.

Despite these limitations, there are many projects trying to integrate ZKPs and Bitcoin. They determined to make Bitcoin more scalable and more capable for smart contracts, ultimately making Bitcoin more economically sustainable and viable even with the diminishing block reward through halving. For examples, B^2 Network [4] and Merlin Chain [23] are working on ZK Rollups to scale Bitcoin; Bitlayer [9] takes a BitVM [26] approach to create a computational layer for Bitcoin, while LumiBit [21] adapts ZKEVM to achieve the same. In [27], ZeroSync has compressed the bootstrapping process (initial block download) into a single ZKP verification using a ZKP-circuit-friendly language called

---

Formerly nChain researcher. Work done while at nChain.

J. Garcia-Alfaro et al. (Eds.): ESORICS 2024 Workshops, LNCS 15263, pp. 309–325, 2025.
https://doi.org/10.1007/978-3-031-82349-7_21

Cairo [13], thus dramatically reducing the time required to start a Bitcoin node. However, in all the examples mentioned above, practically verifying ZKP on-chain has not yet been realised.

sCrypt [31] has implemented ZKP verification (Groth16, [19]) in Bitcoin Script on the BSV, a version of Bitcoin, achieving a script size of 1.2MB [32,33]. However, their implementation is not practical, and it falls short for three reasons. First, it cannot be deployed on the BSV mainnet without a collaborating miner. This is because of a policy that restricts the script size to 500 kB [25], and non-policy-compliant transactions can only be accepted by other miners if the collaborating miner successfully mines a block. Second, it is not a faithful implementation of the Groth16 verifier as they hard-code in the script data which should be revealed at the point of spending, thus greatly limiting the applicability of their code. Third, their approach of using a compiler that converts TypeScript to Bitcoin Script generally leads to scripts of non-optimal size.

Our main contributions are:

- an implementation of bilinear pairings in Bitcoin Script, which has size[1] of 293.6 kB, and that can be readily used on the BSV mainnet;
- an implementation of Groth16 verification in Bitcoin Script, which has size[2] of 466 kB, and that can be readily used on the BSV mainnet;
- an analysis of the trade-off between script size and execution time caused by large number arithmetics (the smaller the script, the larger the numbers, hence the longer execution time);
- a significant reduction in transaction fees for on-chain ZKP verification as the transaction size is significantly reduced.

To achieve this level of optimisation, we use a combination of different techniques, each providing a significant reduction in script size:[3]

- stack management: being aware of positions of elements on the stacks and identifying the best arrangement of data elements and operations that results in the smallest script;
- no computation of inverses: designing the script to verify a candidate inverse instead of computing it;
- sparseness: working with field elements represented by polynomials that have many zero coefficients [30];
- seed choice: choosing an elliptic curve with seed having the smallest Hamming weight.

---

[1] All the sizes are cumulative of the locking and unlocking script size.

[2] The size reported here is for one public input, in Sect. 4 we also report the size for the Groth16 verifier with two public inputs.

[3] It is difficult to pinpoint where exactly the reductions come from, as they are a combination of all the techniques we employed. However, in the body of the text we provide rough estimations for each of the techniques we employ.

Our scripts are publicly available on GitHub.[4]. In the repository, readers can find a Python code used to generate our scripts,[5] another Python code used to generate the test data for benchmarking purposes, and the references to examples of on-chain transactions.

Our results enable, for the first time, practical ZKP verification on the mainnet of a Bitcoin version called BSV.[6] While Ethereum uses ZKPs for scalability, Bitcoin can also use them to enable smart contracts with greater flexibility. That is, in theory, one can run any computation off-chain and generate a ZKP, which is verified on chain, that the computation was done correctly. For example, the computation can be the validation of a token rule set, the enforcement of a financial contract, or the execution of instructions based on business logic and workflows.

The paper is structured as follows. In Sect. 2, we recall the preliminary notions we need in the rest of the paper, and we introduce the notation we use for Bitcoin scripts. In Sect. 3, we detail our implementation of the Optimal Ate Pairing and of the Groth16 verifier instatiated over the curve BLS12-381. Finally, in Sect. 4 we evaluate our scripts according to script size and execution time, and we compare the cost of verifying a ZKP on BSV and on Ethereum.

2 Preliminaries

2.1 Bitcoin

The Bitcoin blockchain [28] parses block data x into an ordered set of transactions $x := (\mathsf{tx}_1, \ldots, \mathsf{tx}_n)$. Each transaction specifies a list of inputs and outputs. An output of a transaction is *spent* if it is referenced as an input of a valid transaction. An output can only be spent once.

Bitcoin uses a non-Turing complete, stack-based programming language in which spending conditions can be coded into *locking* scripts contained in outputs. Each input of a transaction contains an *unlocking* script, with the arguments needed to execute the locking script from the output referenced by the input. The spending is accepted if the execution terminates with true.

We think of the subroutines that make up a locking script as the implementations of functions $f(x_1, \ldots, x_n)$, and of the elements in the unlocking script as the values $(\tilde{x}_1, \ldots, \tilde{x}_n)$ over which the functions are evaluated. The unlocking script is then the implementation of a predicate (a function that returns true or false) whose calculation requires the evaluation of various functions (the subroutines) on the values supplied in the unlocking script.

---

[4] https://github.com/nchain-innovation/zkscript_package.

[5] We generate our scripts as outputs of Python functions, so that they can be composed and shuffled around in an easy way. The approach we take is similar to that of BitVM [12], but they use Rust in place of Python.

[6] For our optimisations to work on BTC, we need large integer arithmetic.

Script Execution. A script is a sequence of opcodes and data objects. It is evaluated in reverse Polish notation by the Bitcoin Script engine, starting by pushing to the stack the arguments specified in the unlocking script.

The set of opcodes available for scripting depends on the implementation of Bitcoin. We will use the BSV implementation [11] because it supports large numbers (of size up to 10 kB) and has the widest opcode support for arithmetic operations.[7] We list the opcodes used in this paper in Table 1; note that they are not all the ones needed in our implementations.

We introduce some notation that will be used throughout this work:

– $\langle\langle l \rangle\rangle$ denotes data hard-coded in the locking script. Thus, we will write

$$[\texttt{foo}] := \langle\langle l \rangle\rangle [\texttt{bar}]$$

  to denote that the locking script $[\texttt{foo}]$ consists of a subroutine script $[\texttt{bar}]$ and hard-coded data $\langle\langle l \rangle\rangle$.
– $[\![x]\!]$ denotes data on top of the stack, i.e., the data we would get if we popped an element from the stack. More generally, $[\![x_0]\!], \ldots, [\![x_n]\!]$ means that x_n is the data on top of the stack, x_{n-1} is the data below x_n (second from the top), and x_0 is the data buried at depth $n + 1$ in the stack.
– $[\![y_0]\!], \ldots, [\![y_m]\!] \leftarrow [\![x_0]\!], \ldots, [\![x_n]\!]$ $[\texttt{foo}]$: Before executing $[\texttt{foo}]$, the top $n + 1$ elements of the stack are $[\![x_0]\!], \ldots, [\![x_n]\!]$, and after executing $[\texttt{foo}]$ the top $m+1$ elements are $[\![y_0]\!], \ldots, [\![y_m]\!]$.

Table 1. Opcodes used in this paper

Opcode	Operation
OP_1SUB	$[\![x_0 - 1]\!] \leftarrow [\![x_0]\!]$ OP_1SUB
OP_DEPTH	$[\![x_n]\!], \ldots, [\![x_0]\!], [\![n + 1]\!] \leftarrow [\![x_n]\!], \ldots, [\![x_0]\!]$ OP_DEPTH
OP_PICK	$[\![x_n]\!], \ldots, [\![x_0]\!], [\![x_i]\!] \leftarrow [\![x_n]\!], \ldots, [\![x_0]\!], [\![i]\!]$ OP_PICK
OP_EQUAL	$[\![x_0 == x_1]\!] \leftarrow [\![x_0]\!], [\![x_1]\!]$ OP_EQUAL
OP_VERIFY	Pop x_0; fail if x_0 is false, otherwise, continue $\leftarrow [\![x_0]\!]$ OP_VERIFY
OP_EQUALVERIFY	OP_EQUALVERIFY = OP_EQUAL OP_VERIFY

2.2   Pairings

Bilinear pairings are the building block of many important cryptographic primitives. The most efficient instantiation of a bilinear pairing is the Optimal Ate pairing [22], which is defined as a map $e : \mathbb{G}_1 \times \mathbb{G}_2 \to \mathbb{G}_T$ such that

$$e(n[A], [B]) = e([A], n[B]) = e([A], [B])^n$$

---

[7] BTC only allows number up to 4 bytes and has disabled various opcodes needed for arithmetic operations [1].

for any $[A] \in \mathbb{G}_1$, $[B] \in \mathbb{G}_2$ and $n \in \mathbb{Z}$. Here, $\mathbb{G}_1$ and $\mathbb{G}_2$ are subgroups of the group of points on some elliptic curves.

The value of e on $(P,Q) \in \mathbb{G}_1 \times \mathbb{G}_2$ is computed in two steps. First, we compute $\mathsf{miller}(P,Q) \in \mathbb{G}_T$, the output of the Miller loop [24], and then we perform a final exponentiation $\mathsf{miller}(P,Q)^\eta$, where η is an exponent depending on the instantiation of $\mathbb{G}_1$, $\mathbb{G}_2$ and $\mathbb{G}_T$. We set $e(P,Q) := \mathsf{miller}(P,Q)^\eta$.

In this paper, we instantiate the Optimal Ate Pairing over BLS12 curves [8] for their robustness against some known attacks [5–7,20] and their efficiency [3].

BLS12 Curves. BLS12 curves have the form $y^2 = x^3 + b \mod q$, where b is a parameter of the curve, and $q = (u-1)^2(u^4 - u^2 + 1)/3 + u$ is a prime dependent on a seed u. We write $E_{b,u}(\mathbb{F}_{q^n})$ to denote set of points of the BLS12 curve with parameters b and u over $\mathbb{F}_{q^n}$.

For BLS12-381, we have $u = -(2^{63} + 2^{62} + 2^{60} + 2^{57} + 2^{48} + 2^{16})$ and $b = 4$. When instantiating the Optimal Ate Pairing over this curve, $\mathbb{G}_1$, $\mathbb{G}_2$ and $\mathbb{G}_T$ are cyclic groups of order $r = u^4 - u^2 + 1$, $\mathbb{G}_1$ is a subgroup of $E_{b,u}(\mathbb{F}_q)$, while $\mathbb{G}_T = \mathbb{F}_{q^{12}}$. To construct $\mathbb{G}_2$, we set $\mathbb{F}_{q^2} = \mathbb{F}_q[t]/(1 + t^2)$, and then $\mathbb{G}_2$ is a subgroup of $E_{b',u}(\mathbb{F}_{q^2})$, where $b' = (1+t)b \in \mathbb{F}_{q^2}$.

2.3 zkSNARKs

Circuits and NP Relations. Let $\mathsf{C} : \mathbb{F}_r^{\ell+h} \to \{0,1\}$ be a polynomial-size arithmetic circuit over a finite field $\mathbb{F}_r$. The NP relation $\mathcal{R}_\mathsf{C}$ for C is defined as

$$\mathcal{R}_\mathsf{C} := \left\{ (\boldsymbol{a}; \boldsymbol{w}) \in \mathbb{F}_r^\ell \times \mathbb{F}_r^h \mid \mathsf{C}(\boldsymbol{a}, \boldsymbol{w}) = 1 \right\}.$$

The vector $\boldsymbol{a} = (a_1, \ldots, a_\ell)$ is the statement of the relation, sometimes also called the instance or public input, and the vector $\boldsymbol{w}$ is the witness or private input. The language associated to $\mathcal{R}_\mathsf{C}$ is $\mathcal{L}_\mathsf{C} := \{\boldsymbol{a} \in \mathbb{F}_r^n \mid \exists \boldsymbol{w} \in \{0,1\}^h \text{ s.t. } (\boldsymbol{a}; \boldsymbol{w}) \in \mathcal{R}_\mathsf{C}\}$.

zkSNARKs. A preprocessing, zero-knowledge, succinct, non-interactive, argument system of knowledge (zkSNARK[8]) for $\mathcal{R}_\mathsf{C}$ is a triplet of algorithms $\Pi := (\mathsf{Setup}, \mathsf{Prove}, \mathsf{Verify})$ such that Setup takes as input a security parameter λ and the description of the circuit C, and it outputs a pair of keys pk and vk. The prover Prove takes pk, the statement $\boldsymbol{a}$ and the witness $\boldsymbol{w}$ and outputs a proof $\pi \in \mathbb{G}_1 \times \mathbb{G}_2 \times \mathbb{G}_1$, that is $\pi \leftarrow \mathsf{Prove}(pk, \boldsymbol{a}, \boldsymbol{w})$. The verifier Verify takes vk, $\boldsymbol{a}$, π and it either accepts or rejects, that is $\{\mathsf{true}, \mathsf{false}\} \leftarrow \mathsf{Verify}(vk, \boldsymbol{a}, \pi)$. The proof purportedly is for the statement "$\boldsymbol{a} \in \mathcal{L}_\mathsf{C}$".

Groth16. Groth16 [19] follows the linear interactive proof paradigm [10] with security in the generic group model, and can thus be instantiated with pairings. Given $\pi = ([A]_1, [B]_2, [C]_1)$, the result of Verify on the public input

---

[8] In this paper, we use ZKP and zkSNARK interchangeably. It is understood that there is a subtle difference which is not relevant to this paper.

$\boldsymbol{a} = (a_1, \ldots, a_\ell)$ and the proof π is the result of an equation of pairings:

$$e([A]_1, [B]_2) = e([\alpha]_1, [\beta]_2) \cdot e\left(\sum_{i=0}^{\ell} a_i[P_i]_1, [\gamma]_2\right) \cdot e([C]_1, [\delta]_2) \tag{1}$$

where $[\alpha]_1, [\beta]_2, [\gamma]_2, [\delta]_2$ and the $[P_i]_1$'s[9] are part of vk, and $a_0 = 1$.

Note that the equation (1) depends on C only via the number of public inputs. This means that a Bitcoin Script implementation of Verify will be independent of the complexity of the calculations happening in C, and will scale only according to the number of public inputs. Furthermore, the size of the proof π is fixed to that of three groups element, once again independent of C.

These properties make Groth16 the best candidate for implementing zkSNARK verification on-chain as it induces the least transaction size and computational complexity, resulting in low fees and fast execution time.

3   Implementation of Pairings and Groth16 in Script

We now outline our implementation of the Optimal Ate Pairing and of the Groth16 verifier in Bitcoin Script. First, we break down the scripts into subroutines. That is, we look at the operations required to compute the Optimal Ate Pairing and to verify a Groth16 proof, and we decompose these operations into simpler ones that we efficiently implement. Second, in constructing the subroutines we assume that the spender (the prover in the zkSNARK framework) supplies to the script (the verifier) additional input data to simplify the proof verification. The script will then verify that the data supplied is the one purported to be, and use it if it is, or fail otherwise. See Sect. 3.1 for an example of the input data supplied by the spender.

Remark 1. In Bitcoin, the prover/verifier framework of zkSNARKs is transposed to that of a payer who constructs the locking script (the Groth16 verifier) and of a spender who shows a zero-knowledge proof to prove they have the right to spend. While in zkSNARKs only the verifier carries the burden of verifying the proof, in our setup we assume that also the prover performs part of the computation required to verify the proof, so to reduce the size of the Bitcoin Script Groth16 verifier. This means that there is an additional burden on the prover, which is quantified by the amount of work required to compute the product of the three Miller loops in (6). This added burden is acceptable as it is easier to increase efficiency of off-chain computations rather than optimising script size.

The Optimal Ate Pairing is computed as $e(P, Q) = \mathrm{miller}(P, Q)^\eta$, see Sect. 2.2. We implement it by first implementing the Miller loop, and then the final exponentiation. That is, we construct a script [millerLoop] that computes

---

[9] The $[P_i]$'s are the evaluations of the QAP polynomials of the public inputs corresponding to the R1CS system of C on the verifier pre-computed challenge (the so-called *toxic waste* generated in the setup), [18].

the function $(P, Q) \mapsto \mathsf{miller}(P, Q)$, and a script $[\texttt{finalExponentiation}]$ that computes the function $(-) \mapsto (-)^\eta$. More precisely, on input data

$$
\begin{aligned}
[\texttt{inputMillerLoop}] &= [\![\mathsf{aux}_{\texttt{miller}}]\!], [\![P]\!], [\![Q]\!] \\
[\texttt{inputFinalExponentiation}] &= [\![\mathsf{aux}_{\texttt{exp}}]\!], [\![x_0]\!]
\end{aligned}
\tag{2}
$$

where $x_0 \in \mathbb{F}_{q^{12}}$, and $\mathsf{aux}_{\texttt{miller}}$, $\mathsf{aux}_{\texttt{exp}}$ is auxiliary data, they compute

$$
\begin{aligned}
[\![\mathsf{miller}(P, Q)]\!] &\leftarrow [\texttt{inputMillerLoop}]\ [\texttt{millerLoop}] \\
[\![x_0^\eta]\!] &\leftarrow [\texttt{inputFinalExponentiation}]\ [\texttt{finalExponentiation}]
\end{aligned}
\tag{3}
$$

Then the script implementing the Optimal Ate Pairing is

$$
[\texttt{pairing}] = [\texttt{millerLoop}]\ [\texttt{finalExponentiation}]
\tag{4}
$$

Indeed, on input $[\texttt{inputPairing}] = [\![\mathsf{aux}_{\texttt{exp}}]\!], [\![\mathsf{aux}_{\texttt{miller}}]\!], [\![P]\!], [\![Q]\!]$, we get

$$
[\![e(P, Q)]\!] \leftarrow [\texttt{inputPairing}]\ [\texttt{pairing}]
$$

We approach the Groth16 verifier in a similar way. By rearranging (1) from Sect. 2.3 using the bilinear properties of e and its definition, we see that Groth16 verification entails verifying the following equation

$$
\begin{aligned}
&\left(\mathsf{miller}([A]_1, [B]_2) \cdot \mathsf{miller}\left(\sum_{i=0}^{\ell} a_i [P_i]_1, -[\gamma]_2 \right) \cdot \mathsf{miller}([C]_1, -[\delta]_2) \right)^\eta \\
&= e([\alpha]_1, [\beta]_2)
\end{aligned}
\tag{5}
$$

Hence, we need a script $[\texttt{multiScalarMultiplication}]$ that computes the function $(a_1, \ldots, a_\ell) \mapsto \sum_{i=0}^{\ell} a_i [P_i]_1$, and a script $[\texttt{tripleMillerLoop}]$ that computes the product of the three Miller loops in (5). Then, the Groth16 verifier is[10]

$$
\begin{aligned}
[\texttt{groth16Verifier}] = &[\texttt{multiScalarMultiplication}] \\
&[\texttt{tripleMillerLoop}]\ [\texttt{finalExponentiation}] \\
&\langle\!\langle e([\alpha]_1, [\beta]_2) \rangle\!\rangle\ \texttt{OP\_EQUALVERIFY}
\end{aligned}
\tag{6}
$$

We now detail the challenges to implement the subroutines the make up $[\texttt{pairing}]$ and $[\texttt{groth16Verifier}]$, and our proposed solutions.

3.1 Optimising the Miller Loop

The value $\mathsf{miller}(P, Q)$ for curves in the BLS12 family is computed according to algorithm (1), where $\mathsf{ev}_{\ell_{T,Q}}(P)$ denotes the evaluation of the line through T and Q at P.

---

[10] Note that $e([\alpha]_1, [\beta]_2)$ can be hard-coded because $[\alpha]_1, [\beta]_2$ are part of vk and are known before the proof is generated.

Algorithm 1. Miller Loop

Inputs: $P \in \mathbb{G}_1$, $Q \in \mathbb{G}_2$, $u = \sum_{i=0}^{n} u_i 2^i$, $u_i \in \{-1, 0, 1\}$, $u_n \neq 0$
Output: miller$(P, Q) \in \mathbb{G}_T$

    out $\leftarrow 1$
    if $u_n = 1$ **then**
        $T \leftarrow Q$
    else
        $T \leftarrow -Q$
    end if
    for $i = n - 1, \ldots, 0$ **do**
        out $\leftarrow$ out^2
        $T \leftarrow 2T$
        if $u_i = 1$ **then**
            out $\leftarrow$ out $\cdot$ ev$_{\ell_{T,Q}}(P)$
            $T \leftarrow T + Q$
        else
            out $\leftarrow$ out $\cdot$ ev$_{\ell_{T,-Q}}(P)$
            $T \leftarrow T - Q$
        end if
    end for

Seed Choice. To obtain the most efficient implementation of [`millerLoop`], we seek to minimise the length of the loop and the cost of performing the operations in each iteration. The length of the loop and the number of operations performed can be minimised by choosing a curve whose seed u has small Hamming weight (number of non-zero bits) and bit-length. Our choice is BLS12-381, for which u has bit-length 64 and Hamming weight equal to 6, see Sect. 2.2.

Sparseness. The number of operations performed in the Miller loop can be further reduced by leveraging *sparseness* as explained by Scott in [29]. Both out and the line evaluations belong to the finite field extension $\mathbb{F}_{q^{12}}$, but many of the coefficients of the line evaluations are zero (that is why Scott calls them sparse). Leveraging this knowledge, we reduce the size of the script required to multiply two line evaluations from 1 kB (the size of our implementation of multiplication over $\mathbb{F}_{q^{12}}$, to 150 bytes (the size of our script for the multiplication of two sparse elements).

Remark 2. When implementing [`tripleMillerLoop`] for (6), instead of computing miller$([A]_1, [B]_2)$, miller $\left(\sum_{i=0}^{\ell} a_i [P_i]_1, -[\gamma]_2 \right)$ and miller$([C]_1, -[\delta]_2)$ one after the other, we parallelise the computation. Namely, as evaluating miller$(-, -)$ means executing algorithm (1), instead of repeating the loop three times, we go through the loop once, and at every iteration we carry out the computations required by each of the three terms appearing in (6). In this way, we can multiply together the sparse elements coming from the various line evaluations, thus amplifying the size optimisation resulting from leveraging sparseness.

Verifying the Gradient. Finally, we look at reducing the cost of performing the various operations required by the Miller loop. To update the value of T, we sum points in $\mathbb{G}_2 \subset E_{b',u}(\mathbb{F}_{q^2})$, while to update out, we need to compute line evaluations. The most inefficient part of these operations is the calculation of the gradient of the line through two points on the curve. The inefficiency is due to the fact that computing the gradient requires inverting an element in a finite field, an operation whose cost in Bitcoin Script is substantial.[11]

To avoid the overhead of computing the gradient on-chain, we verify a candidate provided in the unlocking script as part of the auxiliary data $\text{aux}_{\text{miller}}$. Namely, every time we need the gradient of the line through two points $R_1, R_2 \in \mathbb{G}_2$, we expect the gadient $\lambda \in \mathbb{F}_{q^2}$ to be supplied in $\text{aux}_{\text{miller}}$, and we verify that λ is computed correctely by verifying

$$\lambda \cdot (x_{R_2} - x_{R_1}) = y_{R_2} - y_{R_1}$$

where $R_i = (x_i, y_i) \in \mathbb{F}_{q^2} \times \mathbb{F}_{q^2}$. Note that verification is very efficient, as once λ is verified, it can be used multiple times. Putting it into numbers, verifying the gradient instead of computing it on chain allows us to save roughly $3 \cdot \log(q) = 3 \cdot 381 \sim 1100$ bytes.

3.2 Optimising the Final Exponentiation

Final exponentiation is the same for [pairing] and [groth16Verifier], and it entails raising an element of $\mathbb{F}_{q^{12}}$ to the power η. To minimise the script size of [finalExponentiation], we follow the standard approach in the literature and split the final exponentiation in an easy and a hard part

$$[\text{finalExponentiation}] = [\text{easyExponentiation}] \, [\text{hardExponentiation}]$$

In the hard part, we leverage the Frobenius map $\mathbb{F}_{q^n} \to \mathbb{F}_{q^n}, z \to z^q$, to fix the cost of [hardExponentiation] to (roughly) that of performing five exponetiations to the power u.

For the easy part, we need to compute one Frobenius map, and to invert an element in $\mathbb{F}_{q^{12}}$. Instead of performing inversion on-chain, similarly to what we did in the Miller loop, we verify an inverse candidate supplied in the unlocking script as part of the auxiliary data aux_{exp}. Namely, as we need the inverse of an element $z \in \mathbb{F}_{q^{12}}$, we expect the inverse z' to be supplied in aux_{exp}, and on-chain we verify $z \cdot z' = 1 \in \mathbb{F}_{q^{12}}$. This allows us to fix the cost of [easyExponentiation] to constant (it is independent of the curve parameters).

Remark 3. Even if the Frobenius map entails raising an element to the power q, its implementation is of constant size because it only requires multiplying the components of $z \in \mathbb{F}_{q^n}$ by some constants.

---

[11] If $z \in \mathbb{F}_q$, then inverting z in Bitcoin Script requires $O(\log(q))$ operations using Fermat's Little Theorem.

3.3 Optimising the Multi Scalar Multiplication

The hardest subroutine to optimise in (6) is [multiScalarMultiplication].
The reason is that this subroutine computes $\sum_{i=0}^{\ell} a_i [P_i]_1$, which depends both
on circuit-specific values: the $[P_i]'s$, see Sect. 2.3, and on values supplied by the
prover: the public inputs $a_1, \ldots, a_\ell$.

As the public inputs are supplied by the prover, they are not known when
[multiScalarMultiplication] is constructed, and therefore the script must
take into account the worst case scenario, namely, $a_i = r$.

The cost of computing $\sum_{i=0}^{\ell} a_i [P_i]_1$ scales linearly with ℓ, which is unfortunate as a single multiplication $a_i [P_i]_1$ costs about 35 kB via double-and-add (and
verifying the gradient as in Sect. 3.1). To optimise the size of the script we use
a standard trick: pass the ℓ public inputs a_i of C as witness and a hash of them
as public input. This makes the size of the script independent of the number of
public inputs at the cost of increasing the computational burden of the prover.

More specifically, let $H : \{0,1\}^* \to \mathbb{F}_r^d$ be a cryptographic hash function
where $\mathbb{F}_r$ is the field over which C is defined. Then, the augmented relation for
which we prove satisfiability is

$$\mathcal{R}' := \left\{ ((h_1, \ldots, h_d); (a_1, \ldots, a_\ell, \boldsymbol{w})) \;\middle|\; \begin{array}{l} \mathsf{C}(a_1, \ldots, a_\ell, \boldsymbol{w}) = 1 \\ (h_1, \ldots, h_d) = H(a_1, \ldots, a_\ell) \end{array} \right\}.$$

In this way, we keep the size of the script fixed to that of a Groth16 verifier
for a circuit with d public inputs. Indeed, in a proof for relation $\mathcal{R}'$ the prover
supplies d public inputs $h_1, \ldots, h_d$ for which the circuit corresponding to $\mathcal{R}'$
verifies that $(h_1, \ldots, h_d)$ is the digest of $(a_1, \ldots, a_\ell)$, the original public inputs
that are now passed as private inputs, and that $\mathsf{C}(a_1, \ldots, a_\ell, \boldsymbol{w}) = 1$. The public
inputs $h_1, \ldots, h_d$ are a commitment to the public inputs $a_1, \ldots, a_\ell$.

For example, if $\ell > 2$ we can set H to be the (vector) Pedersen hash over
the JubJub curve [34], whose base field is the scalar field $\mathbb{F}_r$ of BLS12-381. A
Pedersen hash digest is just a single group element of JubJub $h = (h_1, h_2) \in \mathbb{F}_r^2$.
Thus, $d = 2$ and the verification script only needs to compute $h_1 [P'_1] + h_1 [P'_2]$,
instead of an ℓ-multi scalar multiplication.

3.4 Subroutine-Independent Optimisations

In this section we detail some optimisations that we apply to all the subroutines
appearing in (4) and (6).

Stack Management. Stacks are data structures equipped only with push and
pop operations, which means that we can only access the top element of the
stack. This property makes storage and retrieval of temporary variables a task
with great impact on script size.

During script execution, the Bitcoin Script Engine has two stacks at its dis-
posal, the main stack, also referred to as the stack, and the altstack. One can
only push and pull elements from the altstack, which is why it is customary to

use it to store variables. We take a different approach, we use the bottom of the stack instead. As the depth of the stack can be obtained with the opcode OP_DEPTH, the bottom of the stack can be thought to have a fixed position, and can be used to store variables.

The variable we need more often in [pairing] and [groth16Verifier] is q, which we store at the bottom of the stack, and fetch with the following script

$$[\text{fetch}_q] = \text{OP\_DEPTH OP\_1SUB OP\_PICK} \tag{7}$$

In this way, we save ~ 50 bytes compared to pushing q to the stack every time we need it.

Remark 4 (Make fetching secure). As there is no way to efficiently push an element to the bottom of the stack, we assume q is supplied in the unlocking script as part of the auxiliary data. To ensure that it is the one we assume it to be, i.e., the parameter q of BLS12-381, we use the following script

$$[\text{verify}_q] = \text{OP\_DEPTH OP\_1SUB OP\_PICK} \langle\langle q \rangle\rangle \text{ OP\_EQUALVERIFY}$$

Arithmetic over Finite Fields. All the subroutines in (4) and (6) require arithmetic over (a finite field extension of) $\mathbb{F}_q$. The biggest impact of finite field arithmetic on script size comes from modulo operations by q. To efficiently mod by q, we employ two techniques.

First, as taking the residue class modulo q is a homomorphism $\mathbb{Z} \to \mathbb{F}_q$, instead of taking a modulo after every operation, we do it only once in a while. A similar approach was taken in [17], but we improve it by using the *modulo threshold*, i.e., the upper bound on the size of the numbers during script execution, as a parameter of the script. Tuning this parameter we have a trade-off between script size and execution time, see Sect. 4.

Second, we batch modulo operations, so that q must be fetched only once. We explain the technique in the case of addition, but it can be applied to any other operation. As elements of $\mathbb{F}_{q^n}$ are given by tuples $(z_1, \ldots, z_n)$ of elements in $\mathbb{F}_q$, computing $(z_1, \ldots, z_n) + (\tilde{z}_1, \ldots, \tilde{z}_n)$ means computing $z_i + \tilde{z}_i \mod q$ for $i = 1, \ldots, n$. Being Bitcoin Script a stack-based language, we must compute each component $z_i + \tilde{z}_i \mod q$ and place it on top of the stack. Instead of sequentially computing $z_i + \tilde{z}_i \mod q$ for $i = 1, \ldots, n$, we compute $z_i + \tilde{z}_i$ for $i = n, \ldots, 1$, place them on the altstack, and then sequentially take the modulo of each element. With this technique, we save $(n - 1)$ bytes for every modulo operation.

Remark 5 (Preventing overflows). As we remarked in Sect. 2, the BSV implementation supports large numbers. However, policy restrictions dictate that the numbers must fit in 10 kB. To avoid overflows, we proceed as follows. As the operations executed in [groth16Verifier] are fixed, and we know the largest size of the input data fed to the script, when constructing the script we keep track of the size of the numbers we are working with. For example, if we multiply two numbers of bit size at most $|q|$, we know that the result has bit size at most $2|q|$. Then, in the script we reduce modulo q before the numbers overflow.

We go one step further: we introduce a modulo threshold variable that is supplied at the point of script construction and that dictates when to perform modulo operations. See Sect. 4.1 for more information.

4   Script Benchmarking

We now benchmark our scripts according to three metrics: script size, script execution time, and the cost of publishing a transaction with the script on-chain. Based on the first two metrics, we select the optimal modulo threshold, see Sect. 4.1, and then we compare the monetary cost of executing our script to that of executing an equivalent script on Ethereum, see Sect. 4.2.

4.1   Script Size and Execution Time

When constructing the [pairing] and [groth16Verifier], we can choose the threshold after which modulo operations are carried out. Namely, we can choose the largest size the numbers can reach during script execution before we mod by q and bring them back to $\mathbb{F}_q$. Changing the threshold for modulo operations allows us to strike a balance between script size and execution time. Indeed, the more often we mod by q, the bigger the script size, but the lower the execution time of the script, as it will work with smaller numbers.

Below, we plot the threshold for the modulo operations against script size and execution time, respectively, for [pairing] and [groth16Verifier] with one and two public parameters, i.e., $\ell = 1$ and $\ell = 2$. We run our tests in a BSV regtest v1.0.8 on a processor Intel Core i7, 2.6 Ghz, 6-Core.

While BSV can support transactions with arbitrary script size and execution time, and with numbers of length up to 750 kB, current policy restrictions impose that the locking script is at most 500 kB, that it executes in at most 1 second, and that the numbers[12] must fit in 10 kB [25].

Figure 1 shows that the size of [pairing] decreases rapidly when the modulo threshold increases from 50 bytes (which implies that we mod by q after every operation) to 2 kB. Further increases of the modulo threshold result in small further decreases of the script size, but at the cost of a higher execution time. In particular, when the modulo threshold reaches 4 kB, the execution time approaches the policy threshold of 1 s. As there is not a big difference in either script size or execution time when the modulo threshold passes from 2 kB to 3 kB, we take a conservative stance and choose 2 kB as the optimal modulo threshold for the [pairing]. This choice results in a script of size 286 kB and with execution time of circa 0.47 s.

Figure 2 shows that the size of [groth16Verifier] behaves similarly. Namely, the size of the script decreases rapidly when the modulo threshold increases from

---

[12] By numbers we mean elements on the stack that are used in mathematical operations.

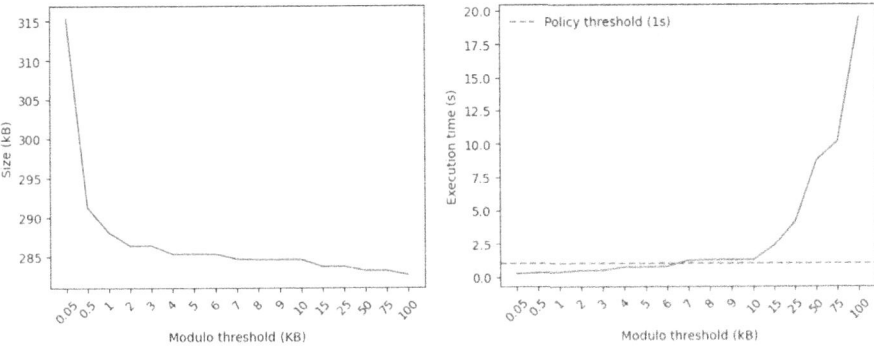

Fig. 1. Size and execution time of [pairing] as functions of the modulo threshold

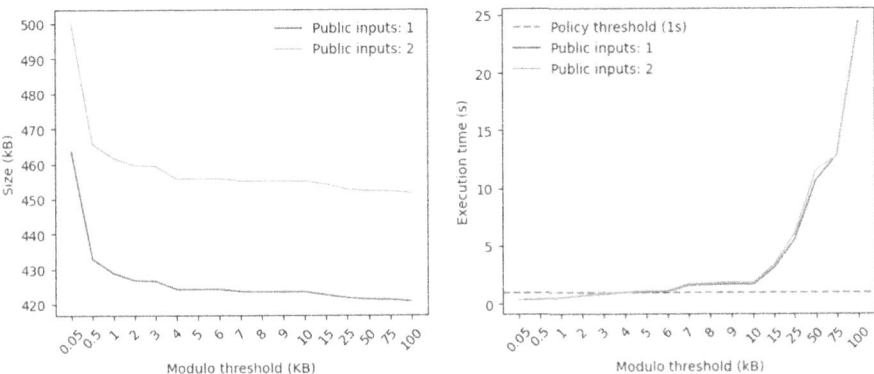

Fig. 2. Size and execution time of [groth16Verifier] as functions of the modulo threshold

50 bytes to 2 kB, but further increases do not decrease the script size too much. For Groth16, we approach the consensus threshold of 1s execution time when the modulo threshold approaches 3 kB. We choose as optimal modulo threshold 2 kB, which results in script of sizes 426 kB and 460 kB, for one and two public inputs, respectively, and with execution times of circa 0.67s and 0.70s, respectively.

Remark 6. In the Figs. 1 and 2, we focus on the size of the locking script because the modulo threshold does not affect the size of the unlocking script. However, in Sect. 4.2 we will take into account both locking and unlocking script, as the cost of publishing of script on-chain depends on both.

4.2   Monetary Cost

In this section, we compare the transaction fees for the Optimal Ate Pairing and the Groth16 verifier on BSV and Ethereum, respectively. For simplicity, the comparison only focuses on the cost for the computation to be done by the nodes in a network. We do not take other factors such as the cost to maintain the respective network or the time it takes for the transaction to be confirmed and published.

The results presented in Table 2 and Table 3 make it apparent that as of May 2024, it is much cheaper to execute bilinear pairings and the Groth16 verifier on BSV than on Ethereum.[13]

In BSV, a miner executes a script $[\mathsf{S}] = [\mathsf{unlock}][\mathsf{lock}]$ if there is a transaction $\mathsf{tx_{lock}}$ with an output $\mathsf{txOut_{lock}}$ that has $[\mathsf{lock}]$ as locking script, and there is a transaction $\mathsf{tx_{unlock}}$ with an input $\mathsf{txIn_{unlock}}$ that spends $\mathsf{txOut_{lock}}$ and that has $[\mathsf{unlock}]$ as unlocking script. In this situation, consensus requires a miner to execute $[\mathsf{S}]$, regardless of what operations are contained in it.[14] Thus, we model the cost of executing a script in BSV as the dollar value of the transaction fees required to publish $[\mathsf{S}]$ on-chain.

From the analysis of Sect. 4.1, we see that the optimal modulo thresholds for the Optimal Ate Pairing and the Groth16 verifier are given by 2 kB in both cases. The script size for $[\mathsf{pairing}]$ and $[\mathsf{groth16Verifier}]$ can be read off from Fig. 1 and Fig. 2, and are 286 kB for $[\mathsf{pairing}]$, and 426 kB, 460 kB for $[\mathsf{groth16Verifier}]$ with $\ell = 1$, $\ell = 2$, respectively; the size of $[\mathsf{unlockPairing}]$, see (2), is 7.6 kB, while the size of the unlocking script of $[\mathsf{groth16Verifier}]$ with $\ell = 1$ is 40 kB, and with $\ell = 2$ is 60 kB.

To estimate fee rates on the BSV blockchain and the BSVUSD conversion rate, we download data from WhatsOnChain.com [35]. We consider the average fee rate and the exchange rate for the period going from 15/03/2024 to 12/06/2024. We trim the series by removing the values below the 5th percentile and above the 95th percentile. Then, we take the 25th, 50th, and 75th percentile from the time series of fee rates as estimates of low, medium and high fee rates. They come out to be: 57, 79 and 120 sats/kB, respectively. As estimate of the exchange rate, we take the average price of the trimmed time series, which is $73 per BSV. The results of the calculations are presented in Table 2 for the Optimal Ate Pairing, and in Table 3 for Groth16 verifier.

The cost to execute an Ethereum contract is proportional to the computational complexity of the underlying code, with computational units measured in terms of gas. Hence, the cost of executing a contract in Ethereum is given by how many units of gas it requires, and gas cost at the time of execution.

Since EIP-1108 [2], the cost of executing one pairing is of 79000 ($= 34000 + 45000$) gas units, whereas the cost of executing the Groth16 verifier is of 153150 ($= 34000\cdot3+45000+6150$, see [2]) gas units for one public statement, and 159300 for two public statements. We estimate the cost of executing the scripts with the same method as for BSV fee rates. We download the data from Etherscan.io [15], and we calculate three fee rates: low: 11 gwei/gas,[15] medium: 16 gwei/gas, and

---

[13] Note that Ethereum uses a different curve. However, their implementation of pairings is state-of-the-art, so the comparison made here can be considered fair.

[14] The only exception is if the script does not abide by the policies set forth by the miner. For the purpose of this analysis we assume that $[\mathsf{S}]$ satisfies such policies.

[15] 1 gwei equates to 10^{-9} ETH.

high: 24 gwei/gas, as well as an estimated exchange rate of $3394 per ETH.[16] The results of the calculations are presented in Table 2 for the Optimal Ate Pairing, and in Table 3 for the Groth16 verifier.

Table 2. Cost of executing the Optimal Ate Pairing in BSV and Ethereum.

Blockchain	Fee rate		
	Low	Medium	High
BSV	$0.012	$0.016	$0.025
Ethereum	$2.95	$4.29	$6.43

Table 3. Cost of executing the Groth16 verifier in BSV and Ethereum.

	Groth16 verifier ($\ell = 1$)			Groth16 verifier ($\ell = 2$)		
Blockchain	Fee rate					
	Low	Medium	High	Low	Medium	High
BSV	$0.018	$0.024	$0.037	$0.0019	$0.026	$0.040
Ethereum	$5.78	$8.32	$12.48	$5.95	$8.65	$12.97

5   Conclusion

We have demonstrated not only that it is practical to implement the Groth16 verifier in Bitcoin Script, but also that the cost of executing it is much cheaper than that of executing an equivalent script in Ethereum, see Sect. 4. As part of our future work, we plan to implement more pairing-based cryptographic primitives in Bitcoin Script so that the Bitcoin blockchain can leverage this fruitful area of cryptography to its full strength.

References

1. Bitcoin (BTC) Wiki, Script. https://en.bitcoin.it/wiki/Script
2. Cardozo, A.S., Williamson, Z.: EIP-1108: Reduce alt_bn128 precompile gas costs. Ethereum Improvement Proposals, no. 1108 (2018). https://eips.ethereum.org/EIPS/eip-1108

---

[16] Note that, even if the exchange rate of BSV per ETH were 1:1, then executing the scripts on BSV would still be much cheaper. For example, at the price of $3394 per BSV, the Optimal Ate Pairing at high fee rate would cost only $1.16.

3. Aranha, D.F., El Housni, Y., Guillevic, A.: A survey of elliptic curves for proof systems. Des. Codes Crypt. **91**(11), 3333–3378 (2023)
4. B Squared: Zero-knowledge proof verification commitment for ZK-rollup on bitcoin. https://docs.bsquared.network/zpvc
5. Barbulescu, R., Duquesne, S.: Updating key size estimations for pairings. J. Cryptol. **32**, 1298–1336 (2019)
6. Barbulescu, R., Gaudry, P., Guillevic, A., Morain, F.: Improving NFS for the discrete logarithm problem in non-prime finite fields. In: Oswald, E., Fischlin, M. (eds.) EUROCRYPT 2015. LNCS, vol. 9056, pp. 129–155. Springer, Heidelberg (2015). https://doi.org/10.1007/978-3-662-46800-5_6
7. Barbulescu, R., Gaudry, P., Joux, A., Thomé, E.: A heuristic quasi-polynomial algorithm for discrete logarithm in finite fields of small characteristic. In: Nguyen, P.Q., Oswald, E. (eds.) EUROCRYPT 2014. LNCS, vol. 8441, pp. 1–16. Springer, Heidelberg (2014). https://doi.org/10.1007/978-3-642-55220-5_1
8. Barreto, P.S.L.M., Kim, H.Y., Lynn, B., Scott, M.: Efficient algorithms for pairing-based cryptosystems. In: Yung, M. (ed.) CRYPTO 2002. LNCS, vol. 2442, pp. 354–369. Springer, Heidelberg (2002). https://doi.org/10.1007/3-540-45708-9_23
9. Bit Layer: Bitlayer: a bitcoin computational layer architecture based on the BitVM paradigm. https://static.bitlayer.org/Bitlayer-Technical-Whitepaper.pdf
10. Bitansky, N., Chiesa, A., Ishai, Y., Ostrovsky, R., Paneth, O.: Succinct noninteractive arguments via linear interactive proofs. In: Sahai, A. (ed.) Theory of Cryptography - 10th Theory of Cryptography Conference, TCC 2013, Tokyo, Japan, 3-6 March 2013. Proceedings (2013)
11. Bitcoin SV: https://github.com/bitcoin-sv/bitcoin-sv
12. BitVM: Official BitVM implementation in rust. https://github.com/BitVM/BitVM
13. Cairo: The Cairo programming language. https://book.cairo-lang.org/title-page.html#the-cairo-book
14. Ethereum Org: ZERO-KNOWLEDGE ROLLUPS. https://ethereum.org/en/developers/docs/scaling/zk-rollups/
15. Etherscan: etherscan.io. https://etherscan.io/
16. Firo: https://firo.org
17. franchfrog42: zkBaguette applied to zkSnarks. https://github.com/frenchfrog42/zk-hackaton
18. Gennaro, R., Gentry, C., Parno, B., Raykova, M.: Quadratic span programs and succinct nizks without PCPS. In: Johansson, T., Nguyen, P.Q. (eds.) Advances in Cryptology - EUROCRYPT 2013, 32nd Annual International Conference on the Theory and Applications of Cryptographic Techniques, Athens, Greece, 26-30 May 2013. Proceedings
19. Groth, J.: On the size of pairing-based non-interactive arguments. In: Advances in Cryptology - EUROCRYPT (2016)
20. Kim, T., Barbulescu, R.: Extended tower number field sieve: a new complexity for the medium prime case. In: Robshaw, M., Katz, J. (eds.) CRYPTO 2016. LNCS, vol. 9814, pp. 543–571. Springer, Heidelberg (2016). https://doi.org/10.1007/978-3-662-53018-4_20
21. LumiBit: LumiBit's ZK-EVM. https://lumibit.gitbook.io/lumibit-gitbook/overview/lumibit-101/lumibits-zk-evm
22. Matsuda, S., Kanayama, N., Hess, F., Okamoto, E.: Optimised versions of the ate and twisted ate pairings. In: Cryptography and Coding, pp. 302–312. Springer, Heidelberg (2007). https://doi.org/10.1007/978-3-540-77272-9_18

23. Chain, M.: ZK rollup on bitcoin. https://docs.merlinchain.io/merlin-docs/zk-rollup-on-bitcoin
24. Miller, V.S.: The weil pairing, and its efficient calculation. J. Cryptol. **17**(4), 235–261 (2004). https://doi.org/10.1007/s00145-004-0315-8
25. Fromberg, P.: BSV consensus limits. https://github.com/bitcoin-sv/bitcoin-sv/wiki/Consensus-Limits
26. Linus, R.: BitVM: computing anything on bitcoin. https://bitvm.org/bitvm.pdf
27. Linus, R., George, L.: ZeroSync: introducing validity proofs to bitcoin. https://zerosync.org/zerosync.pdf
28. S. Nakamoto: Bitcoin: A Peer-to-Peer Electronic Cash System
29. Scott, M.: Pairing implementation revisited. Cryptology ePrint Archive, Paper 2019/077 (2019). https://eprint.iacr.org/2019/077, https://eprint.iacr.org/2019/077
30. Scott, M.: A note on twists for pairing friendly curves. http://indigo.ie/~mscott/twists.pdf
31. sCrypt Inc. https://scrypt.io
32. sCrypt Inc: sCrypt transaction. https://test.whatsonchain.com/tx/2396a4e52555cdc29795db281d17de423697bd5cbabbcb756cb14cea8e947235
33. sCrypt Inc: Tutorial 5: zero knowledge proofs. https://docs.scrypt.io/tutorials/zkp
34. Sean Bowe. https://github.com/zkcrypto/jubjub
35. TAAL: whatsonchain.com. https://whatsonchain.com/
36. zCash: https://z.cash

Homomorphic Encryption Based ECDSA Generation Over Five Party Protocol

Akshit Aggarwal[1(✉)] and Srinibas Swain[2]

[1] Department of Computer Science and Engineering, Indian Institute of Information Technology, Guwahati, India
akshit.aggarwal@iiitg.ac.in
[2] School of Computer and Mathematical Sciences, University of Adelaide, Adelaide, Australia
Srinibas.swain@adelaide.edu.au

Abstract. Secure computation of multiparty protocol (MPP) is being widely used to address privacy issues in various technologies, such as cryptocurrencies, blockchain, and many more. The security of MPP is computed in various steps, mainly via secret sharing of keys, encryption/decryption of messages, and signature generation. However, literature suggests the secure computation of multiparty is arduous in the presence of adversarial nature of parties. In this paper, we propose a notion for achieving ECDSA in a multiparty protocol using an Authentication server A_t. We demonstrate this using four steps: 1. proposal of multiparty (five) protocol (5PP) in which there are parties with adversarial natures. 2. setup of 5PP with A_t that ensures the mutual identification of parties. 3. Encryption of messages in the proposed 5PP. 4. ECDSA signature generation between the parties in the aforementioned setup. We ensure security in all the steps mainly by using modified Paillier cryptosystem and homomorphic encryption.

Keywords: ECDSA · elliptic curve · five-party protocol · full secrecy · Homomorphic encryption · modified Paillier cryptosystem · ZkPok

1 Introduction

Secure communication over multiparty protocol (MPP) is essential to preserve the privacy of each party within the network during message passing. Multiparty protocol enables n parties to ensure security of a system in the presence of x adversarial parties. The more number of adversarial parties can have an adverse affect on the system. Secure computation of parties can be maintained by a MPP (number of parties ≥ 5) that contains at least 2 adversarial parties [1]. The main contribution of this paper is to generate digital signature using ECDSA to ensure authenticity in a multiparty system. We achieve this in four stages.

In the first stage, we setup a multiparty system (where parties can be adversarial in nature) using five parties. Note that a multiparty system cannot be

J. Garcia-Alfaro et al. (Eds.): ESORICS 2024 Workshops, LNCS 15263, pp. 326–339, 2025.
https://doi.org/10.1007/978-3-031-82349-7_22

established in our context with less than five parties [1]. In the second stage, we use the notion of Authentication server A_t introduced by Tsai et al. [2] (as Authentication server ensures the mutual identification of parties). A_t stores the information of all parties. Parties interact with A_t by non-secret keys that helps to verify the identity of users. Latter, in the third stage, we ensure the security of messages in 5PP by using modified Paillier cryptosystem [3]. Finally, we achieve full secrecy (where full secrecy is defined as when no intruder gets the information during the message transmission) in 5PP over a network by using homomorphic encryption. Homomorphic encryption (H_{em}) hides the information of sender and receiver over a network with the help of arbitrary analytic operation [4]. We also show that using elliptic curve cryptography (ECC), one can achieve a high level of security compared to RSA [5]. This implies a more secure system than RSA can be designed using a relatively smaller key by using ECDSA [6]. We first discuss the relevant literature for this study. ECDSA is helpful for maintaining authentic communication between the parties [7]. ECDSA can be mathematically expressed as:

$$\Omega = \alpha^{-1}(h(m) + \delta\gamma) \tag{1}$$

Here $h(m)$ is a hash function, m is a message, δ is a secret key, α is a secret nonce, and γ is public nonce (such that the x-coordinate of $\alpha \cdot \beta$ where β is base point generator of the elliptic curve).

Literature suggests that a limitation of ECDSA signature is that it does not maintain secrecy, mutual identification of parties, and the case when the number of parties are high. Also, ECDSA generation is quite expensive. Chien et al. [2] have proposed the ECC-based blind signcryption to strengthen the high level of security. The main drawback of their work is that they cannot achieve full secrecy. Xu et al. [8] used the signature key by threshold using the concept of Fiat-Shamir paradigm [9]. The main limitation is that their work leaks the information of both the sender and the receiver. Further, a few of the authors have extended the existing work of Xu et al. [8] by considering the Diffie-Hellman native assumptions and homomorphic Paillier encryption [3, 10–12]. The main limitation of their works is that they did not discuss the adversarial nature of any party. Later on, a few authors extended the existing work by considering the five-party protocol with the adversarial nature of parties [13]. The main drawback is that they did not discuss the mutual identification between the parties. Afterwards, a few authors [14–16] proposed mutual identification based scheme to check the authentication of parties by considering trusted third party protocol. The work of [14] used identity based encryption to establish the mutual identification where key is distributed between multiple parties. The main limitation is high computation time for key agreement procedure. Li et al. [15] proposed third party based approach to mutually authenticate the system. The main limitation of their work is dishonest majority when the number of parties are scale up (by considering dishonest parties). Similarly, Sucasas et al. [16] proposed certificate authority (which provides some cryptographic keys to multi parties) to establish mutual identification. The main limitation of their work is complex protocol designing which increases the computation overhead over the parties. Further, Fragkos et al. [17] proposed several artificial intelligence based approach for authentication and encryption of message having limitation of assumed multiple trusted third party protocol which is not mutually identified. Further, Haung et al. [18] have proposed a partial blind ECDSA scheme widely used in bitcoins. The main drawback of their work is that they use the Zero-knowledge Proof of knowledge (ZkPok), which increases the computation complexity. Xue et al. [19] have proposed two-party ECDSA signature generation via re-sharing of the secret key and linear sharing of the nonce. The main limitation of their work is that it does not applicable to more than two parties. Further, Ma et al. [20] have proposed linear secret sharing that does not require recursive operations for access control over message passing. The main limitation is that their work does not maintain full secrecy. Later, Aggarwal et al. [21] proposed homomorphic encryption over message passing with the help of ECDSA signature that maintains full secrecy. The main drawback is that they did not discuss the mutual identification of parties or the case when number of parties are more than two. Further, Aggarwal et al. [22] extended the work of [21] by considering the adversarial nature of parties using the claim of Byzantine agreement but they did not address the mutual identification between the parties.

In summary, we use 5PP as a multiparty protocol that contains adversarial parties. The communication between the parties is maintained by modified Paillier cryptosystem. The modified Paillier cryptosystem efficiently performs the homomorphic operations that provides security to the system as compared to other existing techniques [23,24]. Later on, this work establishes authentic communication with the help of ECDSA signature. ECDSA signature is helpful for generating the authentication in multiparty protocol.

The roadmap for the paper is as follows. Section 2 discusses the preliminaries. Section 3 discusses the proposed methodology. Security of the proposed work is discussed in Sect. 4. Finally, Sect. 5 discusses conclusion and future work.

2   Preliminaries

2.1   Elliptic Curve Cryptography (ECC)

In this work, message passing is performed via elliptic curves (EC). ECC was first introduced by Neal Kobiltz and Victor Miller in 1985 [25]. EC is a non-singular curve defined over a finite field Z_q (where q is the order of EC). EC consists of a set of points that satisfy the following equation, such as:

$$Y^2 = X^3 + AX + B \tag{2}$$

where $X, Y, A, B \in Z_q$, and $4A^3 + 27B^2 \neq 0$.

2.2   Modified Paillier Cryptosystem

The encryption mechanism of this work is based on the modified Paillier cryptosystem, which is taken from the existing work of Xun et al. [3]. The modified Paillier cryptosystem is based on a large sample space, which is helpful for the easy computation of messages.

Consider a large prime number s (which is supposed to be a public parameter of ECDSA). The modified Paillier cryptosystem is discussed as follows.

– Key Generation: Randomly large prime numbers A and B are selected by parties such that the greatest common divisor $gcd(A-1,s) = gcd(B-1,s) = 1$. Afterwards, parties estimate:

$$N = AsB \tag{3}$$

$$M = (1+N)^{AB}(mod\ N^2), \tag{4}$$

and publishes N, and M as public key keeping (A,B) as secret.

– Encryption: Encryption of message m is performed via randomly selecting I (where $m < q$ and $I \in Z_{N^2}$). Parties compute the ciphertext (CP) as:

$$CP = M^m I^N (mod\ N^2) \tag{5}$$

Here I is randomly selected, so the ciphertext looks like a random number.

– Decryption: The decryption (DC) of message is performed via secret key (A,B) such as:

$$DC = CP^{(A-1)(s-1)(B-1)}(mod\ N^2) \tag{6}$$

and message m can be computed as follows.

$$m = \left[\frac{DC-1}{ABN}\right][(A-1)(s-1)(B-1)]^{-1}(mod\ q) \tag{7}$$

2.3 Elliptic Curve Digital Signature Algorithm (ECDSA)

This section highlights the signature generation with the help of elliptic curves. EC plays a crucial role in achieving a high level of security with a smaller key size. The authenticity of messages over EC can be obtained by secret sharing of public key Q, secret key δ, public nonce γ, secret nonce α, and hash function $h(m)$ (where m is a message). EC is defined over a finite field Z_q consisting of an origin generator β such as:

$$Q = \delta\beta, \tag{8}$$

and

$$\gamma = \alpha\beta \tag{9}$$

Here β is also considered as x-coordinate $Q = \delta\beta$ (due to the symmetric properties of elliptic curves with respect to x-axis). Signature (Ω) over message with the help of EC is termed ECDSA, which can be mathematically expressed as:

$$\Omega = \alpha^{-1}(h(m) + \delta\gamma) \tag{10}$$

3   Proposed Methodology

This section indicates the methodology of our proposed work (as shown in Fig. 1). This work is divided into four steps. These steps are essential for generating the ECDSA signature on the messages. The steps are discussed as follows.

----
1. Five party protocol (5PP)

$h^* = 1$

$x = 1$

$2x + h^* < n$

Here $n = 5$

----
2. Setup and Registration phase

(P_i) .... (P_j)

$\delta_i \leftarrow Z_q,\ D_i \leftarrow Z_q,\ \alpha_i \leftarrow Z_q$ $\delta_j \leftarrow Z_q,\ D_j \leftarrow Z_q,\ \alpha_j \leftarrow Z_q$

$Q_i = \delta_i \beta$ $Q_j = \delta_j \beta$

$\pi_i = h_i(iv_i, Q_i)$ $\pi_j = h_j(iv_j, Q_j)$

$D_i = \alpha_i \beta = (x_{D_i}, y_{D_i})$ $D_j = \alpha_j \beta = (x_{D_j}, y_{D_j})$

$CF_i = \alpha_i^{-1}(\pi_i + x_{D_i}\delta_i)$ $CF_j = \alpha_j^{-1}(\pi_j + x_{D_j}\delta_j)$

----
3. Encryption (modified paillier cryptosystem)

(P_i) (P_j)

$A \leftarrow Z_{N^2}$ $A \leftarrow Z_{N^2}$

$B \leftarrow Z_{N^2}$ $B \leftarrow Z_{N^2}$

$s \leftarrow Z_{N^2}$ $s \leftarrow Z_{N^2}$

$N = AsB$ $N = AsB$

$M = (1 + N)^{AB} \ (\bmod\ N^2)$ $M = (1 + N)^{AB} \ (\bmod\ N^2)$

----
4. ECDSA Signature Generation

4.1. Homomorphic Encryption

(P_i) (P_j)

$\delta_i \leftarrow Z_q$ $\delta_j \leftarrow Z_q$

$I_i \leftarrow Z_{N^2}$ $\alpha_j \leftarrow Z_q$

                                                                 $\gamma_j = \alpha_j \gamma$

                                                                 $I_j \leftarrow Z_{N^2}$

Encrypt with hash function $h(m_i)$ Encrypt with public nonce γ
                                                                 with respect to secret key δ

$CP_i = M^{h(m_i)} I_i^N \ (\bmod\ N^2)$ $CP_j = (M^{\gamma_j} I_j^N)^{\delta_j} \ (\bmod\ N^2)$

4.1.1. Generation of CP_o

$CP_o = H_{em}[(CP_1, CP_2), *]$

$CP_o = M^{(h(m_i)+\gamma_j\delta_j)} I_i^N I_j^{N\delta_j} \ (\bmod\ N^2)$

4.2 Signature generation

$$\Omega = \alpha^{-1}(h(m) + \gamma\delta)$$

Fig. 1. Flow diagram of ECDSA generation over five-party protocol (5PP). Here parties P_i and P_j are randomly selected from 5PP (where $1 \leq i, j \leq 5$, and $i \neq j$).

3.1   Multiparty (five) Protocol (5PP) with Adversarial Nature

In this step, for maintaining secure communication, multiparty (where number of parties ≥ 5) protocol with an adversarial nature is used, which was adopted from the work of Alon et al. [1]. Here we remark that the system is not applicable when the number of parties are less than five. They worked on n-party system with an honest majority, which can be mathematically expressed as:

$$2x + h^* < n \tag{11}$$

Here n is total number of parties. h^* is number of semi-honest parties (where a party is considered semi-honest if it follows all the protocol of the proposed network but is curious to get the information of other parties), and x is number of adversarial parties. For attaining minimum multiparty protocol, we assume $x = 1$ and $h^* = 1$, then the minimum possible value for $n = 4$. When $n = 4$, it is difficult for any party to ensure the system's security (as $n = 4$ disobeys the claim of Byzantine agreement [26]). For the sake of simplicity, we assume that $n = 5$ (say 5PP), which ensures the security of multiparty protocols. The proof for 5PP is discussed in Sect. 4.

3.2   Setup of 5PP with Authentication Server A_t

After measuring adversarial nature of parties, this work uses the notion of an Authentication server, A_t. A_t stores information about all parties that helps check the mutual identification. The mutual identification of phases are discussed as follows.

- Firstly, each party computes the value of its public key, such as:

$$
\begin{aligned}
Q_1 &= \delta_1 \beta \\
Q_2 &= \delta_2 \beta \\
Q_3 &= \delta_3 \beta \\
Q_4 &= \delta_4 \beta \\
Q_5 &= \delta_5 \beta
\end{aligned}
\tag{12}
$$

Here $\{\{Q_1, Q_2, \cdots, Q_5\} \in Z_q\}$ are public keys, $\{\{\delta_1, \delta_2, \cdots, \delta_5\} \in Z_q\}$ are secret keys, β is base point generator of elliptic curve for parties $\{P_1, P_2, \cdots, P_5\}$.
- After computing public keys, each party sends its information to the A_t with secret keys and their unique identity values (iv). Then, A_t applies hash function $(h(\cdot))$ and generates the non-secret salt value, π, for verifying identity of each participant. The corresponding hash value is obtained as follows:

$$
\begin{aligned}
\pi_1 &= h_1(iv_1, Q_1) \\
\pi_2 &= h_2(iv_2, Q_2) \\
\pi_3 &= h_3(iv_3, Q_3) \\
\pi_4 &= h_4(iv_4, Q_4) \\
\pi_5 &= h_5(iv_5, Q_5)
\end{aligned}
\tag{13}
$$

Here $\{\{\pi_1, \pi_2, \cdots, \pi_5\} \in Z_q\}$ are non-secret salt values, $\{h_1, h_2, \cdots, h_5\}$ are corresponding hash values with unique identity values. $\{iv_1, iv_2, \cdots, iv_5\}$ for parties $\{P_1, P_2, \cdots, P_5\}$.

- Each party has their own data points, such as $\{\{D_1, D_2, \cdots, D_5\} \in Z_q\}$ on the elliptic curve, with β being the base point generator. Each party selects their secret nonce values $\{\{\alpha_1.\alpha_2, \cdots, \alpha_5\} \in Z_q\}$ and computes the value of data points such as:

$$
\begin{aligned}
D_1 &= \alpha_1 \beta = (x_{D_1}, y_{D_1}) \\
D_2 &= \alpha_2 \beta = (x_{D_2}, y_{D_2}) \\
D_3 &= \alpha_3 \beta = (x_{D_3}, y_{D_3}) \\
D_4 &= \alpha_4 \beta = (x_{D_4}, y_{D_4}) \\
D_5 &= \alpha_5 \beta = (x_{D_5}, y_{D_5})
\end{aligned}
\tag{14}
$$

Here x_{D_i} and y_{D_i} (where $i \in \{1, 2, \cdots, 5\}$) are the coordinates of x-axis and y-axis corresponding to the data points.

- After computing the data points, each party P_i (where $i \in \{1, 2, \cdots, 5\}$) generates the certificates (CF_i) with the help of A_t such as:

$$
\begin{aligned}
CF_1 &= \alpha_1^{-1}(\pi_1 + x_{D_1}\delta_1) \\
CF_2 &= \alpha_2^{-1}(\pi_2 + x_{D_2}\delta_2) \\
CF_3 &= \alpha_3^{-1}(\pi_3 + x_{D_3}\delta_3) \\
CF_4 &= \alpha_4^{-1}(\pi_4 + x_{D_4}\delta_4) \\
CF_5 &= \alpha_5^{-1}(\pi_5 + x_{D_5}\delta_5)
\end{aligned}
\tag{15}
$$

Later on, the A_t computes the certificate value in terms of binary output, that is, 0 or 1. If the obtained value is 1 means party is valid, else for 0 party either is malicious or semi-honest. The corresponding value of certificates helps obtain the nature of the parties. This technique maintains mutual identification among the parties.

3.3 Modified Paillier Encryption

A Paillier cryptosystem is efficient for performing homomorphic encryption, which maintains full secrecy over the network [27]. In this work, we apply the modified Paillier cryptosystem as it is more secure than the Paillier cryptosystem, which is taken from the existing work of Xun et al. [3]. Here parties P_i and P_j are randomly selected (where $i, j \in \{1, 2, \cdots, 5\}$ and $i \neq j$), which works as a sender and a receiver in the encryption mechanism of messages.

As we know, $M_i = (1 + N)^{AB} (mod\ N^2)$, then

$$
M_i^s = (1 + N)^{AsB} = (1 + N)^N = 1 + N^2 = 1\ (mod\ N^2).
$$

Therefore,

$$DC_i = CP_i^{(A-1)(s-1)(B-1)} \ (mod \ N^2)$$
$$= M^{m_i(A-1)(s-1)(B-1)} \alpha^{N(A-1)(s-1)(B-1)}$$
$$= (1+N)^{AB[m_i(A-1)(s-1)(B-1) \ (mod \ s)]}$$
$$\alpha^{N(A-1)(s-1)(B-1)}$$
$$= 1 + AB[m_i(A-1)(s-1)(B-1) \ (mod \ s)]N$$

Here $AB[m_i(A-1)(s-1)(B-1) \ (mod \ s)] < N$. According to Euler theorem, we know for any non-zero integer χ (where $\chi \in Z_{N^2}$), where $\chi^{\phi(N^2)} = 1 \ (mod \ N^2)$, and $\chi \in Z_{N^2}$ [28].

In the competence of this, we have:

$$AB[m_i(A-1)(s-1)(B-1) \ (mod \ s)] = (DC_i - 1)/N$$

Therefore, we have:

$$m_i = \left[\frac{DC_i - 1}{ABN} \right] [(A-1)(s-1)(B-1)]^{-1}(mod \ s) \qquad (16)$$

3.4   ECDSA Signature Generation

The generation of ECDSA is formed in three steps. Firstly, we apply the ZkPok for the reduction of complexity. In the second step, we apply homomorphic encryption (which is helpful for maintaining secrecy over the network). Afterward, the signature is generated to check the authenticity of messages.

Zero Knowledge Proof of Knowledge (ZkPok). As we know, the value of public key Q and public nonce γ can be computed as $Q = \delta\beta$, and $\gamma = \alpha\beta$.

Computing the value of δ and α by the dint of ZkPok is quite arduous. In this proposed work, we compute the values of δ and α with the help of non-interactive Zero-knowledge Proof of Knowledge $(niZkPok)$ using the concept of Fiat-Shamir paradigm [9,29]. This step reduces the computation of the proposed work.

Homomorphic Encryption. In homomorphic encryption, message stays encrypted at all times, which minimises the likelihood that message gets compromised. In this step, parties P_i and P_j are randomly selected (where $i \neq j$). Afterwards, party P_i encrypts the message m_i with respect to hash function $h(\cdot)$, such as:

$$CP_i = M^{h(m_i)} I_i^N (\mathrm{mod} \ N^2) \qquad (17)$$

Later on, party P_j encrypts the message with public nonce γ and secret key δ_j, such as:

$$CP_j = (M^{\gamma_j} I_j^N)^{\delta_j} (\mathrm{mod} \ N^2) \qquad (18)$$

Further, CP_i and CP_j homomorphically encrypt (H_{em}) messages with the help of analytical function *i.e.*, multiplication $(*)$ and generate the ciphertext as follows.

$$
\begin{aligned}
CP_o &= H_{em}[(CP_1, CP_2), *] \\
&= M^{h(m_i)} I_i^N \ (mod \ N^2) * (M^{\gamma_j} I_j^N)^{\delta_j} \ (mod \ N^2) \\
&= M^{(h(m_i) + \gamma_j \delta_j)} I_i^N I_j^{N\delta_j} (mod \ N^2)
\end{aligned}
\tag{19}
$$

Signature Generation. After getting CP_o, the receiver estimates the signature (Ω) with the help of secret random value (α^{-1}) (where α^{-1} is the inverse of secret random value; as we know, the inverse operation is quite difficult for computation) such as:

$$
\Omega = \alpha^{-1}(h(m_i + \gamma_j \delta_j)
\tag{20}
$$

Here, we remark that during the signature generation time for a particular party, we assume that $i = j = 1$. Then, from Eq. 20, the signature can be computed as follows.

$$
\Omega = \alpha^{-1}(h(m_1) + \gamma_1 \delta_1)
$$

The optimised version for the signature can be expressed as:

$$
\Omega = \alpha^{-1}(h(m) + \gamma \delta)
\tag{21}
$$

Finally, receiver receives signature as (δ, Ω).

4   Security of Proposed Work

In this section, we compute the security of our proposed work. In this paper, security is computed in various steps. The steps are discussed as follows.

4.1   Five Party Protocol (5PP)

As from the existing work of Alon et al. [1], $2x + h^* < n$. If we consider the value of $x = 1$ and $h^* = 1$, then the least value of $n = 4$. As the value of $n = 4$, the system is not secure. At $n = 4$, a system has four parties (say, P_1, P_2, P_3, and P_4). These four-party protocols consist of message m (where party P_1 is randomly selected as a malicious party, party P_2 is selected as a semi-honest party, and the rest parties are considered honest). For ensuring security, we assume that any honest party (say P_4) receives m' from P_1 (as P_1 is malicious party), m'' from P_2 (as P_2 is semi-honest), and m from P_3. In that scenario, the selection of message is arduous for P_4.

For sake of simplicity, at $n = 5$, a system has five parties (say, P_1 (malicious party), P_2 (semi-honest party), P_3 (honest party), P_4 (honest party), and P_5 (honest party)) that consist of message m. For ensuring security, we assume that any honest party (say P_5) receives m' from P_1, m'' from P_2, and m from the rest of parties (as all other parties are honest). In that scenario, party P_4 selects the honest majority by considering the claim of Byzantine agreement [26]. The claim of Byzantine agreement selects two-thirds honest majority that ensures the security of a multiparty protocol in the presence of adversarial behavior by parties. Hence, at $n = 4$, the system does not ensure security. So, in this work, five-party protocol (5PP) is applied, which ensures security even in the presence of adversarial parties.

4.2 Modified Paillier Cryptosystem

In this work, we prove the modified Paillier cryptosystem is secure by taking a random oracle (where the oracle always generates the output either Yes or No). We begin this problem by taking large composite residues. The heart of this proof lies in modulus where modulus is performed on squares. As from paillier encryption, we know that $N = AsB$ (where $A, s, B \in Z_{N^2}$).

Definition. An integer λ is said to be the N-th residue modulo N^2 if there exists an integer μ such that $\lambda = \mu^N (mod\ N^2)$.

The N-th residuosity is a multiplicative subgroup of Z_{N^2} of order s, such as:

$$\phi(N) = (A - 1)(s - 1)(B - 1) \tag{22}$$

Here λ has exactly N-th roots of degree N (where exactly one root is strictly less than N). The N-th roots of unity can be mathematically expressed as:

$$(1 + N)^z = 1 + zN(mod\ N^2), \tag{23}$$

(where $z \in Z_q$). Deciding the P-th residuosity is NP-hard. Accordingly, we assume that:

Conjecture. There exists no polynomial time solver for N-th residues modulo N^2 [Sect. 5, [3]].

As we know from Paillier encryption, $M = (1 + N)^{AB}$. We denote it by $\rho(m, v)$ which can be defined as:

$$\rho(m, v) = M^m v^N (mod\ N^2) \tag{24}$$

(where $m \in Z_q$ and $v \in Z_{N^2}$). Assume $\omega = \rho(m, v) \in Z_{N^2}$.

Claim. Random oracle decides the security of modified Paillier cryptosystem when $z = m$.

As we know, $\omega = M^m v^N (mod\ N^2)$ and we can write it as:

$$\omega M^{-z} = M^{m-z} v^N (mod\ N^2) \tag{25}$$

that submits to the random oracle for solving the residue problem. In case of N-th residue, there exists a constant v'^N (where $v'^N \in Z_{N^2}$) such as:

$$\omega M^{-z} = v'^N (mod\ N^2) \tag{26}$$

From Eqs. (25, 26), we can deduce that:

$$M^{m-z}\left[\frac{v}{v'}\right]^{N} = 1(mod\ N^2) \tag{27}$$

(where v, v' are constants). So by raising power of $(A-1)(s-1)(B-1)$ on both sides, we can deduce that:

$$M^{(m-z)(A-1)(s-1)(B-1)(mod\ s)} = 1(mod\ N^2) \tag{28}$$

Further, we can compute it is as:

$$(m-z)(A-1)(s-1)(B-1)(mod\ s) < s \tag{29}$$

Now, consider the claim when $z = m$ Eq. (29) holds good. We can conclude that random oracle solves the problem and provides the outcome Yes. In the above competency, we can deduce that the modified Paillier cryptosystem is secure.

4.3   Elliptic Curve Discrete Logarithmic Problem (ECDLP)

In this step, security is computed in terms of ECDLP [30]. As from Eqs. (8, 9), $Q = \delta\beta$, and $\gamma = \alpha\beta$.

Computation of Q and γ is adequate with the knowledge of δ, α, and β. Consider a situation where an intruder knows the value of Q, γ, and β. Due to inadequate knowledge, it is arduous to compute the value of δ and α. Hence, the discrete logarithmic problem of elliptic curves improves the security of system.

4.4   Homomorphic Encryption

In this work, we homomorphically encrypt the ciphertexts of parties P_i and P_j with the multiplication operation. As we know from Eq. (19):

$$CP_o = H_{em}[(CP_1, CP_2), *] \tag{30}$$

Consider a situation where, at any instance, when an attacker gets the information of CP_1 and CP_2 with respect to CP_o, then due to inadequate knowledge of arbitrary operation, that is, multiplication $(*)$, an attacker cannot get the information of CP_o. Thus, homomorphic encryption makes the proposed work secure.

4.5   Signature Generation

Finally, for the signature generation, we use the value of secret key (α). We are proposing the inverse operation of secret key, which is quite difficult to compute. Hence, inverse operations increase the security of the system (as message is always encrypted throughout the communication channel).

5   Limitations

This work does not verify the designed protocol concerning side channels attacks (or any cryptographic attacks). The proposed work does not discuss the implementation setup.

6   Conclusion and Future Work

In this work, homomorphic encryption-based ECDSA generation over five-party protocol is proposed. We show the mutual identification between the parties with the help of A_t, and the security of messages is ensured by modified Paillier cryptosystem. Finally, our work achieves the authenticity of 5PP with the help of ECDSA signature.

In future, we will extend our work to more than five parties. Another extension of this study is to maintain full secrecy between the adversarial parties.

References

1. Alon, B., Omri, E., Cherniavsky, A.P.: MPC with friends and foes. In: Proceedings of the 40th Annual International Cryptology Conference, pp. 677–706 (2020)
2. Tsai, C.H., Su, P.C.: An ECC-based blind signcryption scheme for multiple digital documents. Secur. Commun. Netw. **2017**, 1–14 (2017)
3. Yi, X., Lam, K.Y.: A new blind ECDSA scheme for bitcoin transaction anonymity. In: Proceedings of the 2019 ACM Asia Conference on Computer and Communications Security, pp. 613–620 (2019)
4. Chauhan, K.K., Sanger, A.K.S., Verma, A.: Homomorphic encryption for data security in cloud computing. In: Proceedings of 2015 International Conference on Information Technology (ICIT), pp. 206–209 (2015)
5. Saadi, M.A., Kumar, B.: A review on elliptic curve cryptography. Int. J. Future Gener. Commun. Netw. **13**(2), 1597–1601 (2020)
6. Roy, A., Karforma, S.: A survey on digital signatures and its applications. J. Comput. Inf. Technol. **3**(1), 45–69 (2021)
7. Johnson, D., Menezes, A., Vanstone, S.: The elliptic curve digital signature algorithm (ECDSA). Int. J. Inf. Secur. **1**(1), 36–63 (2001)
8. Z. Xu, Y. Pan, and Z. Tao, "A Threshold Signature Key Protection Scheme Based on Blind Technology," in *Proceedings of the 2017 International Conference on Information Technology*, 2017, pp. 157–161
9. Fiat, A., Shamir, A.: How to prove yourself: practical solutions to identification and signature problems. In: CRYPTO, pp. 186–194 (1986)
10. Doerner, J., Kondi, Y., Lee, E., Shelat, A.: Secure two-party threshold ECDSA from ECDSA assumptions. In: Proceedings of 2018 IEEE Symposium on Security and Privacy (SP), pp. 980–997 (2018)
11. Gennaro, R., Goldfeder, S.: Fast multiparty threshold ECDSA with fast trustless setup. In: Proceedings of the 2018 ACM SIGSAC Conference on Computer and Communications Security, pp. 1179–1194 (2018)
12. Castagnos, G., Catalano, D., Laguillaumie, F., Savasta, F., Tucker, I.: Bandwidth-efficient threshold EC-DSA. In: Proceedings of 23rd IACR International Conference on Public-Key Cryptography, pp. 266–296 (2020)

13. Koti, N., Kukkala, V.B., Patra, A., Gopal, B.R.: PentaGOD: stepping beyond traditional GOD with five parties. In: Proceedings of the 2022 ACM SIGSAC Conference on Computer and Communications Security, pp. 1843–1856 (2022)
14. Sahu, A.K., Sharma, S.: Lightweight multi-party authentication and key agreement protocol in IoT-based E-healthcare service. ACM Trans. Multimedia Comput. Commun. Appl. (TOMM) **17**(64), 1–20 (2021)
15. Li, X., Zhang, K., Zhang, L., Zhao, X.: A new quantum multiparty simultaneous identity authentication protocol with the classical third-party. Entropy **24**(4), 1–10 (2022)
16. Sucasas, V., Aly, A., Mantas, G., Rodriguez, J., Aaraj, N.: Secure multi-party computation-based privacy-preserving authentication for smart cities. IEEE Trans. Cloud Comput. **11**(4), 3555–3572 (2023)
17. Fragkos, G., Plusquellic, J., Minwalla, C., Tsiropoulou, E.E.: Artificially intelligent electronic money. IEEE Consum. Electron. Mag. **10**(4), 81–89 (2020)
18. Haung, H., Liu, Z.Y., Tso, R.: Partially blind ECDSA scheme and its application to bitcoin. In: Proceedings of the 2021 IEEE Conference on Dependable and Secure Computing (DSC), pp. 1–8 (2021)
19. Xue, H., Au, M.H., Xie, X., Yuen, T.H., Cui, H.: Efficient online-friendly two-party ECDSA Signature. In: Proceedings of the 2021 ACM SIGSAC Conference on Computer and Communications Security, pp. 558–573 (2021)
20. Ma, R., Du, L.: Attribute-based blind signature scheme based on elliptic curve cryptography. IEEE Access **10** 34221–34227 (2022)
21. Aggarwal, A., Swain, S.: Blind two party ECDSA signing based homomorphic encryption over message passing. In: IEEE/ACS 19th International Conference on Computer Systems and Applications (AICCSA), pp. 1–5 (2022)
22. Aggarwal, A., Swain, S.: Poster: correctness of n-parties ECDSA By the claim of byzantine agreement. In: Proceedings of the 2022 ACM SIGSAC Conference on Computer and Communications Security, pp. 3319–3321 (2022)
23. ShenTu, Q., Yu, J.: A blind-mixing scheme for bitcoin based on an elliptic curve cryptography blind digital signature algorithm. arXiv preprint arXiv:1510.05833 (2015)
24. Knirsch, F., Unterweger, A., Unterrainer, M., Engel, D.: Comparison of the Paillier and ElGamal cryptosystems for smart grid aggregation protocols. In: ICISSP, pp. 232–239 (2020)
25. Kobiltz, N.: Elliptic curve cryptosystem. Math. Comput. **48**(177), 203–209 (1987)
26. Lamport, L., Shostak, R., Pease, M.: The Byzantine generals. ACM Trans. Program. Lang. Syst. **4**(3), 382–401 (1982)
27. Fazio, N., Gennaro, R., Jafarikhah, T., Skeith, W.E.: Homomorphic secret sharing from paillier encryption. In: International Conference on Provable Security, pp. 381–399 (2017)
28. Laššák, M., Porubský, Š: Fermat-euler theorem in algebraic number fields. J. Number Theory **60**(2), 245–290 (1996)

29. Blum, M., Feldman, P., Micali, S.: Non-interactive zero-knowledge and its applications. In: STOC, pp. 103–112 (1988)
30. Diem, C.: On the discrete logarithm problem in elliptic curves. Compos. Math. **147**(1), 75–104 (2011)

Benchmarking Post-quantum Cryptography in Ethereum-Based Blockchains

Patxi Juaristi[1] , Isaac Agudo[2]([✉]) , Ruben Rios[2] , and Laura Ricci[3]

[1] Cloud Data Spaces, Ikerlan, Arrasate-Mondragón, Spain
pjuaristi@ikerlan.es
[2] NICS Lab, Universidad de Málaga, Málaga, Spain
isaac@uma.es
[3] Università di Pisa, Pisa, Italy

Abstract. Blockchain technology has significantly transformed various industries by enabling secure and tamper-resistant transactions. However, the rise of quantum computing threatens the cryptographic foundations of blockchain networks, making blockchain vulnerable to signature forgery and transaction manipulation. This raises concerns about the long-term viability of blockchain systems and highlights the need for post-quantum secure solutions.

This paper investigates the feasibility of quantum-resistant blockchain ecosystems. Our research focuses on estimating the cost of the integration of the post-quantum algorithms selected in the NIST standardization competition into Ethereum-based blockchains.

Keywords: Blockchain · post-quantum cryptography · digital signature · Ethereum · ECDSA · Dilithium · Falcon · SPHINCS$^+$

1 Introduction

In recent years, blockchain technology has emerged as a revolutionary technology for secure and decentralized data management, largely due to its ability to provide an immutable and transparent data ledger, which cannot be manipulated. This technology has been adopted in various sectors, with finance being the main application scenario, but also extending to supply chain management and many others.

However, the advent of quantum computers poses a major threat to the foundations of blockchain technology as they could undermine the security of current cryptographic algorithms. Leveraging the principles of quantum mechanics, quantum computers can perform a large number of calculations simultaneously because their basic unit of information representation, the quantum bit or qubit, can exist in a superposition of states. This allows multiple states to be represented at the same time, greatly facilitating efficient parallel processing [1].

J. Garcia-Alfaro et al. (Eds.): ESORICS 2024 Workshops, LNCS 15263, pp. 340–353, 2025.
https://doi.org/10.1007/978-3-031-82349-7_23

As such, quantum computers are capable of solving complex mathematical problems considerably faster than classical computers.

The potential of quantum computing is significantly enhanced by the application of specific algorithms, such as Shor's algorithm [2] for factoring large numbers, and Grover's algorithm [18] for speeding up searches in unstructured data.

These algorithms have direct implications for the security of current cryptographic algorithms, especially public-key algorithms. For example, the security of RSA is based on the impossibility of factoring large prime numbers, but with Shor's algorithm a 2048-bit RSA key could be factorized in approximately 8 h using a quantum computer with 20 million qubits [13].

While this is a clear threat to security, the reality is that we are still far from building quantum computers with this number of qubits. To the best of our knowledge, the largest quantum computers to date have just over a thousand of qubits. IBM's Condor, for example, has 1.121 qubits [14]. On such a computer, the factorization of the above mentioned RSA key would take approximately 142.204 h, or about 5915 d. This value was obtained without differentiating between physical and logical qubits, because otherwise the result would be much higher [3].

Although quantum computers are not an immediate problem, the rapid development of them in recent years, has led to the need for new cryptographic algorithms that can withstand quantum computers. These new cryptographic algorithms are referred to as post-quantum or quantum-resistant algorithms.

Since blockchains rely on public-key cryptography to operate, they are also vulnerable to quantum computers. The main mechanism for interacting with blockchains is through transactions, which are digitally signed to ensure their authenticity. Most blockchains, including Bitcoin and Ethereum-based blockchains, use the Elliptic Curve Digital Signature Algorithm (ECDSA) [15] for this purpose. The main reason is that ECDSA uses short keys and produces short signatures.

In this paper we investigate the threat that quantum computers pose to blockchain systems and whether post-quantum cryptography (PQC) can be integrated into Ethereum-based blockchains to mitigate the risk. The main contribution of this paper is a performance comparison of the PQC algorithms selected from the NIST standarization process against ECDSA using real-time transaction data. It has been focused only on the ECDSA signature algorithm used to sign the Ethereum transactions, not in the BLS signature. The reason for this has been because replacing BLS is much more changeling given that Ethereum consensus uses BLS signature aggregation to store the results of the consensus voting. In the end, the solution has been composed of a modular and scalable system for acquiring, comparing and visualizing the results.

The rest of this paper is organized as follows. Section 2 provides a comparative analysis with related works. Next, Sect. 3 introduces the main existing post quantum cryptography families. The benchmarking architecture is described in Sect. 4. Subsequently, Sect. 5 shows the results obtained from the evaluation of applying ECDSA and NIST selected algorithms to real-time transaction data from an actual blockchain network. Finally, Sect. 6 present the conclusion and outlines potential lines of future research.

2   Related Work

Concerns about the threat of quantum computers to current cryptographic schemes have led to notable research in this area, generating several solutions and surveys.

Regarding survey papers, Buser et al. [4] focus on exotic signature schemes for post-quantum blockchains, exploring the challenges associated with their implementation and proposing research directions. More recently, Yang et al. [21] presented a comprehensive survey and comparison of post-quantum and quantum blockchains, which highlighted the current state of research and identifying possible future directions.

Some papers focus on investigating the application of post-quantum blockchains to particular scenarios. For example, Chen et al. [5] concentrate on studying the practical implications of integrating post-quantum cryptographic schemes into blockchain systems designed for the Internet of Things (IoT) and other smart city infrastructures. Similarly, Yi et al. [22], discuss the application of post-quantum blockchain technology to secure the social Internet of Things (SIoT), proposing a framework that leverages post-quantum cryptography to ensure data integrity and privacy in these scenarios.

Additionally, some authors proposed the use of lattice-based cryptography to make blockchain networks resistant to quantum attacks. The focus of [11] is the creation of a cryptocurrency based on a post-quantum blockchain while [16] proposes a new signature scheme and describes how to apply it to secure blockchain transactions. None of them present a practical implementation.

To the best of our knowledge, the paper that is most similar to ours is [9]. This paper analyses the feasibility of post-quantum algorithms for the blockchain. However, their study does not use the finalists of the PQC competition organized by NIST. Furthermore, their evaluation is not done with real blockchain data.

In contrast, in this paper we provide a modular and scalable tool to facilitate the incorporation of novel post-quantum algorithms as they are developed. In addition, our solution uses real-time transaction data from a blockchain network, making the evaluation results more accurate.

3   Post-quantum Cryptography Families

The threat of quantum computing to today's cryptographic schemes has prompted the US National Institute of Standards and Technology (NIST) to launch a standardization process for post-quantum schemes, which aims to develop and standardize cryptographic algorithms that are resistant to quantum attacks [17]. The competition started in 2016 with 69 candidate algorithms and has progressed through rounds of evaluation. The candidates algorithms can be classified into different families, which are briefly described below.

Lattice-based cryptography relies on the mathematical properties of lattices, geometric structures formed by points in n-dimensional space. It involves solving problems such as the Shortest Vector Problem (SVP) and the Closest Vector Problem (CVP) in these high-dimensional spaces, making brute-force attacks impractical. Lattices are often represented as arrays for easier matrix operations. The main cryptographic schemes include NTRUEncrypt and NTRUSign, which leverage SVP and CVP, and Ring-LWE-based schemes, which use the Ring Learning with Errors (RLWE) problem to perform computations on polynomial rings.

Code-based cryptography is one of the oldest and most studied approaches to post-quantum cryptography. Its security is based on the difficulty of solving the mathematical problems associated with error-correcting codes. These codes ensure reliable data transmission over noisy channels by introducing redundancy, which allows the receiver to detect and correct errors, while attackers without secret knowledge cannot decode the data. The McEliece cryptosystem, created in 1978, is the most famous code-based algorithm. It encrypts messages by encoding them in codewords and adding random errors to make decryption impossible without the private key. Although efficient and secure, the McEliece cryptosystem has large public keys and computationally intensive key generation and management processes.

Multivariate polynomial-based cryptography (MPKC) is a cryptographic scheme that exploits the hardness of solving systems of multivariate polynomial equations, which are computationally very difficult to solve, and have been proven to be NP-Complete, like some other lattice or code problems. These problems are of complexity class NP (non-deterministic polynomial time), which means that if a polynomial-time algorithm exists for solving any NP-complete problem, then polynomial-time algorithms exist for solving all problems in NP, making them essentially equivalent in difficulty.

Hash-based cryptography is a method of encrypting and securing data using hash functions. Before the process begins, it is necessary to determine which values are to be signed, and then to generate a long random string of characters for each of them. This resulting random string will be the private key used to sign the data. Once the private key is ready, this string is hashed using typical hash functions such as SHA-1, SHA-3, SHA-256 or BLAKE2, which produce strings between 256 and 512 bits, which are used as public keys to verify the signature. This is done by hashing the signature (the private key) and comparing it with the public key it has.

Isogeny-based cryptography creates cryptographic systems over finite fields using isogeny graphs of elliptic curves, which are mappings that preserve algebraic structures. An isogeny is a morphism between two elliptic curves, characterized by its homomorphism between the groups of points on the curves. Key generation involves choosing two elliptic curves over a finite field and generating a secret isogeny between them. The private key is the isogeny, while the public key is made of the starting and resulting curves. While the Supersingular Isogeny Diffie-Hellman (SIDH) protocol and its successor, Supersingular Isogeny

Key Encapsulation (SIKE), were initially prominent, they have been found vulnerable to cryptographic attacks. As a result, newer isogeny-based schemes like SQISign and its variants have emerged. SQISign, which has been featured in recent NIST post-quantum cryptography evaluations, represents a more robust approach, addressing the vulnerabilities of earlier protocols and offering promising security in the evolving landscape of post-quantum cryptography.

4   Benchmarking Solution

This section describes the benchmarking tool developed to evaluate the performance of both current and post-quantum cryptographic algorithms in blockchain.

The tool consists of a set of interconnected functional blocks that result in a modular and scalable environment for the evaluation of cryptographic algorithms against real-time transactions from an Ethereum-based blockchain. The tool also provides an interface for the visualization and analysis of the results.

In the following, we present the overall architecture of the benchmarking solution and its building blocks in detail.

4.1   System Architecture

The proposed solution consists of four main components as illustrated in Fig. 1. The first component is devoted to the deployment of a blockchain network. The second component provides all necessary cryptographic algorithms, which will be applied to actual blockchain data in the third component. The fourth component provides a mechanism to display the results.

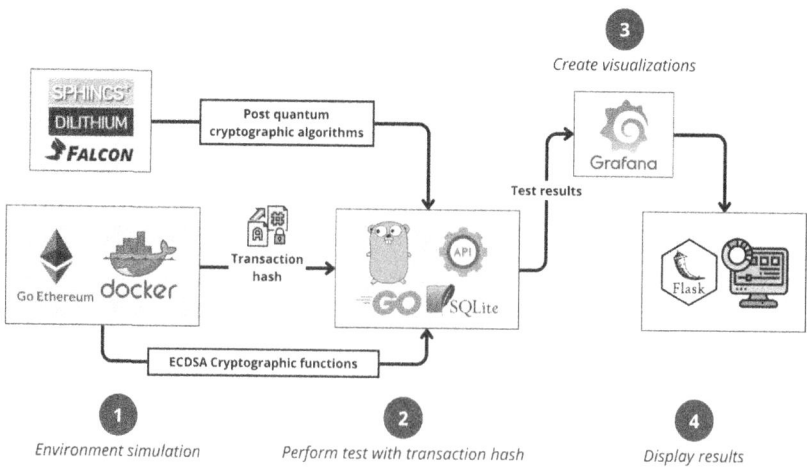

Fig. 1. Benchmarking solution architecture

As shown in the figure, our solution incorporates an actual blockchain network capable of deploying and running a number of Go-Ethereum nodes using a Docker environment. All transactions sent in the blockchain environment are intercepted and their actual payloads are passed to our benchmarking API. The benchmarking component evaluates the performance of both the cryptographic algorithms currently provided by the Go-Ethereum client and the post-quantum cryptographic schemes selected by NIST. The results are stored in a Sqlite database that is read by Grafana, the component in charge of generating graphics for comparing the evaluation results. These graphics are finally included in a web application developed with Flask to facilitate the visualization and analysis of the results.

4.2   Cryptographic Component

This section presents the cryptographic algorithms and libraries incorporated in our benchmarking solution. Currently, it includes the three post-quantum signature algorithms selected by NIST after their standardization competition:

– **CRYSTALS-Dilithium** [7]: Dilithium is a digital signature algorithm based on the hardness of lattice problems over module lattices. It ensures that even with access to a signing oracle, an adversary cannot fabricate a new signature for an unsigned message or a different signature for an already signed message. Dilithium utilizes rejection sampling of Fiat-Shamir with Aborts and the uniform distribution for signature generation, leading to secure yet larger signatures. Despite this, its key size is reduced post-creation with an optimizaiton process, making it the algorithm with the smallest combined public key and signature size among lattice-based schemes. Dilithium offers three modes (Dilithium 2, 3, and 5), with increasing security and resource needs, and includes AES encryption.
  As there is a library that implements this algorithm in GO [6], the necessary test functions have been included directly in the simulation program that has been carried out in GO.
– **Falcon** [10]: As Dilithium, it is a lattice-based digital signature scheme, but uses the Gentry, Peikert, and Vaikuntanathan framework [12], deploying NTRU lattices with a fast Fourier sampling trapdoor sampler. This scheme addresses the short integer solution (SIS) problem over NTRU lattices, which remains computationally challenging even for quantum computers. Falcon offers two modes, Falcon-512 and Falcon-1024, with this benchmark focusing on Falcon-1024 due to its higher security.
  To implement of Falcon, since there is currently no native library for GO, it was necessary to use the CGO library to combine C and GO code, calling Falcon cryptographic functions from C [19] for analysis in GO.
– **SPHINCS+** [20]: Stateless hash-based digital signature scheme using Merkle tree structures. It offers high security with relatively short signatures and fast verification times. SPHINCS+ includes three variants based on the underlying hash functions: SHAKE256, SHA-256, and Haraka, with this benchmark focusing on SHA-256.

The GO library for SPHINCS$^+$ [8] supports 12 modes per hashing method, varying in hash length (128, 192, 256) and mode type (simple, robust). In this case, six modes have been analyzed, covering both simple and robust options for each hashing type.

Although this component only incorporates libraries for the three finalists of the NIST competition, it is designed to facilitate the inclusion of new cryptographic algorithms in the future.

4.3 Measurement Component

The measurement component is one of the core elements of the proposed solution. This component is responsible for receiving, in real time, the transactions of all blocks generated by the Ethereum-based blockchain.

Every time a signature is generated or verified in the blockchain network, an API call is made with the hash of the transaction. This hash is then used as payload to perform the comparisons of cryptographic functions.

The tests, which are performed in every single API call, simulate a key generation, signature generation and signature verification process. These tests are first carried out with the cryptographic code extracted from Go-Ethereum, i.e. with ECDSA, and then compared with the post-quantum cryptographic schemes explained above: Dilithium, Falcon and SPHINCS$^+$.

The metrics measured have been the execution time and the memory usage of the corresponding cryptographic function. All measurements have been carried out directly from GO, with native libraries: `time` for time measurement and `runtime/pprof` for CPU profiling. Both are started just before calling the function to which the parameters are going to be measured.

However, instead of measuring the time directly in the blockchain node, we produce also an ECDSA signature in the backend to ensure that all benchmarked algorithms are run in the same environment. As the backend does not know the private keys used for signatures, we need to generate a new pair in each test iteration. In addition to that, key and signature sizes have also been measured apart from the tests.

Execution Times. The simulations have been carried out several times in a loop and the average execution time of all of them has been calculated, since there have been functions that took extremely low time that were considered as 0ms by the measurement function. This loop was 50 times for the tests performed by API call.

However, the need to perform iterations to obtain more accurate results, increased considerably the time required to complete each test. This has caused another problem, which was that API calls were being received with new block information, while tests were still running with hashes from previous blocks. In short, it took longer for the GO program test to complete than for the private network to validate a new block.

Therefore, it has been essential to implement asynchronous calls in the blockchain network, so that it has not need to wait for the API response and continues its normal operation. At the same time, and more importantly, a queuing system has had to be implemented in the GO program. This has been achieved using GO channels and GO routines. When the application launches, the channel is initialized and a GO routine is started to handle incoming requests. Then for each API call received, the hash information has been added to the channel queue, to be executed one at a time on a first-come, first-served basis.

Memory Usage. In addition to measuring the execution time of cryptographic functions, in order to assess whether an algorithm is suitable or not, it has been very interesting to quantify the memory usage during executions. For this purpose, four metrics have been evaluated:

- **Alloc**: Amount of memory allocated by the Go runtime for live objects, including all reachable objects in the heap, as well as some additional memory used by the garbage collector and other runtime structures.
- **Total alloc**: Cumulative amount of memory allocated since the program started. It covers all allocations, even those that have been freed by the garbage collector.
- **Sys**: Total memory obtained from the operating system, including both the Go heap and any memory allocated by the Go runtime for other purposes (such as stack space, memory-mapped files, and so on).
- **Num GC**: Number of garbage collection cycles that have occurred since the program started. Garbage collection is the process of reclaiming memory that is no longer in use by the program, and each cycle involves scanning the heap to identify and free unreachable objects.

5   Experimental Results

The test results have been divided into three parts: the key and signature sizes, and the execution times and memory usage of the functions under test.

5.1   Key and Signature Sizes

Table 1 shows the comparison of private and public key and signature sizes for each type of cryptographic algorithm. It is worth mentioning that the size of the public key is only the size of the key itself, which in reality would have to be added 1 bit for the signature of the y-coordinate.

Comparing the key sizes of the various cryptographic schemes, there have been notable differences that reflect their security objectives and underlying algorithms. The best values have been obtained by ECDSA and 128-bit SPHINCS$^+$, which with the sum of the public and private key sizes achieve the same size.

Table 1. Key and signature sizes of different algorithms

Algorithm	Public key	Private key	Signature
ECDSA	64	32	64
Dilithium2	1312	2528	2420
Dilithium3	1952	4000	3293
Dilithium5	2592	4864	4595
Falcon 1024	1793	2305	1231
SPHINCS+ SHA256 128bit - Robust	32	64	17088
SPHINCS+ SHA256 192bit - Robust	48	96	35664
SPHINCS+ SHA256 256bit - Robust	64	128	49856

ECDSA has a 64-byte public key and a 32-byte private key, while SPHINCS+ has a 32-byte public key and a 64-byte private key.

In any case, although ECDSA could be considered the best in this aspect, it should be noted that the set of all SPHINCS+ schemes have values very close to ECDSA and therefore, values that could be competitive to it in this aspect. Among SPHINCS+ versions, the higher the security level, the more bits are used and therefore, the key sizes increase. However, using the simplest version, the 128 bit one, it is possible to use the same key sizes as ECDSA.

In contrast, both Dilithium and Falcon have been excessively far from the ECDSA or SPHINCS+ key size values. They should be used in scenarios where security is paramount and large key size is not an issue.

In case of the signatures, it can be seen that the result changes radically compared to the key sizes comparison. Although ECDSA has still been the best, SPHINCS+, which for the keys was the second best option, becomes the worst with a huge difference with the rest.

In this case, the second best option has been Falcon 1024. However, the size have fallen far above of the ECDSA signature size, since the size of a Falcon 1024 signature is equivalent to just over 19 ECDSA signatures.

The size of the signatures generated using Dilithium has also turned out to be considerably larger, doubling the size of Falcon 1024 using Dilithium2, and more than tripling if Dilithium5 is employed.

In general, it can be concluded that there is no scheme that globally (adding the three sizes) comes close to ECDSA, since the second best is Falcon and exceeds it by 33 times. Especially analyzing the sizes of the signatures, it can be clearly stated that all post-quantum schemes are extremely far from the ECDSA values. However, SPHINCS+, in the aspect of the keys obtains a very good result, being even better in the size of the public keys and not much worse in the private ones. In any case, it is clear that using these algorithms, the increase in the size of the keys and especially of the signatures is an inevitable consequence of the improvement in security they offer.

5.2   Execution Times

One of the most important factors when choosing one cryptographic algorithm over another is the time required for the algorithm to execute the cryptographic functions. Therefore, much emphasis has been placed on measuring and analyzing in a precise and detailed way the execution times required by each cryptographic scheme.

The final average results after more than 24 h of running the blockchain network have been those summarized in the Table 2 and also visible in the historical data dashboards of the project.

Table 2. Average execution times by algorithms (ms)

Algorithm	Key generation	Signature generation	Signature verification
ECDSA	90.7	58.6	71.4
Dilithium2	80.5	149	17.3
Dilithium2-AES	102	124	16.5
Dilithium3	144	222	22.7
Dilithium3-AES	171	191	19.5
Dilithium5	201	251	33.6
Dilithium5-AES	254	207	29.6
Falcon 1024	90434	13162	166
SPHINCS$^+$ SHA256 128bit - Robust	5612	120583	7845
SPHINCS$^+$ SHA256 128bit - Simple	3376	72760	4569
SPHINCS$^+$ SHA256 192bit - Robust	8318	198359	11856
SPHINCS$^+$ SHA256 192bit - Simple	4977	118773	6777
SPHINCS$^+$ SHA256 256bit - Robust	26333	483158	14568
SPHINCS$^+$ SHA256 256bit - Simple	13074	240571	6957

Firstly, evaluating the differences in key generation times, it can be concluded that there have been two algorithms that clearly stand out above the rest: ECDSA and Dilithium2 (both in its normal version and in the AES version, which hardly varies). However, it should be noted that all versions of Dilithium have a relatively good execution time that did not deviate that much from the ECDSA times. In fact, the Dilithium2 version improves on the ECDSA result and achieves the shortest execution time of all the algorithms. However, both SPHINCS$^+$, in all its versions, and Falcon, differ exaggeratedly compared to the times of the rest, especially the latter.

Secondly, evaluating the signature generation times, there is no doubt that ECDSA is clearly above the rest of the algorithms, as it is slightly more than twice as fast as the second, Dilithium2-AES. Unlike the key generation, in this section Falcon 1024 (224 times the ECDSA time) has obtained a better result than SPHINCS$^+$ (2057 times the ECDSA time in the simplest mode), but they are still times that are not at all competitive compared to the times of ECDSA or even Dilithium.

However, at this point it must be taken into account the large difference that existed between the signature size of ECDSA and the signature sizes of the post-quantum algorithms, which greatly influences the time of signature generation.

Finally, as far as signature verification times are concerned, it is interesting to note that ECDSA did not obtain the best score on this point, being clearly outperformed by Dilithium in all its versions.

Dilithium2 has been more than four times faster than ECDSA, and Dilithium5, the version with the highest level of security, 2.1 times faster too. Falcon 1024, on the other hand, although it has been more than twice as slow as ECDSA, was not far behind. SPHINCS$^+$, in all its modes, has been the scheme that took an exorbitant amount of time compared to the rest, being 47.3 times slower than Falcon 1024 for example (128bits robust mode). However, although it is not a very considerable difference, a clear difference in times could be observed when using the robust or simple mode of SPHINCS$^+$, regardless of the number of bits used.

Summarizing the results, on the one hand, in key generation, Dilithium obtains a result very close to ECDSA, even improving its time in its Dilithium2 version. The rest of the algorithms need an extremely higher time and are not competitive at all. The same happens in the generation of signatures, although in this case Dilithium does not improve the time of ECDSA in any version, it is very close. The worst here is SPHINCS$^+$, while Falcon improves compared to key generation. The most remarkable thing happens in signature verification, where Dilithium is exceptionally better than the rest, including ECDSA, being between 2.1 and 4.1 times faster than ECDSA depending on the versions used.

Therefore, in the sum of all times, it can be concluded that Dilithium needs a similar amount of time as ECDSA, being practically the same time in the Dilithium2 version. Comparing it with the rest of the post-quantum schemes, it obtains an excellent result, being the only one that could compete in this aspect with the current cryptographic methods.

5.3   Memory Usage

In addition to measuring the execution time of cryptographic functions, in order to assess whether an algorithm is suitable or not, it has been very interesting to quantify the memory usage during executions. Nevertheless, obtained results have not been as interesting and analyzable as those of the execution time, which has led to more extensive conclusions.

The values of total alloc, sys and num GC, have concluded to be very similar between all the executions of the different algorithms in each test. The metric of interest for the analysis has been the alloc, the amount of memory allocated by the Go runtime for live objects, which has led to detect greater variation among the different algorithms.

First, in the memory allocation levels of the key generation, a clear difference has been observed between ECDSA and Falcon compared to Dilithium and

SPHINCS$^+$. Although ECDSA achieved the lowest result, it is less than 1% better than Falcon, which is a negligible difference. The difference to consider exists when compared to the other two post-quantum algorithms, which need about 55–60% more memory than the first two.

Next, the results of the same metric have been analyzed for the signature generation process, and it was observed that in this aspect, Dilithium improves and approaches the values of ECDSA and Falcon, which are still slightly better in that order. SPHINCS$^+$, on the other hand, still requires about 50% more memory compared to the other three algorithms.

Finally, signature verification follows the same pattern as signature generation, with all the algorithms being quite close to each other, except SPHINCS, which continues with much higher values. However, in this case, it can be seen that there is a notable difference between the different modes that has SPHINCS. The robust 192-bit mode gives the best result, while curiously, the simple mode of the same bits is the one that gives the worst result of all, surpassing it by just over 10%. The rest of the algorithms are in between, but except for the 128-bit one, in the other two, it is the simple mode which needs less allocated memory than the robust mode.

6   Conclusions and Future Work

One of the main conclusions was obtained during the research and study process. At present, quantum computers are still a long way from being able to break current encryption schemes easily and quickly. Current quantum computers are not necessarily large enough to break the schemes fast, nor are they anywhere near the size needed at the moment.

The test execution times have been where the most interesting information has been extracted, especially because a similar performance has been seen between ECDSA and Dilithium, and a huge difference has been observed with the other two analyzed schemes.

Analyzing the memory usage, it can be said that even though there is a difference between the schemes, it is not as big as in the case of the execution times. Falcon equals ECDSA in terms of results, followed by Dilithium, which needs more resources in key generation, but in the other two processes it is practically the same as ECDSA. However, SPHINCS$^+$ does require slightly more memory in all processes.

In summary, analyzing all the results, it can be clearly concluded that in terms of performance, Dilithium is currently the best post-quantum cryptographic scheme, being quite close to the performance levels of ECDSA, which has been the present scheme used as a comparison. In the case of the simplest version of Dilithium (Dilithium2), summing all the values of time and memory, it would only need 12% more execution time in the three processes evaluated and 20% more memory. These values, which although on a large scale could make a considerable difference, are values that are not too far off current levels. Therefore, the increase in security level that the integration of this algorithm could entail, could be totally understandable in exchange for the slight decrease in performance.

From the results presented and also during the development, new ideas, questions and improvements have arisen, which will be detailed below.

The main point for improvement would be to integrate the post-quantum cryptographic methods used in the tests into the blockchain network directly, i.e. to include them into the source code of the used Ethereum client, in this case Go-Ethereum. This way, more detailed tests could be performed, with real transactions, enabling the analysis of more factors such as network load for example. It would be possible to analyze the behavior of the methods in a real network, including latency, node distribution, volume of transactions...

Secondly, while current tests only include post-quantum digital signature algorithms selected by NIST, many other post-quantum algorithms could be tested in the future.

Finally, current tests were performed on a local computer with its own computational limitations and concurrent processes, which might affect results. Moving the system to an external server dedicated to testing, free from other tasks, would provide more accurate performance measurements. Additionally, creating a network of multiple systems to run the same tests and share a common database would allow for calculating average values across different systems, offering a broader perspective on performance results.

Acknowledgements. This work has been partially supported by project PID2022-139268OB-I00, financed by MCIN/AEI/10.13039/501100011033FEDER, UE and project TED2021-129830B-I00, financed by MCIN/AEI /10.13039/501100011033/ Next-GenerationEU/PRTR.

References

1. Arute, F., Arya, K., Babbush, R., et al.: Quantum supremacy using a programmable superconducting processor. Nature **574**(7779), 505–510 (2019). https://doi.org/10.1038/s41586-019-1666-5
2. Bhatia, V., Ramkumar, K.: An efficient quantum computing technique for cracking RSA using Shor's algorithm. In: 2020 IEEE 5th International Conference on Computing Communication and Automation (ICCCA), pp. 89–94 (2020). https://doi.org/10.1109/ICCCA49541.2020.9250806
3. Brooks, M.: Quantum computing is taking on its biggest challenge: noise (2024). https://www.technologyreview.com/2024/01/04/1084783/quantum-computing-noise-google-ibm-microsoft/
4. Buser, M., et al.: A survey on exotic signatures for post-quantum blockchain: challenges and research directions. ACM Comput. Surv. **55**(12) (2023).https://doi.org/10.1145/3572771
5. Chen, J., Gan, W., Hu, M., Chen, C.M.: On the construction of a post-quantum blockchain for smart city. J. Inf. Secur. Appl. **58**, 102780 (2021). https://doi.org/10.1016/j.jisa.2021.102780
6. Cloudflare: CIRCL: cloudflare interoperable reusable cryptographic library (2024). https://pkg.go.dev/github.com/cloudflare/circl/sign/dilithium

7. CRYSTALS Team: Cryptographic suite for algebraic lattices (crystals) (2023). https://pq-crystals.org/
8. Daugaard, K.: Sphincsplus-golang (2023). https://github.com/kasperdi/ SPHINCSPLUS-golang
9. Fernández-Caramès, T.M., Fraga-Lamas, P.: Towards post-quantum blockchain: a review on blockchain cryptography resistant to quantum computing attacks. IEEE Access **8**, 21091–21116 (2020). https://doi.org/10.1109/ACCESS.2020.2968985
10. Fouque, P., Hoffstein, J., Kirchner, P., Lyubashevsky, V., et al.: Falcon (2017). https://falcon-sign.info/
11. Gao, Y.L., Chen, X.B., Chen, Y.L., Sun, Y., Niu, X.X., Yang, Y.X.: A secure cryptocurrency scheme based on post-quantum blockchain. IEEE Access **6**, 27205–27213 (2018). https://doi.org/10.1109/ACCESS.2018.2827203
12. Gentry, C., Peikert, C., Vaikuntanathan, V.: Trapdoors for hard lattices and new cryptographic constructions (2007). https://eprint.iacr.org/2007/432
13. Gidney, C., Ekerå, M.: How to factor 2048 bit RSA integers in 8 hours using 20 million noisy qubits. Quantum **5**, 433 (2021).https://doi.org/10.22331/q-2021-04-15-433
14. IBM: IBM's roadmap for scaling quantum technology. IBM (2023). https://www.ibm.com/quantum/blog/ibm-quantum-roadmap
15. Johnson, D., Menezes, A., Vanstone, S.: The elliptic curve digital signature algorithm (ECDSA). Int. J. Inf. Secur. **1**(1), 36–63 (2001). https://doi.org/10.1007/s102070100002
16. Li, C.Y., Chen, X.B., Chen, Y.L., Hou, Y.Y., Li, J.: A new lattice-based signature scheme in post-quantum blockchain network. IEEE Access **7**, 2026–2033 (2019). https://doi.org/10.1109/ACCESS.2018.2886554
17. National institute of standards and technology (NIST): Post-quantum cryptography (2024). https://csrc.nist.gov/Projects/post-quantum-cryptography/selected-algorithms-2022
18. Pati, C.: Search using Grover's algorithm. National Institute of Technology Rourkela (2023). https://doi.org/10.13140/RG.2.2.25842.07369
19. Pornin, T.: Falcon source files (reference implementation) (2021). https://falcon-sign.info/impl/falcon.h.html
20. SPHINCS+ Team: Sphincs+ (2023). https://sphincs.org/
21. Yang, Z., Alfauri, H., Farkiani, B., Jain, R., Di Pietro, R., Erbad, A.: A survey and comparison of post-quantum and quantum blockchains. IEEE Commun. Surv. Tutorials **26**(2), 967–1002 (2024). https://doi.org/10.1109/COMST.2023.3325761
22. Yi, H.: Secure social internet of things based on post-quantum blockchain. IEEE Trans. Netw. Sci. Eng. **9**(3), 950–957 (2022). https://doi.org/10.1109/TNSE.2021.3095192

CyberICPS Papers

Preface to the Proceedings of CyberICPS 2024

This book contains revised versions of the papers presented at the 10th Workshop on Security of Industrial Control Systems and of Cyber-Physical Systems (CyberICPS 2024). The workshop was co-located with the 29th European Symposium on Research in Computer Security (ESORICS 2024) and was held in Bydgoszcz, Poland, on September 20th, 2024.

Cyber-physical systems (CPS) are physical and engineered systems that interact with the physical environment, whose operations are monitored, coordinated, controlled, and integrated by information and communication technologies. These systems exist everywhere around us, and range in size, complexity, and criticality from embedded systems used in smart vehicles, to SCADA systems in smart grids, to control systems in water distribution systems, to smart transportation systems, to plant control systems, engineering workstations, substation equipment, programmable logic controllers (PLCs), and other Industrial Control Systems (ICS). These systems also include the emerging trend of the Industrial Internet of Things (IIoT), which will be the central part of the fourth industrial revolution. As ICS and CPS proliferate, and increasingly interact with us and affect our lives, their security becomes of paramount importance.

CyberICPS 2024 brought together researchers, engineers, and governmental actors with an interest in the security of ICS and CPS in the context of their increasing exposure to cyberspace, by offering a forum for discussion on all issues related to their cyber security. CyberICPS 2024 attracted 17 high-quality submissions, each of which was assigned to 3 referees for single-blind review; the review process resulted in 9 papers being accepted to be presented and included in the proceedings, i.e., the acceptance rate was 53%. An additional paper originally submitted to, reviewed by, and accepted for the SECPRE workshop, which was cancelled, is included in these Proceedings. The chairs and members of the Program Committee were not involved with nor had visibility of the reviewing process of submissions authored or co-authored by them. The accepted papers cover topics related to many aspects of cyber security in cyber-physical and industrial control systems, ranging from threats, to risks that such systems face, to cyber-attacks that may be launched against such systems, to ways of detecting and responding to such attacks.

We would like to express our thanks to all those who assisted us in organizing the event and putting together the program. We are very grateful to the members of the Program Committee for their timely and rigorous reviews. Thanks are also due to the ESORICS Workshop Chairs and to the ESORICS Organizers. Last, but by no means least, we would like to thank all the authors who submitted their work to the workshop and contributed to an interesting set of proceedings.

November 2024

Sokratis Katsikas
Frédéric Cuppens
Nora Cuppens
Costas Lambrinoudakis

Organization

Nikolaos Pitropakis	Edinburgh Napier University, UK
Indrakshi Ray	Colorado State University, USA
Indrajit Ray	Colorado State University, USA
Andrea Saracino	Consiglio Nazionale delle Ricerche, Italy
Georgios Spathoulas	University of Thessaly, Greece
Gabor Visky	Tallinn University of Technology, Estonia

Additional Reviewers

Shwetha Gowdanakatte	Colorado State University, USA
Oluwatosin Falebita	Colorado State University, USA
Andreas Menegatos	University of Piraeus, Greece
Ibrahim Lazrig	Colorado State University, USA

Exploring Anomaly Detection for Marine Radar Systems

Antoine Saillard[1,2], Konrad Wolsing[1,2(✉)], Klaus Wehrle[2],
and Jan Bauer[1]

[1] Cyber Analysis and Defense, Fraunhofer FKIE, Wachtberg, Germany
{antoine.saillard,konrad.wolsing,jan.bauer}@fkie.fraunhofer.de,
{saillard,wolsing}@comsys.rwth-aachen.de
[2] Communication and Distributed Systems, RWTH Aachen University,
Aachen, Germany
wehrle@comsys.rwth-aachen.de

Abstract. Marine radar systems are a core technical instrument for collision avoidance in shipping and an indispensable decision-making aid for navigators on the ship's bridge in limited visibility conditions at sea, in straits, and harbors. While electromagnetic attacks against radars can be carried out externally, primarily by military actors, research has recently shown that marine radar is also vulnerable to attacks from cyberspace. These can be carried out internally, less "loudly", and with significantly less effort and know-how, thus posing a general threat to the shipping industry, the global maritime transport system, and world trade. Based on cyberattacks discussed in the scientific community and a simulation environment for marine radar systems, we investigate in this work to which extent existing Intrusion Detection System (IDS) solutions can secure vessels' radar systems, how effective their detection capability is, and where their limits lie. From this, we derive a research gap for radar-specific methods and present the first two approaches in that direction. Thus, we pave the way for necessary future developments of anomaly detection specific for marine navigation radars.

Keywords: Marine Radar Systems · Maritime Cyber Security · Intrusion Detection Systems · Anomaly Detection · Navico BR24

1 Introduction

Marine navigation has long benefited from marine radar technology, enabling navigators to accurately assert their position, heading, and distance to surrounding hazards. In recent decades, navigational instruments have followed global trends of digitization. Electronic chart display and information systems (ECDISs) have superseded paper charts. Communication equipment, Global Navigation Satellite System (GNSS) devices, and various sensors now interface with each other over shipboard networks [9,35], ultimately leading to increased autonomy of vessels [17,19]. This trend likewise affects Marine Radar Systems

(MRSs), where digital radar displays have replaced their analog predecessors and their networking with other navigation instruments allows them to display a unified view of the vessel's state and surroundings to navigators [8].

Computer networks forming the digital backbone of modern vessels do not come without challenges. Alongside digitization, the maritime industry has seen increased interconnectivity of its assets, with readily available satellite and mobile communication networks allowing for remote maintenance, chart updates, and crew access to the Internet [35]. Thus, the previously "water"-gapped shipboard systems become increasingly connected to the outside world, leading to new cyber threats, a serious concern that the nascent field of maritime cybersecurity research seeks to address. In that regard, the vulnerabilities of fundamental maritime systems on board vessels have been intensively discussed [3,6,9,13] and demonstrated for various maritime systems, such as the automatic identification system (AIS) [1,4], GNSS [7], VSAT [27], and also radar [5,22,34,36], showing their possible impacts on the economy, ecology, and human lives. However, security research on MRSs remains limited, especially regarding techniques to effectively mitigate potential cyberattacks.

With regard to network-based cyberattacks, as for any communication network, securing MRSs' networks consists of two complementary efforts: the *prevention* of attacks in the first place and the *detection* of successful intrusions. On modern vessels, the former is usually implemented through network segmentation, *i.e.* the separation of crew and management IT systems from critical OT systems [15]. Unfortunately, the integrity of radar data exchanged also depends on this segmentation as the often proprietary communication protocols employed are largely unsecured, lacking authentication mechanisms [36].

While preventive measures such as authenticated communication are desirable for the protection of MRS, they may be difficult to implement without the cooperation of radar vendors as modifications to the existing systems incur the risk of voiding mandatory certifications. As complementary approach and topic of this publication, *detecting* the manipulation of a radar image or changes in their communication in time for navigators to react is another viable option.

The suitability of IDSs has long been researched for many domains [2,33]. Yet, despite being a crucial component of shipboard navigation system networks [36], to date, detection mechanisms for MRSs have rarely been considered [23]. Thus, our work aims to address this research gap by investigating the applicability and evaluating the effectiveness of both existing and novel anomaly detection techniques for MRSs by making the following contributions:

- We update existing attack vectors on MRSs reported across different publications into a comprehensive and unified representation.
- To protect against these threats, we assess the effectiveness and capabilities of existing IDS solutions in a marine radar scenario.
- Based on identified limitations, we propose two novel image-based detection approaches to address the gaps in existing Intrusion Detection Systems.

2 Background on Marine Radar Systems

On modern ships, an integrated bridge systems (IBS) combines navigation equipment, controls over steering and propulsion, as well as communication devices in a unified system [3,13] (*cf.* Fig. 1). Typical components include an ECDIS, radar, autopilot, GNSSs, speed logs, gyrocompasses, and AIS. To present a complete picture of the nautical situation to navigators, all these components are interconnected with the help of specialized maritime network protocols such as NMEA 0183 or its IP-based successors IEC 61162-450/460 [14,15], which broadcast updates to the entire network, *e.g.* regular GNSS position updates.

MRSs play a critical role in any IBS as they allow reliably determining the range and bearing to potential hazards, even at night or in adverse weather conditions [8]. Because of radar's importance for collision avoidance, it is mandated by the International Convention for the Safety of Life at Sea (SOLAS) on passenger vessels and any vessel exceeding 300 gross tonnage [32].

Technically, MRSs can be abstracted into three main components [36], *cf.* Fig. 1: First, the transceiver antenna emits short directional electromagnetic pulses and receives the *echo, i.e.* the signal reflection of objects. The measured time difference between the pulse's emission and its echo's reception allows for estimating the distance to the detected object. The echoes of all objects detected by orienting the pulse in a given direction through the rotating antenna constitute a *radar spoke.* Second, a processor unit performs the signal processing. It is typically interconnected to the rest of the IBS to leverage exchanged sensor data, *e.g.* to keep the image in a north-up orientation using data from the gyrocompass. Lastly, the radar display, also called Plot Position Indicator (PPI), is the interface for the operators. It displays the radar image composed of the individual radar spokes and allows settings such as the scan range to be adjusted.

To transmit the radar spokes to the PPI, there exist many vendor-specific network protocols which share common features [36]. In this publication, we will focus on the Navico BR24 radar protocol [11] as it is a simple protocol that still exemplifies the characteristics of most radar communication protocols [36]. Its

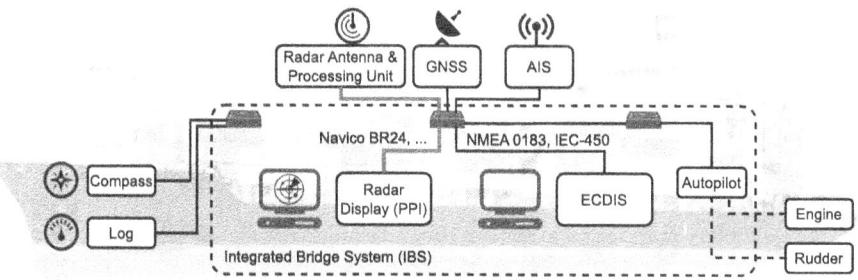

Fig. 1. MRSs, composed of a radar antenna unit and display, are connected via the IBS's backbone network shared with other nautical equipment. Lacking proper preventive measures, the communication path, marked in red, is at risk.

communication is split into three channels, each using a distinct UDP/IP multicast address: (i) the image channel carrying the raw radar image, (ii) the register control channel carrying commands to the processor unit to adjust settings, and (iii) the report channel carrying meta-data from the processor unit [11].

Next, we concentrate on the most important communication channel, the image channel (i). BR24 subdivides the radar image into 2048 scanlines, each corresponding to a radar spoke with a span of about 0.176°. Scanlines are accumulated at the radar processor as generated by the turning radar and sent in aggregates of 32 scanlines per UDP packet. Each scanline carries a header with metadata such as the current angle and the range of the scanline, as well as a payload of 1024 4-bit grayscale pixel values. Rendering each scanline pixel at the proper polar coordinates on the PPI yields the radar image over time. To adjust the image, parameters such as scan range, antenna rotation speed, and processing filters can be modified through the PPI's user interface, which sends the corresponding register messages to the processing unit. For more information, please refer to the publication by Dabrowski *et al.* [11].

Crucially, BR24 and other commonly used protocols lack essential security features, thus making marine radar susceptible to cyberattacks [36]. Figure 2 exemplarily depicts such an attack against the radar image. There, the image is shifted in the direction of travel so that the landmass on the PPI appears further away than it actually is. If carried out skillfully and situationally, *e.g.* during poor visibility, this attack can compromise the safety of vessels.

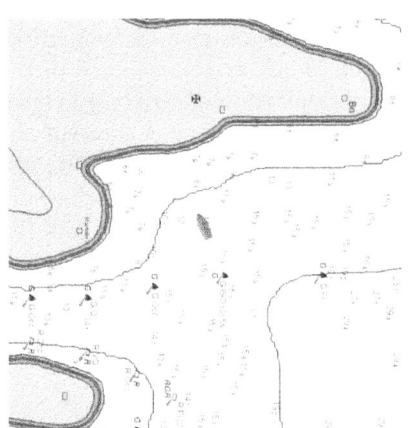
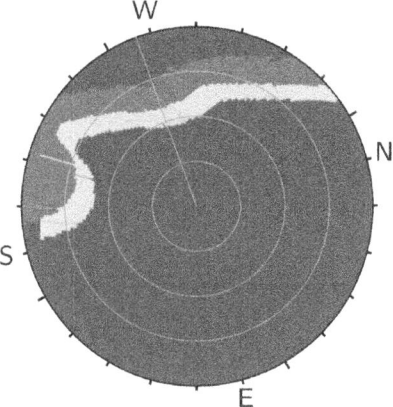

(a) Actual nautical position obtained by GNSS and displayed on the ECDIS.

(b) The shoreline's radar image (yellow) on the PPI is shifted further away (red).

Fig. 2. Exemplary translation attack on the radar image shown by the PPI to the crew to let the shoreline appear further away than it actually is.

3   Cybersecurity for Marine Radar

With the rising awareness of maritime cybersecurity, researchers have begun investigating the vulnerability of MRSs [22,34,36]. In our work, we consider attacks that target the disruption of an MRS for the crew. An elaborated threat model is presented in the following Sect. 3.1. We then lay out different paths to remedy this current situation and state our research question in Sect. 3.2.

3.1   Threat Model

Executing attacks against MRSs is a non-trivial task. Referring to the MaCRA framework [35], we therefore assume any attacker to at least possess the resources of a $Tier_3$ threat actor. Such an attacker has the resources to exploit vulnerabilities to gain access to the IBS and the necessary domain knowledge and testing environments to develop specialized attacks, *i.e.* understanding of protocols in use and the victim's system as a whole. To more precisely specify the threat model MRSs are exposed to, we summarize related work by introducing five axes that distinguish the individual attack types.

0) Attack Type. As proven in related work, MRSs are susceptible to various attack vectors such as hardware- or software-based exploits [34], network attacks [36], and complementary threats from the domain of electronic warfare [22]. In 2020, Svilicic *et al.* conducted an extensive security assessment of radar systems on board two oil tankers [34], detecting many vulnerabilities in their underlying operating system, some of which were critical enough to enable a complete takeover of the system. Likewise, due to the typical lack of confidentiality and authentication mechanisms in the employed communication protocols, attackers may inject malicious commands or image data, as successfully demonstrated for Navico's BR24 protocols [36] or ASTERIX CAT-240 [22,23]. Such attacks can arbitrarily alter the displayed radar image on the PPI and deceive the crew's understanding of the navigational situation (*cf.* Fig. 2).

1) Attack Point. Concerning network-based attacks, which are the focus of this publication, one overarching classification is the attacker's position in the network, *cf.* red path in Fig. 1. In a Machine-on-the-Side (MotS) position, an attacker does not control the communication channel between processor and PPI, and can merely eavesdrop and inject packets. Machine-in-the-Middle (MitM) situation, the attacker has complete control over the communication channel and can prevent messages exchanged between processor and PPI from reaching their destination. The capabilities of MitM depend on the exact position of the attacker in the IBS topology. This publication considers an attacker isolating the PPI from the network with complete control over both the radar system's communication and all the NMEA 0183 traffic exchanged with the PPI.

2) Communication Channel. MRSs have multiple communication channels (*cf.* Sect. 2), *e.g.* the radar image stream, a control channel from the PPI to the radar unit, or a return channel for reports about the radar's state. These channels can all be individually attacked. Generally, the implementation details

of attacks against any channel heavily depend on the radar communication protocol used, the exact layout of the system, and the installed hardware.

3) Manipulation Type. Diving deeper into the attacks against the radar
image, prior work distinguished between three main types of image manipulation [36]. *Denial of Service (DoS)* attacks deny using the radar image, *e.g.* by
blanking the screen. *Transformation* attacks apply geometrical transformations
to the image, affecting the bearing (rotation) or range (scaling) of plotted echoes.
Object manipulation attacks alter the echoes of objects by (re)moving legitimate
echoes or adding artificial ones, *e.g.* to mimic buoys or other vessels.

4) Stealthiness. This axis concerns the degree to which the attack is con-
ceived to remain undetected. On a technical level, mechanisms, such as source
address spoofing, can be implemented to evade trivial protection measures. But,
also the image manipulations itself can be conducted instantaneously, stealthily
over time, or even be supported by external sensor information. For the latter, an attacker needs complementary information about the navigational situation to enhance the effect of their attacks [36]. This might include knowledge
about visibility conditions, time of the day, or position of surrounding vessels
reported by AIS to tailor an attack precisely to a challenging navigation situation. Another avenue is exploiting knowledge of the vessel's speed and turn rate
reported over NMEA 0183 to discreetly manipulate the radar image's orientation during dynamic maneuvers, where minor discrepancies might be harder to
notice [36].

3.2   Methods for Securing Marine Radar

Considering the spectrum of attacks, effective countermeasures are urgently
needed. Optimally, preventive measures such as message authentication address
the cause of the current threats. But in their absence or as additional security
measure for defense-in-depth, we focus on detective measures in this publication.

An IDS alerts the crew about (ongoing) attacks. Since past cyberattacks
against MRSs are currently either not documented or of solely academic nature,
we cannot assume that sufficient samples of attacks exist to train an IDS. Hence,
we consider unsupervised IDSs trained on benign data to obtain a model of
normality. Anomalies, *i.e.* any deviation from these models, are considered an
attack.

Naturally, there exists a vast body of commercial and academic IDS solutions.
In this work, we consider four major classes: i) *rule-based* IDSs matching packets
against a set of rules [31], ii) *timing-based* IDSs, *e.g.* measuring packets' inter-
arrival times [21], iii) IDSs leveraging *machine-learning* to learn complex network
patterns [24], and iv) IDSs that analyze the *application layer* data [23,37], such
as the radar image in our context. However, given the broad threat model, we
believe that a single IDS is unlikely to adequately capture all attack vectors.
Thus, our research question is:

*Which existing IDS solutions are best suited for protecting MRSs, and where
do novel approaches need to be developed to fill in the gaps?*

4 Measurement Setup

To tackle the research question, we apply a selection of existing IDSs to marine radar network traffic and measure their capabilities. This section first details our considered attacks in Sect. 4.1. Then, we present the RadarSec-Lab environment and the IDS framework with which we conduct the experiments in Sect. 4.2.

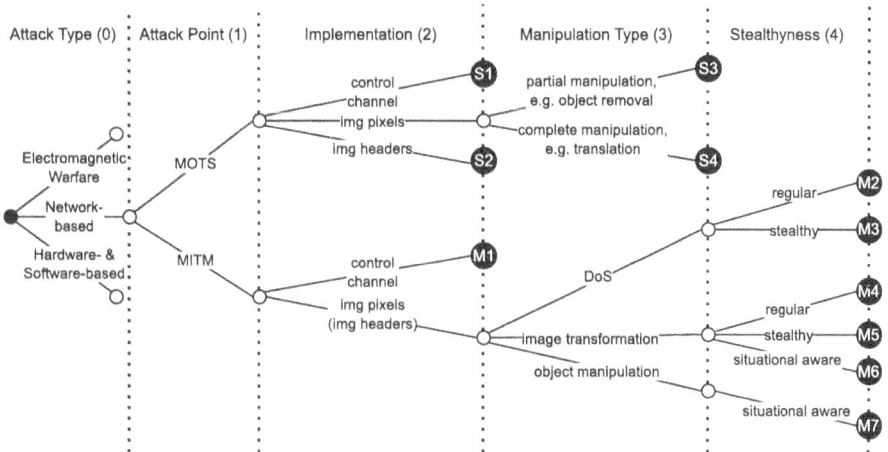

Fig. 3. Selection of network-based attack vectors which we consider in this publication. We include four MotS attacks (S1–S4) and seven MitM attacks (M1–M7).

4.1 Attack Vectors

Combining all axes from Sect. 3.1, a considerable number of attack vectors can be envisioned, especially because axis 4), stealthiness, is versatile. Thus, we restrict our analyses to a meaningful and reasonably sized subset, as listed in Fig. 3, and prune the attack classification tree accordingly. In the following, we briefly discuss our decisions for this selection.

For the attack point axis (1), we consider both variants, MotS and MitM. Regarding the implementation axis (2), our selection depends on the protocol that we analyze. Since Navico BR24 contains explicit control channels between the radar unit and PPI, *cf.* Sect. 2, we distinguish between hijacking the control channel and manipulating the image directly through the streamed pixels or indirectly through image headers. Note that we omit the latter when considering MitM attacks since manipulating a scanline's angle in the packet header or on image-level results in the same effect on the PPI. The manipulation type axis (3) is only meaningful when considering image pixel manipulation. In the MotS case, we distinguish between attacks manipulating the whole image and those only affecting a small number of pixels, as they might influence communication timings differently. The complete distinction between all options is only made in the MitM case. Similarly, variants along the stealthiness axis (4) are only considered for MitM image manipulation to yield the most challenging scenarios. Here, we differentiate between regular stealthiness implementing just source address spoofing, stealthier attacks that apply modifications gradually over time, and even ones leveraging information exchanged via NMEA 0183 to be situational aware, *i.e.* to rotate the image during a maneuver. These eleven attack classes cover a considerable extent of the possible attack vectors that promise to be challenging for IDSs to detect.

4.2   RadarSec-Lab Environment and IDS Framework

Given the attack definition, we still need tools to tackle our research question. First, a simulation environment to implement the derived attacks and second, a selection of IDSs for which we examine their effectiveness, *cf.* Fig. 4.

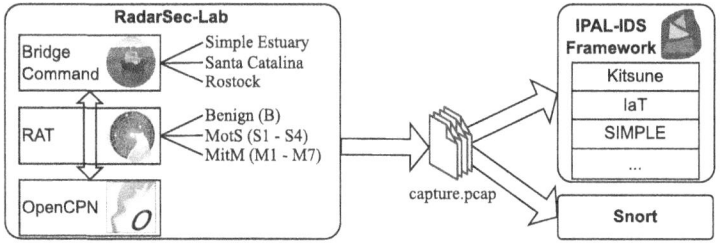

Fig. 4. We utilize the RadarSec-Lab [36] environment, the IPAL IDS framework [38], and Snort [31] to examine the effectiveness of IDSs in a marine radar environment.

Simulation. While conducting our research with a real MRS system would be preferable, we choose a simulation environment for scientific reproducibility and comparability in the future. The RadarSec-Lab was specifically designed to support marine radar cybersecurity research [5,36]. It simulates Navico BR24 radar communication by combining a customized version of the Bridge Command [26] ship simulator with OpenCPN [25], an open-source ECDIS. Finally, the Radar Attack Tool (RAT) [36] carries out various network-based attacks against BR24. In RAT, we added the capability to also conduct MotS attacks.

RadarSec-Lab generates a dataset for the training and evaluation of IDSs. We record one packet capture for each attack type, including a benign scenario without attacks (B). Descriptions of each attack can be found in Table 1 and at https://zenodo.org/records/7188636/files/README.md. Each capture lasts 1100 seconds and contains a randomized number of attacks with randomized duration with at least 70 seconds of benign traffic separating two consecutive attacks. Parameterizable attacks have randomized settings, *e.g.* the angle by which the radar image is rotated or the time it takes to ramp up the rotation to increase stealthiness. Finally, to evaluate environment-specific effects, each scenario is run in three simulated worlds available in RadarSec-Lab (Simple Estuary, Santa Catalina, and Rostock) each with a different type of vessel and with three repetitions (six in the case of scenario B). The resulting dataset contains 117 packet captures, covering all 12 attack scenarios (B, S1–S4, and M1–M7) and totaling about 36 h of simulation.

Table 1. Description of our attack scenarios provided by RAT.

Scen.	Description
B	MRS operates normally without attacks.
S1	Commands the radar to be turned off.
S2	Modifies the protocol header to rotate the radar image.
S3	Adds fake vessels and removes existing vessels from the radar image.
S4	Distort the radar image (random, blank screen, shift image).
M1	Commands the radar to be turned off.
M2	Distort the radar image (random, blank screen, static overlay)
M3	Freezes the radar image to the last received image.
M4	Scales, rotates, or shifts the radar image instantaneously.
M5	Scales, rotates, or shifts the radar image slowly over time.
M6	Scales, rotates, or shifts the image disguised in the vessels movements.
M7	Adds fake vessels and removes existing vessels from the radar image.

Experiment. The packet captures serve as input for the evaluation of various IDSs, including Snort [31] and IDSs of the IPAL IDS framework[1] [38], which offers a plethora of validated (re-)implementation of established IDSs, *cf.* Fig. 4. To train them, we use one benign scenario of the Simple Estuary environment as the training dataset and the second benign repetition of Simple Estuary to adjust the IDSs' sensitivity. Our configuration goal is to minimize the amount of false positives to avoid disrupting the crew during normal operations.

Metrics. To measure the e IDSs' effectiveness, we leverage three metrics. First, we consider an attack to be detected if an alarm is raised during its execution and state the fraction of successfully detected attacks. Second, the false positive rate (FPR) metric counts the number of false positives relative to the number of benign packets. Lastly, an IDS should also ideally detect anomalous behavior in a timely manner. Therefore, we also consider the average time to first detection (TTD). Every metric is calculated individually for each of the twelve attack types but counting all three environments and three repetitions.

---

[1] For the IPAL framework, we added support for the considered Navico BR24 network protocol, *cf.* https://github.com/fkie-cad/ipal_transcriber.

```
alert udp any any    > any 6680 (   :"RadarOps A disabled";
        content:"|00 C1 00|";  depth:3;  sid:6680;)
alert udp any any    > any 6680 (   :"RadarOps B disabled";
        content:"|01 C1 00|";  depth:3;  sid:6681;)
alert udp any any    > any 6678 (   :"Duplicate scanline";
        content:"|00 44 0D 0E 00 00 34 92|";
        threshold:type both,track by_dst,   2,seconds 1;  sid:6678;)
```

Listing 1.1: Our Snort rules for Navico BR24. Rule 1 and Rule 2 alert on setting the MRS to standby, while Rule 3 detects too frequent occurrences of a scanline.

5 Effectiveness of Existing IDSs Adapted to MRS

We now assess which IDS direction of existing works proves promising in detecting which attack type. To this end, Sect. 5.1 introduces the four IDSs used in our analyses, and Sect. 5.2 shows their strengths and deficiencies in protecting MRSs.

5.1 IDS Selection

Research has proposed plenty of IDSs to differentiate benign and malicious behavior. Given the four directions introduced in Sect. 3.2, we select one representative for each and present their core idea as well as how they transfer to MRS

Rule-Based (Snort). A rule-based IDS, such as the prominent software Snort [31] considered here, monitors network traffic and inspects packets for patterns associated with known malware strains and attacks, matching their header and content against a set of rules. Unsurprisingly, a naive application of existing rules, *e.g.* defaults included with the Debian Snort package, is ineffective in detecting any attack in our data. Thus, we exemplarily develop custom rules for Navico BR24 as depicted in Listing 1.1. The first two rules match packets with register commands disabling the radar unit. Rule 3 instead defines a constraint on benign behavior. It assumes a maximum rotation speed on the radar antenna, expecting a scanline with a specific angle to be received not earlier than a certain time threshold (one second here) after the previous one.

Timing-Based (IaT). A second IDS considers the inter-arrival time (IaT) between network packets, leveraging the periodicity of network traffic and raising an alarm when deviations exceed pre-determined thresholds [21]. To this end, IaT's model estimates the mean μ and standard deviation σ of the underlying IaT distribution. These values are the basis of the model's upper and lower thresholds defined as $\mu \pm N\sigma$, where N is a user-defined sensitivity threshold, which we adjust to achieve no false positives on the training data. In the marine radar context, this IDS constructs a model for the radar image stream. Since the rotation speed of the radar antenna is constant, the network packets delivering the image step-by-step are assumed to occur regularly.

Machine-Learning (Kitsune). From the domain of machine-learning, Kitsune is a widely used general-purpose network IDS [24]. It trains artificial neural networks to perform anomaly detection on network traffic. The IDS's ability to apply to any UDP or TCP traffic makes it an interesting candidate. Internally, Kitsune keeps track of multiple features, such as the bandwidth or IaT, and calculates an anomaly score, the Root Mean Square Error (RMSE). The user defines a threshold upon which an alert is raised for each packet exceeding it.

Application-Layer (Steadytime). The last IDS monitors application data, *i.e.* the payload of network packets, which in our case contains the radar image and control commands. Steadytime [37] assumes that monitored features regularly change, such as the radar angle changing with each transmitted radar spoke. It measures the time a feature remains static and compares it to the minimal and maximal static time seen during training. More concretely, we select the following radar features: i) the scanline counter and angle values, as these should change regularly between each transmitted packet, and ii) the sum of each image frame's first scanline's pixels and the sum of pixels in scanlines with angle 0, since given natural noise, perfectly static images can be considered anomalous.

Table 2. Performance of existing IDSs in a MRS context. No IDS raises a false alarm in the benign scenario (B), and they reliably detect the MotS attacks (S1–S4) yet struggle to detect MitM attacks, especially those targeting the radar image.

	Metric	B	S1	S2	S3	S4	M1	M2	M3	M4	M5	M6	M7
Snort	Det. Attacks [%]	–	100	100	100	100	0	2.2	2.3	4.7	2.2	0	7.1
	FPR [%]	0	0	0	0	0	0	0	0	0	0	0	0
	Mean TTD [s]	–	0	1.8	1.2	1.3	–	11.4	1.7	12.3	1.7	–	35.8
IaT	Det. Attacks [%]	–	0	100	100	100	0	0	0	0	0	0	0
	FPR [%]	0	9.0	4.5	4.3	4.3	9.1	0	0	0	0	0	0
	Mean TTD [s]	–	0	3.0	3.1	3.1	–	–	–	–	–	–	–
Kitsune	Det. Attacks [%]	–	100	100	100	100	100	8.9	2.3	0	2.2	0	0
	FPR [%]	0	29.3	6.6	6.2	6.2	27.4	0	0	0	0	0	0
	Mean TTD [s]	–	3.5	0.5	0.5	0.5	4.0	18.4	6.2	–	6.0	–	–
Steadyt.	Det. Attacks [%]	–	0	100	100	100	0	60.0	100	7.0	2.2	9.1	4.8
	FPR [%]	0	0	0	0.1	0.1	0	1.5	1.6	0	0	0	0
	Mean TTD [s]	–	–	0	0.1	0	–	7.4	62.6	20.8	9.4	22.8	19.8

5.2   Evaluation

Applying the IDSs to the recorded data, we obtain the results depicted in Table 2. First, we observe that all IDSs' FPR is 0.00 % if no attacks are present, *cf.*

column B. This is interesting as we trained only on the Simple Estuary world but evaluated in all three worlds. We therefore conclude that no IDS is sensitive to environmental changes in terms of false positives. However, regarding the detected attacks, we find a clear distinction between MotS (S1–S4) and MitM (M1–M7).

The MotS attacks are detected remarkably well by all approaches, except for IaT and Steadytime failing to detect S1. Since S1 deactivates the radar, the IDSs emit the alerts too late namely when the radar is activated again. Next, the TTD is small with 0 to 3.1 s, which is in the order of one full rotation of the radar (about 2.4 s in RadarSec-Lab). During attack conditions, the FPR is generally higher than during benign behavior. While Snort and Steadytime still feature a FPR of 0 to 0.11 % in MotS attacks, IaT and Kitsune reach levels of up to 29.3 %. Both IDSs make use of window mechanisms, where past packets factor into the classification of the current packet, leading to trailing false positives.

This effect is particularly pronounced at the end of attacks in scenario S1, where the resumption of the image stream after a long interruption causes a notable jump in the IDSs' anomaly scores. Figure 5 depicts this phenomenon exemplarily for Kitsune. During attacks the anomaly score (blue curve) steadily rises in absence of packets. At the end of each attack when the radar image stream resumes, the jitter on that communication channel causes a notable jump in the anomaly score, leading to trailing false positives (yellow marker).

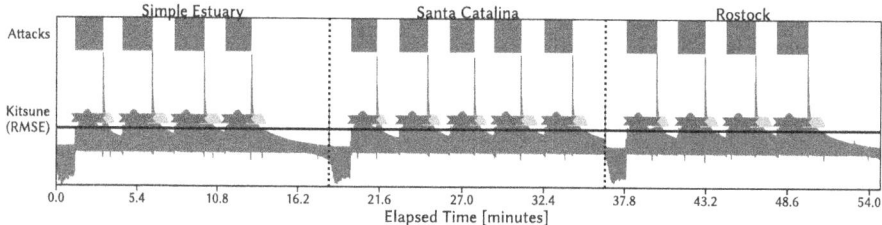

Fig. 5. Performance of Kitsune on the S1 scenario. Attacks are highlighted in red, whereas alerts are indicated with purple (true alert) and yellow (false alert) markers. The blue curve depicts Kitsune's anomaly score, and the black line is the alert threshold. (Color figure online)

We deem these false positive rates to be acceptable due to the approaches' excellent FPR results in the absence of attacks (B). Interestingly, the Snort rules outperform the more complex IDSs but require understanding the protocol's packet format, and might fail in a more dynamic or noise-prone environment.

Despite these promising results, MitM attacks are, for the most part, not reliably detected. The purely network-based IDSs, Snort and IaT, fail to detect any attack sufficiently or do so just by chance. Kitsune can still detect M1, in which the traffic volume drops dramatically in the absence of the transmission of image data, as one of the features Kitsune monitors is the per-host bandwidth. Steadytime, as it also considers the application layer, *i.e.* the transmitted radar image, detects M2 and M3, where the radar image is static. But, this could trivially be circumvented by attackers by adding noise to the image.

Takeaway. Tying back to our research questions, existing IDSs are suitable for MRSs as they effectively detect MotS attacks while raising no false alarms during benign operations. However, it turns out that it is not feasible to detect the broad class of MotS attacks, especially those that change the radar image.

6   Radar-Specific Approaches

Having identified a lack of detection capabilities for MitM attacks, we develop two novel IDSs designed to detect anomalies in the displayed radar image. First, we present and evaluate *Image-Delta*, a rather simple approach (Sect. 6.1), and then consider the more complex *Chart-Diff*, based on nautical charts (Sect. 6.2).

6.1   Radar Image-Delta IDS

According to the International Maritime Organization (IMO), MRS must scan their environment at a rate of no less than 12 rpm [16]. At typical vessel velocities, movement in the short interval between two full radar scans should yield only small differences in consecutive images. In contrast, image manipulation attacks introduce sudden changes, especially if they alter the entire image, *cf.* [36]. Hence, *Image-Delta* determines the amount of change, the *delta*, between subsequent images and raises an alarm if the observed change exceeds the acceptable range.

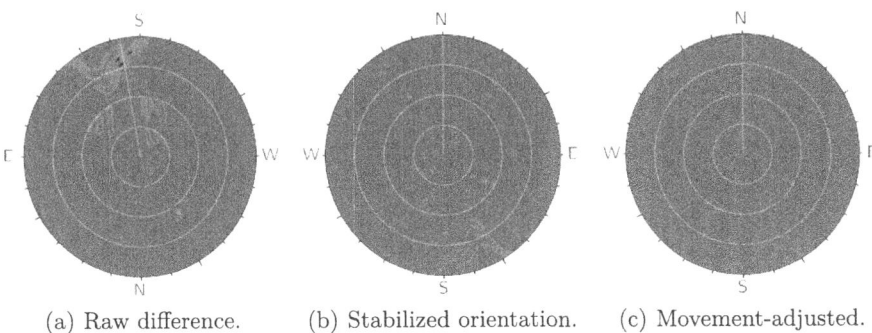

(a) Raw difference.   (b) Stabilized orientation.   (c) Movement-adjusted.

Fig. 6. Stabilizing radar images with the vessel's position and orientation from NMEA 0183 enables *Image-Delta* to remove legitimate differences in the images.

Because most of the difference between two consecutive images is expected to be caused by the vessel's movement (translation and rotation), *Image-Delta* leverages NMEA 1803 reports for compensation, raising the sensitivity of the detector as shown in Fig. 6. The stabilization adds the current heading to each scanline's angle to ensure a north-up orientation, *cf.* Fig. 6(b). Then, each pixel is offset by the recent movement of the vessel reducing even more legitimate differences between the figures, *cf.* fewer red echoes in Fig. 6(c). As a final step, we minimize the influence of noise with a Gaussian blur filter. The difference between all pixel values, *cf.* red parts in Fig. 6(c), is summed up and divided by the total value of pixels occurring in both images, giving a relative change between the images (δ). Scaling the delta in such a manner normalizes the final value, making it independent from radar specifics such as resolution, and reducing the influence of environmental factors such as the prevalence of landmasses.

Finally, this delta serves as the basis for the detection mechanism. During training on the Simple Estuary world, we measure the maximum δ, which multiplied by a sensitivity parameter serves as the detection threshold. During detection, a δ value exceeding the threshold causes an alert.

Table 3. *Image-Delta* outperforms existing IDSs regarding MitM but struggles in sophisticated attacks and performs worse in previously unseen environments.

Metric	B	S1	S2	S3	S4	M1	M2	M3	M4	M5	M6	M7
Det. Attacks [%]	–	0	44.4	0	47.7	0	75.6	61.4	100	31.1	15.9	7.1
FPR [%]	0	0.3	0.6	0	0.8	0.3	1.5	1.9	1.4	1.6	1.1	0.1
Mean TTD [s]	–	–	2.1	–	1.9	–	1.6	7.1	3.0	17.0	14.4	6.9

Results. We subject *Image-Delta* to the same evaluation as before, *cf.* Table 3. Again, we validate the absence of false positives across all benign scenarios B. The purely image-based IDS performs worse in MotS scenarios S1 and S3, where no or little manipulation of the image occurs. Still, substantial modifications to the image (S2 and S4) are detected. As *Image-Delta's* goal is to address the shortcomings of existing IDSs, we focus on the MitM scenarios below.

Scenarios in which *Image-Delta* performs best are those where the image changes rapidly, *i.e.* blanking or randomly overwriting the radar image (M2), freezing the image (M3), or suddenly scaling, rotating, or translating it (M4). The attack types less reliably detected are those that implement mechanisms to increase stealthiness, *i.e.* applying image modifications slowly over time (M5) or scaled with the vessel's measured movements (M6). Note that switching off the radar (M1) is also not detected as no new radar images are generated. Lastly, missing the vast majority of attacks of M7, *Image-Delta* proves ineffective in this scenario. Only the echoes of single ships are manipulated, which is largely indistinguishable to the IDS from noise or inaccuracies in the stabilization and movement compensation process.

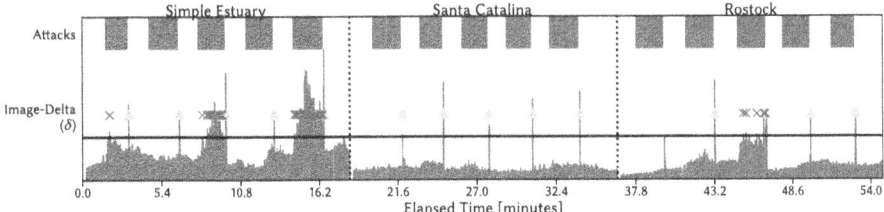

Fig. 7. Performance of *Image-Delta* on the M5 scenario. Attacks are highlighted in red, whereas alerts are indicated with purple (true alert) and yellow (false alert) markers. The blue curve depicts *Image-Delta*'s anomaly score, and the black line is the alert threshold. Note that the false positives at the end of attacks are caused by the sudden return to the unmodified image, resulting in a large delta in all cases. (Color figure online)

Concentrating on the stealthy attacks from M5 in the Simple Estuary world, which was used for training, the IDS detects 9 of the 15 attacks. But the detection performance is diminished on the other two scenarios (Santa Catalina and Rostock), *cf.* Fig. 7. *Image-Delta*'s performance depends on features of surrounding landmasses. Both benign changes and those caused by the attacker's gradual manipulation of the image are much more pronounced in Simple Estuary, causing the learned detection threshold to be inadequate for the two other environments. Depending on training conditions, the IDS can therefore be expected to underperform or cause false positives in unseen environments, a serious impediment to real-world applicability of the approach.

Lastly, we examine the real-time performance of *Image-Delta* as it has to handle large streams of uncompressed radar images. To this end, we measure the processing time for a single run of packet parsing and the detection methodology on a Intel i7-1365U CPU with 16GB of RAM. Parsing an 18.3 minutes long PCAP consisting of 362 724 packets takes about 7.9 minutes, in large part due to the slow pyshark library. Our prototypical and unoptimized implementation of *Image-Delta* processes the parsed PCAP in 6.4 minutes. We therefore consider the approach to be feasible in processing Navico BR24 traffic in real time.

Takeaway. In contrast to previous IDSs, *Image-Delta* effectively detects sudden overlaying and transformation of the radar image even in MitM scenarios. It is significantly less effective in stealthier, gradual variants of the attacks, and inadequate in detecting object manipulation attacks targeting relatively small objects such as ship echoes. One drawback is that its performance can depend on terrain features, *e.g.* the jagged landscape of Simple Estuary represents more opportunities for both benign inaccuracies and deliberate manipulation of the image to increase the anomaly score than the two other simulated world's smoothly rising land. As a result of training *Image-Delta* on the Simple Estuary world, it is therefore not sufficiently sensitive for the two other environments.

6.2   Radar Chart-Diff IDS

Our second IDS aims to improve *Image-Delta*'s lack of environmental aware-ness. The main idea is to obtain some ground truth about the environment, *i.e.* landmasses or buoys, from a trusted source. Since IBSs are obligated to have regularly updated, accurate digital charts on board for the areas in which the ship operates, these can be correlated with the radar image. Hence, the idea is to overlap the radar image with the charts and measure their difference.

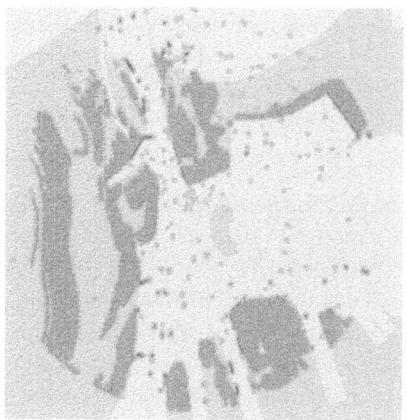
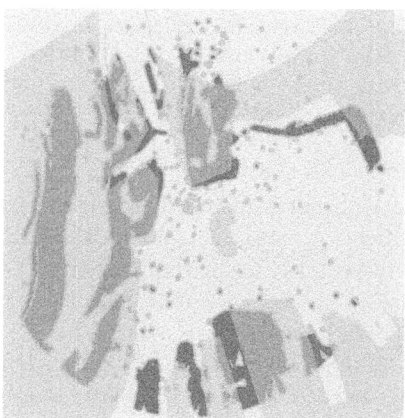

(a) Normal condition.   (b) Anomalous condition (rotated).

Fig. 8. *Chart-Diff* counts the amount of invalid radar echoes (red) that do not cor-respond to the landmasses (gray). Weak echoes are attenuated through the filtering process and discarded as noise (orange), improving the sensitivity of the detector. (Color figure online)

For that purpose, *Chart-Diff* considers each radar echo independently. If an echo's position corresponds to a location that is marked as a landmass on the chart, this pixel is considered valid, *cf.* green pixels in Fig. 8(a). Note that not every pixel on the radar image representing landmasses must contain an echo since landmasses may be shadowed, *e.g.* through mountains. In contrast, invalid (non-verifiable) echoes can fall into four categories for which ground truth is hard to obtain: other vessels, uncharted objects, inaccuracies, or noise. Although information about other vessels can be obtained from AIS, not all ves-sels are equipped with AIS. Also, AIS signals could be tampered by sophisticated attackers [4], and indeed RAT already manipulates them appropriately [36]. Like-wise, uncharted objects or remaining inaccuracies cannot be predicted. Still, we apply a Gaussian blur filter to the image to find and ignore small or weak echoes resulting from noise, *cf.* orange pixels in Fig. 8(b). For detection, *Chart-Diff* learns the maximum proportion of invalid pixels, *i.e.* red pixels, during normal conditions. If an attack tampers with the radar image, *e.g.* rotating it, we expect the number of invalid pixels to increase and exceed the normal maximum, *cf.* Fig. 8(b).

Table 4. *Chart-Diff* is capable of detecting sophisticated manipulations such as translation, or rotation, by having more information available about the area from charts.

Metric	B	S1	S2	S3	S4	M1	M2	M3	M4	M5	M6	M7
Det. Attacks [%]	–	0	100	0	61.4	0	46.7	95.5	81.4	84.4	56.8	2.38
FPR [%]	0	0	0	0	0	0	0	0	0	0	0	0
Mean TTD [s]	–	–	4.6	–	3.9	–	3.2	25.4	7.3	26.2	20.8	9.7

Results. Like *Image-Delta*, *Chart-Diff* is also unable to detect S1, S3, and M1, but performs better in S4, M3, M5, and M6, especially in the scenarios we aimed to improve, such as M5, where the detection rate increases from 31.1 % to 84.4 %. *Chart-Diff* even makes great progress on M6, containing the stealthiest image manipulations conducted during vessel maneuvers, *e.g.* rotating the radar image while the vessel is turning. Lastly, leveraging ground truth from the charts reduces environment-specific influences on the anomaly score: unlike *Image-Delta*'s, surrounding landmasses' features may vary widely as long as the accuracy of the charts remains comparable. In scenario M6 we nonetheless find *Chart-Diff* to underperform in the Santa Catalina world. There, the vessel's few course changes and the relatively short duration of attacks do not provide enough opportunity for the attacker to cause significant rotation of the image. Translation in the direction of travel is also largely undetected as the vessel moves parallel to a relatively straight shoreline of this world.

We again measure the computational performance of our newly proposed IDS with the same methodology as for *Image-Delta*, *cf.* Sect. 6.1. *Chart-Diff* takes 5.7 minutes to process the 18.3 minutes long PCAP thereby being slightly faster than *Image-Delta*. Again, this IDS proves promising for time detection in real-time.

Takeaway. As an alternative radar-specific IDS, *Chart-Diff* outperforms *Image-Delta* on stealthier attacks. Additionally, one advantage of *Chart-Diff* is that its alerts can be visualized to the crew, *e.g.* by highlighting suspicious echos once an alert is raised, *cf.* Fig. 8. Thereby, navigators can validate and reflect the ongoing situation and assess it themselves if necessary.

7   Discussion

Closing our analyses, we present related work and summarize the state of intrusion detection for MRS in Sect. 7.1. Finally, we discuss limitations in Sect. 7.2.

7.1   Related Work and Lessons Learned

Detecting anomalies in radar data caused by cyberattacks has been recently tackled in the aerospace sector [10,20,29,30]. Yet, these works conceptually differ from challenges of the maritime domain as they consider (pre-)processed flight paths of tracked objects in a stationary setting, whereas vessels are constantly changing their location. Beyond tracking ships, navigators are likewise interested in perceiving landmasses. In the maritime domain, radar images combined with charts have been utilized for localization and detection of GNSS tampering [12], similar to *Chart-Diff*, but with a different purpose. The only directly related work we found is presented by Longo *et al.* [23], who propose a policy-based IDS for the ASTERIX CAT-240 radar protocol in a maritime scenario. Their policies enforce a constant rotation speed and a strict monotonicity of message identifiers, which is analogous to detecting the maliciously injected duplicates of image frames in the MotS scenarios S2–S4.

Table 5. Our evaluation on the effectiveness of IDSs reveals that MotS attacks are reliably detectable by established IDSs while lagging in MitM scenarios. Set out to remedy this situation, *Image-Delta* and *Chart-Diff* make progress in that direction, yet still leave room for improvement in the most sophisticated attacks (M6 and M7).

IDS	S1	S2	S3	S4	M1	M2	M3	M4	M5	M6	M7
Snort [31]	✓	✓	✓	✓	✗	✗	✗	✗	✗	✗	✗
IaT [21]	✗	✓	✓	✓	✗	✗	✗	✗	✗	✗	✗
Kitsune [24]	✓	✓	✓	✓	✓	✗	✗	✗	✗	✗	✗
Steadytime [37]	✗	✓	✓	✓	✗	(✓)	✓	✗	✗	✗	✗
Longo *et al.* [23]	✗	✓	✓	✓	✗	✗	✗	✗	✗	✗	✗
Image-Delta	✗	(✓)	✗	(✓)	✗	✓	✓	✓	(✓)	(✓)	✗
Chart-Diff	✗	✓	✗	(✓)	✗	(✓)	✓	✓	✓	(✓)	✗

In a final assessment, shown in Table 5, we summarize the effectiveness of each IDS for the individual attack vectors. In addition to our experiments, we take the results of Longo *et al.* [23] into account, yet marked as grey since we transferred their results to our attack taxonomy without extra evaluations. Concerning our analyses of existing approaches and related work (upper and middle part of Table 5), we conclude that MRS can be effectively protected against MotS attacks using existing IDS approaches when adapted to radar network traffic. Set out to address the gap in MitM attacks, novel radar-specific, image-based IDSs such as *Image-Delta* or *Chart-Diff* provide a remedy in these situations especially for attacks M2–M5. But they still struggle with stealthy attacks that are carefully executed by sophisticated adversaries. Attacks modifying individual echoes, such as a nearby vessel (M7), are currently not covered by any approach. In conclusion, considering the pros and cons of each approach considered in our evaluation, currently, only a combination of multiple IDSs promises effective protection MRSs against most attacks.

7.2   Limitations and Future Work

As a simulation environment, RadarSec-Lab offers the possibility of scientifically reproducible experiments, but falls short in replicating user-induced behavior of real seafarers. Thus, we have not yet considered such behavior, *e.g.* changing the radar resolution or scanned ranges. Our environment also has two other technical limitations. First, while the network traffic patterns are largely comparable to a real network, RadarSec-Lab supports only one of many network protocols (Navico BR24). Still, according to prior work, MRS protocols from different vendors are relatively similar [36]. Second, the radar echoes simulated by Bridge Command lack realism, since compared to real MRS they are of lower resolution, overly sharp, and only approximate physical effects such as reflectivity.

With regard to a deployment of Radar-IDSs, future work still faces challenges. First, we trained and evaluated with little data compared to vessels that operate for weeks. Second, beyond detection performance, giving appropriate advice to the crew about the MRS's state is crucial to be of actual benefit, as proposed in [28]. Here, *Chart-Diff* IDS may be a first step in that direction, *cf.* Fig. 8. Next, the issue of verifying other vessels and AIS signals persists. While Katsilieris *et al.* [18] have validated AIS signals with radar echoes, nowadays both sources have to be considered vulnerable. Finally, the most significant conceptual issue of image-based IDSs is that these are mainly suited for coastal regions. In open waters, where there are virtually no reference signals to determine whether the image is altered, detecting anomalies is much more difficult. This scenario as well as coordinated attacks simultaneously targeting multiple IBS components, *i.e.* radar, AIS, and NMEA 0183, are a challenging field for future research.

8   Conclusion

Modern vessels' integrated bridge systems (IBSs) and thus also their radar systems have experienced increased interconnectivity leading to new cybersecurity challenges. In this publication, we explored the approach of anomaly detection as one possible defense-in-depth solution for protecting the Marine Radar System (MRS). To this end, we evaluated a representative selection of existing approaches and, moreover, presented two novel domain-specific detectors tailored to MRS. Our results show potential for the application of Intrusion Detection Systems (IDSs) for MRS to remedy the current situation. Even if the resilience of MRS network protocols to cyber attacks will be hardened preventively, radar-image-based IDSs could still be beneficial to thwart attacks from the electromagnetic warfare vector. Therefore, the novel detectors we have introduced in this paper promise great value for future systems.

Acknowledgments. This work is part of the project MUM2 and was partially funded by the German Federal Ministry of Economic Affairs and Climate Action (BMWK) with contract number 03SX543B managed by the Project Management Jülich (PTJ). The authors are responsible for the publication's contents. The authors would like to thank Frederik Basels for evaluating the computational performance of the IDSs.

Disclosure of Interests. The authors have no competing interests to declare that are relevant to the content of this article.

References

1. Amro, A., et al.: From click to sink: Utilizing ais for command and control in maritime cyber attacks. In: ESORICS (2022). https://doi.org/10.1007/978-3-031-17143-7_26
2. Amro, A., et al.: Navigation data anomaly analysis and detection. Information **13**(3) (2022). https://doi.org/10.3390/info13030104
3. Awan, M.S.K., et al.: Understanding the Vulnerabilities in Digital Components of an Integrated Bridge System (IBS). JMSE **7**(10) (2019). https://doi.org/10.3390/jmse7100350
4. Balduzzi, M., et al.: A security evaluation of AIS automated identification system. In: ACSAC (2014). https://doi.org/10.1145/2664243.2664257
5. Basels, F., et al.: Demo: Maritime radar systems under attack. Help is on the way! In: IEEE LCN (2024). https://doi.org/10.1109/LCN60385.2024.10639793
6. Bauer, J., et al.: Phish & Ships and Other Delicacies from the Cuisine of Maritime Cyber Attacks. In: MARESEC (2023). https://doi.org/10.5281/zenodo.8406034
7. Bhatti, J., et al.: Hostile control of ships via false GPS signals: demonstration and detection. J. Institute of Nav. **64**(1) (2017). https://doi.org/10.1002/navi.183
8. Bole, A., et al.: Radar and ARPA Manual – Radar and Target Tracking for Professional Mariners, Yachtsmen and Users of Marine Radar. Butterworth-Heinemann Ltd, 2nd edn. (2009)
9. Caprolu, M., et al.: Vessels cybersecurity: issues, challenges, and the road ahead. IEEE Commun. Mag. **58**(6) (2020). https://doi.org/10.1109/MCOM.001.1900632
10. Cohen, S., et al.: RadArnomaly: protecting radar systems from data manipulation attacks. Sensors **22**(11) (2022). https://doi.org/10.3390/s22114259
11. Dabrowski, A., et al.: A digital interface for imagery and control of a Navico/Lowrance broadband radar. In: Robotic Sailing (2011). https://doi.org/10.1007/978-3-642-22836-0_12
12. Dagdilelis, D., et al.: Cyber-resilience for marine navigation by information fusion and change detection. Ocean Eng. **266** (2022). https://doi.org/10.1016/j.oceaneng.2022.112605
13. Hemminghaus, C., et al.: BRAT: a bridge attack tool for cyber security assessments of maritime systems. TransNav **15**(1) (2021). https://doi.org/10.12716/1001.15.01.02
14. IEC 61162-450:2018: Maritime navigation and radiocommunication equipment and systems – Digital interfaces – Part 450: Multiple talkers and multiple listeners – Ethernet interconnection (2018)
15. IEC 61162-460:2018: Maritime navigation and radiocommunication equipment and systems – Digital interfaces – Part 460: Multiple talkers and multiple listeners – Ethernet interconnection – Safety and security (2018)
16. IMO Resolution A.477(12): Performance Standards for Radar Equipment. Resolution, International Maritime Organization (1982)
17. Katsikas, S., et al.: Chapter: Cybersecurity of the Unmanned Ship. Cybersecurity Issues in Emerging Technologies, Taylor & Francis Group, 1st edn. (2021)
18. Katsilieris, F., et al.: Detection of malicious AIS position spoofing by exploiting radar information. In: FUSION (2013)

19. Kavallieratos, G., et al.: Modelling shipping 4.0: a reference architecture for the cyber-enabled ship. In: ACIIDS (2020)
20. Krim Rahaoui, A., et al.: Adaptive threshold for anomaly detection in ATM radar data streams. In: ICPRAI (2022). https://doi.org/10.1007/978-3-031-09282-4_36
21. Lin, C.Y., et al.: Timing-based anomaly detection in SCADA networks. In: CRITIS (2018). https://doi.org/10.1007/978-3-319-99843-5_5
22. Longo, G., et al.: Electronic attacks as a cyber false flag against maritime radars systems. In: IEEE LCN (2023). https://doi.org/10.1109/LCN58197.2023.10223370
23. Longo, G., et al.: Attacking (and defending) the maritime radar system. IEEE Trans. Inf. Forensics Secur. (2023). https://doi.org/10.1109/TIFS.2023.3282132
24. Mirsky, Y., et al.: Kitsune: an ensemble of autoencoders for online network intrusion detection. In: NDSS (2018). https://doi.org/10.14722/ndss.2018.23204
25. OpenCPN: OpenCPN Chart Plotter (2023). https://github.com/OpenCPN/OpenCPN
26. Packer, J.: Bridge Command (2023). https://github.com/bridgecommand/bc
27. Pavur, J., et al.: A tale of sea and sky on the security of maritime VSAT communications. In: IEEE Symposium on Security and Privacy (2020). https://doi.org/10.1109/SP40000.2020.00056
28. von Rechenberg, M., et al.: Guiding ship navigators through the heavy seas of cyberattacks. In: MARESEC (2022). https://doi.org/10.5281/zenodo.7148794
29. de Riberolles, T., et al.: Characterizing radar network traffic: a first step towards spoofing attack detection. In: IEEE Aerospace Conference (2020). https://doi.org/10.1109/AERO47225.2020.9172292
30. de Riberolles, T., et al.: Anomaly detection for ICS based on deep learning: a use case for aeronautical radar data. Ann. Telecommun., 1–13 (2022). https://doi.org/10.1007/s12243-021-00902-7
31. Roesch, M., et al.: Snort: lightweight intrusion detection for networks. In: LISA (1999)
32. SOLAS Chapter V: Safety of Navigation (2009), IMO
33. Spravil, J., et al.: Detecting maritime GPS spoofing attacks based on NMEA sentence integrity monitoring. JMSE **11**(5) (2023). https://doi.org/10.3390/jmse11050928
34. Svilicic, B., et al.: Towards a cyber secure shipboard radar. J. Navigation **73**(3) (2020). https://doi.org/10.1017/S0373463319000808
35. Tam, K., Jones, K.: MaCRA: a model-based framework for maritime cyber-risk assessment. WMU J. Marit. Aff. **18**(1), 129–163 (2019). https://doi.org/10.1007/s13437-019-00162-2
36. Wolsing, K., et al.: Network attacks against marine radar systems: a taxonomy, simulation environment, and dataset. In: IEEE LCN (2022). https://doi.org/10.1109/LCN53696.2022.9843801
37. Wolsing, K., et al.: Can industrial intrusion detection be simple? In: ESORICS (2022). https://doi.org/10.1007/978-3-031-17143-7_28
38. Wolsing, K., et al.: IPAL: breaking up silos of protocol-dependent and domain-specific industrial intrusion detection systems. In: RAID (2022). https://doi.org/10.1145/3545948.3545968

Hunting Vulnerabilities in the Maritime Domain: A Domain Wide Cybersecurity Vulnerability Analysis

Abdullah Zafar and Ahmed Amro$^{(\boxtimes)}$ (iD)

Norwegian University of Science and Technology NTNU, GjØvik, Norway
ahmed.amro@ntnu.no

Abstract. The maritime domain, constituting over 80% of global trade, is a critical component of the world economy, facilitating the transfer of vast quantities of goods across the globe. In this way, the success of other crucial sectors vital to the normal functioning of life relies heavily on the pivotal role of the maritime domain. People have been navigating waterways through ships since ancient times. With technological progress, the structure and functioning of these ships have changed drastically. Modern ships comprise a wide array of interconnected and complicated information and operational cyber physical systems. With increasing connectivity through modern communication technologies, these systems are fast becoming connected to the outside world. Furthermore, the trend of remote-controlled and autonomous ships is expected to increase soon. Hence, assessing the cybersecurity posture of the maritime systems and identifying & fixing the vulnerabilities that comprise those ships is of utmost importance. To achieve these objectives, this research contributes in two ways, 1) proposing a comprehensive vulnerability and threat analysis methodology, named *MaThreX* developed to compile maritime-related known vulnerabilities and gather related threat-related information providing key insights to enhance decision-making and security measures, and 2) results from utilizing *MaThreX* for conducting a domain-wide analysis of the vulnerabilities found in the maritime assets and infer threat-related information to capture the threat landscape in the domain.

1 Introduction

The role of the maritime domain as a critical infrastructure has invited a large body of research and interest among the domain stakeholders to invest efforts for ensuring safe and secure operations and cybersecurity has been identified as a major concern in this regard. According to a recent survey on the state of cyber risk management in the maritime industry, 44% of the 200 industry professionals surveyed reported that their organizations have been the target of a cyber attack. The survey also revealed that shipping companies pay an average of $3.1 million in ransom for cyber attacks [8]. These findings highlight the significant impact of cyber attacks on the maritime sector, making it a crucial factor for change.

J. Garcia-Alfaro et al. (Eds.): ESORICS 2024 Workshops, LNCS 15263, pp. 382–402, 2025.
https://doi.org/10.1007/978-3-031-82349-7_25

In 2017, the International Maritime Organization (IMO) passed Resolution MSC. 428(98) [18] which made it mandatory for ship owners and operators to include cybersecurity in their safety management systems. The resolution was supported with guidelines for cyber risk management [4] which called for continuous risk analysis to be performed, taking into account the threat landscape including current and emerging cyber threats and vulnerabilities. The International Association of Classification Societies (IACS) released revised Unified Requirements (URs) in April 2024. These requirements include UR26 (Cyber Resilience of Ships) [6] and UR27 (Cyber Resilience of On-board Systems and Equipment) [7]. Both documents provide a set of minimum performance and functional criteria that aim to ensure that all new vessels contracted after the 1st of July 2024 are cyber-resilient. They also provide detailed requirements for evaluation and testing, incident response plans, recovery plans, and training and drills. These requirements are expected to have a significant impact on shipowners, classification societies, and manufacturers/suppliers in the maritime industry. The UR27 refers to reducing vulnerabilities through hardening and applying patches to onboard systems and equipment. On the other hand, asset vulnerabilities are a critical element in the risk assessment in the UR26. The document includes a requirement that suggests the application of vulnerability scanning for keeping up-to-date systems during the commissioning phase of ships. Additionally, it discusses the management of software updates during the operational phase by addressing vulnerabilities and cyber risks. Furthermore, there is a requirement for ship cybersecurity and resilience programs to be made to the society which considers "known vulnerabilities".

The importance of identifying, monitoring, and addressing vulnerabilities in the domain is clear and should be seen as a vital and continuous process for all involved stakeholders. While many studies have discussed vulnerabilities in the context of vulnerability scanning, analysis, threat and risk assessment, and management, none have looked at the overall cyber risk using existing Common Vulnerability and Exposures (CVEs) in the domain. Therefore, this paper aims to examine the cyber threat landscape in the maritime domain by considering existing known vulnerabilities.

Our proposed approach differs from the existing literature, which mainly focuses on threats and risks using experimental studies or theoretical scenarios. Instead, we utilize CVEs to make realistic assumptions about system risks and encompass a broad range of them in the maritime domain. This approach will assist various stakeholders in understanding the threat landscape better and offer insights to enhance defences in the maritime domain.

Our methodology which is supported by a tool called Maritime Threat eXplorer (MaThreX), relies on a set of open-source tools to query, validate, and analyze domain vulnerabilities. The query function searches multiple vulnerability databases using a comprehensive list of keywords relevant to the maritime domain. These vulnerabilities are then used to evaluate the overall risk picture and deduce the MITRE ATT&CK tactics and techniques. This process aims to thoroughly address maritime vulnerabilities to accurately depict the threat landscape by eliminating false positives (vulnerabilities detected based on irrelevant string matching). The findings are then summarized to capture the state of cyber vulnerabilities in the domain. The contributions of this paper can be summarized as follows:

- A tool-supported semi-automated vulnerability and threat analysis approach, reflecting the cyber risk landscape in the maritime domain based on existing known vulnerabilities (CVEs).
- Identification of the current cyber threat landscape through the application of this approach.

2   Background

2.1   Maritime Cyber Risks

The maritime infrastructure relies on various Information Technology (IT) and Operational Technology (OT) systems, including the Automatic Identification System (AIS), Electronic Chart Display and Information System (ECDIS), Global Positioning System (GPS), and Operational Technology (OT) Systems. **AIS**, mandated by the International Maritime Organization (IMO), facilitates the exchange of critical voyage information but is vulnerable to attacks due to its unauthenticated and unencrypted radio-based protocol [12,14,16,31]. **ECDIS**, essential for electronic navigation, is susceptible to attacks, especially when running outdated software, which can extend to other connected systems [10,43,44,46]. **GPS**, critical for navigation, is prone to spoofing and jamming attacks, posing operational risks [10]. **OT systems** in modern ships, when integrated with IT systems, expose isolated vulnerabilities to potential exploitation [5,10], raising concerns about potential manipulation of a ship's course or causing collisions.

Furthermore, these systems rely on specific protocols and standards used in maritime operations, such as the National Marine Electronics Association (NMEA) standard and the AIS protocol. The NMEA standard facilitates communication between marine systems by transmitting sensor data through a message-based protocol [40]. AIS, which is based on the NMEA standard, is a specialized message-based protocol that is used in various maritime services including traffic management, search and rescue, and collision avoidance [28].

The majority of academic work related to maritime cybersecurity focuses on a small subset of the domain's systems with AIS, ECIDS, and GPS as the most commonly highlighted. Therefore, broadening the research to include other maritime assets is necessary.

2.2   Threats and Vulnerability Constructs

A wide range of constructs (i.e. terminologies) exist in the cybersecurity domain to communicate aspects related to risks associated with threats and vulnerabilities. This section highlights constructs relevant to this paper, chosen based on their commonality in the literature. Definitions of each construct with examples are provided below.

- **CVE** [36] stands for Common Vulnerabilities and Exposures (e.g. CVE-2023-36857). Cybersecurity vulnerabilities are assigned entries, each including an ID number, a description, and at least one public reference.
- **CPE** [35] stands for Common Platform Enumeration. A nomenclature dictionary is commonly utilized to refer to specific hardware, operating systems, and applications. A CPE refers to a particular product, its vendor, version, and update. CVEs are usually assigned to one or several CPEs. An example is: cpe:2.3:h:bakerhughes:bentley_nevada_3500_system:-:*:*:*:*:*:*:*
- **TTP** [38] stands for Tactics, Techniques, and Procedures which are commonly utilized constructs adopted by the MITRE ATT&CK framework. Tactics refer to adversarial objectives (e.g. "TA0001: Initial Access"). Techniques refer to methods adversaries employ to achieve their objectives (e.g. "T1133: External Remote Services"). Procedures refer to the actual implementation (e.g. malware) employed to realize the adversarial technique (e.g. "S1060: Mafalda").
- **CAPEC** [34] stands for Common Attack Pattern Enumeration and Classification (e.g. CAPEC-555: Remote Services with Stolen Credentials). CAPEC provides a classification for the known attack patterns employed by attackers to exploit known weaknesses in cyber systems. Hence, by definition, it is clear that CAPECs are connected to CWEs.
- **CWE** [37] stands for Common Weakness Enumeration (e.g. CWE-522: Insufficiently Protected Credentials). CWEs are a way of categorizing the underlying weakness that caused the vulnerability (or CVE). Hence, CWEs are linked to one or more CVEs.
- **KEV** [19] standing for Known Exploited Vulnerabilities, is a list of CVEs that have been successfully exploited (e.g. CVE-2024-24919).
- **CVSS** [22] The Common Vulnerability Scoring System is a standard used to assess the severity of a CVE. It helps capture the characteristics of a vulnerability to calculate its severity score. For example, the CVSS score of CVE-2023-36857 is 6.5 (Medium). Not all CVEs have all versions of CVSS available, so this paper uses the latest version for each CVE in the analysis.
- **EPSS** [23] stands for Exploit Prediction Scoring System. It provides a way to assess the likelihood of a vulnerability being exploited. The score gives a numerical value indicating the likelihood of an exploitation attempt of a specific CVE in the next 30 d. For example, the EPSS Score of CVE-2022-3569 is 7.8 (High).

2.3   Open-Source Tools

We have employed two open-source tools for the development of threat exploration methodology in this paper, namely, *CVEMap*, and *BRON*.

CVEMap is an open-source command-line utility which provides a structured and easy way to navigate public CVE sources [2]. The tool uses data from various public sources giving a wide coverage of all reported vulnerabilities. The most important are the National Vulnerability Database (NVD) [39] from NIST and the CISA KEV database. Furthermore, it combines data from other sources such as Hackerone and publicly available exploits from Github. Furthermore, *CVEMap* provides capabilities to search for vulnerabilities by querying the CVE data or by vendor.

BRON [21] is a bi-directional data graph that links different threat constructs, namely, ATT&CK TTP, CWE, CVE, and CAPEC [26]. The CVE records are linked to CWEs, the CWEs are linked to CAPECs, and CAPECs are linked to ATT&CK techniques. These mappings provided by *BRON* for the different threat constructs and the ability to navigate the knowledge graph enable further exploration of the risk picture delineated by the identified CVEs to generate useful insights.

3   Related Work

3.1   Maritime Threat Landscape

The maritime cyber risk picture or what could be referred to as the threat landscape has been captured in the literature through different perspectives, including, incidents (i.e. what has happened) or threats (i.e. what may happen).

The incident perspective provides tangible intelligence and information that can be used to learn lessons to avoid repeating mistakes. Meland et al. [33] captured the threat landscape in the domain by analyzing 46 maritime cybersecurity incidents between 2010–2020. The objectives of their analysis were to understand the types of threats (e.g. misuse of AIS and positioning data) facing the industry and infer the attack points (e.g. GNSS) and techniques (e.g. social engineering) to inform defences.

On the other hand, the threat perspective provides information about what may happen based on theoretical analysis or empirical evidence. Androjna et al. [13] conducted a literature review to capture the cyber trends and challenges from different perspectives including attack types, surface, and impacts. The authors identified a wide range of methods threatening the shipping industry including, among others, ransomware, defamation, and digital piracy. Moreover, Amro and Gkioulos [12] conducted a literature review to capture the threat landscape in the maritime domain based on the observed tactics (i.e. objectives) and techniques (i.e. methods) utilized the MITRE ATT&CK framework [42].

3.2   Vulnerabilities and CVEs in the Domain

Some works in the literature have discussed vulnerabilities in the domain without referring to specific CVEs. Svilicic et al. [45] conducted a vulnerability scan and risk analysis of a ship ECDIS using the Nessus scanner. The authors identified a group of vulnerabilities mostly related to the operating system of the ECDIS. Additionally, Bothur et al. [15] focused on theoretical vulnerability analysis of some ship systems such as Industrial Control Systems (ICS), AIS, and VSAT.

Other literature has discussed specific CVEs in different ways. Amro [11] identified five CVEs related to six marine devices (e.g. GPS) found to be emitting NMEA messages on the Internet. The author relied on vendor-specific messages found using the Shodan scanner to identify the device names and then utilized the NVD to discover their associated CVEs. Bronk and Dewitte [17] referred to a specific CVE in Navis software for railcar hub assignment and train load sequence planning to highlight the challenge in port security in contracts to ship security by having many more points of entry to the interconnected port systems. Hopcraft et al. [27] discussed a specific CVE in VDR software to argue about the existence of unsecured devices in the world fleet. Freire et al. [24] discussed an attack model that can threaten Maritime Monitoring Systems. Among the attacker's capabilities is exploring existing vulnerabilities such as PostgreSQL CVE. Grigoriadis et al. [25] proposed a risk assessment framework targeted for the maritime sector. The framework utilizes the CAPEC attack patterns to describe cyber threats against assets. The framework then uses the CVSS metrics of the CVEs associated with those threats to measure the risk level. The authors demonstrated their approach by discussing the risk in eight situations (e.g. cargo loading & unloading). The risk assessment included 7 different assets across the situations with 7 unique CVEs. Juvonen et al. [29] discussed the CVEs associated with Apache Log4j2 exploitation within aeronautical, maritime, and aerospace communication environments. The authors demonstrated proof of concepts for exploiting those vulnerabilities over mission-critical wireless communication protocols like ACARS, ADS-B, and AIS. Martinie et al. [32] and Kalogeraki et al. [30] applied the supply chain risk assessment methodology (MITIGATE) [41] to assess risks related to cargo manifest files, Maritime Logistics and Supply Chain (MLoSC) respectively. MITIGATE utilizes knowledge obtained from CVEs, CPEs, and CWEs for analyzing threats, vulnerabilities, and their impact. Martinie et al. [32] referred to 6 unique CVEs to demonstrate the knowledge obtained from utilizing CVEs and CWEs for risk assessment while Kalogeraki et al. [30] referenced two CVEs as examples demonstrating their proposed approach. Enoch et al. [20] applied the knowledge of known vulnerabilities for assessing the risks against maritime systems based on the CVSS metrics of their associated CVEs. They demonstrated their work through 8 CVEs identified in 6 systems (e.g. Engine control system and ECDIS).

In summary, the identified works referring to CVEs in the maritime domain or applying them in different cybersecurity functions only highlight a small subset of CVEs not representative of the range of vulnerabilities in the domain. To the best of our knowledge, this paper provides the most comprehensive view of vulnerabilities in the maritime domain in addition to a semi-automated approach allowing continuous monitoring of the domain's vulnerability landscape.

3.3   Examples of Threat Assessment Reports

Norwegian Maritime Cyber Resilience Center (NORMA Cyber) is a hub for cybersecurity in the Norwegian maritime sector [1]. NORMA offers several services to its members, including threat intelligence, by sharing vulnerability information and mitigation advice. It also publishes threat reports every year, reviewing the cybersecurity situation of the past year based on reported incidents, vulnerabilities, etc., and forecasting an assessment for the next year. They also emphasize the importance of vulnerability information for accurate threat assessment in the annual threat assessment report.

The European Union Agency for Cybersecurity (ENISA) [3] also, in its annual threat landscape for 2023, emphasizes the importance of vulnerability information to learn about the trends in cybersecurity. The ENISA threat report uses various metrics related to vulnerabilities like CVSS score, CWEs, and KEV values.

Our tool can automatically gather information about various metrics and generate insights similar to those found in ENISA and NORMA Cyber Threat Reports. Additionally, the tool's scope can be customized based on the input keywords provided for vulnerability searches. This tool is helpful as it automates the provision of vulnerability information. It also links vulnerabilities to products, weaknesses, and attack techniques, providing organizations with a comprehensive understanding of the risk picture. Furthermore, our unique methodology covers a wide range of devices used in the maritime domain by searching for all approved device vendors in the marine industry.

4   Maritime Threat Explorer (*MaThreX*)

4.1   The *MaThreX* Process

In this section, we present the *MaThreX* methodology complete pipeline showing its application in the threat analysis of the maritime domain.

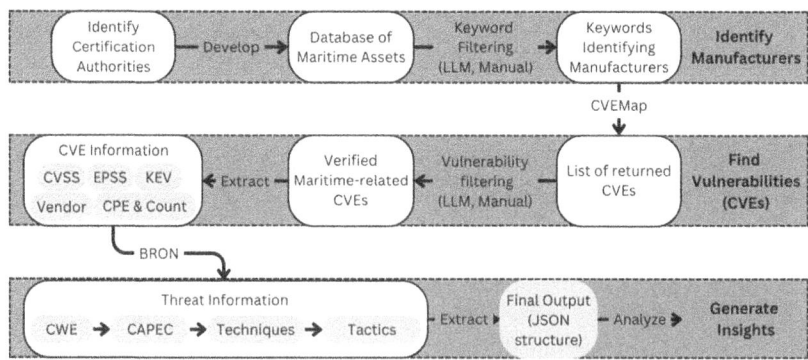

Fig. 1. The flow diagram of the *MaThreX* methodology

As shown in Fig. 1, the methodology be divided into three main stages, namely, 1) listing all maritime equipment manufacturers, 2) finding the known vulnerabilities in the devices manufactured by them, and 3) compiling further information from *CVEMap* and *BRON* data to present insights about the state of maritime cybersecurity. The first stage starts by identifying maritime certification authorities to find databases of maritime equipment. These databases are then filtered to get a searchable keyword list containing maritime equipment manufacturers. The keyword list is passed to *CVEMap* in stage 2 to search for CVEs related to those manufacturers. Upon filtering the CVE list and extracting their information (e.g. CVSS, CPEs), the CVE list is input into the *BRON* tool to extract further information (e.g. CWE, CAPEC) in stage 3. Finally, all the gathered information is compiled into a final output to be analyzed to describe the state of maritime cybersecurity. The keyword and CVE filtering in stages 1 and 2 have been conducted both manually and using Large Language Models (LLM) to evaluate the utility of Artificial Intelligence (AI) in automating this process to facilitate its continuity. In the following subsections, these steps are explained in detail.

Stage 1 – Identify Manufacturers: The manufacturers were identified to compile a list of keywords to be used for searching for known vulnerabilities in the devices and equipment used in the maritime industry.

A novel approach was devised that goes top-down starting with the certification authorities that certify equipment used in the maritime infrastructure (e.g. ships) and then searching for any publicly available database of certified equipment. This led us to DNV (Det Norske Veritas) which serves as a certifying body to assess the equipment used onboard vessels and in other sectors and maintains a list of all certified devices on its approvals website[1]. *Approval Finder* by DNV is a web tool to search and verify the products, manufacturers, and service suppliers approved by DNV. On this site, one can find the certificate number, product name, expiry date, company name, country, city, and approval group of any approved entity. The website has 74,028 products listed in the database at the time of this writing. Out of these, only 41,217 have active certificates. In this paper, the devices with active certificates were considered as those with expired certificates have less chance of being actively used in ships.

Another identified certification body was the European Maritime Safety Agency (EMSA). EMSA has a list of Marine Equipment Directive (MED) applicable to ships flying the flag of an EU country, Norway or Iceland. EMSA provides a portal that keeps the list of MED-approved devices[2]. Hence, this is the most comprehensive list covering the whole EU. This database lists 190,181 different equipment used on ships, along with other information, including the company name and product type. We also found a third database from the Maritime and Coastguard Agency of the UK that contains a list of devices that are approved by the UK[3]. This is rather small compared to the previous database and contains only 2198 entries.

---

[1] https://approvalfinder.dnv.com/.
[2] https://portal.med.emsa.europa.eu/.
[3] https://www.gov.uk/government/publications/uk-marine-equipment-approval-database.

In our testing, we found that using product names to search for vulnerabilities in databases may not yield accurate results. Although it may seem like using product names could reduce false positives, the way products are listed in the databases is not standardized and does not align with the vulnerability search tool. We experimented using *CVEMap* to query CVEs for a small subset of devices made by Furuno, a known maritime equipment manufacturer. The list of devices contained comma-separated models, so we separated these devices to increase the chances of finding vulnerabilities. We compiled a list of 107 keywords by taking the 'Product name' field from all entries containing the word 'Furuno' in the 'Company' column and removing duplicates. Unfortunately, the results did not yield any CVEs. However, when we searched using the company name, we found six vulnerabilities. Hence, keeping in view the discussion above and the results from the preliminary experiment, we decided to proceed with the company names as keywords for the vulnerability search.

In the filtering step, the list of companies is extracted from the databases, and the final keywords list is prepared to be fed into *CVEMap*. First, a preliminary list of companies was manually extracted from each of the three database files using Microsoft Excel. Since the DNV database also stored product categories and product types, this was done by filtering the Excel file based on the product category 'Instrumentation and Automation'. Since we are only interested in devices with cybersecurity vulnerabilities, this category was selected because it contained such devices, e.g. control systems, AIS transceivers, and ECDIS. Furthermore, it was ensured that other categories are irrelevant, e.g. machinery equipment, life-saving equipment, etc. Still, other categories that might be relevant to certain organizations might be easily added to generate the final list of manufacturers.

It is noteworthy to mention that the EU MED database did not provide product categories like DNV. Hence, a different approach based on Excel was used to filter out unwanted products like paints, winches, sewage, etc. This approach was used to remove unwanted equipment while also ensuring that relevant devices are not removed. This resulted in a reduction of products from 190181 to 69214 yielding **3175 unique companies**. This process greatly reduced the search keywords, but the companies' lists need more processing before they can be fed to *CVEMap*. The DNV company list contained many duplicates, e.g. there were 34 variants of the company ABB like ABB AG, ABB AS, ABB Automation, etc. Furthermore, the existence of characters like AS or Gmbh; abbreviations denoting the company liability type, next to company names hinders the search of companies by making it more restrictive. Also, we must be careful in removing keywords that are expected to give many hits, resulting in many false positives, because by removing useful keywords for fear of getting many false positives, we also risk ignoring keywords that would give relevant vulnerabilities too.

During the filtering step, two approaches were considered: a manual approach and an automated LLM-based approach. The manual approach includes analyzing each entry in the complete list (3889 keywords), and based on personal judgment derived from working with search terms, cleaning the list by removing keywords, removing characters, dividing the company name into multiple, making variations of the company name or remove duplicates that are expected to give the same result. On the other hand, when implementing the LLM-based approach, cleaning the keywords list was conducted by employing the GPT-4 model, the latest in the series of Generative Pre-trained Transformer models [9].

Finally, we only considered the keywords from UK MED and DNV databases because they gave a stable list covering a large set of relevant companies. However, the EU MED database list of keywords did not produce a high-quality output. It was found through smoke testing that some very famous companies were not present, and further, due to lack of product category in the data, many irrelevant companies were also present in the list.

Stage 2: Find Vulnerabilities. Once we have the list of equipment manufacturers, the next step is to look for known vulnerabilities in their devices using *CVEMap*.

CVEMap provides multiple ways to look for vulnerabilities. Since we have a list of product vendors as our input, we could have done it in two ways, by querying in the CVE data or by searching through the vendor. The list of equipment could be used to search directly for products but it becomes too restrictive, and the product name in *CVEMap* and our list can vary (e.g. Furuno in our list and Furunosystems in the CVE data) hence there is a good chance that we miss out on a lot of CVEs. So, we instead went for the querying function. This also has a negative point in that it gives many false positives that need to be filtered afterwards which we are going to discuss further on.

As mentioned before, the query-based search through *CVEMap* can result in many false positives. For example, searching for a maritime-related keyword "sonar" gives CVEs related to Jenkins[4] which is an open-source automation tool used in software development and not related to any marine sonar equipment. The false match is due the SonarQube platform for code inspection integrated within Jenkins. Also, our list contains some companies like Siemens, ABB, etc., that manufacture various kinds of IT systems, including those that may not be used in maritime.

Hence, to remove these kinds of CVEs from our list, we employed manual filtering and again decided to test LLM-based filtering. GPT-4 model was employed and given CVE name and its description and asked to return a 'yes' or 'no' based on whether it could be used in a maritime setting or not.

Stage 3: Generate Insights. In this step, set up our instance of the *BRON* tool on a server. The data graph is implemented in a database using ArangoDB, a graph database system. Next, we had to write our scripts to query and traverse the data graph in an automated manner using the list of CVEs. The script output is a JSON file containing arrays of CVEs containing all information found through *BRON* and other important CVE-related data used for analysis. The different fields in the final JSON structure are described in Table 1.

---

[4] https://www.jenkins.io/.

Table 1. Fields in the JSON structure

Field	Description
cveId	The root object that contains details about the CVE
sourceQuery	A string storing the search term used to identify this CVE entry in *CVEMap*
countCPE	An integer representing the number of CPE entries associated with this CVE.
manufacturer	A string indicating the manufacturer or vendor of the product that has the vulnerability in the NVD database
CVSS	A floating-point number representing the CVSS score.
EPSS	A floating-point number representing the EPSS score.
KEV	A boolean indicating whether the CVE is part of the KEV catalogue
cwes	An array of strings representing CWE identifier associated with the vulnerability
capecs	An array of strings listing CAPEC identifiers associated with the vulnerability
techniques	An array of strings listing ATT&CK techniques used to exploit the vulnerability
tactics	An array of strings listing ATT&CK tactics associated with the techniques

Finally, the output JSON structure can be used for visualizing and analyzing the wide range of information extracted from the *MaThreX* tool. Microsoft Power BI[5] is merely an example and it was employed in this paper. Power BI was chosen for its robust visualization capabilities, allowing the creation of interactive and insightful dashboards and reports. With Power BI, it was possible to visually represent various aspects of the data, including trends, patterns, and correlations, thereby facilitating a comprehensive analysis of the information gathered from the tool.

4.2 *MaThreX* results

In this section, we will describe the results obtained by running the *MaThreX* tool against the DNV and UK MED databases. The final vendor list comprised 803 keywords (691 from DNV, 143 from UK MED, and 31 commons). Out of which, 52 gave hits in *CVEMap*, resulting in 928 CVEs. Upon removing duplicates and false positives, 27 keywords and 244 CVEs remained. The next step is to dive deeper into the CVEs and identify details about the vulnerabilities. This involved querying the *BRON* database to identify CPEs, CWEs, CAPECs, Techniques, and Tactics for each vulnerability. Table 2 shows the final number of these threat constructs found during our research. In the following subsections, we will correlate the different constructs related to the CVEs found in maritime assets to gain deep insights into the maritime threat landscape. All the results including the final list of vendors and vulnerabilities (with false positives and filtered) are provided in our online repository[6].

---

[5] https://app.powerbi.com/.
[6] https://github.com/ahmed-amro/MaThreX.

Table 2. Summary of the threat constructs generated by *MaThreX*

Threat construct	CVEs	CPEs	CWEs	CAPECs	Techniques	Tactics
Count	244	1810	94	391	234	14

Trend over the Years. Fig. 2 plots the number of CVEs by year. The plot shows an overall increase in reported vulnerabilities over the years, with the number of CVEs peaking in the year 2023 with 93 vulnerabilities. This healthy trend indicates an increase in scanning for vulnerabilities in these systems.

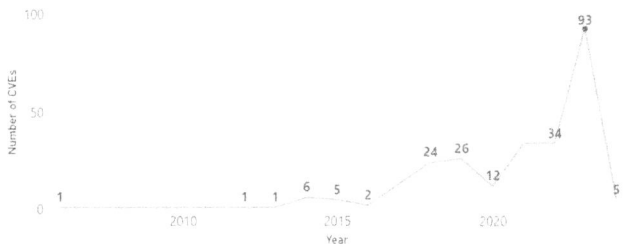

Fig. 2. Reported Vulnerabilities Trend over the years

Severity and Exploitability. Severity and Exploitability combined can help decision-makers prioritize the vulnerabilities that need to be fixed urgently. Figure 3 shows the severity by plotting the CVSS scores of the identified vulnerabilities. Since the CVSS score ranges between 1–10, the scores are divided into bins for this visualization. The figure shows a slight tilt towards the higher CVSS scores, with the topmost bin of CVSS scores 8.9–9.45 having 38 CVEs. Most CVEs (53) lie between the range of 6.7–7.25. This shows that the CVEs affecting the maritime systems are mostly of higher severity.

Regarding the EPSS scores, which reflect the exploitability or likelihood of vulnerabilities being exploitable in the near future. Almost all of the vulnerabilities have a very low value of <0.04, which is expected since no vulnerability was found to be listed in the KEV catalogue as known exploitable CVEs. There is only one outlier with a score of 0.84 for a CVE assigned to Wago. This is a positive indicator regarding the reduced exploitability of maritime vulnerabilities with few exceptions. Still, this metric changes frequently based on the availability of exploits to the found vulnerabilities. This motivates frequent execution of such analysis to maintain an up-to-date threat picture.

Insights About Vendors. A very important use case of CVE data and related information is the insights gathered about different vendors. This information can be helpful in several ways including supply chain management. Figure 4

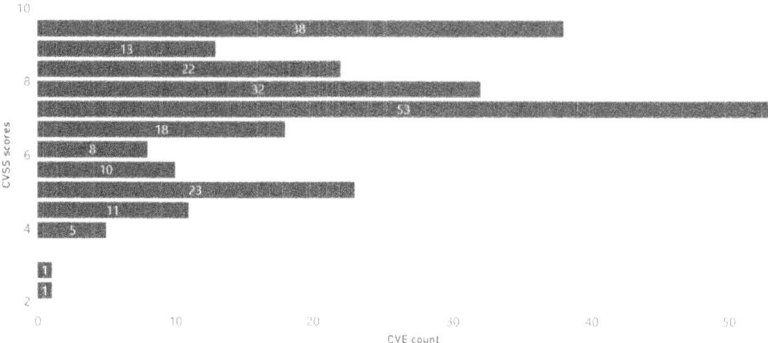

Fig. 3. CVSS scores of identified vulnerabilities

shows the vendors with the most known vulnerabilities and the number of products (i.e. CPEs) affected by those vulnerabilities. Similarly, Fig. 5 shows the average vendor-based CVSS score information.

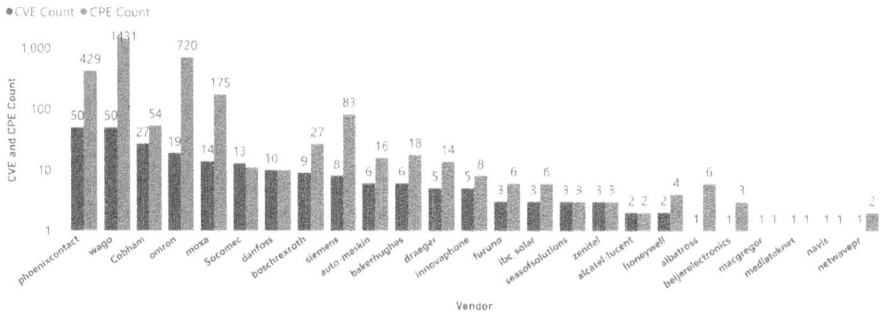

Fig. 4. Number of CVEs and CPEs by vendor on a logarithmic scale

Noteworthy, just seeing a single metric alone might give an incomplete picture. As shown in Fig. 4, Phoenix Contact has the most identified vulnerabilities (along with Wago). However, it is the third regarding the number of product versions affected by these vulnerabilities. Another insight appears when considering the number of CVEs and the average CVSS scores. For example, Navis has only a single reported vulnerability for a single CPE as shown in Fig. 4 while this vulnerability has the highest CVSS score as shown in Fig. 5.

Weaknesses and Adversaries Related Insights. Table 3 shows the top 10 most occurring weaknesses related to the identified CVEs including their description. The finding of CWE-798 weakness as the top weakness emphasizes the threats posed by the use of hardcoded credentials in maritime equipment. This

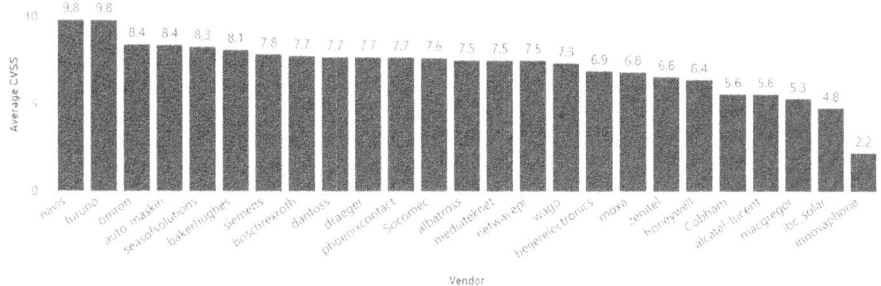

Fig. 5. Average CVSS by vendor

is a very important insight as it provides actionable information to vendors and users of the equipment to focus on weaknesses to make them secure.

Table 3. Top 10 CWEs

ID	CVE Count	(%)	Description
798	19	13.77%	Use of Hard-coded Credentials
79	18	13.04%	Improper Neutralization of Input During Web Page Generation
78	15	10.87%	Improper Neutralization of Special Elements in an OS Command
200	14	10.14%	Exposure of Sensitive Information to an Unauthorized Actor
306	14	10.14%	Missing Authentication for Critical Function
787	12	8.7%	Out-of-bounds Write
80	9	6.52%	Improper Neutralization of Script-Related HTML Tags in a Web Page
20	8	5.8%	Improper Input Validation
732	8	5.8%	Incorrect Permission Assignment for Critical Resource
287	7	5.07%	Improper Authentication

Furthermore, the top 10 CAPEC patterns, ATT&CK techniques, and tactics are presented in Tables 4, Table 5, and Table 6 respectively. These metrics provide key insights into the methods adversaries may use to compromise systems. The information was retrieved by navigating the *BRON* data graph.

As an example, the attack pattern with the highest CVE count is CAPEC-60: Reusing Session IDs (aka Session Replay). Coupled with this, the most often employed technique is T1027.009, which involves the use of obfuscated files or information, specifically through embedded payloads. This attack pattern and technique align with the most prevalent ATT&CK tactics Defense Evasion (TA0005). These metrics together provide a comprehensive understanding that allows for improved threat modelling, vulnerability management, and the implementation of targeted security measures to defend against real-world threats.

Table 4. Top 10 CAPEC IDs

ID	CVE Count	(%)	Description
60	9	5.45%	Reusing Session IDs (aka Session Replay)
22	8	4.85%	Exploiting Trust in Client
55	8	4.85%	Rainbow Table Password Cracking
59	8	4.85%	Session Credential Falsification through Prediction
122	7	4.24%	Privilege Abuse
26	7	4.24%	Leveraging Race Conditions
76	7	4.24%	Manipulating Web Input to File System Calls
79	7	4.24%	Using Slashes in Alternate Encoding
102	6	3.64%	Session Sidejacking
20	6	3.64%	Encryption Brute Forcing

Table 5. Top 10 ATT&CK Techniques

Techniques	CVE Count	(%)	Description
T1027.009	14	7.14%	Obfuscated Files or Information: Embedded Payloads
T1040	10	5.10%	Network Sniffing
T1134.001	10	5.10%	Token Impersonation/Theft
T1499.002	10	5.10%	Endpoint Denial of Service: Service Exhaustion Flood
T1539	10	5.10%	Steal Web Session Cookie
T1110.002	9	4.59%	Brute Force: Password Cracking
T1110.003	9	4.59%	Brute Force: Password Spraying
T1550.004	9	4.59%	Use Alternate Authentication Material: Web Session Cookie
T1558.003	9	4.59%	Steal or Forge Kerberos Tickets: Kerberoasting
T1005	8	4.08%	Data from Local System

4.3   Comparing Manual and LLM-Based Filtering

During the testing of keyword filtering, we used an LLM method with a list of companies from DNV to obtain CVEs and then compared the results with a manual list. The LLM method, although effective in many cases and covering numerous results, was not as effective as manual filtering. It missed some useful keywords, and the keyword-cleaning process was not very effective in some cases. Therefore, we do not recommend it as an effective method for filtering keywords, as skipping important CVEs at this crucial step will lead to an incomplete threat assessment. Additionally, the effort required for manual filtering is manageable in this case and is not needed so frequently when creating a list of manufacturers.

Table 6. Top 10 ATT&CK Tactics

Tactic	CVE Count	(%)	Description
TA0005	56	12.47%	Defense Evasion
TA0003	52	11.58%	Persistence
TA0006	52	11.58%	Credential Access
TA0004	46	10.24%	Privilege Escalation
TA0007	38	8.46%	Discovery
TA0009	36	8.02%	Collection
TA0001	35	7.80%	Initial Access
TA0040	32	7.13%	Impact
TA0008	29	6.46%	Lateral Movement
TA0011	21	4.68%	Command and Control

For CVE filtering, we passed the list of CVEs obtained from *CVEMap* to GPT-4 to filter only maritime-related CVEs. We provided 852 CVEs, along with their descriptions, to the model, which is less than the actual list of CVEs obtained from *CVEMap* (928 CVEs). This is because the list from *CVEMap* contains some duplicate CVEs in cases where two keywords returned the same CVE. Additionally, it was not possible to obtain descriptions for some CVEs with their status listed as 'awaiting analysis'.

The results of the filtering were not very promising. The model returned 'Yes' for 56 and 'No' for 796 CVEs. Upon comparing the CVEs with the list obtained from manual filtering, considered as the ground truth, it was found that the tool correctly identified 35 out of 56 as maritime-related CVEs, while the remaining 21 were incorrectly characterized as such. Similarly, 592 CVEs were correctly classified, while 204 were incorrectly classified as unrelated to the maritime industry. This resulted in an accuracy of 73.6%.

Ideally, the accuracy should be higher. These results suggest that the model can somewhat reason about the CVEs. However, due to the reduced accuracy, the model is insufficient for practical application. Consequently, these results indicate that the current implementation of LLM models is unsuitable for our application. Therefore, based on the available LLM models, this paper suggests a manual approach. However, the model might be improved by providing more training data or context.

5   Discussion

5.1   Maritime Threat Landscape

The *MaThreX* methodology gathers data on vulnerabilities in the maritime industry to understand its cybersecurity state. This is the first work of its kind for this sector. By examining vulnerabilities, we can describe threats based on empirical evidence and understand attackers' abilities. In this section, we examine the threat landscape from the perspectives of adversarial tactics and techniques, and attack patterns. These perspectives are derived from threat-related information associated with discovered vulnerabilities.

We can infer the adversarial objectives the vulnerabilities can support by looking at the ATT&CK tactics. The results suggest that the vulnerabilities can support all 14 enterprise tactics from reconnaissance to impact. We can also infer the methods the attackers can apply to exploit the vulnerabilities by looking at the ATT&CK techniques. The results suggest that the vulnerabilities can support 234 techniques which constitute about 54% of the entire ATT&CK enterprise techniques. Considering the range of both tactics and techniques, attackers have flexibility in developing a variety of multi-stage attacks (i.e. kill chains) within the maritime assets.

We can also infer the attack patterns that adversaries can employ to exploit the vulnerabilities by looking at the CAPEC patterns. The vulnerabilities can be exploited through 391 CAPEC patterns which constitute about 70% of the entire CAPEC list. However, the distribution of patterns relevant to each vulnerability is flat, meaning that 73% of attack patterns can exploit 1 or 2 vulnerabilities. On the other hand, only 27 patterns enable the exploitation of 5 or more vulnerabilities. Those patterns (partially shown in Table 4) can be considered to constitute a higher risk and would be logical to be prioritized for mitigations.

Lastly, this methodology can also be applied to other industries (e.g. energy) or organizational levels to capture the threat landscape by adjusting the keyword list to control the scope of target assets.

5.2   Limitations

Although the *MaThreX* methodology generates robust results and insightful findings, some limitations must be mentioned to further improve the process in the future. Starting with the dataset issues such as including missing product types and categories, incorrect types or categories, and inconsistencies in company naming conventions. These inconsistencies can affect the accuracy and reliability of the tool. Addressing these issues by refining and standardizing the data sources will significantly enhance the tool's performance and the validity of its findings.

Another issue is the manual filtering of keywords and CVEs which can be considered subjective. Different considerations were made while cleaning the companies' keywords list. The addition of a keyword giving false hits does not affect the output of the tool but only makes the next stage which filtering the CVEs harder. However, if a useful keyword is ignored for the fear of getting too many false positives, then as a result, the tool can skip important vulnerabilities. However, it is equally important to be careful while adding or removing CVEs in the next stage because having unrelated vulnerabilities in the final list will skew our view of the state of maritime cybersecurity.

Lastly, in the results section, we have shown the tool's potential by picking some interesting comparisons from the data. For example, the section related to vendors shows how this tool can help make informed decisions while selecting a vendor based on their cybersecurity posture. Similarly, CWEs, CAPECs, and MITRE Tactics and Techniques provide insights into attackers' behaviour. We believe that there can be a lot more interesting comparisons made through this data based on the use case.

6   Conclusions

This research focuses on analyzing vulnerabilities and threats within maritime systems. By analyzing 244 maritime-related vulnerabilities identified by 803 keywords comprising maritime equipment manufacturers, this study provides a detailed understanding of the state of maritime cybersecurity. The identified CVEs affect 1810 CPEs (or product versions). The trend showing an increase in reported vulnerabilities and insights like those about maritime vendors is key in reflecting the state of maritime cybersecurity from the perspective of the reported vulnerabilities. Additionally, the threat of hardcoded credentials has been confirmed in this study as the highest occurring weakness enabling the discovered vulnerabilities. Furthermore, our analysis suggests that the vulnerabilities can enable a range of kill chains due to their association with a large number of tactics, techniques and attack patterns.

Some improvements can be made regarding the *MaThreX* tool. By incorporating more databases into the input, we can improve the coverage of the tool. Furthermore, the tool can be converted to a complete automated analysis framework by incorporating AI or customized LLM-based solutions to replace the manual work related to keyword filtering and CVE filtering. Specialized LLM-based solutions can also be applied in the final step to generate insights from the gathered data. The methodology must also be rigorously tested in different case studies to empirically assess its utility.

In summary, this study provides a method for continuous understanding of the threat landscape in maritime systems, highlighting the potential and limitations of the proposed method for future advancements in maritime cybersecurity. Safeguarding the security and resilience of maritime assets is crucial, and continued research and development will be vital for protecting these critical infrastructures from sophisticated cyber threats.

References

1. Annual threat assessment 2024 — Norma cyber. https://www.normacyber.no/news/annual-threat-assessment-2024. Accessed 21 April 2024
2. cvemap overview - projectdiscovery documentation. https://docs.projectdiscovery.io/tools/cvemap/overview. Accessed 29 April 2024
3. ENISA. https://www.enisa.europa.eu/. Accessed 22 April 2024

4. Guidelines on maritime cyber risk management. http://www.imo.org/en/OurWork/Security/Guide_to_Maritime_Security/Documents/MSC.1-CIRC.1526(E).pdf

5. Maritime cyber security: a comprehensive approach. https://www.missionsecure.com/maritime-security-perspectives-for-a-comprehensive-approach. Accessed 12 July 2023

6. Ur e26 rev1 CR - cyber resilience of ships. https://iacs.s3.af-south-1.amazonaws.com/wp-content/uploads/2022/02/04140503/UR-E26-Rev.1-Nov-2023-CR.pdf. Accessed 21 March 2024

7. Ur e27 rev CLN - cyber resilience of on-board systems and equipment. https://iacs.s3.af-south-1.amazonaws.com/wp-content/uploads/2022/05/29103853/UR-E27-Rev.1-Sep-2023-CLN.pdf. Accessed 21 March 2024

8. Global industry report: the great disconnect (2022). https://cyberowl.io/resources/global-maritime-industry-report-the-great-disconnect/. Accessed 21 March 21

9. Achiam, J., et al.: GPT-4 technical report. arXiv preprint arXiv:2303.08774 (2023)

10. Akpan, F., Bendiab, G., Shiaeles, S., Karamperidis, S., Michaloliakos, M.: Cybersecurity challenges in the maritime sector. Network **2**(1), 123–138 (2022)

11. Amro, A.: Cyber-physical tracking of IoT devices: a maritime use case. In: Norsk IKT-konferanse for forskning og utdanning. No. 3 (2021)

12. Amro, A., Gkioulos, V.: From click to sink: Utilizing AIS for command and control in maritime cyber attacks. In: European Symposium on Research in Computer Security, pp. 535–553. Springer (2022). https://doi.org/10.1007/978-3-031-17143-7_26

13. Androjna, A., Brcko, T., Pavic, I., Greidanus, H.: Assessing cyber challenges of maritime navigation. J. Mar. Sci. Eng. **8**(10), 776 (2020)

14. Balduzzi, M., Pasta, A., Wilhoit, K.: A security evaluation of AIS automated identification system. In: Proceedings of the 30th Annual Computer Security Applications Conference, pp. 436–445 (2014)

15. Bothur, D., Zheng, G., Valli, C.: A critical analysis of security vulnerabilities and countermeasures in a smart ship system (2017)

16. Botunac, I., Gržan, M.: Analysis of software threats to the automatic identification system. Brodogradnja: Teorija i praksa brodogradnje i pomorske tehnike **68**(1), 97–105 (2017)

17. Bronk, C., deWitte, P.: Maritime cybersecurity: meeting threats to globalization's great conveyor. In: Lehto, M., Neittaanmäki, P. (eds.) Cyber Security. CMAS, vol. 56, pp. 241–254. Springer, Cham (2022). https://doi.org/10.1007/978-3-030-91293-2_10

18. Committee, T.M.S.: International maritime organization (IMO) (2017) guidelines on maritime cyber risk management (2017). http://bit.ly/MSC428-98 (2017)

19. Cybersecurity and Infrastructure Security Agency (CISA): known exploited vulnerabilities catalog. https://www.cisa.gov/known-exploited-vulnerabilities-catalog. Accessed 19 June 2024

20. Enoch, S.Y., Lee, J.S., Kim, D.S.: Novel security models, metrics and security assessment for maritime vessel networks. Comput. Netw. **189**, 107934 (2021)

21. Hemberg E., et al.: Github page for bron - link and evaluate public threat and mitigation data for cyber hunting. https://github.com/ALFA-group/BRON. Accessed 19 June 2024

22. FIRST: Common vulnerability scoring system (CVSS). https://www.first.org/cvss/. Accessed 19 June 2024

23. FIRST: Exploit prediction scoring system (EPSS). https://www.first.org/epss/. Accessed 19 June 2024
24. Freire, W.P., Melo Jr, W.S., do Nascimento, V.D., Nascimento, P.R., de Sá, A.O.: Towards a secure and scalable maritime monitoring system using blockchain and low-cost IoT technology. Sensors **22**(13), 4895 (2022)
25. Grigoriadis, C., Laborde, R., Verdier, A., Kotzanikolaou, P.: An adaptive, situation-based risk assessment and security enforcement framework for the maritime sector. Sensors **22**(1), 238 (2021)
26. Hemberg, E., et al.: Linking threat tactics, techniques, and patterns with defensive weaknesses, vulnerabilities and affected platform configurations for cyber hunting. arXiv preprint arXiv:2010.00533 (2020)
27. Hopcraft, R., Harish, A.V., Tam, K., Jones, K.: Raising the standard of maritime voyage data recorder security. J. Mar. Sci. Eng. **11**(2), 267 (2023)
28. IMO: Resolution a.1106(29) revised guidelines for the onboard operational use of shipborne automatic identification systems (AIS) (2015)
29. Juvonen, A., Costin, A., Turtiainen, H., Hämäläinen, T.: On apache log4j2 exploitation in aeronautical, maritime, and aerospace communication. IEEE Access **10**, 86542–86557 (2022)
30. Kalogeraki, E.M., Papastergiou, S., Mouratidis, H., Polemi, N.: A novel risk assessment methodology for scada maritime logistics environments. Appl. Sci. **8**(9), 1477 (2018)
31. Levy, S., Gudes, E., Hendler, D.: A survey of security challenges in automatic identification system (AIS) protocol. In: International Symposium on Cyber Security, Cryptology, and Machine Learning, pp. 411–423. Springer (2023). https://doi.org/10.1007/978-3-031-34671-2_29
32. Martinie, C., Grigoriadis, C., Kalogeraki, E.M., Kotzanikolaou, P.: Modelling human tasks to enhance threat identification in critical maritime systems. In: Proceedings of the 25th Pan-Hellenic Conference on Informatics, pp. 375–380 (2021)
33. Meland, P., Bernsmed, K., Wille, E., Rødseth, Ø., Nesheim, D.: A retrospective analysis of maritime cyber security incidents. TransNav: Int. J. Marine Navig. Saf. Sea Transp. **15**(3), 519–530 (2021)
34. MITRE: Common attack pattern enumeration and classification (CAPEC). https://capec.mitre.org/. Accessed 19 June 2024
35. MITRE: Common platform enumeration (CPE). https://cpe.mitre.org/. Accessed 19 June 2024
36. MITRE: Common vulnerabilities and exposures (CVE). https://cve.mitre.org/. Accessed 19 June 2024
37. MITRE: Common weakness enumeration (CWE). https://cwe.mitre.org/. Accessed 19 June 2024
38. MITRE: MITRE ATT&CK. https://attack.mitre.org/. Accessed 19 June 2024
39. NIST: National vulnerability database (NVD). https://nvd.nist.gov/vuln. Accessed 19 June 2024
40. NMEA: National marine electronics association - nmea0183 standard (2002)
41. Schauer, S., Polemi, N., Mouratidis, H.: Mitigate: a dynamic supply chain cyber risk assessment methodology. J. Transp. Secur. **12**(1), 1–35 (2019)
42. Strom, B.E., Applebaum, A., Miller, D.P., Nickels, K.C., Pennington, A.G., Thomas, C.B.: Mitre ATT&CK. Design and philosophy. Technical report (2018)
43. Svilicic, B., Brčić, D., Žuškin, S., Kalebić, D.: Raising awareness on cyber security of ECDIS. TransNav: Int. J. Marine Navig. Saf. Sea Transp. **13**(1), 231–236 (2019)

44. Svilicic, B., Kamahara, J., Celic, J., Bolmsten, J.: Assessing ship cyber risks: a framework and case study of ECDIS security. WMU J. Marit. Aff. **18**, 509–520 (2019)
45. Svilicic, B., Kamahara, J., Rooks, M., Yano, Y.: Maritime cyber risk management: an experimental ship assessment. J. Navig. **72**(5), 1108–1120 (2019)
46. Svilicic, B., Rudan, I., Jugović, A., Zec, D.: A study on cyber security threats in a shipboard integrated navigational system. J. Marine Sci. Eng. **7**(10), 364 (2019)

Threat Modeling in Satellite Communications for Maritime Operations

Even Kvam Frøseth[(⊠)], Georgios Kavallieratos[(⊠)] [ID],
and Sokratis Katsikas[(⊠)] [ID]

Department of Information Security and Communication Technology (IIK),
Norwegian University of Science and Technology, Gjøvik, Norway
evenkv@stud.ntnu.no, {georgios.kavallieratos,sokratis.katsikas}@ntnu.no

Abstract. The New Space Era and the emergence of high-bandwidth Low Earth Orbit (LEO) satellite constellations have caused a rapid change in the cyber threat landscape for industries reliant on satellite communications. One of these is the maritime sector. This work aims to analyze the threat landscape in satellite communications for maritime operations. To this end, an overview of the systems related to satellite communications in maritime operations is first provided. Then, three threat modelling methods, namely the STRIDE method, the Microsoft Threat Modelling Tool and the SPARTA framework are used to provide a holistic analysis of the threats in satellite communications at different, complementary levels. As an example, a sophisticated GPS spoofing attack that can cause major incidents for ships is analyzed in detail. The results will support the space sector towards improving the system architecture and making ship operations more secure.

Keywords: Space · Cybersecurity · Satellites · Threats · Maritime

1 Introduction

Satellite communications are crucial for the global connectivity as they provide vital links to several industries such as maritime, energy, transportation and supply chain. The increased technological advancements of satellite technology, such as Low Earth Orbit (LEO) satellite constellations, expand the functions and operations of satellite communications. Such technological advancements brought significant opportunities but also came with significant security challenges. The term *New Space Era* describes the increased participation of private companies and commercial ventures in the space sector [14]. This has led to an explosion in the number of satellites in space today[1].

Satellite technology has historically relied on security through obscurity, assuming that limited access to technical details would protect against potential threats. Nowadays, the cybersecurity threats in space have increased and the

---

[1] Orbiting Now: https://orbit.ing-now.com.

J. Garcia-Alfaro et al. (Eds.): ESORICS 2024 Workshops, LNCS 15263, pp. 403–424, 2025.
https://doi.org/10.1007/978-3-031-82349-7_26

analysis of such threats and the identification of the appropriate controls are needed [2].

Nowadays, the maritime industry adopts low-latency, high-bandwidth, and cost-effective Internet through LEO satellite networks such as Starlink and OneWeb, to facilitate the core functions and operations. However, the integration of such technologies in the maritime industry increases the attack surface. A report with relevant cybersecurity incidents in the maritime sector illustrates the vulnerabilities and the threat landscape of the sector [16].

Maritime operations depend on satellite communications. The modern LEO satellite constellations pose a significant risk to the maritime sector and therefore the threat landscape and the potential cyber attacks should be analyzed. By leveraging a systematic analysis of the cyber threats posed by the space sector to the maritime sector, the most critical threats can be identified, analyzed, and mitigated.

This work explores the threats, vulnerabilities, and risks associated with integrating advanced satellite communication systems like Starlink into maritime operations. This is done by employing three distinct threat modeling methodologies, namely the STRIDE method, the Microsoft Threat Modeling Tool and the Space Attack Research and Tactic Analysis (SPARTA) framework. The STRIDE threat model provides a holistic view of the entire satellite communication system, from the ground stations and satellite constellation to a ship's satellite communication equipment and internal networks. The Microsoft Threat Modelling Tool supports the semi-automated implementation of STRIDE and provides threat analysis at a more detailed level than STRIDE itself. The SPARTA framework builds upon the MITRE ATT@CK framework and is used herein to facilitate the investigation of the Software-Defined Radio (SDR) for GPS spoofing to comprehensively analyze specific attack scenarios. The contributions of this work are as follows:

- Identifies the components of a state-of-the-art LEO satellite constellation.
- Analyzes the cybersecurity threats against LEO satellite components.
- Estimates the cyber risks of satellite communication in maritime operations.

The remainder of this article is structured as follows: Sect. 2 presents an overview of the satellite communication infrastructure. Section 3 reviews related work. In Sect. 4 we briefly discuss STRIDE, and the reasons that led us to use it, as well as the results of its application to the satellite communication infrastructure in maritime. In Sect. 5 the summary of the results is provided and finally, Sect. 6 summarizes our conclusions and proposes directions for future work.

2   Satellite Communications for Maritime Operations

Figure 1 provides a high-level overview of a system that uses a modern LEO satellite constellation for Internet through satellite communication. A large vessel is considered, since large ships highly rely on the Internet through satellite communication to operate. The assets of the space infrastructure are divided into four segments; these are the *space*, *link*, *ground*, and *user* segments [12].

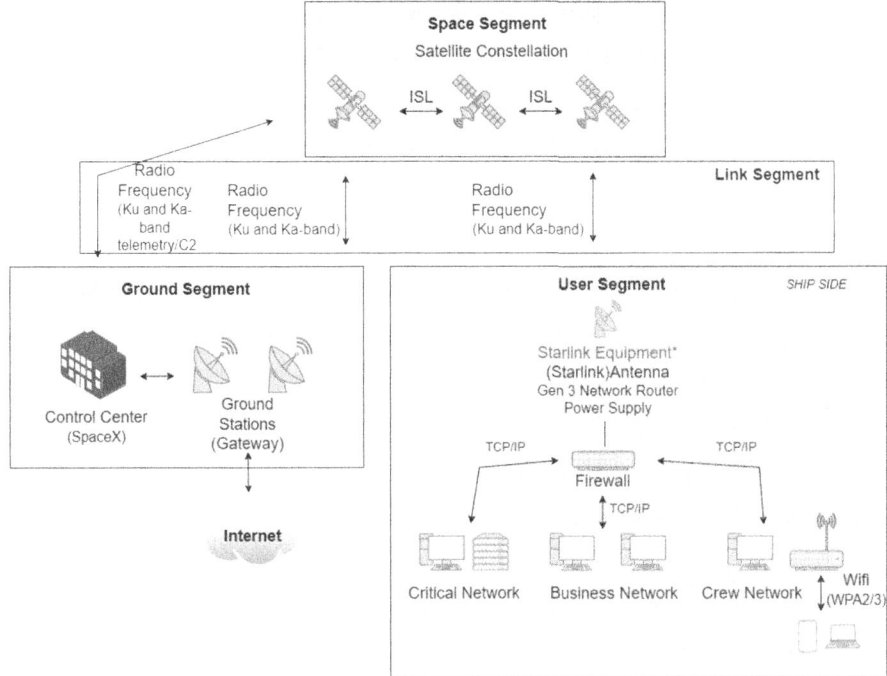

Fig. 1. Satellite Communication Overview.

The *space segment* entails all components designed to operate in space; this can include the following [18]:

– Communication satellites, navigation satellites, scientific satellites and more.
– Spacecrafts including probes, space stations, and telescopes.

For Starlink, the space segment consists of 5313^2 satellites operating at a LEO altitude of 540 to 570 km above earth as of writing this paper [33]. The satellites uplink and downlink operate in the Ku- and Ka-bands, with a frequency range of 10.7–12.7 GHz, 13.85–14.5 GHz, 17.8–18.6 GHz, 18.8–19.3 GHz, 27.5–29.1 GHz, and 29.5–30 GHz [6]. The satellites have multiple antennas and the ability to connect to multiple terminals at the same time, and according to [9], Starlink uses an OFDM modulation technique for signal transmission. Recently, the OFDM modulation and waveform was confirmed by a patent filed by SpaceX [25]. The first versions of the Starlink satellites used a bent-pipe solution for satellite-to-satellite communication, but Inter-Satellite Links (ISL) has been adapted and tested since version 1.5 of the Starlink LEO satellites was launched [35].

---

² Starlink SX: https://starlink.sx/.

The *link segment* provides the communication links to transmit data between the space segment to the ground and the user segments. This can be divided into *uplink*, *downlink*, and *crosslink*. The links can be [12]:

- Radio frequency (RF) communications link.
- Optical communication links. From ground to satellite and from satellite to satellite.

The *ground segment* contains all the terrestrial components and systems needed to properly operate, control, and support space-based assets. There is no publicly available information on Starlink's control centers. We can only assume that they operate as normal command centers, managing the constellation with telemetry and other data points. Ground stations are spread throughout the world to provide the maximum amount of coverage. The specifications of the ground stations are not publicly known, other than the modulation techniques and RF signal usage previously mentioned. Starlink uses a series of point-of-presence (POP) to connect to the internet backbone [27]. This can include [18, pp. 57–59]:

- Ground stations for uplink and downlink with antenna arrays and tracking systems.
- Control centers, including mission control, network operations centers, support infrastructure, and critical personnel for the operation of space-based assets.

The *user segment* entails all the elements that enable an end-user to access and utilize the data and services provided by space-based assets. The user segment is needed to transform the outputs from the space and ground segments to a usable application for the end user. The LEO user segment consists of the user terminal and other hardware and software [26]. This can include [12]:

- User equipment: antennas and satellite dishes, satellite phones and GPS receivers.
- Software applications like navigation and mapping.

The maritime domain is described within the user segment. The user segment consists of a firewall and three internal networks (*critical, business, crew*) on the ship. All the networks use generic standardized network protocols.

- Firewall: A generic firewall that sits between the Starlink user equipment and the three internal networks. The firewall monitors the network traffic and acts as a switch between the networks.
- Critical Network: The critical network contains network reliant systems that are deemed critical. These can include mail servers, database and storage solutions.
- Business Network: The business network contains all the network reliant systems used to conduct daily business on the ship. These can include desktop computers, laptops, and other relevant devices.
- Crew Network: The crew network consists of the crew wifi network solution and all devices connected to that network.

3   Related Work

A systematic literature review examines the cybersecurity aspects in space analyzing the space segment, the ground segment, and the user segment by leveraging the NIST cybersecurity framework, is provided in [12]. Threat modeling specifically focusing on satellites is a research area that has received significant attention. A comprehensive study on the challenges in threat modeling for new space systems is presented in [22]. STRIDE and DREAD are used to analyze the capability of existing threat modeling methods for capturing threats and security requirements from a system-centric approach. In [8], a threat model and security analysis of spacecraft computing systems is performed based on STRIDE and the critical assets in spacecraft systems are identified. In [20], a novel framework is presented that aims to assess the high-level resilience of the space systems considering specific types of threats. Willbold et al. [34] developed a taxonomy of threats against satellite firmware focusing on satellite-specific threat models. Pavur and Martinovic [19] provides a comprehensive analysis of the historical evolution and current state of cybersecurity threats targeting satellite systems. A comprehensive report on applying the NIST Cybersecurity Framework[3] to satellite command and control is presented in [15]. A conceptual model is proposed in [3] to study the space cybersecurity's challenges and opportunities emphasizing on the necessity of a comprehensive approach.

Kavallieratos et al. in [13] investigate cyberattacks against autonomous ships by leveraging the STRIDE methodology. A novel graphical security model named MV-HARM is proposed in [4] to analyze the security of maritime vessel networks. The cyber risks related to ship network infrastructure are discussed in [10]. The security of OPS-SAT CubeSat focusing on an attack targeting the mission's primary payload is provided in [1]. The cascading effects of cyberattacks against the space infrastructure are explored in [7], based on the complex network of interdependencies.

To the best of our knowledge, no previous work has implemented a holistic threat analysis to identify potential attacks against maritime operations that may occur in the space LEO infrastructure.

4   Threat Analysis in Satellite Communications for Maritime Operations

4.1   Methodology

STRIDE is a threat modeling methodology or framework originally created by Kohnfelder and Garg in 1999 and adopted by their employer Microsoft[4] in 2002 [23]. STRIDE is one of the most mature threat modeling frameworks and stands

---

[3] NIST CSF: https://www.nist.gov/cyberframework.
[4] Microsoft   STRIDE: https://learn.microsoft.com/en-us/previous-versions/commerce-server/ee823878(v=cs.20)?redirectedfrom=MSDN.

for the initials of the words *Spoofing, Tampering, Repudiation, Information Disclosure, Denial of Service,* and *Elevation of Privilege* that correspond to the threat types that the method considers.

The STRIDE threat modeling process is usually divided into four steps [21]: *Step 1* consists of modeling a system in a diagram; the diagram type could be a data flow diagram (DFD), state lane diagram, swim lane diagram, or unified modeling diagram (UML). The most widely used diagram type is DFD [24, pp. 44]. *Step 2* consists of mapping the identified DFD elements to the STRIDE threat categories. A DFD element can be susceptible to more than one of the categories [21]. *Step 3* consists in extracting threats. Specific threats are extracted for each of the identified mappings between a DFD element and a threat category. *Step 4* consists of documenting the identified threats in a structured format; this is often done using misuse cases [21].

It is important to note that we implemented STRIDE in the architecture depicted in Fig. 1, considering the four space segments and their components. This allows us to extract results that remain valid despite internal architectural modifications, as long as each system or subsystem of the architecture remains operationally the same. The risk analysis is carried out by considering the likelihood of an attack and its impact. For the risk analysis we employed the risk matrix depicted in Fig. 2 and used the criteria shown in Table 1 and in Table 2 to assess risk.

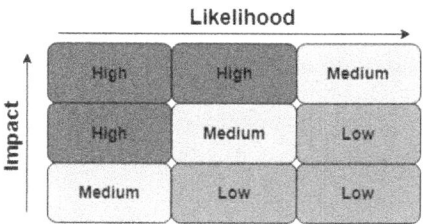

Fig. 2. Risk matrix, based on [13].

4.2 Applying STRIDE to Satellite Communications for Maritime Operations

A full analysis of threats against the Satellite Communication infrastructure as it is depicted in Fig. 1 using STRIDE has been carried out. In the interest of adhering to space limitations, in this section we present a selected subset of the results of [5]. In the tables that follow "I" stands for "Impact", "L" stands for "Likelihood" and "R" stands for "Risk". Tables 3 to 10 show the threat analysis results.

Table 3 shows the results of the STRIDE threat modeling in the Control Center. 4 high risks and 2 medium risks were identified. Table 4 shows the results

Table 1. Impact criteria for satellite communication in maritime operations

Impact Criteria	
High (H)	1. Threats that may lead to the loss of human life. 2. Threats that may cause significant disruption to critical operations. 3. Threats that could result in major financial loss. 4. Threats that could result in unauthorized access to sensitive information. 5. Threats that could cause extensive service outage. 6. Threats that could compromise the integrity of command and control systems.
Medium (M)	1. Threats that could cause partial disruption of services. 2. Threats that may result in data manipulation. 3. Threats that could degrade communication quality 4. Threats that could result in unauthorized network access 5. Threat that could impact business operations. 6. Threats that may cause moderate economic impact.
Low (L)	1. Threats that could cause minor delays or disruptions. 2. Threats that may result in leakage of nonsensitive data. 3. Threats that could temporarily reduce service quality. 4. Threats that could cause brief communication interruptions. 5. Threats that could have minimal operational impact. 6. Threats that could lead to minor economic impact.

Table 2. Likelihood criteria for satellite communication in maritime operations

Likelihood Criteria	
Very Likely (VL)	1. The adversary is highly motivated and capable, with the skills and resources to exploit vulnerabilities, and there are no effective countermeasures deployed. 2. There are widely known and easily executable exploits targeting the system, which can be executed at any time by attackers. 3. The system, including satellite communications and ground stations, has high exposure to the internet and external networks, increasing the risk of attack. 4. There have been frequent past incidents indicating a high likelihood of similar attacks in the future.
Moderate (M)	1. The adversary is motivated and capable, but the system has some countermeasures that can mitigate the risk to a moderate level, but still be vulnerable. 2. The system has known vulnerabilities, but exploiting them requires physical access or specific conditions that are not always met. 3. Systems are indirectly exposed to the Internet or external networks, making it moderately challenging for attackers to reach and exploit them. 4. There have been occasional incidents or attempts indicating a moderate likelihood of similar attacks.
Rare (R)	1. The attacker is not highly motivated or lacks the necessary skills and resources to perform an attack, or the deployed countermeasures are highly effective. 2. An attacker must have administrative rights or specific, hard-to-obtain knowledge to perform the attack. 3. The system is not connected to external networks or systems, minimizing exposure. 4. There have been few to no past incidents, indicating a low likelihood of similar attacks occurring.

Table 3. Control Center in STRIDE

	Control Center			
T	**Threat description**	**I**	**L**	**R**
S	An attacker could spoof the identities of authorized personnel, gaining access to control center systems and issuing unauthorized commands to satellites.	H	M	H
T	An attacker could physically tamper with control center hardware, this can include servers, control terminals, and so on, ultimately installing malicious hardware or firmware, disrupting operations. An attacker could also tamper with the supply chain of hardware and/or software used in the control center to obtain the same results.	H	R	M
R	An attacker could manipulate control center access logs to obscure their actions, making it difficult to trace or prove malicious activities.	H	M	H
I	Sensitive operational information, such as satellite control commands or telemetry data, could be intercepted from the control center, leading to unauthorized access and data breaches.	H	M	H
D	An attacker could launch a DoS attack against control center systems, causing service outages and disrupting communications with the satellite constellation.	H	M	H
E	An attacker could exploit software vulnerabilities in control center systems to gain elevated privileges, allowing them to control or disrupt satellite operations.	H	R	M

Table 4. Ground stations in STRIDE

	Ground Stations			
T	**Threat description**	**I**	**L**	**R**
S	An attacker could spoof the radio frequency signals used by the ground station to communicate with the satellites. This could lead to the ground station accepting false commands or telemetry data, disrupting satellite operations.	H	M	H
T	An attacker could physically tamper with the ground station's equipment, inserting malicious hardware or modifying existing components to disrupt communications or data integrity.	H	R	M
R	An attacker could perform actions within the ground station's network that go unlogged or mislogged, enabling them to deny responsibility for malicious activities and avoid detection.	M	M	M
I	Sensitive information, such as control commands and telemetry data, could be intercepted by an attacker during transmission between the ground station and satellites, leading to potential data breaches.	H	M	H
D	An attacker could launch a DDoS attack against the ground station, overwhelming its systems and causing a denial of service, disrupting communications between the station and the satellite network.	H	M	H
E	An attacker could exploit vulnerabilities within the ground station's software to gain elevated privileges, granting them unauthorized access to critical systems and the ability to issue commands to the satellites.	H	R	M

of the STRIDE threat modeling on ground stations. 3 high risks and 3 medium risks were identified.

Table 5 shows the results of the STRIDE threat modeling on the LEO satellites. 3 high risks and 3 medium risks were identified. Table 6 shows the results of the STRIDE threat modeling on the Starlink equipment on board the ship. 4 high risks and 2 medium risks were identified.

Table 7 shows the results of the STRIDE threat modeling in the generic firewall between the Starlink user equipment and the 3 internal networks on

Table 5. LEO Satellites in STRIDE

	LEO Satellites			
T	**Threat description**	**I**	**L**	**R**
S	An attacker could spoof the satellite communication signals, causing the satellites to accept false commands or telemetry data, potentially leading to incorrect positioning or data transmission errors.	H	M	H
T	An attacker could physically tamper with a satellite if they gain access to it, this could be done in orbit or by tampering with the satellite supply chain. The potential to insert malicious hardware, software, or modifying components is a possibility.	H	R	M
R	An attacker could manipulate logs or telemetry data to hide malicious activities, making it difficult to trace or prove their actions.	M	M	M
I	Sensitive information, such as encryption keys and satellite control data, could be intercepted by an attacker, leading to potential unauthorized access and data breaches.	H	M	H
D	An attacker could launch a jamming attack against the satellite's communication frequencies, causing a denial of service and disrupting communication with the ground stations or the ships Starlink equipment.	H	M	H
E	An attacker could exploit software vulnerabilities in satellite control systems to gain elevated privileges, allowing them to issue unauthorized commands and control the satellite.	H	R	M

Table 6. Starlink Equipment on ship in STRIDE

	Starlink equipment on ship			
T	**Threat description**	**I**	**L**	**R**
S	An attacker could spoof the signals between the ship's antenna and the LEO satellites, causing the antenna to accept false commands or data, leading to incorrect operations or data corruption.	H	M	H
T	An attacker could physically tamper with the antenna or power supply on the ship, inserting malicious hardware or modifying components to disrupt communication or damage equipment.	H	M	H
R	An attacker could manipulate logs or records on the ship network, obscuring their actions and making it difficult to trace or prove malicious activities.	M	M	M
I	Sensitive information, such as encryption keys or operational data, could be intercepted from the ship antenna or network cables connected to equipment, leading to unauthorized access and data breaches.	H	M	H
D	An attacker could launch a jamming attack on the ship antenna, disrupting communication with the satellite and causing a denial of service.	H	M	H
E	An attacker could exploit vulnerabilities on the ship Starlink equipment software, gaining elevated privileges and unauthorized control over the communication system.	H	R	M

board the ship. 3 high risks and 3 medium risks were identified. Table 8 shows the results of the STRIDE threat modeling in the critical network on the ship. 4 high risks and 2 medium risks were identified.

Table 9 shows the results of the STRIDE threat modeling in the business network on the ship. 1 high risk and 5 medium risks were identified. Table 10 shows the results of the STRIDE threat modeling in the crew network on the ship. 5 medium risks and 1 low risk were identified.

Table 7. Generic ship firewall in STRIDE

	Generic ship firewall			
T	**Threat description**	**I**	**L**	**R**
S	An attacker could spoof the source IP address of a trusted network segment, for example the critical network, to bypass firewall rules and gain unauthorized access to sensitive systems and data.	H	M	H
T	An attacker could physically tamper with the firewall hardware, potentially inserting malicious components or modifying firmware to bypass security checks.	H	R	M
R	An attacker could compromise the firewalls logging and auditing mechanisms to alter logs, making it difficult to trace unauthorized activities and attribute malicious activities.	M	M	M
I	An attacker could exploit vulnerabilities in the firewall to intercept and access sensitive data being transmitted between the Starlink equipment and internal networks.	H	M	H
D	An attacker could overload the firewall with traffic (DDoS attack), causing it to fail and disrupting communications between the Starlink equipment and the internal networks.	H	M	H
E	An attacker could exploit software vulnerabilities in the firewall to gain elevated privileges, allowing them to modify rules and control network traffic.	H	R	M

Table 8. Critical network in STRIDE

	Critical network			
T	**Threat description**	**I**	**L**	**R**
S	An attacker could spoof critical network credentials or communication protocols, gaining unauthorized access to critical systems and potentially causing critical disruptions or malicious activities.	H	M	H
T	An attacker could tamper with systems or devices with authorization in the critical network to insert malicious firmware or hardware, leading to disruptions or unauthorized access to data.	H	R	M
R	An attacker could manipulate logs or records within the critical network to obscure their actions, making it difficult to trace or prove malicious activities.	H	M	H
I	An attacker could gain unauthorized access to sensitive information on the critical network, such as navigation data, propulsion system controls, or critical safety system configurations.	H	M	H
D	An attacker could launch a DDoS attack against critical systems or devices on the critical network, causing a loss of availability and potentially disrupting critical ship operations.	H	M	H
E	An attacker could exploit a vulnerability in a critical system or device on the critical network, allowing them to gain elevated access and control over critical ship operations, including the ability to modify configuration settings and inject malware.	H	R	M

4.3   Microsoft Threat Modelling Tool

The Microsoft's Threat Modeling Tool (MTMT) allows the identification of potential threats which target data flows and back-end services of the system under analysis [11]. This tool allows the identification of security problems in processes, data stores and data flows, as the analysis is conducted using DFDs. Hence, DFDs for the satellite communication infrastructure for maritime operations are created.

MTMT comes with templates, and SDL TM Knowledge Base (Core) (4.1.0.11) was used as the base template for this analysis. The templates

Table 9. Business network in STRIDE

	Business network			
T	**Threat description**	**I**	**L**	**R**
S	An attacker could spoof business network user credentials or communication protocols, gaining unauthorized access to sensitive business information and resources.	M	M	M
T	An attacker could tamper with devices like workstation and other devices connected to the business network, to insert malicious software or hardware, leading to data breaches and disruptions.	M	M	M
R	An attacker could manipulate business network logs to obscure their actions, making it difficult to trace or prove malicious activities.	M	M	M
I	Sensitive business information, such as financial data or intellectual property, could be intercepted from the business network, leading to data breaches and competitive disadvantages.	H	M	H
D	An attacker could launch a DoS attack against business network servers, causing service outages and disrupting business operations.	M	M	M
E	An attacker could exploit vulnerabilities in business network software or devices to gain elevated privileges, allowing them to access and manipulate sensitive data and systems.	H	R	M

Table 10. Crew network in STRIDE

	Crew network			
T	**Threat description**	**I**	**L**	**R**
S	An attacker could spoof crew network credentials, gaining unauthorized access to personal information and potentially using the network as a pivot point to access other networks and systems onboard	M	M	M
T	An attacker could gain unauthorized access to a crew device or system on the crew network and modify its configuration or software, allowing them to disrupt or manipulate crew communications or steal personal data.	M	M	M
R	An attacker could manipulate logs or records on the crew network to obscure their actions, making it difficult to trace or prove malicious activities.	M	M	M
I	An attacker could gain unauthorized access to sensitive personal data from the crew on the crew network, such as identifiable personal information, financial data or medical records.	M	M	M
D	An attacker could launch a DDoS attack against crew devices or systems on the crew network, causing loss of availability and potentially disrupting the communication and morale of the crew. A DDoS attack could also lead to potential monetary loss to the crew, due to the limited data plan in maritime satellite Internet.	M	M	M
E	An attacker could exploit vulnerabilities in crew network software to gain elevated privileges, allowing them to access and manipulate personal data and network settings.	M	R	L

come with predetermined assumptions and descriptions and are usually related towards software-specific threat modeling. The main elements and parts of the template have been modified to represent the systems and components of the targeted infrastructure considering the Microsoft's user guide on MTMT [17]. The elements in the DFD are called *stencils* in MTMT. The definition of these five elements had to be adjusted in our STRIDE threat model. These are described in Table 11.

Table 11. MTMT element descriptions

Element	Description
Process	Represents a system component or operational entity involved in the satellite communication process.
External Interactor	Represents an external system or network interacting with the satellite communication system. For example, terrestrial internet backbone.
Data store	Any storage location for data, such as a database or file system.
Data flow	Represents the flow of data between system components or operational entities involved in the satellite communication process.
Trust Boundary	Boundary that defines areas of differing trust levels. Used to indicate where security controls are applied and where data transitions from one trust level to another.

The STRIDE threat modeling process is utilized by creating a DFD-diagram based on the identified assets of Sect. 2. The DFD-diagram is visualized in Fig. 3. The threat model produced a total of 177 threats in the Satellite Communications infrastructure for Maritime Operations. MTMT has an export function that provides a report of the threats identified in the threat model.

In the interest of adhering to space limitations, in this section we present a selected subset of the results of [5]. Figure 4 shows an exported threat in the Denial of Service category, for the RF signal data flow between a ground station and a LEO satellite.

4.4   SPARTA

In the previous analysis a holistic threat modeling approach was provided for the overall infrastructure. By focusing on particular critical assets identified from the STRIDE threat modeling, the Space Attack Research and Tactic Analysis (SPARTA) framework is applied. SPARTA is developed by The Aerospace Corporation to address the information and communication barrier in the space field [30]. SPARTA builds upon MITRE ATT&CK[5] and leverages unclassified research from academia and other credible information sources into cybersecurity matrices consisting of Tactics, Techniques, and Procedures (TPP). *Tactics* in

---

[5] MITRE ATT&CK: https://attack.mitre.org/.

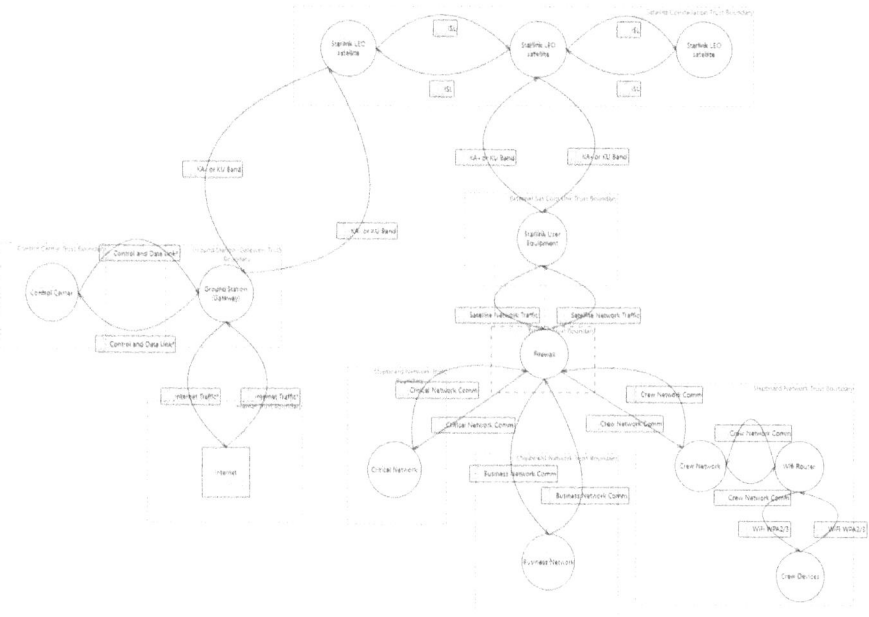

Fig. 3. Satellite Communications for Maritime Operations - DFD-diagram

SPARTA represent the tactical goals of the threat actor. These are: *Reconnaissance, Resource Development, Initial Access, Execution, Persistence, Defense Evasion, Lateral Movement, Exfiltration, and Impact* [31]. *Techniques* are used to explain how a threat actor accomplishes a tactical objective through specific actions [32]. *Procedures* are used as a step-by-step description of the threat actors' use of tactics, techniques, and sub-techniques to achieve their initial tactical goal [29]. SPARTA also defines countermeasures that can be employed to prevent the successful execution of a technique or sub-technique. The countermeasures are made and mapped to standards such as NIST SP 800-53[6] and ISO 27001[7] [28]. The framework is not necessarily a traditional threat modeling framework, but can be utilized as an attack-centric threat modeling framework.

In Fig. 5 a threat actor compromises a ground station connected to the Starlink LEO satellite constellation and uses SDR to spoof GPS signals that are intended for a ship. SPARTA uses IDs to keep track of tactics, techniques, sub-techniques, and countermeasures. Figure 6 illustrates the applied SPARTA matrix.

The SPARTA matrix consists of 9 tactics. *The Persistence* and *Evasive Action* tactics are combined in our threat model because they are relevant to the attack under analysis. Tactic *Exfiltration* is not considered, because it is not

---

[6] NIST SP 800-53: https://csrc.nist.gov/pubs/sp/800/53/r5/upd1/final.
[7] ISO 27001: https://www.iso.org/standard/27001.

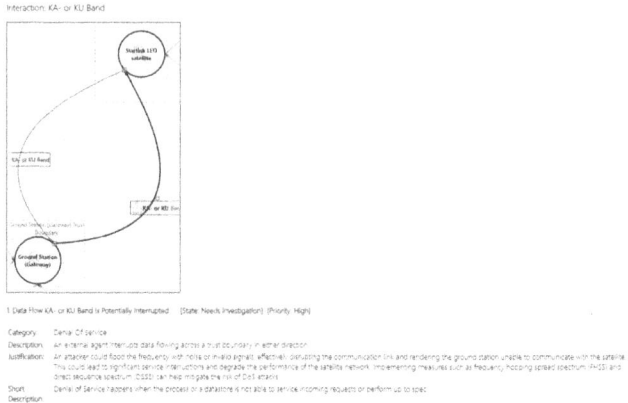

Fig. 4. Interaction between Ka- or Ku-band for Ground Station and Satellite

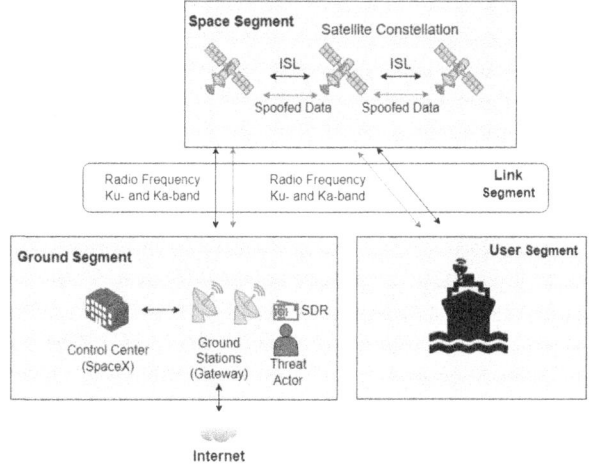

Fig. 5. Ground Station Spoofing Attack Through SDR.

relevant to our scenario. An overview of the tactics with IDs is found in [31], techniques with IDs in [32], and countermeasures with IDs in [28].

The results of using SPARTA to analyze the specific attack follow.

Reconnaissance

- **Tactic ID:** ST0001
- **Tactic objective:** Obtain necessary information about the target ground station or vessel to facilitate further attacks.

The first step of the attack is the reconnaissance phase. The attacker aims to gather intelligence on the ground station or vessel connected to the Starlink

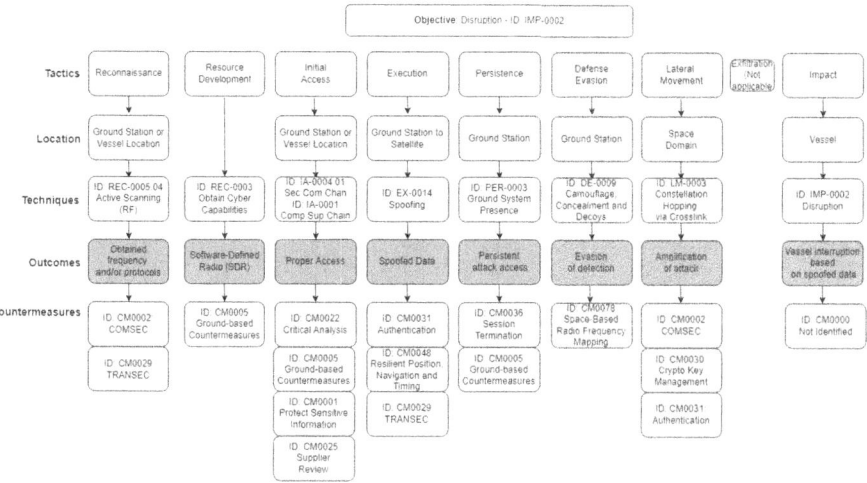

Fig. 6. Spoofing attack through SDR.

LEO satellite constellation. The attacker takes the following steps to achieve the objective:

– **Technique ID:** REC-0005.04 - Active Scanning (RF)

The attacker uses a scanning device to identify and map the frequency and protocols used by the target ground station or vessel. The attacker also checks all available information sources that pertain to the details and security of the ground stations or the vessel.

ST0001 - Countermeasures To mitigate the risk associated with this reconnaissance tactic, the following countermeasures can be implemented:

– **CM ID:** CM0002 - Communications Security. Employ robust communications security measures to protect sensitive information transmitted over communication channels. This includes secure communication protocols that utilize strong cryptographic mechanisms.
– **CM ID:** CM0029 - Transmission Security. Implement transmission security solutions to protect against RF scanning and eavesdropping. Jam-resistant waveforms, frequency hopping, and spread spectrum techniques can be used to obscure the communication signals.

Resource Development

– **Tactic ID:** ST0002
– **Tactic objective:** Develop or obtain the necessary resources and capabilities to support subsequent attack activities.

The attacker needs to acquire or develop tools, technologies, and capabilities required to execute the attack. This includes obtaining the necessary cyber capabilities to compromise the ground station and perform GPS spoofing. The following technique is used:

- **Technique ID:** REC-0003 - Obtain Cyber Capabilities. The attacker acquires or develops SDR technology and other cyber tools needed to spoof GPS signals.

ST0002 - Countermeasures. Protection of terrestrial assets is in focus to protect from physical attacks on the ground station.

- **CM ID:** CM0005 - Ground-based Countermeasures Implement monitoring of suspicious activities and access control to prevent unauthorized access to ground stations. Intrusion detection systems can be used to identify potential threats.

Initial Access

- **Tactic ID:** ST0003
- **Tactic objective:** Gain unauthorized access to target.

In the initial access phase, the attacker aims to breach the security of the target ground station or vessel. Techniques used are:

- **Technique ID:** IA-0004.01 - Secondary/Backup Communication Channel
- **Technique ID:** IA-0001 - Compromise Supply Chain

The attacker could exploit vulnerabilities in secondary or backup communication channels to gain access to the ground station. This may involve targeting less secure backup systems or communication channels that are not as heavily monitored or protected. An attacker could also target the supply chain of components in the ground station, which includes both hardware and software. A supply chain compromise could give an attacker a backdoor into the ground station system.

ST0003 - Countermeasures. Protecting against initial access to a system is a comprehensive task that requires a holistic view of the system to be able to mitigate threats.

- **CM ID:** CM0022 - Critical analysis. Critical analysis and risk assessment of critical components and the data flow of the ground station. This includes secondary and backup systems.
- **CM ID:** CM0001 - Protect Sensitive Information. Clear procedures on how to store and protect sensitive information should be implemented; this includes design and operational information for ground stations.
- **CM ID:** CM0025 - Supplier Review.
- A supplier review should be performed for all critical components of ground stations. This includes components and services of the ground station.

Execution

– **Tactic ID:** ST0004
– **Tactic objective:** Execute actions on the target to achieve intended malicious activity.

The execution phase implements the planned actions to manipulate or disrupt the target's operations. The primary objective in this use case is to spoof GPS signals that are intended for a vessel. The following technique is used:

– **Technique ID:** EX-0014 - Spoofing. The attacker uses the SDR technology from the resource development phase to generate and transmit false GPS signals. The spoofed GPS signals are specifically designed to deceive a vessel GPS receiver. Eventually, this leads to navigation errors, which could lead to operational disruptions or accidents.

ST0004 - Countermeasures. Countermeasures that protect the RF signal from ground to satellite are important in the execution phase, the attacker has already established a foothold and has potentially acquired the necessary capabilities up until this phase.

– **CM ID:** CM0031 - Authentication. Robust authentication mechanisms for GPS signals should be implemented. This can include cryptographic authentication.
– **CM ID:** CM0048 - Resilient Position, Navigation and Timing. Resilient Positioning, Navigation, and Timing (PNT) solutions that can detect and mitigate the effect of GPS spoofing should be implemented. This can include multiple sources of PNT data and employing anti-spoofing and jamming mechanisms.

Persistence and Defense Evasion

– **Tactic ID:** ST0005
– **Tactic ID:** ST0006
– **Tactics objective:** Maintain a persistent presence, avoid detection, and evade defensive measures to maintain access and control over the target system.

The persistence and defense evasion phases are combined in our use case because they overlap to a large degree. In the persistence phase, the attacker focuses on establishing and maintaining a foothold within the target ground station. In the defense evasion phase, the attacker employs techniques to avoid detection by the target's security system and potential personnel. This is done to ensure the longevity of the attack and minimize the risk of being discovered and removed.

– **Technique ID:** PER-0003 - Ground System Presence
– **Technique ID:** DE-0009 - Camouflage, Concealment and Decoys

E. Kvam Frøseth et al.

The attacker establishes persistent access within the ground station's systems or physical location. This can involve installing backdoors, maintaining control over compromised accounts, or leveraging existing vulnerabilities. It can also involve disguising physical access to the location of the ground station's location, eliminating physical security measures, including disabling monitoring and camera surveillance. This leads to the attacker having continuous access to the ground station.

ST0005 and ST0006 - Countermeasures. An attacker who has persistent access to a system is problematic. It is hard to physically protect a ground station just because of the nature of how they have to operate; this includes the fact that they have to be spread around the world.

– **CM ID:** CM0036 - Session Termination. Strict session management and automatic termination of an inactive session should be implemented.
– **CM ID:** CM0078 - Space-based Radio Frequency Mapping. Space-based RF mapping should be implemented to detect anomalies in communication patterns.
– **CM ID:** CM0005 - Ground-based countermeasures. Comprehensive logging and monitoring systems to detect and analyze suspicious activities should be implemented.

Lateral Movement

– **Tactic ID:** ST0007
– **Tactic objective:** Move laterally within the target environment to access additional systems or data and expand the attack's impact.

In the lateral movement phase, the attacker seeks to exploit the Starlink satellite constellations crosslink capabilities to amplify the GPS spoofing attack.

– **Technique ID:** LM-0003 - Constellation Hopping via Crosslink. The attacker leverages inter-satellite links (ISLs) to hop from one satellite to another, with the potential of accessing different parts of the network or additional ground stations. This can amplify the attack to disrupt multiple vessels within a certain area relying on the same spoofed GPS data.

ST0007 - Countermeasures. Potentially being able to move laterally in a compromised system is a major problem and can have a significant impact on the attack, by potentially amplifying spoofed data.

– **CM ID:** CM0002 - COMSEC. Encryption and secure communication protocols should be implemented to avoid compromise in the inter-satellite links.
– **CM ID:** CM0030 - Crypto Key Management. Best-practice cryptographic key management should be implemented to ensure that encryption keys are securely generated, distributed, and stored.
– **CM ID:** CM0031 Authentication. Strong authentication mechanisms should be implemented to verify entities that attempt to communicate or move laterally within the satellite constellation.

Impact

- **Tactic ID:** ST0009
- **Tactic objective:** Cause disruption to target vessel(s) through GPS spoofing.

The impact phase of the SPARTA matrix sets the ultimate goal for the attack.

- **Technique ID:** IMP-0002 - Disruption. The attacker uses the compromised ground station and spoofed GPS signals to mislead the vessel. This results in the vessel receiving incorrect navigation information, which can lead to operational disruptions, navigation errors, or physical accidents.

5   Summary of Results and Discussion

As already mentioned, 177 threats were identified during our STRIDE threat modeling in MTMT. This is consistent with the notion that STRIDE provides a large number of threats for complex systems and should be an iterative process throughout the lifetime of a system [23]. Threats identified through MTMT analysis are similar to the threats identified by the STRIDE methodology. However, the threats identified in the MTMT are more detailed, focusing on specific system/protocol vulnerabilities and complement the STRIDE analysis results. For example, the DoS threat in the ground station is described in STRIDE as *"An attacker could launch a DDoS attack against the ground station, overwhelming its systems and causing a denial of service, disrupting communications between the station and the satellite network"*. This same threat in the MTMT analysis is described in more detail: *"An attacker could flood the frequency with noise or invalid signals, effectively disrupting the communication link and rendering the ground station unable to communicate with the satellite. This could lead to significant service interruptions and degrade the performance of the satellite network. Implementing measures such as frequency hopping spread spectrum (FHSS) and direct sequence spectrum (DSSS) can help mitigate the risk of Dos attacks"*.

An overview of the results of the STRIDE threat model is provided in Table 12. The bottom row of the table shows a total risk score considering the criticality of each scenario (H=3, M=2, and L=1). This overview gives us a good understanding of the threats and risks throughout the system. Spoofing, Information Disclosure, and Denial of Service gathered the highest scores of cyber risk. Tampering, Repudiation, and Elevation of Privilege are at a lower risk than the two aforementioned threats. This makes sense, particularly for Tampering and Elevation of Privilege, because they usually require a more sophisticated attack to materialize, compared to Spoofing, Information Disclosure, and Denial of Service.

The risks for each identified asset are high across the main maritime elements as these are described in Sect. 2. The Business Network and the Crew Network are identified as the assets with the lowest risk, with a total risk score of 13 and 11 respectively. The rest of the assets have a total risk score in the range of

Table 12. Overview of STRIDE threats and risks, based on [13]

	Control Center	Ground Station	LEO Satellite	User Equipment	Ship Firewall	Critical Network	Business Network	Crew Network
	STRIDE overview							
T								
S	H	H	H	H	H	H	M	M
T	M	M	M	H	M	M	M	M
R	H	M	M	M	M	H	M	M
I	H	H	H	H	H	H	H	M
D	H	H	H	H	H	H	M	M
E	M	M	M	M	M	M	M	L
TR	16	15	15	16	15	16	13	11

15-16. This shows that proper management of the ship's network is an important factor in mitigating threats and risks in the user segment.

By leveraging an attack-centric approach, an attack that describes a GPS spoofing attack originating from a ground station, traveling through satellite communication to a target ship is analyzed. SPARTA is based on real-life information and data on space systems, which ensures that the threat model is grounded in reality and reflects the actual risks and vulnerabilities presented in satellite communication systems. The SPARTA matrix tooling also contributes to making the threat modeling process structured and comprehensive. SPARTA showed that a sophisticated GPS spoofing attack can be carried out to disrupt or potentially cause major incidents for ships. It also highlights the importance of securing ground stations, both physically and virtually.

Cybersecurity research in space infrastructure faces several significant limitations, which can impact the development and deployment of secure systems in this critical sector. Space systems operate in harsh environments, leading to unique technical challenges such as radiation effects, latency issues, and limited computational resources. These factors complicate the application of conventional cybersecurity measures. Furthermore, the lack of information regarding technical aspects of the space systems is among the main limitations when analyzing space infrastructure.

6 Conclusions

This work discussed the growing cyber threat landscape for maritime operations caused by the emergence of high-bandwidth, low-latency, and cost-efficient Internet through LEO satellite constellations. The components and cybersecurity threats of state-of-the-art LEO satellite constellations were presented. In addition, the threats and risks to satellite communication in maritime operations were identified. The threat analysis illustrated that LEO satellite constellations are complex systems that span multiple domains. STRIDE identified numerous threats and gave a holistic view of the threats to satellite communications by leveraging the MTMT analysis. Several observations were made through a risk assessment of the assets and threats identified. Spoofing, Information Disclosure, and Denial of Service had the highest risks in terms of threats. STRIDE and SPARTA were used to properly cover an under-researched area and give both a holistic and detailed view of threat modeling. As future work, we aim to further explore the threats against satellites used in the maritime sector by applying an automated tool and examine the propagation of the risks among critical infrastructures.

References

1. Calabrese, M., Kavallieratos, G., Falco, G.: A Hosted Payload Cyber Attack Against Satellites. In: AIAA SciTech Forum and Exposition, 2024. American Institute of Aeronautics and Astronautics Inc, AIAA (2024). https://doi.org/10.2514/6.2024-0270
2. Dark Reading Staff: Satellite Networks Worldwide at Risk of Possible Cyberattacks, FBI & CISA Warn (2022). https://www.darkreading.com/vulnerabilities-threats/satellite-networks-worldwide-at-risk-of-possible-cyberattacks-fbi-cisa-warn
3. Diro, A., Khan, S.K., Molla, A.: Leveraging system dynamic modelling for space cybersecurity conceptualisation and assessment. Available at SSRN 4671343
4. Enoch, S.Y., Lee, J.S., Kim, D.S.: Novel security models, metrics and security assessment for maritime vessel networks. Comput. Netw. **189** (4 2021). https://doi.org/10.1016/j.comnet.2021.107934
5. Frøseth, E.K.: Threat Modeling in Satellite Communications for Maritime Operations. Master's thesis, Norwegian University of Science and Technology (June 2024)
6. Gerber, C.J.: Cybersecurity risk effects of starlink on rural populations in the united states (2023)
7. Hanan, J.T., Fowler, E., Hernandez, S., Niemczyk, M., Tatar, U., Keskin, O.F.: Analysis of satellite systems' dependencies and their cascading impacts. In: 2024 Systems and Information Engineering Design Symposium (SIEDS), pp. 493–498. IEEE (2024)
8. Hasan, R., Hasan, R.: Towards a threat model and security analysis of spacecraft computing systems. In: 2022 IEEE International Conference on Wireless for Space and Extreme Environments, WiSEE 2022, pp. 87–92. Institute of Electrical and Electronics Engineers Inc. (2022). https://doi.org/10.1109/WiSEE49342.2022.9926912
9. Humphreys, T.E., Iannucci, P.A., Komodromos, Z.M., Graff, A.M.: Signal Structure of the Starlink Ku-Band Downlink (2023)
10. Kaminska, N., Kravtsova, L., Kravtsov, H., Zaytseva, T.: Modeling ship cybersecurity using Markov chains: an educational approach. Tech. rep. (2024)
11. Kavallieratos, G., Chowdhury, N., Katsikas, S., Gkioulos, V., Wolthusen, S.: Threat analysis for smart homes. Future Internet **11**(10), 207 (2019)
12. Kavallieratos, G., Katsikas, S.: An exploratory analysis of the last frontier: A systematic literature review of cybersecurity in space. International Journal of Critical Infrastructure Protection **43** (12 2023). https://doi.org/10.1016/j.ijcip.2023.100640

13. Kavallieratos, G., Katsikas, S., Gkioulos, V.: Cyber-attacks against the autonomous ship. Tech. rep. (2019). https://doi.org/10.1007/978-3-030-12786-2_2
14. Kodheli, O., et al.: Satellite communications in the new space era: a survey and future challenges. IEEE Commun. Surv. Tutorials **23**(1), 70–109 (2 2020).https://doi.org/10.1109/COMST.2020.3028247, https://arxiv.org/abs/2002.08811v2
15. Lightman, S., Suloway, T., Brule, J.: NIST IR 8401 Satellite Ground Segment. Tech. Rep. (2022). https://doi.org/10.6028/NIST.IR.8401
16. Meland, P.H., Bernsmed, K., Wille, E., Rødseth, J., Nesheim, D.A.: A retrospective analysis of maritime cyber security incidents. TransNav **15**(3), 519–530 (2021https://doi.org/10.12716/1001.15.03.04
17. Microsoft: Microsoft Threat Modeling Tool (2022). https://learn.microsoft.com/en-us/azure/security/develop/threat-modeling-tool-feature-overview
18. Nejad, B.: Introduction to Satellite Ground Segment Systems Engineering (2023)
19. Pavur, J., Martinovic, I.: Building a launchpad for satellite cyber-security research: Lessons from 60 years of spaceflight. J. Cybersecur. **8**(1) (2022). https://doi.org/10.1093/cybsec/tyac008
20. Plotnek, J., Slay, J.: A threat-driven resilience assessment framework and security ontology for space systems. Tech. rep. (2022). https://www.researchgate.net/publication/370102679
21. Scandariato, R., Wuyts, K., Joosen, W.: A descriptive study of Microsoft's threat modeling technique. Requirements Eng. **20**(2), 163–180 (2013). https://doi.org/10.1007/s00766-013-0195-2
22. Sheik, A.T., Atmaca, U.I., Maple, C., Epiphaniou, G.: Challenges in threat modelling of new space systems: A teleoperation use-case. Adv. Space Res. **70**(8), 2208–2226 (10 2022). https://doi.org/10.1016/j.asr.2022.07.013
23. Shevchenko, N., Chick, T.A., O'riordan, P., Scanlon, T.P., Woody, C.: Threat Modeling: A Summary of Available Methods (2018)
24. Shostack, A.: Threat Modeling: designing for security. Wiley, 1st edition edn. (2014)
25. SpaceX: Modulation and Waveform Patent. Patent No: US 12.003.350 B1
26. Starlink: Flat High Performance Kit Specifications (2024). https://api.starlink.com/public-files/specification_sheet_flat_high_performance.pdf
27. Starlink: Starlink Point of Presence (2024). https://starlink-enterprise-guide.readme.io/docs/peering-with-starlink
28. The Aerospace Corporation: SPARTA Countermeasures (2022). https://sparta.aerospace.org/countermeasures/SPARTA
29. The Aerospace Corporation: SPARTA Procedures (2022). https://aerospace.org/article/understanding-space-cyber-threats-sparta-matrix
30. The Aerospace Corporation: SPARTA: Space Attack Research and Tactic Analysis (2022). https://sparta.aerospace.org/resources/getting-started
31. The Aerospace Corporation: SPARTA Tactics (2022). https://sparta.aerospace.org/tactic/SPARTA
32. The Aerospace Corporation: SPARTA Techniques (2022). https://sparta.aerospace.org/technique/SPARTA
33. Voicu, A.M., Bhattacharya, A., Petrova, M.: Handover strategies for emerging LEO, MEO, and HEO satellite networks. IEEE Access **12**, 31523–31537 (2024). https://doi.org/10.1109/ACCESS.2024.3368503
34. Willbold, J., Schloegel, M., Vögele, M., Gerhardt, M., Holz, T., Abbasi, A.: Space Odyssey: An Experimental Software Security Analysis of Satellites (2023)
35. Zhang, W., Xu, Z., Jyothi, S.A.: An In-Depth Investigation of LEO Satellite Topology Design Parameters (2024)

Cybersecurity Challenges in Industrial Control Systems: An Interview Study with Asset Owners in Norway

Lars Halvdan Flå⬛, Christoph Alexander Thieme⬛, Martin Gilje Jaatun$^{(\boxtimes)}$ ⬛, and Geir Kjetil Hanssen⬛

SINTEF Digital, Trondheim, Norway
{lars.flaa,martin.g.jaatun}@sintef.no

Abstract. This paper presents cybersecurity challenges related to industrial control systems (ICSs), identified through interviews with ICS asset owners. We interviewed participants from 10 companies within the oil and gas, food and beverage, and electricity generation and distribution industries in Norway. The interviews focused on cybersecurity challenges related to the three topics of supply chain, handling of vulnerabilities, and testbeds and digital twins. Thematic analysis of the interviews resulted in identification of 7 challenges, which can serve as inspiration and motivation for future research efforts in the field of ICS and Operational Technology (OT) cybersecurity.

Keywords: Cybersecurity Challenges · Interview Study · Operational Technology (OT) · Industrial Control System (ICS)

1 Introduction

The widespread existence of ICSs in different industries and critical infrastructures necessitates the protection of these assets against cyberattacks. The development and operation of ICSs have traditionally focused on safety and availability, and only to a lesser degree on cybersecurity. Recent trends in digitalization have however caused these systems to become more interconnected and exposed, making them more vulnerable to cyberattacks.

The motivation for this work is to explore the challenges to securing ICSs, and ultimately contribute to overcoming these challenges. The task of securing an ICS is influenced by various aspects, among them, potentially competing interests such as availability and safety, the ICS owner's risk appetite, available security solutions, available competence, and knowledge of the current threat landscape.

In order to identify the challenges and the context surrounding them, we conducted interviews with representatives of 10 companies, within 3 different industries. These industries were oil and gas, food and beverage, and electricity generation and distribution. The companies can be referred to as ICS asset owners as they all owned and operated ICSs in operation. Through analysis of the interviews, we seek to answer the following

J. Garcia-Alfaro et al. (Eds.): ESORICS 2024 Workshops, LNCS 15263, pp. 425–438, 2025.
https://doi.org/10.1007/978-3-031-82349-7_27

research question: *What are the challenges with regards to cybersecurity for ICS asset owners?*

In this work, we identified 7 challenges related to cybersecurity for ICS asset owners. In this paper our primary goal is not to suggest solutions, but we rather intend to provide inspiration and motivation for future research efforts in the field.

The structure of the paper is as follows: In Sect. 2, we give an overview of some of the previous works on interviews with ICS stakeholders. In Sect. 3, we present the methodology of our study. In Sect. 4, we present challenges identified from the interviews. Section 5 briefly discusses these challenges, along with some solutions. Section 6 concludes the paper.

2 Background

In this section we provide a non-exhaustive overview of existing works identifying challenges and needs for ICS security. Most of the works presented in this section refer to Operational Technology (OT), a term we argue can have a wider scope than just ICSs. However, in this case we believe that the presented works primarily refer to ICSs, and throughout the paper, these terms are used interchangeably. We prefer the term ICS, but use the term OT when used by the participants and included in quotes or when this term is used in other works which we refer to.

As part of a larger study commissioned by the Petroleum Safety Authority Norway (PSA) in 2019, Jaatun et al. performed interviews with petroleum sector stakeholders regarding Computer Emergency Response Team (CERT) capacity in the North Sea with an aim to determine the need for a separate CERT for the Norwegian petroleum industry [1]. The conclusion was that there did not seem to be grounds for establishing a separate petroleum CERT, but that the petroleum industry actors rather should join up with one of the existing CERTs such as KraftCERT. This recommendation was later adopted by PSA.

In another study for the PSA, Hanssen et al. interviewed stakeholders regarding increased integration of Information Technology (IT) and OT in the petroleum industry [2] and made several recommendations to the industry. These recommendations included an increased focus on data quality and integrity, since many of the data-intensive services being introduced in the industry are impacted directly by poor-quality data, which clearly has implications for cyber security.

In a similar study for the PSA, Jaatun et al. interviewed petroleum sector representatives to assess the applicability of Norwegian National Security Authority's (NSM) guidelines for IT security in OT-systems [3]. They found that these good-practice guidelines for IT-systems are mostly applicable also for OT-systems, but that allowances must be made for the critical nature of these systems and the priority of availability over confidentiality, implying that, e.g., security patches generally cannot be applied "immediately", and systems that are suspected of being compromised cannot simply be shut down (as in the IT world).

Within the same domain of petroleum, Onshus et al. performed interviews with petroleum industry stakeholders regarding the need for independence between IT and OT systems [4]. They identified 15 challenges for the industry, among them how equipment and working methods can be certified in a cost-effective way. Finally, they provided recommendations to regulatory bodies and the industry, including an increased focus on cybersecurity barrier management.

Specifically targeting the topic of supply chain security, Jaatun and Sæle performed a limited set of interviews on behalf of The Norwegian Energy Regulatory Authority (NVE) to establish how particularly smaller Distribution System Operators (DSOs) in Norway could improve supply chain security [5]. Based on this work they created a checklist for use in procurement processes, where many of the recommendations are related to ensuring that suppliers are located in appropriate geographic locations, and that expectations for suppliers regarding, e.g., participation in exercises are clearly stated in contracts. They also recommend that principles for software security are observed when developing software.

On the topic of security culture in OT, Evripidou et al. conducted 33 interviews with representatives from 25 organizations and as a result identified three barriers to development of a security culture [6]. The first and second of the identified barriers was governance structure and lack of communication. The common denominator for these barriers seemed to be the traditional divide and cultural differences between IT and OT, where operations has resided with the OT/engineering department, while security has resided with the IT department on the enterprise side. The final barrier was lack of expertise, where the authors point to cybersecurity simply being added to existing job descriptions without being accompanied by competence building as one of the factors for this barrier.

Jamail et al. interviewed eleven representatives of nine organizations to explore the use of threat modelling in cyber physical systems (CPS) [7]. Among other, they found that the variety of CPS domains posed a challenge, as several of the participants working in multiple domains found it difficult to have broad knowledge of CPS threats and components.

Lastly, Nüßer et al. performed a study of the state of cybersecurity in 25 manufacturing companies, either through online questionnaires or through interviews [8]. Based on this they present what percentages of their participants perform certain activities, such as performing regular risk assessments, or what percentages experience certain challenges, such as lacking asset inventory.

Most of the work we have summarized in this section has typically focused on one particular domain, e.g., petroleum, or a particular area of cyber security, e.g., security culture. Motivated by an interest in various topics across different industries operating ICSs, we select a wider scope for our study. This is presented in Sect. 3.

3 Methodology

In this section we describe the methodology used to answer the following research question: *What are the challenges with regards to cybersecurity for ICS asset owners?*

We collected data through interviews with ten representatives from ten companies in Norway, all operating ICSs. The companies were distributed across three industries (oil and gas, food and beverage, and electricity generation and distribution). Interviews were performed using Microsoft Teams, with two of the authors as interviewers and

428   L. H. Flå et al.

one participant from the company. The interviews were recorded for analysis purposes. One of the interviewers had the role as lead, while the second asked complementary questions and took notes. The interviews lasted between 48 and 68 min and focused on ICS cybersecurity challenges related to the three topics of supply chain, handling of vulnerabilities, and testbeds and digital twins. The topics were chosen based on the authors' interests.

The interviews were semi-structured, meaning that they allowed the interviewers to deviate from the prepared questions in the interview guide. This format was chosen to allow interviewers to pursue interesting topics, and for the participants to have the freedom to highlight what they perceived as important. Consequently, this contributed to the interviews containing information outside of the three main topics listed earlier. The interview guide is included in the appendix. Due to the semi structured format and limited time, we did not cover all questions in all the interviews.

To enable a detailed analysis of the data, the interviews were recorded and transcribed using a locally executed instance of OpenAI's Whisper[1] software for speech recognition. The transcripts generated by Whisper were then checked against the recorded interview and corrected. These corrected transcriptions of the interviews formed the input to the subsequent analysis.

For the detailed analysis of the interviews, we based our approach on the method for thematic analysis, as outlined by Braun and Clarke [9] and later revisited in Braun and Clarke [10]. We chose this approach as it is claimed to be, among other things, flexible, relatively easy to learn and perform, and accessible to researchers with little experience of qualitative research. The method consists of six steps, as listed below. The steps are named in accordance with Braun and Clarke [10], and the description indicated how we have adapted and performed each step. Although the steps are listed sequentially, it was in practice an iterative process.

1. **Data familiarisation and writing familiarisation notes.** This step was mainly carried out by listening to the recorded interviews and correcting any mistakes made in the transcription process by the Whisper software. The transcriptions were split between two people, who listened through them in parallel and made corrections. A few high-level topics/codes were noted down in this step.
2. **Systematic data coding.** In this step, we assigned codes to data extracts interesting for our analysis, i.e., data extracts relevant for challenges related to ICS cybersecurity. The set of codes were refined and expanded as we went through the process of coding all the interview.
3. **Generating initial themes from coded and collated data.** In this step, we proposed preliminary themes based on the codes, and grouped the codes into themes. Some codes were excluded, either because they did not fit any theme, because we considered the coded information too sensitive, or because they did not contain enough data.
4. **Developing and reviewing themes.** In this step we re-read the interviews to see if the identified themes worked and coded any overlooked segments.
5. **Refining, defining and naming themes.** In this step we renamed themes, changed the mapping of codes to themes, and split and merged themes. As a result, we converged on the themes included as subsections in Sect. 4.

---

[1] https://github.com/openai/whisper

6. **Writing the report.** In this step we identified what we consider to be the main findings related to the research question. This is presented in Sect. 4, structured according to the themes defined in the previous step.

The participants were sent a complete draft of the paper to have the opportunity to check quotes and provide feedback on the content.

4   Results

In this section we present the challenges we identified from the interviews. As we discuss further in Sect. 5, these results should not be interpreted to mean that the following challenges were relevant to all the participants, or that all participants expressed support for all challenges. What is presented is the breadth of challenges identified in the interview material and their relevance may therefore vary among industries and companies.

4.1   Challenge: Limited Insight into Cybersecurity Risks in the Supply Chain

A first challenge for ICS asset owners was a limited ability to verify the state of cybersecurity in their supply chain, both regarding the supplier companies themselves and the products and services they deliver. Most of the participants reported that they trust their suppliers on topics such as installing patches or using the system and equipment provided by the supplier. The factors underpinning this trust relation seemed to differ, but in many cases, it appeared to be the result of an inability to verify patches, systems, and equipment, typically caused by a lack of specific competence and resources.

Instead of verifying the actual products from suppliers, several of the participants stated that they resort to some sort of assessment of the supplier, either performed by a third party, the supplier themselves, or the ICS asset owner. In addition to these methods of verification, some also stated that aspects such as size and reputation influence their confidence in a supplier.

While assessments of suppliers can give insight into the first level of the overall supply chain, it can be challenging to maintain an overview of who they in turn bring in as their suppliers. Several of the participants expressed that it is challenging to acquire an overview of the companies that make up their supply chain, and they were not aware of good tools for estimating the supply chain risk. Some examples of challenges related to supply chain risk mentioned were situations where suppliers changed cloud providers, often triggering a new risk assessment, and the challenge of estimating and following up security culture in a supplier company.

4.2   Challenge: Lack of Cybersecurity Awareness in the Procurement Process

A second challenge was a lack of cybersecurity awareness in procurement processes, both on the part of the suppliers and ICS asset owners. Several participants reported challenges related to most phases of the procurement and supplier requirements process. The very first aspect highlighted by several participants was to get involved in the procurement process. As one participant put it: *"That's been a process that's been mainly done, you know, at the plant, and they're not used to involving IT at all in the procurement process."*

The subsequent stage, formulating or determining requirements for suppliers, was also something several participants found to be a challenge. One participant highlighted the challenge of how requirements are understood by suppliers: *"[...] we can define it, cyber security, what we need but it's kind of a challenging task to give it to the vendors and that they actually understand it so and how they understand it".*

On the topic of whether suppliers were able to meet requirements, responses included that the suppliers were immature, that larger suppliers were typically better than smaller, but also that requirements from the industry had caused a positive trend. Still, several participants also stated that they had experienced that suppliers had been reluctant to comply with requirements, for various reasons.

4.3 Challenge: Establishing Asset Inventory

A third challenge was to establish an inventory of the ICS assets. This topic was one that a majority of the participants highlighted as important but also as challenging. As one participant put it, *"[...] it's not one of the most important, it's the one important task to do [...]"*, while at the same time noting that *"[...] it's kind of challenging to actually establish it in a good practice way".* Adding to this, another participant noted that while their current asset inventory might be up to date, maintaining it and keeping it up to date is a challenge.

Regarding the challenges of establishing and maintaining an asset inventory, it seemed to be harder on the lower levels of the Purdue model (i.e., the part of the ICS closer to the physical process). While several participants reported the use of automated solutions for asset management on servers, routers or components running general operating systems, equipment on lower levels such as Remote Terminal Units (RTUs) and Programmable Logic Controllers (PLCs) seemed to be more challenging and by one of the participants claimed to rely more on manual input. However, while asset overview seemed to be a challenge, several participants expressed satisfaction with network-based monitoring tools and intrusion detection systems and claimed that these had improved the situation. In some cases we were also of the impression that a significant part of the value added by these solutions came from their ability to aid in asset discovery/management. As one of the participants stated: *"So, it identifies all equipment, and it identifies all the communication that's between all equipment, and that is a great tool for us. It gives us insights, which is, before we got that tool, it was like a blur".*

A step beyond obtaining an overview of the components and software running in an ICS is to establish Software/Hardware Bill Of Materials (SBOM/HBOM) to get the full overview of the components and libraries a supplier includes in their products. While several of the participants regarded it as a useful concept, we got the impression that it was not perceived as the most urgent one. As one of the participants put it: *"[...] but of all challenges it is perhaps not be the biggest one right now".* Another noted that one had to consider how this information would improve security.

4.4 Challenge: A Need for Practical Cybersecurity Approaches and Guidance

A fourth challenge was the need or desire for more practical approaches and guidance on how cybersecurity could be implemented and managed. Several of the participants touched on how concrete guidelines or templates could be useful. Specifically, the participants mentioned a template for formulating supplier requirement, examples of security goals for common ICS architectures, list of approved providers of various services, ICS security self-assessments, ICS security dilemma training for engineers and managers, and guidance on how to do risk assessments of a supplier's country of origin. One participant also raised the challenge of knowing whether one is in compliance with laws and regulations.

The interviews revealed that there is a fair amount of variety in the standards and guidelines in use, including Center for Internet Security (CIS) Controls, the IEC 62443 family of standards, in-house made frameworks, the NSM's guidelines for IT security, and guidelines from suppliers. The desire for practical guidelines and templates can further be seen in light of some of the comments regarding some of these standards and guidelines. One participant commended the work the NSM has done for IT: " *So make it easily comprehensible, and that is what NSM, I feel, has made the foundational principles a success is that it is so concrete and easy to understand, and something everyone can start working with from one end. Something similar for ICS would have been golden"*. And another clearly preferred the more practically oriented CIS control: "*The CIS controls framework is specific and prescriptive in the way that it states what to do. I have used it for quite some years, and I am very happy with it.*". At the same time, the same participant found material from ISO too focused on procedures: "*If you look at ISO, it's more procedure oriented. To exaggerate: You can have a thousand procedures and still have terrible security"*, while also stating that "*One easily gets lost paying too much attention to procedure compliance vs. focusing on the underlying controls and objectives. The tradeoff is less flexibility"*.

However, here we also saw differences between the companies and participants, as illustrated by the following comments on the IEC 62443 standard. While one participant stated that "*I would say that related to OT security, this is the standard which we focus the most on*", another argued that " *[…] I wonder how up to date those standards are […]. It seems like they try to do what the ISO 27000 series, among others, have done already*" and a third stated that "*I think it will be extremely hard to verify supplier compliance against that standard"*.

4.5   Challenge: Obtaining Resources and Ensuring Awareness of Cybersecurity

A fifth challenge was to obtain resources and ensure awareness of cyber security. As two of the participants stated, "*In a small company […], one has to achieve a lot with quite limited effort"*, and "*But there are of course those who dream of it [implementing a particular solution/feature], but are we to get our work done, many such things disappear in between everyday tasks"*. On top of this, another participant predicted that the competition for resources would harden in the time to come: "*You will have to prove the risk reducing effect, and security controls will be an economic investment just like any other"*.

Two ways in which this seemed to materialize was limited abilities for in-house testing or for realization of a particular solution. Another was the challenge of monitoring requirements over time. Related to the latter, one of the participants noted that performing cyber security revisions of all their suppliers was challenging, and that it required a certain set of competence. Consequently, the participant had on several occasions communicated internally the benefit of establishing a shared cyber security revision service for the whole organization.

Cybersecurity incidents, or the potential for incidents, seemed in some cases to play a role in attracting attention and resources. As examples, one participant commended others in the industry who had publicly stated that they had been victim of an attack, as it made the job of cybersecurity personnel in other companies easier. Another participant actively used questions such as "what if this goes down for x number of hours" when interacting with plant owners in the company.

4.6   Challenge: Barriers to Testbed and Digital Twin Applicability for Cyber Security

A sixth challenge was related to barriers to testbed and digital twin applicability for cyber security. Most of the participants were positive to having some sort of replica of the ICS, either as a digital twin or some type of test bed. But the degree to which it was used, if at all, varied. For test beds, several of the interviews expressed that either they themselves or the supplier had some sort of testing facilities. These seemed to vary in their degree of realistic representation and could be both physical and virtualized. The degree to which testbeds were used seemed to differ between the three industries represented in the interviews, and in many cases ensuring availability was the main motivation for their use. Digital twins were less widespread, with only one of the participants expressing that this was something they worked on, while simultaneously adding that the technology was immature.

Two aspects of digital twins and test beds reoccurred. The first was that these technologies were perceived as most relevant for testing directed towards reassuring availability and to some degree for maintenance. There seemed to be less interest in building up these capabilities primarily with security in mind. Testing for security seemed instead to be more of a complementary/secondary use case. This is likely due to the consequences of downtime in an ICS. One of the participants argued that "*[…] it is a lot easier for us to acquire resources for testing that the functionality of an ICS works as indented, compared to testing the security. This is likely related to both that I believe it would require less resources to test operational functionality, and that there is a lot more understanding for testing operational functionality in the OT community. So it becomes easier to acquire money for it.*". The second aspect was related to whether it would be possible to create a realistic enough representation of the ICS, exemplified by this response when asked if the participant saw a need for a simple and externally developed test bed: "*No, because I think it will be very difficult to make, like something that is generally applicable. Because I think it will be very supplier specific and production specific*".

Several participants were also somewhat skeptical of test beds or digital twins for various other reasons. One questioned what good use cases for the digital twin would be, and another believed trust in the supplier should be established in other ways than the ICS asset owner performing verification in a test bed.

4.7   Challenge: Establishing Vulnerability Context

A seventh challenge was related to establishing the context of a vulnerability. Several participants highlighted the need for understanding the context of a vulnerability, as exemplified by the following statement: *"Our first action is to understand context [...] do we have the possibility of doing something about it? Is it possible to patch, or should we just accept it, or should we apply some mitigating measures?"*. When establishing such a vulnerability context, the location of the vulnerability in the architecture seemed to be of particular importance. As one of the participants stated: *"We have a need for contextualizing the vulnerabilities to a much larger degree. With regards to where they are placed and what they are a part of. There is nothing wrong with the information, but a CVSS [Common Vulnerability Scoring System] of 9.8 is not a CVSS of 9.8. Being on a sealed off network which is very hard to reach is very different from a software running on an internet exposed server"*. A potential approach to contextualizing such vulnerabilities better, mentioned by several participants, was to construct paths or graphs to reason about potential ways for an attacker to reach certain areas/assets of an ICS.

After establishing context, a more informed decision can be taken as to whether the vulnerability should be patched. The loss of availability was not surprisingly a concern for the patching decision, and this was something that most of the participants explicitly stated.

4.8   Additional Challenges

In this section we present a set of additional challenges, for which we collected less data than is the case for the challenges described above.

Several of the participants bought Security Operation Centre (SOC) services from an external provider, although it was unclear to us what parts of the ICSs and/or IT networks these services covered. With regards to challenges related to SOC services, one participant expressed that the SOC did not understand the ICS context to a sufficient degree. As a result, the task of evaluating and contextualizing an event reported by the SOC fell to the participant. Another participant expressed skepticism regarding the quality of SOCs, mentioning long incident report times as an example.

The majority of participants indicated that they get their information on new vulnerabilities from a combination of sources, where the sources can be the suppliers themselves, CERTs, third party security providers, and government bodies, both national and international. All these various sources did not appear to be merged, and hence the ICS asset owner often has to take more than one source into account, a process that at least in some cases did not appear to be very automized. One of the participants expressed that this process suffered from information overload and a lack of support for extracting vulnerability information from supplier platforms.

Additional topics touched upon to some degree were usage of cloud services and AI. Several participants were skeptical of storing security related information in the cloud. Although we touched on AI in several of the interviews, none of the participants seemed to be heavily invested in AI for cyber security, although they all saw it as an area with potential.

5 Discussion

As shown in Sect. 4, the set of cybersecurity challenges are quite diverse. Furthermore, none of the challenges are supported by all interviews, and we emphasize that we cannot conclude that these challenges will be equally relevant to all ICS asset owners. Aspects such as company size, industry and experience of the security team are likely to affect to what degree the identified challenges are perceived as relevant. Additionally, our methodology likely also contributes to the variety of identified challenges. Because of these aspects, we do not attempt to prioritize them with regards to importance or relevance.

Regardless, it is still interesting to observe the variety in the findings. They indicate that the challenges faced by ICS asset owners are quite diverse, and that there might be slightly varying cybersecurity foci across industries, and across companies within the same industry. An observation which further underlines this point is the answers to a question we asked at the very end of the interviews. The participants were asked to highlight one challenge or problem of particular importance, and hardly any of the participants gave the same answer.

We do however see similarities between some of our findings and the findings of earlier studies, as briefly introduced in Sect. 2. Related to the challenge of cybersecurity awareness in the procurement process, there seems to be room for improving the cybersecurity dimension of the procurement process, a process where both ICS asset owners and suppliers must be included. Asset owners can benefit from establishing procurement processes where cyber security considerations are explicitly included, recognizing the implications cyber security incidents may have on ICS availability and business objectives. At the center of this lies the formulation of cyber security requirements for suppliers. We are of the impression that cyber security maturity among suppliers vary, with supplier size as one of the indicators of maturity. It is however important that both suppliers and relevant personnel at the ICS asset owners (e.g. plant owners or management) both see the mutual benefits of considering cyber security in the procurement and delivery of ICS systems.

The challenge of establishing an asset inventory presents itself as particularly relevant as we found support for it in a majority of the interviews, and especially since asset overview/management was not specifically asked for in the interview guide. We suspect that a reason for its relevance independent of this is the foundational and enabling role an updated asset inventory has. We also note that this finding can be confirmed by the study of security culture in OT by Evripidou et al., where they claim that [...] *asset discovery is a substantial challenge for OT companies [...]* [6]. Having an overview of the assets in an ICS as one of two prerequisites for generating value from an SBOM, since it allows ICS asset owners to know where in their architecture a potential third-party vulnerability is located. The second prerequisite is to have a method for estimating the consequences of a vulnerability, i.e., contextualizing the vulnerability. Our results in this paper indicate that there is generally room for improvement when it comes to both of these prerequisites.

For our identified challenge on the need for practical cybersecurity approaches and guidance, we note that one of the participants in the work by Jamil et al. believed it could be useful for the industry as a whole to have a set of quality threat model patterns [7].

Regarding the challenge of obtaining resources and ensuring awareness of cybersecurity, this can also be related to previous findings in literature. Evripidou et al. found that *"[...] the budget and resources for OT are typically owned by the operations function, which has different priorities on how they should be spent"* [6].

Related to the challenge of barriers to testbed and digital twin applicability for cybersecurity, we should emphasize that we include it as a challenge because some of the participants believed it could be useful in a security context, and that it did not see much use in this context. However, we were of the opinion that those participants saw it more as an opportunity than a currently pressing challenge. There are probably several reasons for these technologies seeing limited use towards cybersecurity, but we present two possible reasons. The first is a matter of resources, as the quote in Sect. 4.6 underlines. It is simply easier to get resources for testing functionality as opposed to security. The second potential reason is that other aspects are seen as more important.

When it comes to our identified challenge on contextualizing vulnerabilities, one method for doing this is through attack graphs, a topic covered among others by Kaynar [11]. In an attack graph, an attacker's privileges can be expressed as a node, and exploitation of a vulnerability can be expressed as an edge. Based on the results in our paper, we are left with the impression that such graphs have not been adapted by the industry. While reasons for this would be speculations form our side, it is evident from the work done by Kaynar that attack graphs rely on very detailed asset inventories (hosts, applications, and associated vulnerabilities), as well as their configurations (which hosts and applications can reach which other hosts and applications), which our results indicate could be a challenge. However, in addition to a need for a detailed asset inventory, Kaynar identifies a number of additional challenges for attack graphs which may also be relevant.

Specifically related to simulating the discovery of new vulnerabilities, as mentioned in Sect. 4.7, some of the existing works appears to have contributed to such an approach. For instance, Wang et al. [12], has, according to Kaynar, defined a metric indicating how many zero-day vulnerabilities an attacker would have to exploit to reach an asset.

Further related to the challenge of contextualizing vulnerabilities, we also note that contextualization is already a part of the CVSS framework. However, the CVSS score found in databases such as the National Vulnerability Database (NVD) is what is referred to as the base score, which in turn should be adjusted with a temporal and environmental aspect. During our interviews, we did not investigate further how the participants viewed this method, and whether it was in use or not.

When it comes to Sect. 4.8, we use this to list additional challenges which we identified. They are grouped together as we did not find enough data for them to be included in separate sections.

5.1 Limitations

A major limitation of our work is that we only performed one interview with every participant, thereby being unable to ask clarifying and follow-up questions once we had done a preliminary analysis of the interviews.

Another limitation of our work is that we only interviewed ICS asset owners, as opposed to also interviewing product developers, system integrators, and other cybersecurity related service providers (e.g., CERT or SOC representatives). As a result, we do in some cases only get one side of the story, for instance with regards to the relationship between ICS asset owners and suppliers.

Finally, we repeat that the results are inevitably influenced by the interview guide, which focused on cybersecurity challenges related to the three topics of supply chain, handling of vulnerabilities, and testbeds and digital twins. The focus of our questions, together with the semi-structured form of the interviews, limit us to only drawing conclusions on what was said, as opposed to what was not said. As an example, while one of the participants questioned the ability the SOC to contextualize vulnerabilities, we cannot be certain what the remaining nine think of this topic.

6 Conclusion

In this paper, we present cybersecurity challenges faced by ICS asset owners, based on ten interviews with representatives from ten companies within the oil and gas, food and beverage, and electricity generation and distribution industries in Norway. Our interview guide focused on cybersecurity challenges related to the three topics of supply chain, handling of vulnerabilities, and testbeds and digital twins. The interviews were performed in a semi-structured manner, and each interview was transcribed, coded, and the combined material was analyzed using thematic analysis. We identified seven challenges, related to limited insight into cybersecurity risk in the supply chain, lack of cybersecurity awareness in the procurement process, establishing asset inventory, a need for practical cybersecurity approached and guidelines, obtaining resources and ensuring awareness of cybersecurity, barriers to testbed and digital twin applicability for cybersecurity, and to establishing vulnerability context. The results further furthermore indicate heterogeneity in the challenges faced by the different companies, a finding we attribute to differences in size, industries, but also to our methodology. We briefly discuss the challenges but make no attempt to prioritize them in terms of importance or relevance.

Acknowledgements. We would like to thank the ten participants and express our gratitude for their participation and for openly sharing their ICS cybersecurity views, experiences, and challenges with us.

Appendix: Interview Guide

What is your role and department within the company?

– What is the size of the organization?

   Can you tell us a little about your production environment?

– Do you have one or several factories/plants, do you use safety instrumented systems, what cyber consequences are you most afraid of?

– Do you use or plan to use IoT or AI in any way, and for what purpose?

Do you experience challenges with defining cyber security requirements for suppliers?

– Do you have adequate tools and methods for defining appropriate cyber security requirement for suppliers?
– What standards/guidelines do you use for this (e.g. IEC 62443)

Do you perceive complex supply chains as a risk, and do you feel you have adequate methods for treating this risk?

– Is supply chain risk affected by the country of origin (domestic, foreign)?
– Do you rely on system integrators for maintenance and changes?

Do you experience challenges with following up requirements on suppliers?

– Do you follow up on suppliers to suppliers?
– Do you have the necessary tools and methods for doing so?

Do you experience challenges with estimating the risk to your operations/integration work/product development stemming from the supply chain?

– Both when selecting integrators and later in the operations phase?

Do you perceive patching of your ICS environment as a security challenge? Are you worried about the integrity and safety of patches?

– Do you have adequate tools and methods to assess and ensure the integrity of patches?
– What tools do you normally use?
– When and how often do you patch?

How do you communicate when it comes to vulnerabilities in your ICS?

– Do you experience any challenges with this? (Lack of trust, lack of technical solutions,…)

On a high level, what are your current approaches to secure ICS / integration phase/ product development phase?

– Do you see a need for an ICS testbed (for instance when it comes to verifying integrity of patches, the safety of new patches, testing effects of countermeasures, testing effects of new configurations)?
– Do you see other needs for a digital replica of your ICS or parts of your ICS

Could ICS test beds be relevant in order to run training scenarios for staff?
What would be your main requirements to ICS Test beds? What do you perceive as hurdles for ICS test beds (cost, availability,..)?
Are you familiar with the Asset Administration Shell concept?

– If not, is the concept interesting for you?
– Is this something you think will become important?
– Are you concerned about the cyber security aspects of this?

Anything else you want to add that we might have forgotten to ask you about?
What are your main challenges related to security?

– Which of them is in your opinion the most important to solve?
– How do you see these changing in the future?
– Any challenges we forgot to ask you about?

Based on the topics we have discussed, do you see a need for ICS-related security research?

References

1. Jaatun, M.G., Bodsberg, L., Grøtan, T.O., Moe, M.E.G.: An empirical study of CERT capacity in the North Sea. In: 2020 International Conference on Cyber Security and Protection of Digital Services (Cyber Security). IEEE, Dublin, Ireland (2020)
2. Hanssen, G.K., Onshus, T., Jaatun, M.G., Myklebust, T., Ottermo, M., Lundteigen, M.A.: Principles of digitalisation and IT-OT integration. SINTEF
3. Jaatun, M.G., Wille, E., Bernsmed, K., Kilskar, S.S.: Grunnprinsipper for IKT-sikkerhet i industrielle IKT-systemer. SINTEF (2021)
4. Onshus, T., et al.: Security and independence of process safety and control systems in the petroleum industry. J. Cybersecur. Priv. **2**, 20–41 (2022)
5. Jaatun, M.G., Sæle, H.: A checklist for supply chain security for critical infrastructure operators. In: The Cyber Science 2023, Copenhagen, Denmark July 3 (2023)
6. Evripidou, S., Ani, U.D., Hailes, S., Watson, J.D.M.K.: Exploring the security culture of operational technology (OT) organisations: the role of external consultancy in overcoming organisational barriers. In: Nineteenth Symposium on Usable Privacy and Security (SOUPS 2023), pp. 113–129. USENIX Association (2023)
7. Jamil, A.-M., ben Othmane, L., Valani, A.: Threat modeling of cyber-physical systems in practice. In: International Conference on Risks and Security of Internet and Systems, pp. 3–19. Springer International Publishing (2021)
8. Nußer, W., Koch, E., Trsek, H., Schumann, R., Mahrenholz, D.: Cyber security in production networks – an empirical study about the current status. In: 2017 22nd IEEE International Conference on Emerging Technologies and Factory Automation (ETFA). IEEE (2017)
9. Braun, V., Clarke, V.: Using thematic analysis in psychology. Qual. Res. Psychol. **3**, 77–101 (2006)
10. Braun, V., Clarke, V.: One size fits all? What counts as quality practice in (reflexive) thematic analysis? Qual. Res. Psychol. **18**, 328–352 (2021)
11. Kaynar, K.: A taxonomy for attack graph generation and usage in network security. J. Inf. Secur. Appl. **29**, 27–56 (2016)
12. Wang, L., Singhal, A., Cheng, P., Noel, S.: K-zero day safety: a network security metric for measuring the risk of unknown vulnerabilities. IEEE Tran. Dependable Secur. Comput. **11**, 30–44 (2014)

Usage of Cybersecurity Standards in Operational Technology Systems

Kristian Kannelønning(iD) and Sokratis Katsikas(✉)(iD)

Department of Information Security and Communication Technology, NTNU -
Norwegian University of Science and Technology, Postboks 191, Gjøvik 2802, Norway
{kristian.kannelonning,sokratis.katsikas}@ntnu.no
http://www.ntnu.edu.iik

Abstract. The escalating frequency of cyber attacks against industrial
installations over the past decade underscores the growing imperative
to fortify cybersecurity in organizations. The advent of Industry 4.0 has
interconnected factories with the external world, intensifying cybersecurity risks. While international standards are advocated as a source
of knowledge to enhance cybersecurity efforts, scant information exists
regarding their applicability and usage in Industry 4.0. Diverse cybersecurity standards are available, either specialized for Information Technology (IT) or Operational Technology (OT) or formulated as universal umbrella standards to guide organizations' efforts. In this paper, two
data sources are deployed - a Semi-Systematic Literature Review (SSLR)
and interviews- to unveil the extent of utilization of cybersecurity standards for OT systems in the Industry and to identify potential barriers
to cybersecurity standard usage. The results indicate a low applicability
of cybersecurity standards within OT systems. Additionally, the size and
lack of practical guidelines in OT cybersecurity standards act as entry
barriers, especially for Small and Medium Enterprises (SMEs) with limited resources. The interviews reveal that the organizations mitigate the
identified barriers by creating bespoke internal OT standards appropriate for the organization's size and goals.

Keywords: Cybersecurity standards · Industry 4.0 · Operational
Technology · IEC62443

1   Introduction

The network connections between factories and the outside world are increasing. A common term for this highly connected integration is Industry 4.0. The
term was first coined in 2011 at the Hannover fair, and [2] defines Industry
4.0 as the connection between production and information- and communication
technologies, ICT. The merging of production- and process data with machine
data enables machines to communicate with each other. The motivation for
this increased adoption of Industry 4.0 with its internet-connected factories and

J. Garcia-Alfaro et al. (Eds.): ESORICS 2024 Workshops, LNCS 15263, pp. 439–452, 2025.
https://doi.org/10.1007/978-3-031-82349-7_28

plants is to improve efficiency and effectiveness [10]. A common term in conjunction with Industry 4.0 is the Cyber-Physical System (CPS). Cyber-physical systems identify anything that integrates computation, networking, and physical processes-binding together the virtual digital world of computers and software and its interaction with the physical analog world. The Industrial Internet of Things (IIoT) is made up of networked CPSs. In these Internet-connected industrial contexts, cybersecurity issues represent one of the most relevant challenges to be dealt with [10]. Another common term that encompasses the terms Industry 4.0 and CPS is Operational Technology (OT). OT includes a broad range of programmable systems and devices that interact with the physical environment. Examples of OT systems are industrial control systems, physical access control systems, and transportation systems. One crucial difference between IT and OT systems is that the latter directly affects the physical world [19].

In the last decade, an increasing number of cyber attacks against industries, including critical infrastructure, highlights the need for organizations, governments, and society to be aware and prepare for unwanted events. Such cyber attacks can potentially inflict severe consequences on organizations and the public. Well-known examples of such attacks are those against the Maroochy County Water System in 2000, the Stuxnet attack in 2010, the power outtake in Ukraine in 2015, the attack on Norsk Hydro in 2019, the attack on the US Colonial pipeline in 2021 and the most recent attack when Russian hackers hit twenty-two Danish power companies. The attack on the Danish power companies began in May 2023 and aimed to gain comprehensive access to Denmark's decentralized power grid. These are a few examples from a much longer list of severe publicly known attacks that grow larger yearly. Threat actors, the perpetrators responsible for these events, range from insiders to criminals and nation-states [17]. In 2022, manufacturing had the highest share of cyber attacks among the leading industries worldwide. During that year, cyber attacks in manufacturing companies accounted for nearly 25 percent of the total cyber attacks.

Given the above, the importance of securing the Industry against cyber attacks is ever-increasing as the number of attacks continues to rise. As cybersecurity risk will persist as a significant challenge for organizations in the coming years, developing and fortifying the organizational cybersecurity posture will be of great importance. Several paths exist toward securing an organization. Organizations can install technical solutions like firewalls, intrusion detection systems, and the like to enhance cybersecurity. However, a holistic perspective addressing technology, processes, and people must be deployed for an organization to be secure and maximize its cybersecurity posture. For an organization to achieve holistic cybersecurity fortification, cross-functional collaboration is required. The effort is not restricted to one person or department; every member must adhere to the organization's prescribed policies.

The knowledge and structure to improve an organization's cybersecurity can be found in international cybersecurity standards. Cybersecurity standards serve as a set of recommendations that specify how organizations should carry out their operations and processes. They are often embraced because they are proven effective in providing well-structured cybersecurity requirements and controls. They provide a multitude of benefits that justify the time and financial resources required to produce and apply them [4]. Some are dedicated to specialized domains, e.g., IT or OT. Others are developed as general umbrella standards to be used anywhere by everyone, regardless of domain or organizational size. The use of cybersecurity standards should be deployed in their intended domain. A multitude of standards exist, and substantial research has classified differences and overlapping features of the most used standards [4,8,9,20].

International standards are highlighted as a path for improved cybersecurity [4]. However, little is known about the applicability or the usage of cybersecurity standards for OT systems in Industry 4.0 organizations. This paper aims to uncover to what degree such standards are used and what the potential barriers to their utilization are. To this end, two separate data sources are deployed, namely, a literature review by means of a Semi-Systematic Literature Review (SSLR) and semi-structured interviews with senior industry personnel responsible for OT.

The remainder of this paper is organized as follows: Section 2 describes the employed research methods, i.e., the SSLR and the interviews. In Sect. 3, the results and the findings are presented. These are further discussed in Sect. 4, while our conclusions and outlines for further research are found in Sect. 5.

2   Methods

A literature review aims to broaden the understanding of where the current knowledge resides and to support the need and significance for future research in contributing to expanding knowledge [6]. As Fink suggested in [6], descriptive reviews are particularly relevant when randomized controlled trials or rigorous observational studies are scarce or unavailable. The results are descriptive synthesizes based on data abstraction from included articles. The validity of the findings from the literature review depends on the reviewer's expertise and critical imagination in combination with the quality of available literature.

On the other hand, interviews are great for understanding the "how" and "why" of a particular contemporary event [21]. An interview lets the participant explain why they answered the questions the way they did [5]. Although interviews, especially with few interviews conducted, cannot be generalizable to populations or universes, they can be generalizable to theories (analytic generalizations) [21]. Furthermore, utilizing two data sources, namely interviews and the analyzed literature, strengthens the results by data triangulation in developing convergent evidence [21].

2.1   Literature Review

The literature review followed the guidelines of the Preferred Reporting Items for Systematic Reviews and Meta-Analysis, PRISMA, by Page et al. [6,13,15]. Even though the review followed the guidelines from PRISMA and [6,15], the most appropriate terminology for this review is Semi-Systematic Literature Review, SSLR. An SSLR is most suited when a topic has been researched by different groups of researchers or within different disciplines; that is, reviewing every article that could be relevant to a topic is simply impossible [16]. The use of specific search words has limited this review, and consequently, the included literature cannot be claimed to be exhaustive for all related research areas.

Firstly, one must investigate if a similar review has already been conducted. No such evidence was found. The benefit of preliminary searches is that they help refine research questions, optimize search strings, and verify that the planned review and the chosen research questions are relevant and valuable to the body of knowledge. A systematic review is, unlike subjective reviews, comprehensible and easily reproducible [6]. Research questions, search strategy, inclusion and exclusion criteria, and the data extraction method are defined before the research commences.

Predefined research questions must be formulated to ensure that relevant knowledge is captured. These must be broad enough to include relevant literature and be precise enough to guide the review [6]. This research aims to better understand how much research has been done within cybersecurity standards in the context of OT systems and to what degree practitioners apply standards. Subsequently, the following research questions have been defined:

- RQ1: What does research report on the applicability of cybersecurity standards for OT systems?
- RQ2: Are there barriers limiting the use of standards, and if so, how can the barriers be reduced?
- RQ3: Are cybersecurity standards perceived as one size fits all? (Small, medium, and large enterprises)

The results in this SSLR stem from searches in the following databases: Scopus, IEEE, Springer, Engineering Village, ScienceDirect, and ACM. Keywords deployed were the same across the databases. However, the search string was modified according to the search database syntax, e.g., (Standard OR Security Standard) AND (Operational Technology OR OT) AND (Cyber security OR Cybersecurity) to capture all relevant publications. The search term OT or Operational Technology was selected instead of the broader terms Industry 4.0 or CPS to limit irrelevant publications to a reasonable amount. Limiting the results with narrower search terms consequently defined the research method as an SSLR instead of an SLR. However, as a precaution and to ensure that the selected terms Operational Technology or OT would yield relevant results, a test was performed on the IEEE and ScienceDirect database, replacing OT with the wider, more encompassing term "Industry 4.0" in the search string. This received a significantly higher number of publications. Searches with OT in the search string received 487 results while replacing OT with Industry 4.0 received 3692 results in the two databases. A review of the first 1636 of the 3692 publications (approximately 44%) did not result in any new relevant publications. Therefore, it is assumed that the searches are exhaustive and all relevant papers have been identified in the context of cybersecurity standards within OT. Searches were restricted to titles, abstracts, and keywords in publications from 2002 until 2023.

After duplicates were removed, the following exclusion and inclusion criteria were applied:

Exclusion criteria:

- Non-peer-reviewed studies from organizational reports, guidelines, and technical opinion reports;
- Research design - exclude reviews, editorials, and testimonials;
- Non-research literature.

Inclusion criteria:

- Written in English;
- Published in (2002–2023);
- Original studies using theoretical or empirical data;
- Studies published in Journals, Conference Proceedings, and books/book sections.

2.2   Interviews

Semi-structured interviews were conducted to unearth a more profound understanding of the application of cybersecurity standards within OT systems. Seven interviews were completed during the spring of 2023. Before conducting the interviews, an interview guide was developed and tested on members from academia and personnel within the Norwegian Industry working with OT systems. The interviews took about one hour and were completed online using Microsoft Teams, with recordings transcribed before analysis.

Four organizations were approached to inquire about participating in the study. To understand how each organization works with cybersecurity, personnel from the OT and IT departments within the same organization were interviewed, except for one organization, where only IT participated. However, this participant was responsible for both OT and IT security. All participants have more than 20 years of experience in their field of expertise and hold cybersecurity responsibilities in their organization within their domain of either OT or IT.

One organization operates in discrete manufacturing, producing finalized end-products; two in process manufacturing, and one in food and beverage. Three organizations are classified as large enterprises with over 1,000 employees, while the smallest currently has around 150 employees.

The interviews and interview guide covered three broad thematic topics; one topic covered the application of standards used in general and cybersecurity standards in particular. The allotted time spent on each topic was dependent upon the responses. The sections tended to be brief for those with little experience or knowledge regarding standards. However, short sessions regarding standards often meant longer sessions on the two other topics, resulting in an approximately equal duration of each interview. The interview guide was pre-tested, and questions regarding standards started wide and in general terms and eventually turned increasingly narrower into cybersecurity standards. Below is an excerpt of the questions:

- Not restricted to cybersecurity; are standards used, and to what extent in your organization?
- If any, within what domain? (Safety, cybersecurity, or others?)
- What standards are you familiar with?
- To what extent do standards contribute to your organization's cybersecurity program?
- When using cybersecurity standards, how would you describe the material's content?
- In your opinion, what are the pros and cons of using standards? Are there better alternatives?

Analysis of the interviews relies on template analysis. The transcripts are coded by using predefined code. These codes are also referred to as a codebook. The start of the analysis relies on the predefined codes. However, codes do not remain static. Modifications or additional codes are allowed as the analysis progresses. The template is organized concerning different themes defined by the researcher and most commonly involves some hierarchical structure [7]. An often-used approach is to sort text with similar codes into separate categories for final distillation into major themes [3]. A significant advantage of template analysis stems from the highly flexible approach that can be modified to accommodate any study in a particular area. It does not come with many prescriptions and procedures, and the principles behind the technique are easily grasped by those unfamiliar with qualitative methods, partly due to the similarities of content analysis [7].

3 Results

Searches from the selected databases resulted in 1183 records after removing duplicates. The first step in conducting the SSLR is to perform an assessment based on the title and abstract [15]. This first assessment removed 1074 articles, leaving 109 records in the second analysis step. The substantial removal of 91% of the records indicates that the search and used search strings fetched a broad result, and it is therefore expected that all relevant records have been included in the results. The second step includes an assessment of the introduction and conclusion of the records. For this SSLR, the records method section was also investigated at this step. The second step reduced the number from 109 to 13 records eligible for full-text analysis. The results from the different databases are listed with the initial search result and records included in the complete text analysis: ScienceDirect (377/5), IEEE (110/7), Engineering Village (333/0), Scopus (246/1), ACM (117/0). The complete process is graphically depicted in Fig. 1.

Of the six articles included in the analysis, three were published in journals and three in conferences, with publication dates ranging from 2017 to 2023.

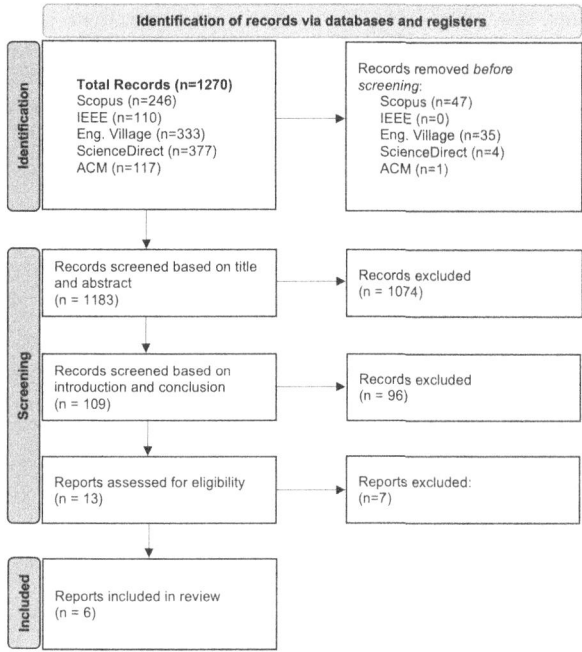

Fig. 1. SSLR Process

3.1 Findings

The results described above lead to the following findings, the presentation of which is structured to follow the research questions defined in Sect. 2.

What Does Research Report on the Applicability of Cybersecurity Standards for OT Systems? Very few articles address the research question regarding the applicability of cybersecurity standards for OT systems. With the word applicability, the goal is to find quantitative results indicating the degree of usage of cybersecurity standards. To what extent do practitioners use standards, and which standards do practitioners use? Several articles, including [20], present exciting quantitative findings, but the results rely on secondary data, e.g., a survey performed by a third party. Such papers are excluded according to the criteria put forth in this review. Only two of the identified articles provide quantitative results that include OT standards.

In [14], Pawar reports on their results from a survey with 115 SME participants from a wide range of industries and geographical locations. Participants also included personnel of organizations within manufacturing. According to [14], 49% of SMEs have no cybersecurity standards or framework in place. The NIST CSF is implemented by 8% of the SMEs. The other standards presented in the results are not OT-specific, and neither is information regarding the participant's main business activities available. However, since an unknown percentage of participants operate within manufacturing, it is reasonable to include the results. One interesting finding in the paper is worth lingering on. Although the application of standards is found to be low, 56% still report having cybersecurity controls implemented [14]. Organizations implement security measures, but the effort is not motivated by compliance to a standard.

The second article providing quantitative results is [12]. The paper reports on results from a survey of 25 organizations, all operating within the German Industry, particularly in or near North Rhine-Westphalia, with 21 of the 25 organizations categorized as operating within discrete manufacturing. Results suggest that cybersecurity standards and best practices are only somewhat implemented. As much as 80% of the large organizations participating in the survey have implemented cybersecurity measures from the German BSI IT-Grundschutz, a standard comparable to IEC27001. At the same time, only 35% of SMEs do the same. The numbers are reduced when focusing on specific OT cybersecurity standards, e.g., IEC 62443. 65% of large organizations report having an IEC 62443-related project already conducted, while the corresponding number for SMEs is less than 25%. The paper does not clarify what an IEC 62443-related project entails.

These two papers indicate a low applicability for using standards, particularly cybersecurity standards for OT. Similar results have been found in a recent unpublished study by the authors. Organizations within the Norwegian Industry were surveyed through a questionnaire regarding the usage of cybersecurity controls. In the survey, the respondents, n=34, also reported, "To what degree has international cybersecurity standards, IEC 62443 or similar, influenced your organization's cybersecurity program?". Of the n=34 respondents, only 32% (n=11) responded that their organization has either a very important- or important influence from international standards. Similar results are found in the interviews conducted in this study. Although the number of interviews is low, only seven, the theme is consistent with the literature and unpublished survey findings. The usage of security standards from the OT-responsible participants is non-existent. Even familiarity with cybersecurity standards is non-existent. A compilation of their responses could be distilled into this statement: "I am focusing on keeping the factory running. I do not know the international cybersecurity standards, so I put my trust into what vendors or machine builders tell me is sufficient for security". Responses from IT responsible favor using standards, and they express a higher knowledge and familiarity towards both IT and OT standards. However, the reported usage of specific OT standards is still low. In contrast, the applicability of adhering to IT-specific standards is high. Three of the four organizations are ISO 27001 certified and hence are compliant with an international IT standard, while the fourth organization is planning for ISO certification in the future.

Are There Barriers Limiting the Use of Standards, and if So, How Can the Barriers Be Reduced? Several of the included articles highlight that the applicability of standards is low, with various reasons for the shortage of usage. Quantitative results are not required to explain why implementation gaps exist and what could potentially bridge the identified gaps.

Both [18,20] find that the lack of comprehensible implementation guidelines also referred to as practical guidelines, is highlighted as one of the reasons for low implementation. Even though a high-level description exists in all standards and guidelines, Staves found in [17], that only 54% of them provide technical guidance when investigating thirty-one such resources in the context of cyber-security incidents and response. The identified lack of practical advice could act as a barrier to the implementation of OT cybersecurity controls [17,18].

The sheer volume and complexity of some cybersecurity standards, particularly IEC 62443, is also an argument for the identified shortage of implementation. In [20], Wagner reports that many resources are needed for an enterprise just to understand which parts in general and which topics in particular of the standard series are relevant for the organization. Staves [17] found through eight interviews that several participants raised concerns regarding the volume and depth of existing standards and guidelines from a usability perspective. This is also confirmed by the interviews conducted in this study. Among respondents familiar or very familiar with the different standards, IEC 62443 was specifically mentioned in this context, and the consensus among respondents is that the content and scope are too extensive. The scope and number of pages make using standards anything but trivial. One respondent highlighted that even after attending seminars to learn about IEC 62443, the material is still too heavy to combine with your day-to-day job, "We are reliant on external consultants to help with this work."

An interesting finding from [17] reveals that OT personnel find available standards and guidelines to be information-focused instead of function-focused, lacking tools and frameworks that adequately cover OT. Participants from IT could see direct similarities between IT and OT and that the separation and need for independent guidance will be counter-productive usage of time and resources. Separation of IT and OT is also presented in [12], who found that about 50% of the organizations applied the same rules for IT and OT regarding incident handling, indicating a desire to standardize the process landscape. The authors of [12] do raise the question, without providing an answer, of whether global rules meet the different requirements of IT and OT devices and processes.

Pawar's and Palivela's article focusing on SMEs states that there exist gaps in the implementation of cybersecurity controls [14]. SMEs cannot relate their cybersecurity efforts or measures against business priorities. Reference [14] proposes a framework called the Least Cybersecurity Control Implementation (LCCI) to bridge this gap. The LCCI will be based on implementing the least cybersecurity controls according to the defense-in-depth concept and the organization's prioritization of the CIA (Confidentiality, Integrity, Availability) triangle for mission-critical assets. The LCCI follows a seven-step process to secure mission-critical assets. It is not transparent which standards are used as the foundation for the development of LCCI, or if the framework is based on standards at all.

Our interviews revealed an interesting path for organizations to bridge the gap of voluminous standards with a lack of practical advice. Development of an organizational bespoke standard. Three of the four organizations in this study have developed these bespoke standards individually. The bespoke standards are developed at the corporate level and distributed throughout the OT department and different locations of the organization. This new bespoke internal standard is based on international standards; however, the organization's employees do not know which standards have been used as the basis. By applying this method, a made-to-order standard is available to the OT responsible that includes practical advice in a smaller format suitable to the organization's size and goals. The organizational standard thereby removes the identified gaps regarding the volume and complexity of interpreting standards, a task given to the organization's few corporate functions.

Are Cybersecurity Standards Perceived as One Size Fits All? (Small, Medium, and Large Enterprises). Cybersecurity standards must be applicable for practical use in their intended domain. Reference [20] compared IEC62443, NIST SP 800-82, and VDI/VDE 2182 in terms of general aspects, process models, and best practice measures. The process model in VDI/VDE 2182 is found to be the most applicable for both SMEs and large enterprises, with relatively detailed steps, practical application examples, and usability for beginners, which are contributing factors to the decision. However, VDI/VDE lacks the coverage found in the comparison of the other two standards. IEC 62443 is most suitable for large organizations as it covers both technical and organizational best practice measures. It also provides coverage and certification opportunities for integration service providers and product suppliers. The downside is the standard's size, making it less desirable for SMEs constrained by resource limitations.

Lack of resources is also pointed out in [1], where they exemplify some obstacles for SMEs when adopting standards. In preparation for using the NIST Framework for Improving Critical Infrastructure Cybersecurity (CSF) version 1.1, a 55-page document has been developed just to describe the implementation process. Additionally, [1] highlights that NIST CSF, although designed for all organizations, regardless of size, states that the framework is very complicated to comprehend and implement. Therefore, a detailed 55-page guidebook is available for readers to learn the new vocabulary for a better understanding of the standard. This is no easy task for an SME with limited resources. The same is found in the interviews. Although only one of the four organizations is classified as an SME, it is apparent and clearly expressed that without a good financial situation and management's interest in hiring external expertise, complying with a cybersecurity standard is nearly impossible.

As referred to in the subsection on RQ1, an unpublished survey by the authors, with responses from organizations within the Norwegian Industry, indicates a low usage of international security standards, with only 32% of organizations having a significant influence from standards in their cybersecurity programs. Of the organizations reported to follow a security standard, all are defined as large organizations with over 250 employees. This result aligns with [20], who found that IEC 62443 is most suited for large organizations. Both the organization's size and the OT department's size are found in the survey to influence an organization's inclination to follow such security standards.

4   Discussion

The results pertaining to RQ1 in the literature review section of this study include very few studies providing quantifiable answers to the degree of application of cybersecurity standards for OT systems. Only [12] is dedicated to OT systems, whereas [14] have included manufacturing organizations as participants and are therefore included. The results indicate low applicability or usage of standards within OT, which corroborates the findings from the interviews in this study. Similar results are found in the aforementioned unpublished survey, where only 32% of the respondents report that cybersecurity standards have significantly influenced their organization's cybersecurity program. With such few references, interviews, and a relative few, n=34, responses for the survey that are limited to a geographical location, a conclusive answer to the widespread usage of standards within OT systems cannot be given. However, there is reason to suspect that the applicability of cybersecurity standards is low. Does a low applicability of standards constitute a low or poor cybersecurity posture for OT? Are organizations inherently vulnerable due to the lack of prescription for dedicated OT cybersecurity standards? Answers to such questions are outside the scope of this study. However, this study can provide some answers and indicative reasons as to why the usage is low, if low applicability eventually would be concluded.

IT standards like the ISO 27000 series or equivalent are present in several of the included articles and in the interviews, where three of the four organizations are ISO 27001 certified. Reference [12] states that 80% of large enterprises adhere to the German BSI IT-Grundschutz, a German standard comparable with ISO 27001, and over 50% of German organizations are ISO 27001 certified according to [11]. When an organization follows or, even better, is certified as ISO 27001 compliant, a set of measures is in place. Governance documents, restricting employees' online behavior, IT security training, incident handling, and recovery procedures to mention a few. These IT-driven processes and procedures will also include parts of the OT section of an organization. i.e., personnel working within OT will have policies regarding their online behavior. So effectively, organizations could have a standard-driven cybersecurity posture even though dedicated OT standards enjoy low implementation.

Reference [11] finds that the key obstacle for organizations to be ISO 27001 certified is time and high cost. Is it then reasonable for organizations to implement two cybersecurity standards that are partly overlapping or have similarities when viewed from an IT perspective [17]? With time and high cost highlighted as key obstacles, would not deciphering and interpreting a voluminous standard like IEC 62443, with its 800 pages and lack of practical guidance [17, 18], drain an organization for resources that have already been highlighted as key obstacles? The decision of whether to comply with one or two cybersecurity standards leads the discussion to the organization of and responsibility for OT cybersecurity.

OT operations are inherently different from IT. It is an area requiring specialized knowledge and experience. Even with the introduction of Industry 4.0 and the integration of IT with OT, there still are vital differences between the two, such as patch management, prioritization towards the CIA triangle, and safety aspects concerning CPS, to mention a few. The technical differences between IT and OT are well documented in research. Running a OT system, requires OT personnel. The interviews revieled an interesting difference between IT and OT personnel regarding familiarity with standards in general and cybersecurity in particular. Employees with IT backgrounds had a much broader understanding of governance and the need for implementing procedures in the organization. In contrast, the focus of OT personnel was explicitly stated to keep the system running and avoid downtime. Several avenues could give answers to this difference. One avenue apparent in the interviews is differences in education. IT personnel with education within IT will typically follow a curriculum that includes at least a basic understanding of governance and policies. In contrast, personnel within OT do not have this knowledge as a baseline from their education. No further investigation has been done to determine if the difference, or to what degree, education contributes to the lower implementation of cybersecurity standards in OT systems. Still, the two groups have distinct differences in this regard. What is apparent is that OT representatives must, due to the distinct differences between IT and OT, be part of implementing and managing cybersecurity efforts designated for OT. Given the differences in priorities and unfamiliarity with standards for OT personnel interviewed, this is not a simple task.

5   Conclusion

Of the substantial number of 1183 records found through searches in the databases, only 13 were found to be eligible for complete text analysis, and of those, only five provided answers to the defined research questions. The limited number of records included in this review can indicate a shortage in research on the defined research questions. Several publications without peer reviews and the rigor deployed in scientific papers, e.g., whitepapers or industry reports, provide interesting insights. Still, such reports are not material for developing empirical truths like scientific papers. This could indicate that the cybersecurity field for OT is pushed forward by industry players rather than research.

However, what is valid for both the number of articles and the degree of applicability towards RQ1 - both are low. Definitive conclusions regarding the usage of standards cannot be based on only two papers, but it is at least an indication of the degree of applicability. Findings in the literature are substantiated by findings from the seven interviews and the survey, with n=34, done in the Norwegian Industry. What is more apparent is that several gaps have been identified and exist. The size and lack of practical guidelines in OT cybersecurity standards appear as entry barriers to application. This is even more true for SMEs with limited resources, highlighted by the fact that exclusively large organizations in the unpublished survey follow a security standard.

As these gaps become apparent, few ways to bridge them have been identified in the literature. However, the interviews uncovered an interesting finding: Organizations create bespoke standards. These organizational bespoke standards are developed and compiled at the corporate level. The work is done without local OT personnel's involvement, and the resulting standard is designed to remove the barriers identified in the literature for practitioners. These bespoke standards provide OT with easy, hazel-free access to an organizational standard based on international standards containing practical advice with a scope that fits the organization.

Following the finding in [17] that from an IT perspective, standards have similarities, applying two, one for IT and one for OT, will be a waste of resources. As found in the interviews and the literature reviewed, many organizations comply with IT standards. If an organization believes that the effort to implement two standards is time not well spent, future research investigating the amount or degree of usage of OT cybersecurity standards will not provide evidence towards questions like "how much cybersecurity effort is put forth by an organization or an industry". Future research should, therefore, investigate what cybersecurity controls organizations implement to improve their cybersecurity posture. As found in [14], organizations have cybersecurity measures in place, even though they do not adhere to a cybersecurity standard. Such research will have significant implications for both researchers and practitioners.

References

1. Benz, M., Chatterjee, D.: Calculated risk? A cybersecurity evaluation tool for SMEs. Bus. Horizons **63**(4), 531–540 (2020). https://www.sciencedirect.com/science/article/pii/S0007681320300392
2. Corallo, A., Lazoi, M., Lezzi, M.: Cybersecurity in the context of industry 4.0: a structured classification of critical assets and business impacts. Comput. Ind. **114**, 103165 (2020). https://www.sciencedirect.com/science/article/pii/S0166361519304427
3. Dicicco-Bloom, B., Crabtree, B.: The qualitative research interview. Med. Educ. **40**, 314–321 (2006)
4. Djebbar, F., Nordström, K.: A comparative analysis of industrial cybersecurity standards. IEEE Access **11**, 85315–85332 (2023)
5. Edgar, T., Manz, D.: Introduction to Science. In: Research Methods For Cyber Security, pp. 3–31 (2017)
6. Fink, A.: Conducting Research Literature Reviews. SAGE Publications (2019)
7. King, N.: Using templates in the thematic analysis of text. In: Essential Guide to Qualitative Methods in Organizational Research, pp. 256–270 SAGE Publications (2004)

8. Leszczyna, R.: A review of standards with cybersecurity requirements for smart grid. Comput. Secur. **77**, 262–276 (2018). https://www.sciencedirect.com/science/article/pii/S0167404818302803
9. Leszczyna, R.: Cybersecurity and privacy in standards for smart grids - A comprehensive survey. Comput. Stand. Interfaces. **56**, 62–73 (2018)
10. Lezzi, M., Lazoi, M., Corallo, A.: Cybersecurity for industry 4.0 in the current literature: a reference framework. Comput. Ind. **103**, 97–110 (2018). https://www.sciencedirect.com/science/article/pii/S0166361518303658
11. Mirtsch, M., Blind, K., Koch, C., Dudek, G.: Information security management in ICT and non-ICT sector companies: a preventive innovation perspective. Comput. Secur..**109**, 102383 (2021). https://www.sciencedirect.com/science/article/pii/S0167404821002078
12. Nüßer, W., Koch, E., Trsek, H., Schumann, R., Mahrenholz, D.: Cyber security in production networks - An empirical study about the current status. In: 2017 22nd IEEE International Conference On Emerging Technologies And Factory Automation (ETFA), pp. 1–4 (2017)
13. Page, M., et al.: The PRISMA 2020 statement: an updated guideline for reporting systematic reviews. BMJ **372**, n71 (2021)
14. Pawar, S., Palivela, D.: LCCI: a framework for least cybersecurity controls to be implemented for small and medium enterprises (SMEs). Int. J. Inf. Manage. Data Insights. **2**(1), 100080 (2022)
15. Silva, R., Neiva, F. Systematic literature review in computer science - A practical guide. Relatórios Técnicos Do DCC/UFJF **1**(8) (2016)
16. Snyder, H.: Literature review as a research methodology: An overview and guidelines. J. Bus. Res. **104**, 333–339 (2019). https://doi.org/10.1016/j.jbusres.2019.07.039
17. Staves, A., Anderson, T., Balderstone, H., Green, B., Gouglidis, A., Hutchison, D.: A cyber incident response and recovery framework to support operators of industrial control systems. Int. J. Crit. Infrastruct. Prot. **37**, 100505 (2022). https://www.sciencedirect.com/science/article/pii/S187454822100086X
18. Staves, A., Maesschalck, S., Derbyshire, R., Green, B., Hutchison, D.: Learning to walk: towards assessing the maturity of OT security control standards and guidelines. In: 2023 IFIP Networking Conference (IFIP Networking), pp. 1–6 (2023)
19. Stouffer, K., et al.: (MITRE), MT: NIST Guide to Operational Technology (OT) security. Tech. Rep. NIST SP 800-82r3, National Institute of Standards and Technology, Gaithersburg, MD (2023). https://doi.org/10.6028/NIST.SP.800-82r3. https://csrc.nist.gov/pubs/sp/800/82/r3/final
20. Wagner, P., Hansch, G., Konrad, C., John, K., Bauer, J., Franke, J.: Applicability of security standards for operational technology by SMEs and large enterprises. In: 2020 25th IEEE International Conference On Emerging Technologies And Factory Automation (ETFA), vol. 1, pp. 1544–1551 (2020)
21. Yin, R.: Case Study Research and Applications: Design and Methods. SAGE Publications (2017)

Deployment Challenges of Industrial Intrusion Detection Systems

Konrad Wolsing[1,2]([✉]) [iD], Eric Wagner[1,2] [iD], Frederik Basels[2], Patrick Wagner[1], and Klaus Wehrle[1] [iD]

[1] RWTH Aachen University, Aachen, Germany
{eric.wagner,patrick.wagner,wolsing,wehrle}@comsys.rwth-aachen.de
[2] Fraunhofer FKIE, Wachtberg, Germany
{konrad.wolsing,eric.wagner,frederik.basels}@fkie.fraunhofer.de

Abstract. With the escalating threats posed by cyberattacks on Industrial Control Systems (ICSs), the development of customized Industrial Intrusion Detection Systems (IIDSs) received significant attention in research. While the existing literature proposes effective IIDS solutions evaluated in controlled environments, their deployment in real-world industrial settings poses several challenges. Adding to known obstructions, this paper highlights two critical aspects that significantly impact IIDSs' practical deployment, i.e., the need for sufficient amounts of data to train the IIDS models and the challenges associated with finding suitable hyperparameters, especially for IIDSs training only on normal ICS data. Through empirical experiments conducted on multiple state-of-the-art IIDSs and diverse datasets, we establish the criticality of these issues in deploying IIDSs in ICS environments. Our findings show the necessity of extensive malicious training data for supervised IIDSs, which can be impractical considering the complexity of recording and labeling attacks in actual ICSs. Furthermore, while other IIDSs circumvent the previous issue by requiring only benign training data, these can suffer from the difficulty of setting appropriate hyperparameters, which likewise can diminish their performance. By shedding light on these challenges, we aim to enhance the current understanding of limitations and considerations necessary for deploying effective cybersecurity solutions in ICSs, which might be one reason why IIDSs see few deployments.

Keywords: Industrial Intrusion Detection Systems · Cyber-Physical Systems · Industrial Control Systems · Hyperparameter · Deployment

1 Introduction

Industrial Control Systems (ICSs), ranging from manufacturing over power grids to water and gas distribution, are facing harmful consequences due to cyberattacks [3,17]. The protection of such facilities is, however, not trivial as many systems rely on insecure legacy communication protocols, replacement of which

J. Garcia-Alfaro et al. (Eds.): ESORICS 2024 Workshops, LNCS 15263, pp. 453–473, 2025.
https://doi.org/10.1007/978-3-031-82349-7_29

is cumbersome, expensive, and often unrealistic due to high uptime requirements [15]. Consequently, recent research focuses on easily retrofittable Industrial Intrusion Detection Systems (IIDSs) specifically designed to take advantage
of the unique characteristics of each ICS by searching for anomalous behavior in
largely predictable networking patterns and physical processes [22].

The foundation of these detection mechanisms is mostly rooted in classical
supervised machine-learning or *One-Class Classifiers (OCCs)* [22,34]. In supervised approaches, the IIDS is trained on labeled samples of normal behavior
and attacks to learn classifiers, e.g., Random Forests (RFs) or Support Vector
Machines (SVMs) [27]. Meanwhile, OCCs are trained only on normal ICS behavior, e.g., to identify the operational boundaries of physical measurements [33],
and deviations from this learned behavior are classified as potential attacks.

Research demonstrates the alleged effectiveness of hundreds of newly proposed IIDSs by evaluating them on dedicated datasets and publishing achieved
detection performances [8,22]. In vitro, these IIDSs achieve excellent results [12,
20,24,33]. However, when it comes to real-world deployments, these solutions
are challenging to configure [10] and then cannot perform as promised [2,30]
and thus do not find their way into practice [29]. Consequently, the performance
derived by current evaluation methodologies seems hardly representative of the
actual quality of an IIDS if deployed in the real world [6]. While the scientific
literature already identifies challenges for transferring IIDSs from research into
practice [2,6,30], we proclaim that two aspects impacting IIDSs' deployability
in ICS environments require additional attention.

First, it remains unclear how much training data is required to maximize
detection performance. This question is especially critical in the case of supervised IIDSs, where the generation of attack samples in a testbed might still be
relatively easy, but collecting or generating real-world attack samples is much
harder [7]. OCCs' training data, on the other hand, is easily collectable, but
they still require hyperparameter tuning [18]. Yet, hyperparameter tuning is
rarely intuitive, especially with often-employed custom classifiers, and it remains
unknown whether it is possible to transfer good hyperparameters between ICS
deployments as considered feasible in other machine-learning domains [28]. In
research, the authors thus may optimize them for a given dataset (with attacks),
which is, however, unfeasible in practice due to lack of attack samples.

Intrusion detection for ICS is especially challenging because of hard to obtain
and labeled *attack samples* from cyberattacks in real systems, as their generation could expose, disrupt, and potentially damage sensitive infrastructure or
facilities. For artificial datasets and testbeds as used in research [8], on the other
hand, it is relatively easy to generate such attack samples. Thus far, IIDS proposals do, however, all require custom training phases for the concrete deployment
with hardly any model transferability across scenarios [11,34]. We thus observe
a large discrepancy between training data availability for research activities and
real-world deployments, which may be the cause for the reported challenging
deployment of current research proposals [2,29]. In this publication, we measure

the severity of these factors on the detection performance of diverse IIDSs to understand how big their influence in potential deployments can become.

Contributions. To investigate the potential influence of training data availability on IIDSs' deployability, we make the following contributions:

- We demonstrate that the amount of attack samples in training significantly influences the performance of IIDSs based on supervised machine-learning.
- We show that the influence of hyperparameters for OCC-based IIDSs varies tremendously. While some IIDSs are susceptible to even tiny changes, others are largely hyperparameter-agnostic and even generalize across deployments.
- Based on our findings, we advocate for more expressive IIDS evaluation procedures to narrow the gap between research and real-world IIDS deployments.

Availability Statement. To facilitate further research, we publish the artifacts from our paper: https://zenodo.org/records/10728074

2 Background on Industrial Intrusion Detection

For readers unfamiliar with the topic of *industrial* intrusion detection, we motivate the rationale of retrofitting such solutions to ICS. We then present one IIDS from the literature in detail, which we evaluate in this publication.

Industrial Control Systems (ICSs) are the foundation of diverse applications such as manufacturing, production, distribution of water, gas, or electricity, and autonomous vehicles [17]. One typical architecture that all these applications rely on are digital control loops measuring the environment with sensors and influencing it through actuators usually interconnected with industrial control networks [15]. Consequently, ICSs are likewise susceptible to regularly occurring threats from cyberspace [3]. For their mitigation, either preventive measures such as authenticated and encrypted communication channels [9] or detective approaches like IIDSs [22] can be implemented. This publication focuses on the latter, which aim at timely indicating malicious behavior to ICS operators before actual harm can be conducted and avoid attacks remaining uncovered.

To detect unwanted behavior, the detection methodologies underlying *industrial* IDSs make great use of domain knowledge and ICS-specific behavior [34]. One key attribute is ICSs' notorious predictability, as they usually perform repetitive tasks [15]. Based on a set of training data, a detection model can be trained and tuned with hyperparameters to indicate unexpected deviations, such as cyberattacks. Note that supervised IIDSs require attack samples while OCC methods solely train on benign data. The goal of each approach and their tuning is to detect as many cyberattacks as possible while emitting few false positive alerts, which would have to be falsified by operators afterward. The performance of an IIDS is ultimately measured with metrics [22] like the F1 score.

One approach to implementing such an OCC-based IIDS is MinMax (cf. Fig. 1) [33]. It is based on the fact that physical values measured by sensors

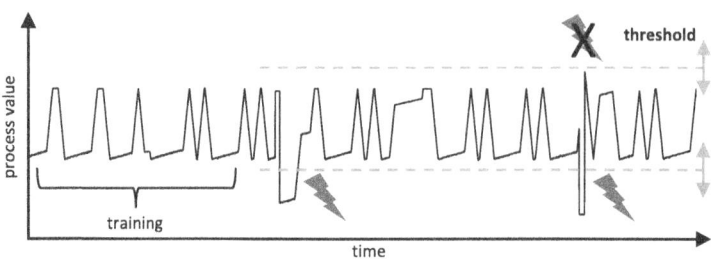

Fig. 1. An IIDS learns the repetitive patterns of an ICS's behavior to indicate anomalies. This requires finding a suitable hyperparameter, such as the threshold for MinMax visualized here [33], which influences the alert decision of an IIDS.

usually reside within precise limits, e.g., a boiler inside an ICS has a lower and upper operational temperature. MinMax extracts these limits from a set of benign training data. Then, since physical measurements can underlie natural variation and noise, the approach enlarges these limits by a configurable hyperparameter to avoid too many false positive alarms. In the end, an alarm is raised if a measurement exceeds or undercuts the trained threshold. Note that MinMax serves as an example and IIDSs generally exhibit complex decision-making algorithms. Finally, the ICS operators are in charge of analyzing the raised alarm and initiating countermeasures.

For OCC-based IIDSs, as depicted here, the training requires benign data recorded, e.g., during normal ICS behavior. Still, for deployment, hyperparameters, i.e., the threshold, have to be adequately selected to reduce the number of false-positives and not miss attacks (cf. Fig. 1). Contrary, while supervised IIDSs can find adequate hyperparameters themselves during training as they also learn on malicious samples, this requires obtaining or generating such (attack) data in an ICS potentially involving actual physical processes [7].

3   Open IIDS Deployment Challenges in ICS

After a short primer on IIDSs, we now highlight deployment challenges of IIDSs along recent related work, reproducibility studies, and meta-reviews (Sect. 3.1). Afterward, we formulate the research questions addressed in this paper (Sect. 3.2).

3.1   Related Work

For IDS research, there exists a body of meta-studies that critically reflect their effectiveness and suitability. In that regard, Sommer et al. [30] argue, not specifically focusing on industrial networks, that machine-learning is better suited for finding similarities than differences, which complicates their application in anomaly detection. Moreover, it is challenging to conduct sound evaluations, which they presume to be the reason why most approaches cannot keep up with expectations in real deployments. Adding to these issues, Ahmed et al. [2] identify scalability, exhaustive system modeling during training, and noisy input data as challenges seldom evaluated in live deployments. Also challenges like operational drift and component aging become only apparent in real deployments [25]. While issues of applying general machine-learning in practice are well-known [6], the effects of training *industrial* IDSs in artificial scenarios and their implications for potential deployments have thus far not been experimentally analyzed.

Moreover, general machine learning research has examined the importance of hyperparameter tuning [6,18]. Here, we are mostly concerned with second-level hyperparameters, i.e., hyperparameters that must be set prior to training [28]. To obtain a general understanding of the tunability of these second-level hyper-parameters, Probst et al. [28] analyzed six supervised machine-learning algo-rithms. They found good default values working on many datasets and iden-tified those hyperparameters worth considering for tuning. In a similar study, Weerts et al. [32] found out that leveraging default hyperparameters was non-inferior to tuning them. However, all these works mostly consider supervised machine-learning and neither look at OCC nor tackle the peculiarities in ICS. Regarding the latter, default values found in these works do not apply to the entirely different and custom OCC-based IIDS algorithms usually found in ICS research. Focusing on ICS, Fung et al. [14] show exemplarily that three consid-ered IIDSs deliver mostly stable performance under different hyperparameters. However, the set of tested hyperparameters is derived from attack samples, which may not be available (in high quantity or quality) for real deployments.

3.2   Research Questions

The deployment of IIDSs in real industrial networks proves challenging, with experimental deployments failing to keep up with promising results from artificial scenarios. We suspect training data availability, especially samples of attacks, to be one potential cause for this situation. Detection algorithms themselves are often applicable to multiple industrial domains [34]. However, they assume to be trained separately for each deployment to learn the expected behavior. For example, the learned boundaries of a water tank's maximum acceptable fill level differ for each IIDS deployment. Consequently, it is inevitable to train an IIDS for a specific target use case. Yet, this challenge of training an IIDS is not critically reflected in research where simply another (existing) dataset can be leveraged. To verify our suspicion and improve future evaluation methodologies of IIDSs to reflect their actual deployability into real-world scenarios, we answer four key research questions within this paper.

Q1 – How many attack samples do supervised IIDSs need? The training of supervised IIDSs requires benign *and* malicious data samples. E.g., one of the most commonly used dataset [22], the Morris Gas dataset [26], consists of 274.628 samples, of which 22% are attacks. For evaluations, authors usually randomly shuffle and split this dataset, leveraging 80% for training and the rest for evaluations [4,27]. With this split, the training data still contains around

48.000 attack samples. Yet, obtaining this amount of labeled attack samples from each ICS an IIDS should be deployed is unrealistic considering the costs and risks associated with their generation leading to our question.

Q2 – How much training data do OCC-based IIDSs need? IIDSs requiring only benign training data can be trained with less difficulty, e.g., even during the regular operation of an ICS. However, this training data must still be collected, and it must be ensured that it reflects *all* possible normal behavior. Hence, we want to understand how much training data is actually necessary and whether large variances exist across detection methods.

Q3 – What is the influence of hyperparameters on performance? Beyond training data, OCC-based IIDSs request hyperparameters, which may significantly impact detection performance. Here, the MinMax IIDS introduced in the background (cf. Sect. 2) uses a fixed threshold across datasets, whereas an optimized threshold could drastically influence detection performance, as evidenced in Fig. 1. However, such hyperparameter tuning is only possible if attack samples for the concrete deployment scenario are available.

Q4 – Can we transfer good hyperparameters across scenarios? To unlock the benefits of tuned hyperparameters in OCC-based IIDSs, we consider the previously proposed concept of transferring good configurations across deployment scenarios [28,32]. Such a step would also allow us to use the extensively available attack samples from artificial scenarios to tune real-world deployments. However, thus far, it remains unclear to what extent such transferability is possible and to what extent this is scenario and IIDS dependent.

4   Deployability of Supervised IIDS

Our initial analysis concerns the deployability of supervised IIDSs w.r.t. the amount of required attack samples. We first describe our experiment design, then analyze our results, and finally summarize the implications of our findings.

4.1   Experiment Setup

For our experiments on supervised IIDSs, we consider a RF and a SVM classifier as used in several proposed IIDSs [4,19,27]. As independently examined by Perez et al. [27] and Anton et al. [4], these classifiers can be adapted to operate on Modbus network traffic via derived features such as the function code or transmitted process values. The classifiers are trained and evaluated on a set of benign and malicious Modbus packets. Our experiment is based on existing re-implementations of these two IIDSs made available in the IPAL IDS Framework [34]. We took care to use the same data preprocessing and hyperparameters as mentioned in the publication [27] (cf. Availability Statement).

Concerning the datasets, we leverage the same dataset originally used to evaluate the two IIDSs [4,27], which is also the most commonly used dataset for supervised IIDSs [22]. This dataset has been recorded in a miniature gas-pipeline ICS lab-environment leveraging Modbus as communication protocol. Within this setup, a total of 60048 attack samples across 35 types of attacks with varying complexity, such as reconnaissance or modifying setpoints, have been collected. Whether accumulating and labeling this amount of attack data outside a lab in the field is actually possible remains questionable.

To understand how many attack samples are necessary to train a supervised IIDS, we reduce the number of attacks contained in the training dataset while keeping the number of benign training data constant. We start with a random 80/20 train/test split as in the original evaluation [4,27] and five folds. We then remove all but one attack sample from the training data and retrain the IIDS while gradually increasing the amount of attacks in the training data. The 20% of the test set remain unchanged after the random train/test split. For each number of learned attack samples, we calculate the average recall (fraction of identified attacks) and precision (fraction of correct alerts) over all folds.

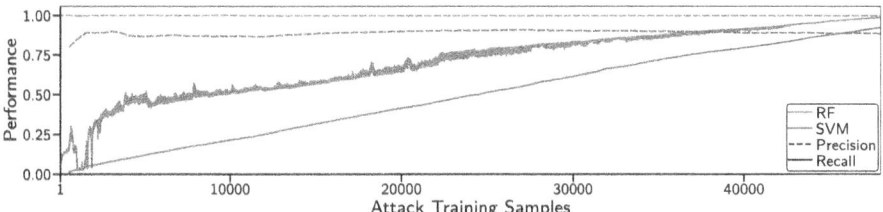

(a) After an initialization phase, the recall increases linearly with more attack samples, while changes in precision are only minimal. To yield high detection scores, more than 40.000 malicious packets are required in training for both supervised IIDSs. Note that the data for SVM was sampled in steps of 500 attacks due to long training times.

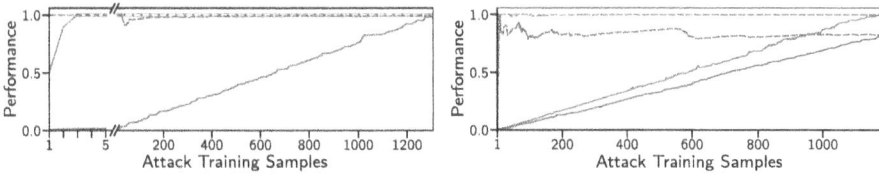

(b) The RF requires few training samples on attack number 19 (clean registers).

(c) Attack 10 (change physical value) requires many samples to be trained.

Fig. 2. Gradually increasing the amount of attack samples within the training data reveals that both RF and SVM require lots of data to yield satisfying detection performance. For a simple attack, cf. Fig. 2(b), the RF requires only about three samples.

4.2   Q1 – How Many Attack Samples Do Supervised IIDSs Need?

Having established our methodology, we can now exemplarily assess the deployability of supervised IIDSs w.r.t. to the amount of attack samples. To this end, Fig. 2 depicts the detection performance of the RF and SVM classifiers. In Fig. 2(b) and Fig. 2(c), we show two exemplary attack types in isolation.

Starting with a broad overview in Fig. 2(a), if the RF is trained on all available attack samples ($x = 48.049$), it reaches a precision of 0.998 and a recall of 0.987. Likewise, the SVM achieves a score of 0.885 in precision and 0.924. As we expect, both IIDSs achieve the best detection performance when trained on all (those in the original train set) available attack samples.

As we reduce the number of attack samples, we observe a nearly linear reduction in recall of both IIDSs. For RF, the performance drops from 0.987 to about 0.44 if provided with just 5000 attack samples. Below this threshold, the recall for RF drops even more drastically. The SVM shows a similar trend with fewer fluctuations. Interestingly, precision remains largely unaffected in both cases, which we presume results from not changing the amount of benign training data.

To better understand these effects, we repeat this experiment only considering a single attack type during training and testing. Exemplarily, we show attack type 19 from the dataset [26] in Fig. 2(b) and attack type 10 in Fig. 2(c). For attack type 19, we observe a vastly diverging behavior between RF and SVM. The RF achieves optimal detection rates after just three attack samples. The IIDS has likely learned to identify that this attack uses a Modbus function code not occurring during normal behavior. In contrast, this generalization does not apply to the SVM. Attack type 10, shown in Fig. 2(c), which manipulates reported sensor readings, proves difficult to learn for both IIDSs. Here, the recall continues to grow linearly as more attack samples are available for training. Overall, we see that only with a high number of malicious training samples can the IIDSs score the excellent detection results reported in the respective publications.

4.3   Conclusion

Looking back at our results, we see that supervised IIDSs can generalize an attack pattern in some cases as observed, for example, for the RF classifier for attack type 19, which introduces an otherwise unused Modbus function code. This attack should thus also easily be detected by simple rule-based IIDSs [13]. In general, however, we observe relatively little generalization for both IIDSs. The linearly increasing recall scores with increasing the number of attack samples rather indicate an overfitting behavior of the classifiers, i.e., only the precise misbehavior observed during training is also later classified as such. These results provide further evidence for prior work by Kus et al. [21], who already identified a lack of generalization during supervised IIDS training.

As proclaimed by Etalle et al. [11], we also find that supervised IIDSs are rather unsuited for deployments in diverse ICS environments due to only performing well with many attack samples, potentially due to overfitting, which aligns with prior research [2,11,21,25]. Yet, these issues are hardly discussed in prior work as publications promoting the use of machine-learning in ICS mainly focus on the final achieved detection performance [4,19,27]. Consequently, novel designs for supervised IIDSs must be critically reviewed to be considered suitable for real ICS deployments.

5 Deployability of OCC-Based IIDS

OCC-based IIDSs promise to avoid these issues of supervised IIDSs by requiring only training data from benign ICS operations. Getting such benign data is easier than collecting or generating attack samples, but it must still be collected, processed, and verified, such that requiring less training data makes an OCC-based IIDS easier to deploy. Moreover, hyperparameter tuning, especially if hyperparameters cannot be transferred across scenarios, can still unrealistically boost an OCC-based IIDSs' performance in research. To understand these effects, we first lay out the evaluation setup underlying our measurements (Sect. 5.1) to then tackle the research questions Q2 to Q4. In the end, we summarize our findings on the deployability challenges of OCC-based IIDSs (Sect. 5.5).

5.1 Experiment Setup

We examine four IIDSs, which were published at top security conferences – MinMax [33], Invariant [12], TABOR [24], and Seq2SeqNN [20]. We make use of available open-source implementations or validated re-implementations within the IPAL IIDS framework [34]. For further details, we refer the reader to Appx. A, the respective publications, or IPAL's public implementation [34]. These four IIDSs, which also feature vastly different numbers of hyperparameters for their configuration, cf. Tab. 1, build the foundation for our analysis.

Table 1. We analyze four state-of-the-art IIDSs with diverse hyperparameters, on three datasets. We aim at 10.000 random samples for each IIDS's hyperparameter space, yet we have reached computational limits, resulting in fewer samples for some.

IIDS	SWaT [16]	WADI [1]	BATADAL [31]	Parameter
MinMax [33]	10 000	10 000	10 000	2
Invariant [12]	703	10 000	1088	10
TABOR [24]	10 000	10 000	10 000	7
Seq2SeqNN [20]	231	182	500	6

To generalize our results, we analyze three datasets, namely the SWaT [16], WADI [1], and BATADAL [31], which are among the most commonly used datasets in this research area [22]. All three datasets come with dedicated training data that is free of attacks. The testing part of SWaT and WADI contains 36 and 14 different cyberattacks respectively while BATADAL provides 12 attacks.

While the previous experiment's design decisions coincide with usual IIDS evaluation methodologies [22], our work differs within the hyperparameter selection we aim to study. Although three of the examined IIDSs' publications contain short discussions about (some) hyperparameters [12,20,33], none defines the precise acceptable range of the hyperparameter space. To this end, we have to come up with our own definition. For nominal and ordinal hyperparameters, we simply enumerated all possible values, and for rational numbers, we had to define a custom range based on our understanding of the proposed system. During their definition, we took special care that the values proposed in the original publications are contained in our analyzed ranges.

Finally, to conduct a parallelized examination of the hyperparameter in a repeatable manner, we leveraged Ray Tune [23], a library to scale hyperparameter search and tuning. Provided with a definition of a hyperparameter search space, Ray Tune selects one hyperparameter configuration uniformly at random at a time and then trains and evaluates the respective IIDS on the dataset. We then calculate the precision, recall, and F1 score metrics, as these are among the most common performance metrics in IIDS research [22].

We aimed to achieve up to 10.000 samples for all IIDS and dataset combinations, building a solid foundation for our subsequent analyses, cf. Tab. 1. In some cases, such as evaluating the Invariant IIDS on SWaT, training a single configuration takes up to eleven days, which explains the reduced number of samples. Similarly, the training of the Seq2SeqNN IIDS requires exclusive access to potent GPUs to train a neural network. To grant other researchers access to the result of these extensive computations for further analyses, we made all collected data publicly available, cf. Availability Statement.

5.2   Q2 – How Much Training Data Do OCC-Based IIDSs Need?

First, we want to understand the impact of the amount of (benign) training data on IIDS performance. Here, we only consider the best hyperparameters found w.r.t. the F1 score for each IIDS and dataset combination. Beginning with the entire training data (100%), we gradually reduced the training data and evaluated the IIDS after each training against the entire test dataset.

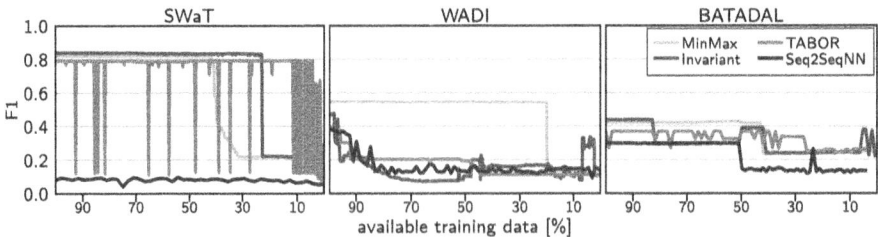

Fig. 3. Reducing the amount of benign training data likewise diminishes the detection rate but not all IIDSs experience an equal performance reduction. The training data Seq2SeqNN on SWaT and WADI is reduced in steps of 10.000 in contrast to 1.000 for the others whereas all IIDSs on BATADAL are sampled in steps of 100.

As shown in Fig. 3, the amount of training data impacts the detection performance of each IIDS differently. E.g., the performance of MinMax on SWaT and BATADAL initially stays high. Only when the data is reduced to about less than 40% does the performance drop significantly. On WADI, this drop occurs much later at about 20% of the overall training data. For Invariant, we observe a similar pattern on SWaT achieving top scores even with about 25% of the data. Yet, on WADI, this approach requires nearly all training data to get close to its optimal score. TABOR on SWaT shows another interesting behavior where instead of a slow reduction, we observe occasional drops in performance, which accumulate toward the end. Upon investigation of TABOR's trained model, we noticed that the drops in between are caused by learning a different model, showing the unstable nature of the trained model. This also occurs in reduced form for BATADAL but not on WADI, where TABOR shows a more continuous reduction as less training data is made available. Seq2SeqNN performs poorly on SWAT and on the other datasets its performance drops significantly as training data is reduced to 50%. Overall, we observe that all IIDSs perform nearly optimally on SWaT and BATADAL with just about half of the training data, while performance on WADI often quickly drops off.

Takeaway. Our data shows that judging upfront whether one has acquired enough training data in a deployment scenario can be challenging. The amount of training data seems to be neither directly dependent on the IIDS nor on the complexity of the concrete scenario. As Invariant and Seq2SeqNN on WADI experience a substantial increase close to 100% training data, this may be an indication that these IIDSs would benefit from even more training data than contained in the dataset. We also see that the performance of the different IIDSs drops suddenly after a certain point, indicating that not observing some specific event during training can be responsible for much of the performance loss. Interestingly, the IIDSs seem to have different events triggering their performance loss. When interpreting these results, dataset characteristics should also be kept in mind. E.g., SWaT contains one attack that is significantly longer than the others, which significantly worsens the F1-score if it is not detected anymore. Hence, the sudden drops of MinMax and Invariant on SWaT could be explained by the sudden inability to identify that specific attack. Overall, determining the amount of training data varies across IIDSs and scenarios, such that a final assessment can only be made on a case-by-case basis. Nonetheless, over all datasets, utilizing more training data does not diminish the detection performance.

5.3 Q3 – What Is the Influence of Hyperparameters on Performance?

Next, for our investigation on the significance of hyperparameters (Q3), we take a broad view of the obtained measurements (cf. Sect. 5.1). To this end, Fig. 4 depicts every IIDS's performance distribution along several metrics and datasets.

At first glance, we observe that hyperparameters have a tremendous effect on the performance of IIDSs. E.g., considering the precision of the MinMax IIDS on the SWaT dataset (cf. ① in Fig. 4), the performance varies between 0.99 at best and 0.13 at worst, which implies that, depending on the chosen configuration, the approach performs close to optimal or is inapplicable. But looking at the

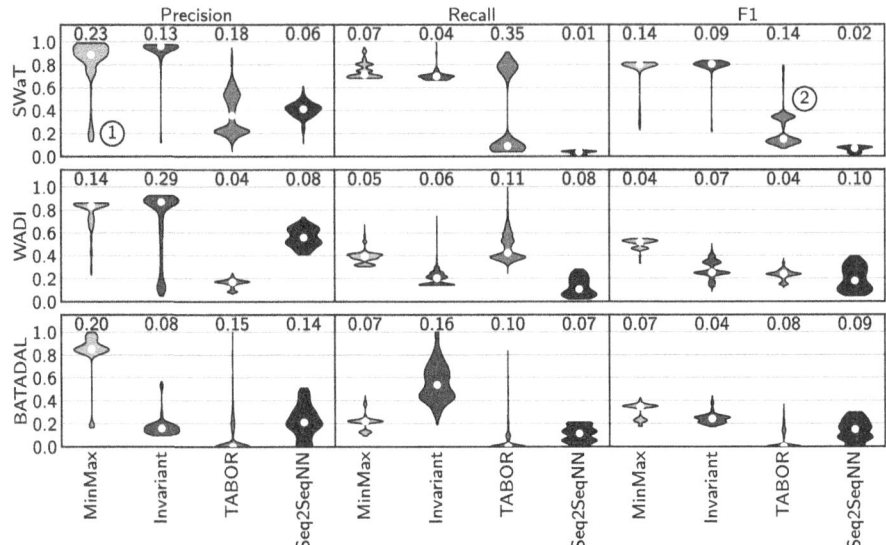

The white dot represents the median and the numbers on top are the standard deviation of each distribution.

Fig. 4. An IIDSs' performance depends on an optimal choice of hyperparameter. While MinMax or Invariant yield satisfying results in F1 score on SWaT for the majority of configurations, obtaining a good configuration for TABOR is challenging. Thus, judging the expectable performance of an IIDS by a single number can be misleading.

entire distribution, it becomes apparent that low values in recall are outliers as the median performance (white dots) is still high at 0.89. Still, the standard deviations around the median is relatively high at 0.23, and thus, performance penalties can be expected for MinMax in recall if not parameterized correctly.

Taking a broader look at the precise distribution of different approaches, not all IIDSs exhibit the same patterns. When considering MinMax and Invariant for SWaT in the F1 score, the majority of configurations perform decently, and bad results are mostly outliers. We call this type of distribution *stable* as it is quite likely to pick a good-performing configuration without having to invest great efforts. In contrast, the opposite is true for TABOR ②, with a median of just 0.15, which is far from what could be achieved at best (0.79) with this approach. Here, unlike MinMax, it is quite unlikely to hit such a good-performing configuration even with expert knowledge. Therefore, there is a qualitative difference between the presumably stable MinMax, which promises to have a straightforward configuration process [33], and TABOR. Note that for MinMax, these observations may be affected by only having two hyperparameters in the first place (cf. Tab. 1). Still, Invariant, despite having the most parameters, features a similar stable distribution as MinMax, at least w.r.t. the F1 score.

Next, we want to understand whether the (in-)stability property is inherent to a specific IIDS. First and foremost, note that the absolute scores achieved between the datasets (cf. lower part of Fig. 4) are sometimes lower compared to SWaT as not all IIDSs were primarily designed for the other datasets. Hence, we only focus on the distributions here. In general, the distributions are loosely similar in each setting. The performance distributions of most IIDSs have roughly the same features on WADI and BATADAL, with some exceptions, such as WADI missing the outliers to the top in some cases. This observation indicates that the stability of an IIDS may be dominantly determined by the underlying detection mechanism rather than the scenario. Consequently, stability seems to be an inherent feature of an IIDS, which could act as a proxy for determining how easy or difficult deploying an IIDS in a new, real application may be.

Considering MinMax, the authors publish their IIDS with a F1 score of 0.78 for SWaT and 0.52 for WADI [33]. W.r.t. our evaluation, these numbers are close to the median (SWaT 0.8 and WADI 0.52) and leave headroom to the maximum (0.82 respectively 0.55). Thus, the published numbers are representative of the expectable performance, which comes as no surprise as the authors stated not to have performed any parameter optimization [33]. In contrast, Feng et al. [12] promote the Invariant IIDS with a recall of 0.79 for SWaT and 0.47 for WADI. Compared to the median performance (SWaT 0.7 and WADI 0.2), the published values are outliers by multiple standard deviation. Therefore, it can be assumed that Feng et al. published optimized performance statistics. Such fine-tuning certainly has value in examining what maximal performance can be achieved by a proposed approach. However, it risks misrepresentation how good a system may perform in a real deployment and may prevent fair comparisons of approaches.

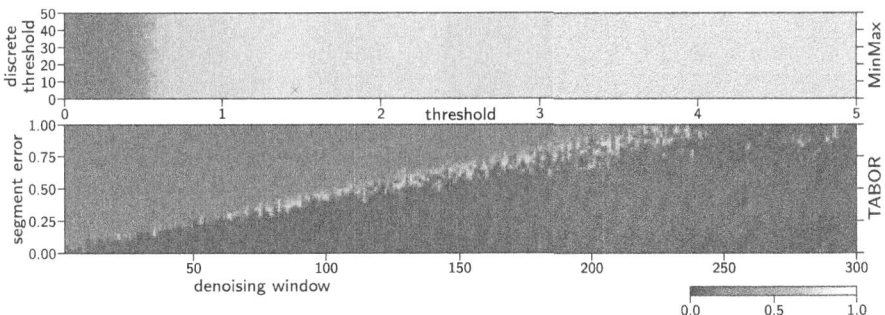

The red cross (×) indicates the optimum found during the experiment.

Fig. 5. The impact of hyperparameters can vary significantly between approaches. While on the SWaT for MinMax (upper plot), one parameter is decisive for the entire performance, suitable configurations for TABOR (lower plot) are more challenging to obtain as several parameters influence each other.

Given the distinct behaviors IIDSs show under varying hyperparameters, we also asked what the reasons for these behaviors might be. Therefore, we take a closer look at MinMax and TABOR on the SWaT dataset and F1 score, as depicted in Fig. 5, where we visualize the detection performance as a heatmap in dependence of two relevant hyperparameters. For MinMax, we identify that the final result mostly depends only on the threshold parameter (cf. Sec. 2). For small values (below 0.6), there is a significant drop in detection performance, but afterward, there are only subtle changes and the threshold has no significant impact anymore. In contrast, for TABOR, we observe more interdependence in two of the seven hyperparameters. Both parameters influence the performance, and changes to one parameter alter the optimal value of the other parameter. Thus, only a combination of correctly set hyperparameters yields good configurations, which complicates setting up TABOR and explains our previous observation where only a few configurations yielded good performance.

Takeaway. We observed that hyperparameters have a tremendous impact on the measured performance of OCC-based IIDSs. Moreover, there exist considerable differences in IIDS stability. The MinMax or Invariant IIDSs yield results that are close to their optimal in a majority of configurations. At the same time, TABOR only achieves optimal performance if multiple hyperparameters are fine-tuned, cf. Fig. 5. Our results stand in contrast to Fung et al., who claimed that reconstruction-based IIDSs can have a good performance over a broad spectrum of hyperparameters [14], likely because our evaluation covered a more diverse set of IIDSs. This (in-)stability w.r.t. hyperparameters complicates scientific comparisons and real-world applicability if the performance of an IIDS is only acceptable for a very confined parameter space. Consequently, we warn that judging an IIDSs' performance by a single configuration, as done currently throughout the literature, can be misleading.

5.4   Q4 – Can We Transfer Good Hyperparameters Across Scenarios?

As we discussed in the previous section, it can be difficult to obtain suitable hyperparameters for an IIDS for a given deployment or dataset. For the selection of suitable hyperparameters, we do, however, not need to start from scratch in most cases. Instead, published parameters or guidelines from previous deployments may help to identify good parameters. Thus, one idea is to reuse these already known configurations and transfer them to a new scenario to hopefully achieve adequate performance. If such hyperparameter transfers are feasible, it would alleviate the problem of (in-)stability discussed before. Previously, Probst et al. [28] found universally good-performing default hyperparameters for supervised IIDSs. However, we consider OCCs-based IIDSs with potentially more intricate hyperparameters that may hinder such transferability.

As the first step in that direction and to examine whether a known, good-performing configuration is also suitable on a different dataset, we conducted the following evaluation. First, we select the top ten configurations according to the F1 score of an IIDS and dataset, e.g., MinMax on SWaT, and measure the performance of these hyperparameters applied to the other datasets, i.e., WADI and BATADAL. Applying this methodology, Fig. 6 depicts the distribution of the obtained ten results on the new datasets. In addition, we mark the globally achievable optimum in a given setting found in the previous analysis from

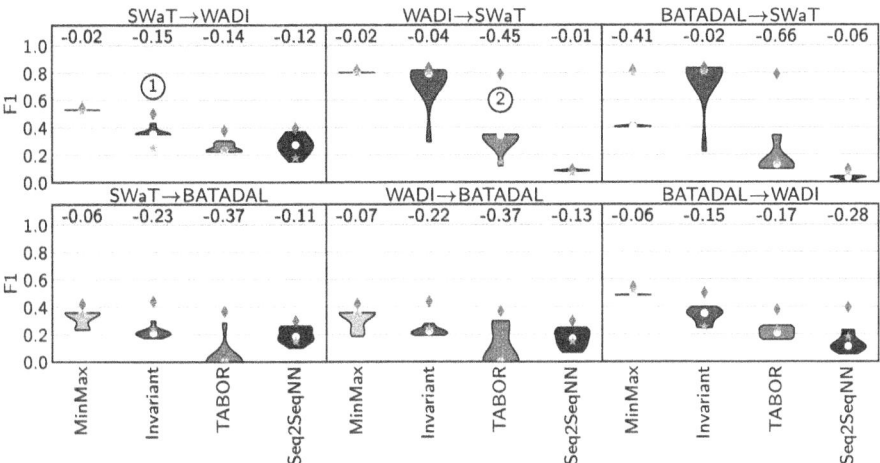

The numbers on top are the difference between the median (white dot) and maximum achievable performance (♦).

Fig. 6. Transferring the top ten configurations found for one dataset to another promises to avoid the problem of parameter optimization in new settings. But, this methodology usually lacks behind the achievable optimum (♦) and does not systematically exceed randomly selected hyperparameters, cf. · marking the median of all hyperparameters in the target dataset.

Sect. 5.3 with an ♦ and the median performance of randomly selected hyperparameters with an ·. This analysis enables assessing how likely a configuration is transferable to another scenario without tuning but also depicts the potential losses in performance along the way. Note that since we sampled all hyperparameters randomly (cf. Sect. 5.1), it is not guaranteed that we measured the precise configuration on the respective other datasets. In that case, we selected the measurement closets to the selected default configuration.

We start considering the Invariant IIDS transferred from the SWaT to the WADI dataset as a case study first (cf. ① in Fig. 6). We see that the transferred configurations achieve decent performance relative to the achievable maximum of 0.5. The median expectable performance from transferring the configurations (white dot) is -0.15 points lower than the maximum achievable. Given that no effort was required to find these configurations, this median of the transferred configurations (0.35) is an improvement over the previous random median performance (0.25, cf. Fig. 4). In contrast to this example, there also exist cases where hardly any transferability is possible. When considering TABOR transferred from the WADI to the SWaT dataset (cf. ② in Fig. 6), there is a large gap between the median of the transferred configurations (0.23) and the achievable optimum (0.79). While in that case, transferring the results is still better than picking a random configuration (0.15), a large potential is left on the table. More generally, the median transferred performance (white dots) is, on average,

0.18 lower than the respective achievable optimum (♦). At the same time, this method is equal to randomly selecting a configuration (no difference to ⋆ on average). Thus, while transferring configurations from one scenario to another seems promising, this concept still proves not be be that advantageous.

Takeaway. On the one hand, OCC-based IIDSs lack guidelines for hyperparameter configuration. On the other hand, if known configurations exist, they only offer limited transferability. On average, good hyperparameters on one dataset do not perform better than randomly chosen hyperparameters on another dataset. Thus, if an IIDS is challenging to configure in the first place, even default configurations or templates from other scenarios do not help much, and, in the worst case, manual efforts are required to tune the approach individually.

5.5 Conclusion

We began with the observation that the amount of data required for training differs significantly between IIDSs (Q2), which complicates providing concrete advice for deployments. Still, as one redeeming feature, more training data does not seem to negatively impact the detection performance. Next, we studied the hypothesis that hyperparameters are a crucial factor for IIDS performance and again observed vastly different behaviors w.r.t. stability. Indeed, it proved difficult for some IIDSs to yield good results on average (Q3), and quick solutions such as generic default configurations that generalize to new scenarios or datasets did not prove promising (Q4). In contrast to the works by Probst et al. [28] and Weerts et al. [32], we found that deriving default values for hyperparameters of OCC-based IIDSs for the ICS domain is challenging for our three analyzed datasets and tuning them manually based on attack samples still brings an enormous performance benefit. Therefore, these effects can explain previously reported problems from related work, e.g., failed reproducibility studies or deploying such approaches in practice [2,11,30]. I.e., Erba et al. [10] tried to reproduce the Invariant IIDS and had troubles finding the hyperparameters to match the publications result. This is in line with our assumption from Sect. 5.3 where we presumed that the authors of the Invariant IIDS have tuned their published parameters. Consequently, current evaluation methodologies in research omit a relevant attribute of IIDSs that is currently not easily measurable.

In general, obtaining a quantitative intuition on an IIDS's training and tuning demands can provide valuable data on the one hand, for ICS operators having to select, set up, and configure an IIDS and, on the other hand, for research to establish fairer and easier comparisons. Note that we do not want to prioritize an IIDS with low training and low tuning demands over ones with excellent detection performance. Instead, we want to create awareness for these challenges and advocate for researchers to scrutinize their work more w.r.t. their deployability.

6 Open Deployment Issues and Limitations

Our results regarding the analysis of research questions Q1 to Q4 prominently show that there exist complex challenges to transferring an IIDS developed in research to an actual ICS that are not captured accurately by the current standard in IIDS evaluations. Hence, the standard procedure of publishing the detection performance for one or multiple datasets [22] is insufficient to capture an IIDS' true value. Concerning these issues, we now discuss new strategies to assess the ease and limitations of an IIDS' deployment already during the research stage.

One significant obstruction in deploying IIDSs is acquiring sufficient training data (Q1 and Q2) whilst avoiding overfitting of supervised IIDS models. From a research perspective, an adopted evaluation methodology that more deeply assesses the capabilities and especially training properties of an IIDS in the lab may be suited to estimate its training demand upfront. In that regard, the evaluation methodologies we presented enable, one the one hand, inferring the learning rate from which the amount of required training data for a deployment can be estimated. On the other hand, by visualizing the learning rate of individual attacks, first signs of overfitting can be revealed. In addition, the methodologies proposed by in related work [5, 21] can answer how well a supervised approach generalizes to unknown attacks, e.g., found during live operations, which are not part of the training data. Together, such enhanced evaluation methodologies can reveal IIDSs that a) require little training samples and b) generalize to a wide variety of (zero-day) cyberattacks beyond the ones seen in training.

With the previous issues addressed, the challenge of configuring an approach (Q3 and Q4) remains. For research, analyzing (new) IIDSs w.r.t. their stability in hyperparameters or ease of configuration, as done by us, can provide additional information for ICS operators on which IIDS may be best suited for a given deployment. Therefore, we ideally need a compact metric that expresses the average performance or stability of performance results. While the data generated in our publication would allow us to compute such values (cf. Fig. 4), how to arrive at a holistic metric that is adequate for scientific purposes is still unclear to us. Another idea for better understanding OCC-based IIDSs is to use a few attack samples from reference attacks to configure hyperparameters. Whether this yields good hyperparameters to detect other attacks remains to be seen.

More generally, while the previously sketched concepts may work well for research, it is not directly apparent how their insights transfer to actual deployments. Also, deployability, in general, involves more than recording training datasets and configuring hyperparameters [6]. E.g., the issue of operational drifts such as wear and tear, which can invalidate once-trained models over time, has been neglected by us [25]. Answering whether an IIDS is ultimately deployable in an actual system thus likely has to involve the expertise of ICS stakeholders as already demanded in meta-surveys, e.g., by Lamberts et al. [22]. Regarding our work, we can, therefore, not finally argue how much training data would still be acceptable or how many false positives and false negatives are tolerable without conducting experiments together with ICS experts within an actual ICS.

7   Conclusion

ICSs become an indispensable building block for our modern society and, with their high level of digitalization, face potentially disastrous cyberattacks. As a reaction, research to automatically detect such intrusions took off within the last decade [22], and nowadays, with plenty of promising IIDSs, the transition to deploying those solutions in real-world ICSs is urgently needed. Yet, this step involves its own challenges, of which we assess and quantify two in detail in this paper. Especially in industrial settings, the acquisition of adequate training data, avoiding overfitting during training, and the configuration of hyperparameters for IIDSs to match their excellent detection performance found in (synthetic) research environments is challenging. As we show, too little training data or tuning of hyperparameters can lead to devastating performance penalties.

While finding solutions to those issues would require the involvement of ICS stakeholders that ultimately deploy IIDSs, we, from a research perspective, recommend taking those properties into account while evaluating novel approaches. Thereby, we can hopefully shift these deployability challenges more into the focus of researchers who design new intrusion detection methods.

Acknowledgments. This work is part of the project MUM2 and was partially funded by the German Federal Ministry of Economic Affairs and Climate Action (BMWK) with contract number 03SX543B managed by the Project Management Jülich (PTJ). This paper was partially supported by the EDA Cyber R&T project "Cyber Electromagnetic Resilience Evaluation on Replicated Environment (CERERE)", funded by Italy and Germany. The authors are responsible for the publication's contents.

Disclosure of Interests. The authors have no competing interests to declare that are relevant to the content of this article.

A   IDS Description

To measure the deployability of OCC-based IIDSs, we examined four existing approaches. In the following, we provide a short description of their concept:

MinMax. The first IIDS, MinMax, learning the minimum and maximum bounds of a sensors' normal values (cf. Sect. 2), serves as a representative for a class of lightweight IIDSs that aim to implement straightforward detection methodologies that do not require complex configuration, technical understanding, or computational resources [33]. Any violation against the learned minimum and maximum values is indicated as an alert to the ICS operators.

Invariant. This IIDS [12] leverages data mining techniques to find mathematical equations that must be fulfilled at all times. E.g., if the inlet valve of a water tank is opened, its water level is expected to rise. Since an invariant is fulfilled all the time during normal behavior, any violation is then reported.

TABOR. This IIDS fuses three detection approaches based on timed automata, Bayesian networks, and out-of-bounds checks [24]. The timed automata component considers a single sensor value and learns a model of its behavior. E.g., the water levels of a tank usually rise for 30 min and then decrease over several hours. Together with the Bayesian network, unknown process states can be determined, such as the inlet valve being still opened despite the water level rising for more than 30 min. To complement their method, an alert is also raised with an out-of-bounds check working similarly to the MinMax IIDS.

Seq2SeqNN. Lastly, Seq2SeqNN [20] trains a neuronal network on GPUs to understand the ICS's behavior and perform predictions for the future. Given a recent history of physical values, the neuronal network is able to perform a prediction for the near future. If these predictions deviate too much from the observed behavior, an alarm is raised.

References

1. Ahmed, C.M., Palleti, V.R., Mathur, A.P.: WADI: a water distribution testbed for research in the design of secure cyber physical systems. In: CySWATER. ACM (2017). https://doi.org/10.1145/3055366.3055375
2. Ahmed, C.M., MR., G.R., Mathur, A.P.: Challenges in machine learning based approaches for real-time anomaly detection in industrial control systems. In: CPSS. ACM (2020). https://doi.org/10.1145/3384941.3409588
3. Alladi, T., Chamola, V., Zeadally, S.: Industrial control systems: cyberattack trends and countermeasures. Comput. Commun. **155** (2020). https://doi.org/10.1016/j.comcom.2020.03.007
4. Anton, S.D.D., Sinha, S., Dieter Schotten, H.: Anomaly-based intrusion detection in industrial data with SVM and random forests. In: SoftCOM (2019). https://doi.org/10.23919/SOFTCOM.2019.8903672
5. Apruzzese, G., Laskov, P., Schneider, J.: SOK: pragmatic assessment of machine learning for network intrusion detection. In: IEEE EuroS&P (2023). https://doi.org/10.1109/EuroSP57164.2023.00042
6. Arp, D., Quiring, E., Pendlebury, F. et al.: Dos and don'ts of machine learning in computer security. In: USENIX Security Symposium (SEC) (2022)
7. Bader, L., Serror, M., Lamberts, O., et al.: Comprehensively analyzing the impact of cyberattacks on power grids. In: IEEE EuroS&P (2023). https://doi.org/10.1109/EuroSP57164.2023.00066
8. Conti, M., Donadel, D., Turrin, F.: A survey on industrial control system testbeds and datasets for security research. IEEE Commun. Surv. Tutorials **23**(4) (). https://doi.org/10.1109/COMST.2021.3094360
9. Dahlmanns, M., Lohmöller, J., Pennekamp, J.: et al.: Missed opportunities: measuring the untapped TLS support in the industrial internet of things. In: ASIACCS. ACM (2022).https://doi.org/10.1145/3488932.3497762
10. Erba, A., Tippenhauer, N.O.: Assessing model-free anomaly detection in industrial control systems against generic concealment attacks. In: ACSAC (2022). https://doi.org/10.1145/3564625.3564633
11. Etalle, S.: From intrusion detection to software design. In: ESORICS. Springer (2017).https://doi.org/10.1007/978-3-319-66402-6_1
12. Feng, C., Palleti, V.R., Mathur, A., et al.: A systematic framework to generate invariants for anomaly detection in industrial control systems. In: NDSS. Internet Society (2019). https://doi.org/10.14722/ndss.2019.23265

13. Fovino, I.N., Carcano, A., De Lacheze Murel, T. et al.: Modbus/DNP3 state-based intrusion detection system. In: AINA. IEEE (2010). https://doi.org/10.1109/AINA.2010.86
14. Fung, C., Srinarasi, S., Lucas, K., et al.: Perspectives from a comprehensive evaluation of reconstruction-based anomaly detection in industrial control systems. In: ESORICS. Springer (2022). https://doi.org/10.1007/978-3-031-17143-7_24
15. Galloway, B., Hancke, G.P.: Introduction to industrial control networks. IEEE Commun. Surv. Tutorials **15**(2) (2013). https://doi.org/10.1109/SURV.2012.071812.00124
16. Goh, J., Adepu, S., Junejo, K.N., Mathur, A.: A dataset to support research in the design of secure water treatment systems. In: Havarneanu, G., Setola, R., Nassopoulos, H., Wolthusen, S. (eds.) CRITIS 2016. LNCS, vol. 10242, pp. 88–99. Springer, Cham (2017). https://doi.org/10.1007/978-3-319-71368-7_8
17. Humayed, A., Lin, J., Li, F., et al.: Cyber-physical systems security-a survey. IEEE Internet Things J. **4**(6) (2017). https://doi.org/10.1109/JIOT.2017.2703172
18. Hutter, F., Kotthoff, L., Vanschoren, J. (eds.): Automated Machine Learning. TSSCML, Springer, Cham (2019). https://doi.org/10.1007/978-3-030-05318-5
19. Junejo, K.N., Goh, J.: Behaviour-based attack detection and classification in cyber physical systems using machine learning. In: CPSS (2016). https://doi.org/10.1145/2899015.2899016
20. Kim, J., Yun, J.-H., Kim, H.C.: Anomaly detection for industrial control systems using sequence-to-sequence neural networks. In: Katsikas, S., et al. (eds.) Cyber-ICPS/SECPRE/SPOSE/ADIoT -2019. LNCS, vol. 11980, pp. 3–18. Springer, Cham (2020). https://doi.org/10.1007/978-3-030-42048-2_1
21. Kus, D., Wagner, E., Pennekamp, J., et al.: A false sense of security? Revisiting the state of machine learning-based industrial intrusion detection. In: CPSS. ACM (2022). https://doi.org/10.1145/3494107.3522773
22. Lamberts, O., Wolsing, K., Wagner, E., et al.: SOK: evaluations in industrial intrusion detection research. J. Syst. Res. **3**(1) (2023). https://doi.org/10.5070/SR33162445
23. Liaw, R., Liang, E., Nishihara, R., et al.: Tune: a research platform for distributed model selection and training (2018). https://doi.org/10.48550/arXiv.1807.05118
24. Lin, Q., Adepu, S., Verwer, S., Mathur, A.: TABOR: a graphical model-based approach for anomaly detection in industrial control systems. In: ASIACCS. ACM (2018). https://doi.org/10.1145/3196494.3196546
25. M. R., G.R., Ahmed, C.M., Mathur, A.: Machine learning for intrusion detection in industrial control systems: challenges and lessons from experimental evaluation. Cybersecurity **4**(1), 1–12 (2021). https://doi.org/10.1186/s42400-021-00095-5
26. Morris, T.H., Thornton, Z., Turnipseed, I.: Industrial control system simulation and data logging for intrusion detection system research. In: SCSS. CAE in Cybersecurity Community (2015)
27. Perez, R.L., Adamsky, F., Soua, R., Engel, T.: Machine learning for reliable network attack detection in SCADA systems. In: IEEE TrustCom. IEEE (2018). https://doi.org/10.1109/TrustCom/BigDataSE.2018.00094
28. Probst, P., Boulesteix, A.L., Bischl, B.: Tunability: importance of hyperparameters of machine learning algorithms. J. Mach. Learn. Res. **20**(53) (2019). http://jmlr.org/papers/v20/18-444.html
29. Seng, S., Garcia-Alfaro, J., Laarouchi, Y.: Why anomaly-based intrusion detection systems have not yet conquered the industrial market?. In: Aïmeur, E., Laurent, M., Yaich, R., Dupont, B., Garcia-Alfaro, J. (eds.) Foundations and Practice of

Security. FPS 2021. LNCS, vol. 13291. Springer, Cham (2022). https://doi.org/10.1007/978-3-031-08147-7_23

30. Sommer, R., Paxson, V.: Outside the closed world: on using machine learning for network intrusion detection. In: S&P. IEEE (2010). https://doi.org/10.1109/SP.2010.25

31. Taormina, R., Galelli, S., Tippenhauer, N.O., et al.: Battle of the attack detection algorithms: disclosing cyber attacks on water distribution networks. J. Water Resour. Plan. Manag. **144**(8) (2018). https://doi.org/10.1061/(ASCE)WR.1943-5452.0000969

32. Weerts, H.J., Mueller, A.C., Vanschoren, J.: Importance of tuning hyperparameters of machine learning algorithms (2020). https://doi.org/10.48550/arXiv.2007.07588

33. Wolsing, K., Thiemt, L., van Sloun, C., et al.: Can industrial intrusion detection be SIMPLE? In: Atluri, V., Di Pietro, R., Jensen, C.D., Meng, W. (eds.) ESORICS. Springer, Cham (2022). https://doi.org/10.1007/978-3-031-17143-7_28

34. Wolsing, K., Wagner, E., Saillard, A., et al.: IPAL: breaking up silos of protocol-dependent and domain-specific industrial intrusion detection systems. In: RAID. ACM (2022). https://doi.org/10.1145/3545948.3545968

A Framework for Applying Digital Twins to Support Incident Response

Sabah Suhail[1]([✉])[iD], Mubashar Iqbal[2][iD], Kieran McLaughlin[1][iD], Brian Lee[3][iD], and Babar Imtiaz[3][iD]

[1] Queen's University Belfast, Belfast, UK
{s.suhail,kieran.mclaughlin}@qub.ac.uk
[2] University of Tartu, Tartu, Estonia
mubashar.iqbal@ut.ee
[3] Technological University of the Shannon, Athlone, Ireland
{brian.Lee,Muhammad.BabarImtiaz}@tus.ie

Abstract. The convergence of information technology (IT) and operational technology (OT) has made manufacturing industries an attractive target for cyberattacks, ranging from industrial espionage to sabotage. Existing security tools, operating alone, are not capable enough to manage cybersecurity operations effectively. Digital twin (DT), as a security-enhancing enabler, can support complementary security measures alongside existing incident response (IR) solutions. DTs have been proposed in different IR phases; however, a comprehensive solution covering the IR lifecycle has yet to be addressed. This paper presents a DT-based IR solution to guide plant operators in modeling security-enhancing DTs for manufacturing industries. Moreover, the DT-based IR solution integrates existing security tools to ensure the effective safeguarding of critical assets and prompt response to cyber incidents. With an automotive assembly line as a cyber-physical production system (CPPS) use case, we examine the applicability of a DT-based IR solution.

Keywords: Digital Twin (DT) · Incident Response (IR) · Cyber-Physical Production System (CPPS) · Industrial Control System (ICS) · Cybersecurity

1 Introduction

In recent years there have been a number of reported cases of cyberattacks on manufacturing industries, where there have been direct effects on the operations of physical processes such as production lines. For instance, Emotet [17] was found to have compromised multiple automotive manufacturers, including Toyota in Japan, which exemplifies the need for securing an industrial control system (ICS) against potential attacks. Similarly, ransomware attacks on Renault-Nissan [15], Saint-Gobain [1], and Norsk Hydro [2] are among other notable cyberattacks on manufacturing ecosystems.

J. Garcia-Alfaro et al. (Eds.): ESORICS 2024 Workshops, LNCS 15263, pp. 474–493, 2025.
https://doi.org/10.1007/978-3-031-82349-7_30

To address the aforesaid cyberattacks in a timely and effective manner, it is essential to adopt solutions that can analyze data and state inconsistencies without causing damage to the physical assets [12]. One such solution is digital twins (DTs). DTs are virtual replicas of their physical counterparts that must *(i)* exhibit sufficient fidelity in terms of attributes and services, *(ii)* maintain a continuous synchronized feedback loop, and *(iii)* provide objective-specific actionable insights while covering entire lifecycle [4,13,31]. Recently, DTs have gained significant attention as security-enhancing enablers to support various phases of incident response (IR) [14]. The existing works emphasizing DT for securing cyber-physical systems (CPSs) cover different IR phases [5]. Nevertheless, a comprehensive approach that covers the entire IR lifecycle is yet to be addressed. Furthermore, the integration of existing IR solutions or tools like security information and event management (SIEM) along with DT-based security solutions is not given due attention.

This work aims to answer the following research questions (RQs) to address IR phases in manufacturing industries using DTs. *(RQ1)* How can critical assets, processes, or services be identified as suitable candidates for developing a security-enhancing DT? *(RQ2)* Given resource constraints, including communication, computation, and storage costs, which DT operation modes can be leveraged to optimize cybersecurity value? *(RQ3)* How can DT-based IR solutions complement existing security solutions? These questions lead to our main contributions:

– To guide plant operators, such as in manufacturing industries, we present a framework for DT-based IR lifecycle phases, including design-and-engineering and operation-and-maintenance.
– As an example of a cyber-physical production system (CPPS), we explore an automotive assembly line as a use case and consider IR lifecycle phases as the underlying security objective. We investigate viable IR solutions applying different DT operation modes (simulation and replication) and consider existing IR solutions, such as SIEM, using assessment criteria, including cost (operational and maintenance), damage (financial or operational), and recovery time.

The paper is organized as follows. Section 2 provides background information and existing works to establish the context of the work. Section 3 showcases an automotive assembly line use case featuring an attack scenario. Section 4 discusses the modeling requirements of a DT-based IR solution, covering how to model and utilize DT-based IR. Finally, Sect. 5 presents the concluding remarks of the paper and future research directions.

2   Background and Related Work

This section provides an overview of essential topics necessary for comprehending the outcomes of this research, e.g., Sect. 2.1 discusses the DT operations modes, Sect. 2.2 provides an overview of IR phases, and Sect. 2.3 presents the related works concerning DT-based IR solutions in manufacturing industries.

2.1   DT Operation Modes

In manufacturing industries, introducing sustainable-by-design or security-by-design at the initial (design) phase can help to *(i)* lower defects such as parameter configuration, *(ii)* support agile product lifecycle management methods, and *(iii)* analyze assets in a virtual environment before real-world operations. A DT can investigate data inconsistencies through a simulation mode that does not connect to the physical asset or a replication mode that involves continuous mapping of the physical and twin environments. Being reproducible and repeatable, simulation mode can enable a plant operator to test and debug design artifacts by (re)running DT instances until the optimal operating conditions are met for a given production process [9,35]. Replication mode allows plant operators to identify data inconsistencies by continuously synchronizing the state and data of the physical system with its twin counterparts [11].

2.2   Incident Response (IR)

IR refers to the structured approach taken by organizations to manage and address security incidents, cyber threats, or disruptions to minimize damage, reduce recovery time, and mitigate the impact on the business [30]. The IR lifecycle comprises the following phases.

Preparation: Creating an IR plan, establishing a response team, defining roles and responsibilities, and conducting training drills.

Identification: Identifying a security incident through various monitoring systems or reports to understand the nature and scope of the problem.

Containment and Eradication: Taking immediate actions to remove the threat and eliminate the incident's root cause.

Recovery: Restoring affected systems, data, and operations to normal functionality while ensuring the security and integrity of the environment.

Lessons learned: Conducting a post-incident review to analyze the incident and improve IR procedures for the future.

2.3   Related Work

DTs as security-enhancing enablers have been proposed to enhance the performance of IR phases, such as staff training, anomaly detection, and system testing [13]. For example, [8,37] utilize DTs as cyber ranges to provide hands-on cyber skills (preparation phase). Works including [8,9,12,24,33] utilize DTs for security posture testing and anomaly-based intrusion detection (identification phase). DTs can help to minimize the impact on live systems (containment phase) as discussed in [7,16,24,26]. For example, virtual segmentation and isolation, access controls simulation, firewall configuration, simulation, and testing of different containment strategies. Using DTs, organizations can accelerate the restoration of affected systems (eradication and recovery phases) while ensuring security, minimizing downtime, and validating the recovery procedures in a controlled environment before implementing them on live systems [7,16]. Additionally, DTs can refine IR strategies based on insights gathered from the recovery process (lesson learned phase), ultimately contributing to a more effective and secure incident resolution [7].

The existing works on DT-based IR focus on either one or two IR phases and lack a coherent view across the entire IR lifecycle. Furthermore, the existing works overlook the integration of security-enhancing DTs with established security tools/solutions. Therefore, the question is how to model DT-based IR and integrate them with existing security measures. In this regard, our work bridges the research gap by highlighting how to model DT-based IR (Sect. 4.1), which DT modes must be leveraged, and how to integrate DT-based IR solutions with existing security solutions (Sect. 4.2).

3   Use Case: An Automotive Assembly Line

This section discusses the physical infrastructure in a typical automotive assembly line (Sect. 3.1) and an attack scenario targeting the welding process in the body shop (Sect. 3.2).

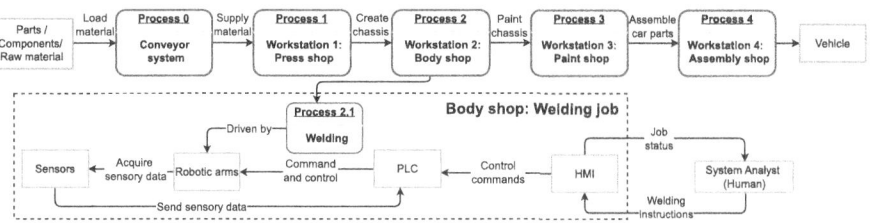

Fig. 1. Data Flow Diagram illustrating automotive manufacturing stages emphasizing the welding process in the body shop (represented by dashed lines).

3.1   Infrastructure in Automotive Assembly Line

We present an automotive assembly line as a CPPS use case where we consider four automotive production stages (as Fig. 1 shows), namely the press shop, the body shop, the paint shop, and the final assembly shop [19]. Each production stage can be represented by a workstation operated on a conveyor system that moves the vehicle chassis or parts between workstations. Each workstation performs a specific set of tasks on the vehicle. To do so, workstations are equipped with physical assets, including (i) control systems such as programmable logic controllers (PLCs), to manage the sequence of operations in the assembly line, human-machine interfaces (HMIs), to provide interfaces for operators to interact with and control the assembly such as robotic arms (to perform tasks including welding, painting, and handling heavy components), feeders and hoppers (to store and supply raw materials, components, or parts to the assembly line), automated guided vehicles (AGVs), to transport heavy or bulk materials, and *(iii)* data acquisition sources (sensors, actuators, vision systems) to measure or monitor operations. Note that we have not considered auxiliary processes such as inventory management or manual inspection. Under such settings, we can achieve two objectives: *(a)* protect critical assets or processes by separating them with less protected/less critical (sub)zones and *(b)* identify physical assets or processes that require twin counterparts to track data inconsistencies.

To simplify the illustration of complex automotive production processes, we focus on the welding process within a body shop as an example (as Fig. 1 shows). The rationale for selecting this process is that the welding process demands precision and accuracy to ensure the alignment of various components in the assembly phase. More specifically, any flaws in the welding process can directly impact the structural integrity, durability, and safety of the manufactured vehicle [10]. In the body shop, the components, including frame sections, panels, or other structural parts, that require welding to create the chassis structure are obtained from the press shop. The HMI communicates voltage, current, wire feed speed, and arc length to a PLC, which then controls the welding robotic arms to weld at predefined joints or designated areas on the components to assemble the chassis [29]. Sensors, such as tactile, temperature, and arc, affixed to robotic arms operate based on predefined configurations for efficient and automated monitoring of the welding process [29]. Note that the welding process may differ based on a specific model, make, individualized parts, or welding approach; however, the fundamental steps remain constant across various welding methods.

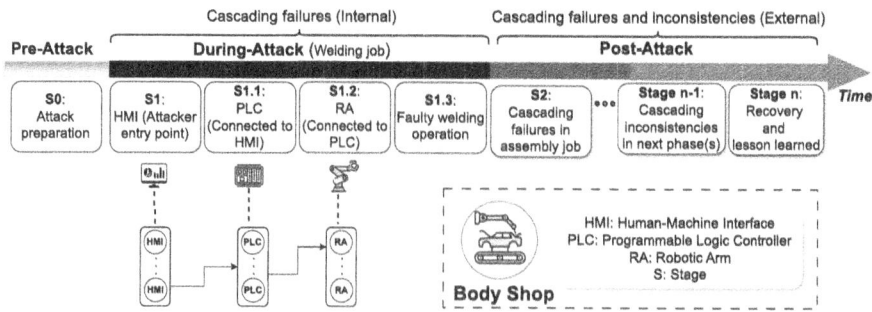

Fig. 2. Illustration of an attack scenario targeting the welding process, highlighting the attack stages and potential internal and external cascading failures.

3.2   Attack Scenario

Visualization tampering at the HMI could be an attractive target for attackers, as evident from Stuxnet and Industroyer incidents [20]. Attackers may conceal critical information, show erroneous data to mislead operators or tamper with data [4]. Following the cyber kill chain (CKC), we have outlined the progression of a cyber attack by classifying the attacker's actions targeting the welding process into three stages: pre-attack, during-attack, and post-attack, as illustrated in Fig. 2. During the pre-attack stage, attackers collect intelligence regarding system infrastructure and operational processes, for example through reconnaissance or phishing techniques, or with the collaboration of insiders. During the attack stage, attackers may exploit vulnerabilities in the HMI to gain entry and manipulate welding parameters. Unauthorized access to the HMI due to default passwords or unpatched software could allow attackers to inject malware into the interconnected systems. The adulterated parameters are passed to the PLC that commands and controls welding robots (see Fig. 1). Improper voltage and current levels can lead to overheating or weak welds. For instance, overheating due to higher voltage or current levels may lead to burn-through or distortion of the chassis, whereas inadequate penetration into the base material due to lower voltage or current levels may create weak joints, thereby jeopardizing the chassis's strength and stability. Thus, during the post-attack phase, such attacks eventually lead to production delays in the automotive production phases (such as the assembly phase in the body shop) because detecting and rectifying poor-quality welds require additional time and resources. Furthermore, inappropriate settings of welding equipment may result in malfunctions of the welding gun or power source, leading to equipment damage, costly repairs, and production downtime. Thus, an attack on one shop or workstation can lead to external cascading failures or inconsistencies in the subsequent automotive production shops (as depicted in the extreme right of Fig. 2). We will revisit this attack scenario in Sect. 4.2, where we will explore effective solutions for resolving such attacks.

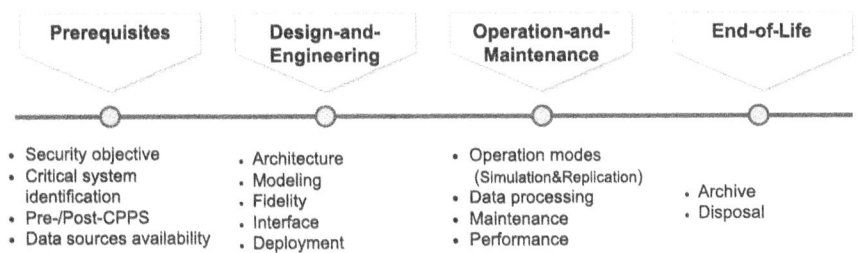

Fig. 3. Illustrating the key steps within security-enhancing DT lifecycle phases.

4   DT-Based IR Framework

In this section, we propose a DT-based IR framework (Sect. 4.1), primarily focusing on the design and operation phases. The framework of DT-based IR provides abstract representations crucial for understanding various DT concepts, illustrating the system's structure and behavior. Following [36], our framework is developed using unified modeling language (UML) class diagrams. Then we analyze the derived IR-based DTs models (Sect. 4.2) based on an attack scenario (discussed in Sect. 3.2), followed by a discussion of insights (Sect. 4.3).

4.1   Designing and Developing DT-Based IR Solutions

We propose that the lifecycle of a DT in tandem with its physical counterpart comprises four main phases: *(i)* prerequisites, *(ii)* design-and-engineering, *(iii)* operation-and-maintenance, and *(iv)* end-of-life (as Fig. 3 shows).

First, the security objective(s) must be determined, including intrusion prevention and detection, cyber deception, digital forensics, testing, and training [14], reflecting the subsequent CPPS-DT lifecycle phases. The reason for determining the security objective at the prerequisite phase is to configure the security-enhancing DT design parameters following the available resources.

Second, depending on the CPPS infrastructure, plant operators may choose to create DTs of a network, system, application, or a combination of these for an underlying use case and security objectives. Due to feasibility limitations in creating a DT for the entire infrastructure [13] as well as the challenge in identifying which CPS sub-systems can be mapped to a DT, we propose that the DT modeling process can be refined by: *(i)* breaking down the infrastructure into sub-components, *(ii)* constructing a data flow diagram to pinpoint critical assets, processes, or services, and *(iii)* selecting which of these critical elements should be modeled as a DT. This step addresses RQ1.

Third, DTs rely on data sources obtained from ongoing physical processes, assets state data, real-time sensory data, historical data, or other sources [35]. Data availability is crucial because DTs rely on the data to accurately represent the physical system they simulate [4,35]. Therefore, it is essential to identify the availability of data sources subject to the pre and post-existence of a specific CPPS instance [34]. For instance, if a CPPS is operational and requires security assessment during its operation-and-maintenance phase, modeling a DT from scratch (i.e., design phase) can utilize historical and real-time data. Conversely, if the CPPS is not yet in existence, DT modeling can draw upon alternative data sources, such as historical data from similar production or manufacturing processes. Upon establishing the prerequisites, the DT can be developed and managed based on CPPS-DT lifecycle phases.

To enforce security by design, DT modeling must cover the IR lifecycle so that the DT instances can be instantiated accurately, exhibiting the functionalities required during an incident. In the following, we mainly discuss the design-and-engineering (Fig. 4) and operation-and-maintenance (Fig. 5) lifecycle phases of DT-based IR.

Design-and-Engineering Phase. Figure 4 illustrates the DT design-and-engineering phase (marked with dotted lines) and its integration with IR phases (marked with dashed lines), including preparation and identification.

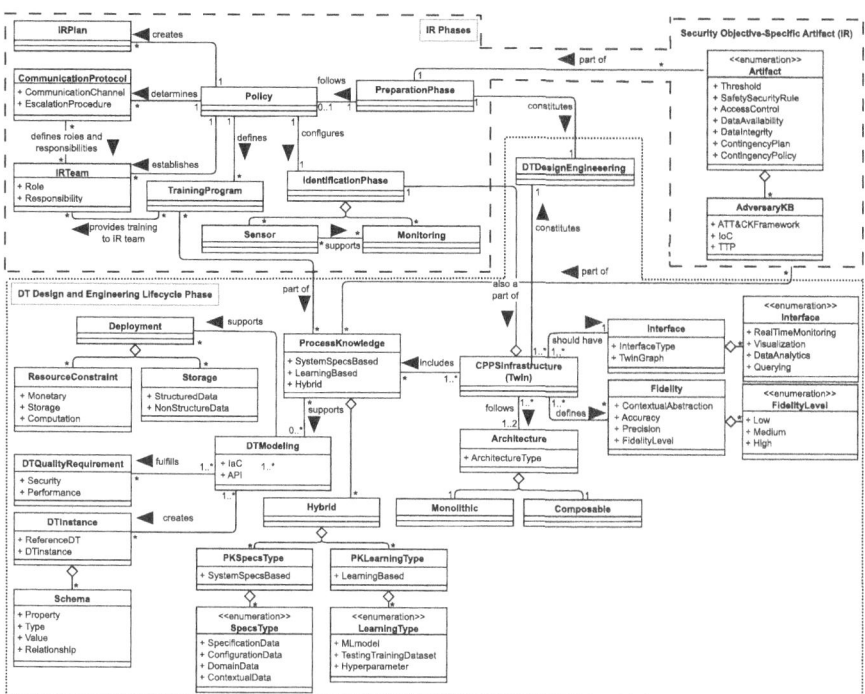

Fig. 4. Design-and-engineering phase of DT-based IR. For illustration purposes, the dashed and dotted lines delineate the IR and DT lifecycle phases, respectively.

For plant operators, Fig. 4 refers to design DT-based IR solutions. *First*, it provides the foundational building blocks necessary for modeling security-enhancing DTs. For instance, selecting a DT architecture, integrating process knowledge (PK), accessing DT artifacts via an interface, and determining sufficient fidelity depending on the underlying security objective. Moreover, it outlines the factors to consider when deploying DT-based IR solutions, such as resource constraints, storage requirements, and quality requirements. *Second*, it integrates IR phases into the DT model, ensuring that DT instances accurately reflect the functionalities needed during the preparation phase, such as establishing the plan for IR team training based on organizational policies, and the identification phase, such as monitoring CPPS twin infrastructure based on predefined thresholds and rules.

The DT-based IR preparation phase comprises plans, protocols, and resources heavily relying on organizational policies (refer to the upper left dashed part of Fig. 4). The policies are derived from security objective artifacts such as data security, access control, and existing adversary knowledge bases (KBs), e.g., tactics, techniques, and procedures (TTPs) and indicators of compromise (IoCs) (refer to the rightmost dashed part of Fig. 4). The preparation phase requirements, such as instantiating simulated training programs, can be translated as DT PK, i.e., data flows, behaviors, connections, and components within a physical system or asset. PK could be learning-based, specification-based, or hybrid [14]. PK is further subjected to fidelity, i.e., the degree of resemblance between the twin and its physical counterpart. Measuring the fidelity levels, such as low, medium, or high depends on DT operation modes, i.e., simulation and replication (as Fig. 5 shows). For instance, a high-fidelity DT model is required for replication mode. Furthermore, high-fidelity DT correlates with higher DT accuracy and precision, albeit at higher deployment costs. Moreover, high-fidelity DTs lead to information leakage [31]. Therefore, a trade-off is required between generalization and contextualization.

The CPPS twinned architecture can be defined as monolithic or composable (refer to the lower right dotted part of Fig. 4). Monolithic refers to asset, system, or process-level twin, whereas composable refers to component-level twin [23, 28]. The diversity among these DT types stems from their granularity levels, ranging from singular representations of parts or components (such as a temperature sensor, which can be termed as a component twin) to more comprehensive twins that encompass entire systems (such as the overall welding process, which can be termed as a process twin). For DT-based IR, composable DTs, i.e., component twins, offer a flexible and modular strategy, thereby facilitating attack localization by analyzing the component-level DT instance. The deployment of DT is constrained by resource availability, including communication, computation, and storage costs (refer to the upper right dotted part of Fig. 4). For instance, long-term data storage may utilize cloud services as a scalable and cost-effective solution. The DT data and models can be stored as structured or non-structured data. The deployed DT models must exhibit security and performance requirements, including confidentiality, integrity, availability, access control, and scalability. A reference DT (blueprint) can be instantiated to generate DT instances with schema having properties, types, values, and relationships. For instance, in manufacturing custom-built luxury vehicles with distinctive chassis designs, DT instances can be tailored to accommodate individualized or customer-specific welding specifications while maintaining consistency with fundamental welding operations outlined in the reference DT blueprint.

To automate the deployment of system configurations, infrastructure as code (IaC) can be used to (re)generate DT instances. The DT modeling can use application programming interfaces (APIs) to support services specific to simulation tools used for DT modeling. For instance, Microsoft Azure DT provides Azure IoT Hub–a cloud-hosted service that facilitates communication between applications and devices [22]. CPPS twins can be accessed through an interface for querying and visualization; additionally, it supports twin graphs (based on DT models) that combine real-time monitoring and data analytics [22] (refer to the lower rightmost dotted part of Fig. 4). During the identification phase, the DT operation mode supports monitoring CPPS twin infrastructure to identify deviations in the replication mode during the digital-physical mapping based on the predefined thresholds or safety and security rules defined in policies or analyze DT instances through reconfigurable and reproducible simulation environments.

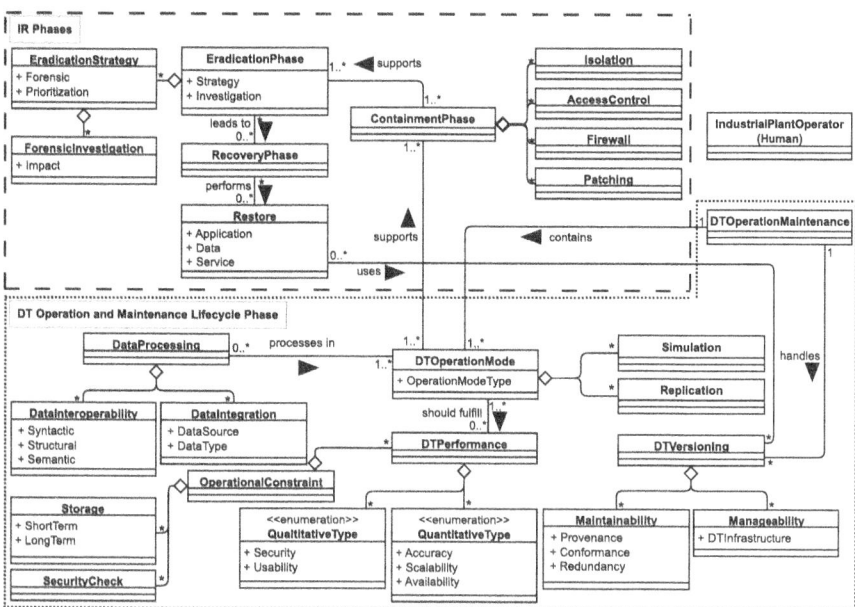

Fig. 5. Operation-and-maintenance phase of DT-based IR. For illustration purposes, the dashed and dotted lines delineate the IR and DT lifecycle phases, respectively.

Operation-and-Maintenance Phase. Figure 5 illustrates the DT operation-and-maintenance phase (marked with dotted lines) and its integration with IR phases (marked with dashed lines), including containment, eradication, and recovery. For plant operators, Fig. 5 serves as a reference to operate DT-based IR solutions. *First*, it outlines DT operation modes (simulation and replication). Moreover, it provides the operational requirements of DTs, such as DT performance requirements essential for the trustworthiness of decisions made by the DT. *Second*, it integrates IR phases into the DT model during the containment and eradication phases to leverage DT modes. For instance, using DT simulation to analyze the propagation of attacks and the effectiveness of various containment strategies. Additionally, DT versioning can aid in restoring compromised applications, data, or services in the recovery phase.

The DT-based IR containment phase limits the impact of an incident by using containment strategies, including isolation, access control, firewall, or patching (refer to the rightmost dashed part of Fig. 5). The eradication phase comprises forensic and prioritization, focusing on removing threats. Forensic investigation involves examining the affected systems, logs, and other digital artifacts to understand the incident or exploited vulnerabilities. Based on the urgency of securing critical assets or systems, prioritization defines which actions need immediate attention. DT simulation and replication modes can be leveraged to carry out containment and eradication phases (refer to the upper rightmost dotted part of Fig. 5). For example, with the simulation mode, plant operators can analyze the asset, process, or service under attack, in isolation from the physical system, to understand the attack scenario and its ramifications, or to localize the compromised node. The data processing during DT simulation and replication modes must comply with data integration, i.e., combining data from heterogeneous sources or formats into a unified format, and interoperability, i.e., enabling systems or devices to exchange and interpret data seamlessly. The recovery phase involves restoring the normal operations of applications, data, or services from backups, repairing compromised systems, and implementing security patches. To restore the system, DT instances managed and maintained through versioning (refer to the lower rightmost dotted part of Fig. 5), can be utilized during the backup process to ensure data integrity and system reliability. Maintenance of DT instances involves keeping track of provenance data, compliance with any relevant standards, and backup that serves as a fail-safe in case of primary system failure. The performance of a DT must adhere to quantitative and qualitative aspects. Quantitative assessments involve metrics, such as accuracy, scalability, and availability, whereas qualitative assessments involve security and usability. These factors may significantly effect the system's recovery time and the trustworthiness of decisions made by the DT.

4.2   Utilizing DT-Based IR Solutions During System Attacks

Based on the attack scenario (Sect. 3.2), in the following, we explore a viable IR solution that leverages *(i)* an existing IR solution (such as SIEM) to address RQ3, *(ii)* DT operation modes (simulation and/or replication) to address RQ2, and/or *(iii)* a combination of both solutions while minimizing cost, reducing response time, and mitigating potential damage. The selection of a cybersecurity solution depends on various factors, including a company's size, security posture, financial constraints, regulatory obligations, or current industry adoption trends in the automotive manufacturing industry. Note that the proposed solution focuses on synergizing DT-based solutions with established IR solutions such as SIEM, considered a key cyber defense platform in the industry [18]. Table 1 summarizes our findings regarding integrating SIEM with DT-based IR solutions across cyber attack stages.

We consider the effectiveness of the IR solution based on two factors, i.e., cost and response time. The following discussion is based on the attack scenario on the welding process (Sect. 3.2). Various costs associated with cybersecurity solutions can be defined as *(i)* initial costs (covering implementation and deployment, licensing), *(ii)* operational costs (utilities, consumables, resource usage such as hardware, servers, or cloud infrastructure), *(iii)* maintenance and manageability costs (scaling and upgrading, debugging, hardware maintenance, software licensing renewals), and *(iv)* others such as training cost (programs and resources for educating employees) [25]. For instance, in the case of a DT-based IR solution, the initial cost may include DT modeling that involves creating multi-fidelity DT instances (ranging from low to high), integration and interoperability with physical system infrastructure, i.e., data sources, and DT infrastructure (computation, communication, and storage) and DT performance requirements. The operational cost of DT may include real-time monitoring tools, analytics platforms, and other allocated resources such as storage. The maintenance cost includes regular updates and security patches. The training cost includes personnel training and resources to educate employees about the DT-based IR solution. Considering initial DT modeling and deployment costs have already been incurred, we focus on operational and maintenance costs. While we have theoretically addressed the cost factor, it is worth noting [6] formulates the problem of deriving cost-effective DT for security tests as a 0–1 non-linear programming problem.

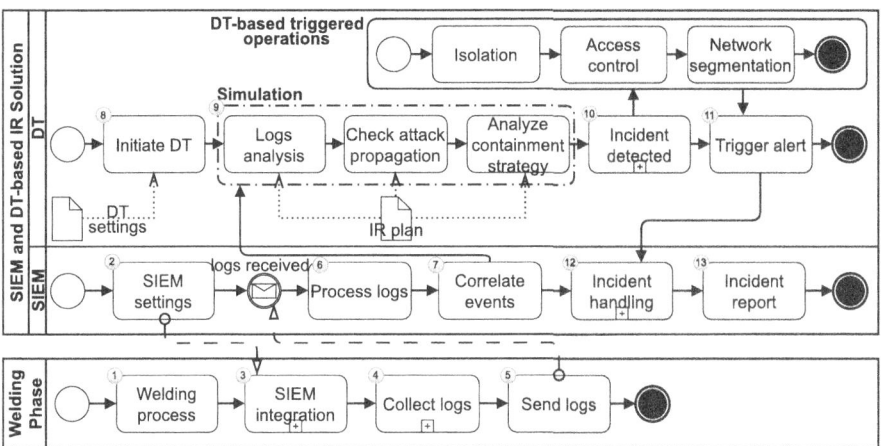

Fig. 6. Illustrating the response to a cyberattack (depicted in Fig. 2) during the containment and eradication phases.

Preparation *Effective solutions: SIEM and DT-Based Simulation and Replication Modes.*
Justification: During the preparation phase, the manufacturing industry must be equipped with the necessary strategies, including developing IR plans, establishing IR teams, conducting regular training programs, deploying tools, and reviewing policies to mitigate the impact of potential security incidents effectively (refer to the preparation phase in the dashed part of Fig. 4). For instance, the DT replication mode continuously synchronizes with physical welding processes to promptly detect data inconsistencies. Furthermore, DT simulation instances can be instantiated to facilitate training and awareness programs, enabling teams to practice response strategies in a risk-free, controlled environment (see Fig. 4). These training initiatives ensure that IR teams are equipped with the necessary skills to effectively respond to incidents, thereby enhancing their preparedness. SIEM can offer real-time monitoring and analysis of security events by collecting, correlating, and logging data for compliance or auditing purposes. For instance,

during the pre-attack stage, login attempts to HMI may be correlated with irregular network traffic patterns or unauthorized alterations to welding parameters. Additionally, it can be used to log access data for the HMI controlling welding robotic arms via PLCs.

Identification *Effective Solution: SIEM.*

Justification: During the identification phase, SIEM can assist plant operators by analyzing network traffic and system logs, providing insights into potential insider threats or compromised credentials, to identifying suspicious activities or deviations from benign behavior (identification phase in the dashed part of Fig. 4). For example, adulteration of welding parameters, unauthorized access attempts, or unusual login patterns providing insights about insider threats or compromised credentials can be flagged as anomalies. Moreover, integrating SIEM with third-party threat intelligence feeds, including threat signatures, profiles, and IoCs, can identify patterns, anomalies, and potential threats.

Assessment: Operational and maintenance costs are primarily associated with SIEM. An additional cost, such as licensing, may be incurred if third-party solutions are used for advanced real-time threat recognition. With SIEM-based solutions, there might be possibilities of burnout due to the lack of context needed by plant operators to understand alerts or false positives [21], particularly if the attacker adulterates parameters at random intervals or within normal variability. Therefore, to minimize damage and reduce response time, the solution must adapt to fine-tuning threshold levels to reduce false positives and use context-aware detection techniques to distinguish malicious and benign activities.

Containment and Eradication *Effective Solution: SIEM and DT-Based Simulation Mode.*

Justification: We assume the welding process has been integrated into the SIEM system. Following our DT-based IR approach, plant operators may utilize a combination of SIEM and a DT-based simulation mode, as Fig. 6 shows. First, the SIEM collects system logs, network traffic, and user activity (see Fig. 6 step 4) from the physical infrastructure, including HMIs, PLCs, and robotic arms operating in the body shop (see Fig. 1). Second, to allow an in-depth incident investigation, DT simulation mode is integrated with the SIEM system using its log analysis and event correlation capabilities. DT instance(s) are instantiated (see Fig. 6 step 8) based on modeling requirements depicted in Fig. 4. To localize the compromised asset, DT simulation mode can facilitate scenario analysis by modeling different attack scenarios and containment strategies to assess *(a)* how the attack might propagate, *(b)* which containment strategies would be most effective, *(c)* what could be the potential impact of containment actions on the physical system, and *(d)* how to systematically eradicate the root cause of the security incident from the affected system (see Fig. 5). For example, simulating containment strategies (see Fig. 6 step 9) involves *(i)* isolation methods (quarantine affected welding process from other workstations or manufacturing networks) to prevent external cascading inconsistencies or failures across

Table 1. Applying an integration of SIEM with DT-based IR solutions across cyber attack stages (depicted in Fig. 2)

Cyberattack stages	IR phase	Response strategy	Details
Pre-attack	Preparation	Simulation, Replication, SIEM	Simulated training environment for plant operators' training and awareness; Replication mode for continuous digital-physical mapping to detect data inconsistencies; SIEM logs and correlates HMI access.
	Identification	SIEM	SIEM detects suspicious activities like parameter tampering, unauthorized access, or unusual logins by analyzing network traffic and system logs.
During attack	Containment and Eradication	Simulation, SIEM	Simulating containment strategies; SIEM monitors network traffic, logs for unauthorized access to the quarantined welding process, and tracks HMI within the zone for compliance and anomaly detection.
Post-attack	Recovery	Simulation, Replication	Simulated DT instance of the welding process validates the integrity of the restored welding process by comparing current welding parameters against benign operational parameters; DT replication mode synchronizes with the recovered welding process.
	Lesson learned	Simulation, SIEM	Simulated training environment for plant operators to prepare against cyberattacks; SIEM conducts postmortem analysis and ensures compliance through reports and dashboards.

other shops, *(ii)* access controls (disable or restrict access to compromised HMI), or *(iii)* network segmentation (to segregate the body shop's network traffic). For instance, SIEM can support simulation mode in applying isolation methods by monitoring network traffic and logs for unauthorized access attempts to the quarantined welding process. Additionally, they can track HMI within the quarantine zone to ensure compliance with isolation measures and detect anomalies or security breaches. Thus, SIEM can correlate event data from HMI logs with DT simulation mode to reconstruct the timeline of events necessary for identifying the root cause. Once the incident of a compromised HMI is detected (see Fig. 6 step 10), the SIEM should assist in executing incident handling (see Fig. 6 step 12), including remediation, patch management, removal of malware and backdoors, and validation of actions taken to eradicate the root cause.

Assessment: Through real-time monitoring and analysis, SIEM systems can collate multiple events and logs from various assets and systems in the welding shop. Such data ingestion and logged events from multiple sources can support DT simulation mode. During simulation mode, isolation methods can be applied to a range of simulated attack scenarios that can leverage SIEM data to detect security breaches or anomalies. Consequently, integrating SIEM and DT simulation modes ensures the timely identification and triaging of security incidents.

Recovery *Effective Solution: DT Simulation and Replication Modes.*
Justification: The plant operators can follow a two-step approach during recovery surveillance, i.e., post-attack stage. First, test patches for a vulnerable asset, i.e., HMI or suspected service in a simulated environment, and monitor the restored system against any anomalies or residual threats. The simulated DT instance of the welding process can act as a sandbox that validates the integrity of the restored welding process by comparing current welding parameters against benign operational parameters. This strategy can help plant operators test, verify, and validate compromised assets before replicating them on the live physical system. Second, upon synchronizing the physical asset or service with DT replication mode, continue monitoring the recovered systems, i.e., HMI through the replication mode to identify the re-occurrence of abnormal behavior or vulnerabilities. The replication mode can be a backup to restore the system to a known stable state in the face of an attack or system failure, thereby minimizing downtime and ensuring resilience.
Assessment: Both DT modes, particularly replication mode, have associated operational and maintenance costs; however, they offer long-term benefits in terms of operational resilience and risk mitigation.

Lesson Learned *Effective Solutions: DT-Based Simulation Mode and SIEM.*
Justification: The plant operators can harness outcomes from both SIEM and DTs as both solutions have been proposed independently or in combination during the earlier IR phases. For instance, the obtained results can be used to *(i)* carry out post-incident analysis and documentation, *(ii)* provide actionable recommendations and remediation plan outlining steps to address identified weaknesses or gaps (such as weak or default credentials of HMIs) in security measures to prevent similar incidents, and *(iii)* summarize key takeaways and insights gained from IR phases and share findings with other manufacturing industry peers to enforce collaborative learning against evolving threats. Such IR reports might be of additional support to gain insights into future incidents in manufacturing industries. DT simulation mode could be realized as a comprehensive gamification platform (as suggested by [34]). With DTs, a simulated and controlled hands-on learning/training environment can help to train operations personnel and prepare for the next threat wave. For instance, DT instance(s) can present diverse challenges based on varying objectives and scenarios from the welding process. SIEM complements the simulation mode by conducting postmortem analysis and ensuring adherence to regulatory requirements and industry standards through the generation of compliance reports, audit trails, and security dashboards. Moreover, training exercises can vary from *table-top* discussion-based sessions (such as workshops on identifying phishing emails and password security of assets) aimed at familiarizing employees with cybersecurity awareness and best practices, to *live-play* role-based exercises (such as simulated

cyberattacks on welding systems followed by IR drills) aimed at enhancing the skill set of security professionals.

Assessment: The investigation results from both security solutions have the potential to identify malicious incidents in a timely manner, minimizing response time and decreasing damage.

4.3   Takeaways

Existing IR solutions like SIEM and underlying technologies such as artificial intelligence/machine learning (AI/ML) or adversary KBs may not suffice independently for effective cybersecurity operations [24]. Consequently, DT as a security-enhancing enabler can serve as complementary security measures alongside existing IR solutions, enhancing the overall security infrastructure and maximizing cybersecurity value. Through the proposed work, such a combined security solution, integrating DTs with conventional IR solutions enables organizations to navigate resource constraints effectively while ensuring the efficacy of their security strategies, thereby enhancing threat visibility, response agility, and defense strategies to fortify the overall security posture.

The capital and operational expenditure on DT-based solutions covers various aspects, including implementation and deployment, operational, maintenance, and training costs. Furthermore, the cost factor in DT modeling is influenced by security objectives such as anomaly detection or cyber deception, which are determined by the required degree of fidelity. For instance, cyber deception demands higher fidelity compared to anomaly detection scenarios [32]. Despite the theoretical nature of the discussion in Sect. 4.2, the insights on the cost of DT-based solutions offer valuable information that can inform decision-making processes, strategic planning, and resource allocation in practical applications.

In this work, regarding the modeling and deployment of DTs, we follow the composable DTs with component twins that allow a flexible, modular, and agile approach [23,28]. Component twins can provide granularity, thereby supporting the identification and localization of attacks. For example, within the manufacturing context, instead of making system-level DT for the entire body shop, which could be complex and resource-intensive, a more practical approach would be to create individual DTs for components such as PLCs, HMIs, sensors, etc., and then aggregate these instances to form a comprehensive DT. On the one hand, replication mode may incur higher costs as it requires *(a)* modeling DT instance(s) with sufficient fidelity and *(b)* time-dependent synchronization consistency with the physical asset. On the other hand, the continuous feedback loops through replication mode can offer varying degrees of autonomy, ranging from human-in-the-loop to human-on-the-loop to fully autonomous systems. Moreover, it can support system resilience by providing a backup to restore system states. However, given that the security of a DT is a critical concern [4,31], replication modes must be carefully executed. In the manufacturing context, the replication services, in the case of critical processes, ensure availability, reliability, and fault tolerance. Therefore, replication mode must be applied for key operations such as welding processes or automated inspection to minimize the risk of failure and enhance system resilience rather than auxiliary processes such as inventory management. Following a pragmatic approach, a triage decision must be based on attack severity, potential impact, and available resources.

We selected the welding process in the body shop of the automotive manufacturing industry to demonstrate a theoretical application of the DT-based IR framework in a realistic practical scenario. Given that the welding process demands precision and accuracy, the DT-based IR framework as compared to existing security solutions, can provide a viable approach to prevent, detect, and mitigate cyber incidents in a timely and effective manner.

The proposed DT-based IR framework can be extended to other use cases, specifically those involving fixed physical environments characterized by machinery and equipment that remain static. Examples include electronics manufacturing, consumer goods manufacturing, and food manufacturing, which face cybersecurity risks due to their reliance on interconnected systems [3]. It is worth noting that, for the given CPPS use case, the DT-based IR design parameters may vary depending on the security-enhancing use case of the DT and available resources.

5   Conclusion and Future Work

Cyberattacks on manufacturing industries have demonstrated severe consequences for business and economic sectors. This work discusses the significance of integrating security-enhancing DTs for effective IR in the manufacturing industries. First, we present a framework for DT-based IR to guide plant operators in manufacturing industries, mainly focusing on the design and operation lifecycle phases. Second, we analyze an attack scenario within the automotive assembly line to illustrate the practical feasibility of a DT-based IR solution. We discuss viable approaches, such as DT operation modes (simulation and replication), and existing security tools, such as SIEM, while considering various assessment criteria, including cost, damage, and recovery time.

We anticipate that Figs. 4 and 5 can be a reference for plant operators to design and operate DT-based IR solutions. Compared to traditional security solutions, such as SIEM, the DT-based IR framework potentially offers a more effective solution due to its close coupling with attributes of the CPS. This is attributed to its capability to reproduce attack scenarios for in-depth analysis through simulation mode, maintain continuous synchronization of feedback loops with their physical counterparts for real-time updates of system state and behavior through replication mode, and employ component-level DTs to identify cascading inconsistencies (dotted line parts in Fig. 4 and Fig. 5). Furthermore, the proposed approach can guide plant operators in utilizing DT-based IR solutions alongside existing security tools when the system is under attack.

When designing security-enhancing DTs, our approach primarily builds on [14] where we add value by integrating DT architecture (monolithic or composable), data processing services (integration, interoperability), DT performance (quantitative and qualitative), operational constraints (storage and security checks), and DT versioning (maintainability and manageability). This extension to security-enhancing DTs provides plant operators with a thorough consideration of the requirements for designing and developing DT-based IR.

As the proposed DT-based IR framework is yet to be implemented, the next steps in this research anticipate proof-of-concept experimentation through a small-scale testbed to explore practical challenges in integration. Attack and response experiments will be conducted to investigate response times required for the DT-based approach to carry out successful IR functions. Subsequent stages of experimentation and development will focus on tuning the approach for accuracy, for a lab-based use case, aiming to provide broader lessons that can generalized across other use cases. Similarly, comparing DT-based IR solutions with other established security solutions or tools to understand how they can complement security-enhancing DTs in cybersecurity operations is also necessary. Such assessment should include evaluating metrics such as cost, damage, and recovery time. Furthermore, we acknowledge the value of broadening our scope with additional resources, such as those from the DT Consortium [27], to fully consider various requirements for DT design and operation.

Acknowledgements. This work was supported by the North-South Research Programme, which is delivered by Higher Education Authority (HEA) on behalf of the Department of Further and Higher Education, Research, Innovation and Science (DFHERIS) and the Shared Island Unit at the Department of the Taoiseach.

References

1. Saint-gobain press release (2017). https://www.saint-gobain.com/sites/saint-gobain.com/files/03-07-2017_cp_va.pdf
2. Cyber-attack on hydro (2019). https://www.hydro.com/en/media/on-the-agenda/cyber-attack/
3. Alamri, A.H.: Dragos industrial ransomware analysis: Q1 2024 Dragos (2024). https://www.dragos.com/blog/dragos-industrial-ransomware-analysis-q1-2024/. Accessed 05 May 2024
4. Alcaraz, C., Lopez, J.: Digital twin: a comprehensive survey of security threats. IEEE Commun. Surv. Tuts. **24**(3), 1475–1503 (2022). https://doi.org/10.1109/COMST.2022.3171465
5. Allison, D., Smith, P., Mclaughlin, K.: Digital twin-enhanced incident response for cyber-physical systems. In: Proceedings of the 18th International Conference on Availability, Reliability and Security. ARES 2023, Association for Computing Machinery (2023). https://doi.org/10.1145/3600160.3600195
6. Bitton, R., et al.: Deriving a cost-effective digital twin of an ICS to facilitate security evaluation. In: Computer Security, pp. 533–554. Springer International Publishing, Cham (2018). https://doi.org/10.1007/978-3-319-99073-6_26
7. Bécue, A., Maia, E., Feeken, L., Borchers, P., Praça, I.: A new concept of digital twin supporting optimization and resilience of factories of the future. Appl. Sci. **10**(13) (2020). https://doi.org/10.3390/app10134482
8. Bécue, A., et al.: Cyberfactory#1 — securing the industry 4.0 with cyber-ranges and digital twins. In: 2018 14th IEEE International Workshop on Factory Communication Systems, pp. 1–4 (2018). https://doi.org/10.1109/WFCS.2018.8402377

9. Dietz, M., Vielberth, M., Pernul, G.: Integrating digital twin security simulations in the security operations center. In: Proceedings of the 15th International Conference ARES (2020). https://doi.org/10.1145/3407023.3407039

10. Doshi, A., Smith, R.T., Thomas, B.H., Bouras, C.: Use of projector based augmented reality to improve manual spot-welding precision and accuracy for automotive manufacturing. Int. J. Adv. Manuf. Technol. **89**(5–8), 1279–1293 (2017). https://doi.org/10.1007/s00170-016-9164-5

11. Eckhart, M., Ekelhart, A.: A specification-based state replication approach for digital twins. In: Proceedings of the 2018 Workshop CPS-SPC, pp. 36–47 (2018). https://doi.org/10.1145/3264888.3264892

12. Eckhart, M., Ekelhart, A.: Towards security-aware virtual environments for digital twins. In: Proceedings of the 4th ACM Workshop CPSS, pp. 61–72 (2018). https://doi.org/10.1145/3198458.3198464

13. Eckhart, M., Ekelhart, A.: Digital Twins for Cyber-Physical Systems Security: State of the Art and Outlook, pp. 383–412. Springer International Publishing, Cham (2019). https://doi.org/10.1007/978-3-030-25312-7_14

14. Eckhart, M., et al.: Security-enhancing digital twins: characteristics, indicators, and future perspectives. IEEE Secur. Priv. **21**(6), 64–75 (2023). https://doi.org/10.1109/MSEC.2023.3271225

15. Eisenstein, P.A.: European car plants halted by wannacry ransomware attack (2017). https://www.nbcnews.com/business/autos/european-car-plants-halted-wannacry-ransomware-attack-n759496

16. Gehrmann, C., Gunnarsson, M.: A digital twin-based industrial automation and control system security architecture. IEEE Trans. Ind. Inform. **16**(1), 669–680 (2020). https://doi.org/10.1109/TII.2019.2938885

17. Hanrahan, J.: Suspected conti ransomware activity in the auto manufacturing sector (2022). https://www.dragos.com/blog/industry-news/suspected-conti-ransomware-activity-in-the-auto-manufacturing-sector/

18. Kinyua, J., Awuah, L.: AI/ML in security orchestration, automation and response: future research directions. Intell. Autom. Soft Comput. **28**(2) (2021)

19. Konstantinidis, F.K., Mouroutsos, S.G., Gasteratos, A.: The role of machine vision in industry 4.0: an automotive manufacturing perspective. In: 2021 IEEE International Conference on Imaging Systems and Techniques, pp. 1–6 (2021). https://doi.org/10.1109/IST50367.2021.9651453

20. Lee, R.M., Assante, M., Conway, T.: CRASHOVERRIDE: Analysis of the Threat to Electric Grid Operations. Dragos Inc. (2017)

21. López Velásquez, J.M., Martínez Monterrubio, S.M., Sánchez Crespo, L.E., Garcia Rosado, D.: Systematic review of SIEM technology: SIEM-SC birth. Int. J. Inf. Secur. **22**(3), 691–711 (2023). https://doi.org/10.1007/s10207-022-00657-9

22. Microsoft: What is azure digital twins? https://docs.microsoft.com/en-us/azure/digital-twins/overview. Accessed 05 Sept 2023

23. Minerva, R., Crespi, N.: Digital twins: properties, software frameworks, and application scenarios. IT Professional **23**(1), 51–55 (2021). https://doi.org/10.1109/MITP.2020.2982896

24. Mohsin, A., Janicke, H., Nepal, S., Holmes, D.: Digital twins and the future of their use enabling shift left and shift right cybersecurity operations. In: 2023 5th IEEE International Conference on Trust, Privacy and Security in Intelligent Systems and Applications, pp. 277–286. IEEE Computer Society (2023). https://doi.org/10.1109/TPS-ISA58951.2023.00042

25. Oettl, F., Eckart, L., Schilp, J.: Cost estimation approach of a digital twin implementation in industry. Procedia CIRP **118**, 318–323 (2023). https://doi.org/10.1016/j.procir.2023.06.055, 16th CIRP Conference on Intelligent Computation in Manufacturing Engineering

26. Redelinghuys, A., Basson, A.H., Kruger, K.: A six-layer architecture for the digital twin: a manufacturing case study implementation. J. Intell. Manuf. **31**(6), 1383–1402 (2020). https://doi.org/10.1007/s10845-019-01516-6

27. van Schalkwyk,P., Sean Whiteley, M.G.: Digital twin capabilities periodic table (2024). https://www.digitaltwinconsortium.org/wp-content/uploads/sites/3/2024/04/DTC_Capabilities-Periodic-Table-User-Guide-v1.1.pdf. Accessed April 2024

28. van Schalkwyk, P., Isaacs, D.: Achieving Scale Through Composable and Lean Digital Twins, pp. 153–180. Springer International Publishing, Cham (2023). https://doi.org/10.1007/978-3-031-21343-4_6

29. Shah, D.N.: Automatic welding and soldering machine using plc in automobile application. In: 2021 Asian Conference on Innovation in Technology, pp. 1–6 (2021). https://doi.org/10.1109/ASIANCON51346.2021.9544774

30. Shinde, N., Kulkarni, P.: Cyber incident response and planning: a flexible approach. Comput. Fraud Secur. **2021**(1), 14–19 (2021). https://doi.org/10.1016/S1361-3723(21)00009-9

31. Suhail, S., Iqbal, M., Jurdak, R.: The perils of leveraging evil digital twins as security-enhancing enablers. Commun. ACM **67**(1), 39–42 (2023). https://doi.org/10.1145/3631539

32. Suhail, S., Iqbal, M., McLaughlin, K.: Digital twin-driven deception platform: vision and way forward. IEEE Internet Comput. 1–9 (2024). https://doi.org/10.1109/MIC.2024.3406188

33. Suhail, S., et al.: Towards situational aware cyber-physical systems: a security-enhancing use case of blockchain-based digital twins. Comput. Ind. **141**, 103699 (2022). https://doi.org/10.1016/j.compind.2022.103699

34. Suhail, S., et al.: ENIGMA: an explainable digital twin security solution for cyber-physical systems. Comput. Ind. **151**, 103961 (2023). https://doi.org/10.1016/j.compind.2023.103961

35. Tao, F., Zhang, H., Zhang, C.: Advancements and challenges of digital twins in industry. Nat. Comput. Sci. **4**(3), 169–177 (2024). https://doi.org/10.1038/s43588-024-00603-w

36. Yue, T., Arcaini, P., Ali, S.: Understanding digital twins for cyber-physical systems: a conceptual model. In: Margaria, T., Steffen, B. (eds.) ISoLA 2020. LNCS, vol. 12479, pp. 54–71. Springer, Cham (2021). https://doi.org/10.1007/978-3-030-83723-5_5

37. Zhou, H., Li, M., Sun, Y., Tian, Z., Yun, L.: Digital twin-based cyber range for industrial internet of things. IEEE Consum. Electron. Mag., 1–11 (2022). https://doi.org/10.1109/MCE.2022.3203202

Automated Side-Channel Analysis of ARM TrustZone-M Programs

Sepideh Pouyanrad[1] , Fritz Alder[1] , and Jan Tobias Mühlberg[1,2(✉)]

[1] DistriNet, KU Leuven, 3001 Leuven, Belgium
fritz.alder@acm.org, jan.tobias.muehlberg@ulb.be
[2] Université Libre de Bruxelles, 1050 Brussels, Belgium

Abstract. ARM TrustZone is a dominant security technology in embedded processors, mobile devices, Cyber-Physical Systems, and the Internet of Things. TrustZone enables software isolation, allowing critical code to execute in a 'secure world' that is protected from direct access by less critical code. However, side-channel vulnerabilities fall outside of this isolation model: secret-dependent behavior in vulnerable programs may be observed from the normal world, compromising the confidentiality of secure-world programs. In this paper we present a tool that uses symbolic execution and static analysis to detect timing side channels in compiled programs for ARM's lightweight Cortex-M processors. We evaluate our approach on previously published benchmarks and attacks, demonstrating that our tool, SCF^{ARM}, exhibits high accuracy in detecting a range of side-channel vulnerabilities, specifically in the TrustZone secure world. To the best of our knowledge, SCF^{ARM} is the first side-channel detection tool tailored for ARM TrustZone, which we make available under an open-source license.

Keywords: Side Channel · ARM TrustZone-M · Symbolic Execution

1 Introduction

With increased connectivity in Cyber-Physical systems (CPS) and the rapid proliferation of Internet of Things (IoT) across domains such as smart homes, healthcare, transportation, and industrial systems, ensuring the security of these interconnected devices has become an utmost concern. IoT systems, consisting of embedded devices and networked components, handle an abundance of sensitive data, making them prime targets for malicious actors who seek to exploit vulnerabilities to extract information or gain control over installations [34,47]. Among the multitude of security threats, timing side-channel attacks have emerged as a significant and pervasive challenge. These side channels leverage timing variations in program execution to compromise the confidentiality and of sensitive data [17,28,30,50,57,64].

ARM-family processors have emerged as a dominant choice for embedded devices, across CPS and IoT, and in mobile phones, capturing a substantial market share of over 60% [63]. To enhance security, ARM has incorporated TrustZone

J. Garcia-Alfaro et al. (Eds.): ESORICS 2024 Workshops, LNCS 15263, pp. 494–513, 2025.
https://doi.org/10.1007/978-3-031-82349-7_31

[10,53], a hardware-based Trusted Execution Environments (TEEs), into their processors. TrustZone ensures the isolation of security-critical software and data from the rest of the system, enabling secure execution of critical tasks and protection of sensitive information. It achieves this by dividing the processor into two separate and concurrent security realms or worlds: the 'Normal World' and the 'Secure World.' These worlds operate independently of each other, possessing distinct memory spaces and execution environments. Thus, developers often rely on the presumption that secrets are protected within the secure world due to the processor's isolation guarantees. However, research [19,37,46,53,57,58,69] reveals the potential vulnerability of the TrustZone secure world to side-channel attacks that can lead to the unintended disclosure of secrets.

The TrustZone technology employed in ARMv8-M processors (such as Cortex-M23/ M33/ M35P/ M55/ M85), do not claim to protect against side-channel attacks [7]. Primary attack vectors here are secret-dependent control flow with measurable timing differences or secret- dependent memory access patterns. Furthermore, TrustZone cannot effectively prevent secret leakage that stems from program implementation flaws, which can arise from weaknesses in protocols or algorithms, as well as mistakes made by developers.

Early detection of side channel attacks enables proactive mitigation measures to be implemented. Researchers and practitioners have proposed various approaches to analyze binary code, or source code employing techniques such as symbolic execution [24,26], type systems [1,2,25,54], and machine learning [45], among others [28]. These approaches aim to identify and mitigate timing side channel vulnerabilities targeting different architectures. However, each approach carries its own limitations and strengths, necessitating a thorough exploration of the existing body of work in this field (cf. Section 3).

In this paper, we present a new and automated approach to detecting timing side-channel leakage in ARM TrustZone-M programs, utilizing symbolic execution-based analysis for the static verification. Our approach and tool targets the ARM Cortex-M23 microcontroller, capitalizing on the predictability of instruction execution times on these microcontrollers. Our objective is to ensure the absence of timing side-channel vulnerabilities, interrupt-latency vulnerabilities (such as Nemesis [64]), DMA-based attacks (i.e. BUSted [57]), and detect any undesired explicit and implicit information flow, which is roughly equivalent to the concept of covert storage channels in later literature [44]. This is particularly relevant in the context of applications that are compartmentalized into a security critical application part (e.g. managing and using cryptographic credentials) and a less critical part (e.g. displaying a user interface) to make use of the ARM TrustZone. For example, in an industrial robotic system, critical tasks such as motion control and safety management are isolated in the secure world, while less critical tasks are handled in the normal world. An attacker who exploits timing side-channel vulnerabilities in the normal world could disrupt time-critical operations or compromise safety, leading to operational failures or even physical harm. Securing these systems against such attacks is vital for maintaining the safety of industrial control systems.

Our proposed approach is implemented in an automated tool, SCF^{ARM} to statically detect the aforementioned vulnerabilities in ARMv8-M binaries. The primary objective of SCF^{ARM} is to track the flow of secret information between the TrustZone's secure world and the non-secure world, detecting and reporting any potential information leakages. SCF^{ARM} stands for "Side Channel Finder for ARM" and is named after earlier tools with similar abilities for the AVR and MSP430 platforms [25,54] but relies on different analysis techniques. To the best of our knowledge, SCF^{ARM} is the first static analysis tool for detecting side-channel vulnerabilities in ARMv8-M binaries. Unlike existing state-of-the-art solutions that focus on general side-channel detection or are tailored to other architectures, SCF^{ARM} uniquely integrates symbolic execution with static analysis to address both timing and storage channels within the ARM TrustZone framework. We leverage the deterministic nature of instruction execution on Cortex-M23 microcontrollers to ensure soundness and precision. Our approach fills a critical gap in the security analysis of embedded systems that utilize ARM and specifically ARM TrustZone.

To establish the efficacy of our approach, we evaluate SCF^{ARM} on a set of benchmarks that spanned a diverse range of synthetic benchmark programs designed to unveil both typical and challenging structures of secret-dependent control flow [66], and by running SCF^{ARM} on code from the BUSted [57] attack. In summary, our contributions include:

- We present a novel approach that relies on symbolic execution and static analysis to conduct sound information flow analysis in compiled ARM-V8 programs. our approach is tailored to detect side-channel vulnerabilities in applications compartmentalization with ARM TrustZone.
- We have implemented our approach in a tool SCF^{ARM}, which we evaluate and show that our approach successfully detects timing side channel attacks, Nemesis attacks [64], BUSted attacks [57], and undesired direct and indirect information flow to unprotected locations. Our results demonstrate a high precision and scalability of SCF^{ARM}, making it useful for real-world security assessments.
- We make SCF^{ARM} and our benchmark datasets publicly available on the GitHub repository at https://github.com/sepidehpouyan/ARM-SDFT.

2   Background: TrustZone and Side Channels

2.1   TrustZone on ARM Cortex-M

ARM TrustZone [48,53,55] is a hardware-based security architecture that essentially divides the ARM processor into two distinct execution environments: the "Normal World" and the "Secure World". The approach assigns two virtual cores to each physical processor, together with the mechanism to securely switch between both realms. The worlds are isolated from each other, and the Normal World is typically where the non-secure, general-purpose operating system and applications run. The Secure World is a more trusted and isolated area where security-critical operations, cryptographic functions, and sensitive data can be processed and stored.

On ARM application processors (Cortex-A) [9,55], a separate processor mode known as the secure monitor handles secure context switching between worlds. ARM microcontrollers (Cortex-M) [10] lack this dedicated secure monitor software. Instead, essential mechanisms integrated into the core logic act as gatekeepers, facilitating the transition between secure and non-secure realms. These two worlds are rigidly separated at the hardware level and possess differing levels of privilege. Non-secure software is explicitly restricted from directly accessing resources in the secure world. This paper focuses exclusively on TrustZone features for Cortex-M processors.

TrustZone for ARMv8-M devices is tailored for ARM microcontrollers, specifically the Cortex-M series, which is optimized for swift context switching and ultra-low power embedded applications. Leveraging specialized hardware integrated into Cortex-M cores along with a dedicated secure instruction set, TrustZone facilitates the establishment of multiple software security domains. These domains enforce strict access controls, allowing trusted software exclusive access to secure memory and I/O, all while maintaining optimal system performance.

Armv8-M Architecture. ARMv8-M features a set of 32-bit general-purpose registers (R0 to R12, Link Register (LR), Program Counter (PC)) and floating-point register (D0-D15) that are shared between secure and non-secure states. TrustZone-enabled ARMv8-M microcontrollers have separate stacks for each security state, with the Stack Pointer (SP) being security-banked, meaning one instance exists in each state. The CONTROL register and some other special-purpose registers are also banked, and the core automatically switches between their instances during state transitions. ARMv8-M architecture introduces a new ISA with additional instructions and features, which enhances code density, reduces interrupt latency, and improves system performance. The architecture includes a two-stage pipeline for instruction execution, providing efficient handling of instructions.

The Secure World. Memory space in the Armv8-M architecture is partitioned into secure and non-secure memory regions. The secure memory space is further divided into two types: secure and non-secure callable (NSC). Secure addresses are exclusively allocated for memory and peripherals that can only be accessed when the core is executing in secure state. The program address, the address of the instruction currently executed, determines the security state of the processor. NSC represents a unique class of secure memory locations that facilitates the transition of software from a non-secure to a secure state, allowing for controlled and secure state changes.

The security state assigned to each memory address are established through either the programmable Secure Attribution Unit (SAU) or by a fixed Implementation Defined Attribution Unit (IDAU). The SAU is always available in ARMv8-M cores, while the IDAU is external to the core and the presence depends on the vendors implementation. In cases where both the IDAU and SAU are available within a system, the SAU's attributions take precedence, unless the IDAU specifies a higher security attribute for a particular address. The SAU can only be programmed in the secure state.

The Nested Vectored Interrupt Controller (NVIC) enables secure and non-secure configuration for each interrupt. The processor seamlessly handles interrupts based on its current security state. Notably, when a non-secure interrupt occurs during secure code execution, the processor securely manages the transition, preserving secure context data and preventing information leakage.

Transitioning Worlds. In ARM TrustZone, transitioning between the secure and non-secure worlds involves three main instructions: Secure Gateway (SG), Branch with Exchange to Non-Secure State (BXNS), and Branch with Link and Exchange to Non-Secure State (BLXNS). The SG instruction switches from the non-secure world to the secure world and is typically found at the start of a secure entry point's veneer, which includes the SG instruction followed by a branch to the secure function. These veneers are located in memory regions attributed to the NSC by the linker. The SG instruction sets the security state to secure, banks registers, and clears bit[0] of the Link Register (LR) to indicate a return to non-secure. To transition back to the non-secure world, as shown in Fig. 1, the BXNS instruction is used to branch to non-secure code. In contrast, the BLXNS instruction allows secure software to call functions in the non-secure world while saving the return address for subsequent use.

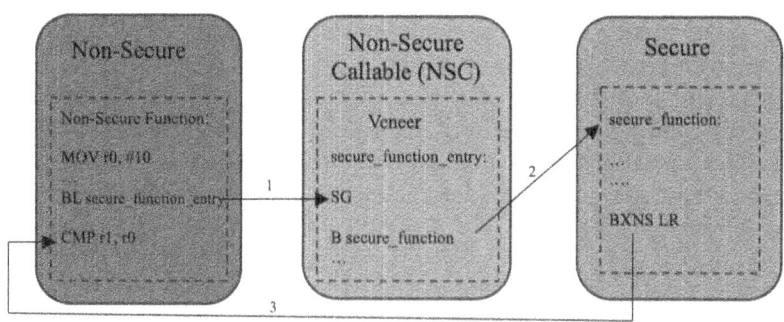

Fig. 1. Secure Function Call in TrustZone-M

TrustZone is not bullet-proof and successful attacks have been published [43,46,53]. The architecture, while designed to provide robust hardware-based security by isolating secure and non-secure worlds, is not immune to microarchitectural side-channel vulnerabilities [19,46,53,57,69]. These vulnerabilities arise due to the shared resources and memory management between the secure and non-secure domains. ARM [7] has acknowledged that the security extensions for the ARMv8-M architecture are not designed to protect against side-channel attacks resulting from control flow or memory access patterns. Besides attacks that abuse architectural and microarchitectural state, sensitive information can be unintentionally leaked through covert channels [44,59].

2.2   Microarchitectural Side-Channel Attacks

A range of attacks aim to uncover confidential information hidden within the shared microarchitectural state by exploiting observable side effects. Notably, observing timing variations is the most prevalent method for observing microarchitectural state changes [65].

Single-purpose embedded processors typically emphasize simplicity, power efficiency, and cost-effectiveness over advanced microarchitectural features like caches, pipelining, and speculative execution, which results in predictable instruction timings, reducing the risk of side-channel attacks. However, research [18,30] has demonstrated that secrets can still be revealed through start-to-end timing side channels. In addition, Nemesis-type interrupt timing attacks [64] can allow highly precise, instruction-granular timing measurements, which can even compromise secrets from branches with balanced start-to-end timings. These side-channel attacks abuse the CPU's interrupt mechanism to reveal microarchitectural instruction timings within TEEs. In recent findings, researchers have identified DMA-based side-channel attacks specifically aimed at embedded TEEs [14,57]. These attacks exploit timing variations arising from contention between a DMA device and the CPU as they access the shared memory bus, enabling the attacker to construct a cycle-accurate memory access trace of a victim program.

BUSted: Microarchitectural Side-Channel Attacks on TrustZone-M MCUs. A class of microarchitectural side-channel attacks that leverage the timing differences in the arbitration logic of the MCUs bus interconnect is called BUSted [57]. It's evident that concurrent access by multiple bus master (e.g., CPU, DMA) to a shared bus slave (e.g., memory controller) leads to time delays for at least one, causing subtle timing variations. By observing the timing drifts on memory transactions, an attacker can extract information regarding the victim's memory access pattern. Consequently, without breaking security isolation boundaries, a malicious bus master can spy on bus activity and determine when another bus master accessed a specific slave.

The code example in Fig. 2 shows a balanced conditional statement dependent on a secret variable, compiled for the ARM Cortex-M23. Since both execution paths have an identical execution time of 5 clock cycles, starting from t + 1 after the *cmp* instruction, an attacker wouldn't observe any difference in execution time. Consequently, distinguishing between these execution paths and subsequently extracting the secret becomes unfeasible. Yet, an observer could still detect divergent memory access patterns between these two execution paths. When the branch (*bne*) isn't taken, it completes within a single clock cycle, causing the *str* instruction to occur at clock cycle t + 3. Conversely, if taken, the branch incurs a two-clock-cycle process, resulting in the *str* instruction taking place at clock cycle t + 4. Overall, this changes the relative position of the *str* instruction to the bne instruction and unveils the secret. By monitoring either 't + 3' or 't + 5' clock cycles, an attacker can potentially deduce the secret by observing the presence or absence of contention on the data memory bus.

Given the nature of this attack, targeting on microarchitectural design issues, comparisons have arisen likening its impact to that of renowned exploits like Spectre. Embedded projects relying on hardware-assisted privilege separation via TrustZone-M must now factor in the potential for information leakage from components operating within the secure world.

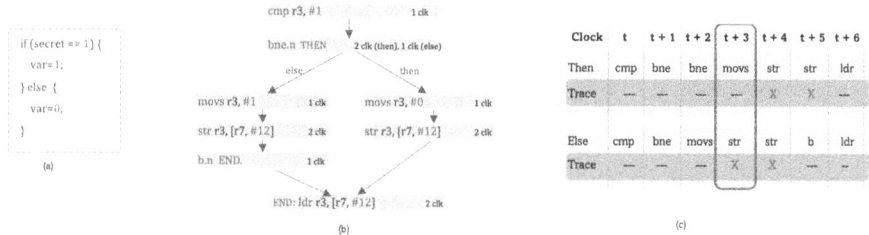

Fig. 2. (a) secret-dependent branch, (b) compiled code CFG for Arm Cortex-M23, (c) memory access pattern and monitoring of clock t+3 and t+5.

2.3   Program Analysis

Our approach relies on *Taint Analysis* that traces the flow of data of interest throughout program execution, utilizing "taint tags" as markers attached to registers and memory. We further employ *Value Set Analysis* to approximates the potential values that each program data object might hold. *Symbolic Execution* is used to explore program execution by substituting variables with symbolic representations, systematically traversing the program.

3   Related Work

Side-channel Attacks on TrustZone-M. Extensive research has been conducted on microarchitectural timing channels [28], notably introduced by Kocher [36], gaining widespread attention following the disclosure of Spectre [35] and Meltdown [41]. However, exploration into side-channel attacks within TEE context is a relatively recent endeavor. Several authors [19,32,37,46,58,65,69] have raised concerns regarding software side-channel vulnerabilities in higher-end TEEs like ARM TrustZone. Additionally, research on microcontrollers [13,14,29,43,51,57, 64] investigated the potential for information leakage through side-channels.

For instance, Gnad et al. in [29] capitalized on the correlation between ADC noise and MCU power consumption in Cortex-M4, utilizing software power consumption traces to extract secret keys from an AES implementation. Similarly,

O'Flynn and Alex Dewar in [51] exploited the ADC in a SAM L11 (Cortex-M23) MCU, executing a remote power side-channel attack to bypass TrustZone-M protection and retrieve a secret key. In contrast to power side-channel attacks, Nemesis attack by Van Bulck et al. [64] exploits the CPU's interrupt mechanism to extract instruction timings from MSP430 MCUs. In [14], the authors leverage minor timing variations in unprivileged DMA requests, arising from contention on the shared memory bus within openMSP430 MCUs, to acquire a memory access trace of a victim program. Likewise, BUSted [57] represents a type of side-channel attack utilizing timing discrepancies on the MCU bus interconnect to bypass the security assurances provided by memory protection primitives in Armv8-M MCUs with TrustZone-M.

Program Analysis. There exists substantial literature on timing side-channel detection employing ML models [5,23,45], dynamic taint analysis [31], fuzzing [49], Abstract interpretation [27,39], Logical reduction [22], type-based solutions [1,25,42,54,56,68], and several other methodologies [3,28,62]. Closely related to our work are the Side Channel Finder tools [25,42,54], which involve type systems for the static detection in Java programs and AVR and MSP430 programs. To enhance the accuracy of our analysis and to expand our capability to trace information flow across TrustZone-provided protection domains, our work employs a symbolic execution-based analysis. This allows for meticulous control over memory operations, refining the precision of our analysis.

Symbolic Execution. Related work [12,15,16,21,24,26,52,61,67] has focused on detecting microarchitectural side-channel vulnerabilities using symbolic execution. For instance, Bang et al. [12] use symbolic execution, string analysis, and model counting to quantify leakage for a particular type of side channel. Pasareanu et al. [52] proposed a symbolic execution approach for side-channels detection and quantification. They measure side-channel leakage by creating specific public inputs that trigger maximum leakage. This is accomplished through Max-SMT solving applied to the constraints derived from symbolic execution. ENCIDER [67] employs dynamic symbolic execution and taint analysis to uncover timing and cache side-channel vulnerabilities within Intel SGX applications. It decomposes side-channel requirements based on the bounded non-interference property and implements byte-level information flow tracking through API modeling. CoCo-Channel [15] employs taint analysis to detect secret-dependent conditional statements within Java programs. It assigns symbolic cost expressions to various program paths and utilizes symbolic execution to identify and report paths demonstrating secret-dependent timing behavior.

Additionally, various other studies [16,21,61] leverage symbolic execution to derive a symbolic cache model and verify that the cache behavior remains independent of sensitive data. Scalability concerns often hinder symbolic execution. Daniel et al. [24] introduced an automatic, efficient binary-level verification method tailored for constant-time analysis. This method conducts both bug identification and bounded verification on practical cryptographic implementations. Employing relational symbolic execution with specialized optimizations in information flow and binary-level analysis, their approach maximizes shared information between executions following the same path. Pitchfork [26] unites symbolic execution and dynamic taint tracking to accurately propagate secret taints across all execution paths.

Our work explores a static method for identifying timing side channels by integrating symbolic execution and taint analysis. To the best of our knowledge, SCF^{ARM} is the first static analysis tool capable of automatically detecting timing side channels, Nemesis, BUSted, and covert storage leakage, in ARM-M binaries.

4 Objectives and Analysis

Our objective is to develop an approach that merges taint tracking techniques with symbolic execution of Trusted Application (TA) binaries to systematically identify undesired information leakage. Subsequently, we notify developers of these identified leakage points for further action and resolution.

Scope. Our focus revolves around small-scale embedded systems and IoT devices that operate using MCUs, such as the Arm Cortex-M family. These MCUs operate within strict constraints, characterized by limited computing power and memory. They feature simplified microarchitectures, lacking components like caches and typically operating with 2–3 pipeline stages. Additionally, they do not support virtual memory. Generally, MCUs consist of a single CPU while offering a diverse array of peripherals, including UART, SPI, timers, DMAs, and I2C, among others. Some devices may incorporate MPUs, and the latest iterations of ARMv8-M MCUs introduce support for dual security states, namely secure and non-secure worlds (known as TrustZone-M). These MCUs are engineered to ensure highly predictable outcomes, consistently delivering identical outputs for specific inputs within defined timing constraints.

Adversary. The adversary's goal is to extract sensitive information from an isolated environment by bypassing the memory isolation security mechanisms in TrustZone. We assume the attacker has access to either the source code or compiled binary code of the victim's program. Additionally, they can monitor the program's execution time and outputs. Furthermore, we consider a more capable attacker who has complete control over the unprotected normal world and its resources. This includes the ability to manage bus masters (e.g., DMA), configure peripherals like timers, and control scheduling decisions. We are not considering side channels arising from cache contention or branch prediction feature, as they fall beyond the scope of this work due to their absence in the targeted MCU architecture.

4.1 An Example: OTP

Consider a secure One-Time Password (OTP) system illustrated in Fig. 3, which could be involved in verifying mobile users accessing web services. An OTP is a dynamically generated string of characters used to authenticate a user for a single transaction with an authentication server. This approach augments the traditional user ID and password authentication by introducing a dynamic password that changes with each authentication attempt. The OTP mechanism operates by generating a code using an internal clock (or counter) and a factory-encoded secret key known as the 'seed.' To maintain the confidentiality of both the generated OTPs and the seeds, the code and data involved in OTP operations inhabit the secure world of TrustZone [60], guaranteeing the integrity and confidentiality by restricting access exclusively to the secure domain.

However, any inadvertent mishandling of the seeds or OTPs—such as storing them in plaintext on unprotected memory, logging them, or exposed via non-secure I/O —or if an implicit flow is triggered by updating a publicly observable variable within the program control flow—an attacker could potentially access the generated OTPs. Furthermore, the attacker might deduce secrets by analyzing time variations within a secret-dependent branch.

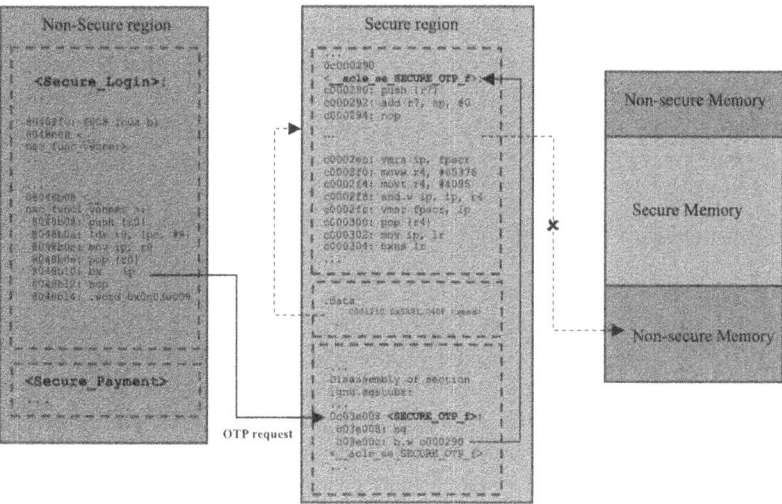

Fig. 3. Sketch of a TrustZone-based implementation of secure OTP generation where seeds are stored and processed in the processor's secure region only.

4.2   Taint Tracking of Function Inputs

Our method involves an information flow analysis that links each value with a security tag indicating its sensitivity level. We categorize these levels into two labels: 'H' for high sensitivity and 'L' for low sensitivity. Each input (initial state of registers, etc.) and output (final state of registers, etc.) of a program is assigned one of these labels. To track and identify both explicit and implicit data flows of high sensitivity during program execution, our approach incorporates a symbolic taint-tracking mechanism.

Specifically, initial register contents and associated memory are transparently substituted with unconstrained symbolic values. We, furthermore, utilize Angr's annotation system [6] to flag sensitive symbolic values as tainted. This taint, conservatively propagated throughout symbolic execution, allows for querying during subsequent analysis to identify potential information leakage.

4.3   Timing-Sensitive Information Flow Policy

An information-flow analysis verifies the absence of undesired information leakage within a program. A timing-sensitive variant of this analysis considers the impact of confidential data on the program's execution time. The intended security assurance is typically defined through information flow policies that prevent secret data from affecting an attacker's observations. We utilize a symbolic taint-tracking strategy to monitor potential policy violations during execution.

Taint tags follow Angr's propagation rules during symbolic program execution, aligning with ARMv8-M instruction semantics. For example, in the case of an instruction like 'ADD dst, src1, src2', a taint propagation rule defines that the resulting tag of 'dst' is determined by performing a bit-wise OR operation on the tags of 'src1' and 'src2'. These rules imposes constraints on the sensitivity of data stored in registers and memory cells throughout program execution.

4.4   Detection of Timing Side Channels

To ensure the absence of timing side channels within a program, our approach involves the initial computation of control-dependence regions for each branch instruction dependent on secret data. This employs Safe Over-Approximation Properties [25]. In particular, our focus lies in comparing the execution times between the 'then' and 'else' branches, distinguishing two distinct control-dependence regions for jumps influenced by confidential information. Afterward, we sums up the execution time of all instructions within each region.

Within ARMv8-M architecture, conditional branch instructions require an extra clock cycle when they are taken: if the total time required for executing the 'then' region plus one equals the time taken for jumping and executing the 'else' region in a secret-dependent branch, it becomes impossible to discern the value of secret data by observing the program's overall execution time.

Identifying the Nemesis vulnerability in an ARMv8-M binary involves pinpointing a jump instruction depending on secret data. Due to the variable execution times of branch instructions in ARMv8-M architecture when taken or not, an attacker can interrupt a branch instruction to capture the secret information. Consequently, the attacker can even execute a Nemesis attack on balanced paths.

To detect the BUSted vulnerability, we traverse every path within a branch dependent on secret information, scrutinizing the execution points of 'str' or 'ldr' instructions. If these instructions execute at different clock offsets on conditional paths, it exposes a potential vulnerability for attackers to exploit distinct memory access patterns and gain access to sensitive information.

4.5 Augmented Taint Flow Directives

Secret-dependent branches introduce variations in the program flow based on confidential information. By observing changes in execution time, logical operations, or other side channel information arising from these branches, attackers can deduce details about the secret data, such as its value or structure. Consequently, when a secret-dependent branch involves an operation where a memory cell or register is written within a particular path, it's crucial to mark that register or memory as tainted.

We employ Angr's MemoryMixin extension, which conducts exhaustive validations on every memory access. When these accesses occur within secret-dependent branches, we annotate the symbolic values as tainted to reflect their elevated sensitivity within that particular context. This approach guarantees the detection of flows from secret information to attacker-observable outputs.

5 SCF^{ARM} Design and Implementation

We have developed the SCF^{ARM} specifically for the static analysis of ARMv8-M binaries targeting Cortex-M23, focusing on identifying timing side-channel vulnerabilities. Our approach, centered around symbolic taint-tracking, enables a rapid, cost-effective, and automated assessment of these vulnerabilities. We have implemented an open source version of SCF^{ARM} built upon Angr [6] and SCF^{MSP} [54]. Specifically, (1) we use Angr for symbolic execution of binaries and conducting Value Set Analysis (VSA) to determine potential register values or symbolic memory addresses; (2) we expand the functionality of the SCF^{MSP} tool to analyze TrustZone-M targeted binaries and ensure program integrity against a novel DMA-based attack termed BUSted [57].

Figure 4 showcases a high-level workflow diagram detailing the components of the SCF^{ARM} tool. The dashed box denotes the core elements implementing our proposed side channel evaluation technique. SCF^{ARM} is built on approximately 1110 lines of Python code and integrates established Python libraries, detailed below. We now briefly describe each element:

Parser. We employ this component to convert the input binary into assembly language. Initially, we utilize the pyelftools Python library [70] to locate the starting point of instructions within the binary. Subsequently, we leverage the Capstone disassembler [20] to translate the binary into ARMv8-M instructions, generating mnemonic codes and symbolic representations of processor instructions. This process allows us to extract essential details such as opcodes, addresses, and instruction lengths. Finally, we determine the required clock cycles for executing each instruction based on the specifications outlined in the ARMv8-M Architecture Reference Manual [8].

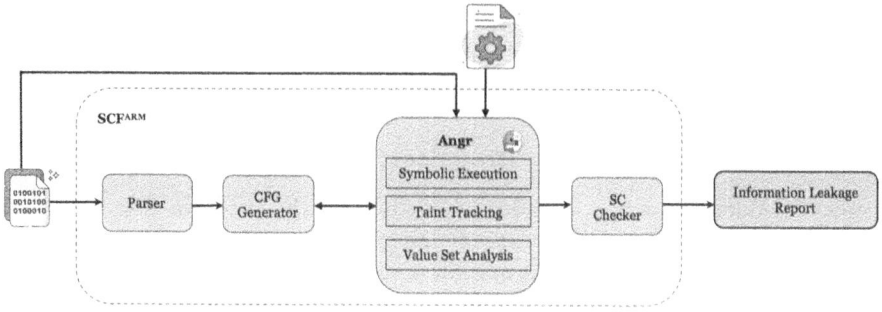

Fig. 4. Overview of SCF^{ARM}

CFG Generator. This component constructs an accurate program Control Flow Graph (CFG) using the NetworkX [33] Python library. This component establishes a mutual connection with the subsequent component, enabling the retrieval of the target address for 'branch and exchange' instruction $BX\ <Rm>$ through VSA in Angr. The resulting graph facilitates the identification of execution point predecessors and successors, aiding in computing control dependence regions for branches and inferring loops within assembly programs.

Angr. Utilizing a JSON-formatted configuration file that lists the starting function's arguments derived from high-level code to determine taint sources (i.e., highly sensitive inputs). This component employs Angr's annotation system to mark registers and memory cells containing confidential data with a taint label. It associates arguments with their corresponding registers following the ARMv8-M calling conventions [8]. These taint tags propagate during symbolic execution. Our taint analyzer tracks both explicit and implicit flows. Upon completion of symbolic execution, the component presents a list of tainted registers and memory cells for subsequent analysis.

SC Checker. This module performs static analysis to identify potential side channel leaks within ARMv8-M assembly programs. Our SCF^{ARM} tool currently detects vulnerabilities falling into four distinct classes:

- Timing Channel: Detected when a program exhibits different execution times depending on the secret input. SCF^{ARM} detects these leaks by measuring the overall running times of if/else regions in secret-dependent branches.
- BUSted Vulnerability: Recognized when a program includes store/load instructions with different time offsets inside the if/else regions of a secret-dependent branch.
- Nemesis Vulnerability: Identified when a program displays varying execution times for at least one instruction within the if/else regions of a secret-dependent branch.
- Storage Channel: Flagged if there is undesired information flow from secret inputs to observable output, such as return registers or memory writes.

6   Evaluation

In this section, we present our assessment of SCF^{ARM}, emphasizing the accuracy of our static analysis in detecting side channels. Our evaluation of SCF^{ARM} uses code from the BUSted attack [57] as a real-world example, and is otherwise relying on benchmarks from [66], featuring programs with a diverse range of patterns for secret-dependent control flow, featuring vulnerabilities and benign code. In the absence of standardized benchmarks for side-channel leakage in embedded systems' code, our evaluation aims to provide a reproducible and comparable assessment of SCF^{ARM}'s effectiveness. The benchmarks consist of C programs compiled using 'arm-none-eabi-gcc,' a cross-compiler toolchain tailored for generating code targeting ARM Cortex-M and Cortex-R processors without an operating system (bare-metal). The compiler is configured with the '-mcpu=cortex-m23' option to generate optimized binary for ARM Cortex-M23 architecture. Here, we provide a brief overview of selected benchmark programs:

- **busted:** This program features a vulnerability to the BUSted attack [57]. The vulnerability arises from the execution of the 'str' instruction at different time offsets within the 'then' and 'else' regions. However, it is free of start-to-end timing leaks due to having a balanced branch.
- **busted-free:** This program uses nop to delay the execution of the 'str' in the 'else' branch of **busted** by one clock cycle. This delay ensures that memory access occurs at the same time offset but results in unbalanced branches.
- **strcmp:** This code performs a character-by-character comparison of two strings (cf. Figure 5 (a)) and includes secret-dependent branches.
- **constant_time_strcmp:** Utilizing a constant-time implementation we fix the timing side channel in our string comparison code (cf. Fig. 5 (b)).
- **diamond:** This program features two branching instructions dependent on secret values and one independent branch.
- **loop:** The program contains a loop that relies on a condition with public data and includes a secret-dependent branch within the loop body.
- **secure loop:** Bitwise operations eliminate the need for the branch.
- **multifork:** In this program, a switch statement evaluates the value of a secret variable and compares it against multiple cases.
- **ifthenloop & ifthenloop_nop_padded:** These programs involve a secret-dependent branch and a loop with a public condition variable, executed if the branch is taken. In the 'padded' version, SPSVERBc1s ensure balanced branches.
- **ifthenlooplooptail:** This program introduces intricate control flow with nested secret-dependent branches and loops.

In Table 1, we present the experimental results of applying SCF^{ARM} to the benchmark. Our results showcases that SCF^{ARM} effectively analyzes intricate binaries designed for ARM Cortex-M23. The tool identifies a spectrum of side-channel vulnerabilities and also demonstrates its efficiency in swiftly and accurately detecting sensitive data leakage. Branch balancing or constant-time programming by itself cannot entirely eliminate the risk of unintended information

```
for (size_t i = 0; i < len; ++i)        for (size_t i = 0; i < len; ++i)
{                                        {
    if (s1[i] != s2[i]){                     result |= s1[i] ^ s2[i];
        return 0;                        }
    }
}                                        return result;

return 1;
```

(a)   (b)

Fig. 5. String comparison with *(a)* branching and *(b)* in constant time.

Table 1. Evaluation results for SCF^{ARM} on the benchmark suite. For each compiled example program, we give an indication for C program complexity (LOC = lines of code, CFG Size = number of nodes in the program's Control Flow Graph), execution time of SCF^{ARM}, and list the vulnerabilities found by SCF^{ARM}.

Benchmark	LOC	CFG Size	SCF^{ARM} exec time	Timing Channel	Nemesis Vulner- ability	BUSted Vulner- ability	Storage Channel
busted	14	20	3.042 s	×	✓	✓	✓
busted-free	15	21	3.725 s	✓	✓	×	✓
strcmp	10	34	4.563 s	✓	✓	✓	×
constant_time_strcmp	13	39	2.564 s	×	×	×	×
diamond	20	35	4.762 s	✓	✓	✓	✓
loop	16	49	3.330 s	✓	✓	✓	✓
secure_loop	22	58	4.902 s	×	×	×	✓
fork	7	19	3.269 s	✓	✓	✓	✓
fork_nop_padded	12	24	3.769 s	×	✓	✓	✓
indirect	20	29	3.460 s	✓	✓	✓	✓
multifork	15	34	4.013 s	✓	✓	✓	✓
branchless_multifork	8	42	2.713 s	×	×	×	✓
ifcompound	22	33	4.480 s	✓	✓	✓	✓
call	19	29	2.762 s	×	×	×	✓
ifthenloop	20	43	4.476 s	✓	✓	✓	×
ifthenloop_nop_padded	25	50	4.608 s	×	✓	✓	×
ifthenloopif	28	74	6.890 s	✓	✓	✓	×
ifthenlooploop	28	67	7.580 s	✓	✓	✓	×
ifthenlooplooptail	38	110	8.136 s	✓	✓	✓	×
multiply	5	12	3.789 s	×	×	×	✓

leakage within a program. In such instances, it becomes imperative to take additional measures, e.g., storing program outputs in protected memory.

6.1 Discussion

Soundness & Path Explosion. In the absence of sophisticated architectural features such as paging, caches, or out-of-order execution, the time taken for instruction execution on the Cortex-M23 is wholly deterministic. Our approach is sound in the sense that it follows the instruction semantics and execution times of the processor documentation. However, our approach is incomplete due to state and path explosion for complex programs, which could lead to early termination of the analysis. Practically this may or may not be a problem depending on the input program, and related work that uses Angr to find side-channel vulnerabilities in enclave runtimes [4] suggests that scalability to realistic code sizes, even more so for embedded systems, can be achieved.

Nemesis & Busted Detection. As of our current knowledge, there have been no reported instances of a Nemesis attack being executed on an ARM Cortex-M microcontroller. Nevertheless, the ARM Cortex-M23 meets the necessary prerequisites for a Nemesis attack, completing the current instruction before handling an interrupt [64]. This introduces timing variations between interrupted instructions, which could be leveraged by an attacker to distinguish between secret-dependent branches. Furthermore, in our attacker model, the adversary has the capability to control a timer device and closely monitor Interrupt Service Routines (ISRs), roughly resembling a configuration conducive to launching a Busted attack [57].

7   Conclusions and Future Directions

We presented SCF^{ARM} as a new tool for the automated detection of microarchitectural side channel vulnerabilities in ARM-M programs that rely on TrustZone. Our work specifically targets timing side channels, Nemesis, BUSted attacks, and information leakage, in TrustZone-M applications. Our work relies on the predictability of execution times on Cortex-M processors, which allowed us to develop a symbolic taint-tracking approach for timing-sensitive information flow analysis with a high degree of precision. We applied SCF^{ARM} to a range of synthetic and real-world benchmarks. The outcomes of these experiments illustrate the tool's capability to identify a spectrum of side-channel vulnerabilities, enabling developers to assess and mitigate these vulnerabilities. To the best of our knowledge SCF^{ARM} is the first side-channel detection tool for compiled ARMv8-M programs and we make our tool and benchmarks publicly available.

Several avenues for future research emerge from this work. Firstly, we aim to enhance the comprehensiveness of our framework by extending its coverage to encompass the entire ARMv8-M instruction set, which involves the formalization of a leakage model for every instruction. We intend to conduct a comprehensive evaluation of SCF^{ARM} by applying it to off-the-shelf TrustZone-M programs and scrutinizing its performance on cryptographic libraries, such as wolfSSL [71]. Moreover, in pursuit of efficiency improvements, the incorporation of state-merging [38] or path prioritization strategies [11,40] would be useful.

Acknowledgments. This research is partially funded by the Research Fund KU Leuven, by the Cybersecurity Research Program Flanders, and by the CyberExcellence programme of the Walloon Region, Belgium. Fritz Alder is supported by a grant of the Research Foundation – Flanders (FWO).

References

1. Barthe, G., Betarte, G., Campo, J., Luna, C., Pichardie, D.: System-level non-interference for constant-time cryptography. In: Proceedings ACM SIGSAC Conference on Computer and Communications Security, pp. 1267–1279 (2014)
2. Agat, J.: Transforming out timing leaks. In: Proceedings ACM Symposium on Principles of Programming Languages (POPL), pp. 40–53. ACM Press (2000)
3. Akram, A., Mushtaq, M., Bhatti, M., Lapotre, V., Gogniat, G.: Meet the sherlock holmes' of side channel leakage: a survey of cache SCA detection techniques. IEEE Access **8**, 70836–70860 (2020)
4. Alder, F., Daniel L., Oswald, D., Piessens, F., Van Bulck, J.: Pandora: principled symbolic validation of intel SGX enclave runtimes. In: Proceedings of the 2024 IEEE Symposium on Security and Privacy (S&P), pp. 93–93. IEEE (2024)
5. Allaf, Z., Adda, M., Gegov, A.: A comparison study on flush+reload and prime+probe attacks on AES using machine learning approaches. In: UK Workshop on Computational Intelligence (2017)
6. Angr. https://angr.io/. Accessed 29 April 2024
7. Arm developer: clarification of timing side channel attacks on TrustZone enabled Cortex. Accessed 29 March 2024
8. Arm Limited or its affiliates.: Armv8-M architecture reference manual (2021)
9. Arm Ltd.: ARM security technology: building a secure system using TrustZone technology (2009)
10. Arm Ltd.: TrustZone technology for ARMv8-M architecture. In: Whitepaper (2017)
11. Baldoni, R., Coppa, E., D'Elia, D.C., Demetrescu, C., Finocchi, I.: A survey of symbolic execution techniques. ACM Comput. Surv. (CSUR) **51**(3), 50:1–50:39 (2018)
12. Bang, L., Aydin, A., Phan, Q.S., Pasareanu, C., Bultan, T.: String analysis for side channels with segmented oracles. In: Proceedings of the 2016 24th ACM SIGSOFT International Symposium on Foundations of Software Engineering (FSE 2016), pp. 193–204 (2016)
13. Barenghi, A., et al.: Exploring cortex-M microarchitectural side channel information leakage. In: IEEE Access, pp. 1–10 (2021)
14. Bognar, M., Van Bulck, J., Piessens, F.: Mind the gap: studying the insecurity of provably secure embedded trusted execution architectures. In: Proceedings of the 2022 IEEE Symposium on Security and Privacy (S&P), pp. 1638–1655. IEEE (2022)
15. Brennan, T., Saha, S., Bultan, T., Pasareanu, C.: Symbolic path cost analysis for side-channel detection. In: ISSTA (2018)
16. Brotzman, R., Liu, S., Zhang, D., Tan, G., Kandemir, M.T.: CaSym: cache aware symbolic execution for side channel detection and mitigation. In: Proceedings of the 40th IEEE Symposium on Security and Privacy (S&P) IEEE (2019)
17. Brumley, B. B., Tuveri, N.: Remote timing attacks are still practical. In: ESORICS, pp. 355–371 (2011)

18. Brumley, D., Boneh, D.: Remote timing attacks are practical. Comput. Netw. **48**(5), 701–716 (2005)
19. Bukasa, S.K., Lashermes, R., Le Bouder, H., Lanet, J.-L., Legay, A.: How Trust-Zone could be bypassed: side-channel attacks on a modern system-on-chip. In: Hancke, G.P., Damiani, E. (eds.) WISTP 2017. LNCS, vol. 10741, pp. 93–109. Springer, Cham (2018). https://doi.org/10.1007/978-3-319-93524-9_6
20. Capstone. http://www.capstone-engine.org/. Accessed 29 April 2024
21. Chattopadhyay, S., Roychoudhury, A.: Symbolic verification of cache side-channel freedom. In: Transactions on Computer-Aided Design of Integrated Circuits and Systems (2018)
22. Chen, J., Feng, Y., Dillig, I.: Precise detection of side-channel vulnerabilities using quantitative cartesian hoare logic. In: Proceedings of the Conference Where the Paper was Presented, pp. 875–890 (2017)
23. Chiappetta, M., Savas, E., Yilmaz, C.: Real-time detection of cache-based side-channel attacks using hardware performance counters. In: Applied Soft Computing, pp. 1162–1174 (2016)
24. Daniel, L.-A., Bardin, S., Rezk, T.: Binsec/Rel: efficient relational symbolic execution for constant-time at binary-level. In: Proceedings of the 2020 IEEE Symposium on Security and Privacy (SP 2020), pp. 1021–1038. IEEE Computer Society (2020)
25. Dewald, F., Mantel, H., Weber, A.: AVR processors as a platform for language-based security. In: Foley, S.N., Gollmann, D., Snekkenes, E. (eds.) ESORICS 2017. LNCS, vol. 10492, pp. 427–445. Springer, Cham (2017). https://doi.org/10.1007/978-3-319-66402-6_25
26. Disselkoen, C., Cauligi, S., Tullsen, D., Stefan, D.: Finding and eliminating timing side-channels in crypto code with pitchfork. In: TECHCON (2020)
27. Doychev, G., Köpf, B., Mauborgne, L., Reineke, J.: Cacheaudit: A tool for the static analysis of cache side channels. ACM Trans. Inf. Syst. Secur. (TISSEC) **18**(1), 1–32 (2015)
28. Ge, Q., Yarom, Y., Cock, D., Heiser, G.: A survey of microarchitectural timing attacks and countermeasures on contemporary hardware. J. Cryptograp. Eng. **8**(1), 1–27 (2018)
29. Gnad, D.R.E., Krautter, J., Tahoori, M.B.: Leaky noise: new side-channel attack vectors in mixed-signal IoT devices. In: Journal of IACR Transactions on Cryptographic Hardware and Embedded Systems, pp. 1–20 (2019)
30. Goodspeed, T.: Practical attacks against the MSP 430 BSL. In: Twenty-Fifth Chaos Communications Congress (CCC), Berlin, Germany (2008)
31. Graa, M., Cuppens-Boulahia, N., Cuppens, F., Lanet, J.L., Moussaileb, R.: Detection of side channel attacks based on data tainting in android systems. In: Proceedings of the Conference Where the Paper was Presented, pp. 205–218 (2017)
32. Gross, M., Jacob, N., Zankl, A., Sigl, G.: Breaking TrustZone memory isolation through malicious hardware on a modern FPGA-SoC. In: Proceedings of the 3rd ACM Workshop on Attacks and Solutions in Hardware Security Workshop, pp. 3–12. ACM (2019)
33. Hagberg, A., Swart, P., Chult, D. S.: Exploring network structure, dynamics, and function using NetworkX. In: Technical Report (2008)
34. Hassija, V., Chamola, V., Saxena, V., Jain, D., Goyal, P., Sikdar, B.: A survey on IoT security: application areas, security threats, and solution architectures. In: IEEE Access (2019)
35. Kocher, P., et al.: Spectre attacks: exploiting speculative execution. In: Proceedings of the 40th IEEE Symposium on Security and Privacy (S&P), pp. 1–19. IEEE (2019)

36. Kocher, P.C.: Timing attacks on implementations of Diffie-Hellman, RSA, DSS, and other systems. In: Koblitz, N. (ed.) CRYPTO 1996. LNCS, vol. 1109, pp. 104–113. Springer, Heidelberg (1996). https://doi.org/10.1007/3-540-68697-5_9

37. Kou, Z., He, W., Sinha, S., Zhang, W.: Load-step: a Precise TrustZone execution control framework for exploring new side-channel attacks like flush+Evict. In: 58th ACM/IEEE Design Automation Conference (DAC), pp. 979–984 (2021)

38. Kuznetsov, V., Kinder, J., Bucur, S., Candea, G.: Efficient state merging in symbolic execution. In: PLDI, pp. 193–204. ACM (2012)

39. Köpf, B., Mauborgne, L., Ochoa, M.: Automatic quantification of cache side-channels. In: International Conference on Computer-aided Verification, pp. 1–15 (2012)

40. Li, Y., Su, Z., Wang, L., Li, X.: Steering symbolic execution to less traveled paths. In: SIGPLAN Notices, vol. 48, no. 10, pp. 19–32 (2013)

41. Lipp, M., et al.: Meltdown: reading kernel memory from user space. In: Proceedings of the 27th USENIX Security Symposium, pp. 1–18. USENIX Association (2018)

42. Lux, A., Starostin, A.: A tool for static detection of timing channels in Java. J. Cryptograp. Eng. **1**, 303–313 (2011)

43. Ma, Z., Tan, X., Ziarek, L., Zhang, N., Hu, H., Zhao, Z.: Return-to-non-secure vulnerabilities on ARM Cortex-M TrustZone: attack and defense. In: 2023 60th ACM/IEEE Design Automation Conference (DAC), pp. 1–6, San Francisco, CA, USA. IEEE (2023)

44. Murray, T., et al: SEL4: from general purpose to a proof of information flow enforcement. In: Proceedings of the 2013 IEEE Symposium on Security and Privacy (S&P), IEEE (2013)

45. Mushtaq, M. et al.: Machine Learning For Security: The Case of Side-Channel Attack Detection at Run-time. In: 2018 25th IEEE International Conference on Electronics, Circuits and Systems (ICECS), pp. 485–488, IEEE (2018)

46. Muñoz, A., Rios, R., Roman, R., Lopez, J.: A survey on the (in)security of trusted execution environments. Comput. Secur. **129**, 103180 (2023)

47. Neshenko, N., Bou-Harb, E., Crichigno, J., Kaddoum, G., Ghani, N.: Demystifying IoT security: an exhaustive survey on IoT vulnerabilities and a first empirical look on internet-scale IoT exploitations. IEEE Commun. Surv. Tutorials **21**(3), 2702–2733 (2019)

48. Ngabonziza, B., Martin, D., Bailey, A., Cho, H., Martin, S.: TrustZone explained: architectural features and use cases. In: 2016 IEEE 2nd International Conference on Collaboration and Internet Computing (CIC), pp. 445–451 (2016)

49. Nilizadeh, S., Noller, Y., Pasareanu, C.: DiffFuzz: differential fuzzing for side-channel analysis. In: Proceedings of the Conference or Journal Name, pp. 1–10 (2018)

50. Osvik, D. A., Shamir, A., Tromer, E.: Cache attacks and countermeasures: the case of AES. In: Cryptographers' Track at the RSA Conference (2006)

51. O'Flynn, C., Dewar, A.: On-device power analysis across hardware security domains: stop hitting yourself. In: Journal of IACR Transactions on Cryptographic Hardware and Embedded Systems, pp. 1–23 (2019)

52. Pasareanu, C., Phan, Q.S., Malacaria, P.: Multi-run side-channel analysis using symbolic execution and Max-SMT. In: Computer Security Foundations Symposium (2016)

53. Pinto, S., Santos, N.: Demystifying ARM TrustZone: a comprehensive survey. ACM Comput. Surv. (CSUR) **51**(6), 1–36 (2019)

54. Pouyanrad, S., Mühlberg, J. T., Joosen, W.: SCF MSP: Static detection of side channels in MSP430 programs. In: Proceedings of the 15th International Conference on Availability, Reliability and Security (ARES) (2020)

55. Pouyanrad, S., et al.: End-to-End Security for Distributed Event-Driven Enclave Applications on Heterogeneous TEEs. In: ACM Transactions on Privacy and Security (TOPS), pp. 1–46. ACM (2023)

56. Rodrigues, B., Pereira, F.M.Q., Aranha, D.F.: Sparse representation of implicit flows with applications to side-channel detection. In: Proceedings of the 25th International Conference on Compiler Construction (CC 2016), pp. 110–120 (2016)

57. Rodrigues, C., Oliveira, D., Pinto, S.: BUSted!!! Microarchitectural Side-Channel Attacks on the MCU Bus Interconnect. In: Proceedings of the 45th IEEE Symposium on Security and Privacy (S&P) IEEE (2024)

58. Ryan, K.: Hardware-backed heist: extracting ECDSA keys from qualcomm's TrustZone. In: CCS 2019: Proceedings of the 2019 ACM SIGSAC Conference on Computer and Communications Security (CCS), pp. 181–194. ACM (2019)

59. Sabelfeld, A., Myers, A.C.: Language-based information-flow security. IEEE J. Sel. Areas Commun. **21**(1), 5–19 (2003)

60. Sun, H., Sun, K., Wang, Y., Jing, J.: Trust OTP: transforming smartphones into secure one-time password tokens. In: Proceedings of the 2015 ACM SIGSAC Conference on Computer and Communications Security (CCS), pp. 976–988. ACM (2015)

61. Sung, C., Paulsen, B., Wang, C.: CANAL: A cache timing analysis framework via LLVM transformation. In: ASE (2018)

62. Szefer, J.: Survey of microarchitectural side and covert channels, attacks, and defenses. J. Hard. Syst. Secur. **3**(3), 219–234 (2018). https://doi.org/10.1007/s41635-018-0046-1

63. Travlos, D.: Arm holdings and qualcomm: the winners in mobile. In: Whitepaper (2013)

64. Van Bulck, J., Piessens, F., Strackx, R.: Nemesis: Studying microarchitectural timing leaks in rudimentary CPU interrupt logic. In: Proceedings of the 2018 ACM SIGSAC Conference on Computer and Communications Security (CCS). ACM (2018)

65. Van Bulck, J.: Microarchitectural side-channel attacks for privileged software adversaries. PhD thesis, KU Leuven, Belgium (2020)

66. Winderix, H., Mühlberg, J. T., Piessens, F.: Compiler-assisted hardening of embedded software against interrupt latency side-channel attacks. In: 2021 IEEE European Symposium on Security and Privacy (EuroS&P), pp. 667–682. IEEE (2021)

67. Yavuz, T., Fowze, F., Hernandez, G., Bai, K.Y., Butler, K.R., Tian, D.J.: ENCIDER: detecting Timing and Cache Side Channels in SGX Enclaves and Cryptographic APIs. In: IEEE Transactions on Dependable and Secure Computing (2022)

68. Zhang, D., Askarov, A., Myers, A.C.: Language-based Control and Mitigation of Timing Channels. In: Proceedings of the 33rd ACM SIGPLAN Conference on Programming Language Design and Implementation (PLDI), pp. 99–110 (2012)

69. Zhang, N. et al.: TruSpy: cache side-channel information leakage from the secure world on arm devices. In: Transactions on IACR Cryptology (2016)

70. pyelftools. https://github.com/eliben/pyelftools. Accessed 29 April 2024

71. wolfSSL (2024). https://www.wolfssl.com/. Accessed 29 April 2024

FRAMED: Toward Automated Identification of Embedded Frameworks in Firmware Images

Jorik van Nielen[1]([envelope]), Andreas Peter[2], and Andrea Continella[1]

[1] University of Twente, Enschede, The Netherlands
{j.j.vannielen,a.continella}@utwente.nl
[2] University of Oldenburg, Oldenburg, Germany
andreas.peter@uol.de

Abstract. In the era of the Internet of Things, firmware security analyses have become tremendously important to protect networks and guarantee safety-critical operations. Indeed, the firmware running on smart devices (which are increasingly adopted also in critical infrastructures) often contains security vulnerabilities, and delivering timely updates proved to be challenging, both from a technical perspective and due to a lack of support from device vendors. In particular, firmware images present difficulties that hinder automated analyses and patching, mostly because their code and data are opaquely intermixed and squashed together on top of embedded development frameworks. In this paper, we propose a new lightweight approach to automatically analyze firmware images and identify the embedded frameworks they are built upon. Our approach facilitates reverse engineering, reducing the scope for security analyses and assisting the vulnerability detection and patching process of embedded devices. We implement our approach in FRAMED, and we evaluate it on a dataset of 536 firmware images from different devices and vendors. Our system identifies embedded frameworks with an accuracy of 83%, and we perform a case study to combine FRAMED with an existing patch injection framework, demonstrating to be a helpful and effective tool for security analysts and reverse engineers.

Keywords: Embedded Frameworks · Firmware · Reversing · IoT

1 Introduction

The adoption of Internet of Things (IoT) devices has grown explosively over the last decade [31]. In fact, IoT devices present an affordable and accessible option to add connectivity to physical objects that were not able to cross the barrier to the digital world before. This feature is attractive for both individuals and organizations, and manufacturers meet this demand with a wide variety of devices, such as thermostats, lighting, and smoke detectors, but also more critical ones such as pacemaker monitors and smart locks. Moreover, smart devices

© The Author(s), under exclusive license to Springer Nature Switzerland AG 2025
J. Garcia-Alfaro et al. (Eds.): ESORICS 2024 Workshops, LNCS 15263, pp. 514–533, 2025.
https://doi.org/10.1007/978-3-031-82349-7_32

are increasingly adopted within critical infrastructures, where they enable the remote management of cyber-physical systems, such as industrial robots and actuators [11].

While the extra connectivity of IoT devices brings value to the users, it also opens up new attack vectors. Attacks on smart devices over the Internet or Bluetooth are nowadays a real and practical scenario [11]. If vulnerable, threat actors can mount attacks against devices to alter their behavior or take full control of them. In fact, the number of cyber-attacks mounted against IoT devices has almost tripled in the last two years [41]. With the popularity of IoT devices in vital industrial processes and critical infrastructures, the security of their firmware is an area of utmost importance. To further highlight the state of (in)security in smart devices, new advances in vulnerability discovery for embedded firmware [6,7,26,33,35,40] has significantly increased the rate of security advisories released and disclosed by researchers and practitioners.

However, the disclosure of vulnerabilities to the vendors does not guarantee a fast deployment of patches to ensure the security of all vulnerable devices. One recurring cause of the long patch latency is vendors dropping support for older devices [16,43]—besides, update mechanisms are themselves often vulnerable [19, 44]. Another critical cause is the complexity of producing and testing patches. Many IoT devices run custom firmware, and generating a patch often requires extensive testing. Since a low patch latency is crucial for IoT devices, especially when deployed in critical infrastructures, researchers investigated approaches to introduce quick "hot" patches before a fully-fledged patch is released by the vendor [16,17,30].

Third-party patching for embedded firmware without the cooperation of the vendor is a significantly challenging task that is made even harder by the wide adoption of development frameworks (known as *embedded frameworks*)—i.e., embedded-specific development frameworks that abstract the development and provide OS-like features to firmware developers. During compilation, the embedded framework and user application are squashed together into a single image (also known as *blob*). Such firmware blobs typically do not contain debugging symbols, are structured in custom binary formats, and have no clear distinctions between code and data segments, making automated analyses hard. Besides, device manufacturers usually do not disclose that their devices are vulnerable before releasing a patch. Therefore, potentially affected organizations need to track if their devices are vulnerable to newly disclosed vulnerabilities, especially taking into account any vulnerabilities that affect libraries and frameworks that the device firmware relies on. Thus, knowing what frameworks firmware images are built upon is of great use for security management. Moreover, with information about the adopted embedded framework, security analysts and reverse engineers know what functions to expect in the firmware. This helps analysts distinguish framework functions from user application functions, which, since frameworks introduce hundreds of functions, significantly eases the reverse engineering process. All in all, the automated identification of the embedded frameworks within firmware images can be of great use to reverse engineers for security analyses. In the academic community, the process of uncovering components and dependencies within software is part of a broader field known as Software Composition Analysis (SCA).

While existing SCA approaches have shown great results, they are unfortunately not directly applicable to the firmware domain. Binary-to-binary SCA approaches, such as FirmSec [48] and Asm2Vec [12], require compiled embedded framework object files. However, the compilation of embedded frameworks involves manual efforts and has shown to be time-consuming at scale [38], hindering automation. Binary-to-source techniques, such as BinaryAI [20] and OSSPolice [13], do not require the compilation. However, these approaches leverage information stored in the binary that is not always present in firmware blobs, such as exported function names. Besides, embedded frameworks often make use of macros to suit the many compilation targets, which can highly impact the semantics on a function level. Current binary-to-source SCA techniques do not account for this dynamic setting.

In this work, we propose a lightweight approach to analyze firmware images and identify the embedded frameworks they are built upon. By identifying the embedded frameworks, our approach assists security analyses by revealing the main firmware component and gives reverse engineers a starting point for recovering function symbols in firmware images. Additionally, our approach can assist in the patching of firmware. For instance, state-of-the-art firmware patching approaches such as HERA [30] and Shimware [16] require a hooking location where additional checks can be performed. Currently, the hooking location has to be manually provided by the analyst. Our approach eases the process of finding a hooking location by giving security analysts information about the structure of the adopted frameworks and facilitating the function symbols recovery process.

To identify embedded frameworks, our approach leverages the strings embedded within firmware blobs to produce fingerprints—the intuition is that strings carry significant semantic information to characterize software components. In fact, previous work showed the effectiveness of using strings for library detection [13,18,20,27,45], but to the best of our knowledge, we are the first to apply this method to embedded framework identification. More specifically, our approach first recognizes and filters out irrelevant strings, and then compares the remaining ones to string literals identified in the source code of embedded frameworks. To improve the accuracy, we take into account the existence of framework clones and third-party library reuse.

We implement a proof-of-concept of our approach in FRAMED. In our experiments, FRAMED shows promising results, correctly identifying 83% of the frameworks in a labeled dataset of 536 firmware images, spanning eight different frameworks. Moreover, for four of the most popular embedded frameworks, including Mbed [25], our system achieves correct identification for all of the tested firmware samples.

To demonstrate the real-world applicability and practicality of FRAMED, we describe a real-world use case. We combine FRAMED with Shimware [16], an existing patch injection tool, to identify the framework adopted by a firmware image and use this information to find a suitable location for a patch, ultimately fixing a security flaw in the firmware image.

In summary, our contributions are as follows:

- We propose a new lightweight, string-based approach to characterize embedded frameworks.
- We implement our approach in FRAMED, a pipeline to automatically identify the frameworks used in real-world firmware images.
- We evaluate our approach on a dataset gathered from four prior works, containing 536 labeled firmware samples. Additionally, we demonstrate a use-case where we combine FRAMED with an existing patch injection tool to ease the patching process.

In the spirit of open science, our source code is publicly available at https://github.com/utwente-scs/frameD.

2 Background and Challenges

In this section, we provide background information on the firmware structure and types, and how such structure and the adoption of embedded frameworks affect the analysis and reversing processes. Then, we present the challenges in the firmware domain for embedded framework identification.

2.1 Firmware Analysis

Firmware Structure and Types. The low processing power and long battery lifetime requirements of embedded devices make it sometimes infeasible to run full operating systems (OS) like Linux or Windows. Instead, firmware features embedded operating systems, or even embedded frameworks without a logical separation between kernel and application code. In the literature, these two types of firmware are referred to as Type-2 and Type-3 firmware, respectively [29]. While detecting the use of Linux in firmware images is an explored topic [4], the identification of Type-2 and Type-3 frameworks is not. In this paper, we refer to both embedded operating systems and embedded frameworks as embedded frameworks.

Embedded Frameworks. To take away the complexity of the hardware programming from the programmer, various abstractions are used in practice. As a basis, Hardware Abstraction Layers (HALs) provide functions to developers to perform hardware operations without knowledge of the underlying hardware. HAL functions are small functions that specifically target one hardware configuration. In most cases, HAL functions are provided by chip vendors directly. Besides ease of communication with the hardware, developers might want to simplify the development further with a higher level of abstraction. Another highly demanded feature is OS-like capabilities such as scheduling of processes or tasks. Embedded frameworks provide such functionalities in varying degrees of sophistication. Some frameworks, like FreeRTOS [15], solely provide a couple of simple operating system functionalities, while, for instance, RIOT [34] adds more functionalities such as a full system shell and a complete file system implementation. To simplify the development process even further, developers turn to libraries for performing higher-level tasks. Popular libraries provide functionalities such as communication protocols (e.g., HTTP), data processing (e.g., compression), and user interface capabilities. In this research, we consider *embedded frameworks* in a broad sense as any embedded-specific development framework that aims to abstract the development and provide OS-like features to firmware developers. Some frameworks purely implement the HAL with the option to add third-party libraries, while others feature a more complete embedded OS with ad-hoc libraries. Figure 1 visualizes the different components of the embedded framework in the context of the complete firmware image.

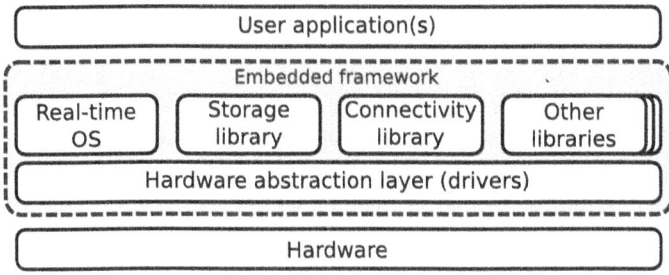

Fig. 1. An embedded framework consists of several components or a subset thereof. The hardware abstraction layer features hardware-specific functions that provide access to hardware resources. The real-time OS component enables process scheduling and resource management. A storage library adds file system functionality to the firmware. A connectivity library implements a network protocol, such as Bluetooth. Additionally, embedded frameworks can include libraries for cryptographic functions, data handling, etc. The user application is not part of the embedded framework. It implements the process logic and operates on top of the provided embedded framework functionality.

Firmware Analysis and Reversing. Non-general-purpose OS-based firmware is difficult to analyze and patch. In fact, the projects are mostly compiled into a single executable file, without any distinction between data, operating system functions, and user application functions. Also, firmware images are compiled without debugging symbols. Thus, analyzing such firmware is a daunting task. The use of embedded frameworks further increases the difficulty of reversing firmware images. Not only introduce frameworks more functions, they also add custom abstraction layers and sometimes apply object-oriented programming techniques. Thus, it becomes more labor-intensive to determine the semantics of functions and identify the relevant ones, creating challenges for automation.

However, if the framework can be identified, the process becomes much simpler. Equipped with knowledge of the framework, the analyst can consult the documentation of the framework to learn more about the firmware structure. Additionally, the analyst can use existing SCA techniques to locate important functions in the firmware image.

2.2 Challenges for Firmware Composition Analysis

The properties of the firmware domain pose several challenges for the identification of embedded frameworks.

Firmware Blobs are Stripped and use Opaque Binary Formats. Existing binary-to-source SCA techniques leverage various features for fingerprinting. Two examples are the exported function names and the data present in data segments. However, with the opaque binary format used for firmware images, many of these normally easily retrievable fingerprinting sources are either very hard to extract or not present at all. For instance, OSSPolice [13] uses exported function names to identify present libraries. This information is however not present in firmware blobs. To successfully identify frameworks in firmware images, the solution must rely solely on features that can be reliably extracted.

Embedded Framework Functions are Semantically Different, Depending on the Build Target. Embedded frameworks have been designed to support many architectures and microcontrollers. To achieve this portability, embedded frameworks widely use macros to differentiate the behavior for each platform. Unfortunately, existing binary-to-source SCA techniques do not take this into account. As a result, many of the features used by the state-of-the-art cannot be used reliably for identifying the frameworks present in firmware images. For instance, SCA techniques frequently use the number of basic blocks contained in a function as a fingerprint for that function. However, in the firmware domain this might not be a reliable feature. For example, TCP/IP implementation functions are semantically different for boards that support IPv6, and as a result have different basic block counts. Consequently, matching functions based on features such as basic blocks is more challenging in the domain of embedded frameworks.

Embedded Frameworks are Hard to Compile in an Automated Fashion. Binary-to-binary SCA techniques require the compilation of all components that you want to identify. In our scenario, this requires the compilation of all embedded frameworks. Previous works mentioned the extensive manual effort required for the compilation task [38]. With hundreds of embedded frameworks available on GitHub and many of them receiving continuous updates, manual compilation becomes a significant limitation that hinders automation.

Embedded Frameworks Might Contain Third-Party Libraries. It is common for embedded frameworks to use open-source libraries to facilitate certain features. For example, Contiki [8] uses a third-party library for the FAT file system implementation. A solid approach to identifying embedded frameworks should ensure that the identification of a third-party library does not result in the incorrect identification of the embedded framework.

Existing SCA approaches have not been designed to address the challenges that occur when identifying embedded frameworks. Therefore, a new, embedded framework-specific SCA technique is required.

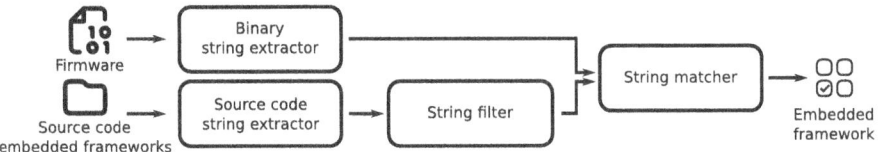

Fig. 2. Simplified representation of FRAMED. The arrows represent the flow of data between the different components.

3 Methodology

We present FRAMED, our approach to identifying embedded frameworks in firmware images. At a high level, FRAMED takes as input an embedded firmware image and a set of embedded frameworks (including their source code) and evaluates whether the given image is built on top of any of the user-provided frameworks. Figure 2 shows a high-level overview of the complete pipeline.

3.1 Frameworks Collection and Processing

The first step of our methodology is to build a large collection of embedded frameworks to identify within firmware images. Embedded frameworks are generally released as open-source code to the public, and they can be easily found online. Two popular examples are Mbed [25] and RIOT [34]. After building a satisfactory complete collection, the `Source code string extractor` extracts the hardcoded strings from each project.

As a second step, the `String filter` applies multiple filters to the strings extracted from the open-source projects. A first filter removes common and short strings. Very short strings are removed since they are not strong indicators and would increase the number of false positives. They include omnipresent strings such as a single format string specifier, e.g. *"%d"*. Moreover, very common strings, like *"error"*, should have a lower impact on matches than for example *"Error: new serial object is using same UART as STDIO"*, a string only found in Mbed. Furthermore, some strings are present across firmware samples, also when no framework is used. Examples are *"0123456789abcdef"* and *"localhost"*. Thus, we filter out popular strings to reduce false positives. Additionally, FRAMED filters out strings that are found in common firmware libraries. Since many open-source frameworks use common third-party libraries in their source code, these strings could result in false positives when a firmware image uses a library that is also used by an embedded framework. By filtering out the strings found in common embedded libraries the number of false positives is reduced.

While the construction of a complete string collection of all embedded frameworks is easily automated, it is still a time-consuming process. Luckily, this process only has to be conducted once. Thereafter, we can use the local string database to evaluate any number of firmware samples.

3.2   Framework Identification

After the construction of the embedded framework string collection, the `Binary string extractor` extracts the strings from the given firmware image. The extracted firmware strings and filtered source code strings are then handed to the `String matcher`. For each framework, the `String matcher` computes how many exact string matches are present. An additional step is required to accurately identify embedded frameworks. This is because many open-source frameworks are clones of more popular frameworks, with minimal changes. These clones often contain the same signatures as the original repository, impacting the performance of our tool. To limit the negative impact of clones, we cluster the potentially matching frameworks based on whether the matching strings are the same. A `String score` is calculated for each cluster using Equation (3). To calculate the `String score`, we first calculate the `String popularity` for each string present in the cluster, by counting how many clusters in total contain this string (Eq. 2). The `String score` of the cluster is then calculated as the sum of the inverse `String popularity` of all the strings present in the cluster. The `String score` ensures that unique strings have a bigger impact on the final result, since unique strings are strong indicators for an embedded framework. Finally, the cluster with the highest `String score` is selected as the matching cluster. If the `String score` of the selected cluster is higher than a predetermined threshold, the most popular framework in that cluster is returned as the identified framework.

$$I(\text{string s}, \text{cluster c}) = \begin{cases} 1 & \text{if } s \in c \\ 0 & \text{otherwise} \end{cases} \tag{1}$$

$$\text{String popularity}(\text{string } s) = \sum_{c \in \text{clusters}} I(s, c) \tag{2}$$

$$\text{String score}(\text{cluster } c) = \sum_{\text{string } s \in c} \frac{1}{\text{String popularity}(s)} \tag{3}$$

Employing the clustering technique in a more general SCA approach might result in clustering together two libraries that are both present, and returning only one. In the domain of embedded framework identification such cases of false negatives are not expected, since only one framework is used to build the firmware image around. The embedded framework can be seen as the operating system of the firmware image, thus it is not practical to use multiple frameworks in the same image. This is why FRAMED looks for one framework, and not multiple ones.

3.3   Implementation Details

To implement the `Source code string extractor`, FRAMED uses the `ANTLR` lexer [1]. For our proof-of-concept implementation, we provide `ANTLR` with C and C++ grammars. However, FRAMED can easily be extended to other languages by providing additional grammars. For example, adding Rust support only requires providing a Rust grammar, which can be easily found online.

For the implementation of `Binary string extractor`, FRAMED uses the Linux utility `strings`. This utility scans through the binary looking for subsequent bytes that represent valid ASCII characters, and returns them as strings.

In the final step of the `String matcher`, FRAMED clusters similar frameworks together. We then use the GitHub star count as a popularity metric to select the final framework from the cluster.

4   Evaluation

In this section, we describe the process we follow to build our database of frameworks, and we evaluate the performance of our tool in identifying frameworks in embedded firmware.

4.1   Database Creation

To assess the performance of FRAMED, we start by constructing the local string database. We use the GitHub API to query for open-source embedded frameworks and collect their source code. To search for embedded frameworks, we use six different queries:

- Embedded operating system;
- Operating system microcontrollers;
- Internet of Things operating system;
- OS IoT;
- OS Internet of Things;
- RTOS.

These specific queries have been selected to ensure that all firmware framework projects we found on GitHub through a manual search are present in the final list. For each query, we search in the description of all GitHub repositories and select the top 100 C/C++ repositories based on star count. We clone the resulting 404 repositories locally. We add one additional framework manually, namely the Arduino framework. While Arduino is a widely adopted framework, it cannot be found on GitHub using our queries since it only has a very short description. The `String filter` reduces the number of strings extracted from the source codes in multiple steps. First, we remove string duplicates and decode escape sequences, to match how strings are stored in the firmware images. Then, we remove strings that are less than 6 characters long. This filters out strings that do not contain a lot of information about the repository, such as *"bytes"*, *"done"*, and also single characters. Next, we filter out the most popular strings. The popularity of strings in our dataset is shown in Fig. 3. In our dataset, we notice many strings occurring 22 times. This turned out to be strings from Mbed clones, which we do not want to filter out. This is why we decided to filter out strings with more than 22 occurrences. A few strings that are filtered out this way are *"failed"*, *"abcdefghijklmnopqrstuvwxyz"*, and *"%s%s%s"*. Filtering out popular strings has shown to be effective in prior works [27]. The final step we perform is filtering out strings from common libraries that are used for embedded systems. We found that many frameworks use common third-party libraries. Without filtering out library strings, FRAMED would raise many false positives. To filter out library strings, we locally cloned all library repositories listed in a popular reference collection called "awesome-embedded-software" [3]. We extracted the strings in a similar fashion to how we extracted the framework strings.

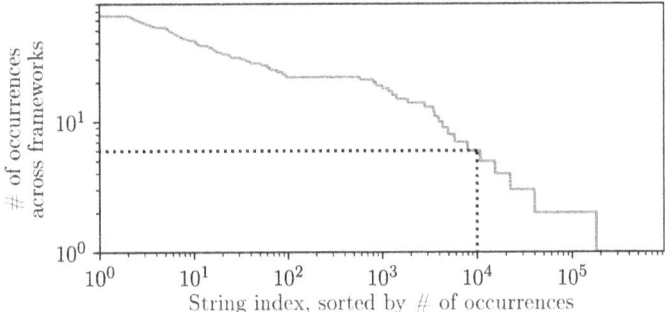

Fig. 3. String popularity in our framework string database, with double logarithmic axes. E.g., as depicted with the black dotted line, the 10,000th most frequently occurring string is present in 6 embedded frameworks in our collection.

4.2   Pipeline Performance

We evaluate the performance of FRAMED on a dataset of 536 labeled firmware images. We construct the dataset by combining the datasets from four prior works. We specifically select collections with firmware samples that use popular embedded frameworks, to ensure the experiments are similar to real-world scenarios. Our dataset features eight different embedded frameworks and a variety of target microcontrollers. Besides, twelve of the samples do not use a framework. Each firmware sample has either been labeled with a framework by the source, or we manually reverse engineer the firmware images to determine the adopted

Table 1. Sources, frameworks, and counts of firmware samples that we used in our evaluation.

Dataset	Framework	No. Samples
Feng et al. (P2IM) [14]	Arduino [2]	5
	RIOT [34]	1
	FreeRTOS [15]	1
	None	3
Clements et al. (HALucinator) [7]	Contiki [8]	2
	None	9
Scharnowski et al. (Fuzzware) [35]	Zephyr [47]	10
	Contiki-NG [9]	2
	Mbed [25]	10
Shen et al. [37]	Zephyr [47]	193
	Mbed [25]	32
	NuttX [32]	188
	FreeRTOS [15]	80
Total		536

frameworks. The complete list of sources, frameworks, and sample counts of the firmware samples is shown in Table 1.

To examine the capabilities of our pipeline, we measure its performance on the 536 labeled firmware images. The framework identification takes 3 s per firmware sample on average, in a single-threaded environment.

Figure 4 shows the performance for the framework detection compared to different string score thresholds. At a threshold of 3.5, 83% of the samples are labeled correctly. At a lower threshold of 2, 18% of the framework identifications are false positives, while at a higher threshold of 5 results in only 1% false positives, but more than 20% false negatives. For Mbed the accuracy is 100% at lower thresholds. Only at thresholds starting from 6, do false negatives start occurring. Both NuttX and Zephyr achieve 90%+ accuracy at String score thresholds under 4. Interestingly, for both frameworks we notice that from the threshold of 4, false positives are reducing, and false negatives are increasing.

The detection results per framework and for three different threshold values are shown in Table 2.

Using a low threshold (e.g., 2) results in few false negatives for all frameworks. This can be a useful metric to detect the use of a framework. Although the wrong framework might be detected, the security analyst can use the result to further research the used framework. Samples that do not use a framework can be discarded early. Using a higher threshold such as 5, on the other hand, can be useful in scenarios where one wants to be sure that the detected framework

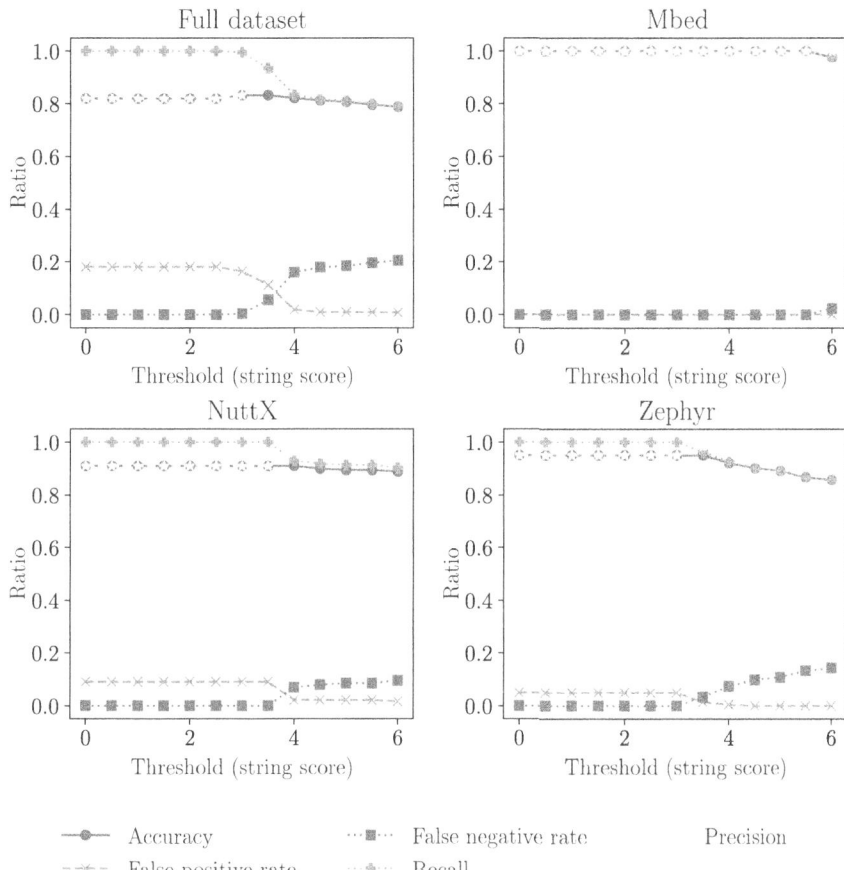

Fig. 4. FRAMED detection performance metrics on the 536 firmware samples.

is correct. For example, at the threshold of 6 only 4 of the 536 samples were incorrectly labeled with a framework. However, there are 110 false negatives at this high threshold. As a result, a firmware blob that has not been identified with a framework might still use a framework.

For the cases where the framework identification is incorrect, we see a few trends. First, we notice that some frameworks use a low number of hard-coded strings, limiting the effectiveness of FRAMED for these specific frameworks. As a result, Arduino and FreeRTOS are harder to detect with FRAMED, and have high false negative rates independent of the string-score threshold. On the other hand, larger frameworks that feature many strings are accurately identified by FRAMED, across firmware samples. Second, we observe a low number of false positives with a balanced threshold (3.5) in place. We manually investigated the false positive cases. We found that the matches mostly occur due to the use of libraries, which are not present in our library collection that is used for string filtering.

Table 2. The results of FRAMED when running over 536 labeled firmware samples, with different string score thresholds.

	Framework	TPs	FPs	TNs	FNs
Threshold = 2	FreeRTOS	27	54	N/A	0
	Zephyr	193	10	N/A	0
	Mbed	42	0	N/A	0
	NuttX	171	17	N/A	0
	Arduino	0	5	N/A	0
	RIOT	1	0	N/A	0
	Contiki	2	0	N/A	0
	Contiki-NG	2	0	N/A	0
	None	N/A	11	1	N/A
	Total	438	97	1	0
Threshold = 3.5	FreeRTOS	27	35	N/A	19
	Zephyr	193	3	N/A	7
	Mbed	42	0	N/A	0
	NuttX	171	17	N/A	0
	Arduino	0	1	N/A	4
	RIOT	1	0	N/A	0
	Contiki	2	0	N/A	0
	Contiki-NG	2	0	N/A	0
	None	N/A	4	8	N/A
	Total	438	60	8	30
Threshold = 6	FreeRTOS	24	0	N/A	57
	Zephyr	174	0	N/A	29
	Mbed	41	0	N/A	1
	NuttX	167	3	N/A	18
	Arduino	0	0	N/A	5
	RIOT	1	0	N/A	0
	Contiki	2	0	N/A	0
	Contiki-NG	2	0	N/A	0
	None	N/A	1	11	N/A
	Total	411	4	11	110

We recognize that using an absolute cut-off threshold is a rather naive method. However, we found that for our dataset, which is diverse in nature, it performs well. Nonetheless, we envision future research on the design of a more accurate approach to identifying embedded frameworks.

5 Case Study

We conduct a case study to demonstrate the application of FRAMED to assist in reversing and patching IoT firmware. Specifically, we focus on the Atmel 6LoWPAN Sender firmware image from the HALucinator paper [7] and study how FRAMED can be integrated with Shimware [16] to enhance its I/O function tracking, ultimately leading to patch injection. Shimware uses an approach called IOFinder to determine I/O functions in firmware images. IOFinder combines static and dynamic analysis to find functions that perform I/O functions. One limitation of IOFinder is that it is not designed to process firmware images that use a larger embedded framework. In the case of the Atmel image, due to the use of a large embedded framework Contiki, IOFinder is unable to detect several relevant I/O functions. As a result, Shimware fails to locate the function where the patch should be introduced [16].

In the practical scenario where we want to patch the Atmel 6LoWPAN Sender firmware image, we can leverage FRAMED to discover the use of the Contiki embedded framework. As we detect the use of a large framework, we know that the results of IOFinder are likely to be incomplete. Therefore, we decide not to use IOFinder. Instead, to recover the function symbols, we can now compile a Contiki example project and use existing binary-to-binary SCA techniques to recover symbols in the binary. For this example, we use Libmatch from HALucinator [7] and reveal the locations and names of 170 functions. Next, the analyst looking to apply the patch can now go over the functions, determine which functions handle the relevant input, and subsequently identify the location for Shimware to inject the patch. Depending on the specific vulnerability, it is possible to apply patches in higher-level functions than the I/O functions. For example, assume that we want to apply a patch to incoming network traffic to filter malicious payloads. We can locate the `tcpip_input` function, which is a Contiki function called by the network driver when a new TCP/IP packet is received, and which represents a perfect hook for our patch. With the knowledge of the address of the `tcpip_input` function, in combination with the Shimware tooling, we insert the patch into the original firmware image.

6 Discussion

We discuss the limitations of FRAMED and directions for future research.

Frameworks with Few Strings. The fundamentals of our approach rely on the presence of strings in the framework and in the firmware image. Generally, all frameworks do contain these strings, but this does not guarantee that they will be present in the final firmware image. To reduce the final image size, unused functions are often left out during the linking phase. As a result, also the strings used in these functions are not included in the final firmware image. This explains why FRAMED has low detection rates for samples using some specific frameworks. An example is FreeRTOS [15], a minimal framework that does not contain much more than HAL functions and some basic scheduling. Since minimal frameworks mostly provide the HAL functions, other approaches are potentially a better fit to detect these types of frameworks. Compiling HAL functions automatically is less challenging than more advanced frameworks, as has been shown and used for a similar approach before (e.g., Libmatch [7]). Thus, one could automatically compile a database of HAL objects and apply Libmatch or a similar approach to detect the HAL functions in the firmware. In the context of firmware patching, IOFinder as used by Shimware [16] is a technique to find relevant IO functions, but only works for smaller frameworks. To summarize, FRAMED provides an approach to aid reverse engineers recover symbols and assist in the patching process of larger embedded frameworks, whereas prior works have shown approaches that are effective for smaller embedded frameworks.

Completeness of Framework Database. To construct our list of frameworks, we used various GitHub queries. While this covers a large portion of the available frameworks, it is not complete. For instance, Software Development Kits (SDKs) for embedded firmware often come with their own frameworks preinstalled. While these frameworks are often open source, you will not necessarily find them on GitHub, or we found them to have short descriptions and are hard to query for. FRAMED does currently not have the capability to detect these frameworks. However, they can be added manually to the database with ease. One other set of frameworks that are currently absent and more difficult to add are private frameworks developed and used by device manufacturers.

Completeness of Library Database. To reduce false positives, we filtered out strings present in commonly used third-party libraries. Selecting the libraries for this list has to be done carefully, as it can easily remove true positives. We chose to use a curated list, as described in Sect. 4. However, in our evaluation, a false positive occurred due to a library missing from our collection. The accuracy of FRAMED relies partly on creating a good list of libraries.

Automation in Function Matching. Our pipeline is fully automated when it comes to creating the string database and identifying the used frameworks. However, the next step in the pipeline would be to recover the symbols fully automatically. To achieve this goal, we have explored the idea of automated compilation of the framework, followed by binary-to-binary SCA. However, fully automating this process requires more research. One of the main challenges for achieving this automation is the nature of the framework projects. They have been developed to ease the development for embedded devices, and provide configuration files and build specifications to adjust the environment for specific hardware. Compiling the object files without the configuration enabled will often fail. Thus, it is required to manually set up a build environment. The alternative is binary-to-source matching. While this is a more complicated approach and no existing projects match our requirements, we see this as the most feasible way forward. Additionally, binary-to-source matching could also be used to resolve the limitations of the lower performance for frameworks that use fewer strings.

Compressed firmware images. Like any other static firmware analysis app-roach, FRAMED struggles with compressed firmware images, as compression can result in failure to extract strings from firmware images. To resolve this, one could integrate FRAMED with existing solutions that unpack known formats (e.g., Binwalk [5]).

7 Related Work

Many previous works have been conducted with similar goals to ours. In this section, we discuss their benefits, downsides, limitations, and assumptions.

There have been various efforts to simplify the reverse engineering and anal-ysis of firmware. Muench et al. [29] focussed on grouping firmware images into types of operating systems. Thomas et al. [42] use both static and dynamic analysis to improve the disassembly quality. Firmline [4] provides a pipeline to automatically detect the architecture and base addresses of non-Linux-based firmware images. With FRAMED, we contribute to the area of firmware analysis by identifying embedded framework usage.

Several studies have been conducted in the area of patching of embedded devices. HERA [30] and RapidPatch [17] both apply hot-patches to running embedded devices, without rebooting the device. However, the focus of both HERA and RapidPatch is solely on how to inject the patch, not where. Dis-patch [23] proposes an approach to patching the firmware of Robotic Aerial Vehicles. They target controller component functions and locate them through the identification of trigonometric functions. This approach does not transfer to a more generic case of function identification. Shimware [16] presents a set of tools to ease the patching of non-Linux based firmware images. The main contributions are the automated locating of I/O functions, finding a location to insert the patch without breaking the functionality of the device, and finding and fixing firmware validity checks. To locate the I/O functions, a hybrid approach combining static and dynamic analysis is used. While it has proven effective for general firmware images, it tends to miss functions if the firmware uses a larger embedded framework. Moreover, the identified I/O functions are not labeled and still require manual reverse engineering to reveal their exact purpose.

Software Component Analysis can be divided into approaches using binary-to-binary matching or binary-to-source matching:

Binary-to-binary SCA. Libmatch [7] combines static and dynamic analysis to locate Hardware Abstraction Layer functions. Asm2Vec [12] uses machine learning to match functions across architecture and compiler optimization lev-els. FirmSec [48] detects third-party component usage in both Linux-based and non-Linux-based firmware images. However, none of these approaches is directly applicable to the challenge of framework identification, due to the manual effort required to compile embedded frameworks.

Binary-to-source SCA. BAT [18] uses strings to get an estimate of code reuse, but does not address further challenges such as cloning. OSSPolice [13] leverages strings, in combination with exported function names to detect the reuse of open source software. Exported function names are however not present in firmware images. Bigmatch [27] identifies the use of open-source libraries in binary executables solely based on strings, but does not take into account the presence of shared third-party libraries between repositories, nor does it tackle software clones that have not been marked as such on GitHub. B2SFinder [45] matches source code to binaries by using 7 binary features that can be extracted with extra knowledge of the binary format. Most of these features are however not present in firmware images.

When it comes to finding vulnerabilities in embedded firmware, various research directions have been explored. First, fuzzing with devices in the loop was a popular topic of research a couple of years ago [10, 21, 24, 46]. While these approaches have good results, they are limited to small-scale experiments and analyses since the device has to be both available and set up. Recently, many rehosting approaches have been proposed. There is a clear divide between papers targeting Linux-based firmware images [16, 22, 28, 40] and monolithic firmware images [7, 14, 35, 36, 39, 49]. Most of these approaches focus on providing valid inputs for MMIO addresses in memory or hardware abstraction layer functions.

8   Conclusion

With FRAMED, we presented an automated pipeline to identify embedded frameworks within firmware images. FRAMED combines string matching and insights in embedded frameworks to provide meaningful semantic annotations that facilitate reverse engineering and security analyses. We evaluated the performance of FRAMED on a labeled dataset of 536 images, obtaining an accuracy of 83%. By changing the threshold, our tool can be adjusted to fit scenarios where either a low number of false positives or a low number of false negatives are required. We envision our tool being used to assist both reverse engineers and automated security pipelines that perform firmware analyses such as vulnerability discovery and patching.

Acknowledgements. We would like to thank our reviewers for their valuable comments and inputs to improve our paper. This work has been partially supported by the Dutch Ministry of Economic Affairs and Climate Policy (EZK) through the AVR project "FirmPatch" and by the project P6 (Open Technology Programme No. 20475) funded by the Dutch Research Council (NWO).

References

1. ANTLR. https://www.antlr.org/. Accessed 14 Feb 2024
2. Arduino. https://www.arduino.cc/. Accessed 17 June 2024
3. Awesome embedded resources for developers. https://github.com/iDoka/awesome-embedded-software. Accessed 14 Feb 2024
4. Balgavy, A., Muench, M.: Firmline: a generic pipeline for large-scale analysis of non-Linux firmware. In: Proceedings of the Workshop on Binary Analysis Research (BAR) (2024)
5. Binwalk. https://github.com/ReFirmLabs/binwalk. Accessed 14 Feb 2024
6. Chen, L., et al.: Sharing more and checking less: Leveraging common input keywords to detect bugs in embedded systems. In: Proceedings of the USENIX Security Symposium (2021)
7. Clements, A.A., et al.: HALucinator: firmware re-hosting through abstraction layer emulation. In: Proceedings of the USENIX Security Symposium (2020)
8. Contiki. http://www.contiki-os.org/. Accessed 17 June 2024
9. Contiki-NG. https://www.contiki-ng.org/. Accessed 17 June 2024
10. Corteggiani, N., Camurati, G., Francillon, A.: Inception: system-wide security testing of real-world embedded systems software. In: Proceedings of the USENIX Security Symposium (2018)
11. Cyber risks to critical infrastructure are on the rise. https://news.microsoft.com/en-cee/2023/06/26/cyber-risks-to-critical-infrastructure-are-on-the-rise/. Accessed 14 Feb 2024
12. Ding, S.H., Fung, B.C., Charland, P.: Asm2Vec: boosting static representation robustness for binary clone search against code obfuscation and compiler optimization. In: Proceedings of the IEEE Symposium on Security and Privacy (2019)
13. Duan, R., Bijlani, A., Xu, M., Kim, T., Lee, W.: Identifying open-source license violation and 1-day security risk at large scale. In: Proceedings of the ACM Conference on Computer and Communications Security (CCS) (2017)
14. Feng, B., Mera, A., Lu, L.: P2IM: Scalable and hardware-independent firmware testing via automatic peripheral interface modeling. In: Proceedings of the USENIX Security Symposium (2020)
15. FreeRTOS. https://www.freertos.org/index.html. Accessed 14 Feb 2024
16. Gustafson, E., et al.: Shimware: toward practical security retrofitting for monolithic firmware images. In: Proceedings of the International Symposium on Research in Attacks, Intrusions and Defenses (RAID) (2023)
17. He, Y., et al.: RapidPatch: firmware hotpatching for real-time embedded devices. In: Proceedings of the USENIX Security Symposium (2022)
18. Hemel, A., Kalleberg, K.T., Vermaas, R., Dolstra, E.: Finding software license violations through binary code clone detection. In: Proceedings of the Working Conference on Mining Software Repositories (2011)
19. Ibrahim, M., Continella, A., Bianchi, A.: AoT - attack on things: a security analysis of IoT firmware updates. In: Proceedings of the IEEE Symposium on Security and Privacy (2023)
20. Jiang, L., et al.: BinaryAI: binary software composition analysis via intelligent binary source code matching. In: Proceedings of the IEEE/ACM International Conference on Automated Software Engineering (ASE) (2024)
21. Kammerstetter, M., Platzer, C., Kastner, W.: Prospect: peripheral proxying supported embedded code testing. In: Proceedings of the ACM Conference on Computer and Communications Security (CCS) (2014)

22. Kim, M., Kim, D., Kim, E., Kim, S., Jang, Y., Kim, Y.: FirmAE: towards large-scale emulation of IoT firmware for dynamic analysis. In: Proceedings of the Annual Computer Security Applications Conference (ACSAC) (2020)
23. Kim, T., et al.: Reverse engineering and retrofitting robotic aerial vehicle control firmware using dispatch. In: Proceedings of the ACM International Conference on Mobile Systems, Applications, and Services (MobiSys) (2022)
24. Koscher, K., Kohno, T., Molnar, D.: SURROGATES: enabling near-real-time dynamic analyses of embedded systems. In: Proceedings of the USENIX Workshop on Offensive Technologies (WOOT) (2015)
25. Mbed. https://os.mbed.com/. Accessed 14 Feb 2024
26. Melotti, D., Rossi-Bellom, M., Continella, A.: Reversing and fuzzing the Google Titan M chip. In: Proceedings of the Reversing and Offensive-Oriented Trends Symposium (ROOTS) (2021)
27. Montesel, P.: Big Match - how i learned to stop reversing and love the strings. https://conference.hitb.org/hitbsecconf2023hkt/materials/D1. Accessed 10 Dec 2023
28. Muench, M., Nisi, D., Francillon, A., Balzarotti, D.: Avatar 2: a multi-target orchestration platform. In: Proceedings of the Workshop on Binary Analysis Research (BAR) (2018)
29. Muench, M., Stijohann, J., Kargl, F., Francillon, A., Balzarotti, D.: What you corrupt is not what you crash: Challenges in fuzzing embedded devices. In: Proceedings of the Symposium on Network and Distributed System Security (NDSS) (2018)
30. Niesler, C., Surminski, S., Davi, L.: HERA: hotpatching of embedded real-time applications. In: Proceedings of the Symposium on Network and Distributed System Security (NDSS) (2021)
31. Number of Internet of Things (IoT) connected devices worldwide from 2019 to 2021, with forecasts from 2022 to 2030. https://www.statista.com/statistics/1183457/iot-connected-devices-worldwide/. Accessed 20 March 2024
32. NuttX. https://nuttx.apache.org/. Accessed 17 June 2024
33. Redini, N., et al.: KARONTE: detecting insecure multi-binary interactions in embedded firmware. In: Proceedings of the IEEE Symposium on Security and Privacy (2020)
34. RIOT. https://www.riot-os.org/. Accessed 14 Feb 2024
35. Scharnowski, T., et al.: Fuzzware: using precise MMIO modeling for effective firmware fuzzing. In: Proceedings of the USENIX Security Symposium (2022)
36. Seidel, L., Maier, D.C., Muench, M.: Forming faster firmware fuzzers. In: Proceedings of the USENIX Security Symposium (2023)
37. Shen, M., Davis, J.C., Machiry, A.: Towards automated identification of layering violations in embedded applications. In: Proceedings of the ACM SIGPLAN/SIGBED International Conference on Languages, Compilers, and Tools for Embedded Systems (LCTES) (2023)
38. Shen, M., Pillai, A., Yuan, B.A., Davis, J.C., Machiry, A.: An empirical study on the use of static analysis tools in open source embedded software. arXiv preprint arXiv:2310.00205 (2023)
39. Srinivasan, J., Tanksalkar, S.R., Amusuo, P.C., Davis, J.C., Machiry, A.: Towards rehosting embedded applications as Linux applications. In: Proceedings of the IEEE/IFIP International Conference on Dependable Systems and Networks (DSN). IEEE (2023)

40. Tay, H.J., et al.: Greenhouse: single-service rehosting of Linux-based firmware binaries in user-space emulation. In: Proceedings of the USENIX Security Symposium (2023)
41. The tipping point: exploring the surge in IoT cyberattacks globally. https://blog.checkpoint.com/security/the-tipping-point-exploring-the-surge-in-iot-cyberattacks-plaguing-the-education-sector/. Accessed14 Feb 2024
42. Thomas, S.L., Van den Herrewegen, J., Vasilakis, G., Chen, Z., Ordean, M., Garcia, F.D.: Cutting through the complexity of reverse engineering embedded devices. IACR Trans. Cryptogr. Hard. Embedd. Syst. **2021**, 360–389 (TCHES) (2021)
43. What happens when the sun sets on a smart product?. https://www.ftc.gov/business-guidance/blog/2016/07/what-happens-when-sun-sets-smart-product. Accessed 22 Dec 2023
44. Wu, Y., et al.: Your firmware has arrived: a study of firmware update vulnerabilities. In: Proceedings of the USENIX Security Symposium (2023)
45. Yuan, Z., et al.: B2SFinder: detecting open-source software reuse in cots software. In: Proceedings of the IEEE/ACM International Conference on Automated Software Engineering (ASE) (2019)
46. Zaddach, J., Bruno, L., Francillon, A., Balzarotti, D., et al.: Avatar: a framework to support dynamic security analysis of embedded systems' firmwares. In: Proceedings of the Symposium on Network and Distributed System Security (NDSS) (2014)
47. Zephyr. https://www.zephyrproject.org/. Accessed 17 June 2024
48. Zhao, B., et al.: One bad apple spoils the barrel: Understanding the security risks introduced by third-party components in IoT firmware. IEEE Trans. Dependable Secure Comput. **21**, 1372–1389 (2023)
49. Zhou, W., Guan, L., Liu, P., Zhang, Y.: Automatic firmware emulation through invalidity-guided knowledge inference. In: Proceedings of the USENIX Security Symposium (2021)

Leveraging the Domain Experts: Specializing Privacy Threat Knowledge

Laurens Sion$^{(\boxtimes)}$ ⓘ, Dimitri Van Landuyt ⓘ, and Wouter Joosen ⓘ

DistriNet, KU Leuven, 3001 Leuven, Belgium
{laurens.sion,dimitri.vanlanduyt,wouter.joosen}@kuleuven.be

Abstract. The design and development of privacy-preserving software systems remains a challenging endeavor, especially with the wide-spread adoption of potentially privacy-harmful technologies such as ML/AI, LLMs, telemetry, etc. Current privacy threat knowledge consolidation efforts mainly focus on the ontological generalization of threat knowledge. The generic encoding of privacy threat knowledge is useful for increasing overall awareness of the diversity and scope of privacy threats and promoting broader application of privacy threat analysis. However, it also inhibits reuse of threat knowledge that is more tailored to the organization context or application domain. There is thus an emerging need to encode, manage, and share specialized privacy threat knowledge that may be more domain-, technology-, or organization-specific.

In this position paper, we outline a vision and roadmap towards improved support for the overall management of privacy threat knowledge, and particularly we envision advanced knowledge modeling support for capturing specialized threat knowledge, supporting evolution, customization, and reuse.

1 Introduction

Engineering privacy-preserving software-intensive systems remains a non-trivial task that requires substantial expertise to assess and strengthen the privacy properties of the system under development. Furthermore, several legislative initiatives (such as the GDPR) stress the importance of considering privacy and data protection in the design and development of systems, and even impose a strong obligation to proactively consider these issues [1].

To assist privacy engineers and developers in this task, diverse approaches such as privacy threat modeling [13], and supporting resources, such as threat trees [38], and other taxonomies [4,8,40] have been created. These resources provide support in two complementary dimensions. First, they provide methodological support [17] for the users to perform the actual privacy analysis of the system under design (process dimension). Second, they provide consolidated and refined threat knowledge to assist users in considering diverse threats in the system they are working on (knowledge dimension).

Even with these supporting resources, privacy experts with relevant domain- or application-specific knowledge remain a scarce resource [44]. Existing efforts to

J. Garcia-Alfaro et al. (Eds.): ESORICS 2024 Workshops, LNCS 15263, pp. 534–541, 2025.
https://doi.org/10.1007/978-3-031-82349-7_33

capture relevant knowledge are generally focused on abstracting specific threats (or weaknesses) for the purpose of making the resulting information more broadly available and applicable across applications and domains (Sect. 2). While such a generalization is definitely useful to enable wider re-use, it also tends to abstract away important details that are no longer available to the user [42].

This position paper argues for and envisions new mechanisms for specialization of privacy threat knowledge that can provide compelling benefits on three fronts. (1) Explicitly capturing specialized privacy threat knowledge enables the construction of organization-specific repositories that capture and propagate earlier experiences and best practices; this allows organizations to emphasize or prioritize specific types of threats that have to be explicitly considered across its products. (2) Specializing the threat knowledge can be performed to accommodate the particularities of specific application domains. (3) A consolidated form of privacy threat knowledge can contribute to the overall practice of cyber threat intelligence (CTI) sharing which entails that diverse players active within the same domain or ecosystem (e.g., supply chain) more readily and freely share information about incidents, vulnerabilities, and encountered attack patterns.

The specialization of threat knowledge enables the construction of, for example, specialized threat libraries. However, the threat modeler not only has to interpret this threat knowledge correctly, but also has to translate that to the relevant application domain. This additional translation step further complicates the use of this knowledge. The specialization of privacy threat knowledge to specific domains can already include this translation step and can enrich the threat knowledge with concrete domain-specific examples to make it much more convenient to use.

2   Related Work

We discuss the availability of different types of threat knowledge resources and the extent of their specialization. Section 2.1 and Sect. 2.2 first elaborate on security and privacy threat knowledge resources. Next, Sect. 2.3 assesses the support in current threat modeling tools. Finally, Sect. 2.4 covers domain-specific and application-specific resources. Figures 1a and 1b visualize the results.[1]

2.1   Security Threat Knowledge Resources

Security threat modeling approaches offer several threat trees [18,38] that capture generic threat knowledge along the STRIDE threat type mnemonic. These trees capture generic ways in which the STRIDE threats can manifest themselves to help threat modelers to instantiate threats.

---

[1] Note that the exact coordinates are not important; the figures serve to draw attention to the quadrant in which the resources are located (i.e. abstract and generic, abstract and application specific, generic and concrete, or application-specific and concrete).

In addition to those resources, there are more generic resources that capture security knowledge. Examples of these are the Common Attack Pattern Enumeration and Classification (CAPEC) [22] that provides attack patterns, Common Weaknesses and Exposures (CWE) [24] for identifying the underlying causes of vulnerabilities [23], the Common Architectural Weaknesses and Exposures (CAWE) [32] that abstracts these to common architectural design flaws, and finally the Top 10 Secure Design Flaws [5] again focusing on more high-level flaws.

Overall, these resources focus on abstracting, for example the CWE catalog is based on an extensive effort to abstract and generalize specific vulnerability reports (CVE) to construct a model of the root causes. They do not provide domain-specific threat knowledge and lack support for refinement. Section 2.4 provides more details on these.

2.2   Privacy Threat Knowledge Resources

In the space of privacy threat knowledge, there are fewer resources. We extend Wuyts' earlier overview [48] with resources that have been published since [7, 9, 14, 47]. One of the main resources in this area are the LINDDUN threat trees that have undergone several iterations [13, 14, 46] with more detail and refinements in threat examples. While these enrichments increase the level of concretization in support of applying the knowledge, LINDDUN itself remains generic in the sense that it is application domain-agnostic, in analogy with STRIDE. A variant of the LINDDUN knowledge is LINDDUN GO [47] which makes the examples more concrete, but again is not domain-specific. The LINDDUN GO-inspired Plot4AI cards [7], on the contrary, focuses specifically on the domain of AI. A recent newly-introduced knowledge source is the MITRE's PANOPTIC [36]. PANOPTIC uses two taxonomies: privacy contextual domains and privacy activities, and is constructed from knowledge about FTC/FCC privacy attacks. Finally, CNIL's methodology for privacy risk [11] also includes a generic list of threats. While the methodology focuses on privacy risk, the provided threats are generic and focus on security (confidentiality, integrity and availability). In other work, a technique for making specific domain refinements of LINDDUN threat knowledge [49] mainly involved tagging or annotating specific branches of the threat trees with domain information. This mechanism is predominantly suited to express domain-specific *selections* from the broader knowledge, i.e. to indicate that some threat types or sub-types are (or not) applicable or relevant to the specific application domain. It however does not support true *specialization* in the sense that newer subtypes (or leading examples) can be introduced of the generic threat types encoded in the threat library.

2.3   Threat Modeling Tools

In additional to the generally-available resources on security and privacy threat knowledge, several threat modeling tools also embed threat knowledge and may allow different forms of customization or specialization of this knowledge. This

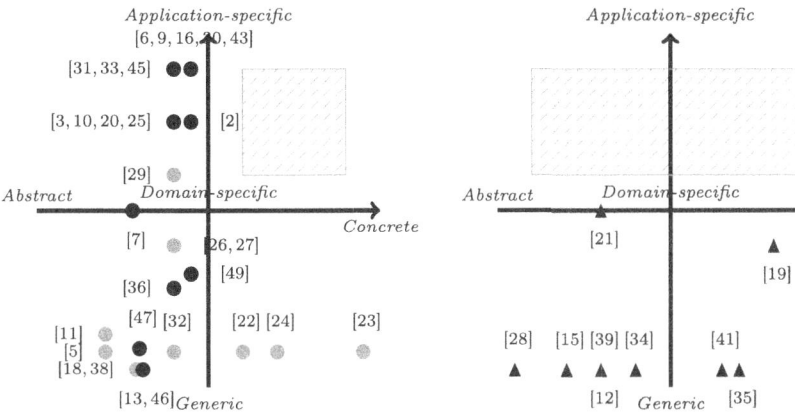

(a) Overview of knowledge resources
This diagram situates security (◐) and privacy (●) knowledge resources on a high-level. Most resources provide generic and abstract knowledge (high-level guidance). Furthermore, most domain- or application-specific resources are research results not readily available for practitioners to apply. The marked area highlights the gap.

(b) Overview of tool support
This diagram situates threat modeling tools. Most provide generic and abstract knowledge (high-level guidance). This confirms the observations from Figure 1a in which the domain- and application-specific resources are not available in tools. The marked area highlights the gap.

Fig. 1. Overview of knowledge and tool support

section outlines the extent of support in existing tools. Shi et al. [37] analyzed several open source and freely available commercial tools. They observe tools to either have a self-defined library (based on STRIDE/LINDDUN or fully custom) or leverage existing resources (CVE, CWE, or CAPEC). Microsoft Threat Modeling Tool [21], ThreatDragon [28], pyTM [41], OVVL [34], threagile [35], and Irius-Risk [19] all rely on such generic sources. Other tools such as threats manager studio [12] and SPARTA [39] provide similar support for automated elicitation of threats based on similar catalogs of threat types. Finally, CAIRIS [15] also supports DFD creation and documenting threats. IriusRisk and Microsoft's Threat Modeling Tool offer additional support for AWS and Azure, with the Microsoft Threat Modeling Tool even having a threat catalog for medical devices.

2.4 Domain and Application-Specific Resources

In addition to the generic resources outlined in Sects. 2.1 and 2.2, there are several resources that offer more scoped and concrete threat knowledge. OWASP publishes several top 10 security risk rankings for mobile [27], web [26], and LLM applications [29]. While these resources focus on security, taxonomies for website privacy vulnerabilities are also available [4]. Listing all potential domain-specific and application-specific resources is not possible. Instead, a few domains are highlighted to illustrate the where these types of knowledge resources can be situated in Fig. 1a. In this case, we highlight the areas of machine learning [3, 10, 20, 25], automotive [6,9,16,30,43], IoT [2], and social networks [31,33,45]. These examples illustrate the range between more generic technologies and highly-specific application domains. However, this specialized knowledge can be mainly found in papers, not in reusable catalogs or tools.

2.5   Observations

The following three observations can be made from the presentation of the different security and privacy threat knowledge resources and threat modeling tool support visualized in, respectively, Figs. 1a and 1b.

First, construction of security and privacy threat knowledge happens mainly through abstraction of concrete vulnerabilities, threats, attacks, etc. to create more generally-applicable resources (CWE, top 10 s, taxonomies, etc.).

Second, this pattern re-appears in tool support. Several tools [19,21] make steps towards providing more specific knowledge, for example, for cloud platforms (e.g., AWS or Azure) or specific domains (e.g., medical devices).

Third, a lot of specialized knowledge is available in particular domains (illustrated through the overview in the areas of machine learning, automotive, IoT, and social networks) but this knowledge is not readily available for practitioners.

This is also confirmed by a mapping study of privacy threat analysis assumptions [42] that has pointed out that a number of assumptions can be attributed to a mismatch between the generic information in the resources and the specific domain, resulting in generic and redundant assumptions (e.g., *threat type X does not apply in our domain*), illustrating the issue when specialization falls short.

3   Roadmap Towards Threat Knowledge Specialization

To bridge the highlighted gap (Figs. 1a and 1b), we argue that more extensive support is needed for domain- and application-specific knowledge. This requires modeling support to capture these domain-specific details in a single threat knowledge representation. In such a representation, domain- or application-specific variants could be realized as filtered views of that threat knowledge [49]. This requires support for encoding information at different abstraction levels (from high-level domain-specific threat types to very concrete example threats). Realizing this requires overcoming a number of key challenges.

Structured and extensible knowledge representation. The first challenge is expanding the modeling support in existing threat libraries to support the representation of domain- and application-specific threat types, characteristics, annotation, and examples. This is necessary for: (1) capturing the application- and domain-specific knowledge at various abstraction levels, and (2) annotating this knowledge with the relevant domain or application to enable filtering and selection support.

Specialization and refinement. Here, the aforementioned mechanisms are leveraged to expand existing threat libraries with more specialized types, characteristics, and examples. To create these resources, existing domain- and application-specific resources (Sect. 2.4) can be encoded. This provides an opportunity to verify whether existing generic resources are expressive enough to cover them and extends the threat library with more concrete information.

Evolution and versioning. To support continuous evolution and extension (when adding new domain- and application-specific knowledge) requires support for evolution and versioning. Modifications to the existing knowledge representation may be necessary in the future to express new types of knowledge that cannot be accurately captured with previous versions.

Reuse and customization. Specialized privacy threat knowledge bases provide the opportunity for organizations to customize the knowledge for internal reuse.

Community interaction. Finally, the model-driven representation of specialized threat knowledge provides a structured format for exchanging this type of information. This raises opportunities for community interactions and collaborations to pro-actively share their knowledge, examples, and potential improvements.

We presented our vision towards more principled support for encoding domain-, technology-, and organization-specific threat knowledge to address this limitation. The specialization of the threat knowledge offers compelling benefits in: (1) helping threat modelers to apply that knowledge in their applications, (2) encoding and reusing organization-specific threat knowledge in a more systematic fashion, (3) increasing efficiency in eliminating and filtering out irrelevant threat knowledge, and (4) supporting and encouraging inter-organizational sharing of privacy threat knowledge. More structured support for specialized privacy threat knowledge creation will support more efficient encoding and knowledge sharing and help organizations to develop privacy-preserving software systems by comprehensively and systematically assessing the privacy threats.

Acknowledgments. This research is partially funded by the Research Fund KU Leuven and Cybersecurity Research Program Flanders.

Disclosure of Interests. The authors have no competing interests to declare that are relevant to the content of this article.

References

1. Regulation, P.: Regulation (EU) 2016/679 of the European Parliament and of the Council of 27 April 2016. Official J. Eur. Union **59**(L 119), 1–88 (2016)
2. Abdulghani, H.A., Nijdam, N.A., Collen, A., Konstantas, D.: A study on security and privacy guidelines, countermeasures, threats: IoT data at rest perspective. Symmetry **11**(6), 774 (2019)
3. Al-Rubaie, M., Chang, J.M.: Privacy-preserving machine learning: threats and solutions. IEEE Secur. Priv. **17**(2), 49–58 (2019)
4. Antón, A.I., Earp, J.B.: A requirements taxonomy for reducing web site privacy vulnerabilities. Requir. Eng. **9**, 169–185 (2004)

5. Arce, I., et al.: Avoiding the Top 10 Software Security Design Flaws. Technical report, IEEE Center for Secure Design (2014)
6. Asuquo, P., et al.: Security and privacy in location-based services for vehicular and mobile communications: an overview, challenges, and countermeasures. IEEE Internet Things J. **5**(6), 4778–4802 (2018)
7. Barberá, I.: PLOT4ai - Privacy Library Of Threats 4 Artificial Intelligence, February 2024. https://plot4.ai/
8. Barker, K., et al.: A data privacy taxonomy. In: Dataspace: The Final Frontier: 26th British National Conference on Databases (2009)
9. Chah, B., Lombard, A., Bkakria, A., Yaich, R., Abbas-Turki, A., Galland, S.: Privacy threat analysis for connected and autonomous vehicles. Procedia Comput. Sci. **210**, 36–44 (2022)
10. Chang, S., Li, C.: Privacy in neural network learning: threats and countermeasures. IEEE Netw. **32**(4), 61–67 (2018)
11. CNIL: Methodology for Privacy Risk Management: How to implement the Data Protection Act. Technical report (2012)
12. Curzi, S.: Pytm (2024). https://threatsmanager.com/
13. Deng, M., Wuyts, K., Scandariato, R., Preneel, B., Joosen, W.: A privacy threat analysis framework: supporting the elicitation and fulfillment of privacy requirements. Requir. Eng. **16**(1), 3–32 (2011)
14. DistriNet: LINDDUN Website (2024). https://linddun.org
15. Faily, S.: Designing usable and secure software with IRIS and CAIRIS. Springer, Cham (2018). https://doi.org/10.1007/978-3-319-75493-2
16. den Hartog, J., Zannone, N., et al.: Security and privacy for innovative automotive applications: a survey. Comput. Commun. **132**, 17–41 (2018)
17. Hernan, S., Lambert, S., Ostwald, T., Shostack, A.: Threat modeling: uncover security design flaws using the STRIDE approach. MSDN Mag. **6**, 68–75 (2006). https://msdn.microsoft.com/en-us/magazine/cc163519.aspx
18. Howard, M., Lipner, S.: The Security Development Lifecycle. Microsoft Press (2006)
19. IriusRisk: IriusRisk (2024). https://www.iriusrisk.com/
20. Lyu, L., Yu, H., Zhao, J., Yang, Q.: Threats to federated learning. Federated Learning: Privacy and Incentive, pp. 3–16 (2020)
21. Microsoft Corporation: Microsoft Threat Modeling Tool 7. http://aka.ms/tmt (2023)
22. MITRE: Common Attack Pattern Enumeration and Classification (2024). https://capec.mitre.org
23. MITRE: Common Vulnerability Enumeration (2024). https://cve.mitre.org
24. MITRE: Common Weakness Enumeration (2024). https://cwe.mitre.org
25. Mo, K., Ye, P., Ren, X., Wang, S., Li, W., Li, J.: Security and privacy issues in deep reinforcement learning: threats and countermeasures. ACM Comput. Surv. **56**, 1–39 (2024)
26. OWASP: Top 10 Web Application Security Risks (2021). https://owasp.org/www-project-top-ten/
27. OWASP: Mobile Top 10 (2024). https://owasp.org/www-project-mobile-top-10/
28. OWASP: Threat Dragon (2024). https://owasp.org/www-project-threat-dragon/
29. OWASP: Top 10 for Large Language Model Applications version 1.1 (2024). https://owasp.org/www-project-top-10-for-large-language-model-applications/
30. Raciti, M., Bella, G.: How to model privacy threats in the automotive domain. arXiv preprint arXiv:2303.10370 (2023)

31. Rodrigues, A., Villela, M.L.B., Feitosa, E.L.: Privacy threat modeling language. IEEE Access **11**, 24448–24471 (2023)
32. Santos, J.C., Tarrit, K., Mirakhorli, M.: A catalog of security architecture weaknesses. In: 2017 IEEE International Conference on Software Architecture Workshops (ICSAW), pp. 220–223. IEEE (2017)
33. Sanz, B., Laorden, C., Alvarez, G., Bringas, P.G.: A threat model approach to attacks and countermeasures in on-line social networks. In: Proceedings of the 11th Reunion Espanola de Criptografıa y Seguridad de la Información (RECSI) (2010)
34. Schaad, A., Reski, T.: Open weakness and vulnerability modeler (OVVL): an updated approach to threat modeling. In: Proceedings of the 16th International Joint Conference on e-Business and Telecommunications. SciTePress (2019)
35. Schneider, C.: Threagile (2024). https://threagile.io/
36. Shapiro, S., et al.: The PANOPTIC™ Privacy Threat Model. Technical report V1, December 2023
37. Shi, Z., Graffi, K., Starobinski, D., Matyunin, N.: Threat modeling tools: a taxonomy. IEEE Secur. Priv. **20**(4), 29–39 (2022)
38. Shostack, A.: Threat Modeling: Designing for Security. John Wiley & Sons, Indianapolis, Indiana (2014)
39. Sion, L., Van Landuyt, D., Yskout, K., Joosen, W.: Sparta: Security & privacy architecture through risk-driven threat assessment. In: 2018 IEEE International Conference on Software Architecture Companion (ICSA-C), pp. 89–92 (2018)
40. Solove, D.J.: A taxonomy of privacy. Univ. Pa. Law Rev. **154**, 477 (2005)
41. Tarandach, I.: Pytm (2024). https://github.com/izar/pytm
42. Van Landuyt, D., Joosen, W.: A descriptive study of assumptions made in LINDDUN privacy threat elicitation. In: Proceedings of the 35th Annual ACM Symposium on Applied Computing, pp. 1280–1287 (2020)
43. Vasenev, A., et al.: Practical security and privacy threat analysis in the automotive domain: long term support scenario for over-the-air updates. In: VEHITS (2019)
44. Verreydt, S., Yskout, K., Sion, L., Joosen, W.: Threat modeling state of practice in Dutch organizations. In: SOUPS 2024: Proceedings of the Twentieth USENIX Conference on Usable Privacy and Security (2024)
45. Wang, Y., Nepali, R.K.: Privacy threat modeling framework for online social networks. In: 2015 International Conference on Collaboration Technologies and Systems (CTS), pp. 358–363. IEEE (2015)
46. Wuyts, K.: Privacy Threats in Software Architectures. Ph.D. thesis, KU Leuven, January 2015
47. Wuyts, K., Sion, L., Joosen, W.: LINDDUN GO: a lightweight approach to privacy threat modeling. In: 2020 IEEE Security and Privacy Workshops (2020)
48. Wuyts, K., Sion, L., Van Landuyt, D., Joosen, W.: Knowledge is power: systematic reuse of privacy knowledge for threat elicitation. In: 2019 IEEE Security and Privacy Workshops (SPW), pp. 80–83 (2019). https://doi.org/10.1109/SPW.2019.00025
49. Wuyts, K., Van Landuyt, D., Hovsepyan, A., Joosen, W.: Effective and efficient privacy threat modeling through domain refinements. In: Proceedings of the 33rd Annual ACM Symposium on Applied Computing, pp. 1175–1178 (2018)

Author Index

J. Garcia-Alfaro et al. (Eds.): ESORICS 2024 Workshops, LNCS 15263, pp. 543–545, 2025.
https://doi.org/10.1007/978-3-031-82349-7

The manufacturer's authorised representative in the EU is Springer
Nature Customer Service Centre GmbH, Europaplatz 3, 69115 Heidelberg,
Germany. If you have any concerns regarding our products, please
contact ProductSafety@springernature.com

Printed and bound by CPI Group (UK) Ltd, Croydon, CR0 4YY

06/05/2026

02103601-0005